P9-CDJ-210

Thomas Jefferson
An Intimate History

BY THE SAME AUTHOR

The Devil Drives
A LIFE OF SIR RICHARD BURTON

Thaddeus Stevens
SCOURGE OF THE SOUTH

No Man Knows My History
THE LIFE OF JOSEPH SMITH THE MORMON PROPHET

EDITOR :

*The City of the Saints
and Across the Rocky Mountains to California*
BY RICHARD F. BURTON

Bust of Thomas Jefferson by Houdon, 1789. New York Historical Society. Photo by Nina Leen. Courtesy *Life*.

Thomas Jefferson

An Intimate History

FAWN M. BRODIE

W. W. Norton & Company
New York • London

Copyright © 1974 by Fawn M. Brodie

First published as a Norton paperback 1998

Library of Congress Cataloging in Publication Data
Brodie, Fawn (McKay) 1915-
Thomas Jefferson, an intimate history.
Bibliography: p.
1. Jefferson, Thomas, Pres. U.S., 1743-1826.
E332.B787   973.4′6′0924 [B]   73-11348
ISBN 0-393-31752-8 pbk.

All rights reserved
Printed in the United States of America

This book was designed by Robert Freese.

Typefaces are Electra and Century Nova,
set by Spartan Typographers.
Printing and binding were done by Vail-Ballou Press.

W. W. Norton & Company, Inc.
500 Fifth Avenue, New York, N.Y. 10110
www.wwnorton.com

W. W. Norton & Company Ltd.
Castle House, 75/76 Wells Street, London W1T 3QT

5 6 7 8 9 0

to Bernard
ever a young gardener

Contents

Illustrations

Foreword

Lionel Trilling, in giving the first annual Jefferson lecture in 1972, chose to speak on Jefferson and the life of the mind. He thus carried forward a tradition set in 1826 by William Wirt, who when delivering in Congress the funeral eulogy on Jefferson concentrated on his vision of liberating "the imprisoned intellect" of man throughout the world. Almost every scholar who has since written about this philosopher-statesman has centered upon his luminous mind and its impact on society. This is a book about Jefferson and the life of the heart.

Before his death Jefferson tried to discourage those contemporaries who wished to be his biographers. "I do not think a biography should be written, or at least not published, during the life of the person the subject of it," he wrote to Robert Walsh on April 5, 1823. "It is impossible that the writer's delicacy should permit him to speak as freely of the faults or errors of a living, as of a dead character. There is still a better reason. The letters of a person, especially one whose business has been chiefly transacted by letters, form the only full and genuine journal of his life; and few can let them go out of their own hands while they live. A life written after these hoards become opened to investigation must supersede any previous one."

The "hoards" of Jefferson letters and his meticulous plantation records are now available as never before. The magic of microfilm brings them to the desk of any serious student, and the scholarship of Julian Boyd has provided, with masterly notes, printed volumes of letters written to Jefferson as well as those written by him, up to 1791. It is now possible to discover with some exactness which Jefferson letters have been lost or destroyed, and while exasperating to the biographer, these very lacunae are sometimes peculiarly meaningful.

Though this volume is "an intimate history" of Thomas Jefferson, it attempts to portray not only his intimate but also his inner life, which is not the same thing. The idea that a man's inner life affects every aspect of his intellectual life and also his decision-making should need no defense today. To illuminate this relationship, however, requires certain biographical techniques that make some historians uncomfortable. One must look for feeling as well as fact, for nuance and metaphor as well as idea and action.

Most of this book is based on Jefferson's own exhaustive records, long available to scholars with access to great libraries, especially the Library of Congress, the University of Virginia, the Massachusetts Historical Society, and the Henry E. Huntington Library. What is new here consists in good part of what in these library collections has been passed over, or ignored because it did not fit into the traditional notions and preconceptions of Jefferson's character. I have also found important material in newspapers, especially those published during Jefferson's presidency, but also elsewhere, such as the two illuminating narratives written or dictated by former Monticello slaves, Madison Hemings and Israel Jefferson, which are here republished for the first time since their initial appearance in the obscure *Pike County (Ohio) Republican* in 1873.

A trip which included a visit to Lodi, Italy, to examine the manuscripts there in the Collegio di Maria SS. Bambina, and to the Bodleian Library at Oxford, brought rewards of hitherto unused material on Maria Cosway, the little artist Jefferson fell in love with in Paris in 1786. She it was who prompted the writing of the most revealing of all his letters, the famous "dialogue between my Head and my Heart," which is reproduced in full in Appendix II of this book.

No one can seek to explore the inner life of Jefferson without feeling awe, affection, and occasionally shock and sorrow. My own special experiences and intentions are reflected in the words of the Lady Murasaki in eleventh century Japan, who wrote gently of her prince-hero in *The Tale of Genji*:

"I should indeed be very loath to recount in all their detail matters which he took so much trouble to conceal, did I not know that if you found I had omitted anything you would at once ask why, just because he was supposed to be an Emperor's son, I must needs put a favourable showing on his conduct by leaving out all his indiscretions? And you would soon be saying that this was no history but a mere made-up tale designed to influence the judgment of posterity. As it is I shall be called a scandalmonger; but that I cannot help."

Acknowledgments

I must acknowledge several different kinds of indebtedness in this volume. First of all, I owe an obvious intellectual debt to Jefferson scholars Dumas Malone and Merrill Peterson, whose writings have illuminated Jefferson's political genius. My portrait of Jefferson the man differs, however, in important respects from theirs, and differs also from the shorter but provocative analysis by Winthrop Jordan in *White over Black*. I also found particularly useful the eighteen volumes of the Jefferson *Papers*, edited by Julian Boyd, and the special volumes of Jefferson letters edited by James A. Bear, Jr., and Helen Bullock.

For new information on the life of Maria Cosway, I am grateful to Superiora Suor Enrica Cozzi for permission to examine the Cosway papers at the Collegio di Maria SS. Bambina, Lodi, Italy, and to the librarians at the Bodleian Library, Oxford, for permission to consult the Douce manuscripts. For many personal courtesies at the University of Virginia and at Monticello I am indebted to Dumas Malone, Merrill Peterson, James A. Bear, Jr., William H. Runge, and William G. Ray. My special thanks go to Roy P. Basler, Director of Manuscripts, Library of Congress, for rushing a special copying of three hundred letters from Jefferson to his son-in-law. For additional aid I wish to thank Natalie Schatz of the Harvard College Library; J. A. R. Wilton of the British Museum; Mary Isabel Fry and Ray Billington of the Henry E. Huntington Library; Stephen T. Riley of the Massachusetts Historical Society; Alfred Bush of the Princeton University Library; Allen T. Price of the Ohio Historical Society; Ray O. Hummel of the Virginia State Library; and the photoreproduction department of the Virginia Historical Society.

John Maass traced the whereabouts of the original of Adriaen van der Werff's painting, *Sarah, Abraham, and Hagar*. Harold J. Coolidge kindly gave me permission to quote a portion of a letter written by Ellen Randolph Coolidge.

I am grateful to Page Smith, as well as Winthrop Jordan and Bernard

17

A. Weisberger, for friendly support at a critical period during this study, and to Peter Loewenberg at UCLA for a sympathetic and sensitive reading of most of the manuscript. This volume was read in part also by members of a seminar on leadership, which included Peter Loewenberg, Victor Wolfenstein, and Bernice Eidelson of UCLA, and also psychoanalysts Ernst Lewy, Robert Dorn, Alfred Goldberg, Maimon Leavitt, and Gerald Aronson. The special insights of these friends, all of whom were deeply interested in Jefferson, served as a spur and reinforcement to my own writing, and enriched the volume. Thanks to Erik and Joan Erikson, I cherish memories of a five-hour discussion of Jefferson at their home, and I am grateful for their sympathetic reading of a portion of the manuscript. My continuing indebtedness to Erikson's own writings needs no underlining here.

From members of my own family I have received the usual warm support and their continuing tolerance of that consuming preoccupation without which no biography can be written. To my son and daughter-in-law, Bruce and Janet Brodie, graduate students at the University of Chicago, I am particularly indebted for their research in Ohio, which uncovered the hitherto overlooked and important Israel Jefferson memoir, reproduced here in Appendix I, and also additional factual data on Madison Hemings. My husband, Bernard Brodie, gave the manuscript several readings, in each case improving it with his expert editorial pencil. Finally, I wish to thank an excellent typist, Carol Steffensen, and a gifted copy editor, Thelma Sargent.

A summary of some of the evidence concerning the Sally Hemings liaison appeared in my article, "The Great Jefferson Taboo," *American Heritage*, June 1972.

FAWN M. BRODIE

Thomas Jefferson
An Intimate History

CHAPTER I

The Semi-Transparent Shadows

Thomas Jefferson of all our great presidents was the most orderly and the most acquisitive. He was also the most controlled. The celebrated equanimity of his temper, crystallized in his pronouncement "Peace is our passion," extended to his private as well as his public life; his daughter Martha described how he lost his temper in her presence only two times in his life. Once was when a long trusted slave twice defied an order concerning the use of a carriage horse, the second when two quarreling ferrymen let the boat in which Jefferson and his daughter were being carried across a river drift dangerously toward some rapids. Then, Martha said, her father, "his face 'like a lion' told the ferrymen 'in tones of thunder' to row for their lives or he would pitch them into the stream." [1]

Jefferson's acquisitiveness particularly in regard to books was legendary in his own lifetime. All his friends knew how he accumulated one of the great private libraries of the young United States, how he sold it far below its value to replace the Library of Congress when the British army burned it in the War of 1812, and then promptly began building up another library to match the old. Few, however, knew that he was so enraged by the senseless act of military vandalism that he suggested paying incendiaries in London to set British buildings afire in return.[2] The rage was momentary; he had believed from the beginning that the war was unnecessary and after initial acquiescence came to see it as a disaster for his country, but he was too loyal to his intimate friend and successor, James Madison, to say so publicly. During his own presidency, faced with the same European imbroglio that sucked Madison into his fatal declaration of war against the British, Jefferson had lived by his own admonition concerning peace, and had avoided war in the face of exasperating provocation. To John Langdon he had written in 1808, when war seemed imminent, "I think one war enough for the life of one man." And to a group of citizens in Maryland, speaking briefly on his way home to retirement in 1809, he had said, "The care of human life and happiness, and not their destruction, is the first and only legitimate object of good government." [3]

Still, in the same year, 1808, Jefferson was capable of issuing an order for one private act of destruction. When he learned that dogs were killing his prize Merino sheep at Monticello he wrote to his overseer: "To secure wool enough, the negroes dogs must all be killed. Do not spare a single one. If you keep a couple yourself it will be enough for the whole land. Let this be carried into execution immediately." And in a letter to a friend he suggested that the world would be better off were the whole canine species to be exterminated. [4]

Jefferson had a superb sense of history and an exact understanding of his own role in it. He preserved a legacy of over 25,000 letters from his friends and acquaintances, as well as copies of his own letters, made with letter presses and on the polygraph machines he delighted in, that numbered 18,000. These letters he indexed in his extraordinary Epistolary Record, extending from 1783 to 1826, which in itself numbered 656 pages. Still, he destroyed what would have been among the most revealing letters of his life, his correspondence with his mother and with his wife. He never finished his autobiography, and halfway through this mere fragment of his life numbering only 120 pages, he complained, "I am already tired of talking about myself." [5]

His orderliness reached such proportions that it can be properly called compulsive. He began his famous *Garden Book* in 1766 with the cheerful line, "March 20. Purple hyacinth begins to bloom," and continued this record of flowering and planting for fifty-eight years. His early biographer Henry Randall was confounded at the discovery among Jefferson's papers of a neatly made chart, "A Statement of the Vegetable market in Washington, during a period of 8 years, wherein the earliest & latest appearance of each article within the whole 8 years is noted." Jefferson had taken the time to note the exact beginning and ending of the season for twenty-nine vegetables and seven fruits. "Never was there a more methodical man from great matters down to the merest seeming trifles," Randall wrote, "never so diligent a recorder of them!" It is in his fantastically detailed account books, however, that Jefferson's orderliness and passion for recording details begin to seem compulsive. Here in these books he listed almost every expenditure of his adult life. Still, this attention to detail did not prevent his going steadily ever deeper into debt. In a careful reading one can follow the intricate path leading him ever more certainly into the final swamp—owing over $100,000—in which he was hopelessly mired when he died.

Jefferson kept a *Farm Book* with intermittent records of fifty-two years of plantation management, including inventories and distribution lists concerning more than a hundred slaves. In this enormously valuable source book, which tells us how much fish and beef, how many beds and blankets, were doled out to each slave and in what year, and which gives the date of almost every slave's birth, and often the date of his death, one can learn more about detailed relations between Jefferson and his slaves than in any other document. It is also a record of extraordinary concealment. Nowhere is there any hint, for example, that the two slaves Harriet and Beverly, listed in the *Farm Book* on page 130 as runaways in 1822, and believed by many of his neighbors and slaves to be his own children, were treated with any special indulgences. This we learn from other sources. And Beverly and Harriet's famous mother, Sally Hemings, celebrated in bawdy ballads during Jefferson's presidency as his slave mistress, is nowhere in the *Farm Book* treated with special attention, as she is in his account books. She is not even given a last name, simply appearing as "Sally" in over thirty listings.

Even though the total record of Jefferson's writings, and the letters written to him, promise to reach fifty-two volumes, there are many mysterious lacunae. This every previous historian or biographer, whether idolatrous or critical, protective or scurrilous, has sensed quickly once he let himself be drawn into the labyrinth of Jeffersonian literature, lured by the mysteries, baffled by Jefferson's ambivalences, and captured by his special genius. Unlike Lincoln's image, which emerges solid, well-defined, a great craggy statue whose proportions are familiar and whose lineaments defy distortion, Jefferson's image remains unfinished. He is like one of Michelangelo's great marble slaves, emerging but still partly trapped in the unchiseled marble. If a biographical portrait of Lincoln is at variance with the true man, it is the biographer who is pitilessly exposed, not Lincoln. And thanks to the industry of an unending parade of Lincoln scholars, there are almost no important mysteries left.

Jefferson, for all his prodigious industry in writing, collecting, indexing, and preserving his personal record in what he understood perfectly to be a "heroic age," and so described it to John Adams,[6] has always defied definitive portraiture. Biographer Albert J. Nock, writing in 1926, stated that Jefferson "was the most approachable and the most impenetrable of men, easy and delightful of acquaintance, impossible of knowledge." Nathan Schachner called him "the delight and despair of biographers," of all the great American statesmen "the most fascinating" and "the most difficult." [7] Dumas Malone, who has come closer than anyone with his expert biographical brush, admitted ruefully after finishing the first of his volumes, "In my youthful presumptuousness I flattered myself that sometime I would fully comprehend and encompass him. I do not claim that I have yet done so, and I do not believe that I or any other single person can." [8]

Merrill Peterson's *Jefferson Image in the American Mind* is as much a mirror of the evolution of American emotions concerning Jefferson as the American intellect. After winnowing what Peterson calls significantly "the massive record of America's affair with Jefferson," he writes, "Jefferson himself has always been an elusive subject; his shadow must prove more elusive still," and concludes that Jefferson's image was "a sensitive reflector, through several generations, of America's troubled search for the image of itself." And after writing his massive political biography, *Thomas Jefferson and the New Nation*, Peterson made a still stronger confession of frustration: "Of all his great contemporaries Jefferson is perhaps the least self-revealing and the hardest to sound to the depths of being. It is a mortifying confession but he remains for me, finally, an impenetrable man." [9]

Bernard Bailyn too has written of Jefferson's "hard glazed surface, so difficult to penetrate." Jefferson, he says, "is all things to all men. He emerges now a culture hero, a god-like luminous presence known only and in some misty way to be wise, good, and difficult to comprehend. The man himself, the personality, has vanished." [10] Henry Adams in writing long ago about Jefferson referred, like Merrill Peterson, to shadows. Few persons, he said, were permitted to share Jefferson's life. He "could be painted only touch by touch, with a fine pencil, and the perfection of the likeness depended upon the shifting and uncertain flicker of its semi-transparent shadows." [11]

Jefferson's secrecy about his intimate life pervades every kind of document he left behind. Although as attentive to the preservation of the early records of his young republic as to his own, he did not keep a diary, as did John and John Quincy Adams, and was persuaded only with great difficulty to embark on his autobiography. "Nothing could be more repugnant to my feelings," he wrote on his retirement from the presidency in 1809, than writing "the history of my whole life." [12] What he wrote down at age seventy-seven was a confounding exercise in concealment, containing only skeletal hints of one of the most richly endowed men in our history. Why he abandoned his memoir at the precise point he did—after describing his five years in France—is in itself a clue to his continuing need for secrecy concerning his private life. Moreover, he did not feel the necessity of amplifying his reputation with a long memoir, as did Ulysses S. Grant, Herbert Hoover, Harry Truman, Dwight Eisenhower, and Lyndon Johnson, or even the necessity of leaving a political statement. This he had done already in his Virginia constitution, Declaration of Independence, and Statute of Virginia for Religious Freedom, the latter two of which he asked to be mentioned on his tombstone.

Like Lincoln and Franklin Roosevelt, Jefferson kept his intimate feelings hidden from the public, either in triumph or in crisis. All three in this respect were unlike Andrew Jackson, who paraded his affections and his hatreds, or Theodore Roosevelt, who articulated almost everything openly in terms of grand adventure. The essential nature of Lincoln's melancholy still resists analysis; during his life he disguised it and ameliorated it by his storytelling and remarkable gift for political parable. "Were it not for these stories I should die," he once confided, "they are vents through which my sadness, my gloom and my melancholy escape." [13] A sensitive study of the Lincoln marriage will not always defy biographers, just as the truth about Franklin Roosevelt's feelings toward the several women who served importantly to shape his life must one day be captured in print, as Joseph Lash succeeded in capturing the feelings of his remarkable wife.

Despite hundreds of volumes about Jefferson, there remain unexpected reserves of unmined ore, particularly in relation to the *connections* between his public life and his inner life, as well as his intimate life. There is important material which has been belittled; controversial material flatly rejected as libelous, and abundant psychological material which is dismissed as "unhistorical" or simply not seen at all. Still, one must admit that what Henry Adams called the "semi-transparent shadows" particularly defy the biographical brush. With Jefferson there is always a shadow behind the obvious. Jefferson was ambivalent not only about love but also about revolution, religion, slavery, and power. He abominated slavery but continued all his life— in Peter Gay's phrase—to "live with, and off it." He was never truly comfortable with power, and his avowal that "that government is best which governs least" was a personal as well as a political statement. Yet he had the habit of command, an instinct for leadership, and a superb capacity for political writing. He despised clergymen all his adult life, and was as contemptuous as Thomas Paine of the idea that God truly interfered in the lives of men, yet whenever he wrote of the failure of emancipation we see the specter of Jehovah armed with thunderbolts virtually at Jefferson's elbow.

Though enormous amounts of research have gone into analyses of the intellectual sources of Jefferson's revolutionary ideas—into what

Daniel Boorstin has described as America's "paroxysm of rebellion against the past"—no attention has been paid to the impact of his parents as energizing sources contributing to that rebellion, whether positively or negatively. Also generally overlooked is the fact that his zeal for the Revolution was interrupted by periods of tormenting doubt. The coincidence can be noted that Jefferson, like several other great revolutionary figures, before he had truly reached manhood saw his father die. George Washington's father died when his son was eleven; Lenin's and Gandhi's fathers died when their sons were sixteen. The impact of the early death of a father upon the revolutionary son has already been a subject of thoughtful study.[14] Except, however, in the writings of Erik Erikson on Luther and Gandhi, the impact of their mothers upon sons destined to lead a revolution has largely been ignored. So little is known about Jefferson's parents that any speculation is hazardous, but there is evidence that there was great conflict in Jefferson over being a revolutionary, and that this conflict had something to do with his seemingly hostile relationship with his mother.

Jefferson has often been condemned for his behavior in defeat. Eric McKitrick describes it as a "superb capacity for washing his hands when failure was clear and manifest . . . with scant sense of the imperatives of salvage," dumping "all the pieces in the lap of a successor." [15] Only when one assembles all the details available of his private life, hidden and scattered like an ancient, partially buried mosaic floor, does it become apparent that Jefferson was neither callous nor self-serving in defeat. He was in deep conflict, and the compelling decisions —especially his resignation as war governor of Virginia during the Revolution—resulted most of all from tragedies in his own family, particularly the death of a small daughter when his military fortunes were at their absolute nadir.

In his *Autobiography* Jefferson writes but fleetingly of "the cherished companion of my life, in whose affections, unabated on both sides, I had lived the last ten years in unchecquered happiness," and one must turn to the account by his daughter Martha to learn with what stupor of mind and counterfeiting of death on his own part did Jefferson react to the lingering death of his wife after the birth of their sixth child. Dumas Malone is convinced that Jefferson had a deep sense of privacy, a reluctance to "gratify the curiosity of posterity," a determination to veil his affection for his wife "from the vulgar gaze." He notes that Jefferson even had the tender epitaph on her gravestone inscribed in Greek rather than in English. The translation reads, "If in the House of Hades men forget their dead, Yet will I even there remember my dear companion," importantly a reference to a pagan rather than to a Christian hereafter.

The Jefferson marriage in all earlier biographies is described as a tender and tragic idyll. In these pages it emerges as something more complicated. It seems likely that Martha Jefferson, unlike stout revolutionists Abigail and Betsey Adams, discouraged the democrat in Jefferson and encouraged the Tory and aristocrat, and that she was jealous of what he called his "passion for politics." There is even some evidence, attenuated and delicate though it be, to suggest that had she lived Jefferson might well have never become president of the United States.

A passion for politics stems usually from an insatiable need, either for power, or for friendship and adulation, or a combination of both. Any man who leaves a legacy of 18,000 letters written in his own hand, most of them written with a wrist that was crippled and stiffened in an accident, has a desperate need for friendship. Jefferson begged for letters, from his wife and daughters as well as his friends, and wrote in bitter protest when they were not forthcoming as often as he expected. His letters to his two adult daughters, Martha and Maria, are so affectionate and so innocently seductive that they become an open window letting us look into a house where the drapes are otherwise resolutely drawn. His letters to his friends are a cornucopia of giving, surely a reflection of his capacity for giving in the art of friendship itself. The very munificence of this giving won to him men as varied as the formal and formidable George Washington and the precocious adolescent, John Quincy Adams, the latter of whom confided to his diary in Paris in 1785, "Spent the evening with Mr. Jefferson, whom I love to be with." [16] Senator William Maclay of Pennsylvania described his face as having "a sunny aspect." Though Jefferson's figure, he said, had "a loose, shackling air," and "a laxity of manner seemed shed about him," still "he scattered information wherever he went, and some even brilliant sentiments sparkled from him." [17] Young Margaret Bayard Smith, wife of a Washington editor, and talented observer in her own right, wrote of her first meeting with Jefferson, "There was something in his manner, his countenance, and voice that at once unlocked my heart." [18] And Jefferson's granddaughter, Ellen Randolph Coolidge, wrote of him, "As a child, girl, and woman I loved and honored him above all earthly beings." [19] John and Abigail Adams in particular learned that they could not abandon Jefferson without a deep sense of loss. And Jefferson himself wrote to James Monroe, "I know that the dissolutions of personal friendship are among the most painful occurrences in human life." [20]

Still, Jefferson, like all great men, was a good hater. The particular Federalists he detested knew it; Gouverneur Morris found him "cold as a frog," and the malicious editor Joseph Dennie called him "sullen and retired." [21] Jefferson's hatred of Hamilton was complicated by jealousy of Washington's affection for the younger man. Theirs was the special hatred of two sons jockeying for the favored position in the eyes of a powerful father, with each son in the end unable either to make his peace with the other brother or to live comfortably with the surrogate parent. Both young men resigned from Washington's cabinet before the end of his second term. The continuing intellectual debate over the Jeffersonian and Hamiltonian rival systems of government takes on a new and richer dimension if seen against the backdrop of the personal drama of this remarkable triangle.

No one can understand the special capacity of Jefferson for friendship without reading the gravely formal, almost lifelong correspondence with James Madison, with whom he never quarreled, and comparing these letters with his sparkling correspondence with John Adams, where the friendship was interrupted by eleven years of bitter silence. Nor can one comprehend the complexity of the triangle comprising Jefferson, his daughter Martha, and her husband, Thomas Mann Randolph, Jr., without reading the four hundred letters exchanged between Jefferson and this difficult son-in-law, who moved in and out of psychosis several times in his turbulent life.

One of the important reasons that Jefferson's true nature has remained elusive is the insistence of all his previous biographers that after the death of his wife he never felt any lasting affection again for any woman. Gilbert Chinard stated the theme in 1928 when he wrote bluntly that though Jefferson corresponded with many women "there is no indication that he ever fell in love again." [22] Biographers and historians almost universally described him as a somewhat monkish, abstemious, continent, and virtually passionless president. Even Winthrop Jordan, the first historian to ask truly exacting questions about Jefferson's intimate life, holds that "with women in general he was uneasy and unsure; he held them at arm's length, wary, especially after his wife's death, of the dangers of over-commitment. Intimate emotional engagement with women seemed to represent for him a gateway into a dangerous, potentially explosive world which threatened revolution against the discipline of his higher self." [23]

But does a man's sexuality atrophy at thirty-nine, especially if he has already demonstrated that he was capable of very great passion? And if he is by nature or upbringing cold and impotent, is not this significantly reflected in his entire personal and political life? All the clinical evidence of our own time suggests a negative answer to the first question, and an affirmative answer to the second. It is true that Jefferson never married again, and the reasons why have been a subject of careful searching in this book. But this searching has been based on the premise that a man's sexuality remains largely undiminished through the years unless it has been badly warped in childhood. Of such warping there is no evidence in Jefferson's life.

There is, on the contrary, overwhelming evidence of his continuing capacity to love, though it was always—save for his first passion at twenty-one—directed toward women who were in some sense forbidden. If one discounts as relatively unimportant his conventional and rather timid affection for Rebecca Burwell, there were altogether four: Betsey Walker, wife of his good friend and neighbor John Walker; Martha Wayles, forbidden in the sense that she was a widow with a child, and possibly not wholly approved of by Jefferson's mother; Maria Cosway, the unhappy wife of the foppish English miniaturist Richard Cosway; and Sally Hemings, slave girl at Monticello who was also half-sister to Jefferson's wife. The importance of the romances with Betsey Walker and Maria Cosway has been consistently diminished by biographers, and the liaison with Sally Hemings passionately denied as libelous. One wonders why.

That something of significance happened in Paris has been known for many years, ever since the publication on August 23, 1828, of Jefferson's first and best-known letter to Maria Cosway, the "Dialogue between My Head and My Heart." [24] But the Jefferson heirs kept hidden until 1944 the rodent-nibbled packet of twenty-five additional letters exchanged between Jefferson and Mrs. Cosway, missives of such ineffable tenderness that they constitute the most remarkable collection of love letters in the history of the American presidency. Even after their publication with impressive annotation by Helen Bullock in 1945, these letters were casually dismissed by almost all Jefferson scholars as evidence of little more than a flirtation, a "love affair," in Winthrop Jordan's words, "in which the 'love' was partly play and the 'affair' non-existent." Merrill Peterson is certain that "Jefferson's feelings toward Maria, while no doubt sexual in origin, had an airy quality that leaves no suggestion of ardent desire. . . . flirting at love, with neither choosing to embrace it." [25] Only Dumas Malone and Marie Kimball are willing to concede the possibility of sexual intimacy during the first autumn in Paris, though they join all the other scholars in that they diminish to zero the importance of Maria's second visit—when she returned from England to spend four months in Paris without her husband.

So overwhelming is the evidence that Jefferson's affection for Maria Cosway was not casual at all that one must conclude that the historians and biographers referred to refuse to believe the evidence only because they do not want to. It upsets their conviction that Jefferson was a man whose heart was always rigidly controlled by his head; it destroys their image of the supreme man of reason; and, more important, it shatters the tenacious myth out of childhood that the father loves only the mother, and the corollary sentimental legend that one great passion fills a whole life until death. Jefferson is made out to be something less than a man, and Alexander Hamilton's ancient canard that Jefferson was "feminine" is perpetuated even in our own time. The ancient accusation in a Federalist newspaper that he was a man "whose blood was snow-broth" lives on, reemphasized recently by Eric McKitrick's description of Jefferson as having "the brooding mentality of a celibate Irish clergyman holding down the lid in the parish." [26]

Freud warned long ago:

> Biographers frequently select the hero as the object of study because for personal reasons of their own emotional life, they have a special affection for him from the very outset. They then devote themselves to a work of idealization, which strives to enroll the great man among their infantile models, and to relive through him, as it were, their infantile conceptions of the father. For the sake of this wish they wipe out the individual features in his physiognomy, they rub out the traces of his life's struggle with inner and outer resistances, and do not tolerate in him anything savoring of human weakness or imperfection; they then give us a cold, strange, ideal form instead of a man to whom we could feel distantly related. It is to be regretted that they do this, for they thereby sacrifice the truth to an illusion, and for the sake of their infantile phantasies they let slip the opportunity to penetrate into the most attractive secrets of human nature.[27]

This kind of canonization dominated nineteenth-century biography, and even today the Jefferson scholars wary of the impulse to sanctify are nevertheless often its victim; they glorify and protect by nuance, by omission, by subtle repudiation, without being in the least aware of the strength of their internal commitment to canonization. This we see particularly in their treatment of the story of Sally Hemings. This liaison, above all others in Jefferson's life, is unutterably taboo. Merrill Peterson repudiated the story in both of his volumes on Jefferson, and Dumas Malone devoted a five-page appendix in his *Jefferson the President* to a detailed denial, which would be more convincing had he not almost totally ignored the most important single document, the reminiscences of Sally Hemings' son Madison.* Black historians, however, have long accepted the story as accurate, and it is one of the most ironic aspects of the Jefferson image today that the blacks who repudiate him as a hero, because of his ambivalence over slavery, nevertheless believe the historical Jefferson to have been

* See Appendix I, pp. 471–76.

a man of great sexual vitality. Many believe that descendants through his slave women dot the country from Cambridge, Massachusetts, to San Francisco. Some even continue to accept the dubious story that a black mistress and two of Jefferson's slave daughters were sold at an auction in New Orleans, a tale that was immortalized in William Wells Brown's novel, *Clotel; or, The President's Daughter*, in 1853.[28]

The story of the slave mistress was first published in detail by scandalmonger and libeler of presidents James Thomson Callender in the *Richmond Recorder* in 1802–3. Callender, who had learned from neighbors of Jefferson the gossip that he had fathered five children by Sally Hemings, wrote of her in some detail, and stated that the features of the oldest, Tom, "are said to bear a striking although sable resemblance to those of the president himself."[29] For several years the Federalist press echoed with ballads and public scoldings about the yellow children at Monticello. Jefferson, who never replied directly to the charge, thus became the first president whose intimate life was used as a political bludgeon by his enemies. True, there is a myth that the British, to discredit George Washington during the Revolution, had forged a letter having him describe the charms of his slave women at Mount Vernon, but no historian has seen the actual letter, and few patriots heard of it at the time. Not till long after Washington's death did Americans learn of his tender affection for his neighbor's wife, Sally Fairfax.[30]

Andrew Jackson was denounced as an adulterer, though the woman in question was his own beloved wife Rachael, and though the charge grew out of a misunderstanding of a legal technicality concerning her previous divorce. Eventually the idea would become a part of the folklore of the American presidency that there must surely be a mistress, if not in the White House then in some dark closet of the president's past. Cleveland frankly acknowledged his illegitimate child in advance of his election. With Warren Harding the mistress in the closet was real enough, and the closet was inside the White House, but he was spared public revelations during his lifetime. Franklin Roosevelt was allowed a decent interval after his death, and biographers waited until both Eleanor Roosevelt and Lucy Mercer Rutherford were dead before publishing the discreet evidence saddening to those who had thought the Roosevelt marriage in every aspect rewarding.

The persistence of the folklore about the mistresses of the presidents is so tenacious, even when there is no foundation for it, that one suspects that there is something here beyond the normal malice and envy inevitably directed toward the powerful and the great. Europeans always delighted in the amours of their kings, just as the poorest Moslems who could not afford even the four wives permitted by

Mohammed gloried in the sheer numbers of their rulers' concubines. The American insistence on punishment would seem to be the inevitable heritage of Puritanism and democracy. Still, whereas the punishers are shrill, others more compassionate frankly and quietly enjoy what seems to be evidence of masculinity in their leaders. Though there has always been protest at love or sexual liaison outside marriage among presidential candidates, there is no good evidence that rumors of it ever cost the presidents many votes. This we shall see with Jefferson.

If the story of the Sally Hemings liaison be true, as I believe it is, it represents not scandalous debauchery with an innocent slave victim, as the Federalists and later the abolitionists insisted, but rather a serious passion that brought Jefferson and the slave woman much private happiness over a period lasting thirty-eight years. It also brought suffering, shame, and even political paralysis in regard to Jefferson's agitation for emancipation.

Eric McKitrick has written perceptively that "the values of Thomas Jefferson's career are basic to the entire system of American culture," and "the way you think about Thomas Jefferson largely determines how you will think about any number of other things." [31] But the way one thinks about Thomas Jefferson is conditioned as much by what others have written about him as by the inner needs of the reader in search of a hero. It makes some difference to the hero-seeker whether, on the one hand, he is convinced by the so-called historical record that Jefferson was indeed a brooding celibate Irish clergyman "holding down the lid in the parish"—in Carl Becker's words, "a man whose ardors were cool, giving forth light without heat" [32]—or whether, on the other hand, he considers him a casual debaucher of many slave women, as some blacks today believe. There remains, however, a third alternative: that he was a man richly endowed with warmth and passion but trapped in a society which savagely punished miscegenation, a man, moreover, whose psychic fate it was to fall in love with the forbidden woman. The fault, it can be held, lay not in Jefferson but in the society which condemned him to secrecy.

Once one accepts the premise that a man's inner life has a continuing impact upon his public life, then the whole unfolding tapestry of Jefferson's life is remarkably illuminated. His ambivalences seem less baffling; the heroic image remains untarnished and his genius undiminished. And the semi-transparent shadows do tend to disappear.

CHAPTER II

The Parents

The tradition in my father's family was, that their ancestor came to this country from Wales, and from near the mountain of Snowdon, the highest in Great Britain.

Thomas Jefferson, *Autobiography*

Like George Washington, whose father died when he was eleven, Jefferson lived all his life with memories of his father as a young and vigorous man, against whom he had never pitted his own strength. Jefferson's father died when he was fourteen, before he had come to terms with him as an equal in adulthood, before he could match his weight as giant against giant. That Peter Jefferson was a giant at least in physical stature we learn not from Jefferson's *Autobiography*, with its scant but important paragraph of definition, but from anecdotes passed down from Jefferson's grandchildren. Biographer Henry Randall, who interviewed several of them, and Jefferson's own great-granddaughter Sarah Randolph, wrote that Peter Jefferson was a man of extraordinary height and such prodigious strength that when standing between two hogsheads of tobacco lying on their sides he could "head" them both up at once.[1] Whether the hogshead of the time weighed "nearly a thousand pounds apiece," as Randall said, or the standard 560 pounds of today is not important. What counts is Jefferson's memory of his father's prowess and his own relation to it, neither of which is easy to document.

It is not difficult to conjure up a picture of the gangling freckled son—who though eventually six foot two and called "Tall Tom" would never be the giant his father was—watching the slaves and neighbors gather round, like the ancient Hebrews around Samson, as Peter Jefferson seized first one hogshead with the right hand and a second with the left and, with the veins standing out in his forehead, pulled them slowly upright. And one can add to this small drama a similar one. Peter Jefferson, it is said, once directed three slaves to pull down a ruined shed which had been girdled with a rope. When after repeated straining they failed, he "bade them stand aside, seized the rope, and dragged down the structure in an instant." So the Samson legend was enhanced. "A cardinal maxim with him," Randall wrote, "was 'Never ask another to do for you what you can do for yourself,' a text his son often afterward preached from." And he often said, "It is the strong in body who are both the strong and *free* in mind." [2] Jefferson made no great fetish of physical strength in his own writings, but he did acquire a machine for measuring strength, and visitors to Monticello who pictured the President as a languid philosopher were often startled to see him matching himself against the younger men.[3]

Thomas Jefferson resembled his father in face, Randall wrote, "but his slim form and delicate fibres were those of his mother's family." [4] When the son came to write about his father in his *Autobiography*, he made no mention of his prowess, although he had described it to his children. When he wrote that the tradition in his father's family was that their ancestors came to this country from Wales, "and from near the mountain of Snowdon, the highest in Great Britain," the reference to height was not to his father but to the mountain—higher than any mountain in England, as every Welshman would tell you then as now. And Jefferson in his turn would contrast the immensity of many things in America against their puny European counterparts. So intent was he in proving the falsity of the naturalist Georges de Buffon's contention that mammals degenerated in size in the New World that he went to great expense to have the skeleton of a seven-foot moose and the bones of American caribou, elk, and deer sent to Paris to prove him wrong. He was elated with the discovery of fossil remains of the American mammoth, and eventually secured a jaw-bone for display at Monticello.

Although Jefferson wrote nothing of his father's physical stature, and never mentioned his local status as member of the Virginia House of Burgesses, justice of the peace, sheriff of Albemarle County, judge of the Court of Chancery, and lieutenant colonel of the militia, he did write significantly about his character. "My father's education had been quite neglected; but being of a strong mind, sound judgment, and eager about information, he read much and improved himself, insomuch that he was chosen, with Joshua Fry, Professor of Mathematics in William and Mary College, to run the boundary-line between Virginia and North Carolina. . . . He died, August 17, 1757, leaving my mother a widow, who lived till 1776, with six daughters and two sons, myself the elder." [5]

"Strong mind, sound judgment, and eager after information, he read much and improved himself." This could apply equally to the son, and one suspects that since it was the only judgment on his father Jefferson ever put in writing, it was an important assessment. In these critical respects young Jefferson imitated his father and improved upon him mightily. None of our presidents had so prodigious a scientific curiosity; none read as much; no other "improved himself" to the extent that he became one of the most learned men in American political history.

Like all responsible fathers in what was essentially a wilderness area, Peter Jefferson taught his son, in Randall's words, "to sit his horse, fire his gun, boldly stem the Rivanna when the swollen river was

'Rolling red from brae to brae.' " [6]

That young Thomas Jefferson yearned to impress his father one learns from the memoirs of a grandson. "Mr. J," Thomas Jefferson Randolph wrote, "urged Manly sports for boys. . . . He advised that boys but ten years old should be given a gun and sent into the forest alone to make them self-reliant. At that age he was so sent by his father. Inexperienced, he was unsuccessful: finding a wild Turkey caught in a pen, he tied it with his garter to a tree, shot it, and carried it home in triumph." [7]

If the details of this story are true, it would seem that Jefferson as a boy lied to impress his father, and that he told the story of the lie without shame to his grandson. He was comfortable with the memory, and no doubt amused by it, which suggests that his father, on finding out the truth, felt the same way. In any case, there is nothing in the remembered anecdotes to indicate that Peter Jefferson was either a tyrannical or punishing parent. We do not know how he treated his slaves, which at his death numbered sixty, but we do know that Jefferson forbade his overseers to use the whip upon his own.

Peter Jefferson read Addison, Swift, Pope, and Shakespeare, and left a small but select library of forty-two volumes. He hired a tutor for his children and turned young Thomas over to him at age five. That the father sensed the rich intellectual promise in this son is suggested by the terms of his will. Here he singled him out to inherit "my mulatto fellow Sawney, my Books, mathematical Instruments & my Cherry Tree Desk and Book case." Jefferson wrote nothing of his father's politics, but Randall in the 1850s uncovered the fact that he had been a Whig, active in many aspects of local government, and had "adhered to certain democratic (using the word in its broad, popular sense) notions and maxims, which descended to his son."[8] He was a prominent member of the Virginia gentry, a friend of the Indians, and a well-known surveyor and map maker. After making several arduous surveying expeditions in the mountains, he and Joshua Fry made a map of Virginia, then much more extensive than it is today, and included adjacent parts of Pennsylvania, New Jersey, and North Carolina. Published in London in 1751, this map remained standard for many years.

Thomas Lewis accompanied Peter Jefferson on the first of these expeditions in 1746, exploring and surveying the "Fairfax Line," the limits of an immense grant from the King to Lord Fairfax. Peter Jefferson kept a journal of their weeks in the mountains, but it burned with the plantation house in Shadwell in 1770.[9] Fortunately, Lewis also kept a journal, so we have a vivid description of horses "tumbling over Rocks and precipices," of cold, rain and near starvation, of exultation over killing "one old Bair & three Cubs." Lewis described one mountain area where they were so "often in the outmoust Danger this tirable place was Calld Purgatory," and the river so treacherous they named it Styx, "from the Dismal appearance of the place Being Sufficen to Strick terror in any human Creature."[10]

Jefferson learned some surveying from his father, and in turn taught Meriwether Lewis. He began his first and only book, *Notes on the State of Virginia*, like a surveyor: "Virginia is bounded on the East by the Atlantic: on the North by a line of latitude, crossing the Eastern Shore through Watkin's Point, being about 37° . 57' North latitude," etc. In this book he used a map based on the one drawn by his father. He showed it with pride to the Hessian officers who were prisoners near Charlottesville in 1779, and, as William Peden has noted, "frequently declared that his map was of more value than the book in which it appeared."[11] All this suggests that as a child he was convinced that his father's exploits were altogether unmatchable.

Peter Jefferson was described in family tradition as "grave and taciturn," and we do not know if he seemed to his small son greatly eloquent, though it takes no special talent to overwhelm a child with stories of bears and near starvation. Jefferson himself was never eloquent in speechmaking, only in writing, in committees, and in quiet conversation. For some reason, perhaps having to do with a fear and tension that began in childhood, when he began to speak in public his voice "sank into his throat" and became "guttural and inarticulate."[12] Surprisingly, in view of his great popularity as president, he gave almost no public speeches save for his inaugural addresses, which he read in a low mumble that the audience barely heard.

He greatly admired eloquence, writing of one of Patrick Henry's early speeches, "He appeared to me to speak as Homer wrote." [13] And though in all his thousands of letters he related almost no anecdotes concerning his parents or his childhood, he did write to John Adams at sixty-nine a remarkable story with eloquence as its theme. It had to do with an Indian chief, Ontasseté, made famous in 1762 by a visit to London, where he was painted by Sir Joshua Reynolds and received by the King. Jefferson's father had known him and his Cherokee followers well.

> Before the Revolution they were in the habit of coming often and in great numbers to the seat of government, where I was very much with them. I knew much the great Ontasseté, the warrior and orator of the Cherokees; he was always the guest of my father, on his journeys to and from Williamsburg. I was in his camp when he made his great farewell oration to the people in the evening before his departure for England. The moon was in full splendor, and to her he seemed to address himself in his prayers for his own safety on the voyage, and that of his people during his absence; his sounding voice, distinct articulation, animated action, and the solemn silence of his people at their several fires, filled me with awe and veneration, altho' I did not understand a word he uttered.[14]

It is odd that Jefferson should have written so detailed an account of the speech of an Indian chief whom he could not understand, and neglect to make any mention of the dangerous adventures of his father, whom he did. Thus is it likely to be with gifted sons. It was the measure of the father that he succeeded in defining the boundaries of Virginia colony in 1751. And while the son never scaled the Allegheny range as did his father, still he annexed with a stroke of his pen as president a million square miles, and he organized an expedition which in 1805 would take the measure of the continent.

Peter Jefferson, like his son after him, had a faculty for friendship. His best friend was his wife's kinsman, William Randolph of Tuckahoe, and like all the other enterprising young married men in Virginia colony these two were madly acquiring the King's good land as fast as possible. Peter had his eye on a choice acreage on the Rivanna River; so did his friend Randolph. When Peter went to file on a thousand acres, he discovered that Randolph had two days earlier filed on 2,400 acres, including the four-hundred-acre area that Peter had coveted most and on which he hoped to build a house. Randolph, learning of Peter's dismay, promptly sold him the four hundred acres, the price— as specifically written in 1736 into the still extant deed—being "Henry

Weatherbourne's biggest bowl of arrack punch." [15] In this spirit of jovial kinship the problem was settled; Peter built a house on the site of his heart, and it was here on April 13, 1743, that his first son, Thomas, was born.

Peter Jefferson called his plantation Shadwell, after the parish in London where his wife had been baptized. The naming could be a token of affection for a woman about whom we know almost nothing, or a gesture of nostalgia on her part, for she was born in London and it is not clear how old she was when she came to Virginia colony. In his will Peter Jefferson wrote, "I give and devise to my Dear & Well beloved Wife Jane Jefferson for and Dureing her Natural Life or Widdowhood the use and profits of the House & plantation whereon I now live." The will, as all wills do, suggests foreboding of early death. And despite his prodigious strength Peter Jefferson was cut down when he was forty-nine; the power in his shoulders made him no less vulnerable than the frailest woman to whatever infection or epidemic carried him off. Thomas Jefferson at fourteen became the head of the family with six sisters, two older than himself, and a younger brother. A father's death always means release from a certain parental despotism, benevolent though it may be. But when the liberation comes too young, and is accompanied by sudden responsibility without real power—for Jefferson inherited no property or slaves till twenty-one—there is likely to be disconcerting experience of inadequacy if not outright youthful failure. Jefferson was ambivalent about power all his life, seeking it out and embracing it, and then abandoning it for reasons his friends found inexplicable. It is possible that this ambivalence had its roots in his difficulties with power at age fourteen, when responsibility was thrust upon him without decision-making rights.

Not only was he subject to the implicit authority of his mother, who could not be fought without arousing guilt, but he was also responsible in the smallest financial matters to the executors of his father's estate, John Harvie, Peter Randolph, Thomas Turpin, John Nicholas, and Dr. Thomas Walker. Jefferson turned to none of these men as mentor or intimate friend. One learns of his sense of abandonment and loss at fourteen from an important letter he wrote many years later to his grandson, when he learned that he was going away to school for the first time. Remembering then the early crisis in his own life, Jefferson wrote:

> But thrown on a wide world, among entire strangers, without a friend or guardian to advise so young too and with so little experience of mankind, your dangers great, and still your safety must rest on yourself. . . .

When I recollect that at 14 years of age the whole care and direction of myself was thrown on my self entirely, without a relative or friend qualified to advise or guide me, and recollect the various sorts of bad company with which I associated from time to time, I am astonished I did not turn off with some of them, and become as worthless to society as they were. I had the good fortune to become acquainted very early with some characters of very high standing, and to feel the incessant wish that I could even become what they were. Under temptations and difficulties, I could ask myself what would Dr. Small, Mr. Wythe, Peyton Randolph do in this situation? What course in it will ensure me their approbation? I am certain that this mode of deciding on my conduct tended more to it's correctness than any reasoning powers I possessed. . . .

From the circumstances of my position I was often thrown into the society of horseracers, cardplayers, Foxhunters, scientific and professional men, and of dignified men; and many a time I asked myself, in the enthusiastic moment of the death of a fox, the victory of a favorite horse, the issue of a question eloquently argued at the bar or in the great Council of the nation, well, which of these kinds of reputation should I prefer? That of a horse jockey? A foxhunter? An Orator? Or the honest advocate of my country's rights?[16]

Dr. William Small, professor of natural philosophy at William and Mary College, was Jefferson's most influential teacher; George Wythe was his law teacher and lifelong friend; Peyton Randolph was active with him in revolutionary politics. But none became a force in Jefferson's life until he was nineteen. Someone much earlier had made him feel that being "worthless to society" was a kind of sin, and instilled the "incessant wish" to model himself after greatness. It is no doubt Peter Jefferson—"honest advocate of my country's rights"—whose giant shadow looms behind this letter, like the ghost of Hamlet's father.

When Jefferson was inaugurated as president of the United States in March 1801, and messages of congratulations were streaming into Washington City, he wrote an elated letter of thanks to his old friend John Dickinson: "No pleasure can exceed that which I received from reading your letter of the 21st ultimo. It was like the joy we expect in the mansions of the blessed, when received with the embraces of our forefathers, we shall be welcomed with their blessing as having done our part not unworthily of them." [17] At this moment of Jefferson's supreme triumph his "forefather" Peter Jefferson was no mere shadow but in the forefront of the son's exultation.

The one person truly kept in the shadow in Jefferson's writings was not his father but . his mother. To return again to Jefferson's letter to his grandson, one sees that where Peter Jefferson is present though not explicitly portrayed, his mother is left out altogether. Even more significant, Jefferson here expresses by indirection what may well have been his lifelong conviction, that his mother was *not* qualified "to advise or guide." This brings us to an examination of Jefferson's mysterious silence about Jane Randolph Jefferson.

If one searches through the scanty documents illuminating the relationship between the great men of American history and their mothers, one finds less about Jefferson and his mother than about any of the others. George Washington's mother was an unloving, parsimonious woman who begrudged her son his successes, who greatly embarrassed him during the Revolution by complaining publicly that he was permitting her to starve when actually he was providing for her adequately, and who had the reputation for being something of a Tory. James T. Flexner, Washington's excellent biographer, tells us that though she lived into his second term as president, she did not appear at either inauguration, and there are extant letters showing her "depreciating her son's achievements." Flexner concludes that "History does not always draw noble men from noble mothers, preferring sometimes to temper her future heroes in the furnace of domestic infelicity." [18]

Franklin wrote little about his mother, but it was unmistakably positive. "My mother had likewise an excellent constitution," he noted in his *Autobiography*, "she suckled all her ten children." And he had engraved on her tombstone, "She was a discreet and virtuous woman." [19] * Lincoln wrote little about his parentage, saying nothing of his mother, Nancy Hanks, except to clarify her lineage, which was cloudy, but there is abundant folklore testifying to his affection and anguish at her death when he was nine. He looked upon the coming of his stepmother, Sarah Bush Johnston, as providential, and wrote of her as "a good and kind mother to A." [20] When his stepbrother suggested selling land which would have cut her income, he wrote with barely restrained anger, "I am not satisfied with. it on *Mother's* account. I want her to have her living, and I feel it is my duty, to some extent, to see that she is not wronged." Although he refused to visit his father in 1851 when he was dying, writing to his stepbrother, "Say to him that if we could meet now, it is doubtful whether it could not be more painful than pleasant," [21] he went out of his way to visit his stepmother in 1861 shortly before leaving for Washington and the presidency.

---

* Franklin was the eighth of ten children and the youngest son. His next oldest brother was accidentally drowned in a tub of suds at eighteen months. It is worth reporting that the first poem Franklin ever published was a ballad about a drowning; in this case the drowning of a lighthouse keeper—a figure, it will be noted, whose duty is to prevent drownings.

As for Jefferson, the astonishing fact is that though he lived with his mother—save for the months he was away at school and studying law—till he was twenty-seven, he did not mention her specifically in the thousands of letters and documents that have come down to us except on two occasions, and these references, one in a letter to his uncle and one in his *Autobiography*, are laconic and virtually without feeling. There are in addition four references to her in his account books which are at least as tantalizing as they are illuminating.[22] Henry Randall, surprised at the barrenness of the record, concluded that Jefferson was "singularly shy" about writing of the females in his family, and that this shyness "reached to positive aversion." Still, Randall conjectured piously that "his mother was in every way worthy of his highest respect and deepest love, and she received them." He reported that she possessed a most amiable and affectionate disposition, a lively cheerful temper, and a great fund of humor, and that she was fond of letter writing. He wrote further that she came from "an abode of refinement and elegant hospitality," that a hundred slaves "waited in and about it." [23] Ellen Randolph Coolidge, who never knew her great-grandmother, also added to the legacy of family lore, writing that Jane Jefferson was "mild and peaceful by nature, a person of sweet temper and gentle manners." [24]

Jefferson's earliest account book, preserved in the Huntington Library, tells us that so long as he lived at home with his mother there was a complicated sharing of slaves, income, food, and other goods. Jefferson itemized everything, and there are frequent listings under the formal heading "Mrs. Jane Jefferson." There are two curious items under this heading in 1768. On May 12 Jefferson wrote, "pd Doct Ellis for attending you £8–0–9. On August 10 he wrote, "Pd Giles Allegre for you £4." Does the inadvertent use of the word "you" tell us that Jefferson's mother was in the habit of checking every one of her son's expenditures, even though he had reached the age of twenty-five? Was this a sterile dialogue between them; was it an important communication, or an infuriating one? All we can be sure of is that Jefferson kept these elaborate lists until his death at eighty-three, and that somehow early in his life he found such records vital and came to believe that to destroy them would bring about the gravest consequences. Jefferson preserved all his own account books, and also those kept by his wife, though he destroyed her letters. No account book exists today in the handwriting of his mother.

There seems to be, in fact, no trace of her handwriting at all. A fire destroyed her Shadwell house in 1770, which would explain the loss of most of the family records and correspondence. Still, she lived for six years after the burning, and during these years Jefferson spent long periods in Williamsburg and Philadelphia. One can be fairly certain that some letters were exchanged. Shortly after the Shadwell fire, Jefferson wrote to his friend John Page:

> My late loss may perhaps have reached you by this time, I mean the loss of my mother's house by fire, and in it of every paper I had in the world, and almost every book. On a reasonable estimate I calculate the cost of the books to have been 200 sterling. Would to god it had been the money; then had it never cost me a sigh! To make the loss more sensible it fell principally on my books of common law, of which I have but one left, at that time lent out. Of papers too of every kind I am utterly destitute. All of these, whether public or private, of business or amusement have perished in the flames. I had made some progress in preparing for the succeeding general court, and having, as was my custom, thrown my thoughts into the form of notes, I troubled my head no more with them. These are gone, and "like the baseless fabric of a vision, Leave not a trace behind." [25]

In what is a very long letter Jefferson made no mention of his mother or of her loss, only "my mother's house." The burning of Shadwell seems to have ended with special finality whatever was the nature of his dependence upon his mother. He was then twenty-seven. At the time of the fire he was building his own house on Monticello. When a single room was finished he moved into it, and two years after the burning took his bride, Martha Wayles Skelton, into what was then a small cottage on a largely barren hilltop.

On March 31, 1776, six years after the burning and four years after his marriage, Jefferson wrote tersely in his pocket account book: "My mother died about eight o'clock this morning, in the 57th year of her age." Two months after her death Jefferson wrote the news of it to his uncle, William Randolph, one of Jane Jefferson's brothers who had chosen to live in England. The letter begins with some discussion of Randolph's business complaints resulting from hostilities which had broken out between England and her American colonies. Only then comes the brusque announcement: "The death of my mother you have probably not heard of. This happened on the last day of March after an illness of not more than an hour. We supposed it to have been apoplectic."

There was little more save "affectionate wishes to Mrs. Randolph and my unknown cousins," with an expression of hope that the quarrel with England would not "ever interfere with the ties of relation. Tho' most heartily engaged in the quarrel on my part from a sense of the most unprovoked injuries, I retain the same affection for individuals which nature or knowledge of their merit calls for." [26]

The coldness and failure to express any nuance of grief are striking—the associations are all to quarreling, hostility, and injury. The only clue in the letter that his mother's relatively early death had made a profound impact is his casual noting that he had been "taken sick myself" at the end of March. We know from other sources that the malady was an agonizing headache that lasted six weeks. Such headaches struck Jefferson several times in his life, generally at intervals of seven or eight years. Usually it is possible to correlate them with acute personal loss—loss that on most occasions was laced with conflict, complicated by indecision and deeply buried rage. They did not come, apparently, with the tragic deaths of his children.

Another reference to Jefferson's mother in his pocket account book, "Pd Mr. Clay for preaching my mother's funeral sermon 40/ [shillings]," would seem to be of no especial interest except for the date, April 11, 1777. For a payment that was usually made quickly, why had Jefferson waited more than a year?

The most revealing of Jefferson's surviving references to his mother he put in his *Autobiography*. Here the overtone is ironic if not unmistakably negative. Jane Randolph Jefferson, he wrote, was "the daughter of Isham Randolph, one of the seven sons of that name and family settled at Dungeness, in Goochland. They trace their pedigree far back in England and Scotland, to which let every one ascribe the faith and merit he chooses." [27]

It may have been this obscure and faintly contemptuous reference to her pedigree, plus the lack of any other data, that prompted Merrill Peterson to write of Jefferson and his mother, "By his own reckoning she was a zero quantity in his life." [28] No mother is a zero quantity in any son's life, and the fact that Jefferson, whether deliberately or not, managed to erase all traces of his opinion and feeling for her seems evidence rather of very great influence which he deeply resented, and from which he struggled to escape.

The reference to the pedigree may be an important clue. Peter Jefferson, of Welsh descent, was already a third-generation colonial in the New World and an independent hostage to its future. Heir as he was to centuries of Welsh hatred and distaste of British rule, had he lived he might well have been in the forefront of the Revolution. But his wife was English-born with strong family ties in the Old World. Her father, Isham Randolph, was a sea captain who had been educated in Virginia colony at William and Mary College. After the death of his first wife he went back to London to find a second, Jane Rodgers,[29] and they lived there for a considerable period. Jane, the first of eleven children, was born in 1720. Eventually Randolph came back to Virginia, and his daughter at nineteen married Peter Jefferson.

By then Isham Randolph was active in the slave trade and by Virginia standards quite rich, with a spacious house and a hundred slaves. Dumas Malone writes that Jane Randolph brought "extensive and influential family connections" to the marriage, and a £200 dowry, but no land. There seems to have been in the family tradition some feeling that in moving to Shadwell, "a small clearing in dense and primeval forest," she had come down in the world.[30]

The Randolphs, Randall tells us, claimed among their ancestors "the powerful Scotch Earls of Murray, connected by blood or alliance with many of the most distinguished families in the English and Scotch peerage, and with royalty itself." We do not know if Jane Randolph Jefferson felt superior to her husband because of her English birth and legendary lineage, whereas Peter Jefferson knew nothing of his own ancestry beyond a Welsh grandfather named Thomas Jefferson. Certainly the slight slur in Jefferson's *Autobiography* about his mother's ancestors hints at such a conflict. And in his *Notes on the State of Virginia* he expressed fear that if great numbers of immigrants continued to come to America they would bring their affection for monarchy, "imbibed in their early youth," and transmit this to their children.[31]

Perhaps with the hope of impressing his future wife, who was something of an heiress, Jefferson, when he was about to be married, wrote to his English agent, Thomas Adams, asking him in slightly ironic tones to search in London for the arms of his family. "I have what I have been told were the family arms," he said, "but on what authority I know not. It is possible there may be none. If so, I would with your assistance become a purchaser, having Sterne's word for it that a coat of arms may be purchased as cheap as any other coat."[32] Later in life he wrote fiercely and contemptuously against men who assumed the right to tyrannize over others because of the accident of their gentle birth. And in the end he devised a coat of arms for himself bearing the inscription "Rebellion to Tyrants Is Obedience to God."[33]

If we know little about Jefferson's relations with his mother, we do have illuminating evidence of what he thought of women in general and of certain women in particular. Jefferson liked women who were gentle, feminine, and yielding. To his daughter Martha he wrote upon her marriage, "The happiness of your life depends now on the continuing to please a single person. To this all other objects must be secondary; even your love to me . . ."[34] In one of his scrapbooks he pasted a newspaper clipping: "A Secret How to Keep a Husband and True—an Address to Married Ladies," which said in part: "Nothing more effectually lessens a man or wife in the eyes of the world, than when they publicly differ in opinion. . . . Modesty and diffidence are the greatest ornaments of a married woman. . . . Anger and violence and rage deform the female figure, and a turbulent woman disgraces the delicacy of her sex." [35]

Jefferson detested women who interfered in their husband's politics, which he later found common in revolutionary France. "The tender breasts of ladies were not formed for political convulsions," he wrote to a friend, "and the French ladies miscalculate much their own happiness when they wander from the field of their influence into that of politicks." [36] He deplored Marie Antoinette's meddling in affairs of state, writing to Madison from Paris, June 20, 1787: "The king loves business, economy, order and justice. He wishes very sincerely the good of his people. He is irascible, rude and very limited in his understanding, religious bordering on bigotry. He has no mistress, loves his queen, and is too much governed by her." [37] Later he came to hold the Queen responsible for the French Revolution, and in his *Autobiography*, which is otherwise largely free from hostility to anyone, painted a most venomous portrait:

> The King was by now become a passive machine in the hands of the National Assembly, and had he been left to himself, he would have willingly acquiesced in whatever they should devise as best for the nation. . . .
> But he had a Queen of absolute sway over his weak mind and timid virtue. . . . This angel, as gaudily painted in the Rhapsodies of Burke, with some smartness of fancy, but no sound sense, was proud, disdainful of restraint, indignant at all obstacles to her will, eager in the pursuit of pleasure, and firm enough to hold to her desires, or perish in their wreck. Her inordinate gambling and dissipations . . . her inflexible perverseness, and dauntless spirit, led herself to the Guillotine, drew the King on with her, and plunged the world into crimes and calamities which will forever stain the pages of modern history. I have ever believed, that had there been no Queen, there would have been no revolution.[38]

Marie Antoinette and Jane Jefferson may have been as unlike as any two women in the eighteenth century, but we know that expressions of intense feelings about reigning sovereigns—even elected ones—are sometimes clues to feelings about the sovereigns of one's childhood. A detailed account of Jefferson's reaction to his mother's death, and the mysterious three-month period preceding it, when he totally abandoned revolutionary politics and his duties in the Continental Congress, will be given in a later chapter. There are hints that his mother opposed Jefferson's revolutionary activities. Few would quarrel with the speculation that Jefferson's father looked to the west, and to nationhood. That Jefferson's mother looked instead back across the sea to England and to perpetual dependency seems likely, though the evidence is scanty.

Certainly Jefferson's failure to mention his mother save in the most noncommittal and cryptic fashion indicates feelings deeply hostile. Once, in praising the sunny climate of Virginia, Jefferson wrote, "It is our cloudless sky which has eradicated from our constitutions all disposition to hang ourselves, which we might otherwise have inherited from our English ancestors." [39] The fact that he continued to live with his mother till he was twenty-seven may suggest that he felt enslaved—he once described his youthful years to John Adams as "the dull monotony of a colonial subservience," and told him that if he had the choice of living his life over again he would not go back before the age of twenty-five.[40] Still there must have been something in him that acquiesced in the enslavement. He must also have passionately loved her, albeit unconsciously, and loved Shadwell, or he would not, at twenty-one, have planted there its plane and locust trees.[41]

CHAPTER III

A Sense of Family

Be you, my dear, the link of love, union, and peace for the whole family. The world will give you the more credit for it, in proportion to the difficulty of the task.

Thomas Jefferson to his daughter Martha, July 17, 1790

One might assume that Thomas Jefferson as the eldest son with six sisters and a younger brother grew up in the most favored family position, the potential heir and young aristocrat, treated by his family, his friends, and numerous slaves with all the deference due his status and obvious promise. The real childhood was more complicated. Jefferson gives us a clue to the complication by passing on to his grandchildren his first childhood memory. As Henry Randall heard it, "He used to mention as his first recollection his being handed up and carried on a pillow by a mounted slave, as the train set off down the river towards Tuckahoe." [1] The earliest memory of any person is usually significant, even though distorted by feeling and enshrouded by time. How old was Jefferson, what was the journey, and why did he remember it?

William Randolph, who had helped shape Thomas Jefferson's destiny by giving his father the site for the Shadwell home in which he was born, had remained an intimate family friend. Randolph's wife died sometime before 1742, leaving two daughters and a son. Ill himself, and full of baleful premonitions, Randolph made Peter Jefferson one of the executors of his estate and begged him, in the case of his own death, to move with his family to the commodious Randolph estate at Tuckahoe and raise both families of children together. Peter agreed.

47

Randolph died soon afterward, age thirty-three. True to his promise, Peter Jefferson uprooted his family in 1745 and moved them the fifty arduous miles to Tuckahoe. It was this first ride through the forest that Jefferson remembered; he was two years old, an unusual age from which to preserve even a fleeting memory intact.

There was more than fatigue and fear to crystallize this memory of separation. In Tuckahoe he moved into a strange house with two girls, age nine and seven, and with a boy of four who bore his own first name. These children were old enough to bully and tyrannize, and they would have been most unusual children if they had not done so. Jefferson's own elder sisters, Jane and Mary, were five and four; Elizabeth was a baby still in his mother's arms. Instead of being the eldest son Thomas Jefferson was suddenly the youngest, and would so remain for seven years.

At fifty Jefferson would write of the other Thomas: "We have had together the intimacy of brothers from 5 or 6 years of age, and the affection of brothers." [2] But this was when Thomas Mann Randolph lay dying and reminiscences were expected to be gentle. Actually there was much hostility between them as adults, and trouble over property. If Jefferson was bullied by the older boy in Tuckahoe, as is likely, it seems also likely that he was mothered by his older sister Jane, since she was the favorite of all his sisters, and his affection for her, later explicitly expressed, was very tender.

A year after moving to Tuckahoe his mother bore a new daughter, Martha, and young Thomas was now hopelessly outnumbered by rivals old and young. He must have learned painfully, too, at Tuckahoe, something of the ambiguity of ownership. For this plantation house, though spacious and gracious far beyond the simplicities of his Shadwell home, big enough with its two wings to provide for separation of the Randolph and Jefferson children at night, still clearly belonged to the Randolphs. And this they probably made decisively clear to their "intruder" cousins. All we know for certain, however, is that regret at separation from home, and hunger to return home, are two of the most ubiquitous and passionately expressed themes in all of Jefferson's intimate letters.

At Tuckahoe Thomas Jefferson learned about the death of a mother by moving in with the motherless. It was there, also, at age five, that he learned that children too could die. His brother Peter Field was born in 1748, only to die within five weeks. How old Jefferson was before he became conscious of the fact that his sister Elizabeth, twenty months younger than himself, was mentally retarded one can only guess, as we must guess, too, at the degree of her affliction.

There were over a hundred slaves at Tuckahoe. Jefferson was one of a big family of whites ruled by his parents, and of a far bigger family of blacks ruled by a handful of whites, and it is important to remember that until Jefferson was nine he lived in a community where the blacks outnumbered the whites by at least ten to one. Whether a black woman assisted in his essential mothering, as was common too on such plantations, he does not say, but one may take it for granted that black children of both sexes were among his earliest friends. He was a part of a highly ordered community, bound together by elaborate plantation rituals, laced through inevitably by coercion and fear. When he was five years old, a slave named Eve on a plantation in nearby Orange County, accused of poisoning her master, was burned at the stake. It was not a lynching; the sheriff carried out the order of the local court.[3] Whether Jefferson as a small boy heard of this atrocity is unknown, but the slaves at Tuckahoe could hardly have missed learning of it.

Children on plantations everywhere became aware of the subtle hierarchies of power without conscious teaching, and Jefferson learned very early that whites ruled over blacks even as children. That something about this disturbed him we see in his *Notes on the State of Virginia*, where he wrote, with remarkable sensibility, a description of the white child's tyranny on the plantation:

> The whole commerce between master and slave is a perpetual exercise of the most boisterous passions, the most unremitting despotism on the one part, and degrading submissions on the other. Our children see this, and learn to imitate it; for man is an imitative animal. . . .
>
> The parent storms, the child looks on, catches the lineaments of wrath, puts on the same airs in the circle of smaller slaves, gives a loose to his worst of passions, and thus nursed, educated, and daily exercised in tyranny, cannot but be stamped by it with odious peculiarities. The man must be a prodigy who can retain his manners and morals undepraved by such circumstances.[4]

Jefferson learned also, very early, that one difference between white and black children was that only the whites went to school. At age five he was ordered to join the older children in a small house in the courtyard, where a tutor managed what was called "the English school." Disliking it in the beginning, he slipped out one day, hid behind an outbuilding, and recited the Lord's Prayer with the request that the school be ended. Every child is sooner or later disillusioned by the impotence of his own prayers; what gives this story point is that Jefferson remembered it, and perhaps by way of warning not to expect too much of Heaven, told it to his grandchildren.[5]

It is impossible to say how early he felt the injustice of the fact that none of his black friends could go to school with him, mingled, as such feeling must have been, with regret that he had to study when they did not. Certainly he outraged and dismayed the Virginia gentry when as an adult he proposed in his *Notes* the radical heresy that all black youths be educated "to tillage, arts or sciences" till twenty-one, and all black girls to eighteen, and this "at public expense."

Still, along with this early sense of racial injustice, Jefferson as a small child somehow developed a feeling he was never able wholly to escape, that blacks and whites must be kept carefully separate. One of the many evidences of his ambivalence about blacks as an adult is that along with his proposal for black education he also proposed black colonization. The young slaves, once educated and freed, he said, "should be colonized to such place as the circumstances of the time should render most proper, sending them out with arms, implements of household and of handicraft arts, seeds; pairs of the useful domestic animals, &c. to declare them a free and independent people, and extend to them our allegiance and protection, till they shall have acquired strength." [6]

Such a proposal of education plus colonization, at public cost, of the majority of the labor force of the South was not a total fantasy when Jefferson wrote it. In 1781, when he penned his *Notes on the State of Virginia*, he was reckoning with the revolutionary upheaval which had seen many thousands of slaves flee to the British with the hope and promise of freedom, and as many as twenty thousand evacuated from slaveholding America in British ships.[7] But Jefferson's plan even in his own time also had the overtones of Robinson Crusoe and Noah's Ark. However naïve from a pragmatic sense, it marked in his own writing a personal recognition of the inequalities and brutalities suffered by the adult slaves who were his protectors and by the slave children who were his friends.

Peter Jefferson left a "body servant" to each child, so Jefferson had a personal valet at age fourteen, and would have one all his life. The role of Negro as subservient was thus further reinforced; it became a bone-deep feeling. Still, his affection for and dependence upon these men, especially Jupiter, who accompanied him to William and Mary, James Hemings, his valet in Paris, and Burwell, who attended him to his death, represented a special relationship the exact nature of which largely defies definition.

When Jefferson was nine, his father decided to return to Shadwell; perhaps the ambiguity of ownership after seven years became his problem too, as the Randolph children approached maturity. Back on the old plantation he built a new house and stable, a mill, tobacco houses, and slave quarters. But young Thomas was left behind to go to school. His father, determined that he should have a classical education, sent him to Dover Church, five miles from Tuckahoe, where a Reverend William Douglas taught Latin, Greek, and French. Once again there was an uprooting, and this time a total separation from his family. He was now some fifty miles from home, isolated from both the big family and the greater plantation family. He boarded with the Douglas family for eight or nine months of each year for five years, the annual cost £16. He did not return to Shadwell except during the summers, until the death of his father in 1757.

Of these five years we know nothing. All the letters Jefferson exchanged with his family were destroyed, either deliberately or in the Shadwell fire in 1770. Because, however, most adults in bringing up their children cannot avoid imitating the cautionary devices of their own parents, and because even those who despise their own upbringing often inadvertently fall into the ancient maternal and paternal patterns, we may look to the letters of Jefferson to his own children for clues to the kind of admonitions he got from his mother, and possibly also from his father, during these formative years.

In 1783, when eleven-year-old Martha Jefferson left Monticello for the first time to live in a strange family, Thomas Jefferson wrote to her as follows:

> I expect you will write to me by every post. Inform me what books you read, what tunes you learn, and inclose me your best copy of every lesson in drawing. . . . Take care that you never spell a word wrong. . . . It produces great praise to a lady to spell well. I have placed my happiness on seeing you good and accomplished, and no distress which this world can now bring on me could equal that of your disappointing my hopes. If you love me then, strive to be good under every situation.[8]

There is affection in this letter; there is also the heaviest burden a parent can place on a child: Be good, be obedient, improve yourself (above all, learn to spell!)—*lest I love you less.*

Again and again Jefferson cautioned his daughters against anger and indolence, the supreme vices in the eyes of this controlled and compulsively busy man. "Anger only serves to torment ourselves," he wrote to Martha. And, "Of all the cankers of human happiness, none corrodes it with so silent, yet so baneful a tooth, as indolence. Body and mind both unemployed, our being becomes a burthen, and every object about us loathesome, even the dearest. Idleness begets ennui, ennui the hypochondria, and that a diseased body. No laborious person was ever yet hysterical. . . . If at any moment, my dear, you catch yourself in idleness, start from it as you would the precipice of a gulph." [9]

This was not unlike the fierce admonition of Abigail Adams to her eldest son, John Quincy, age eleven: "I would rather see you find a grave in the ocean you have crossed than see you an immoral profligate or graceless child." [10] But with Jefferson the admonitions were tangled with an accompanying subtle parental seduction. "Nobody in this world," he wrote to Martha, "can make me so happy, or so miserable as you." [11] So her burden was compounded.

We have only to look at Jefferson's lifelong record of control and equanimity in the public handling of even his nastiest political enemies, and a record of incredible industriousness that stopped only with his death, to see that Jefferson as a child must have been molded in this same fashion. But he paid a penalty. What happens to a child who finds that love is made conditional upon good behavior, upon keeping his temper at all costs, and avoiding indolence like "the precipice of a gulph"? Any child so subtly tormented is likely to develop a continuing hunger for love that is never quite fulfilled, and also to confuse affection with esteem. So it would be with Jefferson. Few presidents have been so thin-skinned, few made so wretched by expressions of political and personal antipathy. He could not himself quarrel openly, and he was distressed beyond measure by newspaper attack.

With his daughters there was in his letters this chronic wistful appeal: Love me—I need you—"Do it for the additional incitement of increasing the happiness of him who loves you infinitely. . . . Continue to love me with all the warmth with which you are beloved." [12] Many men and women throughout his life felt this yearning and this hint of desperation. And because he was gracious and intelligent and generous in giving, as well as in need, they loved him in return.

During the five years Thomas Jefferson went to school at Dover Church his family continued to burgeon. His mother bore three more children, including twins, Anna Scott and Randolph, the only brother to survive infancy. Though the Randolph cousins were no longer with them, Peter Jefferson still acted as guardian, so there were altogether eleven children for whom the Welsh giant was in every way responsible. Of the jealousies, tensions, and pressures, of the camaraderie and affection, we have no record. But Thomas Jefferson emerged from his years at Shadwell, Tuckahoe, and Dover Church with a sense of family that was in every way extraordinary.

Like his father, he would take in the fatherless. When his sister

Martha ran into financial difficulties some years after the death of her husband, Dabney Carr, he brought her to Monticello and for a time raised her six children along with his own. Privacy and solitude, which as an adult he seemed desperately to crave, were not privacy and solitude from family, or at least they were secondary to his need for the big family of his childhood. His letters to his daughters after they were married are full of enticements to them to come and live with him at Monticello. Martha, as we shall see, succumbed to his blandishments, and that decision rocked her own already unstable marriage.

Jefferson encouraged his daughters to marry "within the family." Martha married her distant cousin, Thomas Mann Randolph, son of the "older brother" Thomas at Tuckahoe. Maria married John Eppes, the son of her mother's half sister. Jefferson's younger brother Randolph married his first cousin, Anne Jefferson Lewis. Today it all looks faintly incestuous, but no one then seems to have been in the least troubled by the inbreeding. Jefferson even wrote of his slaves in terms of an extended family, and encouraged them to marry within it. "Nobody feels more strongly than I do the desire to make all practicable sacrifices to keep man & wife together who have imprudently married out of their respective families," [13] he wrote, and he occasionally bought and sold slaves to keep marriages intact.

Hunger to return to "the family" as symbolized in later life by Monticello became chronic with Jefferson. As a boy the Shadwell area meant vacation from school, reunion with his kin, hunting, fishing, daydreaming. When he was a man, Monticello came to mean the Elysian fields, a haven from the brutalities of politics. Typical of many nostalgic letters he wrote his daughter when he was president was one written February 15, 1801: "The scene passing here makes me pant to be away from it: to fly from the circle of cabal, intrigue, and hatred, to one where all is love and peace." [14]

Jefferson was trapped in his family and by his family; and the full measure of this entrapment can best be seen in the fact that when he decided to build a home of his own it was only four miles distant from Shadwell. Even as an old man he spoke of Virginia as his "country." Monticello, "the little mountain" he selected as the site for his own home, was clearly the capital, and he its reigning prince.

Jefferson did not inherit all his father's property, though as the eldest son in Virginia colony, where primogeniture was still legal; it would not have been surprising if he had. Peter Jefferson did not believe in it, and his son later led the fight to get it abolished in the state altogether. Peter Jefferson's will provided that Jane Jefferson should inherit the Shadwell plantation and one-sixth of the household goods and slaves, who numbered at his death about ninety. Each of his six daughters was promised six slaves and £200, payable when she was married or upon reaching the age of twenty-one. The remainder of the land was to be divided between Thomas Jefferson and his younger brother, with Thomas when he was twenty-one getting the preferred choice. This meant at least 2,500 acres on the Rivanna River and about thirty slaves. The will further provided that on the death of his mother Thomas would inherit Shadwell, again about 2,500 acres. He was to be responsible, however, for the education of the younger children, and for the payment of his sisters' "portions." Until age twenty-one, however, he was subject to dictation from the executors of his father's will for all his expenditures. Thus, as we have said, he was given responsibility, but denied power.

For the first two years after his father's death he went to school in Fredericksville, which was near enough to Shadwell so that he could return home on weekends. For two days each week he was the man of the family and the titular heir, with six sisters and a brother who ranged in age at their father's death from seventeen to two. The five weekdays he spent with a dour Anglican clergyman, James Maury, who had eight children of his own and boarded a half dozen students to keep his family solvent. Jefferson wrote nothing of this teacher in his *Autobiography* save to say that he was "a correct classical scholar," but when one compares this comment with the warm praise he showered on his teachers at William and Mary College, it becomes by contrast a clear indication of his dislike.

Maury was an exceptional Virginia clergyman on several counts: he wrote tolerably well, left a considerable record of memorabilia, and counted himself a descendant of French royalty. He was hotly aggressive in defending the rights of the Anglican clergy, believing them to be "a necessary and essential part of the political system of the nation." [15] He was the plaintiff in the celebrated Penny Parsons court case demanding more money from the colony of Virginia for clerical pay, in which the opposing lawyer was Patrick Henry. Henry lost the case, but won immediate fame as an anticlerical rebel. We know from a pamphlet Maury wrote attacking the Anabaptists, and from several letters his family fortuitously preserved, that he was self-righteous and bigoted, and that Patrick Henry may well have had him in mind when he wrote of the clergyman—"rapacious as a harpie" who would "snatch from the hearth of every honest farmer his last hoe-cake, nay, take the last blanket from a woman in childbirth."

Maury hated the Scots in Virginia colony, calling them "raw, surly and tyrannical," and abominated as "dupes, deceivers, and madmen" the New Light ministers, leaders of small evangelical sects that were threatening the power of the state church. In daring to insult divine authority, he said, they were no better than the false priests of the Old Testament who had been swallowed up by an earthquake. It is clear that he would cheerfully have duplicated this miracle in Virginia if he could.[16]

Jefferson lived with this clergyman when he was fourteen and fifteen, the great adolescent rebellion years. All the hostility that would normally have been expended, and with great guilt, against his father, could now be recklessly concentrated on Maury and the whole Anglican Church. And the contrast between this clergyman, who called the speeches of dissident ministers "the frantick ravings of fanaticism, or artful fictions of imposture," and his own father, who had believed in freedom of the mind, generated a hostility that had permanent consequences in America. No other statesman of his time would match Jefferson in his hatred of the established faith. He never really exorcised this hatred. We cannot be sure if it began with James Maury, or with William Douglas before him. But Jefferson's repudiation of every standard of Maury's life was total.

Maury despised the Indians as barbarians; Jefferson, like his father, found them fascinating objects of study, and fighting men worthy of respect. Maury had no faith in what he called the "vulgar herd," and quoted in his speeches, "Cursed be the man who trusteth in. man, and maketh flesh his arm, and whose heart departeth from the Lord." Jefferson, the first of the great democrats in our history, said, "The steady character of our countrymen is a rock to which we may safely moor." [17] Maury preached that "all enjoyments and possession of the world" become "a temptation to evil." "The grand purpose of life," he said, "is to prepare for death, and that is preparing for eternity." Jefferson would live under the benign beacon, "The earth belongs to the living."

The destruction of the power of the Anglican Church became one of Jefferson's chief goals during the Revolution, and one of his first acts as governor of Virginia and as member of the Board of Visitors of William and Mary College in 1780 was to rout out the divines and turn the school over to the professors of science, mathematics, and modern languages. His distrust of clergymen as factionalists, schismatizers, and imprisoners of the human spirit continued to his death.

Still, it would be a mistake to assume that this Anglican clergyman had only a negative impact on Thomas Jefferson's youth. From Maury he learned not only a "correct" knowledge of Greek and Latin, but an affection for languages not only as tools for communication and the unlocking of secrets, but also as a beckoning path into history and mythology. Jefferson mastered Greek so well he was able to write to Dr. Joseph Priestley in 1800, "I enjoy Homer in his own language infinitely beyond Pope's translation. . . . I thank on my knees, Him who directed my early education, for having put into my possession this rich source of delight. . . ." [18]

Where in his reading of the classics he first encountered the story of Jason and his Argonauts one cannot be sure. Certainly this legendary hero caught his imagination as no other in Greek history. At nineteen Jefferson built a flatboat, actually suitable for sailing only on Virginia rivers, but he fantasied himself sailing in it to "England Holland France Spain and Italy (where I would buy me a good fiddle) and Egypt and return through the British provinces to the northward home." [19] "Argonauts" became his word for the leaders of the Revolution, and "Argo" his lifelong metaphor for the nation of which he had been a master builder.

At fourteen and fifteen, mastering Greek grammar under the inflexible discipline of the Anglican divine, Jefferson could escape in two directions, either home to Shadwell, and the family to which he was so deeply committed, or to the world of heroes. He would be torn between these two directions throughout his life. For all his delight in the bewitching wooded countryside of Albemarle, and his affection for the family of his childhood, he could not live with them for long periods without restlessness, boredom, and even depression. Back he would go to what he once described to James Monroe as "that passion," the political life.[20] Once immersed in it he would begin to pine for the bucolic life, for the cultivation of trees, for planting flowers, and for counting the purple hyacinths in bloom. This perpetual yearning for the other of the two lives he could be leading ended only with his final retirement to Monticello after eight years as president. He was then sixty-five.

CHAPTER IV

A Capacity for Involvement

As I grow older I set a higher value on the intimacies of my youth, and am more afflicted by whatever loses one of them to me.

Thomas Jefferson to Alexander Donald, July 28, 1787 [1]

It was rare for a man to know Thomas Jefferson well and not cherish the friendship all his life. This was as true of his early youth as during his manhood. James Maury had four students besides Jefferson who were age fourteen to sixteen, one his own son. All became intimate friends. Jefferson corresponded with two of the four until his death—James Madison (cousin of the president), later president of William and Mary College, and James Maury, Jr., who abandoned Virginia colony to become a British merchant. The latter would lament, at Jefferson's death in 1826, "on hearing my antient class mate had left me the sole survivor of the *five* who were together somewhat more than *three score and ten* years ago." Dabney Carr, the closest of all his youthful friends, married Jefferson's sister Martha. "Never had man more of the milk of human kindness," Jefferson wrote of him, "of indulgence, of softness, of pleasantry, of conversation and conduct." [2]

There were difficulties only with John Walker, son of one of the executors of his father's will. When young Walker married Elizabeth Moore, he invited Jefferson to be one of the "bridemen" at his wedding. He set up housekeeping on a nearby plantation, and even made Jefferson executor of his estate in his will. But years later in an explosive and bitter assault, he privately accused Jefferson of having on numerous occasions tried to seduce his wife.

Most Virginia plantations were isolated from each other by stretches of dense forest and wretched roads. Shadwell, however, was near a public highway and "the stopping place for passers-by." [3] There was in Jefferson's youth much visiting and party going. Dancing master Alexander Ingles taught him and four of his sisters to dance; someone taught him the violin and the cello and his sisters the harp. Eventually, when an Italian musician moved into the area, Jefferson took violin lessons regularly. "I suppose," he told Nicholas Trist many years later, "that during at least a dozen years of my life, I played no less than *three hours* a day." [4] Music became one of the enduring pleasures of his life, and undoubtedly the fact that Martha Wayles and Maria Cosway were both players of the harpsichord enhanced their attractiveness in his eyes.

He did not play by ear, as did Patrick Henry, who as a young man was in great demand at parties. Jefferson first encountered Henry, then a country storekeeper and law student, when he was fiddling at a Christmas holiday gathering at the home of Nathan Dandridge in Hanover in 1759. Though he was only sixteen, Jefferson remembered the party with peculiar vividness, describing it to both William Wirt and Daniel Webster when he was past seventy. Henry was seven years older than Jefferson, and clearly not a member of the Virginia gentry. "Mr. Henry had a little before broke up his store," Jefferson told Wirt, "or rather it had broken him up. . . . His manners had something of the coarseness of the society he had frequented; his passion was fiddling, dancing and pleasantry. He excelled in the last, and it attached every one to him." [5] One sees a certain envy along with contempt enduring undiminished by the passage of fifty-six years, and Jefferson's envy was for that capacity in Patrick Henry in which he himself became supremely gifted—the capacity for "attaching everyone to him." The contempt would harden into hatred when Jefferson and Henry became political rivals and enemies. But in 1759 Henry quite captured the younger man. "I was once sincerely affectioned towards him," Jefferson wrote in 1795. [6]

As it turned out, the holiday season of 1759 was a significant time for decisions. After consulting on New Year's Day with his mother's cousin, Peter Randolph, he decided to go to William and Mary College, and on January 14, 1760, wrote a letter asking formal permission from his guardian, John Harvie. This is the earliest of all Jefferson's letters to survive:

SIR

    I was at Colo. Peter Randolph's about a Fortnight ago, and my Schooling falling into Discourse, he said he thought it would be to my

Advantage to go to the College, and was desirous I should go, as indeed I am myself for several Reasons. In the first place as long as I stay at the Mountains the Loss of one fourth of my Time is inevitable, by Company's coming here and detaining me from School. And likewise my Absence will in a great Measure put a Stop to so much Company, and by that Means lessen the Expences of the Estate in House-Keeping. And on the other hand by going to the College I shall get a more universal Acquaintance, which may hereafter be serviceable to me; and I suppose I can pursue my Studies in the Greek and Latin as well there as here, and likewise learn something of the Mathematics. I shall be glad of your opinion.[7]

That it was really Jefferson's mother who was complaining about "so much Company" and "the Expences of the Estate in House-Keeping" seems likely. There had been two weeks of parties at the holiday season, and Jefferson's sister Mary would be married to John Bolling on January 24. If, however, Jefferson was truly disturbed about all the festivities taking up "one fourth of my Time," and "detaining me from School," this is surely evidence that parental admonitions about work and duty had already marked Jefferson for life with a sense of guilt about having fun.[8] Later, his friend John Page would report that Jefferson in college "could tear himself away from his dearest friends, to fly to his studies." [9]

Once installed in Williamsburg, where he matriculated surprisingly late in the spring, March 25, 1760, he was quickly caught up in a circle of young people, where pairing off and passionate exchanges of confidence were commonplace. It was not only the young men and women who delighted in the company of this tall, sandy-haired youth, with an imperturbable temper, evident kindness, and slight shyness with its hint of vulnerability. Older men too were captivated.

William Small, professor of mathematics and natural philosophy, one of the seven men who made up the faculty, was a Scot with an instinct for smelling out greatness. Later, in England, where he went to study medicine after a bureaucratic dispute with the college authorities, he would number among his friends Erasmus Darwin, James Watt, Joseph Priestley, and Josiah Wedgwood.[10] During Jefferson's first year at William and Mary, Small taught him rhetoric, *belles-lettres*, and ethics as well as mathematics and natural philosophy. Almost at once he discovered or generated in the young student a fervor for learning. Nor was the attraction one-sided, as Jefferson recorded with pleasure at seventy-seven in his *Autobiography*: "It was my great good fortune, and what probably fixed the destinies of my life, that Dr. William Small of Scotland, was the Professor of Mathematic, a man profound in most of the useful branches of science, with a happy talent of communication, correct and gentlemanly manners, and an enlarged and liberal mind. He, most happily for me, became soon attached to me, and made me his daily companion when not engaged in the school; and from his conversation I got my first views of the expansion of science, and of the system of things in which we are placed." [11]

Jefferson wrote to one friend that Small was "as a father" [12] to him. And in a graceful and grateful phrase he pointed out that Small "filled up the measure of his goodness to me" by introducing him to two good friends, George Wythe, who became his law teacher, and Francis Fauquier, British governor of Virginia colony—in Jefferson's words, "the ablest man who ever filled that office." There developed an extraordinary friendship. Fauquier, "Dr. Small and Mr. Wythe, his *amici omnium horarum* [friends of all hours] and myself," Jefferson wrote, "formed a *partie quarée*, and to the habitual conversations on these occasions I owed much instruction." [13] Fauquier, almost sixty, a country gentleman from Hertfordshire and Fellow of the Royal Society, had a passion for music, a curiosity for scientific studies, and a fatal fascination with gambling. According to Virginia rumor he had lost his whole inheritance in a single night to Lord Anson (the famous admiral), who out of compassion saw to it that he was given an appointment as governor in the New World. [14] When he first arrived in Virginia, he witnessed with astonishment on July 9, 1758, a hailstorm that broke every window on the north side of the Palace, and left enough ice on the ground for him to cool his wine and freeze cream the following day. He measured the hailstones and sent an account to his brother, who published the story in the *Philosophical Transactions* of the Royal Society. [15] Fauquier thereafter kept a diary record of the Williamsburg weather—Jefferson would do the same for long periods at Monticello and in Washington.

Fauquier was happy to have the gifted young fiddler play in his weekly concerts, and he soon found Jefferson rewarding also in other respects. At their frequent dinners together with Small and Wythe, Jefferson wrote, "I have heard more good sense, more rational and philosophical conversation than in all my life besides." [16]

Small returned to England in 1764; Jefferson never saw him again, and it is not certain if Small wrote to him. But when the Revolution broke out, Jefferson felt compelled to explain his own position, and this letter has come down to us. Writing to Small on May 7, 1775, he deplored the Battle of Lexington, fought by "our brethren of Boston," against the King's troops, noting that a "phrenzy of revenge seems to have seized all ranks of people." Like a good patriot, however, he deplored King George's "incendiary" declarations and "haughty deportment." Then to make clear that for him their cherished friendship was in no way impaired by the political dissensions, he sent six dozen bottles of Madeira—on two different boats to insure their arrival— Madeira he had kept aging in his cellar for eight years.[17] Thus he expressed his gratitude, and demonstrated what would be a lifelong habit for keeping his friendships in repair.

Fauquier died after a lingering illness in March 1768, before the Revolution could strain his friendship with Jefferson. Scientifically curious to the end, uncertain of the cause of his own "tedious" illness, he provided in his will that his body might be dissected for the benefit of medicine. It was not done.[18] Of the uncommon trio comprising Jefferson's mentors in college, only Wythe was left. By every standard he was the most important. Jefferson described Wythe in his *Autobiography* as "my faithful and beloved mentor in youth, and my most affectionate friend through life." In letters to friends he was more explicit, calling Wythe "my second father," "my antient master, my earliest & best friend" to whom "I am indebted for first impressions which have had the most salutary influence on the course of my life." [19]

Wythe was a fine Greek and Latin scholar, and when at thirty-five he accepted the nineteen-year-old Jefferson as a law student, he was one of the most respected lawyers in Virginia. Jefferson biographers express astonishment that the apprenticeship with Wythe lasted five full years, 1762–67, at a time when almost no one studied law for more than two. Patrick Henry studied "not more than six weeks," or so at least he told Jefferson, and Wythe for one was so convinced of the inadequacy of Henry's training he refused to sign his license.[20] Jefferson's years under Wythe, years of virtually uninterrupted reading, not only in the law but also in ancient classics, English literature, and general political philosophy, were not so much an apprenticeship for law as an apprenticeship for greatness.

In the beginning Jefferson disliked the study of law. To his friend John Page he wrote on December 25, 1762, of Edward Coke, author of the standard text on property and tenure: "I do wish the Devil had old Cooke, for I am sure I never was so tired of an old dull scoundrel in my life." [21] And after seven years of practicing law he cheerfully abandoned the profession for politics. But reading became a necessity for Jefferson, like music and gardening, a special nutrient without which he withered.

Wythe was a collector of books; under his influence Jefferson began collecting too, and their friendly rivalry shortly assumed staggering proportions. Neither was a bibliomaniac; they read what they purchased. Jefferson read avidly, with a hunger of such magnitude that one can only marvel at the gargantuan capacity. He copied great quantities of quotations into his commonplace books, commenting freely with exhilaration or contempt. Years later he sent samples of his notes to Thomas Cooper, apologizing for his youthful arrogance: "They were written at a time of life when I was bold in the pursuit of knowledge, never fearing to follow truth and reason to whatever results they led, and bearding every authority which stood in their way. This must be the apology, if you find the conclusions bolder than historical facts and principles will warrant." [22] Within three years of the burning of his library in the Shadwell fire he had accumulated a new one of about 1,250 volumes, and went on to build a collection of 6,500. As evidence of his great affection, Wythe, unknown to Jefferson, eventually bequeathed him his own superb library in his will. Jefferson would learn of this with mingled gratitude and anguish in 1806, when Wythe was poisoned by a malignant grandnephew who resented being cut out of a portion of property which Wythe in his will had bequeathed to a mulatto youth believed to be his son. [23] Thus Jefferson's "second father" willed him his books, as had the first.

As Small and Wythe ignited in Jefferson a passionate affection for books, so he in turn tried to kindle a similar fire in his friends, his nephews, and later his grandson. When young Robert Skipwith asked him in 1771 to suggest a list of books "amounting to about 30 lb. sterl.," Jefferson spent hours devising instead an ideal collection, so we know the books he thought important when he was twenty-eight. The list included "Percy's reliques of antient English Poetry," Chaucer, Shakespeare, Milton, Dryden, Spenser, Thompson, Gray, Prior, Gay, and Pope, plays by Steele, Congreve, and Addison, novels by Smollett, Richardson, Langhorne, and Sterne. He included the works of Swift, the nine-volume *Spectator*, the five-volume *Tatler*, Locke's "conduct of the mind in search of truth," Bolingbroke's five-volume "political works," Burke in eight volumes, and Hume's *History of England*. Molière was on the list, and Voltaire and Montesquieu, along with Buffon's natural history. From the classics he recommended Xenophon, Epictetus, Seneca, Cicero, Livy, Sallust, Tacitus, Caesar, Plutarch. The Bible was included, though Jefferson was already critical of it, and Josephus. There were books on gardening, husbandry, painting, history, and law, Franklin's *Electricity*, and "A compendium of Physic & Surgery by Nourse." Anyone studying this list, and the commonplace books, would find it difficult to take seriously what Jefferson wrote to William Duane on October 1, 1812: "When I was young, mathematics was the passion of my life." [24] One is reminded of the ironic comment of Bertrand Russell, "When I was young I liked mathematics. When this became too difficult for me I took to philosophy and when philosophy became too difficult I took to politics." [25]

Jefferson had many passions in his youth, and obvious among them was the passion to make all knowledge his province. His delight in mastering everything, which only a young man can experience, led to an astonishing regimen of self-discipline which came close to being obsessive. When another young friend, Bernard Moore, shortly after entering law practice, asked him to prescribe a proper reading list for him, Jefferson replied with a letter—now famous among law students in America—which mirrored his own past. Jefferson rose always at dawn, or sunrise,[26] and he began by telling young Moore what he should read *before* 8 A.M. "Employ yourself in physical studies, Ethics, Religion, natural and sectarian, and natural law," he wrote, and suggested a list of books to be consulted before breakfast. From hours eight to twelve he prescribed reading in law, from twelve to one in politics. The afternoon, he said, should be occupied by history, and "From Dark to Bed-time," *belles-lettres*, criticism, rhetoric, and oratory.[27]

One of Jefferson's friends stated that "when young he adopted a system, perhaps an entire plan of life from which neither the exigencies of business nor the allurements of pleasure could drive or seduce him. Much of his success is to be ascribed to methodical industry." Jefferson's five years of "methodical industry" can best be described in Erik Erikson's happy phrase as an "adolescent moratorium," a deferring of decision-making in preparation for possible future greatness. In his *Young Man Luther* Erikson describes how such a moratorium served to prepare Luther for his great revolutionary period. With Luther it was his years in the seminary, when he strove with such fanatical intensity to be the ideal monk that even his superiors recognized there was some pathology in it. With Jefferson, between nineteen and twenty-four, when most of his friends were hunting, gambling, cockfighting, speculating, marrying young, or wenching among slaves, he seems to have been largely buried in books, and in the kind of books most of his friends avoided as difficult or esoteric. Patrick Henry, who often moved in with Jefferson when he came to Williamsburg to court, once looked over his library and said, "Mr. J., I will take two volumes of Hume's Essays, and try to read them this winter." When Henry returned them, Jefferson remembered later with some contempt, he said, "he had not been able to get half way into one of them." [28]

Jefferson's abnormally prolonged postponement of entering the profession of law suggests in part a reluctance to accept maturity, to abandon the role of son and student which he was enjoying under Wythe. But with the postponement came a consciousness of inner worth, a consciousness common to great men. What it was that Jefferson was preparing for he could not know, but he did it with such industry and conscientious zeal that one must believe he had serious fantasies about one day becoming great. Such fantasies must surely have been stimulated by the trio of extraordinary men in Williamsburg, Small, Fauquier, and Wythe, who accepted him as one of them with affectionate admiration when he was only nineteen.

Jefferson delayed not only his going into law but also his entering into marriage. Though his friendships with men during his early twenties were richly rewarding, serving as a catalyst to his learning and a spur to his ambition to become a political philosopher and man of science as well as a lawyer, his friendships with women were troubled and frustrating. We know a good deal about his first love because he wrote seven recklessly frank letters about it to his good friend John Page, and two less candid but still revealing ones to William Fleming. They were speckled with puns, nonsense, and Latinisms. Page and Fleming preserved them, one suspects, not because of any magical prescience about their future value but rather because they described an anguished affection for one Rebecca Burwell.

Jefferson was fearful of their being read widely, and becoming, as he wrote, "the subjects of a great deal of mirth and raillery." Page wrote his confessions of love for Nancy Wilson in Latin, but this device did not satisfy Jefferson. "We must fall on some scheme of communicating our thoughts to each other, which shall be totally unintelligible to everyone but to ourselves."[29] He employed various devices to disguise Rebecca's name, giving her code names like Adneleb, Becca, Belinda, and writing her name as an anagram, *campana in die* (that is, *bell in day*), all of which was perfectly obvious to George Tucker, Jefferson's first biographer, who published these early letters in 1837.[30]

When they met in 1762, Jefferson was nineteen and Rebecca sixteen. She and her brother Lewis were orphans, and lived with an uncle, William Nelson of York. The only description we have of her comes from an old cleric, who was told by Rebecca's daughter that she was extremely pious, which gives us no idea whatever of what special charms she radiated at sixteen.[31] We know that she gave Jefferson a silhouette of her profile, and that he was desolate when a leaking roof permitted rain water to drip upon his watch, in the back of which he had placed the cutout. In endeavoring to extricate the soaked silhouette, Jefferson told Page, "My cursed fingers gave them such a rent as I fear I never shall get over." The "dear picture" was hopelessly torn. "And now although the picture be defaced," Jefferson continued, "there is so lively an image of her imprinted in my mind that I shall think of her too often I fear for my peace of mind."[32]

In reading later letters to Page, one is immediately struck with Jefferson's advance certainty of failure in this romance. "Had I better stay here and do nothing," he wrote from Shadwell on January 20, 1763, "or go down and do less? . . . Inclination tells me to go, receive my sentence, and be no longer in suspence; but, reason says if you go and your attempt proves unsuccessful you will be ten times more wretched than ever." Either way, it will be seen, he expected to lose. He grumbled of his boredom at home. "For I do not conceive that anything can happen in my world which you would give a curse to know, or I either. All things here appear to me to trudge on in one and the same round." He urged Page to sail with him to England in the boat he was then building, which he had named *Rebecca*. "This, to be sure, would take us two or three years and if we should not both be cured of love in that time I think the devil would be in it." He kept the letter almost two months before sending it, adding postscripts which showed an ever deepening melancholy. "I verily believe Page that I shall die soon, and yet I can give no other reason for it but that I am tired with living. At this moment when I am writing I am scarcely sensible that I exist." [33]

Page from Williamsburg warned him of what he apparently already knew, that there was a rival on the scene, and urged him "to go immediately and lay siege in form." [34] But Jefferson remained morosely home in Shadwell with his mother, staying for nine months, from early January to October 1, 1763, despite the fact that during this period he was supposed to be studying law with Wythe. Like Miles Standish, he begged Page to intercede with Rebecca on his behalf, explaining to her why he must visit England before approaching her uncle about the possibility of marriage. "I should be scared to death at making so unreasonable a proposal as that of waiting untill I returned from Britain, unless she could be first prepared for it." [35] Whether Jefferson's mother was discouraging the courtship, and using as a device agitation for the trip to England where she had relatives, one cannot know, but she did keep him under watch.

When, finally, on October 6, 1763, Jefferson danced with Rebecca in the Apollo Room of the Raleigh Tavern at Williamsburg, he found himself tongue-tied, stammering, and inept. "I had dressed up in my own mind," he told Page, "such thoughts as occurred to me, in as moving language as I knew how, and expected to have performed them in a tolerably creditable manner. But, good God! When I had an opportunity of venting them, a few broken sentences, uttered in great disorder, and interrupted with pauses of uncommon length, were the too visible marks of my strange confusion!" [36] Later he saw her again, and elaborated more fully on the necessity of his going abroad. "I managed in such a manner that I was tolerably easy myself," he confessed to Page. But he could hardly have been surprised that Rebecca looked upon this kind of courtship with incredulity. Though Page had urged him to make another visit to her, he refused, and in words indicating he had by then lost all hope: "A visit could not possibly be of the least weight." [37]

At eleven o'clock at night on March 20, 1764, racked by "a violent head ache" with which he had been afflicted for two days, Jefferson wrote of the finality of his loss to William Fleming. "With regard to the scheme which I proposed to you some time since, I am sorry to tell you it is totally frustrated by Miss R. B.'s marriage with Jacquelin Ambler which the people here tell me they daily expect: I say, the people here tell me so, for (can you believe it?) I have been so abominably indolent as not to have seen her since last October." He tried to pass it off lightly. "Well the lord bless her I say! . . . Many and great are the comforts of a single state. . . . For St. Paul only says that it is better to be married than to burn. Now I presume that if that apostle had known that providence would at an after day be so kind to any particular set of people as to furnish them with other means of extinguishing their fire than those of matrimony, he would have earnestly recommended them to their practice." [38]

In April he barely missed seeing the new Mrs. Ambler at a party at the home of Frances Burwell (later the bride of John Page), to which he had been invited. "What a high figure I should have cut had I gone!" he wrote to Page. "When I heard who visited you there I thought I had met with the narrowest escape in the world. I wonder how I should have behaved? I am sure I should have been at a great loss." [39] The deprivation for Jefferson in losing Rebecca Burwell was more anguishing than has been acknowledged by some of his biographers. Malone holds that "Jefferson carried on this rather absurd affair mostly in his imagination." [40] Nathan Schachner believes "his passion could not have been too unmanageable, for he made no move to journey down to see her," and labels his melancholy "sentimental *Weltschmerz.*" Merrill Peterson put it more perceptively: "He did not wish to lose her, still less was he ready to take her." [41] Whatever the intensity of his own fire, Jefferson was by nature so thin-skinned that the merest hint of Rebecca's indifference to his love would have brought mortification and withdrawal. Most of his life he would react to criticism and rejection with silence if not with flight, deeply burying his rage. If he was unaggressive in this courtship, it may have been because he felt his love to be unrequited, or feared that it might be if made too visible. Especially in the young the overvaluation of the beloved is a commonplace, and with it goes the feeling of one's unworthiness.

He was eminently eligible, a member of the Virginia gentry, a fine musician, a superb horseman, and a capable dancer. He was over six feet two inches tall, lean, sinewy, with a personable if not handsome face. His first biographer tells us that his contemporaries agreed he was "not handsome in his youth," that he was thin and rawboned, with skin that freckled badly and burned in the sun; nevertheless "such a vein of pleasantry ran through his discourse, that he was even then a favourite" with the ladies.[42] There were those who found his manners graceful and his conversation remarkable. However, this may not have been his own opinion of himself. We do not know whether Rebecca actually spurned him, because he seemed not to give her a chance. Perhaps, too, there was an uneasy feeling in him that he was not ready for marriage.

Significantly, after her wedding, Jefferson abandoned all plans to go to England. This heightens the possibility that the proposed trip was a device, either unconscious on his part, or deliberate on the part of his mother, to prevent the marriage. Two years later Jefferson made a leisurely three-month voyage to Annapolis, Philadelphia, and New York, partly to seek out a physician who would inoculate him against smallpox. Once returned, he settled into seemingly perennial bachelorhood. John Page may well have believed that Jefferson had really meant it when he wrote to him in 1763 that "if Belinda will not accept of my service it shall never be offered to another." [43]

As for Rebecca, she has won her page in history as one of the numerous girls who have turned down men destined to be presidents. As Mrs. Jacquelin Ambler she bore two daughters, one of whom wrote a letter mocking Jefferson, which found its way into the *Atlantic Monthly* in 1899.[44] The other married John Marshall, a man destined to be one of Jefferson's most tenacious political enemies.

CHAPTER V

A Problem with the Forbidden

I have often heard my grandfather say that he considered moral deformity as rare as personal deformity.

Ellen Randolph Coolidge, Memoirs [1]

For several years after Rebecca Burwell's marriage Jefferson seems to have been hostile to all women, if one is to believe certain diatribes he copied into his notebooks. Extracts from Latin poets and from *Paradise Lost* (telling title!) berated the female sex for its lack of goodness, fidelity, and intelligence. From Thomas Otway's *The Orphan; or, The Unhappy Marriage* he copied the following:

> I'd leave the world for him that hates a woman,
> Woman the fountain of all human frailty!
> What mighty ills have not been done by woman?
> Who was't betray'd the capitol? A woman.
> Who was the cause of a long ten years war,
> And laid at last old Troy in Ashes? A woman.
> Destructive, Damnable, Deceitful woman!

And in one of his several scrapbooks he pasted "To My Coy Mistress," a translation of a bitter Spanish lyric:

> Ah Chloe, too well does your Corydon know
> That your bosom, so fair yet so frigid resembles

In more points than one, two cold hillocks of snow;
See Cupid close by how he shakes how he trembles
And tho' he is naked, he feels not so bold
To fly to a bosom he knows is so cold! [2]

Later he confessed that when he suffered from insomnia as a young
man, he would lie awake formulating a "love and murder novel." It
worked capitally; before getting past three pages he was fast asleep.[3]

But the scrapbooks contain tender love lyrics as well as these ironic
verses, and since dating many of the extracts is impossible, it is easy
but treacherous to select out those which prove the disillusionment
with women and to ignore those which suggest the contrary. Between
the failure in 1764 of his courtship of Rebecca Burwell and his marriage on January 1, 1772, to Martha Wayles Skelton, Jefferson was
not uninvolved with women. We know of two. Importantly, both
were forbidden. After Rebecca all the women to whom Jefferson was
attracted were in one sense or another interdicted. Never again
would he fall in love with a virgin with whom marriage would be in
every sense socially acceptable.

The first involvement, a natural and long-continuing one we have
not yet noted, was with his oldest and favorite sister Jane. His second sister Mary had married at nineteen, as did his younger sister
Martha. The latter had wed his most intimate friend, Dabney Carr.
The two youths had gone to school together, and had roamed the
Shadwell woods and hills. They had constructed a bench on an out-
look where Jefferson later built his house, and had selected a great oak
tree under which each had agreed to bury the other in case of an early
death. Jefferson would write enviously of Carr in 1770: "This friend of
ours, Page, in a very small house, with a table, half a dozen chairs,
and one or two servants, is the happiest man in the universe." [4]

Jane had not married, however, and at the time of her sister Martha's wedding on July 20, 1765, was a spinsterish twenty-five. Randall
reported Jefferson's memories that she was "a singer of uncommon
skill and sweetness," and wrote that on "many a soft summer twilight,
on the wooded banks of the Rivanna, [one] heard their voices, accompanied by the notes of his violin, thus ascending together." [5] She
died ten weeks after Martha's marriage. Jefferson never wrote directly
about this loss, though his granddaughters reported that as an old man
he occasionally spoke of Jane "in terms of as warm admiration and
love as if the grave had but just closed over her." [6] But he left singular
evidence in his own hand of how this death, the first in his family
since that of his father, had scarred him.

When in 1771 he was planning the hilltop house and acreage he called Monticello, he included a family cemetery. His detailed notes indicate that though Jane's body had by then been six years buried, he intended to have it exhumed and transferred to his hill. Over her burial spot he planned to build an elaborate grotto-temple of meditation. His description of this temple, neatly penned at the end of an account book, has a certain lyric melancholy:

> choose out for a Burying place some unfrequented vale in the park, where is, 'no sound to break the stillness but a brook, that bubbling winds among the weeds; no mark of any human shape that had been there, unless the skeleton of some poor wretch, Who sought that place out to despair and die in.' let it be among antient and venerable oaks; intersperse some gloomy evergreens. . . .
> in the center of it erect a small Gothic temple of antique appearance. . . . in the middle of the temple an altar, the sides of turf, the top of plain stone. very little light, perhaps none at all, save only the feeble ray of an half extinguished lamp.

> Jane Jefferson
> "Ah! Joanna, puellarum optima!
> Ah! aevi virentis flore praerepta!
> Sit tibi terra laevis!
> Longe, longeque valeto!" [7]

Jefferson began keeping his *Garden Book* in the spring following Jane's death. His first notation, March 20, 1766, is famous: "Purple hyacinth begins to bloom." On April 6 he wrote, "Narcissus and Puckoon open," and on April 13, his own twenty-third birthday, "Puckoon flowers fallen." The puckoon, or bloodroot, had lasted one week. This sequence of notations is the first evidence of Jefferson's preoccupation with the beginning and ending of the flowers in his life. Later his fascination with the first day and last day in the life of a bloom extended to many growing plants, to the wheat and tobacco crops he grew in Virginia, to the vegetables in his own garden. This special obsession with timing—with the beginning and end of the life of a fragile flower or succulent berry—suggests a preoccupation with the fragility of life itself, an anxiety made less burdensome by being shifted away from the people he loved, where death was final, to the plants, where every spring meant a renewal of life.

When Jane Jefferson died in 1765, there were still four younger children for whom Jefferson felt responsible. Lucy was thirteen, and the twins, Anna Scott and Randolph, ten. His retarded sister Elizabeth, twenty-one, was an increasingly exasperating burden, as difficulties in keeping a separate expense account for her reveal. Even as an adult Jefferson was forced to check expenditures with the executors of his father's estate—to get their sanction, for example, in seeing to it that Elizabeth as a young woman "should be well dressed." She remained a charge for Jefferson and his mother until she died at thirty. Jefferson's account book for February 21, 1774, records an earthquake so intense "everybody ran out doors." On March 1 he wrote, "My sister Elizabeth was found last Thursday being Feb. 24." On March 7 he recorded her funeral. Except for what is suggested by these sparse, melancholy details, there is no explanation for her dying. How Jefferson felt about this sister is suggested only by a clipping in one of his scrapbooks, "Elegy on the Death of an Idiot Girl." It said in part: "Poor guileless thing! just eighteen years. . . . Heaven took thee spotless to his own." [8]

Even the most cursory examination of Jefferson's account books before his marriage reveals countless financial complications resulting from his being head of a family over which he had no real control. His slaves mingled with those of his mother and sisters; the records show that quarters of beef and sides of pork were given to his mother from his own estate. Eventually he provided a regular allowance of £10 a year for his older sisters and £6 for the younger children.[9] And he was responsible for his sisters' inheritances at twenty-one of £200 each. Jefferson's reluctance to pursue a vigorous courtship of any kind until he was twenty-seven may well have been reinforced by anxieties that he could barely manage the family responsibilities he already had.

Still, if Albemarle County, Virginia, was a prison for a young genius, in the sense that it offered no catapult or even pedestal for his potential greatness, it was a prison he passionately loved. His trip to Philadelphia and New York in 1766, instead of whetting his appetite for further travel, served only to intensify his affection for the undulating Virginia landscape. He was utterly lost to the land.

Exactly when he first decided to build a house on the five-hundred-foot hill near Shadwell is uncertain. When he was in love with Rebecca Burwell, he wrote to John Page of his plans to build in Williamsburg: "I think to build. No castle though I assure you, only a small house which shall contain a room for myself and another for you, and no more, unless Belinda should think proper to favour us with her company, in which case I will enlarge the plan as much as she pleases." [10] But it was not until his long apprenticeship with George Wythe had finally come to an end early in 1767 and he was formally admitted to the Virginia bar that he began detailed plans for a house. By then it was no small cottage in the city he envisioned but something approaching a Renaissance manor, with elaborate gardens, orchards, and a park for a herd of deer. Importantly, the site was only four miles from his mother.

His first mention of the word "Monticello" appears in his *Garden Book* August 3, 1767: "inoculated common cherry buds into stocks of large kind at Monticello." By this time he had perfected plans for leveling the top of the hill and had worked out the problem of sinking a deep well. Why he had abandoned his original name, Hermitage, and changed it to Monticello he never bothered to explain. While he was waiting for the difficult and expensive leveling process, he began to plant like a man possessed. On a single April day, in the gardens of his mother's home at Shadwell, he sowed "Carnations, Indian pink, Marygold, Globe amaranth, Auricula, Double balsam, Tricolor, Dutch violet, Sensitive plant, Cockscomb, a flower like the Prince's feather, Lathyrus, Lilac, Spanish broom, Umbrella, Laurel, Almonds, Muscle plumbs, Cayenne pepper, and 12. cuttings of Gooseberries." [11]

This rage for planting, and his explosion of planning for a magnificent house on one of the most beguiling sites in America, all culminating in 1767, suggest that something important was happening in Jefferson's affections. And what was happening served as a reinforcement of his commitment to the area, a commitment determined certainly by his increasing sense of duty to his family. Building at Monticello anchored him in Albemarle County, close to his mother. It anchored him also to the Virginia gentry, to the planter class, to the life of the slaveholder, to the special delights of country living. But it also subjected him to the limitations of rural life, to the rigidity of thinking among his neighbors, the paucity of good newspapers, and the intellectual stagnation that usually accompanies too great a preoccupation with the land.

Monticello was over a hundred miles from Williamsburg, almost seventy from Richmond. Jefferson's law practice would take him over wretched roads in all directions, and net him less than he expected because so many of his clients never paid their fees. But he chose not to settle in the Virginia capital, the intellectual center of the colony, or even in the smaller Richmond, rapidly burgeoning into a substantial trading center. Thirteen years after he first grafted cherry trees on Monticello slopes he wrote fervently: "Those who labour in the earth are the chosen people of God, if ever he had a chosen people, whose breasts he has made his peculiar deposit for substantial and genuine virtue. It is the focus in which he keeps alive that sacred fire, which otherwise might escape from the face of the earth. Corruption of morals in the mass of cultivators is a phaenomenon of which no age nor nation has furnished an example." [12] Later he wrote another line that became equally celebrated: "I view great cities as pestilential to the morals, the health, and the liberties of man." [13] His equating the

life of the planter and farmer with the life of virtue eventually became
so celebrated a part of Jefferson's philosophy that the ideal agrarian
life became almost synonymous in America with the word "Jeffersonian."

But if one looks at the private life of Thomas Jefferson in precisely
those years in which he committed himself totally to the rustic life,
some curious contradictions emerge. What exactly did Jefferson mean
by virtue, by corruption, and by morality? For if Jefferson truly believed, as he wrote in 1781, that laboring in the earth kept a man's
morals free from corruption, how do we square this with the fact that
the finality of Jefferson's settling into rural living in 1767–68 coincided
with his attempt, or attempts, at the seduction of the wife of his good
friend and near neighbor John Walker? This is an episode that is
still somewhat obscure, and somewhat comic. Its importance need
not be exaggerated, and indeed cannot be, inasmuch as the evidence
is so controversial and the details of what happened so scanty. One
may look at the Jefferson–Betsey Walker "affair" for questions that
have not been asked before. Did it serve to anchor him further to the
Albemarle area? Did it set a new pattern of secrecy for Jefferson in
matters of the heart, a secrecy that remained with him to the end of
his life? Did it represent the beginning of his separation of chastity
from morality, which also continued to the end of his life? Even if
none of these questions can be answered with assurance, the "affair"
does seem to illuminate what we shall see repeatedly in Jefferson's
life—that a preoccupation with planting often seemed to coincide with
an episode of lyric happiness, or with an attempt to recapture lyric
happiness, just as his abandonment of planting often coincided with
loss, death, and depression.

When John P. Foley in 1900 published *The Jefferson Cyclopedia*,
he combined under one heading everything that Jefferson wrote about
"morality," and the accumulation reached almost three thousand
words. For the heading of "virtue" he found about five hundred. But
the *Cyclopedia* does not have a heading for "chastity." Jefferson in his
writings stayed clear of the word, though the idea was implicit in an
occasional discussion of morality. Shortly after he passed the Virginia
bar, at age twenty-four, Jefferson took on a case involving adultery,
and entered the facts of the scandal in his casebook with earthy exactness: "David Frame (Augusta) directs me to issue writ in Scandal
agt James Burnside (Augusta). Burnside said he caught Frame (who
is a married man) in bed with Eliza Burkin put his [hand] on Frame's
as he lay in bed with the girl and felt it wet, and then put his hand
on his [*erased and inked through*] and felt it wet also." [14]

There was never again either such explicit sexual description or such candor in Jefferson's writings. On the four or five occasions in the remainder of his long life when he wrote about adultery, it was always with circumlocution, and always with compassion. He did write on occasion of "good passions" and "bad passions" in letters from France, but there he came to take a positively playful attitude toward violations of the marriage code. At sixty-six, when writing to a friend about the relation between religion and morality, he referred indirectly to the Ten Commandments—"Reading, reflection and time have convinced me that the interests of society require the observation of those moral precepts only in which all religions agree (for all forbid us to steal, murder, plunder, or bear false witness)"—omitting the injunction against adultery and several others.[15] From age twenty-six to sixty-six many things happened to condition Jefferson's feelings about the value or nonvalue of continence and chastity. Certainly his law practice must have provided an education in violations of the prevailing sexual code among whites, and he could hardly have escaped in his youth hearing many stories and perhaps witnessing or participating in the easy sexual contact so common among white men and slave women. Jefferson, however, as we shall see, fell in love only a few times in his life, and apparently always with great intensity. There is no evidence of which we have definite knowledge that he was ever promiscuous, or even simply casual about the affections. This must be kept in mind when looking at the "Mrs. Walker story."

John Walker was one of Jefferson's four best friends, and when he married Betsey Moore in June 1764 Jefferson stood as one of the "bridemen" at the ceremony. At William and Mary College Walker had been capable of enough youthful mischief to get himself "rusticated for a month," as Jefferson put it,[16] but after his marriage he became quickly domesticated, moving to a plantation called Belvoir, close to Jefferson at Shadwell, and assuming various civic responsibilities. By 1768 both he and Jefferson were planning to run for the House of Burgesses. By this time Betsey had borne her husband a daughter.

During the summer of 1768 Walker went off to Fort Stanwix to help conclude a treaty with the Indians, relying upon Jefferson to look after his wife and child. He even took the precaution of writing a will and naming the attractive bachelor his executor. He was gone four months, surely a hazard for the best of marriages, and an invitation to fantasies of adultery on his wife's as well as Jefferson's part, if not to adultery itself. Almost twenty years passed before Betsey made some kind of confession to her husband, and more than another decade would go by before Walker, goaded by the fact that political enemies of Jefferson had leaked rumor of the alleged seduction to the press in 1802, wrote down the details of what happened when he was off in Indian country and thereafter. This he did in 1805 in a letter to Jefferson's enemy, Light-Horse Harry Lee, who had married Walker's niece. The letter is by turns wistful, indignant, farcical, and improbable. There is no easy way to paraphrase it without loss, and since Jefferson's account of what happened so contradicts it, there is no alternative but to reproduce both and suggest that each version be read with caution.[17]

I was married at Chelsea the seat of my wifes father on the 6th of June 64. I was educated at Wm & Mary where was also educated Mr. J.

We had previously grown up together at a private school & our boys acquaintance was strengthened at college. We loved (at least I did sincerely) each other.

My father was one of his fathers exr & his own guardian & advanced money for his education, for which part of an unsettled act my father gave me an order on him returning from France & is the act to which he refers in our correspondence—

I took Mr. J. with me the friend of my heart to my wedding. He was one of my (bridemen).

This as I said above took place in 64.

In 68 I was called to Fort Stanwix being secretary or clerk to the Virginia commission at the treaty with the Indians there held by Sir W Johnson which was composed of Gen'l A Lewis & my father.

I left my wife & infant daughter at home, relying on Mr. Jefferson as my neighbor & fast friend having in my will made before my departure, named him first among my executors.

I returned in Novr. having been absent more than 4 months.

During my absence Mr J conduct to Mrs W was improper so much so as to have laid the foundation of her constant objection to my leaving Mr J my exct telling me that she wondered why I could place such confidence in him.

At Shadwell his own house in 69 or 70 on a visit common to us being neighbors & as I felt true frds. he renewed his caresses placed in Mrs W! gown sleeve cuff a paper tending to convince her of the innocence of promiscuous love.

This Mrs W on the first glance tore to pieces.

After this we went on a visit to Col. Coles a mutual acquaintance & distant neighbor. Mr. Jefferson was there. On the ladys retiring to bed he pretended to be sick, complained of a headache & left the gentlemen among whom I was.

Instead of going to bed as his sickness authorized a belief he stole into my room where my wife was undressing or in bed.

He was repulsed with indignation & menaces of alarm & ran off.

In 71 Mr J was married and yet continued his efforts to destroy my peace until the latter end of the year 79.

One particular instance I remember.
My old house had a passage upstairs with a room on each side &
opposite doors.
Mr J and wife slept in one. I & my wife in the other.
At one end of the passage was a small room used by my wife as her
private apartment.
She visited it early & late. On this morning Mr. J's knowing her cus-
tom was found in his shirt ready to seize her on her way from her
chamber—indecent in manner.
In 83 Mr J went to France his wife died previously.
From 79 Mr J desisted in his attempts on my peace.
All this time I believed him to be my best *frd* & so felt & acted
toward him.
All this time I held him first named in my will, as exct. ignorant of
every thing which had passed.
Soon after his sailing for France was known *Mrs* W then recurred
to my will & being as before asked her objections, she related to me
these base transactions apologizing for her past silence from her fear of
its consequence which might have been fatal to me.
I constantly wrote to him. You have our correspondence & you go
now to Mr. J. My injury is before you. Let my redress be commensurate. It cannot be complete & therefore ought to be as full as possible.[18]

Jefferson never responded publicly to accusations concerning ir-
regularities in his intimate life. He did, however, tell his presidential
secretary, William Burwell, in 1805, that "the affair had long been
known," and that Alexander Hamilton himself "had threatened him
with a public disclosure." He told Burwell further that the seduction,
or attempted seduction—Burwell does not make clear which was involved—was but a single attempt and was "without premeditation &
produced by an accidental visit." [19] There is in addition to this story,
which appears in Burwell's unpublished memoir, a single admission of
slight guilt written in Jefferson's hand; this is a letter to his Secretary
of the Navy, Robert Smith, in 1805, when he said, "You will perceive that I plead guilty to one of their charges, that when young and
single I offered love to a handsome lady. I acknolege its incorrectness." [20]

"Incorrect" is a mild word, suggesting that Jefferson felt no overwhelming remorse. He had committed a breach of decorum, not a sin.
He did not compound the breach by insinuating that Mrs. Walker
had encouraged him; such an admission would have served only to
damage them both, and as we shall see in a later chapter, Jefferson
promised Walker he would do what he could to minimize the publicity,
and went to great pains to avoid a duel. But one might guess from
Walker's letter that Betsey had indeed been seductive on her own

part, and over a long period. That it actually extended into the period of Jefferson's own marriage seems less likely, unless it consisted simply of harmless teasing on the part of both. But of this one cannot be certain.

Jefferson did not meet Martha Wayles Skelton until he was past twenty-seven. From twenty-four to twenty-seven he was exuberantly planting and building only a few miles away from the Walker plantation, and there is no evidence that he courted anyone except his neighbor's wife. He may, as he told Burwell, have tried seduction only once, and thereafter solaced himself with cultivating the earth. "It is incredible," biographer Schachner wrote, "that Betsey could have submitted to so many assaults on her virtue over a period of years without telling her husband, or ceasing to afford Jefferson opportunities to molest her." [21] Dumas Malone called the Walker letter "a disgusting tale which bore the marks of wilful exaggeration, whatever may have been the cause. . . . such an incredible story cannot be accepted in detail. All we can be sure of is that Jefferson made advances of some sort to his friend's wife, while he himself was single, that he deeply regretted his actions, afterwards, and that he accepted all the blame. . . . He was much more in character as a devoted husband and kind father than as an aggressive lover, and it is hard to believe that he would have persisted in the face of rebuffs at any age." [22]

Merrill Peterson believes "the seduction yarn was bawdily elaborated until it read like a chapter in a Richardsonian novel." [23] With all this lighthearted romping in nightshirts, pretended headaches, and verses in favor of adultery thrust into sleeves, the yarn reads much more like the novels of Henry Fielding, whose *Tom Jones* is at least as representative of eighteenth-century courtship as Richardson's sentimental volumes. Malone protests that "such gaucherie, and such personal aggressiveness in the face of rebuffs, were not characteristic of him as a man." [24] Perhaps he was not rebuffed unequivocally, or at all, and Betsey's confession was a farrago of half-truths. Or perhaps Walker wrote his own version of the confessions, insisting on his wife's innocence, to lessen public snickering at his own expense.

Jefferson himself in his famous letter to Maria Cosway called "My Head and My Heart" has his head counseling him in mild exasperation: "These are the eternal consequences of your warmth and precipitation. This is one of the scrapes into which you are ever leading us." [25] Why have Jefferson biographers been so intent on minimizing these "scrapes," or indeed effacing them altogether?

One of the curiosities in this story is that Betsey Walker waited until she was in her forties to confess that Jefferson had tried unsuccessfully to seduce her over a period of ten or eleven years. However she told it, John Walker could hardly believe that it happened exactly as he wrote it to Henry Lee. Thomas Paine would crystallize in an epigram the incredulity most Americans felt when the newspaper disclosures first appeared: "We have heard of a ten year siege of Troy, but who ever heard of a ten year siege to seduce?" [26]

What precipitated Betsey Walker's confession? It cannot really be, as Jefferson biographers have implied, that it was all blown up by Henry Lee for political purposes in 1802. For Walker wrote of the confession privately to Jefferson in Paris, May 15, 1788, and kept it secret for some years thereafter.[27] What appalled Jefferson, according to his secretary, William Burwell, was that Betsey herself in 1805 "countenanced the publications" in Hamilton's newspaper, the *New York Evening Post*. The *Post*, at its most flamboyant, stated that Jefferson "stole to the chamber of his absent friend at dead of night and attempted to violate his bed—and had not the shrieks of the out: raged female awakened an attendant who slept in the room, which obliged him to slink away, probably the crime of Tarquin had here been perpetrated." [28] This may suggest that by then she wanted terribly for the country to know that the attractive President of the United States had once madly pursued her. Countless women fantasy themselves the mistress of a president, and some succeed in turning the fantasy into reality. Whether Betsey Walker had been Jefferson's mistress or not did not matter in the end; most Americans believed she could have been. This might have been triumph enough for her.

Let us remember that George Washington as a young man fell overwhelmingly in love with his neighbor's wife, Sally Fairfax, and that she was a woman of wit, talent, and inner strength, married to what biographer James Flexner describes as "a punctilious and anxious husband," who "must certainly have seemed, in comparison with his powerful junior, a quivery white rabbit." There is no indication that she ever was so tactless as to show her husband Washington's letters, with his references to his "recollection of a thousand tender passages," and his reminiscence, written twenty-five years after her departure for England, of "those happy moments, the happiest of my life, which I have enjoyed in your company." But the letters were never destroyed, and became a part of the intimate Washington record, along with such wistful items described by Flexner as that Washington had bought at auction, when the Fairfax furnishings were sold, the bolster and pillows from Sally's bedroom. Saved, too, was a letter from Washington to his stepgranddaughter in 1795 that Jefferson might well have savored: "Beware of an involuntary passion. . . . In the composition of the human frame there is a great deal of inflammable matter, however dormant it may lie for a time, and . . . when the torch is put to it, *that* which is *within you* must burst into a blaze." [29]

The exact nature of Thomas Jefferson's affection for Betsey Walker, and hers for him, is simply nonrecoverable. There is no real evidence other than the jaundiced listings of the poor husband, hounded as a cuckold in the press from 1802 through 1805, and Jefferson's denials, which would seem to contradict them, but which might only have been conventional gallant efforts to preserve Betsey Walker's reputation and lessen what must have been her painful difficulties with her husband. It is worth noting that when all the publicity and passion were spent, and John Walker in 1809 was dying, he and his wife intimated to James Monroe that they would consider it an act of kindness to be visited by Thomas Jefferson. But Jefferson, then newly retired from the office of president, chose not to go. He sent instead a basket of figs.[30] This was early September, a time of harvest for numerous vegetables and fruits. If it occurred to Jefferson that the fig had an ancient symbolic history, relating to both love and sin, the recognition did not deter him in his choice of gifts.

CHAPTER VI

Martha Jefferson

> . . . the cherished companion of my life, in whose affections, unabated
> on both sides, I had lived the last ten years in unchecquered happiness.
>
> Thomas Jefferson, *Autobiography*

Little of significance is known about Thomas Jefferson's wife except for the passionate attachment she excited in her husband, and the fragility of her body when it came to bearing children. There are no portraits, not even a cutout silhouette, and only one letter, a conventional appeal to Eleanor Madison having to do with raising money and making clothing for soldiers of the Revolution. The letter is remarkable only for a tightness and rigidity of the calligraphy so extreme as to suggest great tension in the writer.[1] We are told by Jefferson's great-granddaughter that she was "very beautiful," "a little above middle height, with a lithe and exquisitely formed figure . . . a model of graceful and queenlike carriage." She had hazel eyes, auburn hair—a deeper red than Jefferson's sandy-colored hair—and exquisite skin. A family slave described her daughter Maria as "low like her mother and longways the handsomest, pretty lady jist like her mother."[2]

Martha Wayles Skelton was a passable harpsichordist and a sweet singer, as Jefferson's sister Jane had been, and music was an immediate bond between them. There is a story that two suitors met accidentally in the hall of her father's house, each believing himself favored, but upon hearing the sound of Jefferson and Martha singing together in the drawing room, they "exchanged a glance, picked up their hats and left."[3] Jefferson fell in love with her in 1770, when he was twenty-seven. There was general happiness over the courtship, except possibly for Jefferson's mother; a hint of her possible disapproval of her daughter-in-law surfaces in a portrait sketch written by Jefferson's granddaughter, who could not have known either of the two women:

> My grandmother Jefferson had a vivacity of temper which might sometimes border on tartness, but which, in her intercourse with her husband, was completely subdued by her affection for him. . . . She was a very attractive person and my grandfather was tenderly attached to her. She commanded his respect by her good sense and domestic virtues, and his admiration and love by her wit, her vivacity, and her most agreeable person and manners. She was not only an excellent housekeeper and notable mistress of a family, but a graceful, ladylike and accomplished woman, with considerable powers of concentration, some skill in music, all the habits of good society, and the art of welcoming her husband's friends to perfection. She was greatly liked by them all. She made my grandfather's home comfortable, cheerfully pleasant, just what a good man's home should be.
>
> She had been a favorite with her husband's sisters (we all know that this is a delicate and difficult situation) with his family generally and with her neighbors.[4]

The omission of reference to Jefferson's mother in the last sentence and the phrase "delicate and difficult situation," may suggest that she lacked enthusiasm for the marriage, though it is slight evidence. It is possible, as with many widows, that she would have unconsciously opposed any marriage for her eldest son.

Robert Skipwith, who married Martha's half sister Tabitha, in writing his happy approval of Jefferson's forthcoming wedding on September 20, 1771, described Martha as having "the greatest fund of good nature," and "that sprightliness and sensibility which promises to ensure the greatest happiness."[5] Jefferson for his part rejoiced also in Tabitha, writing of her to Skipwith as "dear Tibby . . . the first in your affections, the second in mine."[6] He described his father-in-law John Wayles in his *Autobiography* as "a most agreeable companion, full of pleasantry and good humor, and welcomed in every society." Wayles in turn thought highly enough of Jefferson to make him an executor in his will.

Much has been made of the fact that Martha was a widow, and that when Jefferson wrote out the marriage-license bond he described her first as "spinster" and then crossed the word out and wrote "widow" above it.[7] This tells us little except that he did not want to think of her as a widow, but as wholly his own. That he was enraptured is evident from an early letter: "In every scheme of happiness she is placed in the fore-ground of the picture, as the principle figure. Take that away, and it is no picture for me."[8] But Martha did come to Jefferson as the widow of his former friend, Bathurst Skelton, matured by marriage, sexually experienced, and also scarred by the tragedy of her husband's death. She had been married twenty-two months—November 20, 1766, to September 30, 1768—and brought to her new marriage a four-year-old son, John. She was, moreover, the product of a complicated family heritage that has never really been described.

John Wayles had seen three wives die. The first, Martha Eppes Wayles, had died within three weeks of her daughter Martha's birth. The second wife, a Miss Cocke, bore four daughters, three of whom, Elizabeth, Tabitha, and Anne, grew to maturity. After she died, Wayles married for the third time, one Elizabeth Lomax, widow of Reuben Skelton, but she survived only eleven months. At her death Martha Wayles was thirteen. Five years later, then eighteen, Martha married the younger brother of her second stepmother's first husband. Her half sister, Elizabeth Wayles, married Martha Wayles' mother's nephew, Francis Eppes.[9] The complications reflected the intimacy of rural Virginia life, where family gatherings were a major stimulus to matchmaking.

But there was an added complication. After the death of his third wife, John Wayles had turned for solace to a mulatto slave within his own household. This was Betty Hemings, who had already borne six children to a slave father. She bore John Wayles six more, and after his death two additional children, one to a white man, the other to a black slave.[10] Here was a woman of extraordinary vitality, resistant to all the infections of childbirth that carried off Martha Wayles' mother, and whatever diseases killed Wayles' other wives. All but three of her fourteen children would grow to maturity, their ages recorded in Jefferson's *Farm Book*, and she herself would survive at Monticello until 1807, age seventy-three.

A romantic story had followed her birth, which her grandson Madison Hemings wrote in detail:

> I never knew of but one white man who bore the name of Hemings. He was an Englishman and my great grandfather. He was the captain of an English trading vessel which sailed between England and Williamsburg, Va., then quite a port. My [great-]grandmother was a full-blooded African, and possibly a native of that country. She was the property of John Wales, a Welchman. Capt. Hemings happened to be in the port of Williamsburg at the time my grandmother was born, and acknowledging her fatherhood he tried to purchase her of Mr. Wales who would not part with the child, though he was offered an extraordinary large price for her. She was named Elizabeth Hemings. Being thwarted in the purchase, and determined to own his own flesh and blood, he resolved to take the child by force or stealth, but the knowl-

edge of his intention coming to John Wales' ears, through leaky fellow servants of the mother, she and the child were taken into the "great house" under their master's immediate care. I have been informed that it was not the extra value of that child over other slave children that induced Mr. Wales to refuse to sell it, for slave masters then, as in later days, had no compunctions of conscience which restrained them from parting mother and child of however tender age, but he was restrained by the fact that just about that time amalgamation [i.e., miscegenation] began, and the child was so great a curiosity that its owner desired to raise it himself that he might see its outcome. Capt. Hemings soon afterwards sailed from Williamsburg, never to return. Such is the story that comes down to me.

Elizabeth Hemings grew to womanhood in the family of John Wales, whose wife dying she (Elizabeth) was taken by the widower Wales as his concubine, by whom she had six children—three sons and three daughters, viz: Robert, James, Peter, Critty, Sally and Thena. These children went by the name of Hemings.[11]

Madison Hemings' memoir, of which this extract forms the beginning, has been in part repudiated by Jefferson biographers because Hemings claimed to be Jefferson's own son by Elizabeth's daughter Sally, and this claim they found insupportable. The reminiscences are most competently related; it is possible they were corrected by the editor who printed them. The details, insofar as they can be checked for accuracy in Jefferson's *Farm Book* and in the reminiscences of his overseer Edmund Bacon, show few errors of fact. Hemings described the saga of his grandmother's birth unpretentiously as "the story that comes down to me," and one must guess that it came directly from his mother, since he was too young to have remembered hearing it from Elizabeth Hemings herself.

"My very earliest recollections are of my grandmother Elizabeth Hemings," he wrote. "That was when I was about three years old. She was sick and upon her death bed. I was eating a piece of bread and asked her if she would have some. She replied: 'No; granny don't want bread any more.' "

Isaac, a slave at Monticello, whose reminiscences were dictated to Charles Campbell in 1847, described Elizabeth or Betty Hemings as "a bright mulatto woman," and differentiated her children as "bright" and "darker" mulattoes. "Folks said that these Hemingses," Isaac related, "was old Mr. Wayles's children." [12] We know from birth dates in Jefferson's *Farm Book* that Robert and James Hemings were born in 1762 and 1765, before Martha Wayles left home to be married to Bathurst Skelton. She could hardly have been unaware of their paternity, or that of four more "bright mulattoes"—three daughters and another son—who were born to Betty Hemings after her own departure.[13]

Winthrop Jordan has suggested that Martha Jefferson was "almost certainly ignorant of the situation," though he believes Jefferson was not.[14] But such painful secrets are precisely those that children are certain to sense, though they often repress the knowledge, and Martha could hardly be called a child. To discuss such miscegenation, at least in writing, even diary writing, violated one of the most dominant of all southern taboos. Mary Boykin Chesnut represented the exception to the taboo when a good many years later she wrote with ironic precision in her celebrated *Diary from Dixie*: "God forgive us but ours is a monstrous system, a wrong and an iniquity! Like the patriarchs of old, our men live all in one house with their wives and concubines; and the mulattoes one sees in every family partly resemble the white children. Any lady is ready to tell you who is the father of all the mulatto children in everybody's household but her own. Those, she seems to think, drop from the clouds." [15]

Eighteen months after Martha Skelton married Thomas Jefferson, her father died and she inherited 135 slaves. Among them were Betty Hemings and ten of her twelve children. Unlike almost all the other slaves in Jefferson's *Farm Book* they were accorded a last name, Hemings. Most of them became favored house servants. The darker Hemingses, Mary, Martin, and Bett, were brought to Monticello as early as 1774, one year after Wayles' death, along with two of the light mulatto boys "Jamey" (James), then nine, and his twelve-year-old brother Bob.[16] The "concubine," Betty Hemings, apparently came to Monticello in 1775. She was given a cabin, and there are references in Jefferson's account book of payments to Betty Hemings for "pullets" and "fowls," which indicate considerable independence and special treatment.[17] In 1775 Betty bore a son, John; Madison Hemings said his father was John Nelson, a white carpenter at Monticello.[18] In 1777 she bore a daughter, Lucy, said to be the daughter of a slave. As Madison Hemings wrote of his grandmother, "She had seven children by white men and seven by colored—fourteen in all." [19]

Betty Hemings' childbearing, and the cheerful giving of her body, spanned twenty-four years. Edmund Bacon, Monticello overseer after 1806, reported the story handed down among the slaves that Betty Hemings was among those who attended Martha Jefferson in her last illness.[20] If true, it would seem to reflect a friendship between the mistress of Monticello and the slave woman who had for so many years been mistress to her father. The fact that Martha, rather than any of her three white half sisters, had taken the whole Hemings family as part of her inheritance, and welcomed the children as house servants, suggests warmth and affection rather than repudiation, though it may have taken some years to develop.

What Jefferson thought of the miscegenation of his father-in-law must remain largely a mystery, no less than the attitude of his wife. Jefferson detested slave trading, but nine months after his marriage had to face the fact that John Wayles was advertising in the *Virginia Gazette*:

> Just arrived from *Africa*, the Ship Prince of Wales, *James Bivins* Commander, with about four Hundred five healthy *Slaves*: the Sale of which will begin at *Bermuda Hundred* on *Thursday* the 8th of October, and continue until all are sold.
>
> *John Wayles*
> *Richard Randolph* [21]

Jefferson's own grandfather, Isham Randolph, had made money in the same fashion. Within two years after his marriage Jefferson was actively agitating not only for an end to the slave trade but also for the gradual abolition of slavery. But he remained fond of his father-in-law, and took his slave children cheerfully into his own house. Betty Hemings' son Martin, dour and forbidding as Jefferson's grandchildren remembered him, was Jefferson's personal valet for many years. He would "voluntarily suffer no fellow-servant to do the least office for his master." He "watched his glance and anticipated his wants, but he served any other person with reluctance, and received orders from any other quarter with scarcely concealed anger." [22] When Jefferson went to France he took the "bright mulatto" James Hemings, hoping to make of him a fine French chef. But it is Jefferson's final involvement with Sally Hemings that suggests, as we shall see, that in matters of miscegenation John Wayles was an important parental model in his life.

Martha and Thomas Jefferson were married at her home, The Forest, in Charles City County, a few miles west of Williamsburg, on New Year's Day, 1772. After two weeks, leaving her small son behind, they set out on the hundred-mile journey to Monticello, visiting en route the Randolph home at Tuckahoe. Caught by a snowstorm, they abandoned the phaeton at Colonel Carter's house at Blenheim, and set out on horseback for Monticello, where Jefferson had erected a single-room structure somewhat apart from what was to be his palatial home. Jefferson's eldest daughter later wrote of what happened:

> They left it [Blenheim] at sunset to pursue their way through a mountain track rather than a road, in which the snow lay from eighteen inches to two feet deep, having eight miles to go before reaching Monticello. They arrived late at night, the fires all out and the servants retired to their own houses for the night. The horrible dreariness of

such a house, at the end of such a journey, I have often heard both relate.[23]

This account of a cold and cheerless honeymoon probably represents the unconscious deception daughters are likely to fall into. A different account has come down from friends to whom Jefferson also described the arrival in the snow. They reported to Randall that the bridegroom had a bottle of wine hidden behind some books and the "young couple refreshed themselves with its contents, and startled the silence of the night with song and merry laughter." [24]

It was all very symbolic. There would always be books at Monticello, their numbers increasing to thousands. There would always be a well-stocked cellar, with wine of notable quality imported from France. There would always be music—Purcell, Handel, Corelli, Vivaldi, and Boccherini, and later the works of Haydn. Even though his skill was then impaired by a broken wrist, Jefferson as a very old man would play the violin for his grandchildren.

On the morning after his arrival with his bride Jefferson recorded in his *Garden Book*: "the deepest snow we have ever seen. in Albemarle it was about 3 f. deep." [25] The pronoun "we" thus quickly crept into his writings. And so began the "ten years in unchecquered happiness." That Jefferson gave himself up totally to the privacy and passion of a good marriage is evident from the fact that he did not go back to Williamsburg to take his seat in the House of Burgesses, and missed the entire February session. This was the first but not the last time that Jefferson would put his wife before his politics.

The first year, however, brought the special kind of tragedy that would plague the whole decade they lived together, and make one wonder how Jefferson could possibly have described their marriage as he did. Little Jack Skelton died in June 1772, and three out of six of their own children would die before Martha's own calamitous death in 1782. Still, the phrase "unchecquered happiness" was in a special sense exact, for their affections, as Jefferson put it in his *Autobiography*, remained "unabated on both sides," and sorrow may well have served to deepen them.

There is some mystery about the date of Jack Skelton's death; for a long time biographers believed it had happened before the Jefferson marriage. But Jefferson's *Fee Book* in the Huntington Library makes clear that he was making purchases for the boy on February 26, and since his death date was June 10 (mistakenly copied as 1771 instead of 1772), it seems possible that he came to live out his last months at Monticello. Still, he was not buried at Monticello, and it is also possible that he remained with his grandparents instead of following his mother.[26]

The next three years saw the births of two daughters, Martha on September 27, 1772, and Jane Randolph on April 3, 1774. Martha, who was called Patsy, did badly till "a good breast of milk" was found for her in a slave wet nurse, and then she grew into a sturdy, healthy child.[27] There are no reported difficulties with either birth, as there were to be later.

The beginning years of his marriage transformed Jefferson into what Dumas Malone called "a deeply domestic being," and also into what seemed to be a very rich man. With the death of Wayles in 1773 he inherited not only 135 slaves but also 11,000 acres. He already had over 5,000 acres and about fifty slaves. Though a considerable debt rode upon his father-in-law's bequest, Jefferson sold about half the 11,000 acres and thought he thereby cleared his wife's share of the debt, which was £3,749.[28] He retained three plantations, Poplar Forest (in Bedford County), Elk Island, and Elkhill (in Goochland), as well as Monticello, and distributed the new slaves among them. Later, much to his chagrin, the notes given him in payment for the land and deposited in the Virginia Land Office during the Revolution were refused by Wayles' British creditors because of depreciation in American currency, and eventually he had to pay the debt twice. But in the early years of his marriage he thought himself rich, and moved easily into a pattern of gracious living that was always somewhat beyond his means.

Monticello was Jefferson's first creation, by Virginia plantation standards only moderately extravagant but certainly original. Though he went to books for his models, notably Andrea Palladio's Four Books of Architecture, and the works of British architects who had rejected the popular baroque for the simpler designs of antiquity, Jefferson was no slavish imitator. He was pragmatic, experimental, willing to revise and if necessary to tear apart in order to perfect. He was a measurer, a designer, an engineer, and a draftsman, fascinated by detail as much as by the total creation. He made mistakes, but instead of acquiescing and living with the perpetual evidence of his error, eventually he tore the house apart at great inconvenience and cost, redesigning and rebuilding until he had the perfection of the Monticello Americans know today, a miracle of light, elegance, and symmetry.

Some but not all of this was accomplished during the ten years of his marriage. During the first two years his slaves molded and fired thousands of bricks, blasted and dug great cellars in clay. Jefferson had planned an impressive central house with forty-eight-foot wings containing the service quarters. But these quarters, the kitchens, storerooms, wine cellars, and slave bedrooms, were to be covered with terraces and open outward in only one direction so that they remained largely unseen. Here he followed the architect Palladio, who suggested that a house, like a man's body, should be partly hidden.[29] The result was that the "great house," when first finished, as when later remodeled, appeared smaller, lighter, and more graceful than it really was.

Jefferson as an architect has been described as a classicist. But this does not mean he was a conservative. He built like no other man in Virginia in his time; his taste, if not revolutionary in architectural history, was nevertheless an expression of total independence of the architecture he had seen in American cities. When the Marquis de Chastellux, member of the French Academy, visited Monticello in 1780, he was captured by both the man and his house. "Mr. Jefferson is the first American," he wrote, "who has consulted the Fine Arts to know how he should shelter himself from the weather." [30]

Jefferson's garden and orchard plans recall the great gardens of England in their extent and informality; many of his plantings remind one of the magnificent orchards of the Italian Riviera and of southern France—figs, acacias, pomegranates, almonds, olives, nectarines, and oranges—as well as the more conventional walnuts, filberts, peaches, cherries, apples, plums, and pears. Hoping to stock a fenced-in forest park with deer, in the tradition of the great houses in England, he purchased "a deer and fawn" in 1776, and added "a buck and fawn" in 1778.[31] In 1782 Chastellux watched a score of deer eating out of Jefferson's hands.

Before his marriage he had ordered a "forte-piano" for his bride. "Let the case be of fine mahogany, solid, not vineered," he wrote. "The compass from Double G to F in alt. a plenty of spare strings; and the workmanship of the whole very handsome, and worthy the acceptance of a lady for whom I intend it." [32] Now he invited Francis Alberti, an Italian musician who had come to Williamsburg with a troupe of players and had stayed to be a music teacher, to come to Monticello and help improve his violin technique and to instruct Martha on the harpsichord. That he practiced three hours a day tells us something about his leisure as well as his musicianship.

True, he spent many hours at his law practice, on which he also made numerous trips. But, as his earlier biographers have pointed out, very few Virginians paid in cash, and many paid not at all. During Jefferson's first six years as a lawyer he earned £2,177, but collected only £692.[33] The number of delinquent clients in Virginia was so numerous that Jefferson in 1773 joined five other lawyers, including Patrick Henry, and published an announcement that they would give no opinion on any case without the payment of "the whole Fee," nor "prosecute or defend any Suit or Motion unless the Tax, and one half of the Fee, be previously advanced, excepting those Cases only where we choose to act *gratis*." [34] Jefferson had 941 cases in seven years, but the law was never his passion, and he abandoned it cheerfully for politics and revolution.

The law was an open door to politics, and no real barrier to revolution. Most of the hot-blooded young Virginians first ready to break with England were of this profession. But life at Monticello was the life of a baron. When Jefferson wrote that he planted olive trees and pomegranates, one must be reminded that he wielded no shovel but simply directed his slaves. His entire life style in these first years of his marriage pointed to aristocracy. He lived with the grace and elegance of many British lords; his house slaves alone numbered twenty-five. He loved fine wine, blooded horses, exotic orchards, manicured gardens, a great library, and the leisure for reading philosophy, playing music, and recording the vagaries of the weather. He had seen something of this kind of life at Williamsburg, in the place of the Governor, with Fauquier as his model. And he may well have had an important legacy from his mother in the folklore of the English great. Very early he copied from Euripides into his commonplace book, "To be of the noble born gives a peculiar distinction clearly marked among men, and the noble name increases in lustre in those who are worthy." [35]

What is really astonishing is that he became a revolutionary at all. How could this young aristocrat, master of over a hundred slaves, owner of thousands of acres, adored by an amiable and deferential wife, have come very early in his life to risk hanging? What were the promises of the Revolution? And what was his special need? Moreover, after the Revolution he did not slide quickly, as did Patrick Henry, into conservatism and money-making, nor even, like John Adams, into friendly admiration for the British monarchy. Instead he moved forward steadily to become, with Thomas Paine, the most consistent revolutionary of all the founding fathers, so consistent that he was for years denounced by many as an anarchist and a Jacobin.

There is no evidence that Martha Jefferson influenced the direction of her husband's political thinking, though there is a good deal to indicate that she was an extraordinary complication in his political life. There was a mighty and continuing struggle within Jefferson between aristocrat and democrat; and Monticello, to which he had brought this spirited and amiable widow, came to symbolize the aristocratic way of life. Chastellux caught the essence of Jefferson's aristocracy when he wrote in 1782 that "no object had escaped Mr. Jefferson; and it seemed as if from his youth he had placed his mind, as he had done his house, on an elevated situation, from which he might contemplate the universe." [36]

CHAPTER VII

The Revolutionary

As long as we were young and weak, the English whom we had left behind, made us carry all their wealth to their country, to enrich them;
and, not satisfied with this, they at length began to say we were their
slaves, and should do whatever they ordered us. We were now grown up
and felt ourselves strong; we knew we were as free as they were.

Jefferson to Jean Baptiste Ducoigne,
Kaskaskia Indian chief, June 1781 [1]

John Adams as a young man kept a diary, in which one can see his
fascination with politics as early as 1759, and his progressive explosions in ever increasing crescendo against British encroachments on
colonial power. But with Jefferson, though his evolution into a revolutionary is clear enough in his actions, the indignation and rage that
fired these actions have to be ferreted out. Merrill Peterson, noting
that Jefferson was "remarkably inarticulate about the process of thought
that conducted him to the revolutionary event," believed he found
the secret in Jefferson's extraordinary intellectuality, holding that he
"approached the world through his understanding rather than his
feelings." [2] But no man escapes the inexorable though often hidden
commands of his emotions. It is true that Jefferson more than most
men did seek to guide his actions by intellect and reason, but he was no
less pulled by affection or driven by indignation and rage than the other
revolutionaries of his time. As he put it in a celebrated letter, "If our
country, when pressed with wrongs at the point of the bayonet, had been
governed by it's heads instead of it's hearts, where should we have
been now? hanging on a gallows as high as Haman's." [3] Though much

90

of his indignation against the British crown was shared by thousands of other eager patriots, it nevertheless was highly personal with him, guided by the *Zeitgeist* rather than triggered by it. Moreover, there were in these years special other objects of indignation for Jefferson. He held attitudes and suffered emotions not appreciably shared by his fellow Virginians. These had to do with injustices against blacks and Indians, and his rhetoric against the enslavement and persecution of these peoples was very similar to that he employed in defending the colonists against England. Very likely the same rage engendered this rhetoric no matter what its target. That rage could have related to fears of his own enslavement, deriving from his sense of being controlled and manipulated by his parents, particularly his mother. One sees in his fragment of *Autobiography* written in old age how tenaciously entangled were his feelings concerning emancipation of the slaves and emancipation of the colonists from the mother country:

> In 1769 I became a member of the legislature by the choice of the county in which I live. . . . I made one effort in that body for the permission of the emancipation of slaves, which was rejected; and indeed, during the regal government, nothing liberal could expect success. Our minds were circumscribed within narrow limits, by an habitual belief that it was our duty to be subordinate to the mother country in all matters of government, to direct all our labors in subservience to her interests, and even to observe a bigoted intolerance for all religions but hers.[4]

The bill Jefferson refers to here was his first legislative act, at age twenty-four. Virginia law at the time permitted emancipation only for "meritorious services," whereas in North Carolina and Georgia a slaveholder could free a slave simply by registering the act in the county court. Jefferson asked that the right of emancipation by free choice of the slaveholder be granted to all Virginians. For reasons of courtesy he asked his older kinsman, Richard Bland, to offer the bill, with himself seconding it. Later he wrote bitterly of the explosion of opprobrium that followed, for Bland "was denounced as an enemy of his country." [5]

Instead of retreating, however, Jefferson within five years moved into the far more radical position of denouncing slavery as "an infamous practice." He insisted that its abolition was "the great object of desire" in the American colonies—this almost a year before the first abolition society was organized in America.[6] Still, when it came to his own private action there was a kind of seesawing, obvious uncertainty, and also evidence of great ambivalence in Jefferson about black people. In the same year that he suffered failure and abuse in the Virginia assembly for asking for the right to emancipate any of his slaves, a mulatto shoemaker and carpenter belonging to him named Sandy stole one of his horses and ran away. The escape did, to be sure, involve a theft. Still, Jefferson in the *Virginia Gazette* of September 7, 1769, offered a reward for his capture—forty shillings if he were taken in Albemarle County and £10 if caught in another colony. He described the man with distaste:

> He is greatly addicted to drink, and when drunk is insolent and disorderly, in his conversation he swears much, and in his behavior is artful and knavish.

Sandy was caught, and three years later Jefferson sold him for £100.[7]

With one hand Jefferson would in these years continue to shackle a slave who greatly desired freedom; with another he would reach out to unshackle another slave. In April 1770 he undertook the defense of a mulatto who sought freedom on the ground that his grandmother had been the daughter of a white woman and a slave father. The idea of a white woman bearing a child to a black man was abhorrent to all white Virginians, and was conventionally attributed to rape.* But such occurrences were more common than most whites were willing to admit, and consent of the white woman was far less rare than rape by the black man.[8] Jefferson took the case because he believed that the original daughter born to the white mother was legally free—for the status of the slave was determined under Virginia law not by color but by the status of the mother—and that her descendants should therefore also have been free.

Jefferson argued in this case that the sins of the father (or mother) should not be visited upon the child to the third generation, and certainly not to a "generation without end." He said daringly that "under the law of nature, all men are born free, and every one comes into the world with a right to his own person, which includes the liberty of moving and using it at his own will." For 1770 this was such inflammatory heresy in Virginia that the judge peremptorily cut Jefferson's argument short and gave the judgment to the mulatto youth's owner. George Wythe, Jefferson's law teacher—who would later be involved in miscegenation on his own part—had been attorney for the owner, and one wonders what he thought of Jefferson's radical approach, which surely cost the slave any chance of freedom.[9]

Thus, from the beginning of Jefferson's life as a political man and as a lawyer he was caught up not only in the slavery problem but also

---

* It was part of the folklore of the ignorant that a white woman who voluntarily bore a black child would have nothing but black children thereafter.

in the psychological complexities and ambivalences provoked by the issue of miscegenation. Moreover, it deserves notice that his phrase "all men are born free," which appeared six years later in his Declaration of Independence, and which has been traced with such zealous scholarship to men of the Enlightenment, first came to his lips publicly in the legal defense of a black man.

Jefferson was revolted not only by the idea of slavery but also by the casual slaughter of Indians, which had become commonplace on the Ohio frontier. In April 1774 a group of whites led by Thomas and Michael Cresap murdered a group of inoffensive Indians, including several women, one of them, as Jefferson wrote, "very big with child." As it turned out, the murdered Indians consisted of the entire family of a chief, Logan, long known as a friend of the white man. Logan took revenge by having his Shawnees kill a good many white settlers, including women and children. Virginia's governor, Lord Dunmore, led a group of militia into the area and defeated the Indians in the Battle of Point Pleasant. Logan, who escaped, sent a remarkable speech in his own defense that was widely reported in the Virginia press in 1775. Jefferson was so electrified by this speech that he copied it immediately on the only paper he had at hand—the blank pages of his pocket account book (the *Virginia Almanack* of 1775),[10] and later reproduced it in his *Notes on the State of Virginia* as an example of Indian eloquence, thus refuting Buffon's insistence that the American Indian was genetically degenerate. The speech became justly famous:

> I appeal to any white man to say, if ever he entered Logan's cabin hungry, and he gave him not meat: if ever he came cold and naked, and he cloathed him not. During the course of the last long and bloody war Logan remained idle in his cabin, an advocate for peace. Such was my love for the whites, that my countrymen pointed as they passed, and said, "Logan is the friend of white men." I had even thought to have lived with you, but for the injuries of one man. Colonel Cresap, the last spring, in cold blood, and unprovoked, murdered all the relations of Logan, not even sparing my women and children. There runs not a drop of my blood in the veins of any living creature. This called on me for revenge. I have sought it: I have killed many: I have fully glutted my vengeance: for my country I rejoice at the beams of peace. But do not harbour a thought that mine is the joy of fear. Logan never felt fear. He will not turn on his heel to save his life. Who is there to mourn for Logan?—Not one.[11]

Let us take a hard look at this Shawnee chieftain, for if ever Jefferson selected a hero, other than scholars like Bacon, Locke, and Newton, it was he. Here was a man of peace and conciliation, taunted for cowardice, but goaded by senseless slaughter into becoming a fierce and implacable warrior. The whole series of bloody episodes was reported in detail in the Virginia press in 1774–75, the most critical years in Jefferson's evolution into a revolutionary. Though he never condoned Indian killings of whites, yet he held the red man the more shockingly abused, and he paid special homage to the man of reason who had been turned by tragedy into a man of steel and vengeance.

Jefferson's first heady experience with the rhetoric of treason and revolution against the King of England came when he was twenty-two, when he stood at the door of the Virginia House of Burgesses and heard Patrick Henry storm against the Stamp Act. Every school child in America would eventually learn that Henry had cried "Caesar had his Brutus—Charles the First his Cromwell and George the Third—" only to be interrupted with cries of "Treason!," at which point he concluded calmly, "may profit by their example."

"I well remember the cry of treason," Jefferson wrote, "the pause of Mr. Henry at the name of George III., and the presence of mind with which he closed his sentence, and baffled the charge vociferated." [12] So Jefferson added to the imperishable folklore of the revolutionary beginnings of the United States.

Historians are now agreed that the outbreak of rage against the Stamp Act was not so much a reaction to a blatant act of British tyranny, for the tax by modern standards was trivial, but rather evidence of the extraordinary freedom to which the colonists had become accustomed. Andrew Burnaby, visiting America in 1759–60, had described Virginians particularly as "haughty and jealous of their liberties, impatient of restraint, and can scarcely bear the thought of being controlled by any superior power." [13] Americans did not object to taxes for building their own roads, but the Stamp Act revenues were shipped to England, as many protesters said, simply to fatten the pockets of the "debauched" men of Parliament. The revoking of the Stamp Act seemed a remarkable victory to the colonists—Jefferson watched the hysterical celebration in Annapolis in 1766—and served to intensify his own as well as the general American conviction of autonomy. As Gordon Wood puts it, "There was none of the legendary tyranny of history that has so often driven desperate people into rebellion." The colonists, Samuel Eliot Morison insists, were then "the freest people in the world, and in many respects more free than anyone today." [14]

Several of Jefferson's relatives were in the forefront of the revolutionary protest, notably his mentor, Peyton Randolph. It was his mother's first cousin, Richard Bland, whose pamphlet, *An Inquiry into the Rights of the British Colonies*, had served to reinforce the impact of Patrick Henry in 1766. There is also good evidence that Jefferson turned to the literature of Welsh protest—the legacy of his father—for revolutionary ammunition. He copied into his commonplace book from Simon Pelloutier's *Histoire des Celtes* stories of ancient Celtic peoples who elevated or deposed their kings as they wished, and who decided by a majority vote "all matters which affected the well-being of the state." [15] When Edmund Burke denounced the harsh treatment of the American colonies in Parliament on March 22, 1775, he likened the folly to ancient British efforts to "subdue the fierce spirit of the Welsh," noting that the only result was that Englishmen traveling in Wales "could not go six yards from the high-road without being murdered." [16] He was pointing to a history that many a Welshman's son in America would have learned at his father's knee.

Exactly what the royal power could mean to him personally Jefferson did not experience firsthand until 1769, ten days after he became a member of the Virginia assembly. The colonial legislators were considering how best to protest new British taxes on paper, glass, paint, and tea—the Townshend duties—which had served to dispel the complacency resulting from the victory over the Stamp Act. Parliament had dispatched two regiments of British regulars to quiet the wildly protesting Boston area, a political blunder that incensed the whole Atlantic seaboard. "To have a standing army. Good God!" Andrew Eliot wrote to Thomas Hollis, "What can be worse to a people who have tasted the sweets of liberty." [17] Those like George Washington who were veterans of the war that had driven the French from the continent for the further glory of the British crown saw the coming of the British regulars as a personal affront. But when Washington and other members of the Virginia assembly voted to make common cause with Massachusetts colony in protesting British tyranny, the new royal governor of Virginia, Lord Botetourt, ordered the assembly doors shut. So Jefferson was silenced after only ten days of service as a public man.

Lord Botetourt failed to see that every man in the Virginia House of Burgesses counted himself already a kind of monarch. Shut out from their regular meeting place, they simply moved to the Apollo Room of the Raleigh Tavern, elected Peyton Randolph moderator, and proceeded to take the first decisive step toward revolution. George Mason drew up the "Nonimportation Resolution," an agreement to boycott either by nonpurchase or nonconsumption practically all British or foreign goods, including wine and slaves. George Washington introduced it; Jefferson's name was number sixteen on the list of signers.[18] In the preface the colonists vowed "inviolable and unshaken

Fidelity and Loyalty" to the crown, but protested that Parliament was reducing Virginians "from a free and happy People to a wretched and miserable slavery." After signing it, the men all drank toasts to the King.

This agreement and similar ones reached in other colonies had far-reaching consequences. They brought about a repeal of all the Townshend duties save the tax on tea, and made Jefferson a convert to economic coercion.[19] But they also started a curious propaganda barrage. Virginians who every day exercised the power of life and death over blacks, who forbade slave gatherings save for worship, and who silenced dissent with whips and dogs, now began to chant of enslavement. The irony was noted at once in England. Dr. Samuel Johnson asked wryly, "How is it that the loudest yelps for liberty come from the drivers of slaves?" Horace Walpole wrote, "I should think the souls of the Africans would sit heavy on the swords of the Americans." And Edmund Burke pointed out that the urge for independence was fiercer in Virginia and the Carolinas than anywhere. "Freedom to them is not only an enjoyment," he said, "but a kind of rank and privilege." [20]

The word "enslavement" became a widespread shibboleth and rallying cry. John Dickinson in Philadelphia wrote in 1768, "Those who are taxed without their consent expressed by themselves or our representatives are *slaves*." Joseph Quincy cried out in 1774, "I speak it with grief—I speak it with anguish—Britons are our oppressors . . . *we are slaves*." Washington wrote in the same year that the English government was "endeavoring by every piece of art and despotism to fix the shackles of slavery upon us." And Jefferson himself wrote in 1774 of "a deliberate, systematical plan of reducing us to slavery." [21]

The enslavement of blacks was still legal in all of the thirteen colonies, and serious agitation against it was just beginning. Among the slaveholders who shouted "enslavement" at Parliament and King George, there were some who saw the hypocrisy. Many colonists had read John Locke and had come to believe with him in the natural rights of man to life, liberty, and property. They agreed with him also that slavery was a "vile and miserable estate of man." But in confronting their guilt about their own slaveholding, they found a solution in the simple psychological device of projection. "It is the British who are the enslavers," they told themselves and others. Their own enslavement of blacks and the fancied British efforts to enslave them stayed neatly separated in two compartments of feeling unbridged by any form of logic. But for Jefferson there was no such easy way out of the emerging national dilemma and contradiction, which was also for him a profoundly personal dilemma. When in 1769 he demanded of his peers in the Virginia assembly that he be given the right to free his own slaves, he was asking for something very close to a sovereign right. The right to free a black slave was bound up with the right to be free from the tyranny of a king or of Parliament. Most Virginians did not see this yet, and never would. But Jefferson did.

At least he saw it clearly in 1774. Between 1769, when he was locked out of the Virginia assembly, and 1774, when he wrote his first great revolutionary pamphlet, A Summary View of the Rights of British America, he had worked through the complexities of the problem intellectually. The emotional complexities he would never resolve. As Peter Gay has written, he might denounce slavery vigorously, "but could still live with, and off it." [22]

The period of relative quiet between the revocation of the Townshend duties and the Boston Tea Party on December 16, 1773, enlivened chiefly by the burning of the British revenue cutter Gaspee in June 1772, deceived many in both England and America into thinking that the American problem was settled. Washington, who knew the carnage of war and had been appalled at the thought of armed insurrection, happily subsided at Mount Vernon to work on plans to expand his acreage in the West. But like a great many other land speculators he was outraged at the new British land policy of 1768, which made it impossible for colonials to stake out easy claims beyond the mountains and which demanded instead their filing through agents of the crown. These agents favored the few large speculators who were friends of the King. So the annoyances festered.

Jefferson, as we have seen, began during this period to build Monticello, brought his bride there, and began also the long inner struggle of priorities in his life—between political agitation and grafting cherry trees. But he, like many other Americans from 1766 onward, began to read treatises on government, and there began in his life as in the lives of other key men what Bernard Bailyn has called "the most creative period in the history of American political thought." [23] Immediately after being shut out of the Virginia assembly he sent away to England for Locke's On Government, Jean Jacques Burlamaqui's Le Droit naturel, Warner's History of Ireland and History of Civil Wars, Stewart's Political Oeconomy, and the works of Montesquieu.[24] Whereas earlier he had read as a dilettante, now he read with a purpose that was almost obsessive, and he copied great sections on government into his commonplace books. From Abraham Stanyan's Grecian History he abstracted examples of Greek colonies that had revolted from tyranny. The Scottish Lord Kames became along with Locke his master and guide to the theory of natural rights. As Gilbert

Chinard has pointed out in his edition of Jefferson's *Commonplace Book*, Jefferson became an encyclopedia of historical precedents for the federative system of government, studying the Union of Utrecht, the governments of the Helvetic body, Denmark, Sweden, and Poland, and drawing up a long list of cases "showing conclusively, as he thought, that the crown of England was never hereditary nor testamentary and that, in fact as well as in law, the British kings derived their power from the consent of the governed." [25]

John Adams had begun in 1759 reading the works of the great men of the Enlightenment, admonishing himself in his diary in January of that year:

> Aim at an exact Knowledge of the Nature, End, and Means of Government. Compare the different forms of it with each other and each of them with their Effects on the public and private Happiness. Study Seneca, Cicero and all other good moral Writers. Study Montesque, Bolinbroke. [26]

Jefferson had some catching up to do, for after the Stamp Act there had been a phenomenal outpouring of pamphlets having to do with the Anglo-American problem, written not by professional journalists but by clergymen, farmers, merchants, lawyers, and plantation owners. By 1773 John Locke's natural rights theories had become as commonplace for discussions as the Epistles of St. Paul, and for a surprising number of colonists the science of Newton and the political and legal teaching of Locke, Voltaire, Burlamaqui, Rousseau, Beccaria, Grotius, Pufendorf, and Vattel had edged out John Calvin altogether. For Jefferson the old Trinity was replaced by a new trinity, Newton, Locke, and Bacon. As Bernard Bailyn has pointed out, "The colonists had no doubt what power was and about its central role in any political system," and there was a mushrooming consciousness of America's destiny in the context of world history. [27]

How the temporary peace was destroyed by the conspicuous and somewhat comical act of violence known as the Boston Tea Party was described immediately by John Adams, who wrote in his diary the next day, December 17, 1773:

> Last Night 3 Cargoes of Bohea Tea were emptied into the Sea. This Morning a Man of War sails.
> This is the most significant Movement of all. There is a Dignity, a Majesty, a Sublimity, in this last Effort of the Patriots, that I greatly admire. The People should never rise, without doing something to be remembered—something notable and striking. This Destruction of the Tea is so bold, so daring, so firm, intrepid and inflexible, and it must

have important Consequences, and so lasting, that I cant but consider it as an Epocha in History.[28]

Though there was nothing majestic or sublime in the spectacle of white men disguised as Indians and Negroes shrieking with delight as they heaved chests into the harbor, Adams was right; it was "an Epocha in History." It became so because a foolish British government chose to regard the Tea Party not as mere mob violence but as an act of insurrection. The subsequent actions—the blockade of the port of Boston, the abolition of all local government down to and including the office of sheriff and justice of the peace, the forbidding of peaceful assembly for political debate—and their impact on the remaining colonies need no description here. The impact on Jefferson was profound.

It took two forms, one a small action, persuading a group of Virginia radicals to ask the House of Burgesses to appoint a day of fasting and prayer asking "divine Interposition" to avert "the Evils of civil war," a political tactic he described later with satisfaction as being as effective as "a shock of electricity." [29] The other was more important; the crisis sent Jefferson to his desk. Thus, when the members of the Virginia assembly, having been repeatedly dismissed for trivial causes by the British governor Lord Dunmore, decided to meet illegally on August 1774 to elect delegates to a genuinely "Continental" Congress, Jefferson had prepared a remarkable revolutionary document for their inspection.

No one asked him to write it; the composition was in itself an act of arrogance, the kind of arrogance common in young men in revolutionary times, especially if they are greatly gifted. A *Summary View of the Rights of British America*, a closely reasoned statement of colonial grievances, has many times been dissected by scholars, and its intellectual sources traced backward with great skill by Gilbert Chinard, Dumas Malone, Daniel Boorstein, and Merrill Peterson. Max Beloff has noted of this forerunner of the Declaration of Independence: "One hundred and fifty years before Lord Balfour framed for the Imperial Conference of 1926 the famous definition of the status of the self-governing Dominions of the British Commonwealth, subsequently embodied in the Statute of Westminster, Jefferson laid down precisely the same principle. It is an interesting example of the permanent character of the major problems of politics and of the relatively narrow margins within which their solutions can be found." [30]

Though he did not ask for independence, Jefferson phrased the basic problem which Thomas Paine the following year would crystallize in the question, "Should an island govern a continent?"

Can any one reason be assigned why 160,000 electors in the island of Great Britain should give law to four million in the states of America, every individual of whom is equal to every individual of them in virtue, in understanding, and in bodily strength? Were this to be admitted . . . we should suddenly be found the slaves, not of one, but of 160,000 tyrants.[31]

The *Summary View* was Jefferson's first serious piece of writing. It was also, therefore, in an important sense autobiographical. The first substantial writing of any man opens windows on his private conflicts, and the *Summary View* can be studied for clues to the inner grievances of the man as well as the open grievances of America. There is great rage in it, rage that reflected the resentments of thousands, rage that was to be tempered in the polished cadences of the Declaration of Independence. But some of the rage was specific to the problems of Thomas Jefferson. In addition to the intellectual and economic grievances and the problems of deference and power which helped to bring on the American Revolution, there was a primitive generational problem. The normal conflict between generations, the fierce assertation of the young that they have the same rights as the old—which until the 1770s had been contained within the colonies—now became polarized between the "enslaved children" of America and the "mother country" and the King.

This can be seen best in Jefferson's *Summary View* if one peers through the intellectual content to the bare-knuckle feeling underneath. The *Summary View* becomes then, in intent and in feeling, a document not unlike the Ninety-five Theses Martin Luther nailed on the castle church door at Wittenberg. These, too, had been a personal statement—Luther against the Pope—also communicating tremendous rage, part of which, as Erik Erikson has brilliantly demonstrated, should have been properly directed not at the Holy Father but at Luther's own father. As Erikson has concluded, "The matter of indulgences set off the time bomb which had been ticking in Luther's heart."[32] So the destruction of political liberty in Massachusetts colony set off the time bomb that had long been ticking in Jefferson's heart. Let us look at his list of grievances, seeking their more primitive elements:

1. *You do not listen to us*—Of all our petitions "to none of which was ever even an answer condescended."
2. *You gave us nothing*—"Their [our] own blood was spilt in acquiring lands for their settlement, their own fortunes expended in making that settlement effectual."
3. *You are cheating us*—You "have raised their commodities called

for in America to double and treble of what they sold for before such exclusive privileges were given."

4. *You are unfair*—"Justice is not the same thing in America as in Britain."

5. *You take back what you have given us*—"One free and independent legislature hereby takes upon itself to suspend the powers of another, free and independent as itself."

6. *You punish the innocent*—"Without attempting a distinction between the guilty and the innocent [in Boston] the whole of that antient and wealthy town is in a moment reduced from opulence to beggary."

7. *You play favorites*—You sacrifice "the rights of one part of the empire to the inordinate desires of another."

It is obvious that these are common complaints of young people against their parents, and may well suggest something of the nature of Jefferson's deeply felt grievances against his mother, and perhaps even long buried and distorted resentments against his dead father. The *Summary View* struck a chord in countless young men in the colonies, many of whom felt great guilt at taking up arms against the mother country and the King. John Dickinson, a Pennsylvania lawyer whose "Farmer's Letters" beginning in 1767 urged negotiation without violence, frankly described himself and other colonials as children. "Let us behave like dutiful children," he wrote, "who have received unmerited blows from a beloved parent. Let us complain to our parent; but let our complaints speak at the same time the language of affection and veneration." Thomas Bradbury Chandler deplored radical agitation in 1774 as "disrespectful and abusive treatment from children," and conservative Isaac Hunt in his *Political Family* in 1775 also insisted that the colonies were children who owed obedience and deference to the mother country.

British statesmen from arch-Tory Charles Townshend to pro-American Lord Chatham, the elder Pitt, echoed the same theme. Townshend in the Stamp Act debate had described Americans as "children planted by our care, nourished by our indulgence . . . protected by our arms." And Chatham indulged in the same metaphor:

> I love the Americans because they love liberty, and I love them for the noble efforts they made in the last war. . . . [but] they must be subordinate. In all laws relating to trade and navigation especially, this is the mother country, they are the children; they must obey and we prescribe.[33]

Even the conciliatory Burke spoke of America as "in the gristle, and not yet hardened into the bone of manhood." [34]

No other figure of speech was better calculated to enrage the radical young men of America. John Adams wrote in his diary on September 24, 1775: "Ld. North is at his old Work again. . . . He rocks the cradle, and sings Lullaby, and the innocent Children go to Sleep, while he prepares the Birch to whip the poor Babes." Later, when the Declaration of Independence was finally signed, he wrote of it to his wife, triumphantly, including an extraordinary anti-maternal metaphor: "Farewell! farewell, infatuated besotted Stepdame. Independence at last." [35]

Thomas Paine, newly arrived from England and thrust into the revolutionary ferment of 1774, was quick to sense the nature of the colonial fury. "We may as well assert," he wrote, "that because a child has thrived upon milk that it is never to have meat, or that the first twenty years of our lives is to become a precedent for the next twenty." This sentiment, published in his great tract *Common Sense*, he reinforced later in an open letter to British commissioners in New York:

> Your failure is, I am persuaded, as certain as fate. America is above your reach. She is at least your equal in the role, and her independence neither rests upon your consent, nor can it be prevented by your arms. . . . Nothing hurts the affections of both parents and children so much as living too closely connected, and keeping up the distinction too long. . . . had you studied the domestic politics of a family, you would have learned how to govern the state; but instead of this easy and natural line, you flew out into everything which was wild and outrageous.[36]

Among the more "outrageous" suggestions was one Benjamin Franklin brought from England in 1775. He had overheard General Clarke say "that with a thousand British grenadiers he would undertake to go from one end of America to the other, and geld all the males, partly by force and partly by a little coaxing." [37]

Perhaps the most remarkable aspect of Jefferson's *Summary View*, considering his largely conventional and aristocratic life up to 1774, was his courage—effrontery in British eyes—in telling King George what he could and could not do in America. He wrote, in effect: You have no right to land a single armed man on our shores; you have no right to grant lands; you have no right to dissolve our legislatures. "Let not the name of George the third be a blot in the pages of history," he said. "The whole art of government consists in the art of being honest. Only aim to do your duty, and mankind will give you credit where you fail." It was all very highhanded and impudent for an unknown subject of thirty-one years.

Then he compounded the impudence with a threat: "Should the people take upon them to lay the throne of your majesty prostrate, or to discontinue their connection with the British empire, none will be so bold as to decide against the right or the efficacy of such avulsion." Again the figurative language is remarkable. "Laying the throne prostrate" gives a suggestion of rape as well as treason. And the word "avulsion" suggests a tearing away, as a piece of land in a great flood, in a catastrophe of natural violence. All of which was accompanied by a pious note about the mother country: "It is neither our wish nor our interest to separate from her. We are willing on our part to sacrifice every thing which reason can ask to the restoration of that tranquility for which all must wish." [38]

Jefferson started out for the revolutionary gathering at Williamsburg carrying this obviously treasonable document in his pocket, but was stricken with dysentery so severe he had to return to Monticello. He sent two copies on to the convention, one to Patrick Henry, who ignored it, the other to Peyton Randolph, who saw that it got a respectful hearing. Malone ironically calls the dysentery "unheroic." If the illness was psychosomatic, as it may well have been, Malone was indeed speaking truly.

Merrill Peterson acknowledges that Jefferson's body responded to extreme tension with severe headaches, and both Peterson and Malone note that Jefferson suffered grievously from diarrhea when he first became president.[39] There is abundant evidence in modern medical literature that diarrhea, like migraine, is a common ailment of persons who always contain their rage, and the two ailments frequently may be seen in the same victim. Jefferson must have known that his *Summary View* invited hanging. The published version was in fact sent promptly to England, where according to Jefferson it "ran rapidly through several editions," and got his name, along with that of Samuel and John Adams and John Hancock, on a proscribed list in a bill before Parliament.[40] George Washington would later admit that he and his men fought the Revolution "with halters about their necks."

The penalty for treason, as read by British judges sentencing Irish rebels in 1775, was as follows:

> You are to be drawn on hurdles to the place of execution, where you are to be hanged by the neck, but not until you are dead; for, while you are still living your bodies are to be taken down, your bowels torn out and burned before your faces, your heads then cut off, and your bodies divided each into four quarters, and your heads and quarters to be then at the King's disposal; and may the Almighty God have mercy on your souls.

CHAPTER VIII

Jefferson and Independence— The Domestic Problem

> Great leaders become great and they become leaders precisely because they themselves have experienced the identity struggle of their people in both a most personal and a most representative way.
>
> Erik Erikson

Jefferson was in the audience at St. John's Church, Richmond, March 23, 1775, when Patrick Henry made his celebrated speech in favor of arming the Virginia militia, concluding with the phrase that echoed around the world as certainly as the first shot fired at Lexington less than four weeks later, "Give me liberty or give me death!" The son of Henry's physician later wrote of what was apparently whispered about at the time but was afterward forgotten, "Whilst his towering and master-spirit was arousing a nation to arms, his soul was bowed down and bleeding under the heaviest sorrows and personal distress. His beloved companion had lost her reason, and could only be restrained from self-destruction by a strait-dress." The poor mad wife was "confined in a basement room . . . a trapdoor in the hall, near the entrance, where Henry went downstairs to feed her." [1]

Though it seems likely that any man with a psychotic wife would be thinking in terms of liberty or death, no biographer has suggested that something of Henry's misfortune might have influenced at least the intensity and flavor of his rhetoric. Defining the degree to which personal trauma subtly influences political action is one of the most difficult and hazardous of all biographical problems. But once one is alerted to the tragedy of Patrick Henry's strait-jacketed wife, who was to die within a year, one cannot but be struck with the extraordinary degree to which his speech reflected anguish on a personal as well as a political level:

> Suffer not yourselves to be betrayed with a kiss. . . . Have we shown ourselves so unwilling to be reconciled, that force must be called in to win back our love? . . . Shall we try argument? Sir, we have been trying that for the last ten years. . . . Shall we resort to entreaty and humble supplication? What terms shall we find, which have not been already exhausted? . . . We have petitioned—we have remonstrated—we have supplicated—we have prostrated ourselves before the throne . . . we have been spurned, with contempt, from the foot of the throne. . . . There is no longer any room for hope. I wish to be free. . . .
>
> Is life so dear, or peace so sweet as to be purchased at the price of chains and slavery? Forbid it Almighty God! I know not what course others may take, but as for me give me liberty or give me death! [2]

One can speculate too, in examining the impassioned pleas of Tom Paine for separation of America from Britain, that the intensity of this passion had something to do with the recent breakup of his marriage to Elizabeth Ollive. When Paine's first wife died in childbirth, old women of Thetford, England, blamed him, saying that he had demanded that his wife get out of bed too soon to cook for him. When he married again he was impotent. His new wife complained of this publicly, and he soon found himself "despised by the women, jeered by the men, and charged with want of virility." [3] Wretched and bankrupt, Paine went to London, where after a fortuitous encounter with Benjamin Franklin in 1774 he decided to come to America, leaving his wife behind forever. His "Reflections on Unhappy Marriages," published in the *Pennsylvania Magazine* in 1775,[4] in a most important way foreshadowed his *Common Sense*, the definitive argument for a total break with England. Very quickly Tom Paine adopted America as his mistress. Later he would write that "every thought of my heart was on the wing for the salvation of my dear America," and in 1793, as a revolutionary in France, he would argue against the execution of Louis XVI because he had "helped America, the land of my love, to burst her fetters." [5]

Washington's mother, as has been noted, was a termagant and a Tory, though his wife was a jewel of affability and charm who endured the rigors of winter encampments with her husband through the war and sustained him through periods of ravaging pessimism.[6] The danger of generalizing about either the wives or the mothers of the founding fathers becomes apparent, however, when we discover that John Adams' mother was very much a patriot. Still, she was frantic with fear for her son's safety, and pestered him with letters when he was in the Continental Congress. He wrote back saying he was more likely to die of dysentery than a cannon shot, and predicted, wrongly, that the British could no more take Philadelphia than capture the moon. His wife Abigail was as hot for the Revolution as her husband, remaining fearless through the occupation of Boston and fierce in her hatred of the British. In November 1775, when it was treason in Boston to talk openly of abandoning the crown, she disdainfully refused to sign a petition for reconciliation with the King.

"Let us separate," she wrote to John in Philadelphia, "they are unworthy to be our Brethren. Let us renounce them and instead of supplication as formerly for their prosperity and happiness, let us beseach the almighty to blast their counsels and bring to Nought all their devices." [7] Betsey Adams, wife of the volatile Sam Adams, the second most wanted American in England for hanging, described Tory Boston under the heel of the British army in 1775 as "a den of thieves, a Cage of Every unclean Bird." [8] John Adams was proud of his wife's spunky martial spirit, and reported to her with some pity the dilemma of the weak-kneed and bedeviled John Dickinson, who was always counseling caution and negotiation in the Continental Congress:

> His mother said to him, "Johnny you will be hanged, your estate will be forfeited and confiscated, you will leave your excellent wife a widow, and your charming children orphans, beggars and infamous." From my soul I pitied Mr. Dickinson. . . . I was happy that *my* Mother and *my* Wife . . . and all her near relations, as well as mine, had been uniformly of *my* Mind, so that I always enjoyed perfect Peace at home.[9]

What Martha Jefferson thought of the Revolution is a continuing mystery, and there are almost no clues. In destroying his correspondence with his wife, Jefferson made it forever impossible for anyone to sculpture an accurate image of her, and blotted out altogether her response to the crisis of 1775–76. In destroying the record of her personal feelings, he also blotted out his own. So we are left with inconclusive and tantalizing fragments, as with regard to his mother. The very destruction, however, is in itself a clue, and may indicate that he did not want her letters read any more than his mother's because there was something in them that troubled him. No president has been more sensitive about the judgment of history on his own life than Jefferson. Still, he preserved almost everything else. What happened in his domestic life in 1775 and 1776 to make him fearful that history might raise an eyebrow if it knew too much?

During early 1775 Jefferson served on committees to negotiate with the inept and fumbling royal governor of Virginia. But Lord Dunmore finally panicked, and in fear of the hot-blooded young rebels fled with his family to a British ship in Norfolk harbor, leaving the Virginians triumphantly in charge of their own destiny. Jefferson was elected to the Continental Congress, and set forth for Philadelphia, arriving on June 21, 1775. George Washington had just been made commander of the continental forces, elected, as Flexner puts it, "by an illegal junto representing thirteen mutually jealous and independent sovereignties," the commander in chief of a " 'Continental Army' in which he was, at the moment, the only soldier." [10]

Martha Washington burned all but two of her husband's letters to her, and all but one of hers to him, thereby not only rendering a disservice to history but also opening the door to rumors of rifts in her marriage. But she did keep one letter of surpassing significance, which tells us exactly how Washington felt when he committed himself wholly to the Revolution:

> You may believe me, my dear Patsy, when I assure you, in the most solemn manner, that, so far from seeking this appointment, I have used every endeavor in my power to avoid it, not only from my unwillingness to part with you and the family, but from a consciousness of its being a trust too great for my capacity, and that I should enjoy more real happiness in one month with you at home than I have the most distant prospect of finding abroad, if my stay were to be seven times seven years. But as it has been a kind of destiny that has thrown me upon this service, I shall hope that my undertaking it is designed to answer some good purpose.[11]

One cannot but regret that there is no comparable letter from Thomas to Martha Jefferson.

Washington was already a hero to Jefferson, who was eleven years younger, and who at a most impressionable age had heard the stories of his exploits in the French and Indian War. Having missed the dinner in honor of Washington's new appointment, Jefferson rode out with him for some distance when he left with a contingent of militia for the Boston area several days later. There were drums and martial music in this parade of departure. Ballad makers already had begun their songs of praise:

> We have a bold commander, who fears not sword nor gun
> The second Alexander—his name is Washington.

His men are all collected, and ready for the fray.
To fight they are directed—for North Americay.[12]

Jefferson was now caught up in the excitement of being for the first
time at the revolutionary center. He met the celebrated Benjamin
Franklin, John and Samuel Adams, John Hancock, and many others
whose names would grace his Declaration of Independence, all of
them veterans of Congress's multitudinous difficulties. John Adams
had come a long way from the anxious days of 1774, when after his
own election he had written in his diary:

> I wander alone, and ponder.—I muse, I mope, I ruminate.—We
> have not Men, fit for the Times. We are deficient in Genius, in Edu-
> cation, in Gravel, in Fortune—in every Thing. I feel unutterable Anxi-
> ety.—God grant us Wisdom, and Fortitude!
> Should the Opposition be suppressed, should this Country submit,
> what Infamy and Ruin! God forbid. Death in any Form is less
> terrible.[13]

How long before Adams acknowledged Jefferson as "fit for the times"
is not clear. Samuel Ward, delegate from Rhode Island, who had
read Jefferson's *Summary View*, wrote home on July 22, 1775: "Yesterday the famous Mr. Jefferson a Delegate from Virginia in the Room
of Mr. Randolph arrived. I have not been in Company with him yet,
he looks like a very sensible, spirited, fine Fellow and by the Pamphlet
which he wrote last Summer he certainly is one." [14] Almost at once
Jefferson was put to work rewriting a committee report "on the Necessity of Taking up Arms," and then served with Franklin and John
Adams writing a draft of "Resolutions of Congress on Lord North's
Conciliatory Proposal." Like Franklin he almost never took part in
open debate, but quickly became known for his excellence in committees, and served altogether during 1775–76 on thirty-four.[15]

Like many young men thrust into legislative work, he felt himself
to be, despite his prodigious industry, of no real consequence. He
was thirty-two, the second youngest man in the Continental Congress,
and had no idea that he was making any impression on his older peers,
or that he was leaving so much as a thumbprint on the proposals
that had anything to do with power. Adams, for one, was watching
him with enthusiasm, and commented on his erudition in his diary
on October 25, 1775: "Duane says that Jefferson is the greatest Rub-
ber off of Dust that he has met with, that he has learned French,
Italian, Spanish and wants to learn German." Later Adams wrote that
Jefferson brought to the Congress "a reputation for literature, science,
and a happy talent of composition. . . . he was so prompt, frank,
explicit, and decisive upon committees and in conversation—*not even*

Samuel Adams was more so—that he soon seized upon my heart." [16]
So there began one of the great friendships in political history. It
would suffer vicissitudes, collapse for a long period, and then be rescued
for an old age of magical understanding and communication.

In Philadelphia, Adams as well as Jefferson pined audibly for home
and family. "I had rather build stone Wall upon Penns Hill, than be
the first Prince in Europe, the first General, or first senator in America," Adams wrote to his wife on August 18, 1776, and later, "I lead
a lonely melancholy life, mourning the loss of all the Charmes of Life,
which are my family, and all the Amusement that I ever had in Life
which is my farm." [17] But such moods with Adams were transient. He
was wholly addicted to politics and the Revolution; and he wanted
very much to be the "first senator in America."

Jefferson, on the other hand, showed an almost frenetic vacillation
from his political enthusiasm in the early weeks of 1775 to his surprising but determined resignation from the Congress on September
2, 1776. His first trip home to Monticello came two months after his
arrival, when Congress went into a brief recess in late August 1775.
Thus it happened that he was home in September when his younger
daughter died. Little Jane Randolph had lived eighteen months, long
enough to become greatly loved, and her death must have compounded
Jefferson's reluctance to leave his wife. One might surmise that in
view of Martha's delicate health and the increasing chances of
invasion and widespread fighting along the coast, Jefferson would not
ask her to accompany him to Philadelphia, though the wives of other
Virginia delegates, like that of Peyton Randolph and Thomas Nelson,
Jr., had followed their husbands over the bad roads and bridgeless
rivers to America's largest city and revolutionary center. Actually
Martha Jefferson was well enough to travel to The Forest in Charles
City, much nearer to the coast and the British men-of-war than Monticello, and more immediately exposed than Philadelphia. She spent
some weeks there with her sister, Elizabeth Eppes.[18] That she turned
to her sister instead of her husband in this period of mourning is, one
suspects, important evidence that she had no enthusiasm whatever for
Philadelphia and all it represented. It may be simply that she could
not bear the thought of continuing her mourning among strangers,
but when Jefferson tried to persuade her to accompany him on a later
occasion, he was again without success.

During his sad visit home Jefferson learned firsthand that his Randolph relatives were being torn apart by the revolutionary controversy.
His mother's kin, John Randolph, Virginia's attorney general, was so
outraged by what he counted the treason of his Virginia peers that
he was selling his lands and possessions and taking his family to England. Long ago John Randolph and Thomas Jefferson had made a

formal agreement of affection, signing a document which stipulated that should Thomas die first John would inherit £100 sterling worth of his books, and that should John die first Jefferson would inherit his violin and his music. Now, with John about to leave for Europe, Jefferson elected to purchase the coveted violin, and Randolph sold it to him for £13. The exchange of letters between these cousins has the same melancholy overtones we see in letters where families were similarly divided by the American Civil War. Randolph's hot-blooded young son Edmund refused absolutely to go to England with his father, and Peyton Randolph, now Speaker of the Continental Congress and one of the foremost men of the Revolution, promised to adopt him as his own. Jefferson's mother must certainly have been an anguished observer of this family disintegration. We cannot be absolutely certain that she was hostile to the Revolution, but she could hardly have failed to suffer anxieties about her son being hanged, and the departure of her cousin for England could have served only to heighten them.

Jefferson's first letter to his Tory kinsman, written from home on August 25, 1775, reveals that his return to Monticello had brought a temporary revulsion against the whole revolutionary upheaval. "I hope the returning wisdom of Great Britain will e'er long put an end to this unnatural contest," he wrote, and described himself as one of those "who still wish for a reunion with their parent country." Still he gave way, in the end, to sudden and violent belligerence: "But I am one of those too who rather than submit to the right of legislating for us assumed by the British parliament, and which late experience has shewn they will so cruelly exercise, would lend my hand to sink the whole island in the ocean." [19]

Shortly after John Randolph went to England, Jefferson was dining with Peyton Randolph in a restaurant outside Philadelphia when the older man was stricken with a paralytic stroke. He died within five hours. Of all Jefferson's kin, this man had been closest to a replacement for his father, and though he never designated him as his second father as he did George Wythe, Jefferson acknowledged Randolph, along with Wythe and Dr. Small, as the three most influential mentors in his life. Jefferson now wrote to his cousin in England "the melancholy intelligence of the death of our most worthy Speaker," and described briefly the military events that had occurred since his departure, especially in Virginia, where Lord Dunmore's attempt to burn the town of Hampton had raised the countryside "into perfect phrensy." The letter was explosive, bitter, and burning for "separation."

> Beleive me Dear Sir there is not in the British empire a man who more cordially loves a Union with Gr. Britain than I do. But by the

god that made me I will cease to exist before I yeild to a connection on such terms as the British parliament propose and in this I think I speak the sentiments of America. We want neither inducement nor power to declare and assert a separation. It is will alone which is wanting and that is growing apace under the fostering hand of our king. One bloody campaign will probably decide everlastingly our future course; I am sorry to find a bloody campaign is decided on. . . .

we must drub you soundly before the sceptered tyrant will know we are not mere brutes, to crouch under his hand and kiss the rod with which he deigns to scourge us.[20]

It can be seen that the last violent metaphor echoed the cruelty of plantation punishment for blacks. Jefferson truly felt the colonists were being lashed, like slaves. He was also, in the contradictory fashion of most revolutionary slaveowners, disturbed at rumors that Lord Dunmore, in addition to harassing settlements along the coast by bombardment, had promised freedom to any slave who would flee his rebel master to join the standard of the King, and was urging the slaves generally to insurrection. John Adams noted in his diary on September 24, 1775:

These Gentlemen give a melancholy Account of the State of Georgia and S. Carolina. They say that if 1000 regular Troops should land in Georgia and their commander be provided with Arms and Cloaths enough, and proclaim Freedom to all the Negroes who would join his Camp, 20,000 Negroes would join it from the two Provinces in a fortnight. The Negroes have a wonderful Art of communicating Intelligence among themselves. It will run severall hundreds of Miles in a Week or Fortnight.[21]

Thus it is not surprising that when Jefferson, who wrote regularly to his wife once a week, heard nothing from her or her relatives at The Forest from September 30 to November 7, 1775, he became frantic with anxiety. In a letter to his brother-in-law, Francis Eppes, on the latter date, he protested: "I have never received the scrip of a pen from any mortal in Virginia since I left it. nor been able by any enquiries I could make to hear of my family. . . . The suspense under which I am is too terrible to be endured. If anything has happened for god's sake let me know it." [22]

On November 7, 1775, Lord Dunmore officially proclaimed freedom to any Negro who would enter "His Majesty's Troops," and by November 24 John Page was writing to Jefferson that "Numbers of Negroes, and Cowardly Scoundrels" were flocking to his standard. Dunmore, he said, was "now so much reinforced that he is become not only very secure but formidable," and he predicted that the militia companies under Patrick Henry would be helpless against a general

"Insurrection of the Negroes." By early December Dunmore had nearly 300 slaves in military garb, the inscription "Liberty to slaves" emblazoned on each breast.[23] Robert Carter Nicholas reported more alarmingly to Jefferson that British ships were "plying up the Rivers, plundering plantations and using every Art to seduce the Negroes. The Person of no Man in the Colony is safe, when marked out as an Object of their Vengeance; unless he is immediately under the Protection of our little Army." [24] Jefferson urged his wife and Eppes to move further inland—"I have written to Patty a proposition to keep yourselves at a distance from the alarms of Ld. Dunmore"—and promised to join them.[25] Although Congress decided to sit in continuous session, having abandoned plans for adjournment in late December, Jefferson set off for Monticello on December 28, 1775.

Then an extraordinary thing happened. Jefferson dropped out of sight for four months. Other biographers have slurred over this episode. Schachner finds the reasons "obscure," but notes that other delegates "came and went with considerable nonchalance." Malone says that "his fears about his wife's health had started. Also there were many things he wanted to do at Monticello. It was high time that he went home." Peterson notes that Virginia delegates had only one vote in any case, so that any single delegate could represent his colony, which was true enough, and Chinard holds that Jefferson, who had been made commander of the Albemarle County militia on September 26, 1775, went home to organize for the safety of his family.[26]

None of these explanations, or even all of them together, quite explain the length of the absence or the more surprising fact that during this period Jefferson wrote no letters.[27] Thomas Nelson, Jr., another Virginia delegate and a good friend, wrote on February 4, 1776, begging him to bring Martha to Philadelphia, telling him his own wife would nurse her should she use the opportunity to be inoculated against smallpox. This pressure could hardly have been lost on Jefferson, but he did not even answer Nelson for over three months. By then he had returned to Philadelphia and, finding Nelson away, wrote tersely, "I am here in the same uneasy anxious state in which I was last fall without Mrs. Jefferson who could not come with me." [28]

What kept Jefferson in this curious isolation? Washington on New Year's Day 1776 had raised the new American flag; Congress had authorized a force under Benedict Arnold to invade Canada. The war was on in earnest. Jefferson's *Garden Book*, astonishingly, has no entries in 1776, though he was in Monticello through most of the period of spring planting. (His account book does mention that on February

20 he bought a deer for stocking his park.) In his *Autobiography* he skips from July 22, 1775, to May 15, 1776, leaving a total blank for this mysterious interruption in his political life.

Nathan Schachner has written that Jefferson "was never capable of prolonged and sustained political effort," and that his flights to Monticello, especially in defeat, served as periods of regeneration. "He seemed to draw Antaeus-like sustenance from the soil; and the problems he had incontinently quit welled once more in his mind and ripened to reflective solution. When that occurred, he returned to the hustings." [29] Though there is some truth in this, one must note that the flights to Monticello were often periods of intense conflict. Whenever Jefferson returned home, he moved in the direction of prudence and restraint, but never without guilt. This four-month period was one of palpable political regression.

He wrote only one paper, "Refutation of the Argument that the Colonies Were Established at the Expense of the British Nation," so bookish and feeble even in its author's mind that he seems never to have considered publication. It consisted mostly of a description of the early settlement of Virginia drawn from Hakluyt's *Voyages*. His attack on the King was ambiguous, his thesis disorganized, confused, and obscure. "Kings are much to be pitied," he wrote, "who, misled by weak ministers, and deceived by wicked favourites, run into political errors, which involve their families in ruin." [30] One suspects that it was the fear of ruin of his own family, should the Revolution fail, that was holding Jefferson in thrall, and that someone at home was frantic about his own "political errors."

In February Jefferson received from Thomas Nelson a copy of Tom Paine's explosive pamphlet *Common Sense*. Paine smashed like a village pugilist at George III, "this wretch. . . . with the pretended title of father of his people":

> . . . a thirst for absolute power is the natural disease of monarchy.
> . . . In England a King hath little more to do than to make war and give away places; which in plain terms, is to impoverish the nation. . . .
> A pretty business indeed for a man to be allowed eight hundred thousand pounds sterling a year for, and worshipped into the bargain! Of more worth is one honest man to society, and in the sight of God, than all the crowned ruffians that ever lived.

The whole folklore of kingship—the encrustation of superstition, the residue of the ancient belief that he who touched the king must die, and the corollary notion that he who was touched by the king would be healed—all of this Paine shrugged aside as idiocy. Though he had been brought up by his Quaker father in a strong tradition of dissent, his daring was nevertheless remarkable. Europeans fled to America, Paine said, "not from the tender embraces of the mother, but from cruelty of the monster"—which reminds one that Paine as a boy had run away to sea, and had been brought back by his father, only to run away again. Like Jefferson, Paine wrote well of his father but not of his mother; the latter emerges from the Paine documents as a carping woman with a desiccated soul.

Paine's rage against George III is obvious not only in *Common Sense* but also in his later revolutionary tracts. He was the first pamphleteer to call openly for a break with the King, using not only British history but also the Bible with great adroitness to destroy the idea of this sanctity of monarchy. He wrote about America's future with such clarity and prescience that this pamphlet captured Washington at once, and the many other American soldiers to whom the latter in his enthusiasm distributed copies.

> We have it in our power to begin the world over again. . . . 'Tis not the concern of a day, a year, or an age; posterity are virtually involved in the contest, and will be more or less affected even to the end of time, by the proceedings now. Now is the seed-time of the Continental union.[31]

Jefferson read the great tract, but did not move from Monticello. Washington meanwhile scored a victory of enormous psychological importance, moving into Dorchester Heights and forcing the evacuation of the British forces from Boston. Abigail Adams, who had written to her husband on March 2, "The canon continued firing, and my heart beat pace with them all night," reported the departure of the British on March 16 with a kind of ecstasy: "Shurely it is the Lords doing and it is Marvelous in our Eyes." By March 31 she was urging a final snapping of the ancient cords: "I long to hear that you have declared an independency." [32] The same sentiment was sweeping through Virginia. John Page, unaware that Jefferson had abandoned the Continental Congress, wrote to him from Williamsburg on April 6, 1776, "For God's sake declare the Colonies independent at once, and save us from ruin." [33] Still, weeks went by and Jefferson did not return to Philadelphia, and his friends increasingly came to believe that he had given himself up, if not to Toryism, certainly to affectionate abandon with his wife.

Jefferson was about to return at the end of March—so at least he intimated later to Thomas Nelson—when his mother died unexpectedly after an illness lasting "not more than an hour." Whereupon Jefferson was struck by an incapacitating headache that kept him away from Philadelphia for a further six weeks, until May 14.[34] Of all Jefferson's terrible headaches this was the longest. He suffered such headaches, "paroxysms of the most excruciating pain," he said, once every seven or eight years before they finally disappeared altogether after he left the presidency. They came on "every day at sunrise, and never left me till sunset." [35]

In the clinical literature of our own time one reads that migraine sufferers, including the many who share the "sunup-to-sundown syndrome," are generally "anxious, striving, perfectionist, order-loving, rigid persons, who, during periods of threat or conflict, become progressively more tense, resentful, and fatigued. The elaboration of a pattern of inflexibility and perfectionism to deal with feelings of insecurity begins early in childhood. The person with migraine attempts to gain approval by doing more and better work than his fellows, by 'application' and 'hard work' . . . at a high cost of energy." Most such attacks cease after age fifty.[36]

All of this describes Thomas Jefferson. Since he had so few major attacks, and since his whole life has been charted almost day by day, these headaches become a reliable indication of when he was most suffering from tension, and an almost infallible clue to what kinds of problems shattered the stability of this compulsively controlled man. There had already been occasional brief and odd encounters with migraine. When he had looked down from the summit of Virginia's famous Natural Bridge, which he would describe in his *Notes on the State of Virginia* as "the most sublime of Nature's works," it gave him "a violent head ach." Although the sides of the bridge, he said, "are provided in some parts with a parapet of fixed rocks, yet few men have resolution to walk to them and look over into the abyss. You involuntarily fall on your hands and feet, drop to the parapet and peep over it." But the arch itself, as seen from below, "so elevated, so light, and springing, as it were, up to heaven," brought on a "rapture . . . really indiscribable!" [37] Jefferson eventually purchased the Natural Bridge to be his very own property, and took many guests the long ride on horseback to share in its wonder.

Word of the severity of Jefferson's headache in April 1776 went all the way to Williamsburg. At least Edmund Pendleton had heard about it, though he seems to have missed the news of Jefferson's mother's dying.

> Your return to Virginia and my continued hopes of the pleasure of seeing you, postponed my writing 'til I heard you had resumed your charge in Congress. . . . I am sorry to hear your pleasure at home was interrupted by an inveterate head ach, (I don't remember the hard name for it) which I hope you travelled off.[38]

There would seem to be a hint in this letter of negative feelings in Williamsburg about Jefferson's "pleasure at home." If so, it was not the last.

Before setting out for Philadelphia Jefferson, like a prudent husband, left an account of his debts, and the money owed him, and gave £10 to his wife, all jotted down in his account book. Nevertheless he left one duty undone. It would be eleven months, as we have noted, before he would write in his account book, April 11, 1777, "Pd Mr. Clay for preaching my mother's funeral sermon 40/."

Return to Philadelphia brought a sense of rebirth. "I have been so long out of the political world," Jefferson wrote to John Page on May 17, "that I am almost a new man in it." [39] The six weeks after his return from Monticello saw a phenomenal burst of productivity, the most spectacular in Jefferson's life. Between May 17 and June 28, 1776, he wrote his two most famous political documents, the constitution for Virginia, and the Declaration of Independence. Gone was his lethargy, gone forever his misgivings about the Revolution, and in this light his phrase, "I am almost a new man" takes on a special significance.

The writing of the Virginia constitution has been overshadowed by two hundred years of acclaim for the Declaration of Independence. But this constitution, as Julian Boyd has emphasized, contains "indeed most if not all of the leading principles to which Jefferson's entire career was dedicated" [40]—the rights of the citizen against totalitarian control, the importance of a broad-based suffrage, the development of the West in the hands of independent farmers, decent treatment of the Indians, abolition of primogeniture and entail, and the control of military authority by elected civilians. And it was a document of such elaborate political sophistication that it could hardly have sprung, Athena-like, from Jefferson's head without the intellectual preparation that had been going on for several years. Still, there is no evidence that the four months at Monticello saw active and deliberate advance work for either of these great documents of state. On the contrary, all the evidence indicates that he jumped hastily into the constitution writing only after he returned to Philadelphia, when he learned for the first time what was going on in Williamsburg. Moreover, in May 1776 he had no expectation of being asked to write the Declaration of Independence and almost missed the writing of it altogether.

On his return Jefferson had been appalled to read a letter from John Page in Williamsburg saying he hoped that the new Virginia constitution would be written to resemble the old one as nearly as "Circumstances, and that Merit of that Constitution will admit of." Realizing belatedly that the political structure of Virginia was about

to be remade, and remade badly, unless he could be on hand to prevent it, he wrote immediately to Thomas Nelson, Jr., hinting that he
be released from his congressional duties to go to Williamsburg to
work on the new constitution.

> It is the work of the most interesting nature and such as every in-
> dividual would wish to have his voice in. In truth it is the whole object
> of the present controversy; for should a bad government be instituted
> for us in the future it had been as well to have accepted at first the
> bad one offered to us from beyond the water without the risk and
> expense of contest.[41]

The argument was eminently sensible; unless we get a good government in Virginia why fight a war? Jefferson also wrote to Edmund
Pendleton, president of the Virginia Constitutional Convention, asking for a formal release from his Philadelphia duties. He asked Dr.
Gilmer to explain his reason, and gave as one excuse the delicate
health of Martha Jefferson. The Convention found this excuse
frivolous and turned his request down.[42] Meanwhile Jefferson speed-
ily perfected his own version of a constitution, writing three drafts
in thirteen days. The last draft he sent on to Williamsburg with
George Wythe, but it arrived too late. The Convention, working with
less sophisticated models drawn up by John Adams, George Mason,
and Richard Henry Lee, had already finished. It did, however, reopen
the debate and incorporated a portion of Jefferson's draft. This was
not enough for Jefferson, who wrote that the constitution "had many
very vicious points," and who hammered off and on at revising it
through much of his life.[43]

The last-minute nature of Jefferson's rescue operation, and the total
failure of his timing, suggest that the four preceding months in Monticello ending with his mother's death and in his own illness had been
neither a halcyon period of connubial pleasure, as his Virginia patriot
friends intimated, nor a fruitful regenerative period of intellectual
reflection and constitution planning. It had been rather a period of
obscure but intense personal conflict which had included real, if
temporary, abandonment of the revolutionary scene. He emerged from
it "almost a new man," and it is difficult to avoid the conclusion
that his mother's death had been in a most critical respect not so
much a loss as a liberation. The migraine would seem to be important
evidence of the intensity of his conflict over the whole process of
mourning and the finality of the separation. In his first draft of the
Declaration of Independence, after listing grievances against England,
Jefferson wrote and then crossed out the following remarkably personal lines: "This is too much to be borne even by relations. enough

First draft of the Declaration of Independence.
The Papers of Thomas Jefferson, Julian Boyd, ed., I, 414.
Courtesy of Princeton University Press.

be it to say we are now done with them." Then he went on, even further illuminating the nature of his conflict, to write, "We must endeavor to forget our former love for them."

Later, in numerous of Jefferson's references to England as the mother country, one sees nuances in the metaphorical language that hauntingly remind one of the personal crisis of death in 1776. So, in his *Notes on the State of Virginia* in 1781, he would write:

> America, though but a child of yesterday, has already given hopeful proofs of genius. . . . The present war having so long cut off all communication with Great-Britain, we are not able to make a fair estimate of the state of science in that country. . . . The sun of her glory is fast descending to the horizon. Her philosophy has crossed the Channel, her freedom the Atlantic, and herself seems passing to that awful dissolution, whose issue is not given human foresight to scan.[44]

In 1787 he described Americans as affectionate toward France but bound by habit to England. "Chained to that country by circumstances, embracing what they loathe, they realize the fable of the living and dead bound together." [45] And it is worth noting that in January 1793 Jefferson described France as America's "true mother country since she has assured to them their liberty and independence." [46]

CHAPTER IX

The Flight from Power

Circumstances very peculiar in the situation of my family . . .

Jefferson to John Hancock, October 11, 1776

Had Jefferson won his demand to be released from the Constitutional Congress to go to Williamsburg to help write the Virginia constitution, who would have written the Declaration of Independence? John Adams perhaps, for Benjamin Franklin was crippled with gout, and Roger Sherman and Robert R. Livingston, also on the committee, were obviously lesser men. But when on June 11, 1776, Congress elected five men for the task, the thirty-three-year-old Jefferson, surely to his astonishment, received the largest vote. Deferential to the father of the Revolution and what he called "our colossus" on the floor of Congress, Jefferson asked Adams to write the document. He declined.

"Why will you not?" Jefferson asked. "You ought to do it."

"Reasons enough."

"What can be your reasons?"

"Reason 1st. You are a Virginian, and a Virginian ought to appear at the head of this business. Reason 2d. I am obnoxious, suspected, and unpopular. You are very much otherwise. Reason 3d. You can write ten times better than I can."

"Well, if you are decided I will do as well as I can." [1]

This is John Adams' famous version, written forty-six years later, and though Jefferson remembered the occasion somewhat differently, no one can quarrel with its essential validity, for Adams even then could look ruefully at his own weaknesses, and he knew well enough in 1776 that Jefferson had "a peculiar felicity of expression."

No other document in American history has been subjected to the monumental exegesis bestowed upon the Declaration. Historians have traced not only the sources of every idea, but also the degree to which they were commonplace at the moment, so much so that one who reads these monographs may be misled into agreeing with the denigrating Timothy Pickering, who wrote in 1822, "There is not an idea in it but what had been hackneyed in Congress for two years before." [2] When Jefferson learned of this charge he wrote dryly to James Madison: "Pickering's observations . . . may all be true. Of that I am not to be the judge. Richard H. Lee charged it as copied from Locke's treatise on Government. . . . I know only that I turned to neither book nor pamphlet while writing it. I did not consider it as any part of my charge to invent new ideas altogether and to offer no sentiment which had ever been expressed before." [3] To Richard Henry Lee he had written that "it was intended to be an expression of the American mind." Ezra Stiles in 1783 said of the Declaration that Jefferson had poured into it "the soul of the continent."

Still, it is a legitimate question. What was there in the Declaration that was uniquely Thomas Jefferson's aside from his "peculiar felicity of expression," which is in no small measure responsible for the document's continuing impact? There are at least three "essential Jefferson" statements in the Declaration as he originally wrote it; two were edited out. A major deletion was Jefferson's indictment of the King because of his refusal to end the slave trade. Jefferson had accused George III of waging "cruel war against human nature . . . captivating & carrying them into slavery in another hemisphere or to insure miserable death in their transportation hither," of perpetuating an "execrable commerce," and "assemblage of horrors." Then the King had compounded his villainy, Jefferson said, by exciting these same slaves to rebellion and murder, "thus paying off former crimes committed against the *Liberties* of one people, with crimes which he urges them to commit against the *lives* of another." [4]

The passage was cut at the insistence of South Carolina and Georgia delegates, though Jefferson noted wryly, "Our northern brethren also I believe felt a little tender under those censures; for tho' their people have very few slaves themselves, yet they had been pretty considerable carriers of them to others." [5] Although George III had in truth vetoed attempts to stop the slave trade, he was hardly responsible for slavery in colonial America, and Jefferson's attack on him for countenancing emancipation as a war measure would seem to have clouded the moral issue, as many critics later pointed out. [6]

The Congress deleted also the highly personal passage, part of which we have already quoted. The Revolution for Jefferson had not only coincided with the death of his mother; it also threatened to sever ties with his uncle and cousins and a much loved teacher in England. Moreover, he was surrounded by thousands with similar overseas ties of blood and friendship, and in the original of his Declaration he felt compelled to say something about this general loss. This he did in three lines that gave to all humanity a sense of the magnitude of the tearing asunder, and a memorable expression of the sorrow of it all: "These facts have given the last stab to agonizing affection, and manly spirit bids us to renounce forever these unfeeling brethren. We must endeavor to forget our former love for them, and to hold them as we might hold the rest of mankind, enemies in war, in peace friends. We might have been a free & great people together." [7]

This went out under the slashing congressional pen. There remained, however, Jefferson's preamble, with its great revolutionary line, justly called immortal by countless men: "We hold these truths to be self-evident, that all men are created equal, that they are endowed by their Creator with certain unalienable Rights, that among these are Life, Liberty and the pursuit of Happiness." Many have noted that these truths were not self-evident then or later, that men were not equal, that the lines expressed not reality but a challenge to oppressive government.[8] Lincoln perhaps expressed it best, saying the lines were "applicable to all men and all times . . . a rebuke and a stumbling-block to the very harbingers of reappearing tyranny and oppression."

Scholars have been so intent, too, on demonstrating that Jefferson's phrase "the pursuit of happiness" was a commonplace eighteenth-century idea that some have overlooked the fact that the substitution from Locke's "life, liberty, and property" changed the whole thrust of revolutionary thinking in his time, and that the change is still reflected in our own. One may point out, too, that this substitution reflects something of significance in Jefferson's personal life. He believed profoundly in pursuing happiness. When politics threatened to destroy his own, he pushed politics aside. This we can see in two decisions he made in the first four months after writing the Declaration; both related to the precarious health of his wife.

Of all the patriots celebrating the signing of the Declaration of Independence Jefferson was perhaps the least able to enjoy it. He was angered by what he called the "mutilations" of his document, and sent copies of the original to his friends asking if they did not prefer it to the emasculated version. Later, describing his agony during the congressional cutting, he told how Franklin had comforted him with the story of a young hatter who asked his neighbors to criticize the wording of his first advertising sign, "John Thompson, *Hatter, makes and sells hats* for ready money." After the neighborly hackings, which Franklin drolly described in detail, the sign ended up reading only "John Thompson," with the picture of a hat.[9]

Nobody outside Congress save a few friends knew that Jefferson had written the Declaration—the fact, astonishingly, did not appear in an American newspaper till 1784 [10]—and he lived through all the bell ringing and speechmaking without any personal commendation in the press. The response to the Declaration had been extraordinary. In New York colony debtors were freed from prison; in New York City Washington and his troops stood approving as a crowd smashed into a thousand pieces a gilded statue of George III. Revolutionists in Baltimore burned the King in effigy; in Savannah they formally buried him. Store signs bearing the royal arms were ripped down and burned in many cities, or torn in shreds and carried off triumphantly by the people. As Winthrop Jordan put it, in describing these symbolic killings, "The American people had not only declared their independence but had taken to themselves the power of their king." [11]

Many lively stories have survived about the final dramatic moments in Congress, when the obstinate opposition to the signing of the Declaration melted away—how John Dickinson ostentatiously left the hall so that his more radical neighbors would carry Pennsylvania —how Hews of North Carolina, a consistent voter against the Declaration, "started suddenly upright, and lifting up both his Hands to Heaven as if he had been in a trance, cry'd out, 'It is done! and I will abide by it.' " [12] Jefferson took careful notes of the proceedings of the Congress during the two months preceding the signing, which provide an invaluable record of the intellectual content of the debates but tells us almost nothing of how the patriots felt. We have no record of his own moment of exultation when the vote on Richard Lee's resolution carried, July 2, 1776.

John Adams poured out his elation in a letter to his wife:

> Yesterday, the greatest question was decided, which ever was debated in America, and a greater perhaps, never was nor will be decided among men. . . .
> The Second Day of July 1776, will be the most memorable Epocha, in the History of America.—I am apt to believe that it will be celebrated by succeeding Generations, as the Day of Deliverance by solemn Acts of Devotion to God Almighty. It ought to be solemnized

with Pomp and Parade, with Shews, Games, Sports, Guns, Bells, Bonfires, and Illuminations from one End of this Continent to the other from this Time forward forever more.[13]

We do not know whether Jefferson was standing in line at the official signing along with Benjamin Rush, and heard the monstrously fat Benjamin Harrison, in a grisly attempt at humor, say to the slightly built Elbridge Gerry: "I shall have a great advantage over you, Mr. Gerry, when we are all hung for what we are now doing. From the size and weight of my body I shall die in a few minutes, but from the lightness of your body, you will dance in the air an hour or two before you are dead." [14] We do not even know for certain if Jefferson signed on the fourth of July, when twelve states agreed to the resolution, or on the fifteenth, when the action became unanimous. Julian Boyd makes out a good case for the fourth. The broadsides of the time heralded the fourth rather than the second as the great day of the century.[15] All that we can be absolutely certain of about Jefferson's activities on the Fourth of July 1776 is that he recorded the temperature at 6 A.M. as 68° Fahrenheit, that he purchased a thermometer, and recorded the highest temperature of the day as 76°, and that he paid for seven pairs of women's gloves, in the happy expectation, it would seem, of a return to Monticello.[16] For what is missing on this day above all others in Jefferson's life we must especially regret the destruction of his letters to his wife.

John Page wrote to Jefferson on July 20, "I am highly pleased with your Declaration. God preserve the United States. We know the Race is not to the swift nor the Battle to the Strong. Do you not think an Angel rides in the Whirlwind and directs this Storm?" [17] But Jefferson left nothing to indicate either his immediate comprehension of the importance of what he had written, or, like John Adams, some prescience of the destiny of the infant nation at whose birth he had been the most important attending physician. Having finished his congressional assignment, he seems to have had one overpowering impulse, to get out of Philadelphia and back to his wife.

On June 30, two days after having finished writing some of the most memorable political phrases of all time, Jefferson wrote to Edmund Pendleton in Virginia begging him to find a substitute for him in Congress. He would serve in Philadelphia "with cheerfulness," he said, only "till the expiration of our year." [18] Not a word about the Declaration! The next day he did mention it, but only in a defensive letter to William Fleming. "If any doubt has arisen as to me, my country will have my political creed in the form of a 'Declaration &c' which I was lately directed to draw. This will give decisive proof that my own sentiment concurred with the vote they instructed us to give." [19] So he said, in effect, to his patriot friends who suspected his loyalty to the Revolution, "Let this be proof that I am with you." Indeed it was.

Jefferson was optimistic at the moment that the war would be over and won in three months. But his chief reason for wanting to return to Virginia, as he hinted in his letters, was that his wife was pregnant again, and it would seem that he was determined to be in Monticello for her confinement. To Edmund Pendleton he explained somewhat ambiguously: "I am sorry the situation of my domestic affairs renders it indispensably necessary that I should sollicit the substitution of some other person here in my room. The delicacy of the house will not require me to enter minutely into the private causes which render this necessary." [20] But other men's wives were also pregnant. Abigail Adams would bear a stillborn child while John was in Philadelphia, and many a soldier would die in battle without ever having seen the child he had begotten before he left home.

Pendleton, who was fond of Jefferson, wrote back to him in exasperation: "I can but lament that it is not agreeable and convenient to you, for I do not Assent to your being unqualified, tho' I readily *do* to your usefulness in the Representative body [at Williamsburg] where having the Pleasure of Mrs. Jefferson's Company, I hope you'l get cured of your wish to retire so early in life from the memory of man, and exercise Your talents for the nurture of Our new Constitution." [21]

It is clear that Pendleton—with his slur about "the Pleasure of Mrs. Jefferson's Company"—did not know about the nature of Martha Jefferson's health problem, nor in fact does anyone, with all the documents of history at our disposal. If she suffered from debilitating monthly hemorrhaging, or from a tendency to miscarry when pregnant, or from dangerous anemia after childbirth, or from all three, one would understand why Jefferson could not bring himself to explain even in private letters the nature of any of these problems. Such was the commonplace taboo.

A failure to receive his usual weekly letter from her during these months in Philadelphia was enough to send Jefferson into a panic of apprehension. He wrote to his brother-in-law Francis Eppes, with whom his wife was staying, on July 23, 1776, "I have received no letter this week, which lays me under great anxiety. I shall leave this place about the 11th of next month. Give my love to Mrs. Eppes, and tell her that when both you and Patty fail to write to me, I think I shall not be unreasonable in insisting she shall." [22] Six days later he wrote desperately to the unsympathetic Henry Lee, who at the moment was the only one who could vote in his stead as delegate from Virginia, "For god's sake, for your country's sake, and for my sake, come. I receive by every post such accounts of the state of Mrs. Jefferson's health, that it will be impossible for me to disappoint her expectation of seeing me at the time I have promised. . . . I am under a sacred obligation to go home." [23]

To John Page he wrote on July 30, "Every letter brings me such an account of the state of her health, that it is with great pain that I can stay here." [24] But Lee was delayed, and the major crisis of his wife's illness passed without Jefferson's being near her. That she had suffered a miscarriage seems likely; a letter from Jefferson to his brother-in-law on August 9 lacks any sense of urgency and indicates that his wife by then had improved enough to think of returning to Monticello. Jefferson had concluded, "My love to Mrs. Eppes. I hope my letter by last post got there time enough to stay Patty with her awhile longer." [25] Edmund Pendleton wrote Jefferson a cheerful letter on August 26: "I wish you as pleasant a journey as the season will permit and hope you'l find Mrs. Jefferson recovered, as I had the pleasure of hearing in Goochland she was better." [26]

But Jefferson had had enough of anxiety. Without waiting to the end of the year, as he had earlier promised, he resigned his seat in the Congress on September 2, 1776. Despite repeated pleas from his friends, he would not return to national politics for six years, not, in fact, until after his wife's death. And, as we have suggested, it is quite possible that had she lived longer he would never have been president of the United States.

Jefferson abandoned the Continental Congress in 1776, but it did not abandon him. As the war took a turn for the worse, and French aid became a burning necessity, members of the Congress looked about for possible commissioners to Paris. They settled on Benjamin Franklin, an obvious choice, on Silas Deane, who was already involved in getting private aid in France, and on Jefferson, admired for his skill with words, and his knowledge of French, as well as his intelligence and discretion. Richard Henry Lee wrote to him he was confident "that distinguished love for your country that has marked your life, will determine you here." [27] This request, and a similar letter from John Hancock, reached Jefferson in Williamsburg. He was attending the Virginia assembly, happily planning a legislative program to liberalize and reform what he considered the still antiquated and tyrannous machinery of his state. He had, moreover, performed a small miracle; he had persuaded Martha Jefferson to come with him.[28] George

Wythe had made this possible by offering them his pleasant home on the Williamsburg Common.

Jefferson anguished for three days over the summons to go to Paris, and then replied to Hancock: "No cares for my own person, nor yet for my private affairs would have induced one moment's hesitation to accept the charge. But circumstances very peculiar in the situation of my family such as neither permit me to leave nor to carry it, compel me to ask leave to decline a service so honorable and at the same time so important to the American cause." [29]

When Richard Henry Lee, whose own wife had been ill a good deal, learned from Hancock that Jefferson had refused to go on this account, he was enraged: "I heared with much regret that you had declined both the voyage, and your seat in Congress. No Man feels more deeply than I do, the love of, and the loss of, private enjoyments; but let attention to these be universal, and we are gone, beyond redemption lost in the deep perdition of slavery." [30] So Lee hurled in his teeth the charge that Jefferson was abandoning the vital work of the Revolution for "private enjoyments." Benjamin Rush wrote later that once in discussing with Jefferson the possibility of his going to France, the young Virginian had said that "he would go to hell to serve his country." [31] And so sensitive was Jefferson to criticism about his own refusal, which had indeed shocked his friends, that he even explained it in his *Autobiography*: "Such was the state of my family that I could not leave it, nor could I expose it to the dangers of the sea, and of capture by the British ships, then covering the ocean."

The reason for his refusal, which has been totally overlooked, was that Martha Jefferson was again pregnant, but barely, and it is possible that when the summons came to go to France the certainty of the pregnancy was not wholly established. Jefferson had returned briefly with Martha to Monticello on September 10; on October 1, he had paid a Dr. Brydon twenty shillings for a professional visit to his wife.[32] Eight months later, on May 28, 1777, Martha Jefferson would bear a son. One can see why, by October 11, 1776, with the August illness an anguishing memory, and the new pregnancy almost certain, that Jefferson found the idea of going to France inconceivable, and told Hancock no.

Jefferson and his wife seem to have known by now that she had better reason than most women to fear dying in childbirth. But almost no one else knew it. Thus it happened that his characteristic delicacy and secrecy served only to intensify the now widespread gossip that he put "private enjoyments" above the good of the new nation. Later Jefferson wrote somewhat wistfully to Benjamin Franklin, "I wish my domestic situation had rendered it possible for me to have joined you in the very honorable charge confided to you. Residence in a polite Court, society with literati of the first order, a just cause and approving god, will add length to a life for which all men pray." [33] One sees here the barely discernible surfacing of resentment against his "domestic situation" as well as a concern with death. For the expressed wish, that an approving God would add "length to a life for which all men pray," directed at the aging Franklin, could equally well apply to his own wife, with her special vulnerability. So there are hints of a deeply repressed conflict. Jefferson was trapped more than most men of his time, not only by his wife's ill health but also by the intensity of his affection for her. It is possible that already he dared not leave her because he could not face, in fantasy, the reproaches of his own conscience should she die in his absence.

His conflict could have only been deepened when he received reproachful letters from his friends. John Adams, bedeviled with the difficulties of paying for the revolutionary army, and working out the details of the Articles of Confederation that would keep the thirteen colonies decently bound together like the staves in a barrel, sorely missed Jefferson, resented his "retirement," and tactfully told him so. "We want your Industry and Abilities here extreamly. . . . Pray come and help Us, to raise the Value of our Money, and lower the Prices of Things. . . . Your Country is not yet, quite Secure enough, to excuse your Retreat to the Delights of domestic Life. Yet, for the soul of me, when I attend to my own Feelings, I cannot blame you." [34]

Actually, far from enjoying the "Delights of domestic Life," Jefferson had thrown himself into a fury of legislative activity in Williamsburg, introducing a whole galaxy of reforms to make Virginia a thoroughly democratic state.[35] He hoped to extend the suffrage, to abolish primogeniture and entail, to make land acquisition easy for the independent yeoman in the west, thus smashing at the power of the Virginia gentry, of which he was himself so conspicuous a member. Almost singlehanded he worked out a revision of the harsh, antiquated criminal code of the colony, abolishing except for murder and treason the death penalty which had been freely used against horse thieves and minor felons.

Remembering with dissatisfaction his years in private schools with Anglican clergymen, he proposed a state-wide system of tax-supported elementary schools for boys and girls, secondary schools for the ablest students, and a system of scholarships for the highly talented, and their education at the college level. He proposed a state library, and the reform of the curriculum at William and Mary College to transform it from a divinity school to a modern college, with emphasis on science, mathematics, and modern languages.

As we have seen, Jefferson never spoke specifically of the bigotry of the clergymen of his adolescence; his hatred of the Anglican church was generalized rather than specific, but no less deadly. As a lawyer, and new critic of the whole Virginia legal code, he had learned if he did not know it as a child that heresy to the Church of England could be punished by death, that denial of the Trinity was punishable on the third offense by three years in prison, that freethinkers and Unitarians could be declared unfit parents and deprived of their children. Though such laws were dead letters at the moment, he knew they could be revived with a different "spirit of the times." He had come to believe, with John Locke, that religion consists in the *inward* persuasion of the mind, that "the care of every man's soul belongs to himself," that no man should be abused because his "hair is not of the right cut," or because he follows "a guide crowned with a mitre & cloathed in white." [36]

Destruction of the power of the Anglican clergymen now became a private crusade occupying enormous reserves of his energy. It was the toughest of all his battles in the Virginia assembly, and winning it, which took some years, gave him such special satisfaction that he counted it one of the three greatest achievements of his life. The measured cadences of his famous Bill No. 82 demanding the total separation of the anciently meshed powers of church and state rank second only in world impact to those of his Declaration of Independence.

> Almighty God hath created the mind free. . . . To compel a man to furnish contributions of money for the propagation of opinions which he disbelieves and abhors, is sinful and tyrannical. . . . Our civil rights have no dependence on our religious opinions, any more than our opinions of physics or geometry. . . .
>
> *The opinions of men are not the object of civil government, nor under its jurisdiction.* . . . Truth is great and will prevail if left to herself . . . She is the proper and sufficient antagonist to error, and has nothing to fear from the conflict unless by human interposition disarmed of her natural weapons, free argument and debate; errors ceasing to be dangerous when it is permitted freely to contradict them.[37]

Jefferson was consumed with a sense of urgency. Recognizing that great reform can come only in the white heat of revolution, he worked fanatically for clarification, purification, and democratization. Later, in 1781, he would write, "The time for fixing every essential right on a legal basis is while our rulers are honest and ourselves united. From the conclusion of this war we shall be going down hill. It will not then be necessary to resort every movement to the people for support. They will be forgotten, therefore, and their rights disregarded. They will forget themselves, but in the sole faculty of making money. . . . The shackles, therefore, which shall not be knocked off at the conclusion of this war, will remain on us long, will be made heavier and heavier." [38]

If one looks at the record of reform as finally enacted, one stands in awe at the Jeffersonian impact on his own state, and subsequently upon the democracies of the world. No one since has left much more than a fingerprint in comparison with his massive hand. But one must remember that this phenomenal record of legislative reform was not enacted in the Virginia assembly which Jefferson attended from October 1776 to June 1779. One by one in these years his great reform bills went down to defeat.

His only real success was the passing of a bill abolishing primogeniture and entail, making possible, as he said, "instead of an aristocracy of wealth, of more harm and danger, than benefit, to society . . . an opening for the aristocracy of virtue and talent." The landholder could now, Jefferson wrote somewhat ambiguously, "divide property among his children equally, as his affections were divided." [39] (Peter Jefferson, it will be remembered, had not divided his property equally, but had won permission to divide "as his affections were divided," with Thomas Jefferson getting the preferred land over his brother, and his sisters getting none at all.)

Aside from this success, his immense labors resulted only in the passage of a bill partly curtailing the power of the established church to stifle dissenting sects. The conservatives under Benjamin Harrison remained in the saddle, and when Jefferson's name was put up for Speaker in May 1778, he lost by an ignominious 23 to 51. His legal reforms with which he himself was not satisfied were splintered and adopted piecemeal; his land reform program, badly conceived, was manipulated into a windfall for speculators. Church and state were not to be sundered in Virginia till 1786, and his program for state-wide free schools would not be enacted until after the Civil War. His cautious plan for gradual emancipation and colonization of slaves was considered so revolutionary it was not even introduced.

It would be easy to surmise why Jefferson, seeing these enlightened blueprints pigeonholed and mutilated by his own revolutionary patriot friends, living with the recognition that he wielded influence but no power, turned his back on the whole Virginia political scene in disgust.[40] He did abandon it for long periods and his record of legislative innovation is all the more astonishing if one counts up how many days he was absent from the Williamsburg sessions. He was extremely conscientious about attendance when Martha was with him in the autumn of 1776, but in the spring of 1777, when she was not, he remained in the legislature only sixteen days out of the eight-week total. Again, however, the abandonment had to do with personal tragedy. Martha bore a son on May 28; he lived only until June 14, and was buried without even being given a name. Jefferson's wife had now lost three children, two sons and a daughter. Only the sturdy Patsy, age six, had survived.

We know nothing of the impact of these deaths upon Jefferson except that he stayed closer to his wife than ever. When the Marquis de Chastellux came to Virginia seeking out Jefferson in April 1782, he stayed at the tavern of a Mr. Boswell whose wife had seen fourteen children die under the age of two.[41] It was enough to record this stupefying loss; Chastellux made no attempt to describe the state of mind of the woman who had suffered it. The deaths of children, commonly attributed to the will of God, came to all classes. Britain's Queen Anne, who had died early in the century, had had fifteen pregnancies, ten of them miscarriages. Only one of her children had survived infancy and he died at age eleven. That the loss of one's children, however related to God's judgments, sometimes brought on "insanity" in the mother was an eighteenth-century psychological insight with which Jefferson had to reckon. Less than a year before the death of his son, he received a letter from his sister, Martha Carr, with a sad and cryptic account of Polly Ambler, daughter of Rebecca Burwell, who had married John Marshall at fourteen: "Mrs. Marshal, once Miss Ambler, is Insane, the loss of two children is thought to have occationed it." Marshall's "Dear Polly" would move in and out of psychosis all her life.[42]

The coming of inoculation against smallpox, which Jefferson advertised with enthusiasm, had proved a frightening blessing to religious men, disturbing as it did the age-old concept that illness was still a manifestation of God's intentions, if not a punishment for sin. "Why should the 'Vaccine' have been concealed from all eternity, and then instantaneously revealed?" John Adams would ask himself, and then reply: "Worm! ask no such questions! do justly, love mercy, walk humbly. This is enough for you to know, and to do." [44] But Jefferson, who had ardently embraced the new science, could not and would not hide his head in the sand in this fashion. If death from smallpox could be avoided by a simple application of a bit of "pus" in a scratch, what did the will of God have to do with death, whether from smallpox or in childbirth or any other cause? This was a question Jefferson certainly faced head on, as his new deism robbed him of one of man's oldest consolations in the perennial trauma of mourning.

Jefferson's abandonment of the Virginia assembly during the crisis of his son's death did not escape the increasingly hostile Richard Henry Lee, who wrote to him insultingly on August 25, 1777: "It will not perhaps be disagreeable to you in your retirement, sometimes to hear the events of war, and how in other respects we proceed in the arduous business we are engaged in." [44] Jefferson did not reply. He, did however, return to Williamsburg in November 1777 and remained faithfully through the session to January 24, 1778, and was back again in the spring. Martha Jefferson was pregnant again, and bore a daughter on August 1, 1778, who mercifully survived the first terrifying weeks. This was Mary [or Maria], Polly, who would bless Jefferson's years until she was twenty-five.

That Martha's recovery was slow seems probable, for Jefferson stayed in Monticello well into the autumn, missing most of the fall session of the legislature. Whether his wife was exacting and demanding, obsessed with a fear of dying, or truly gravely ill after Polly's birth there is no record whatever, though the last seems most likely, in view of what happened after the birth of her sixth child, in 1782. In any case, during most of 1778 Jefferson stayed in Monticello, where he gave himself up to a new period of enthusiastic planting and building. If one studies his *Garden Book* for this year, with its record plantings of fruit and nut trees, the elaboration of his gardens, his ordering of 90,000 red bricks, and then an additional 100,000, one gets the impression that he had abandoned not only Philadelphia and the making of the nation, but also Williamsburg and the making of Virginia, that he had withdrawn from reform and revolutionary ferment, and even the war. Actually Jefferson did a good deal of his codifying and reforming of Virginia's legal code when he was at home. And what might be thought revulsion was really complacency. The British, who had occupied Philadelphia in September 1777, evacuated it in June 1778, and Washington had won the Battle of Monmouth. A French fleet under d'Estaing had reached the Delaware capes on July 8, and on July 10 France had formally declared war on Britain. The four thousand British and Hessian soldiers under Burgoyne who had surrendered at the Battle of Saratoga on October 17, 1777, had been marched to Charlottesville for safe incarceration in January 1779, and Jefferson had this palpable evidence of victory practically next door. Moreover, he was not alone among the radical Virginia gentry relaxing in the conviction that peace was near.

Washington, who knew the vulnerability of the whole Atlantic coast to British men-of-war, and who was appalled at the British capture of Forts Mifflin and Mercer in late November 1778, which meant control of the Delaware, wrote with great bitterness to Benjamin Harrison on December 20, "I am alarmed and wish to see my Countrymen roused. I have no resentments, nor do I mean to point at any particular characters. . . . but in the present situation of things I cannot help asking: Where is Mason, Wythe, Jefferson, Nicholas, Pendleton, Nelson, and another I could name; and why, if you are sufficiently impressed with your danger, you do not . . . send an extra Member or two [to Congress] for at least a certain limited time till the great business of the Nation is put upon a more respectable and happy establishment." [45]

A British force under General John Campbell captured Savannah, Georgia, on December 29, and Augusta on January 29, 1779. Edward Rutledge, writing from Charleston, South Carolina, reported in despair to Jefferson that the Georgia colony had been reduced to "the Condition of a Conquer'd Province." He begged bitterly for Virginia assistance, "when you have condescended to come down from above and interest yourself in Human Affairs." [46] But Jefferson seemed content to leave all such matters to the state's first governor, Patrick Henry. He busied himself with the problems of the war prisoners, making suggestions for vegetable planting and barracks buildings to aid the officers and men in their wretchedness. He fraternized freely with the German soldiers, discussing philosophy with Captain Johan Ludvig de Unger and Baron Friederich von Riedesel. He played duets with Baron de Geismar, arranged living quarters for Baroness von Riedesel when she joined her prisoner husband, and shared with them both the hospitality of Monticello. Eventually he sold his pianoforte to von Riedesel for £100. [47]

It was all very civilized, very characteristic of eighteenth-century warfare. Russian aristocrats would entertain their British officer prisoners who were of noble blood in similar fashion even in the Crimean War. After Jefferson became Governor of Virginia, one of his German prisoner friends, shortly before being exchanged, wrote a letter back to Germany which was published in a Hamburg newspaper. It was later translated and sent to Jefferson:

> I have free Access to a Copious and well chosen Library of Colo. Jefferson's Governor of Virginia. The father of this learned Man's was also a favourite of the Muses. There is now a Map of his of Virginia extant, the best of the Kind. The Governor possesses a Noble Spirit of Building, he is now finishing an elegant building projected according to his own fancy. In his parlour he is creating on the Cieling a Compass of his own invention by wich he can Know the strength as well as Direction of the Winds. I have promised to paint the Compass for it. He was much pleased with a fancy Painting of mine and particularly

admired the Paper Money brought on in the piece, and in Joke often rebuked me for my thoughtlessness to shew him counterfeit money for wich I knew many had been hanged allready. As all Virginians are fond of Music, he is particularly so. You will find in his House an Elegant Harpsichord Piano forte and some Violins. The latter he performs well upon himself, the former his Lady touches very skilfully and who, is in all Respects a very agreable Sensible and Accomplished Lady.[48]

Had Jefferson continued to live in this fashion, he might have gone through his whole life with a total misconception of war's savagery. But a brutal awakening lay ahead.

CHAPTER X

Jefferson and the War

I am always mortified when anything is expected from me which I cannot fulfill.

Jefferson to James Monroe, May 20, 1782 [1]

Jefferson, with some kind of intuitive self-knowledge, had kept himself isolated from real military involvement in the Revolution. In no sense a soldier, with little interest in military history or strategy, he was preeminently a builder, educator, legislator, and tree planter. He could plan for growth and flowering, but not for pillage and killing. Unlike Alexander Hamilton, who as an adolescent had pined for war to open up roads to glory, Jefferson's fantasies seem to have been channeled in peaceful directions. For this and other reasons he was ill equipped to face personal failure in war. His hatreds were generalized. He hated England, not Englishmen. He hated Tories—which he defined as traitors in thought, not in deed [2]—but only in the abstract. He gave orders as governor of Virginia that any loyalist taken for "treason" should be committed "with no Insult or Rudeness, unnecessary for their safe Custody." [3]

There were two exceptions, one the British governor of Detroit, Henry Hamilton, who had encouraged the Indians to barbarous atrocities against men, women, and children on Virginia's far western frontiers. When "the scalp buyer" was captured by George Rogers Clark and brought to Williamsburg, Jefferson had him put in irons and forbade him either writing materials or visitors. A letter from Washington got him to relax these orders. Similarly he hated Benedict Arnold and wrote secretly to J. P. G. Muhlenberg suggesting that he be kidnaped, and that a $5,000 reward be offered if he were taken alive. In the original draft of this letter he wrote of American "satisfaction" at seeing Arnold "exhibited as a public spectacle of infamy," but he cut this out before sending it, reluctant to betray hatred of such unlovely proportions, even of a traitor.[4] Thus he disciplined his own fantasies of revenge. Instead of releasing his hatreds in real killing or in verbal assault, he turned them inward and flagellated himself. And his political enemies, sensing this vulnerability, whipped him for his errors of military judgment far beyond what he justly deserved.

It was the great misfortune of his life that Jefferson was elected war governor of Virginia in June 1779. In early May, when he was talking of retirement from politics, Edmund Pendleton had written to him sharply, "You hurt [our] feelings when you sometimes speak of retiring. You are too young to Ask that happy quietus from the Public, and should at least postpone it 'till you have taught the rising Generation, the reforms as well as the Substantial principles of legislation."[5] Given such pressure, Jefferson did not object when his name was entered in the race, though it meant running against two good friends, Thomas Nelson and John Page. The final vote in the Virginia assembly was 67 to 61, so Jefferson became governor without such a vote of confidence as might have sustained him in the hazardous times ahead.

Unlike Patrick Henry, he had the misfortune to take office after the British had shifted their major military effort to the South. In May 1779 Sir Henry Clinton threatened Charleston, and just before Jefferson's election a small naval force seized Portsmouth and spent sixteen days plundering the Virginia coast. Jefferson was expected to raise and maintain a militia large enough to defend a land area bigger than the British Isles, and protect an indefensible coastline with generous harbors and rivers inviting invasion at any point. He had a potential of 50,000 militiamen, but only 4,000 serviceable muskets, and he faced increasingly despairing demands for men and supplies for "the Virginia line," the state's component of the regular army, to prevent the British invasion of the South under Cornwallis from becoming a general disaster.

Inflation plagued Virginia as it did all the states; there were those who held that Patrick Henry had done little in his two one-year terms in office but turn out paper money, first £500,000 and then £1,000,000. Virginia had only a tiny arms industry. Its yeomanry was hostile to taxes—the Revolution after all began as a reaction to taxation—and to any militia draft extending beyond two months. A disastrous crop failure greeted Jefferson's first summer in office. And an incipient Tory rebellion simmered in the southwestern counties.

Jefferson in his *Autobiography* reduced the wretched two years of his governorship to two paragraphs, where he did not defend his record. The governorship was his only major failure, but our concern here is not with the military and economic aspects, which have been meticulously explored, but with the personal problems that contributed to that failure, his reaction to it, and the merciless exploitation of it by Federalists later in his life. He learned mightily from this failure, though this did not become apparent till he was president.

The Virginia constitution had crippled the executive authority; not until late in his second term did Jefferson have the right even to call out the state militia without the approval of an eight-man council, which Madison called "eight governors and a councilor . . . the grave of all useful talents." [6] Less than a month after taking office—apparently without any sense of impropriety—Jefferson confessed to the British prisoner of war Major General William Phillips, whom he had entertained at Monticello, "The appointment . . . is not likely to add to my happiness."[7]

Still, though seeming to hate the office, Jefferson embraced its duties with feverish intensity. Hundreds of his letters attest that he worked ceaselessly through the two years to master what were basically insoluble problems. To check the inflation, which among other things made the soldiers' pay almost worthless, he instituted a system of tax payments in wheat and tobacco. A new currency was adopted, but because the British blockade prevented the sale of tobacco abroad no hard money was available to shore it up; in the end both currencies remained in circulation, the second of no more value than the first. The inflation spiral was reflected in Jefferson's account book. By September 28, 1780, Mrs. Jefferson was paying £84.6 for a pair of shoes. The payment for a midwife for delivering a slave woman had been £3 in February 1779; in March 1781 it was £60. Ducks and chickens which in 1779 had cost a few shillings by August 1781 were costing £45 to £50.

The arms factory Jefferson planned on the James River foundered for lack of the skilled personnel he had hoped to get from France. The Prussian, Baron von Steuben, whom Washington sent to Virginia, though contemptuous of Jefferson, also blamed the "indolence" of the Virginians, and Jefferson himself confessed to Lafayette that his militiamen "were not used to war and prompt obedience." [8] His faith that the militia could be counted on at least to defend home and family was shattered as time and again the raw troops broke ranks and ran from seasoned British regulars. He was sickened to learn that when Cornwallis at Camden, South Carolina, on August 16, 1780, smashed the army of General Horatio Gates—who had 1,400 regulars and 2,000 militiamen—a third of the men who panicked were Virginia militiamen.

Actually the militia served a vital function even when they fought badly, for they acted as a deterrent to invasion beyond a certain depth, as well as a force against Tory counterrevolution.[9] Cornwallis, who called the interior of South Carolina "a damned hornet's nest," would find that winning battles was not conquering a continent, and that major engagements served to bleed him into ever debilitating weakness. Jefferson for all his lack of interest in military history had some sound strategic ideas, and he believed with good reason that the British raids served to strengthen the will to resist rather than to drive the colonists back into the arms of the King.[10] He had small difficulty discouraging a threatened Tory uprising in Montgomery County and a secessionist movement in Kentucky. And he worked out with George Rogers Clark an audacious strategy for securing an enormous area in the West by conquering the British stronghold of Detroit. For a time Clark was successful, but when Jefferson tried to augment his force with 2,000 new militiamen from nine western counties, many officers flatly refused to march. Clark's forces dwindled and the expedition failed. Few in the nation besides Washington, who had been won over to Jefferson's plan after an initial period of coldness, understood that the Virginia governor had a truly continental view.[11]

One aspect of Jefferson's governorship that is almost impossible to document is his attitude toward the use of black troops. In 1775 Washington had been appalled by Lord Dunmore's proclamation offering to free any slave who joined his forces. He wrote to Richard Henry Lee that Dunmore must be crushed "instantly," lest he become "the most formidable enemy America has." [12] But black soldiers were recruited in New England—Rhode Island soon had enough for what was called a "black battalion"—and Massachusetts promised freedom to any slave who enlisted, with compensation for the master. New York promised land grants as compensation, and even Maryland permitted slave enlistments after 1777. The revolutionary ferment in Pennsylvania, stimulated by Benjamin Franklin and Thomas Paine in particular, resulted in March 1, 1780, in the first state action toward total emancipation. The legislature agreed that every black child born after that date would be free at age twenty-eight.

Washington came to have great respect for the black soldiers, lost his fears of slave insurrection, and strongly encouraged the gifted young colonel, John Laurens of South Carolina, in his efforts to raise Negro troops in the Deep South. The hardships of Valley Forge provided added inducement. By this time, Lord Dunmore's slave recruits had been decimated by smallpox, and a vigorous propaganda campaign started by Patrick Henry was warning the slaves that British promises were fraudulent, and that ultimately they would all be sold in the West Indies. Thanks largely to Laurens, Congress recommended on March 22, 1779, that 3,000 black troops be raised in South Carolina and Georgia, and that their owners be paid up to $1,000 for each slave.[13]

Laurens' mission to Charleston and Savannah to encourage this movement met with loathing and contempt. The last thing the slave-owners wanted in this area was to see 3,000 free blacks trained in military arts and returning after the war zealous in the spirit of revolution. The young colonel was killed in a skirmish in June 1782, and so died the most promising of all the young idealists in the Deep South. Madison in Virginia also favored liberating slaves and making soldiers of them, but he was not yet a man of great influence.[14]

Virginia never officially permitted slave enlistments; nevertheless free blacks fought as soldiers and sailors—Luther Jackson estimates the forces as about five hundred—and were being drafted as early as November 1777.[15] As the recruitment problems increased, the state authorized the purchase of slaves for service as laborers with the Virginia militia, but few slaveholders were willing to be paid in inflated currency. The hiring of slaves was considered too costly. Instead of recruiting slaves through the promise of freedom and compensating their owners, the Virginia legislature in October 1780 voted to give every white recruit who would serve till the end of the war "300 acres of land plus a healthy sound Negro between 10 and 30 years of age or £60 in gold or silver." [16]

How Jefferson felt about this is obscure. Worried by his increasing failure to recruit militiamen, he begged the legislature on May 10, 1781, to set up a program for impressing male slaves to work as laborers along with the soldiers, pointing out bluntly, "Money will not procure Labourers." Still, he did not urge the arming of slaves. "Slaves are by the laws excluded from the Militia," he said, "and wisely as to the Part of a Souldiers Duty which consists in the Exercise of Arms." [17] Though he deferred in this fashion to the continuing fear of the slave with a gun, his plea resulted in Virginia's being the state which recruited more Negroes for war service than any other save in New England. There was no talk, however, of freedom for these slaves, despite the fact that many of them who aided in building entrenchments faced the danger of enemy fire.

Not surprisingly, thousands of slaves in Virginia fled to the British side. Twenty-two of Jefferson's own slaves were among these fugitives, eleven of them women. Jefferson wrote bluntly in his *Farm Book* that these slaves "joined enemy." [18] Others were forcibly abducted. Small Isaac, son of "Great George" and Ursula, favorite house slaves whom Jefferson had taken to Richmond with him in 1781, remembered the British soldiers coming to the house and demanding "the Governor," saying they "didn't want to hurt him, only wanted to put a pair of silver handcuffs on him." The soldiers searched the house for silver, which Great George had successfully concealed in a bedtick, and plundered the corncrib, meathouse, and wine cellar. Isaac himself was carried off, leaving his mother "cryin' and hollerin'." The British treated him well, he said, giving him "plenty of fresh meat and wheat bread." He watched the Battle of Yorktown from behind the British lines, and afterward was sent back to his mother at Monticello.[19]

Of the twenty-two slaves who fled twelve died, and of the six who returned four died shortly, either of "camp fever" or of smallpox, which now became epidemic at Monticello and killed eight additional slaves.[20] Jefferson soberly recorded all the details in his *Farm Book*. His own moral dilemma we learn about most concretely from a letter he wrote some years later in Paris. Here he described how Cornwallis "carried off" thirty of his slaves, adding:

> Had this been to give them freedom, he would have done right, but it was to consign them to inevitable death from small pox and putrid fever then raging in his camp. This I knew afterwards to have been the fate of 27 of them. I never had news of the remaining three. . . .
>
> I supposed the state of Virginia lost under Ld. Cornwallis's hands that year about 30,000 slaves, and that of these about 27,000 died of the small pox and camp fever, and the rest were partly sent to the West Indies and exchanged for rum, sugar, coffee and fruits, and partly sent to New York, from whence they went at the peace either to Nova Scotia, or England. From this place I believe they have been lately sent to Africa.[21]

What Jefferson felt during the war's turmoil, torn as he must have been between rage at his own slaves who ran away to the enemy and recognition that he was doing nothing to encourage their staying by promises of emancipation for war service, as were governors of the northern states, he never recorded. That he felt as Madison did, that it was far better to compensate a slaveowner who permitted his slave to enlist with a promise of freedom than to bribe a white recruit by promising him a healthy black, one can be fairly certain, considering what he wrote in his *Notes on the State of Virginia* in 1781. But he dared not agitate for this kind of legislation.

Jefferson's political life during the war continued to be punctuated by domestic tragedy. Martha reluctantly joined him in the Governor's Palace in Williamsburg in September 1779, bringing Patsy, now seven, and Polly, a little over a year. Whatever pleasure he took in moving into the charming residence in which he had played chamber music years earlier was spoiled now by fears that Williamsburg was vulnerable to British attack. For this, and other reasons having to do with the relations between the tidewater aristocracy and yeomanry of the up-country, Jefferson persuaded the assembly to move the state government inland to Richmond. He settled with his family in a brick house owned by his uncle, accompanied by several Monticello slaves.

An examination of Jefferson's account book for 1779 shows that throughout the first nine months of the year Jefferson did not give any money for "household expenses" to his wife. Instead the money went to his trusted valet, Martin (son of Betty Hemings), who apparently did the purchasing for the family. In October 1779 one sees again the usual sums to "Mrs. Jefferson" for household expenses, "sundries," and clothes. Since the same happened again in the months before Martha Jefferson's death, this would seem to be evidence that she was ill, and for a very long period.[22]

Early in 1780, in Richmond, Martha again became pregnant. In August she was asked by Martha Washington to participate in a ladies' drive to raise money and make clothing for soldiers, and responded by writing a formal note enlisting the aid of Eleanor Madison, wife of the Reverend James Madison, Jefferson's old schoolmate, and the one Anglican clergyman he counted a friend. This letter, the only one of Martha Jefferson's to survive, tells us little about its author, though her phrase "I cannot do more for its promotion" may suggest that she was in no physical condition to lead the drive.

Richmond August 8, 1780

MADAM

Mrs. Washington has done me the honor of communicating the in-closed proposition of our sisters of Pennsylvania and of informing me that the same grateful sentiments are displaying themselves in Mary-land. Justified by the sanction of her letter in handing forward the scheme I undertake with chearfulness the duty of furnishing to my country women an opportunity of proving that they also participate of those virtuous feelings which gave birth to it. I cannot do more for its promotion than by inclosing to you some of the papers to be disposed of as you think proper.

I am with the greatest respect Madam Your most humble servant,

MARTHA JEFFERSON [23]

She was ill for a time during this pregnancy; Jefferson apparently wrote some details to Baron von Riedesel, who replied on October 2, 1780, two months before the baby's birth was due, congratulating him on her recovery.[24] But Jefferson's anxiety brought thoughts of retirement from the governorship. "I have determined to retire . . .

at the close of the present campaign," he wrote Richard Henry Lee on September 13.[25] Lee did not reply. John Page, to whom Jefferson also hinted of retirement, gave him back the special combination of scolding and praise best calculated to keep him in office. "I know your love of Study and Retirement must strongly solicit you to leave the Hurry, Bustle, and Nonsense your station daily exposes you to. I know too the many Mortifications you must meet with, but 18 Months will soon pass away. Deny yourself your darling Pleasures for that Space of Time. . . . All who know you know how eminently qualified you are to fill the station you hold." [26]

On October 20, 1780, the Virginia militia went into a frenzy of activity when they heard that Major General Alexander Leslie had invaded the James estuary and occupied Portsmouth. Despite exaggerated reports of 4,000 British soldiers, Jefferson refused to believe it to be a major invasion, and he was proved right when Leslie, who had done little but seize colonial cattle, sailed away on November 20. Relaxed and happy, Jefferson was content to order a study sent to the assembly of possible gun emplacements on the Virginia rivers,[27] and took time out to answer in detail an inquiry from the French government about the history, commerce, agriculture, and people of his state. This was the beginning of what would be his famous *Notes on the State of Virginia*. "I take every occasion which presents itself of procuring answers," he wrote to a French friend on November 30, 1780.[28]

It was on this same date, at 10:45 P.M., that his daughter Lucy Elizabeth was born. The birth seems to have gone well, though many entries of purchases for "milk" in Jefferson's account book indicate that his wife could not nurse the baby. But within a month he was giving her money, which shows that she was well enough to make purchases on her own.[29]

On December 9, 1780, Washington wrote to Jefferson that a British fleet carrying grenadiers, light infantrymen, Hessian grenadiers, and light dragoons had left New York, "supposed to be destined Southward." [30] But when word came to Richmond on December 31 that twenty-seven sail had been sighted off the Virginia capes, the optimistic Jefferson refused to become alarmed. Still holding to a naïve conviction that any invasion force would become bogged down in the lowland swamps, he was content to order General Thomas Nelson, head of the Virginia militia, to go to the coast, and with what he admitted later was "a fatal inattention" waited two full days before calling a meeting of the Virginia Council. It was January 2 before the order went out calling up 4,600 militiamen. The two-day delay indeed proved fatal, and was one of several evidences that Jefferson lacked the reflexes of a wartime leader.

The traitorous Benedict Arnold, who led the invasion force, finding the winds unexpectedly favorable, sailed all the way up the James River to Westover and landed 1,500 men. Then in an audacious sixty-six-mile raid he left a trail of damage that astounded the Virginians, humiliated Jefferson, and permanently clouded his reputation as war governor. When Arnold arrived at Richmond, burning and pillaging at will, only two hundred Virginians were assembled to defend the capital. With a jauntiness close to contempt he burned mills, foundries, war stores, and state papers, and even took the time before leaving the city to retrieve five pieces of artillery the fleeing militia had thrown into the James to prevent their capture. He missed abducting Jefferson, who had sent his wife and daughters off to Tuckahoe for safekeeping and who for two days rode frantically about the area trying to establish communications with Baron von Steuben, whom he had appointed at the last moment to defend the city. It was altogether a sorry episode, as his biographers have generally admitted, save for Randall, who tried valiantly to paint Jefferson the hero, describing how he rode one horse till it died under him and then carried his saddle stubbornly to the nearest farmhouse, where he procured another.[31] In reading these details, which serve only to heighten the picture of ineptness and frantic frustration, no one can be surprised that Jefferson afterward cherished fantasies of Benedict Arnold's being "exhibited as a public spectacle of infamy."

He wrote a frank avowal of failure to Washington, who treated the affair with great gentleness, but who recognized its potential serious-ness sufficiently to send 1,200 regulars to Virginia under Lafayette.[32] This changed the whole strategic picture. Lafayette arrived in Williams-burg on March 16, 1781, and for a brief period there was a possibility of his bottling up Arnold on the cape and trapping him in a victory similar to that which would take place at Yorktown six months later. But the French fleet under Admiral Destouches, so essential to the victory, was in a brief engagement driven off the cape by Admiral Arbuthnot, and the opportunity to capture Benedict Arnold and his troops was lost. Had the French fleet arrived as planned, Jefferson would have shared not only in the glory of victory but also in the public humiliating of the nation's most celebrated traitor. The opportunity was lost, and Virginia was left vulnerable to suffer a second disastrous invasion in April 1781.[33]

Even before this invasion, however, Jefferson had decided to retire from the governorship on June 2, 1781, the end of his second term, though the law permitted him a third. What triggered this decision? Though his confidence in himself had been shaken by Arnold's invasion, still his subsequent letters indicate that by April he had recovered much of his old buoyancy. On April 14 he wrote ten letters, none of them reflecting pessimism or despair. Though admitting to Oliver Towles that Virginia was "open to insult and depredation even to the smallest force," he expressed a guarded optimism, and he suggested to others that even the worst enemy depredations would "tend to produce irremovable hatred against so detestable a nation and thereby strengthen our Union." [34]

Jefferson's baby daughter, Lucy Elizabeth, then four and one-half months old, died the next day. On the following morning, April 16, Jefferson wrote a note to David Jameson, "The day is so very bad that I hardly expect a council, and there being nothing that I know of very pressing, and Mrs. Jefferson in a situation in which I would not wish to leave her, I shall not attend to-day." [35] His account book reflected the melancholy happening: "April 15. Our daughter Lucy Elizabeth died about 10 o'clock a m on this day." On April 17, he wrote, "for medicine—£108," and on May 12, "pd Dr Gilmer £9." On April 18 he wrote to Timothy Matlack, "I mean shortly to retire." [36] There was to be no shaking this resolve.

Shortly after his daughter's death he received word from Kentucky Territory of new Indian atrocities calculated to augment Jefferson's own sorrow and sense of guilt. "Infants are torn from their Mothers Arms and their Brains dashed out against Trees," his informant wrote.[37] Had there been no war these infants might well be still alive; had he been home in Monticello so might be his own small daughter. Such thoughts he could hardly have escaped. Later Jefferson wrote to James Monroe, "I think public service and private misery inseparably linked together." [38] But there was an added burden. The death of her baby apparently threw Martha Jefferson into such a state of melancholy that she ceased to function at least as a housewife and a hostess. As during the nine-month period of 1779, she stopped spending money altogether. Jefferson's account book, normally peppered with references to sums for "Mrs. Jefferson" now fails to make any mention of her for an entire year save on two occasions, when it is she who gives money to him:

July 15, 1781: "recd of Mrs. Jefferson £240."

September 25, 1781: "recd of Mrs. Jefferson £120."

Once more the house slaves took over the buying. And as far as this aspect of her life is revealed in Jefferson's tiny daily notations, it would seem that Martha Jefferson spent no money from the death of

Lucy Elizabeth in April 1781 to her own death seventeen months later in September 1782.

Fate would continue to deal Thomas Jefferson one nasty blow after another before he could take refuge in resignation from executive office on June 2, 1781. On April 18 a new British force landed at the mouth of the James with 2,300 men. Benedict Arnold was back, together with Major General William Phillips, whom Jefferson had entertained at Monticello with uncommon courtesy when he was a prisoner of war. Phillips, whom Jefferson described as "the proudest man of the proudest nation on the earth," [39] had been exchanged and was now leading the new expedition. Lafayette was wildly eager to engage him, for Phillips many years before at the Battle of Minden had been in command of the artillerymen whose cannon had killed his father.[40] But Phillips' invasion was no ordinary raid for purposes of plunder and humiliation. Cornwallis, then moving slowly upward through North Carolina, intended to join forces with Phillips, destroy Lafayette's army, and crush the Revolution in Virginia as he thought he had crushed it in the states to the south.

Lafayette had only 900 regulars, but 2,000 muskets had arrived from the North in time to equip the destitute Virginia militia. Though sensibly avoiding a direct battle with the superor British forces, Lafayette did save Richmond from a second plundering by taking up a strategic position near the capital, and Jefferson at this date, April 29, 1781, moved the Virginia government further inland to Charlottesville. It was a going home, not only for himself, but especially for his sick and grieving wife.

The dreaded juncture of the Cornwallis and Phillips forces took place in Petersburg on May 20, 1781. This meant 7,000 British regulars against Lafayette's army, which, though augmented by Pennsylvania regulars under General Anthony Wayne, still numbered only 3,000. Jefferson wrote Washington a desperate letter begging him to come personally to Virginia, describing the military situation exactly, and warning that Cornwallis' devastation of Virginia might "lead the minds of the people to acquiescence under those events which they see no human power prepared to ward off." He also admitted frankly that within three days he would relinquish his own post "to abler hands," [41] though he did not write that he hoped also to see the governorship go to Thomas Nelson, Jr., who had had experience as a soldier.

If Washington was dismayed at Jefferson's refusal to run for reelection at a moment of great calamity, he kept his sorrow to himself.

Perhaps he agreed in his heart with Jefferson, that someone else could do better. But he replied with all gentleness, praising Jefferson's readiness and zeal, and assuring him his friendship. He hinted at the strategy he was planning with the French, which he believed would force the British to evacuate their forces from Virginia, but dared not write it in detail; in any case the letter would have come too late, and would hardly have persuaded Jefferson to try to stay on in office.[42]

On May 28 Jefferson received from Baron von Steuben a copy of a report he was sending to the Virginia legislature, blaming the Virginia government for letting desertion go unpunished and laws go unexecuted, for failing to recruit militiamen, for permitting "shameful evasions and impositions." Though he never mentioned Jefferson by name, von Steuben had written the document as a savage personal indictment.[43] Happier news from Lafayette that General Greene had recently forced the British to evacuate Camden and had recaptured several forts in North Carolina never reached Jefferson, for the letter was intercepted by the British.[44]

Jefferson was at Monticello on June 2, sheltering several legislators. Election for the governorship had been postponed two days because the second fell on a Saturday, so he was still technically in office for the final humiliation. No story in his life has been told more often than how he was awakened at sunrise by young Jack Jouett, who at Cuckoo Tavern had overheard Banastre Tarleton, leading a raiding force of British dragoons, plan to capture the Virginia legislature and Jefferson himself. Jouett had ridden all night through the brush to sound the alarm, and had cuts across his face, legend has it, that left him scarred for life. Jefferson sent his wife and daughters and friends off to safety, meanwhile had a leisurely breakfast, and periodically scanned the landscape through his telescope. Once he saw the green and white uniforms begin the Monticello ascent, he started off on his horse through the woods toward Carter's Mountain, and made his escape.

His behavior was cool, and could certainly be described as brave, but the flight over Carter's Mountain was eventually turned by Jefferson's political enemies into a legend of military ineptness and cowardice. The fact that everyone in the Virginia civil government was fleeing— "Governor, council, everybody scampering," in the words of Betsey Ambler[45]—did not serve to spare Jefferson abuse in his presidential years. And the charge of cowardice, like an evil shadow, would follow him through his life. Light-Horse Harry Lee, writing in 1812 the history of the Virginia campaigns, would describe Cornwallis as "burning tobacco, destroying . . . scattered stores, and chasing our governor from hill to hill, and our legislature from town to town."[46] Jefferson

retaliated by calling Lee's work "an amusing historical novel," and in 1816 at age seventy-three finally attacked the canard in a rare ironic outburst. "That it has been sung in verse, and said in humble prose that, forgetting the noble example of the hero of La Mancha, and his windmills I declined a combat, singly against a troop, in which victory would have been so glorious? Forgetting, themselves, at the same time, that I was not provided with the enchanted arms of the knight, nor even with his helmet of Mambrino. These closet heroes forsooth would have disdained the shelter of a wood, even singly and unarmed, against a legion of armed enemies." [47]

Jefferson fled from Monticello in an agony of apprehension that upon his return he would see nothing but a pile of ashes. His slaves later described how Martin Hemings collected the family silver for Caesar, who was hiding it under the plank floor of the front portico when the dragoons broke through the trees. Martin slammed down the plank, leaving Caesar in the dark recess. One soldier put a pistol to Martin's breast and threatened to fire if he did not reveal the direction in which his master had fled. "Fire away then," Martin replied.[48] But Captain McCleod, heading the raiding party, marveling, one must believe, in the gemlike quality of the setting, gave word that the house and its contents and presumably also the slaves should remain undisturbed. After eighteen hours, the slaves were left in charge.

Cornwallis had no such compunction. With what Jefferson described as "that spirit of total extermination with which he seemed to rage over my possessions," he burned the barns, fences, and growing crops of corn and tobacco at Jefferson's Elkhill plantation, carrying off slaves, cattle, sheep, hogs, and horses, and cutting the throats of the colts too young for service.[49] In the next few weeks Virginia was similarly ravaged wherever Cornwallis moved across her face. But Jefferson, personally crushed by the invasion and his own sense of ineptitude, was ultimately right in his old optimism. For every rebel the British captured and for every barn they burned a dozen patriots sprang out of the Virginia fields. Lafayette too was right when he wrote to Jefferson, "Over running a Country is not to conquer it, and if it was construed into a right of possession, the french could claim the whole German Empire." [50] Cornwallis' order that "every militia man who has borne arms with us and afterwards joined the enemy, shall be immediately hanged"—punctuated by the execution of the patriot colonel Isaac Hayne [51]—served only to kindle Virginia outrage. And when the British general finally settled in at Yorktown, the militia that Jefferson had despaired of ever welding into a decent fighting force had finally become formidable.

Though Jefferson was forgiven for his retirement by Washington, his own enemies in the Virginia legislature, meeting in Staunton on June 12, 1781, voted a resolution of inquiry into his performance as governor. The move was started by a brash young delegate named George Nicholas, but behind him was Patrick Henry, who Jefferson believed coveted the role of dictator. Nicholas asked some searching questions, some of which were not easy to answer.[52] Sick at heart, Jefferson retired with his family to his plantation at Poplar Forest, ninety miles from Monticello and far from British raiders.

Shortly after his arrival there, Jefferson was riding Caractacus, a spirited horse he had himself named and raised from a colt. Though a superb horseman who rode often and often dangerously, he was thrown and injured so seriously that it was six weeks before he could ride again. The cost of two visits from a doctor, in the paper money of the moment, was £600.[53] Later some of his enemies wrote that he had fallen from his horse in his flight over Carter's Mountain, adding to the folklore of his failure and fright. The fall was indeed symbolic, if not an act of self-punishment, for Caractacus was the name of an ancient British king.

During his convalescence Jefferson received a letter from the Continental Congress which should have helped dispel his shame. His friends in Philadelphia, who clearly did not look upon his resignation as unpardonable, seized upon the opportunity to elect him on June 14, 1781, together with John Adams, John Jay, John Laurens, and Benjamin Franklin, as ministers plenipotentiary to aid in securing peace through the intercession of the Empress of Russia. Receiving the letter July 9, Jefferson suffered an agony of indecision he did not resolve for four weeks.[54] That he longed to go to Europe is obvious in a letter he wrote to Lafayette. Not going, he said, meant losing the chance "of combining public service with private gratification, of seeing countries whose improvements in science, in arts, and in civilization, it has been my fortune to admit at a distance but never to see . . ." [55]

But he turned the offer down. His wife was not pregnant; neither was she well. And he wrote frankly to the Congress that for a post of such great consequence he felt himself to be unfit. To Lafayette, who carried this letter of rejection to Philadelphia, he admitted that turning down the offer "has given me more mortification than almost any occurrence of my life." [56] The young French soldier, who had by now come to know Jefferson and to be drawn irresistibly into the magic circle of his friends, understood, though somewhat imperfectly, the nature of his malaise and replied in a friendly letter: "I feel a sincere pleasure in this opportunity to Continue our Correspondence. The Honor of Hearing from you Shall Ever be Wellcome. . . . My affectionate Regard." Later Lafayette wrote to Washington that "Jefferson has been too severely charged." [57] In the following year a letter arriving from Franklin in Paris must have trebled Jefferson's regret: "I was in great Hopes when I saw your Name in the Commission for treating of Peace, that I should have had the Happiness of seeing you here, and of enjoying again in this World, your pleasing Society and Conversation. But I begin now to fear that I shall be disappointed. . . ." [58]

In explaining to his kinsman Edmund Randolph why he had declined the diplomatic assignment, Jefferson wrote, "I have taken my final leave of everything of that nature, have retired to my farm, my family and books from which I think nothing will ever more separate me." He would go to defend his record at the next meeting of the Virginia assembly and then resign from politics forever.[59] But this flight brought no liberation, only the taste of ashes in his mouth. On October 28, 1781, after learning of Washington's victory at Yorktown, Jefferson wrote him his congratulations. His excuse for missing the bonfires, salutes, and speeches of the celebration, and for failing to pay his respects to the commander in chief in person, is one of the most self-revealing in the whole Jefferson-Washington correspondence. He would have come, Jefferson wrote, except for "the state of perpetual decrepitude to which I am unfortunately reduced." [60] Where every other patriot in the thirteen united states felt the exhilaration of victory, Jefferson at thirty-eight felt only a sense of being prematurely old, a defeated and decrepit man.

CHAPTER XI

Jefferson Writes a Book

In literature nothing new; for I do not consider as having added anything to that field my own Notes of which I have had a few copies
printed.

Jefferson to Charles Thomson, July 21, 1785 [1]

Jefferson had retired from office at the worst moment in his state's
history, and at the absolute nadir of his own career. "While an enemy
is within our bowels," he wrote shortly afterward, "the first object is
to expel him." [2] But it was when the enemy was within the bowels of
Virginia that Jefferson retired from office, and it was this retirement,
far more than his mistakes when Arnold first invaded Virginia or his
own flight over Carter's Mountain, that cost Jefferson the esteem of
some of his countrymen and stimulated the humiliating inquiry into
his record.

Virginia was saved and Cornwallis defeated because American and
French regulars blocked off the British forces at Yorktown, and the
French fleet of Admiral de Grasse cut off his escape by sea. But the
very necessity that forced Cornwallis to settle in at Yorktown had to
do with his failure to subdue the American interior. All his ravaging
had resulted not in increased attachment to the crown, but in either a
totally hostile countryside area, or at best a divided one, with Americans engaged in savage encounters with each other. The terrain and
constantly reinvigorated guerrilla patriots helped defeat the British,
and to the extent that Jefferson contributed to this guerrilla effort, as
well as to "the Virginia line," he could rightly claim some credit for
the military victory.

That Jefferson understood the strategic role of the militia is evident from a letter of protest he wrote to James Monroe, who had suggested just before the Yorktown surrender that in view of the certainty of victory they discharge some of the Virginia militia, who were eating up more supplies than they were worth. Jefferson replied stiffly that were it his decision he would not do so. "As an American, as a Virginian, I should covet as large a share of the honor in accomplishing so great an event as a superior proportion of numbers could give." [3] He did indeed "covet" the honor, and had he defended his own conduct and minimized his failures, he might well have stayed on in office the extra five months that would have made it possible for him to share in the heady celebration at Yorktown. But he was unnecessarily defensive about his record, writing that he had been "unprepared by his line of life and education for the command of armies," and that he "believed it not right to stand in the way of talents better fitted than his own . . ." [4] He measured himself against his own ideal rather than against the performance of others. The death of his daughter, coming at the worst possible moment, had compounded his sense of starcrossed destiny, and had made his impulse to flee from responsibility irresistible.

From the time of his flight over Carter's Mountain to the end of September 1781, almost four months, he wrote apparently only seven letters.[5] But in this period, unlike the unproductive three months before his mother's death which had seen even fewer letters, he began to write a book. His *Notes on the State of Virginia* has been described by William Peden, who brought out a richly annotated edition in 1955, as "probably the most important scientific and political book written by an American before 1785 . . . one of America's first permanent literary and intellectual landmarks." It was also an exercise in autobiography and therapy. During the writing he recovered from the sprains and bruises he owed to Caractacus. How quickly he regained his old ebullience is not so certain, though a strong body, creative spirit, and infinite capacity for work are almost certain restoratives to depression, provided there exists as a basic reservoir a sense of inner worth.

During these four months his wife became pregnant again, and no doubt was happy to be making up the loss of Lucy Elizabeth—the new baby daughter would indeed be given the same name. Jefferson mentioned his wife in a letter to James Monroe on October 5, 1781: "Mrs. Jefferson joins me in wishes for a safe and pleasant voiage and return." [6] But as we have said, she was too weak to assume any household duties, as the record of expenditures in Jefferson's account book indicates. Since she had weathered six pregnancies, there was reason for hope that she would survive the seventh. Jefferson had to believe this. But except for a fortnight in Richmond when he defended his name in the Virginia legislature, he did not dare leave his wife for more than a day during the whole nine months.

In his first weeks at Poplar Forest he set himself to answering the twenty-one queries of François de Barbé-Marbois concerning Virginia, upon which he had begun gathering information in November 1780. The answers grew into essays; the digressions expanded into chapters, until the writing adventure became a volume which was not only "Notes on the State of Virginia," but also "Notes on the state of Thomas Jefferson." He wrote of boundaries, rivers, seaports, population, and "Productions Mineral, Vegetable and Animal." He also digressed to discuss the tyranny of the clergy, the necessity of public education, the essential nature of blacks, the origin of the Indians, and the complicated structure of their language. He identified the social and political aspirations of Virginia with those of America. Importantly, too, he identified Virginia with himself.

The book is as wise, thoughtful, and accurate as Jefferson at his best. It is also intermittently angry and indignant, and occasionally shockingly biased and mistaken. Perhaps because originally he did not write with publication in mind, he ceased for a time being a secretive man. But once finished he became deeply suspicious of what he had written. He sent a copy to Marbois on December 20, 1781, describing it as "very imperfect and not worth offering but as a proof of my respect for your wishes." [7] Though several of his friends who read the manuscript begged him to publish it, he did not take pains to correct and enlarge the Notes until his arrival in Paris four years later. Even then, when he permitted publication in 1785, it was in an edition of only two hundred copies, and he refused to have his name appear on the title page.

This reluctance to acknowledge authorship is very like that of Jefferson's great interpreter, Henry Adams, who published his novels under pseudonyms and his Education as a private printing for his friends. Both men seem to have felt singularly vulnerable, fearful of exposing their own feelings as if they were certain to provoke derision. Jefferson in letters to his friends disparaged the first edition of the Notes as of little value, and warned them not to allow their copies to fall into the hands of publishers, though he suggested, in a contradictory letter to Madison, that he would like to send a copy to each student at William and Mary College. "But there are sentiments on some subjects which I apprehend might be displeasing to the country perhaps to the assembly or to some who lead it," he wrote, and begged Madison for advice on the matter. He would send over from Paris, he wrote, only "a very few copies to particular friends in confidence and burn the rest." [8]

To entertain the idea of burning one's own book suggests enormous conflict over its contents. Jefferson was not only uncertain over the value of what he had written, but also apprehensive about the public reaction to what he had said about religion and slavery. Here his instincts were sound enough, for what he wrote on these subjects would be quoted for good and evil in his name for the next two hundred years. He sent John Adams one of the two hundred copies. When Adams wrote to him, "The Passages upon Slavery are worth Diamonds," he replied sadly, "But my country will probably estimate them differently. A foreknowledge of this has retarded my communicating them to my friends for two years." [9]

To prevent the pirating of the book by a French publisher in 1785, he agreed to a French edition, and worked over the translation, which he found execrable. Even here he forbade the use of anything but his initial on the title page. But once this volume was in print he realized the truth of what Madison pointed out to him: "Your notes having got into print in France will inevitably be translated back and published in that form, not only in England but in America unless you give out the original." [10] So he contracted with John Stockdale in London for a British version, with his name for the first time printed with the volume.

To a friend in America, to whom he sent fifty-seven copies for distribution, he wrote that it was "a bad book. . . . the author of which has no merit than that of thinking as little of it as any man in the world can." [11] But this was a mere conceit, defensive if not playful. Jefferson took pride in what he had written, or he would not have sent copies to his friends, but he had constant need to be shored up and sustained, and often demeaned his book by way of an unconscious invitation to such support. He lacked the faith—or arrogance—for authorship. Once quotations from the book began to be used against him in an increasing crescendo of attack, he abandoned further authorship for publication save for his reasoned and prudent political papers, until age seventy-seven, when he began his *Autobiography*. By that time his habit of secrecy had become so rigid he found it impossible to share any of his emotional life, or even to give himself up to reminiscence, as he did on rare occasions in his letters.

But in 1781 he was bursting with grievances and consumed with a sense of failure. The inner ferment resulted—despite the confining organizational structure, which consisted of answers to the twenty-one queries of Marbois—in a surprisingly personal book. There is one passage written in white heat having to do with the Virginia political scene of June 1781. The state legislature instead of holding a routine election to replace Jefferson as governor had permitted a near coup by Patrick Henry, who had hoped to take advantage of the military crisis by becoming dictator. Jefferson was appalled by the narrowness of the vote that prevented it, and still more by the realization that at any time in the future Virginians might "by a single vote be laid prostrate at the feet of one man!"

"In God's name," he wrote passionately, "from whence have they derived this power? . . . Necessities which dissolve a government do not convey its authority to an oligarchy or a monarchy. . . . A leader may offer, but not impose himself, nor be imposed on them. Much less can their necks be submitted to his sword, their breath be held at his will or caprice." Though he did not mention Patrick Henry by name, no one in Virginia needed to be told whom he was writing about, and Henry never forgave Jefferson for his writing that in Virginia government must be "kept in a plurality of hands" so that "the corrupt will of no one man might in the future oppress him." [12]

Most of the book, however, was nonpolitical. It was essentially a guidebook, but one written by a man of genius. He began the book like a surveyor, as we have noted, calmly bounding his state. But he shortly burst out of the confines of Virginia, with descriptions of territories going as far west as Santa Fe. In writing about rivers, which he loved, his writing became excited and sensuous, especially in describing "the passage of the Patowmac through the Blue ridge," which he said was "perhaps one of the most stupendous scenes in nature."

> You stand on a very high point of land. On your right comes up the Shenandoah, having ranged along the foot of the mountain an hundred miles to seek a vent. On your left approaches the Patowmac, in quest of a passage also. In the moment of their junction they rush together against the mountain, rend it asunder, and pass off to the sea . . .
>
> For the mountain being cloven asunder, she presents to your eye, through the cleft, a small catch of smooth blue horizon, at an infinite distance in the plain country, inviting you, as it were, from the riot and tumult roaring around, to pass through the breach and participate of the calm below.

This phenomenon, together with Virginia's great Natural Bridge, he described in an extraordinary metaphor as "monuments of a war between rivers and mountains, which must have shaken the earth itself to its center." [13] Then he went on to write of "the height of our mountains," speculating that the Alleghenies might well be the highest on the continent. Jefferson seldom indulged in such hyperbole, in imagery so rich, in nuances so mysterious, in language that may have pointed, however obliquely, to the earthquakes of psychic discovery in his childhood.

Much in the *Notes* was defensive, and had to do with size. He

bristled at Buffon's odd observation that American mammals were
smaller than those in the Old World, and constructed comparative
tables showing triumphantly that where there were "18 quadrupeds
peculiar to Europe," America had seventy-four, that "of 26 quadrupeds
common to both countries, 7 are said to be larger in America, 7 of
equal size, and 12 not sufficiently examined." [14] The feeling underneath the scientific observations was primitive—I am bigger than you
are—and one suspects that what stimulated all these complications of
weights and heights and comparative sizes had not only to do with the
crisis of his current shame and failure, but also with a much earlier
time when he had been beaten by men or boys much bigger than
himself. The new shame reawakened a sense of earlier shames, and
he worked at resolving them all by pointing out the idiocies of a
French naturalist whom he had never seen.

So too he attacked the statement of Abbé Raynal that America had
never produced "one good poet, one able mathematician, one man of
genius in a single art or a single science." In war, Jefferson wrote,
America had produced a Washington, in physics a Franklin, in mathematics a Rittenhouse. As for the lack of a great poet, he answered
thus:

> When we shall have existed as a people as long as the Greeks did
> before they produced a Homer, the Roman a Virgil, the French a
> Racine and Voltaire, the English a Shakespeare and Milton; should
> this reproach be still true, we will enquire from what unfriendly causes
> it has proceeded . . .

America, he insisted, "though but a child of yesterday, has already
given hopeful proofs of genius." [15]

He was enraged at Buffon's smug omniscience in writing that
American Indians "lack ardor for females," that they "love their parents and children but little," that they have "small organs of generation," and "little sexual capacity." The Indian, he replied, "is neither
more defective in ardor, nor more impotent with his female, than the
white reduced to the same diet and exercise . . . he is brave, when an
enterprise depends on bravery; education with him making the point
of honor consist in the destruction of an enemy by stratagem, and in
the preservation of his own person free from injury. . . . His sensibility is keen, even the warriors weeping most bitterly on the loss of
their children." [16]

Here Jefferson, who had himself so recently been occupied in "preservation of his own person free from injury," and who had grieved
"most bitterly" over the recent loss of a child, wrote with the overtones
of autobiography. So something of his private suffering and guilt were

dissipated and expiated in the seemingly intellectual exercise of writing a superior guidebook to Virginia. What seems to be a chauvinistic affirmation of the preëminence of America was really an exercise in rebuilding faith in himself. For as the book unfolded, he wrote not only about Virginia as it was, but as it must one day be. Here he wrote of his plans for emancipation of the blacks, for general education in a state where a large proportion of the whites were then illiterate, for a vastly improved legal system, for a perfected constitution. Even Virginia architecture, which he pronounced execrable, he vowed would be changed.

He wrote of the superiority of the pastoral life, uncorrupted by the evils of the city, where "dependence begets subservience and venality suffocates the gem of virtue, and prepares fit tools for the designs of ambition."

> Those who labour in the earth are the chosen people of God, if ever he had a chosen people, whose breasts he has made his peculiar deposit for substantial and genuine virtue. . . . While we have land to labour then, let us never wish to see our citizens occupied at a work-bench, or twirling a distaff. Carpenters, masons, smiths, are wanting in husbandry: but, for the general operations of manufacture, let our workshops remain in Europe. . . . The loss by the transportation of commodities across the Atlantic will be made up in happiness and permanence of government. The mobs of great cities add just so much to the support of pure government, as sores do to the strength of the human body.[17]

This passage became justly famous, and many today mistakenly believe it represented Jefferson's thinking all his life. It was written just after Jefferson had renounced the political—and therefore urban—life, and the renunciation had come after a profound inner struggle. This struggle Jefferson defined in a candid letter to James Monroe on May 20, 1782:

> Before I ventured to declare to my countrymen my determination to retire from public employment I examined well my heart, to know whether it were thoroughly cured of every principle of political ambition, whether no lurking particle remained which might leave me uneasy when reduced within the limits of mere private life. I became satisfied that every fibre of that passion was thoroughly eradicated.[18]

The struggle was not over, as the letter itself betrays. "Reduced within the limits of mere private life," carries the overtones of slavery, or at least of his being fenced in. He had by no means purged his "passion" for politics. His paean to country living, written during this period in which he "examined well his heart," was not so much an expression of conviction as a justification and solace. Jefferson was like a defeated noble who retires to his castle to nurse his wounds, and who vows never to return to battle.

That Jefferson had not abandoned the battle at all we see in the *Notes*, especially in his arguments for an end to religious slavery and chattel slavery. If he could not fight Cornwallis, or argue in the legislative arena, he could at least pursue the struggle for liberty with his pen. At the time he was writing the *Notes* Jefferson's proposed legislation to separate church and state forever in Virginia had not yet passed, and he was not sanguine that it ever would. His emancipation proposal had not even been introduced. In urging that the church be curbed he pointed out that it was still legal to burn a heretic in Virginia. And he went on to argue for the right of nonconformity in language that for pious Anglicans had the shock effect of an artillery piece:

> Millions of innocent men, women and children, since the introduction of Christianity, have been burnt, tortured, fined, imprisoned; yet we have not advanced one inch towards uniformity. What has been the effect of coercion? To make one half the world fools, and the other half hypocrites.

As if this rhetoric were not brave enough, he also wrote the two lines which would be quoted against him for the rest of his life as proof that he was an atheist: "But it does me no injury for my neighbor to say there are twenty gods, or no god. It neither picks my pocket nor breaks my leg." [19] So the man who had been accused of cowardice, and who had only recently come very near to breaking his leg when thrown from his horse, charged like Don Quixote against his ancient enemies.

Still, there was contradiction. For Jefferson went on to urge that the tyrannical laws be repealed at once, before the rulers become corrupt and the people careless. But in the very act of retiring Jefferson was doing exactly that which he warned others against, breaking up the unity of the revolutionary government before "every essential right" was "fixed on a legal basis." [20] He was still debating with his own decision to retire, and the eloquence of his protest against anyone's abandoning the politics of this revolutionary time attested to the strength of his passion for that politics.

What Jefferson wrote in the *Notes* about "the blot of slavery," the nature of black men and their abuse by white men, has caused more controversy among Jefferson admirers and detractors than anything else he ever wrote. Writers of every political complexion and every attitude on race can find something to quote approvingly or disapprovingly from this volume. It is not easy to step back into the Virginia of

1781, and even more difficult to reconstruct Jefferson's feelings about blacks, without bringing to bear the judgments of our own time. Scientists of the late eighteenth century were writing about the races of men as if their genetic differences had just been discovered; liberation from the dogmas of the church among men of the Enlightenment had resulted in an avalanche of speculation about racial origins.[21]

When Jefferson came to distinguish among blacks, whites, and Indians, he was echoing the fashion set especially by Buffon whose multivolume *Histoire naturelle*, which began publication in 1749 and extended to 1804, he had begun to read before going to Paris.[22] Buffon's ideas clearly excited Jefferson to correction and contradiction once he arrived. But none of the great men of the Enlightenment wrote about blacks with the personal experience of Thomas Jefferson. He had lived with slaves since childhood, and now was master of several plantations. So far as we know he had not yet met an educated black, but several of the Hemings family slaves had either learned to read and write or were in the process of learning under Jefferson's mastership.[23] Jefferson did know about the poems of Phyllis Wheatley, African-born slave in Massachusetts, whose *Poems on Various Subjects, Religious and Moral* had caused a mild sensation when published in London in 1773, and would see five editions before 1800. But he held her talent in contempt. "Religion indeed has produced a Phyllis Whately," he wrote, "but it could not produce a poet." [24] The contempt, however, may well have been induced by the heavily religious content of her poems, which Jefferson would have found offensive in any writer, black or white.

Many of Jefferson's observations about blacks seem today to be contemptuous and racist. Actually Jefferson was trying to write about Negroes as would a budding scientist, looking at them, he said, "as subjects of natural history." His detachment can be seen as remarkable, provided one refuses to become indignant over obvious errors, which were the errors of the eighteenth century. For a white to concede that blacks were superior to whites in any quality, as did Jefferson, set him apart in his own time in Virginia as either radical or quixotic. For a white to plead for total emancipation in Virginia, as Jefferson did, was an invitation to social ostracism.[25]

Jefferson wrote that whites were superior in "reason" and in beauty. But he wrote of the Negroes that "in memory they are equal to the whites," and that they are "at least as brave, and more adventuresome." In music, he said, "they are more generally gifted than the whites with accurate ears for tune and time," high praise from a man who for years had practiced three hours a day with his violin. His most negative comments were nonetheless deplorable: "Among the blacks is misery enough, God knows, but no poetry . . . in imagination they are dull, tasteless, and anomalous. . . . They secrete less by the kidnies, and more by the glands of the skin, which gives them a very strong and disagreeable odour." He assumed, moreover, that where the red man was truly equal to the white in natural endowment, the blacks were not. Jefferson advanced this "as a suspicion only," and would write later in a letter to Chastellux that "equally cultivated, for a few generations," the blacks might well become the white man's equal.[26] Such theorizing was far more radical as "science" than that of many men of the Enlightenment, who believed in the great Chain of Being, with the Negro securely fastened at the bottom among the races of man, and the American Indian slightly above him.[27] But the sentiments Jefferson wrote to Chastellux in 1785 were never incorporated in his Notes on the State of Virginia, and the damage done in the future to the cause of emancipation and civil rights for Negroes by the negative comments in his few published pages on the nature of the Negro would be appalling.[28]

The science of genetics was not yet born, but Jefferson already had convinced himself that the white slaves of Roman times could be superior as artists and even scientists to their masters, something he would not concede to the slaves at Monticello. Though refusing to concede equality in intellect, in matters "of the heart," he wrote, nature had "done them justice," equally with the whites. And "the disposition to theft with which they have been branded," he added, "must be ascribed to their situation, and not to any depravity of the moral sense." [29]

Could the Negro improve genetically without miscegenation? This question Jefferson never answered precisely. With the talented Hemings family slaves as a model, it is not surprising that he wrote, "The improvement of the blacks in body and mind, in the first instance of their mixture with the whites, has been observed by everyone, and proves that their inferiority is not the effect merely of their condition of life." [30] Like all whites, he found it difficult to believe that the talents of the mulatto might have come from the black ancestors as well as the white.

Nevertheless he did believe that the blacks were capable of self-government in an all-black society, and, as we have already noted, he proposed in his Notes that young black girls be educated at public expense to age eighteen, and the black youths to age twenty-one, and that they be freed and sent off to Africa, or the West Indies, or beyond the Mississippi, with all the tools and capital necessary to start a new state. One wonders if Jefferson ever asked Martin or Robert Hemings their opinion of the idea. He seems not to have understood that such expulsion would mean great psychic as well as economic hardship. And he did not see that the whites would never tolerate the expense of educating their own labor force only to lose it.

Jefferson did ask himself the question, "Why not retain and incorporate the blacks into the state?" His answer was a classic statement of fear. In Virginia as a whole there were ten blacks for every eleven whites; at Monticello the ratio, as in his childhood at Tuckahoe, was around ten to one.

> Deep rooted prejudices entertained by the whites; ten thousand recollections, by the blacks, of the injuries they have sustained; new provocations; the real distinctions which nature has made; and many other circumstances, will divide us into parties, and produce convulsions which will probably never end but in the extermination of the one or the other race.[31]

One can look at this whole concept of emancipation and colonization as a fantasy, which served some important purpose in Jefferson's life. But was it a fantasy in 1781? Slaves by the thousands had fled to the British army, and had been transported from America in British ships, 4,000 from Savannah, 6,000 from Charleston, 4,000 from New York, to say nothing of the thousands carried off by the French.[32] Why else would his own slaves have "joined enemy," except for the promise of freedom? What was possible in war for the hated British must surely be made possible under the enlightened government of the new United States. Pennsylvania was pointing the way, the first of the states to pass emancipation legislation.

> I think a change already perceptible, since the origin of the present revolution. The spirit of the master is abating, that of the slave rising from the dust, his condition mollifying, the way I hope preparing under the auspices of heaven, for a total emancipation.[33]

Still, he let Martin Hemings search out a slave near Williamsburg he thought to be a runaway from his own plantation, enlisting one slave to catch another.[34] Everyone in Virginia at the moment was hunting down his property, and the new United States government would put great pressure on the British to return the blacks who had either been captured or who had voluntarily run their way.[35] Jefferson was too sensitive not to see the contradiction in his own life between theory and action. In the *Notes* he wrote about the moral depravity of the statesman who permits "one half the citizens thus to trample on the rights of the other, transforms those into despots, and these into enemies, destroys the morals of the one part, and the *amor patriae* of the other." And in so writing he seems to have been

seized with an anxiety that came to him rarely, the anxiety of a punishing and avenging God. Should such a God decree that there be "a
revolution of the wheel of fortune," there was no doubt in Jefferson's
mind He would be on the side of the slaves.

And can the liberties of a nation be thought secure when we have
removed their only firm basis, a conviction in the minds of the people
that these liberties are the gift of God? That they are not to be violated
but with his wrath? Indeed I tremble for my country when I reflect
that God is just: that his justice cannot sleep for ever: that considering numbers, nature and natural means only, a revolution of the wheel
of fortune, an exchange of situation, is among possible events: that it
may become probable by supernatural interference! The Almighty has
no attribute which can take sides with us in such a contest.[36]

CHAPTER XII

The Two Marthas

I am born to lose everything I love.

Jefferson to Maria Cosway, July 1, 1787 [1]

When the Virginia legislature convened in November 1781 the members had so forgotten the panic and despair of the previous June that they cheerfully elected Jefferson a delegate to the Continental Congress. But Patrick Henry, by now not only a rival but also an enemy, quietly insisted that the inquiry into Jefferson's record as governor, voted the previous June, should not be rescinded or ignored, and a committee was chosen to hold hearings on the matter. "The inquiry," Jefferson confessed later, "was a shock on which I had not calculated." He felt himself "suspected and suspended in the eyes of the world without the least hint then or afterwards made public which might restrain them from supposing I stood arraigned for treasons of the heart and not mere weaknesses of the head." The injury, he said, "inflicted a wound on my spirit which will only be cured by the all-healing grave." [2]

Though the original inquiry had been set in motion by young George Nicholas, Jefferson was certain he was a mere puppet in the hands of Patrick Henry, "a trifling body . . . below contempt" whose "natural ill-temper was the tool worked with by another hand." Nicholas was, Jefferson wrote, "like the minners which go in and out of the fundament of the whale. But the whale himself was discoverable enough by the turbulence of the water under which he moved." [3]

Jefferson had already complained to Nicholas that he seemed to want "to stab a reputation by a general suggestion under a bare expectation that facts might be afterwards hunted up to boulster it." [4] And when he appeared at the legislature on December 12 to defend himself against the charges the shamed young man was nowhere to be seen. Actually no defense was necessary, for the committee report, as read by John Banister, stated that no information had been brought in save rumors, and "the said rumors were groundless." [5] Nevertheless Jefferson insisted on having the Nicholas list of charges read, and he answered them one by one.

Why did he undertake this unnecessary probing of old wounds, with a defense that was not always effective but sometimes weak and petulant? To the quite legitimate question asking why there had been no "lookouts" to warn of Benedict Arnold's invasion, he replied, "There had been no cause to order lookouts more than has ever been existing. This is only in fact asking why we do not always keep lookouts." [6] There may have been a need for self-punishment here, which Patrick Henry was only too willing to exploit.

Jefferson's friends, who deplored the inquiry as invidious party caviling, saw to it that the legislature voted a resolution of thanks and confidence in his "Ability, Rectitude, and Integrity as chief Magistrate of this Commonwealth." But even this came after wrangling over the wording of the resolution, and the insistence on the part of Jefferson's admirers of the deletion of several phrases that might count against his reputation.[7] It was all in notable contrast to the enthusiastic resolutions of thanks which Jefferson heard voted on December 17 for the heroes of Yorktown: Washington, Rochambeau, de Grasse, and Lafayette.

Once he heard the amended resolution of thanks for himself voted on in the House, December 19, 1781, he not only resigned from the Virginia legislature but also formally declined to serve in the Continental Congress.[8] To the great chagrin of his friends he thus gave notice that he was leaving politics forever. He seems to have confided in no one, at least in writing, about the continuing weakness and ill health of his wife. His friend Edmund Randolph, indignant at what he called Jefferson's "unpardonable rage for retirement," believed it stemmed from what he frankly called the "impeachment" proceedings,[9] and was shortly working to get him back into harness. And it is true that the "rage for retirement" had much to do with his rage against Patrick Henry toward whom he had been "sincerely affectioned long ago." This rage remained slow-burning and inextinguishable. He wrote to Madison three years later, "While Mr. Henry lives another bad constitution would be formed and saddled forever on us. What we have to do I think is devoutly to pray for his death . . ." [10] And contempt for Henry surfaced even at age seventy-seven in the pages of

Jefferson's *Autobiography*, though his enemy had by then been dead for twenty-one years.

Retirement to Monticello this time brought cheerful entries in his *Garden Book*, though the previous desperate summer had seen only a single entry. In February he reported seeing "a flock of wild geese flying to N.W.," in March "Almonds & peaches" in blossom, and in May the sighting of an aurora borealis. He recorded sending apricot, cherry, and apple trees to be planted at Poplar Forest, along with carnations and white strawberries. And he even wrote in a recipe for currant jelly.[11] For a time he took into his home his sister Martha Carr, who had never remarried since the death of Dabney Carr in 1773. She had six children, including two daughters of marriageable age who were beginning to be expensive. Jefferson virtually adopted her eldest son, Peter, who had been living with him since the previous March. He was a handsome, promising youth, whose education Jefferson supervised, and whom he came to love as his own son.

Still, he felt isolated. On March 16 he wrote to one legislator, "You will probably be surprised at the receipt of a letter from one who has been so long withdrawn from your notice." [12] So long? It had been less than three months since his resignation. To Madison, who had been asking his help on the controversial western boundaries of Virginia, he wrote in self-depreciation on March 24: "I shall always be glad to hear from you; and if it be possible for me, retired from public business to find any thing worth your notice, I shall communicate it with pleasure." [13] When the Marquis de Chastellux, a major general in Rochambeau's army, sought him out at Monticello in April 1782, Jefferson encouraged him to stay four days.

Chastellux, a member of the French Academy, who was keeping a journal of his American experiences, was captivated by the house, which he described as elegant and in the Italian taste, though not without fault. But it was Jefferson who left a lasting impact. "It is with himself alone," he wrote, "I ought to bestow my time."

> Let me describe to you a man, not yet forty, tall, and with a mild and pleasing countenance, but whose mind and understanding are ample substitutes for every exterior grace. An American, who without ever having quitted his own country, is at once a musician, skilled in drawing, a geometrician, an astronomer, a natural philosopher, legislator, and statesman. . . .
>
> I found his first appearance serious, nay even cold; but before I had been two hours with him we were as intimate as if we had passed our whole lives together; walking, books, but above all a conversation always varied and interesting, always supported by that sweet satisfaction experienced by two persons, who in communicating their sentiments and

opinions, are invariably in unison, and who understand each other at the first hint, made four days pass away like so many minutes.

Discovering that both were fond of Ossian—"It was a spark of electricity which passed rapidly from one to the other"—each took turns quoting the passages he had memorized. Then Jefferson sent for the book and a bowl of punch, and they talked far into the night. "Sometimes natural philosophy," Chastellux wrote, "at others politicks or the arts were the topicks of our conversation, for no object had escaped Mr. Jefferson." It surely detracts nothing from this affecting scene to note that the poetry both admired was not the work of the third century Gaelic poet but a fraudulent "translation" by their Scottish contemporary, James Macpherson.

The one thing Chastellux missed, but which is implicit in the whole scene, was Jefferson's loneliness. Like everyone else the Frenchman was puzzled by his abandonment of public life, but Jefferson gave him only an evasive explanation. He is "a philosopher, in voluntary retirement from the world, and public business," Chastellux explained, "because he loves the world, inasmuch only as he can flatter himself with being useful to mankind; and the minds of his countrymen are not yet in a condition either to bear the light, or to suffer contradiction." That the health of Jefferson's wife was critical he was not told, though he knew she was expecting to "lie in" at any moment. He described her as "mild and amiable," with "charming children." He did note that Jefferson refused to leave her to accompany him on the eighty-mile trip to the "Bridge of Rocks, which unites two mountains." [14]

Martha Jefferson gave birth to a daughter on May 8, 1782. Jefferson wrote in his account book, "Lucy Elizabeth (second of that name) born at one o'clock AM." On May 20 he wrote to Monroe, "Mrs. Jefferson has added another daughter to our family. She has ever since and still continues very dangerously ill." [15] What kind of medical help she had is not known. Jefferson had come to distrust the practices of bleeding and purging, perhaps after his experience in having a Lieutenant Hayer "cup Mrs. Jefferson" back in 1779.[16] These medical barbarities, at least, seem not to have been employed to hasten her dying. The callousness of Jefferson's admirers and friends in refusing to heed the impending tragedy seems now almost incomprehensible. In the same week of the birth the voters of Albemarle County, without Jefferson's permission, elected him again to the Virginia legislature. Moreover, there was a rule that if a delegate did not appear in Richmond and obtain official permission to leave he could technically be arrested and dragged thither by the sergeant at arms. Though

Jefferson formally refused to serve in a letter of May 6, he was nevertheless covertly threatened with this kind of arrest in the same weeks his wife lay dying.

John Tyler, Speaker of the House of Delegates, who had himself precipitately resigned from the Governor's Council during the British invasion, wrote severely:

> I suppose your reasons are weighty, yet I wou'd suggest that good and able Men had better govern than be govern'd . . . if the able and good withdraw themselves from Society, the venal and ignorant will succeed. . . . I cannot but think the House may insist upon you to give attendance without incuring the Censure of being seized.[17]

It was at this point that Jefferson wrote a raging letter to James Monroe in which he described the gravity of his wife's illness, the crushing impact of the legislative inquiry, and his indignation at being harassed into going back to Richmond. "Offices of every kind, and given by every power, have been daily and hourly declined and resigned from the declaration of independence to this moment," he wrote. No state has "a *perpetual* right to the services of all it's members . . . This would be slavery." [18] It was in this letter, too, that he described the inquiry into his governorship as inflicting "a wound on my spirit which will only be cured by the all-healing grave."

Jefferson's daughter later wrote that in the last four months of her mother's life her father "was never out of calling: when not at her beside, he was writing in a small room which opened immediately at the head of her bed." [19] Word spread through Virginia in late June that Martha Jefferson had died,[20] though she lingered on until September. Edmund Randolph wrote to Madison on July 5, 1782: "Mrs. Jefferson has been too near her flight to a happier station, to suffer her affectionate husband to do more than lament the prospect of a separation." [21]

In this fatal spring of 1782 Jefferson had begun a calendar in which he indicated the beginning dates of the bloom of each of the different flowers in his garden. The first entry was March 17, when a narcissus burst open. Later he noted faithfully the dates of the flowerings of the first jonquil, hyacinth, ranunculus, iris, nasturtium, tulip, peony, lily, hollyhock, and calicanthus.[22] His baby daughter too, was blooming. But by June 25, when he noted the opening of the first Crimson Dwarf rose, his wife was so close to death he had no more heart to continue.

Sometime during these months, perhaps before the summer waned and the harvest lay in the fields, Martha Jefferson came to accept the finality of her own dying. One day she opened the pages of *Tristram*

Shandy, one of her husband's favorite volumes, and began to copy lines of such poignant relevance that in every reading they wrench the heart. That she singled these out for copying, omitting what was not appropriate to her own condition, tells us much about her intelligence, her sensitivity, and above all her necessity to communicate her own feelings with an eloquence she could not herself command but felt compelled to express:

> Time wastes too fast: every letter I trace tells me with what rapidity life follows my pen. The days and hours of it are flying over our heads like clouds of windy day never to return—more everything presses on—

At this point her hand must have faltered, for the remainder of the passage, copied in darker ink, is in Jefferson's clear, firm hand:

> —and every time I kiss thy hand to bid adieu, every absence which follows it, are preludes to that eternal separation which we are shortly to make!

Jefferson put the paper away for safekeeping, later adding to it a lock of his dead wife's hair.[23]

There is a story handed down among the Monticello slaves, and recorded by Edmund Bacon, who became overseer in 1806, that the house slaves "Betty Brown, Sally, Critta, and Betty Hemings, Nance, and Ursula" were in the room when Mrs. Jefferson died.

> They have often told my wife that when Mrs. Jefferson died they stood around the bed. Mr. Jefferson sat by her, and she gave him directions about a good many things that she wanted done. When she came to the children, she wept and could not speak for some time. Finally she held up her hand, and spreading out her four fingers, she told him she could not die happy if she thought her four children were ever to have a stepmother brought in over them. Holding her hand in his, Mr. Jefferson promised her solemnly that he would never marry again. And he never did. He was quite a young man and very handsome, and I suppose he could have married well; but he always kept that promise.

Israel, one of the younger Monticello slaves, said in his reminiscences, "I know that it was a general statement among the older servants at Monticello, that Mr. Jefferson promised his wife, on her death bed, that he would not again marry." [24]

There is a tenacity about deathbed stories that can carry them correctly over many years of retelling. Yet the trauma of death also excites invention. One obvious error shows in the Bacon account: Martha had three children, not four, at the time of her dying. Still, it is possible that her fingers inadvertently spoke of the four dead babies rather than the three living ones. Or Bacon may simply have remembered the number wrongly—when he reminisced to Hamilton W. Pierson, he was an old man of seventy-six. Moreover, he described the slaves as "old family servants and great favorites," reflecting his own experience, but in 1782 Martha Jefferson's half sisters, Critta and Sally Hemings, were thirteen and nine. Betty Hemings was forty-seven.[25]

What of the deathbed promise? Such exactions can be supremely selfish; they can also be pathetic bids for a measure of immortality. If Martha Jefferson, herself a widow when she married Jefferson, truly exacted the promise from her husband that he would never marry again, this could indicate that she may have been as possessive of him in death as she seems to have been possessive of him in life, as jealous of any future wife as she had been jealous of his "passion" for politics. If so, this tenacity reached out beyond the grave with a resulting spoiling he could never shake off. Or it may be that in this gesture she was simply revealing her terrible sadness in relinquishing him together with life.

On September 6, 1782, Jefferson wrote in his account book, "My dear wife died this day at 11:45 a m," The day earlier he had written, "lent to Dr. Gilmer 5 lbs sugar." There is no record that this good friend and physician ever accepted anything for his four-month ministrations; even the valued sugar he would accept only as a loan. Jefferson's eldest daughter, then ten, wrote a meticulous account of what happened after her mother's dying, but not till the passage of over forty years. Still, the details of her recollections, like those of the Hemings family slaves, carry a formidable authenticity. "A moment before the closing scene," she wrote, Jefferson "was led from the room almost in a state of insensibility by his sister Mrs. Carr who with great difficulty got him into his library where he fainted and remained so long insensible that they feared he never would revive."

> The scene that followed I did not witness but the violence of his emotion, of his grief when almost by stealth I entered his room at night to this day I dare not trust myself to describe. He kept his room for three weeks and I was never a moment from his side. He walked almost incessantly night and day only lying down occasionally when nature was completely exhausted on a pallet that had been brought in during his long fainting fit. My Aunts remained constantly with him for some weeks. I do not remember how many. When at last he left his room he rode out and from that time he was incessantly on horseback rambling about the mountain in the least frequented roads and just as often through the woods; in those melancholy rambles I was his

constant companion, a solitary witness to many a violent burst of grief, the remembrance of which has consecrated particular scenes of that lost home beyond the power of time to obliterate.[26]

One sees here a grief that bordered on the pathological, a truly symbolic dying, followed by a binding of father and daughter. When Jefferson's friends heard about the violence of his grief they found it troubling. Edmund Randolph, who had always been contemptuous of Jefferson's running away from politics for his wife's sake, wrote to Madison, "Mrs. Jefferson has at last shaken off her tormenting pains, by yielding to them, and has left our friend inconsolable. I ever thought him to rank domestic happiness in the first class of the chief good; but scarcely supposed that his grief would be so violent as to justify the circulating report of his swooning away whenever he sees his children." Madison replied with indignation that he found the story "altogether incredible." [27]

When someone is long in dying, there is usually preparation and advance secret mourning that steels one for the inevitable ending and lessens the final grief. Jefferson seems to have had no such inner fortification. His wife's many illnesses, inevitably associated with pregnancy, had been in the most literal sense caused by him. With every illness he must have feared her death, and also fought off the guilty reflection that certain freedoms would come to him if she did die. The greater his love the more guilt about these intrusions. Jefferson paid for such conflict first in absolute insensibility, then in insomnia and in a total incapacity for work.

He had written nothing in his *Garden Book* after June 25, 1782. But on September 11, five days after Martha's dying, he made a grisly entry:

W. Hornsby's method of preserving birds.

Make a small incision between the legs of the bird; take out the entrails & eyes, wipe the inside & with a quill force a passage through the throat into the body that the ingredients may find a way into the stomach & so pass off through the mouth. fill the bird with a composition of ⅔ common salt & ⅓ nitre pounded in a mortar with two tablespoonfuls of black or Indian pepper to a pound. hang it up by it's legs 8 or 10. weeks, & if the bird be small it will be sufficiently preserved in that time. if it be large, the process is the same, but greater attention will be necessary.[28]

So he transmuted the inevitable imaginings of the dissolution of his wife's body into a scientific account of how to preserve for display a beautiful dead bird. Such was one of the defenses of a sensitive man who could not handle his grief as other men did.

Belief in a heaven, which he had long since theoretically abandoned, could be no comfort. "If there be beyond the grave any concern for the things of this world," he wrote wistfully to Martha's sister, Elizabeth Eppes, "there is one angel who views these attentions with pleasure and wishes continuance of them while she must pity the miseries to which they confine me." And he hinted that were it not for his daughters he would think of suicide. "This miserable kind of existence is really too burthensome to be borne, and were it not for the infidelity of deserting the sacred charge left me, I could not wish it's continuance a moment." Then, as if abashed at what he had written, he begged forgiveness for afflicting his sister-in-law with his sorrows. "I will endeavor to correct myself," he wrote, "and keep what I feel to myself." [29] To Chastellux, ten weeks after the death, he described his feelings as "a stupor of mind which has rendered me as dead to the world as she was whose loss occasioned it." [30] Only three or four times during the remainder of his life did he again refer to his wife in any letter, and at some point he destroyed all her letters to him and his to her.

What of his three small daughters? Martha, freckled, redheaded, and large-boned, with promise of being very tall like her father, had become his shadow. Her whole life at this point was dedicated to replacing her mother and lessening her father's grief with her sturdy, ubiquitous presence. She did not mourn, nor did her sisters. This Jefferson noted with some consternation. "They are in perfect health," he reported to Elizabeth Eppes, "and as happy as if they had no part in the unmeasurable loss we have sustained. Patsy rides with me 5 or 6 miles a day and presses for permission to accompany me on horseback to Elkhill whenever I shall go there." [31]

Children rarely mourn the loss of their parents with obvious grief. Instead they deny the death with daydreams of the dead parent's return, and so fortify themselves against the reality they are ill equipped to face.[32] Little Polly, who was soon given over to Elizabeth Eppes for mothering, betrayed the scarring of her mother's death only later, when she fought with almost tigerish passion against being torn from her aunt to join her father in Paris. Lucy Elizabeth, the new daughter, knew her mother scarcely at all, being mothered from the beginning, it seems likely, by a slave woman, and then given over to Elizabeth Eppes when Jefferson went to France.

Martha for some time had no real mothering. Jefferson took her with him almost everywhere, and she became for him an object of infinite value, to be educated swiftly, to be matured before the natural time of her maturing, into a companion who would in some measure replace the amiable woman he had lost. Not until he moved to Philadelphia in 1783 did he place her with a substitute mother; this was Mrs. Thomas Hopkinson, mother of one of his own good friends. Here too he arranged for tutors in French, dancing, and painting. When he had to go to Annapolis on November 28, 1783, he wrote her his first letter. It was formidable, with a scheduling of her time in study from 8 A.M. to bedtime, with scarcely a moment even to enjoy a meal. "The acquirements which I hope you will make under the tutors I have provided for you," he wrote formally, "will render you more worthy of my love, and if they cannot increase it they will prevent its diminution." As for Mrs. Hopkinson:

> Consider her I say as your mother, as the only person to whom, since the loss with which heaven has pleased to afflict you, you can now look up; and that her displeasure or disapprobation on any occasion will be an immense misfortune which should you be so unhappy as to incur by any unguarded act, think no concession too much to regain her good will.

If incurring the displeasure of Mrs. Hopkinson was "an immense misfortune," even more so was incurring the displeasure of her father.

> If you love me then, strive to be good under every situation and to all living creatures, and to acquire those accomplishments which I have put in your power, and which will go far towards ensuring you the warmest love of your affectionate father.
>
> TH. JEFFERSON

He added a postscript: "Keep my letters and read them at times that you may always have present in your mind those things which will endear you to me." [33] She kept all his letters. With their publication in 1966 anyone who cared about Jefferson could become privy to the exacting apprenticeship of his daughter. But young Patsy endured it, flourished under it, and in a most important sense held her positions over all rivals up to her father's death.

CHAPTER XIII

The Return to Politics

It seemed rather that his mind, accustomed to the unalloyed pleasure of the society of a lovable wife, was impervious since her loss to the feeble attractions of common society, and that his soul, fed on noble thoughts, was revolted by idle chatter.

van Hogendorp on Jefferson, April 1784 [1]

The death of his wife altered the whole rhythm and direction of Jefferson's life. There was no more pendulumlike swinging between domestic life and politics, with all its attendant conflicts. Eight weeks after Martha's dying he was back in public service, and except for a critical lapse from 1794 to 1797 he was committed to it until the end of his second term as president, altogether twenty-six years. Though his nostalgia for Monticello remained powerful, permeating his letters to his daughters and intimate friends, it was no longer the dominating magnet of his life. The enchantment was gone; so too was the enchainment.

That the whole constellation of wife-plantation-children-illness-happiness-sorrow had served as a chain is evidenced by the alacrity with which he embraced public life as soon as the period of intensive mourning was behind him. More important, he never married again. Most men would have remarried quickly, to provide a mother for the small daughters and to assuage personal needs and loneliness. Jefferson set up defenses against the obviously flirtatious, and sought female companionship, if at all, only with married women who befriended Patsy, such as Elizabeth House Trist, with whose mother he and Patsy boarded for a time in Philadelphia in January 1783. He avoided parties, often pleading illness, and did not go to a ball until Madison's inauguration in 1809, when his wife had been dead for twenty-seven years.[2]

For four years he managed to avoid any entanglement. Then, in that extraordinary window opening a full view of his emotional life, the letter to Maria Cosway called "My Head and My Heart," he wrote the following, under the guise of advice to himself from his "Head":

> Do not bite at the bait of pleasure till you know there is no hook beneath it. The art of life is the art of avoiding pain: and he is the best pilot who steers clearest of the rocks and shoals with which it is beset. Pleasure is always before us; but misfortune is at our side: while running after that, this arrests us. The most effectual means of being secure against pain is to retire within ourselves, and to suffice for our own happiness. . . .
>
> Hence the inestimable value of intellectual pleasures. Ever in our power, always leading us to something new, never cloying, we ride, serene and sublime, above the concerns of this mortal world, contemplating truth and nature, matter and motion, the laws which bind up their existence, and that eternal being who made and bound them up by these laws. Let this be our employ.[3]

So Jefferson disciplined himself from September 1782 to August 1786.

On December 19, 1782, Jefferson made a laconic entry in his account book, "Set out from Monticello for Philadelphia, France." When Congress in November had appointed him minister plenipotentiary to help in the negotiations for peace in Paris, he had accepted instantly. Patsy would accompany him; his two smaller daughters he would leave with their aunt, Elizabeth Eppes. He hoped to take passage on the same French ship as General Rochambeau and the Marquis de Chastellux, but there were exasperating delays. When finally he and Patsy arrived in Baltimore in the unusually bitter January cold, they found the French frigate *Romulus* trapped in the harbor ice, and waited vainly almost a month for the expected thaw.

"I am exceedingly fatigued with this place," Jefferson wrote to Madison on February 14, "as indeed I should be with any other where I had neither occupation nor amusement." He found good company only with General La Vallette, he said, "who obliges me to take refuge in his quarters from the tedium of my own, the latter half of every day."[4]

In Baltimore Jefferson learned, surely with some private chagrin, that a provisional peace treaty had been signed in Paris on November 30, 1782. For the third time he was forced to abandon dreams of

Europe, and went back to Monticello. He spent two weeks in Richmond, reestablishing his political contacts. He permitted Madison a glimpse of his continued alienation from Patrick Henry, who, he wrote, "as usual is involved in mystery: should the popular tide run strongly in either direction, he will fall in with it." [5] Almost at once he became involved in his old project, revising the Virginia constitution, but the state assembly elected him to Congress, and on June 6, 1783, he became head of the Virginia delegation.

The four months before Congress opened he spent at Monticello with his daughters, his sister Martha Carr, and her six children. Here a preoccupation with orderliness, what Julian Boyd calls his "instinct for classification," for a time became preeminent in his life. He drew up a catalogue of all the books in his library, numbering 2,640 volumes, classifying them very much as Francis Bacon had done with his own books, into sections headed Memory (civil and natural history), Reason (moral and mathematical philosophy), and Imagination (fine arts—gardening, architecture, sculpture, painting, poetry, oratory, and criticism). He decided henceforth to keep a summary record of all his future correspondence, and began the preparation of an index to his letters, the "SJL," [6] later augmented by press copies, and copies made on polygraph machines. This became a meticulous espitolary record lasting forty-three years, from November 11, 1783, to June 25, 1826. In his *Farm Book* he made the second inventory of his slaves, which now numbered 204.

That this attention to detail was a kind of remedy for loneliness and despair Jefferson himself recognized. When Madison wrote to him unhappily of the failure of his romance with young Catherine Floyd, Jefferson, who had tried to help further the match, expressed regret, adding cryptically, "Of all machines, ours is the most complicated and inexplicable." As solace he recommended "firmness of mind and unremitting occupations." [7] But he had clearly lost all interest in his garden, and even in his house, which he was preparing to close up altogether for the winter, save for a caretaker, John Key. His *Garden Book* has only one entry for 1783, written three days before the anniversary of the death of his wife:

> 2d. & 3d. September. White frosts which killed vines in this neighborhood, killed tobo * in the N. Garden, fodder & latter corn in August, & forward corn in Greenbriar

Randall was the first to note the symbolism of the entry. "Frost, too," he wrote, "had fallen on the life and happiness at Monticello." [8]

In October 1783 Jefferson settled Patsy in Philadelphia with Mrs. Hopkinson, but had to follow Congress first to Princeton and then to

* Tobacco.

Annapolis, and so saw very little of his daughter, upon whom he had come to depend more than he realized. Like most fathers watching their daughters show the first signs of physical maturity, he thought with anguish of the time she must one day marry. "The chance that in marriage she will draw a blockhead I calculate at about fourteen to one," he wrote pessimistically to Marbois, whose advice he had sought concerning a French tutor.[9] But he proceeded to plan for her education as if she were to be the lifelong companion of a man like himself. In addition to the tutoring that was routine for fashionable young girls of the day, he set up a reading program that promised to make her the best educated woman in America. "The plan of reading which I have formed for her is considerably different from what I think would be most proper for her sex in any other country than America," he told Marbois. "With the best poets and prosewriters I shall therefore combine a certain extent of reading in the graver sciences." He considered her at age eleven mature enough to be trusted with "Gil Blas and Don Quichotte." [10] And he ordered a harpsichord for her from England, "the very best kind . . . with Merlin's forte-piano Stop and other modern Improvements." [11]

Now began that series of letters to Patsy, many of which we have already quoted, with their overwhelming parental exactions. He asked for the best copy of each of her drawings, for the names of the tunes she was playing, and insisted over and again that she write to him once a week. She must learn to spell; she must "never do or say a bad thing." [12] Though he was insistent, repetitive, and constantly hinting at the lessening of his love, Patsy never let herself be bullied. Certain of his affection, she sometimes let as much as two months pass without writing, and Jefferson, like other lonely parents, learned finally to expect less than he wanted. He did not scold her when her art teacher abandoned her because she had "no Genius." [13] And he wrote to her harshly only once, in what became a celebrated letter "on the subject of dress," which, he said, "I know you are a little apt to neglect."

I do not wish you to be gayly clothed this time of life, but that what you wear should be fine of its kind; but above all things, and at all times let your clothes be clean, whole, and properly put on. You will be the last who will be sensible of this. Some ladies think they may under the privileges of the dishabille be loose and negligent of their dress in the morning. But be you from the moment you rise till you go to bed as cleanly and properly dressed as at the hours of dinner or tea. A lady who has been seen as a sloven or slut in the morning will never efface the impression she then made with all the dress and pageantry she can afterwards involve herself in. Nothing is so disgusting to our sex as a want of cleanliness and delicacy in yours. I hope therefore the moment you rise from bed, your first work will be to dress yourself in such a stile as that you may be seen by any gentleman without his being able to discover a pin amiss, or by any other circumstance of neatness wanting.[14]

More than anything he ever wrote, this letter gave rise to the word "fastidious" in descriptions of the character of Thomas Jefferson. But he had grown up with a mother and six sisters, and had lived for ten years with a wife who was very often very ill. Sometimes, perhaps often, he had seen a "sloven or slut in the morning." Bathing daily was not an eighteenth-century habit. Though Jefferson himself may have been far more cleanly than most men, he did not mention his own bathing practices; the most he admitted to was washing his feet in cold water every morning—this for reasons of health. But he wanted his daughter to be neat, clean, and sweet-smelling at all times and bluntly told her so.

At Annapolis Jefferson had to defend himself against the importunities of friends who hoped he would soon marry again. That he was giving some thought to the techniques of courtship, despite his continuing mourning, is suggested by a candid letter he wrote to his nephew Peter Carr, then in school under the tutelage of Walker Maury:

I wish you to be particularly attentive to Mrs. Maury. Nothing can be more unmanly than to treat a lady superciliously. It is in her power to make your time more comfortable, and should you be sick from whom else are you to expect assistance? Besides it is proper for you now to begin to learn those attentions and that complaisance which the world requires you should be shewn to every lady. . . . You will find that on rendering yourself agreeable to that sex will depend a great part of the happiness of your life: and *the way to do it is to practice to every one all those civilities which a favourite one might require.*[15]

The formula I have italicized sounds surprisingly calculating; one would have thought that Jefferson behaved in this fashion by instinct rather than by artifice. He knew exactly what he was doing when he treated women with that courtliness, gentleness, and grace that instantly won their hearts. But since Jefferson insisted on reserving these "civilities which a favourite one might require" for married women, this suggests not only that he was defending himself against remarriage but also that he continued to be attracted only by married women. Understandably, several wives responded with an affection for the young widower that they could not easily conceal, notably Maria Cosway and Lucy Paradise in Paris, and later Margaret Bayard Smith during Jefferson's presidency. That Eliza House Trist was the first of these is evident from a letter she wrote to him when en route to visit her husband on the Mississippi.

> When ever I see any thing out of the common way if they are beautiful prospects my sensations are very singular I believe for I can hardly suppress the tears starting from my eyes and I am lost in wonder but a Philosophical mind like yours can gather information from all you see. . . . It would be one of the greatest pleasures of my life if I cou'd be one of your Company on such a tour but that will never happen.[16]

When Jefferson learned that her husband had died, he wrote a commiserating letter—"Time and occupation," he said, are "slow physicians indeed, but they are the only ones" [17]—and continued a tender but formal correspondence intermittently for many years. He once described her as "a rare pattern of goodness, prudence, and good sense." [18] She never remarried, but happily one of her grandsons married one of Jefferson's granddaughters, and in the end she went to live with them for a time at Monticello.

During the twenty-month period after his wife's death before he went to France, Jefferson found companionship chiefly with three men, all considerably younger than himself: James Madison, thirty-one, James Monroe, twenty-four, and William Short, twenty-three. All had uncommon intelligence and rectitude, and at least in their letters showed a kind of purity bordering on innocence. Importantly, all were looking for wives, and Jefferson's turning to these young Virginians was a kind of returning to the old courtship days at Williamsburg, when there was much seeking among the young men but no quick commitment.

Madison, already Jefferson's legislative collaborator as well as ardent disciple, was a small man; at five foot four he was ten inches shorter than his friend. Though reserved and inhibited in public, he could be droll, bawdy, and satirical, as several of his college ballads recently published by Ralph Ketcham demonstrate. These President John Witherspoon of Princeton must not have seen, or he would not have told Jefferson that he never knew Madison to do or say "an improper thing." [19] Madison, who grew up on a plantation not far from that of Jefferson, was equally antislavery. Though he had considered briefly the idea of becoming a clergyman, once he began to read in the literature of the Enlightenment he abandoned the notion. By 1784 he was as much a deist as Jefferson. During these months together in Congress their friendship took on a kind of Damon and Pythias quality, and the groundwork was made permanent for their political collaboration, astonishingly free of bickering and disaffection, which became the most sustained and fruitful in American history.

Few knew that Madison in his adolescence had suffered from what his brother-in-law described as "a constitutional liability of sudden attacks, of the nature of epilepsy," and what Madison himself described as "somewhat resembling Epilepsy, and suspending the intellectual functions." He lived for many years with the fear of the return of this supposedly incurable ailment, and this may have been the primary reason he remained a bachelor so long. One of Madison's biographers, Irving Brant, diagnosed it as "epileptoid hysteria," and wrote that it finally disappeared with increasing self-confidence and maturity.[20] That Jefferson knew of these attacks, which kept Madison out of the revolutionary army, seems likely; his purchase of a book *Catalepsie* by a famous French physician S. Tissot, would suggest more than a passing interest in the subject. Jefferson at this time owned three other of Tissot's medical treatises, *Santé des gens de lettres*, *Santé des gens du monde*, and one titled *Onanisme*, which trumpeted the dangers of masturbation. He sold them all to James Monroe, along with other books, shortly before departing for France.[21]

Madison suffered other disabilities, including a slight speech defect, and a voice which like Jefferson's was almost inaudible from the platform. Far more inhibited than Jefferson, he did not marry till at forty-four he met the marvelously warmhearted widow, Dolley Todd. During these months with him in Philadelphia and Annapolis, Jefferson kindled his interest in science and natural philosophy; as Brant put it, he freed Madison's mind for exploration.[22] Madison was soon making detailed measurements of small mammals like the weasel, opossum, and mole, leaving Jefferson, appropriately, to collect the bones of giants—moose, elk, and mammoth.

James Monroe was also a member of Jefferson's inner circle, which came very close to being a family. As a young soldier he had had an artery severed by the Hessians in the Battle of Trenton, and Washington had commended him as "a brave, active, and sensible officer." Although he quickly recovered he nevertheless abandoned the northern army midway through the war and unsuccessfully sought a command in the armies of Virginia. After writing rather mysteriously to Jefferson of "inconveniences w'ch have nearly destroyed me," [23] he was taken under Jefferson's wing as a law student. By 1782 he had become one of the two or three men in his life to whom Jefferson would sometimes unburden his heart in letters. Monroe was a stiff, rather formal young man, without any of Madison's sly humor and of such obvious virtue that Jefferson would write of him to Madison,

"Turn his soul wrong side outwards and there is not a speck on it." He repeated the metaphor to another friend, "He is a man whose soul might be turned wrong side outwards without discovering a blemish to the world." [24] There was no mockery here, but just the faintest hint of astonishment at so much goodness. Later William Wirt would write pointedly of Monroe: "Nature has given him a mind neither rapid nor rich, and therefore he cannot shine on a subject which is entirely new to him. But to compensate him for this he is endued with a spirit of restless emulation, a judgment strong and clear, and a habit of application which no difficulties can shake, no labours can tire." [25] If Monroe wanted to emulate anyone it was assuredly Thomas Jefferson. For such discipleship Jefferson had a compelling need.

Of the three most important disciples in Jefferson's life these two were to follow him in the presidency, and his approval would be like the magic touch of a monarch. The third disciple, William Short, we know the least about. A student of William and Mary College, he entered Virginia politics in 1783. Exactly how he found his way into Jefferson's life during this period of mourning and loneliness is not clear. Jefferson urged that he be sent as a delegate to Congress, and then arranged that he be sent to Paris as his private secretary. There John Adams' eighteen-year-old daughter described him as "a well-bred man, without the least formality or affectation of any kind." [26] More than any of the many young men who attached themselves to Jefferson without benefit of kinship, Short became the son which his fate had so far denied him.

In February 1784 Jefferson was urging all three of these young men to buy land near Monticello. He wrote to Madison:

> Monroe is buying land almost adjoining me. Short will do the same. What would I not give you could fall into the circle. With such a society I could once more venture home and lay myself up for the residue of life, quitting all its contentions which grow daily more and more insupportable. Think of it. To render it practicable only requires you to think it so. Life is of no value but as it brings us gratifications. Among the most valuable of these is rational society. It informs the mind, sweetens the temper, chears our spirits, and promotes health.

To be surrounded by "rational society" within easy distance of Monticello was part of Jefferson's dream of utopia. He had long ago enticed Philip Mazzei, Florentine grape grower and friend of princes, to settle as a neighbor. Mazzei had wanted to buy land from Thomas Adams in the Shenandoah Valley, but with Adams had spent a night at Monticello before crossing the Blue Ridge. Jefferson, finding Mazzei excellent company as well as an expert on exotic trees and plants, had taken him on a walk the following morning. When they returned, Adams looked quizzically at the pair. "I see by your expression that you've taken him from me," he said to Jefferson. "I knew you would do that." Mazzei would eventually return to Florence, but his wife, an irascible Englishwoman, would remain behind, and be buried in the Monticello graveyard.[27]

The companionship of these and other male friends, however, was no substitute for that of his wife. Depression clung to him, taking its toll, as so often, on his body. During the six months he was in Congress at Annapolis in 1784, he was for the first time since his college years living apart from any member of his family for an extended period. He now became prey to fevers, and his old migraine headache, which seems not to have plagued him since the death of his mother, came back to torment him. He complained to Patsy he had been "able scarcely to read, write or do anything else," and to William Short he reported, "Having to my habitual ill health . . . lately added an attack of my periodical headach, I am obliged to avoid reading writing and almost thinking." [28]

One would get the impression from these and similar complaining letters that Jefferson was so afflicted he could have been of little use to Congress. Actually in six months he drafted thirty-one essential papers, including the most important legislation of the entire session. A young Dutchman, G. K. van Hogendorp, then touring America watched Jefferson at work and declared he was busier than anyone else. His memoir and his letters to Jefferson put the whole picture of debilitation, fever, and migraine in illuminating perspective. "Retired from fashionable society, he concerned himself only with affairs of public interest, his sole diversion being that offered by belles lettres. The poor state of his health, he told me occasionally, was the cause of this retirement; but it seemed rather that his mind, accustomed to the unalloyed pleasure of the society of a lovable wife, was impervious since her loss to the feeble attractions of common society, and that his soul, fed on noble thoughts, was revolted by idle chatter." [29]

Van Hogendorp, like so many others drawn to Jefferson after a single encounter, begged to see him again. Curious about his melancholy, he succeeded in breaking through what he called Jefferson's "cool and reserved behaviour," and described this later in an effusive but perceptive letter: "At the same time I became acquainted with Your state and with yourself, I grew fond of your benevolent character. . . . I pitied Your Situation, for I thought you unhappy. Why, I did not know; and though you appeared insensible to social enjoyments, yet I was perfectly convinced you could not have been ever so. One evening I talked of love, and then I perceived that you still could feel, and express your feelings." [30]

Jefferson replied stiffly but with obvious emotion:

> Your observation on the situation of my mind is not without foundation: yet I had hoped it was unperceived, as the agreeable conversations into which you led me, often induced a temporary inattention to those events which have produced that gloom you remarked. I have been happy and cheerful. I have had many causes of gratitude to heaven, but I have also experienced it's rigours. I have known what it is to lose every species of connection which is dear to the human heart: friends, brethren, parents, children—

It will be seen that even at this date, in listing his losses, he could not bring himself to write the word "wife." "The sun of life," he continued, has "with me already passed his meridian." [31]

During Jefferson's stay in Annapolis, Washington formally resigned as commander in chief, putting an end to all the fearful talk about his becoming a Caesar. Jefferson was on the committee for the farewell arrangements, which included an elegant public dinner with two or three hundred dignitaries at Mann's Tavern on December 23, 1783, and a ball at the State House, where every window blazed with candles. "The General danced every set," one witness wrote, "that the ladies might have the pleasure of dancing with him, or as it has since been handsomely expressed, *get a touch of him.*" [32] Jefferson missed the ball, but listened to the farewell speech on December 23. "The spectators all wept," one congressman wrote to his wife, "and there was hardly a member of Congress who did not drop tears. The General's hand which held the address shook as he read it." The President of the Congress then read a formal reply, which, in Madison's words, "showed the shining traces" of Jefferson's pen. He praised Washington's wisdom and fortitude, then went on with grace and prescience to pay tribute not only to the man but also to the symbolic gesture so crucial to the young republic, the voluntary relinquishment of power. "Having defended the standard of liberty in this new world: having taught a lesson useful to those who inflict and to those who feel oppression, you retire from the great theatre of action with the blessings of your fellow citizens—but the glory of your virtues will not terminate with your military Command. It will continue to animate remotest ages." [33]

Jefferson could hardly have failed to contrast the homage accorded Washington with the humiliation accorded himself when he retired as governor of Virginia. For if Washington, as James Flexner insists, "sought power not for its own sake but in order to earn love and praise," and if he held to his conviction that the greatest of earthly rewards was "the approbation and affections of a free people," [34] the same was true of Thomas Jefferson. The difference in December 1783 was that Washington had won this approbation, but Jefferson had not.

During the succeeding four months, despite his gloom and manifest ill health, Jefferson drove himself relentlessly. Sorely missing Washington and Franklin, who, he said, "never spoke over ten minutes," and then "laid their shoulders to the great points, knowing that the little ones would follow of themselves," he was appalled at the waste, indolence, and garrulity of most of his congressional colleagues. He described this in his *Autobiography*:

> Our body was little numerous, but very contentious. Day after day was wasted on the most unimportant questions. A member, one of those afflicted with the morbid rage of debate, or an ardent mind, prompt imagination, and copious flow of words, who heard with impatience any logic which was not his own, sitting near me on some occasion of a trifling but wordy debate, asked me how I could sit in silence, hearing so much false reasoning, which a word should refute? I observed to him, that to refute was indeed easy, but to silence impossible.[35]

Jefferson now demonstrated, as in June 1776, his phenomenal capacity for concentrating on the "great points." He managed with difficulty to round up enough members to ratify the treaty of peace with England—the apathy seems today incomprehensible—and he rescued the nation from an appallingly complicated currency bill planned by Robert Morris. "The bulk of mankind are schoolboys through life," [36] he remarked, and succeeded in persuading Congress to base its national coinage on a decimal system with the dollar as the standard unit. He failed, as everyone regrets, to carry out the same reform in weights and measures, and two hundred years later the nation still pays heavily for the absurdities of the British system. He wrote the truly momentous legislation for the government of the western territories, setting forth the principle that new states must be created republican in form, with universal manhood suffrage, and subject to federal taxation. To make possible what was really the orderly development of the whole continent, he set a precedent by cheerfully acquiescing in the loss of a great portion of Virginia. As Boyd points out, "no other state, then or since, ever yielded so great a natural resource to the domain of the whole people." [37]

His legislation further provided that after 1800 there should be "neither slavery nor involuntary servitude" in any newly created state. Significantly, he did not call for colonization and expatriation of the blacks, as in his Notes on the State of Virginia, but for a simple blanket prohibition. No single legislative proposal in American history had so much promise for preventing future mischief from escalating into calamity. But southern delegates swarmed to protest with invective of singular violence. Though every delegate from every state including and north of Pennsylvania voted aye, though Jefferson of Virginia and Williamson of North Carolina also voted aye, every other Southerner voted no. New Jersey, which would have voted aye, lost its vote because a single delegate, John Beatty, was ill. It took seven states to carry the vote; Jefferson got but six. Had the measure passed in this period of great reform, when emancipation measures were sweeping through the legislatures of the North, the slave states would have been cordoned off. Slavery then would have been put, as Lincoln later phrased it, "in the course of ultimate extinction."

Beatty's illness did the country incalculable damage. On April 19, 1784, a minority of delegates in Congress carried the decision for slavery; a minority would carry similar decisions again and again, in a dreary repetition that led inexorably to civil war.

Jefferson even at the time was sickened by the failure, and especially by the votes of his own Virginia delegates. "South Carolina Maryland and !Virginia! voted against it," he wrote to Madison on April 25, 1784.[38] Theoretically Jefferson had long since abandoned the primitive belief that God interfered personally in the affairs of men. But as he saw slavery spreading into the Southwest, and as the consequences of this accidental defeat were borne in upon him, he could not bear to shoulder the total burden of this calamitous failure. In describing it to the French historian Démeunier he wrote with immense sadness:

> The voice of a single individual . . . would have prevented this abominable crime from spreading itself over the new country. Thus we see the fate of millions unborn hanging on the tongue of one man, and Heaven was silent in that awful moment! [39]

When Démeunier needled him by noting that Virginia had failed to enact any kind of legislation for emancipation in 1785, Jefferson was forced again to examine the contradictory behavior of his friends. His own feelings were complicated, no doubt, by the realization that he himself would not unilaterally free his own slaves as a symbolic personal gesture. So again, as in his Notes, Jefferson turned to the avenging deity of his childhood, the God of justice who would right all wrongs, including his own:

What a stupendous, what an incomprehensible machine is man! Who can endure toil, famine, stripes, imprisonment or death itself in vindication of his own liberty, and the next moment be deaf to all those motives whose power supported him thro' his trial, and inflict on his fellow men a bondage, one hour of which is fraught with more misery than ages of that which he rose in rebellion to oppose. But we must await with patience the workings of an overruling providence, and hope that that is preparing the deliverance of these our suffering brethren. When the measure of their tears shall be full, when their groans shall have involved heaven itself in darkness, doubtless a god of justice will awaken to their distress, and by diffusing light and liberality among their oppressors, or at length by his exterminating thunder, manifest his attention to the things of this world, and that they are not left to the guidance of a blind fatality.[40]

CHAPTER XIV

Restlessness and Torment

Tell me who die . . . who marry, who hang themselves because they
cannot marry.

Jefferson to Eliza House Trist,
August 15, 1785 [1]

France for Jefferson was in every sense a liberation. It freed him from
provincial notions about the ultimate superiority of American life
and ameliorated his prejudice against great cities, for Paris was a
city to which he fondly hoped to return. It broadened his understanding of international finance and trade and sharpened his instincts
about the sources and nature of national power. And it gave him an
opportunity to share in a second revolution that had enormous political
consequences. Most importantly for his domestic life, it helped to free
him from the bondage of his dead wife. In Paris he embraced the
philosophy, "the earth belongs to the living; the dead shall have no
power over it." All the dammed-up resources of affection, trickling over
from the moment of his arrival at Le Havre, began to pour out during
his first Paris spring, and then, totally released in his love affair with
the ethereal little artist-musician Maria Cosway, flowed henceforth in
a flood of affection for France, for its countryside, its artists, its scientists, even for Louis XVI, whom at least in the beginning he counted
an amiable monarch, with "an honest heart." [2]

Had he been sent home as he expected within a few months, he
might have returned totally enchained as before by the memories at
Monticello. He recognized this bondage in writing wistfully to Eliza
Trist, "Tell me who die that I may meet these disagreeable events in

detail, and not at once when I return; who marry, who hang themselves because they cannot marry." [3] Even after being appointed minister to replace Benjamin Franklin, who retired in agonies of pain from gout and bladder stone, he could not guess that he would stay altogether five years. The experience destroyed any lingering puritanical legacy from his childhood, broadened his compassion for anyone caught up in the delights and difficulties of extramarital adventure, and confirmed his private conviction that a man is master of his own body and may govern it as he pleases. [4] Almost none of this was obvious in his own time, and is evident today only if one scrutinizes letters which Jefferson's heirs for many years took pains to hide. Here if anywhere one finds the answer to the question whether Jefferson embraced the monastic and continent life ascribed to him by so many, or whether his vital sexuality, instead of atrophying, reasserted itself to make possible a new, if hidden, happiness.

Jefferson sailed for France on the *Ceres* on July 5, 1784, at 4 A.M. Patsy, now twelve, but as tall and self-possessed as a fifteen-year-old, found the sea voyage a delight. "We had a lovely passage in a beautiful new ship that had made only one voyage before," she wrote to Elizabeth Trist. "There were only six passengers, all of whom Papa knew, and a fine sunshine all the way, with the sea which was as calm as a river." [5] Jefferson's account book tells us that he watched the gannets, petrels, and hagdons skimming close to the sea, fished for cod, and watched the sharks and whales. He improved his Spanish by reading *Don Quixote* in the original, and consumed with his friends the four dozen bottles of wine he had prudently brought aboard. Years later, teasing, he told young John Quincy Adams that Spanish was so easy he had learned it in nineteen days at sea. Adams noted the remark in his diary, adding, "But Mr. Jefferson tells large stories." [6]

At Le Havre, Jefferson suffered the usual fate of Americans who flatter themselves that they can speak French only to discover total incomprehension on the part of shopkeepers and porters. He was roundly cheated in the first hour—"It cost Papa as much to have the bagadge brought from the shore to the house, which was about a half square apart, as the bringing it from Philadelphia to Boston," Patsy wrote. The phaeton he had brought with him, driven by the light mulatto slave James Hemings, aroused a curiosity he did not cherish, especially from beggars. "One day," Patsy wrote, "I counted no less than nine while we stopped to change horses." [7]

James Hemings suffered so little from culture shock that Jefferson entrusted him with seventy-two francs and sent him on ahead to make arrangements for an inn at the cathedral town of Rouen, where

Jeanne d'Arc had been tried and burned.[8] From Rouen to Gaillon, through the ancient fortified town of Vernon, to Mantes, Meulon, and Triel, they made their way toward Paris. Patsy was enchanted with the ancient churches. "All the winders are died glass of the most beautiful colours that form all kinds of figures," she wrote, and described the area as "the most beautiful country I ever saw in my life, it is a perfect garden." [9]

The first few months were plagued with the inevitable difficulties of settling into a foreign place, and this an enormous labyrinthine city of great antiquity and appalling density. Paris was still encircled by walls, and inner rings of more ancient walls still stood, though battered by the sieges of centuries. There was no Arc de Triomphe, and the Champs Elysées, upon which Jefferson eventually settled, was then noncommercial, lined with pleasant villas and private gardens. The street was blocked near his own Hôtel de Langeac at the rue Neuve de Barry with the ancient Grille de Chaillot, at which point every peasant bringing in rabbits, vegetables, or chickens was stopped for a toll.[10]

Jefferson struggled with the feelings of an ardent republican set down in the most conspicuously extravagant court in Europe. He was made to feel immediately that he was badly dressed, and that his daughter must not set foot in the streets until, as she put it, they had sent "for the stay maker, the mantua maker, the milliner, and even a shoe maker." [11] Though fascinated by the art, architecture, and especially the music in the city, he was nevertheless for a time homesick and melancholy. With the onset of winter he was quite ill for six weeks. "I relapsed into that state of ill health in which you saw me in Annapolis," he wrote to G. K. van Hogendorp. "I have had few hours wherein I could do any thing, and these were devoted of duty to public business." [12]

He selected a fashionable convent school, the Abbaie de Panthemont, for Patsy's education, and his friend Chastellux persuaded the Comtesse de Brionne to act as her sponsor. Though criticized in America for putting her into a Catholic school, Jefferson was persuaded that she would not be indoctrinated, and noted that the school had many Protestants.[13] Martha wrote later that her father visited her every day of her first month in school "till in fact I recovered my spirits." [14] Soon the motherless girl found herself the object of so much devoted mothering she became quite lost to it. In a long letter to Eliza Trist after being in Paris a year, she wrote, "At present I am charmed with my situation. . . . I am very happy in the convent." [15] John Adams' daughter Nabby described her in this first Paris summer as "a sweet girl, delicacy and sensibility are read in every feature, and her manners are in unison with all that is amiable and lovely; she is very young." [16]

After becoming minister Jefferson entertained a stream of Americans living in Paris, including the Virginia heiress Lucy Paradise, unhappily wed, who became enamored of Jefferson and badgered him with demands to solve her financial problems and marital crises with her Athens-born husband John. Here he renewed his friendships with Philip Mazzei and Thomas Paine. But in the first difficult months he depended heavily on the Adams family, as they did upon him. Forty years later, when John Quincy Adams was elected president, his proud father reminded Jefferson nostalgically of this Paris period. "I call him our John, because, when you were at the Cul de sac at Paris, he appeared to me to be almost as much your boy as mine." [17] Abigail Adams arrived in Paris a week after Jefferson did, enjoying a tender reunion with her husband and seventeen-year-old son, whom she had not seen for four years. Jefferson had never before met a woman with such wit and vivacity as Abigail Adams; he quickly opened his heart.

She advised him about purchases of clothes, dishes, linen, silver, and draperies. "To be out of fashion," she wrote to a friend in America, "is more criminal than to be seen in a state of nature, to which the Parisians are not averse. . . . Poor Mr. Jefferson had to hie away for a tailor to get a whole new black silk suit made up in two days; and at the end of eleven days should another death happen, he will be obliged to have a new suit of mourning cloth, because that is the season when silk must be left off." [18] She commiserated with him about the embarrassing lack of financing accorded American diplomats; neither family could follow the court to Versailles in the summer, for a single month's rent there would have used up a whole year's salary. She advised him about French servants, whom she called "lazy wretches who eat the bread of idleness."

Though at first shocked by the flirtatiousness of the French women, who, she wrote, put their arms "wrapterously . . . around a gentleman," Abigail came eventually to envy and admire them. They are "easy in their manners, eloquent in their speech, their voices soft and musical and their attitude pleasing," she admitted. "I fancy they must possess the power of persuasion and insinuation beyond any other females." [19] Not surprisingly, she could not forgive the French the casual taking of mistresses and lovers which affected every layer of society. She was appalled by a visit to the Hôpital des Enfant-Trouvés, which received 6,000 abandoned children a year. There she learned that half the children born in Paris were illegitimate, and so common was their abandonment that boxes were placed in special sites in Paris especially to receive them for collection.

Deeply Protestant, she and her daughter Nabby were disturbed by a visit with Jefferson to Patsy's school, where they watched the ceremony of two novices taking the veil. Nabby, who wrote an account in her journal, described how the two girls, dressed in loose flowing white robes, their heads shaven and covered with a white cap and bridal veil, lay prostrate on their faces for half an hour, while the priests held a black pall crossed with white over them as the candle-holding nuns chanted prayers. When the novitiates arose and went to the abbess, who put the nun's habit on each and pinned wreaths of flowers upon their heads, Nabby wept. Awed and indignant, she described the girls as victims, but Patsy Jefferson, already more Catholic than her father realized, assured her the nuns were cheerful and happy.[20]

John Adams no less than Abigail warmly welcomed Jefferson into his family. He totally discounted a letter from the envious Arthur Lee, who had written of Jefferson, "His genius is mediocre, his application great, his affection greater, his vanity greater than all." And he wrote back to Lee a warm defense on January 31, 1785, that Jefferson was "an old friend and coadjutor whose character I studied nine or ten years ago and which I do not perceive to be altered. The same industry, integrity, and talents, remain without diminution." [21]

Jefferson served as gentle mediator between Franklin and Adams, who grated on each other, and who now, for the first time—in Adams' words—served "in utmost Harmony." [22] Later Jefferson wrote to Madison that though he had originally remembered Adams as guilty of "a degree of vanity" and altogether too "attentive to ceremony," and though he still found him "vain, irritable and a bad calculator of the force and probable effect of the motives which govern men," still this was "all the ill which can possibly be said of him." "He is as disinterested as the being which made him: he is profound in his views: and accurate in his judgment except where knowledge of the world is necessary to form a judgment. He is so amiable, that I pronounce you will love him." [23] This was as close as the reticent Jefferson could come to saying in a letter that he himself loved Adams.

He envied Adams especially his toughness and imperviousness to attack. When Abigail complained to him from London that her John was the victim of the "blackest slanders" in the British press, Jefferson replied with an oblique reference to his old war-governor wounds:

> Indeed the man must be of rock, who can stand all this; to Mr. Adams it will be but one victory the more. It would have illy suited me. I do not love difficulties. I am fond of quiet, willing to do my duty, but irritable by slander and apt to be forced by it to abandon my post. These are weaknesses from which reason and your counsels will preserve Mr. Adams.[24]

Here too one can discern the faintest hint that he was comparing the strength of Abigail the indomitable with the pathetic weakness and illnesses of his dead wife.

The whole Adams family suffered with Jefferson when Lafayette brought him news in January 1785 that his youngest daughter in Virginia had died the previous October. Whooping cough had ravaged all the children in the Eppes household, killing not only Jefferson's two-year-old Lucy, but also Lucy Eppes, close enough in age to be her twin. Nabby Adams wrote sadly in her journal on January 27, 1785:

> Mr. J. is a man of great sensibility, and parental affection. His wife died when this child was born, and he was almost in a confirmed state of melancholy; confined himself from the world, and even from his friends, for a long time; and this news has greatly affected him and his daughter.[25]

Lafayette had brought two letters, one from Francis Eppes, describing the children as extremely ill, the other from Dr. James Currie, which confirmed the death:

> I am sincerely sorry my dear friend now to acquaint you of the demise of poor Miss L. Jefferson, who fell a Martyr to the Complicated evils of teething, Worms and Hooping Cough which last was carried there by the Virus of their friends without their knowing it was in their train. I was calld too late to do any thing but procrastinate the settled fate of the poor Innocent, from the accounts of the family, a Child of the most Auspicious hopes and having among other early Shining qualities an ear nicely and critically musical. . . . Mr. Eppes lost his own youngest Child from the same Cause.[26]

The despairing Jefferson, tortured by the desire to learn more details, wrote to his brother-in-law begging him to send letters by "the French packet," a fast boat that would bring him a letter in seven weeks. "It is in vain to endeavor to describe the situation of my mind," he said, "it would pour balm neither into your wounds nor mine." [27] Incredibly, the two letters that finally came from Elizabeth and Francis Eppes took six months in passage. They had been written on October 13 and 14, 1784, and did not arrive until May 6, 1785. Elizabeth Eppes had written:

> It is impossible to paint the anguish of my heart. . . . A most unfortunate Hooping cough has deprived you, and us of two sweet Lucys, within a week. Ours was the first that fell a sacrifice. She was thrown into violent convulsions linger'd out a week and then expired. Your dear angel was confined a week to her bed, her sufferings were great though nothing like a fit. She retain'd her senses perfectly, calld me a

few moments before she died, and asked distinctly for water. Dear Polly has had it most violently, though always kept about, and is now quite recovered. . . . Life is scarcely supportable under such severe afflictions.[28]

By now Jefferson's sorrow was mingled with rage at his wife's kin. As soon as he learned of the tragedy he thought of sending for Polly but delayed, believing he would be returning shortly.[29] Then when he learned in May 1785 that he was to replace Franklin as minister he determined to send for his daughter even though it meant a long and possibly hazardous voyage with strangers. Though she was past six, she had not sent him a single letter, and he knew that were he not to reclaim her shortly she would count Francis and Elizabeth Eppes as her true parents the rest of her life. This he found unendurable. "It would be unfortunate thro' life both to her and us," he wrote to Elizabeth Eppes, "were those affections to be loosened which ought to bind us together. . . . This would be too probably the effect of absence at her age." [30] That she was already largely lost he learned when he first wrote asking that she be sent to Paris. There came back a single defiant sentence, "I want to see you and sister Patsy, but you must come to Uncle Eppes's house." [31]

There followed a wooing of his daughter that lasted over a year. Here Jefferson was maladroit. Though he coaxed her with the promise of "as many dolls and playthings as you want for yourself, or to send to your cousins," he also laid down exactions for her behavior that could have served only to deepen her anxieties about pleasing a father she had by now largely forgotten.

I hope you are a very good girl . . . that you never suffer yourself to be angry with any body, that you give your playthings to those who want them, that you do whatever any body desires of you that is right, that you never tell stories, never beg for anything, mind your book and your work when your aunt tells you, never play but when she permits you, nor go where she forbids you.

Then, to this small girl whose face broke out in freckles in the sun, he added, "Remember too as a constant charge not to go out without your bonnet because it will make you very ugly and then we should not love you so much." [32] It is no wonder that she continued to fight fiercely against leaving the parents she knew, whose exactions she did not fear, and it appears that the Eppes family supported her in this. It was not until May of 1787 that they finally put her on a ship bound for Europe, and this was accomplished only with the cruelest kind of deception.

With the coming of spring, in 1785, Jefferson's ill health and melancholy disappeared. In May the Adamses went off to London, where John became the first minister from the United States to the Court of St. James's. Abigail wrote sadly to her sister, "I shall really regret to leave Mr. Jefferson. He is one of the choice ones of the earth." [33] They started a lively correspondence, full of wit, tenderness, teasing, and domestic details of purchases—she bought British clothes for Jefferson and he ordered French gloves, corsets, and *objets d'art* for her.

In the spring and summer of 1785 he raged against the failure of his friends and relatives in America to write to him. "Monroe, I am afraid, is dead," he wrote to William Short on May 2, 1785, "for three packets have now come without bringing me a line from him or concerning him." [34] Monroe was courting Elizabeth Kortright in these months. "Pray write to me, and write me long letters," Jefferson begged Elizabeth Eppes, when desperate for more news of his daughter Polly. "Scribble on as long as you recollect any thing unmentioned, without regarding whether your lines are straight on your letters even." [35] And to Dr. Currie he wrote bitterly:

> Of political correspondence I can find enough. But I can persuade nobody to beleive that the small facts which they see passing daily under their eyes are precious to me at this distance: much more interesting to the heart than events of higher rank. Fancy to yourself a being who is withdrawn from his connections of blood, of marriage, of friendship, of acquaintance in all their gradations, who for years should hear nothing of what has passed among them, who returns again to see them and finds one half dead. This strikes him like a pestilence sweeping off the half of mankind. . . . Continue then to give me facts, little facts, such as you think every one imagines beneath notice, and your letters will be most precious to me.[36]

He begged both Madison and Monroe to come to Paris. "It will make you adore your own country, it's soil, it's climate, it's equality, liberty, laws, people and manners. My god! How little do my countrymen know what precious blessings they are in possession of, and which no other people on earth enjoy." [37]

At first he sorely missed the Adams family. Their departure, he wrote, had left him "in the dumps," and his afternoons hung heavily on him. Thrust into the circles Franklin had abandoned, he believed he would never supplant the most popular American in Europe, renowned as a wit, diplomat, and man of science. Jefferson himself called Franklin "the greatest man and ornament of the age and country in which he lived." [38] But he soon found that as the author of the Declaration of Independence he had achieved a fame of his own, and

Courtesy of the Henry E. Huntington Library and Art Gallery

Left, Thomas Jefferson, 1787, painted by John Trumbull in Paris for Jefferson's daughter Martha. *Above*, Richard Cosway's miniature of Maria Cosway, painted on ivory

Estate of Mrs. Edmund Jefferson Burke

Courtesy of the Bavarian State Collections of Art

Richard and Maria Cosway, engraved by Richard Cosway, 1786

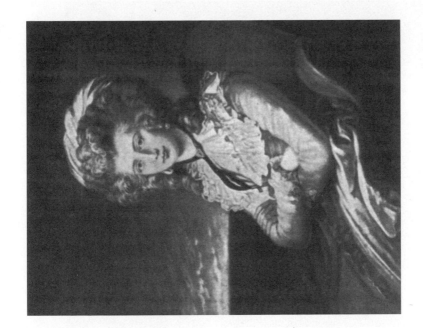

Above, Maria Cosway, a self-portrait, from a rare mezzotint by Valentine Green. *Left*, Sarah, Abraham, and Hagar, by Adriaen van der Werff, much admired by Jefferson in Düsseldorf, Germany, in 1788

Courtesy of the Collegio di Maria SS. Bambina, Lodi, Italy

New York Historical Association

Abigail Adams, 1785, portrait by Mather Brown

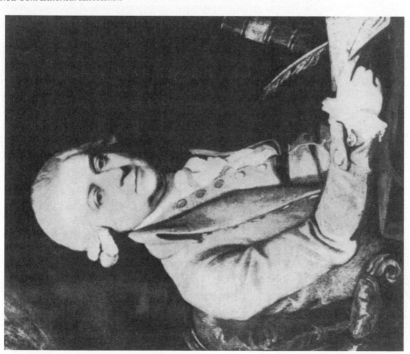

Courtesy of the Boston Athenaeum

John Adams, portrait by Mather Brown, sent to Jefferson in 1788

Courtesy of the Pennsylvania Academy of Fine Arts

George Washington, portrait by Charles Willson Peale

Alexander Hamilton, portrait by Jacques Reich

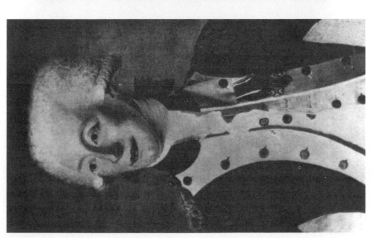

Marquis de Lafayette, by Joseph Boze
Painted for Jefferson, 1790

Courtesy of the Massachusetts Historical Society

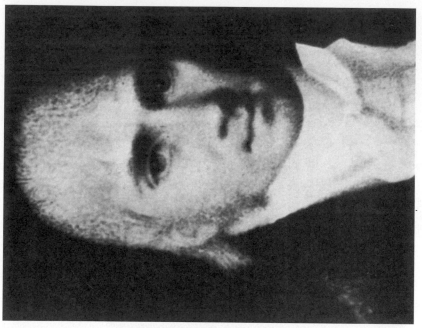

Courtesy of the James Monroe Memorial Foundation, Fredericksburg, Va.

James Monroe, portrait by Madame G. Busset, Paris, 1794–97

Courtesy of the New–York Historical Society

James Madison, after an original portrait by Gilbert Stuart

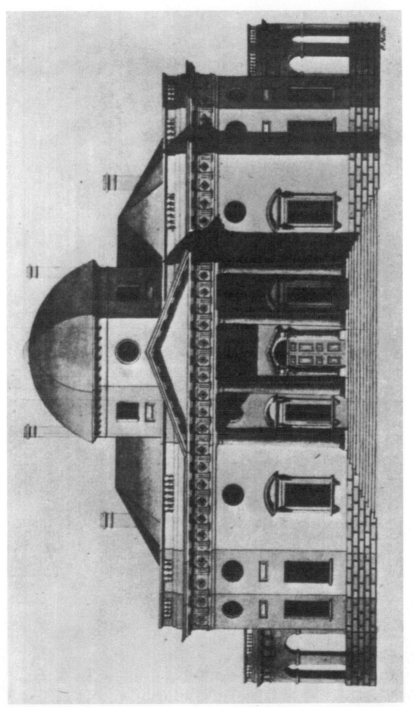

Design for the remodeling of Monticello, drawn by Robert Mills, 1803

Courtesy of the Massachusetts Historical Society

Courtesy of the Worcester Art Museum

Left, Thomas Jefferson in 1800, painted by Rembrandt Peale *above,* Jefferson in 1804, portrait drawn with the aid of a physiognotrace by C. B. J. F. de Saint-Mémin

White House Collections

Aaron Burr, after a painting by J. Vandyke

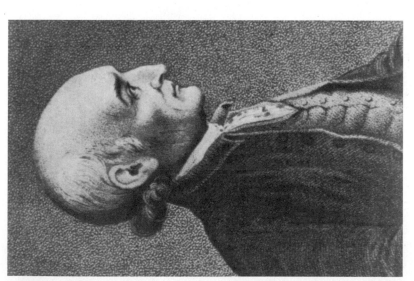

Courtesy of the Virginia State Library

George Wythe, drawn and engraved by J. B. Longacre

Thomas Mann Randolph

Courtesy of the Virginia Historical Society

Martha Jefferson Randolph, portrait by Thomas Sully

Courtesy of the Thomas Jefferson Memorial Foundation, Monticello

Courtesy of the American Philosophical Society

The University of Virginia, drawn by William Goodacres in 1824

Courtesy of the American Philosophical Society

Jefferson at Monticello, age seventy-eight, portrait by Thomas Sully

he was astonished at the favorable publicity in France accorded his bill for establishing religious liberty. Lafayette, who quickly became his best friend among the French aristocracy, wrote to Washington, "Liberal ideas are cantering about from one end of the kingdom to another," and to another friend, "Mr. Jefferson . . . is one of the most amiable, learned, upright and able men who ever existed, and is much beloved in France for his amiable disposition and much respected for his abilities." [39]

An unconscious aristocrat himself, accustomed as were most slaveholders to the habit of command, Jefferson quickly lost his self-consciousness and mingled with the French nobility and members of the diplomatic corps as if he did indeed have that trace of royal blood his mother's family boasted about. But Jefferson's aristocracy was of the spirit. He sought out as friends the scientists and philosophes, the artists and musicians. "Were I to tell you how much I enjoy their architecture, sculpture, painting, music, I should want words," he wrote to a friend.[40] And he held in contempt Americans like William Bingham who "had a rage for being presented to great men" and who, he wrote to Madison, "will make you believe he was on intimate footing with the first characters in Europe and versed in the secrets of every cabinet." [41] Jefferson did not even trouble to describe to anyone his first meeting with Louis XVI. David Humphreys, secretary of the American commission, who watched the ceremony when Jefferson presented his credentials at court, wrote of the King as "rather fat and of a placid, good tempered appearance," attended by one hundred Swiss guards. He found somewhat ridiculous the rituals of bowing and hat removing, noting that every time Jefferson mentioned the name of either King or Queen in his prepared paper he took off his hat and the King and all his courtiers did the same.[42] Though Jefferson was ever mindful of the King's aid in the American Revolution, he understood perfectly that he had been motivated not by love of Americans but by spite and fear of England. Of Foreign Minister Vergennes, Jefferson wrote shrewdly:

> His devotion to the principles of pure despotism render him unaffectionate to our governments but his fear of England makes him value us as a make weight. He is cool, reserved in political conversation, free and familiar on other subjects. . . . It is impossible to have a clearer, better organised head but age has chilled his heart.[43]

Jefferson as a diplomat, as Bernard Bailyn has written, was "unconventional, as imaginative, resourceful and tough as the best, or worst, of the Old World politicians, and more adroit than most." [44] He successfully concluded a consular convention; he wrote a detailed study on whale fishing and reopened the French market for American whale oil, though he was less successful in breaking the monopolistic control of French imports of American tobacco. Most important, he helped to keep the credit of the young republic good, and the nation solvent, by his negotiations, along with John Adams, with the bankers of Holland.

Marie Kimball has described in detail his friendships with some of the most beguiling men in Paris, the Baron de Grimm, the Abbés Chalut and Arnaud, the Duc de la Rochefoucauld-Liancourt, the Duc de Noailles, the Abbé Morellet. Mazzei introduced Jefferson to scientists Lavoisier and Condorcet. He dined with Buffon, and took an almost malicious pleasure in presenting him skins and skeletons of American deer, elk, and moose which he had had shipped to him from America at great expense, proof to the celebrated naturalist that he had been in error when he wrote that mammals degenerated in size in the New World. He met the renowned sculptor Houdon, and arranged for him to make a statue of George Washington, which had been com-missioned by the Virginia assembly, with a promise of 1,000 English guineas as payment. He had Houdon make a bust of Lafayette, also commissioned by the Virginia assembly, and gave it to the city of Paris. It was placed in the Great Hall of the Hôtel de Ville with a proper ceremony. Not unmindful of his own role in history, Jefferson pri-vately commissioned Houdon to make a bust of himself. So he mingled in elite circles, endearing himself to men and women alike. It was all very exhilarating to this forty-two-year-old grandson of an obscure Welshman, who had not himself seen a city with more than 2,000 citizens until he was twenty-three.

When Abigail Adams wrote to him glowingly of London in June 1785, he replied with lines that showed that in eleven months he had become quite lost to France:

> I consider your boasts of the splendour of your city and of it's superb hackney coaches as a flout, and declaring that I would not give the polite, self-denying, feeling, hospitable, good-humoured people of this country and their amability in every point of view, (tho' it must be confessed our streets are somewhat dirty, and our fiacres rather in-different) for ten such races of rich, proud, hectoring, swearing, squibbing, carnivorous animals as those among whom you are; and that I do love this *people* with all my heart.[45]

Charmed as he was by the gentle manners of the French aristocracy, Jefferson was appalled at the misery and squalor of the French masses. "Of twenty millions of people supposed to be in France," he wrote back to America, "I am of opinion there are nineteen millions more wretched, more accursed in every circumstance of human existence, than the most conspicuously wretched individual in the whole United States. . . . The truth of Voltaire's observation offers itself perpetually, that every man here must be either the hammer or the anvil." [46]

His contempt for the institution of monarchy, escalating with passing months, was further exacerbated by a trip to London. John Adams had been received coldly at the Court of St. James's, as what man would not who had once been the most notorious rebel in the British empire? The King had accepted his presence stiffly, as he would the ministers from any nation with whom England had been at war. It was a sign he accepted the adulthood of America and Adams recognized it as such. Adams did not consider it a special act of arrogance to take to court for an introduction to the King the man who had written the Declaration of Independence. But George III did. Though Jefferson was an accredited diplomatist at the court of Louis XVI, deserving of the same minimum courtesy as John Adams, the King of England caused a sensation in the court when he ostentatiously turned his back on them both.

The memory of the public humiliation still burned in Jefferson when he wrote his *Autobiography* at seventy-seven:

> On my presentation, as usual, to the King and Queen, at their levees, it was impossible for anything to be more ungracious, than their notice of Mr. Adams and myself. I saw at once that the ulcerations of mind in that quarter, left nothing to be expected on the subject of my attendance.[47]

His anger at the time was more bluntly expressed: The British, he wrote, "of all nations on earth . . . require to be treated with the most hauteur. They require to be kicked into common good manners." [48]

What had been an amiable and friendly feeling toward the King of France gradually changed into contempt. "The king goes for nothing," Jefferson wrote to John Jay on October 8, 1787. "He hunts one half the day, is drunk the other, and signs whatever he is bid." To Washington he wrote in 1788, "I was much an enemy to monarchy before I came to Europe. I am ten thousand times more so since I have seen what they are." [49] In his "Hints to Americans Travelling in Europe," which Jefferson wrote in 1788, apparently with wide circulation in mind, he suggested that the courts of London and France be seen "as the tower of London or Menagerie of Versailles with their Lions, tygers, and Hyaenas and other beasts of prey." [50]

In Paris Jefferson for the first time in his life met women who wielded political power, and in the beginning was not offended by the phenomenon, except as he watched it exercised by the Queen. He frequented the salons of the Comtesse d'Houdetot, the Julie of Rousseau's *Confessions*, that of Madame Necker and her still more celebrated daughter, Madame de Staël. He became a good friend of the Comtesse de Tessé, aunt of Lafayette, and later sent her many plants from America for her garden. He became the friend of the Duchesse d'Anville, mother of the Duc de la Rochefoucauld, whom Franklin had described as "a lady of uncommon intelligence and merit," and whom the awed Abigail Adams described as "the most learned woman in France." [51] He was welcomed at the home of Madame Helvétius, who adored Franklin. In these elegant salons, Jefferson wrote to Charles Bellini, "it seems that a man might pass a life without encountering a single rudeness." [52] But of Marie Antoinette he wrote in August 1787, "The queen is detested and an explosion of some sort is not impossible." By September of 1788 he looked with an increasingly jaundiced eye on petticoat influence in politics at any level. "The French ladies miscalculate much their own happiness," he wrote to Angelica Church, "when they wander from the field of their influence into that of politics." [53]

In his first year in Paris he professed to be as shocked as Abigail Adams by the handsome prostitutes beckoning on the streets, by the total lack of inhibition in all levels of society. "The domestic bonds here are absolutely done away," he wrote to Eliza Trist. "And where can their compensation be found? Perhaps they may catch some moments of transport above the level of the ordinary tranquil joy we experience, but they are separated by long intervals during which all the passions are at sea without rudder or compass." But he went on to concede whimsically, with a covert return to his language in the Declaration of Independence, that "fallacious as these pursuits of happiness are, they seem on the whole to furnish the most effectual abstraction from a contemplation of the hardness of their government." [54]

He wrote somewhat priggishly to young John Banister, Jr., in October 1785 that he would never encourage a young American to get his education in Europe because, among other things, "he is led by the strongest of all the human passions into a spirit for female intrigue destructive of his own and others happiness, or a passion for whores destructive of his health, and in both cases learns to consider fidelity to the marriage bed as an ungentlemanly practice and inconsistent with happiness: he recollects the voluptuary dress and arts of the European women and pities and despises the chaste affections of those of his own country." [55]

Still, Jefferson's very preoccupation with the "strongest of all the human passions," and the "voluptuary dress and arts" of the women of France, suggests that his own immunity was fast wearing thin.

To Chastellux, to whom he wrote in September 1785 describing personality distinctions between those who lived in the northern part of the United States and those like himself who lived in the South, he used adjectives which suggest that he was giving way to a whole new concept of himself as a passionate man and voluptuary.

In the North they are	In the South they are
cool	fiery
sober	voluptuary
laborious	indolent
persevering	unsteady
independent	independent
jealous of their own liberties, and just to those of others	zealous for their own liberties, but trampling on those of others
interested	generous
chicaning	candid
superstitious and hypocritical in their religion	without attachment of pretentions to any religion but that of the heart.[56]

He began using the word "savage" to describe himself in various letters. On September 6, 1785, he wrote moodily to Baron Geismar, whom he had befriended in the prisoner-of-war camp in Charlottesville, "I am now of an age which does not easily accomodate itself to new manners and new modes of living: and I am savage enough to prefer the woods, the wilds, and the independence of Monticello, to all the brilliant pleasures of this gay capital." [57] Three weeks later in a candid letter to Charles Bellini, he described himself as "a savage of the mountains of America," then went on to compare the "tranquil permanent felicity" of his countrymen with the frenetic French search for happiness: "Conjugal love having no existence among them, domestic happiness of which that is the basis, is utterly unknown. In lieu of this are substituted pursuits which nourish and invigorate all our bad passions, and which offer only moments of extasy amidst days and months of restlessness and torment." [58]

At the same moment that he paid tribute here to the superiority of American marriages, he was betraying more than a passing curiosity in "bad passions" and "substituted pursuits." All around him he saw a cheerful giving up to "moments of extasy" outside the conventional marriage pattern. His secretary William Short would soon be deeply involved with the wife of the young Duc de la Rochefoucauld.[59] Lafayette had had a passionate affair with Madame de Hunolstein.[60] Franklin, at seventy-nine, was openly in love with Madame Helvétius, and had even proposed marriage. This frank, intelligent, and warmly sensuous Frenchwoman had acknowledged her own affection for him, though as Franklin complained to one friend, "it seemed ungrateful in her" that though he had given her so many of his days, "she has never given him a single one of her nights." [61] Jefferson, tired of "days and months of restlessness and torment," was ripe with longing.

CHAPTER XV

My Head and My Heart

What a mass of happiness had we travelled over!

Jefferson to Maria Cosway, October 12, 1786 [1]

Thomas Jefferson and Maria Cosway spent their first afternoon together at a most unlikely spot for the beginning of a romance. This
was the Halle aux Bleds, the big, new, noisy Paris grain market,
crowded with peasants and merchants, and smelling of hay, flax, and
barley. It was, nevertheless, one of the attractions of the day, famous
for its giant dome—130 feet across—constructed of wooden ribs in
such a fashion that the interior was flooded with light. Outside rose
an old Renaissance column with circular steps inside, where visitors
who climbed to the top were told that it had been built for Catherine
de Medici, wife of Henry II, who climbed it often with her astrologer
to learn the will of the stars.

Jefferson had mixed feelings about going on the excursion at all.
"The Halle aux bleds might have rotted down before I should have
gone to see it," he later wrote.[2] But John Trumbull, the young American artist Jefferson had recently met in London who was presently
staying with him as he worked out the design of his planned canvas of
the signing of the Declaration of Independence, persuaded him to go,
promising him amusing company. It consisted of two artists from
London, Richard Cosway and his wife. Thinking that he might at least
see architecture worth copying for a market in Richmond, Jefferson
acquiesced. What he saw there, he wrote later to Maria, was "the most
superb thing on earth." But he was not writing "of a parcel of sticks

and chips put together in pens," but the lady "to whom we had been presented." [3]

Maria Louisa Catherine Cecilia (Hadfield) Cosway was a fragile, languorously feminine woman of twenty-seven, with luminous blue eyes, exquisite skin, and a halo of golden curls. Though of English parentage, she spoke with a marked Italian accent, having been born and educated in Florence, and must have seemed to Jefferson exotic in a way that most Englishwomen were not. Her husband was a small man, shorter even than his wife, invariably dressed with foppish elegance. He was forty-four, close to Jefferson's age, and had been married for only three years. He was bouncy and cheerful; in his wife's words, "toujours riant, toujours gai," [4] but also fulsome and sycophantic. English critics would describe him as "an absurd little coxcomb," "a preposterous little Dresden china manikin." James Northcote dismissed him as "one of those butterfly characters that nobody minded, so that his opinion went for nothing." [5]

Though he was mocked for his pretentiousness in dress, especially a mulberry silk coat ornamented with strawberries, and was described as having a face like a monkey, Cosway in painting self-portraits not surprisingly showed a handsome man, with no trace in his face either of dandyism, or of the cruelty with which he treated his wife. Everyone in the bohemian London court circle in which they moved knew that Maria was wretchedly unhappy. James Northcote, who said she married out of necessity when her mother's money was exhausted, wrote that "she always despised him." And Jefferson, with the special sensitivity of a man in need of love, must have seen this the first afternoon.

Trumbull had told Jefferson in advance of "the merits and talents" of the Cosways, so he must have known that the husband was the most skillful miniature painter in England and that his wife presided over one of London's most fashionable salons. Cosway's Schomberg House was full of European paintings and exotic furniture—Japanese screens, escritoires of ebony inlaid with mother-of-pearl, exquisitely enameled and jeweled boxes, mosaic tables set with jasper, bloodstone, and lapis lazuli, tortoise-shell musical clocks, and Persian carpets—many of which were discreetly sold to the wealthy Londoners who frequented the celebrated Sunday-night musicals, when Maria entertained by playing and singing Italian songs. Whether Trumbull knew that Cosway also secretly painted pornographic pictures on snuffboxes which sold at exorbitant prices is not clear, though it was common enough knowledge in the lively gambling and libertine circle of the Prince of Wales.[6]

After the death of her father in Florence, Maria had wanted to join a nunnery, but her mother, who was Protestant, would have none of it.

Upon coming to England, she had been sheltered by the artist Angelica Kauffmann, then the toast of London. Sir Joshua Reynolds admired Maria's drawings, and like everyone else was charmed by the gentle simplicity of her manner. She was taught by the artist Henry Fuseli, and was said to have been engaged for a time to a composer, a Dr. Parsons. But it was Cosway in the end who in the very crassest sense finally purchased her, settling upon her £2,800, and promising to care for her mother until her death.[7] "As I meant to be a nun," Maria wrote later, "I found the convent I had chosen would have taken me without a fortune; and also found a *husband* who did the same."[8]

After the marriage Cosway improved Maria's English and painting technique, and then set her up as the leading ornament in his grandiose mansion. She told her friends she was afraid of him at first but came to love him, a genteel fiction few believed.[9] Bitter unpublished letters from Maria to her husband written years after their estrangement and still buried in her papers in the convent school in Italy which she founded suggest that there had been an initial period of some happiness, followed by her despairing realization that he was having affairs with men as well as women. One of them reads as follows:

> Remember my good Mr. Cos: how many years we were happy. My wishes were to second and follow yours. . . . until you began to divied Your thoughts, first with occupations in Bedford Square, & a Miss P. Afterwards with Hammersmith and then L. . . . Lastly with the Udneys and this ended our happiness.[10]

But in the first years after their marriage she had been flattered by the continuing publicity; Allan Cunningham wrote that for a time "nothing was talked of but the great youth and talent of Mrs. Cosway; one half of the carriages who stopped at her husband's door contained sitters ambitious of the honours of her pencil."[11] James Boswell, one of her admirers, accused her of treating men like dogs.[12] Cosway saw to it that his wife's pictures were exhibited in the Academy, along with those of Mary Moser, who would one day be his mistress, and of Angelica Kauffmann. No reputable art critic took any of this female talent seriously. "It was not that women were not often very clever (cleverer than many men)," William Hazlitt wrote, "but there was a point of excellence which they never reached." Even Angelica Kauffmann, he said, had "an effeminate and feeble look in all her works. . . . There was not a man's hand in it . . . something with strength and muscle."[13]

Horace Walpole composed for the *Morning Chronicle* a poem of mixed derision and praise, "Verses on Seeing Mrs. Cosway's Pallet":

Behold this strange chaotic mass,
Where colours in confusion lie,
Where rival tints commix'd appear,
Here tints for water, *there* for sky.
Kept in imagination's glow,
See now the lovely artist stand!
Grand visions beaming on her mind,
The magic pencil in her hand.[14]

John Wolcott, writing under the pseudonym Peter Pindar, would write maliciously of both the Cosways:

What vanity was in your skulls
To make you act so like two fools,
To expose your daubs tho' made with wondrous pains out
Could Raphael's angry ghost arise,
He'd catch a pistol up and blow your brains out.[15]

Actually Cosway had a formidable talent, deserving something of George C. Williamson's appraisal that he was "the most brilliant miniature painter" of eighteenth-century England. George III detested him—"Among *my* painters there are no fops," [16] he said—but the Prince of Wales admired his talent and commissioned him to paint miniatures of two of his mistresses, Perdita Robinson and Mrs. Fitzherbert. (The latter miniature he was said to be clutching when he died.) Perdita, whose lovely face was immortalized by Gainsborough and Sir Joshua Reynolds as well as by Cosway, had become a friend to Maria Cosway and they planned to publish a book together, with Maria as illustrator. Abandoned by the Prince of Wales for the more seductive Mrs. Fitzherbert, Perdita had captured the affection of Colonel Banastre Tarleton, whose dragoons had very nearly captured Jefferson at Monticello. She was in Paris with Tarleton in the same September that Maria Cosway met Jefferson, helping with the memoirs of his American campaign, and it is one of the entertaining minor coincidences of history that Jefferson and Tarleton in 1786 were both in Paris and in love with two women who eventually published a book together.[17]

Whether Jefferson ever heard that a secret passage ran from Schomberg House to the quarters of the Prince of Wales and that the Prince had seduced, or tried to seduce, Maria Cosway must remain a mystery.[18] That Trumbull or Maria herself had brought word of the Prince's libertine habits is clear enough from a letter Jefferson wrote to Abigail Adams a week after he met the Cosways. He had heard a rumor of an attempted assassination of George III and wrote to her in some alarm, "No man upon earth has my prayers for his continuance of life more sincerely than him. . . . The Prince of Wales on the throne, Lansdowne and Fox in the ministry, and we are undone!" [19] Jefferson never recognized that the Prince was one of the wittiest and cleverest of all the princes of Europe. Later he described his entourage to John Jay as that of "the lowest, the most illiterate and profligate persons of the kingdom, without choice of rank or merit, and with whom the subjects of the conversation are only horses, drinking-matches, bawdy houses, and in terms the most vulgar." The young nobility, who begin by associating with him, he said, "soon leave him, disgusted with the insupportable profligacy of his society." [20]

What Jefferson was told in advance about Maria Cosway is irrelevant, for if ever a man fell in love in a single afternoon it was he. Though he had a dinner invitation from the Duchess d'Anville, he canceled it with a note, pleading the pressure of newly arrived correspondence, and the visitors to the Halle aux Bleds all drove off happily in a carriage to the Parc de St. Cloud, where they dined, strolled through the gallery, past the cascading fountains in the garden, and then came back to Paris to see the fireworks display, *Spectacle Pyrrhique des Sieurs Ruggieri*, on the rue St. Lazare. Having learned that Maria played both harp and harpsichord, and still loath to say goodbye, Jefferson persuaded them to go on to the home of Johann Baptiste Krumpholtz, whose wife, Julie, a distinguished harpist, entertained them to a late hour. "If the day had been as long as a Lapland summer day," Jefferson wrote to Maria later, he would "still have contrived means . . . to have filled it. . . . When I came home at night and looked back to the morning, it seemed to have been a month gone." [21]

Maria Cosway, like Martha Wayles, was small, exquisite, and feminine as well as being a musician. Importantly too, she seemed to be in need of rescue, trapped like a delicate butterfly in a monstrous web of lascivious intrigue spun by the Prince of Wales. That she was genuinely in need of rescue we know by what happened to her later in life, but when she and Jefferson first met the necessity for rescue was already an old theme in Maria Cosway's life. Maria's mother had had five children born to her before Maria, of whom four had inexplicably died in the night. Charles Hadfield, her father, certain that there had been foul play, though the nurses had been different with each child, hired a governess to watch the nurse when Maria was born.

"One day," Maria wrote, "a Maid servant went into the nursery, took me in her Arms, & said pretty little Creature, I have sent four to heaven, I hope to send you also." The governess, "struck at this extraordinary speech, ran to my father, proper enquiries were made," and the girl went to an asylum for the insane.[22] Maria wrote of her father not only as her rescuer, but also as a man who "had a great taste & knowledge of the Arts & sciences," and who had "in every way contrived to furnish my mind. . . . Everybody knows what my father was and the education he gave me. My gratitude has never ceased." [23] The resemblance in this respect to Jefferson and his own daughter is striking. James Northcote, who had met Maria in Rome in 1778 when she was eighteen, said "she had been the object of adoration of an indulgent father, who, unfortunately for her had never checked the growth of her imperfections." Northcote had found her "not unhandsome" and talented, but also "active, ambitious, proud, and restless." [24] Jefferson saw only "music, modesty, beauty, and that softness of disposition which is the ornament of her sex." [25]

In the first few days after their meeting Jefferson wrote no letters, spending his days in a dizzying round of visits to the Louvre, the Palais Royal, the Bibliothèque du Roi, the "new church of Ste. Geneviève" (converted during the Revolution into the Pantheon), and to Versailles. Accompanying Trumbull and Jefferson in the Cosway entourage was an aging scholar, Pierre François Hugues, known as d'Hancarville, who followed Maria about in humble adoration, and whose legacy of scores of affectionate letters Maria preserved, along with the first note Jefferson sent her, an envelope later inscribed by him to her husband, and a portrait painted of Jefferson by John Trumbull.[26] The Cosways introduced Jefferson to the Polish hero Thaddeus Kosciusko, and to Jacques Louis David, whose enormous canvases Maria greatly admired. They visited the salons of sculptors Jean Antoine Houdon and Augustin Pagou. So the shy diplomat, who had been describing himself as a "savage from Virginia," and who had been consorting with scholars and diplomats, found himself thrust into the insouciant, bohemian life of the artists.

When Richard Cosway began serious work on his miniatures for the Duchesse d'Orléans, and Trumbull went off on a tour of Germany, Jefferson and Maria began to see each other alone. Jefferson's duties as minister were not onerous; they left him free the better part of every afternoon. He saw his daughter chiefly on Sundays, and his evenings were almost always his own. Later he reminded Maria of their expeditions together:

How beautiful was every object! the Port de Neuilly, the hills along the Seine, the rainbows of the machine of Marly, the terras of St. Germains, the chateaux, the gardens, the statues of Marly, the pavillion of Lucienne. Recollect too Madrid, Bagatelle, the King's garden, the Dessert.[27]

Maria Kimball, in *Jefferson: The Scene of Europe*, reconstructed with loving detective work descriptions of what all these gardens, grottoes, intimate restaurants, and inns were like in 1786, and one can see in reading her pages that Jefferson sought out some of the most idyllic spots in all the environs of Paris. What he wrote of as "the Dessert" was really the Désert de Retz, an elaborate *anglo-chinois* garden four miles from St. Germain, containing a grotto, a replica of a ruined Gothic church, a Chinese *orangerie*, a *temple de repose*, and a *temple au dieu Pan*. It also included an enormous column, sixty-five feet in diameter and four stories high, built to look like a ruin, which especially excited Jefferson. "How grand the ideas excited by the remains of such a column!" he wrote to Maria. "The spiral staircase too was beautiful. The wheels of time moved on with a rapidity of which those of our carriage gave but a faint idea, and yet in the evening, when one took a retrospect of the day, what a mass of happiness had we travelled over!" [28]

He could not contain this new happiness, which spilled over in letters to his friends. To Abigail Adams he wrote on August 9, 1786, when he had been seeing Maria Cosway for less than a week:

> Here we have singing, dauncing, laugh, and merriment. No assassinations, no treasons, rebellions nor other dark deeds. When our king goes out, they fall down and kiss the earth where he has trodden; and then they go to kissing one another. And this is the truest wisdom. They have as much happiness in one year as an Englishman in ten.[29]

To the Adamses' new son-in-law, William Stephens Smith, he wrote a long letter on August 10, tedious with business details, but containing a cheerful, totally irrelevant aside, "for beauty is ever leading us astray." [30] And in a letter to George Wythe on August 13 in which he launched into his usual strictures about the malevolence of the kings, nobles, and priests, he nevertheless described the French people as having "the most benevolent, the most gay, and amiable character of which the human form is susceptible." [31]

In these weeks he turned also to reading and writing about the poetry of love. The poems a man chooses to copy or memorize usually speak to him in some special fashion, and under the guise of a scholarly inquiry into patterns of meter and rhyme, later titled "Thoughts on English Prosody," Jefferson caressed a great many beautiful lines. As he himself wrote of these selections, mostly from Milton, Gray, Collins, Shenstone, and Pope, "I chose, too, the most pregnant passages, those wherein every word teems with latent meaning." [32] Some were reflections on his dead wife:

Ye who e'er lost an angel, pity me!

O how self-fettered was my groveling soul!
To every sod which wraps the dead . . .

But most were appropriate to the new love:

He sung and hell consented
To hear the poet's prayer
Stern Proserpine relented
And gave him back the fair

. . .

And I loved her the more when I heard
Such tenderness fall from her tongue.

. . .

With her how I stray'd amid fountains and bowers!
Or loiter'd behind, and collected the flowers!
Then breathless with ardor my fair one pursued,
And to think with what kindness my garland she view'd!
But be still, my fond heart! this emotion give o'er;
Fain would'st thou forget thou must love her no more.[33]

Near the end of his compilation, as Maria Cosway's return to London became certain, he included the melancholy lines:

I mourn
I sigh
I Burn
I die
Let us part—
Let us part
Will you break
My poor heart? [34]

Maria Cosway was as sensitive to Jefferson's loneliness as he was to her unhappiness, and almost from the beginning she felt the power of the clutching hand of his dead wife. After her return to London she wrote to him: "Are you to be painted in future ages sitting solitary and sad, on the beautiful Monticello, tormented by the shadow of a woman who will present you a deform'd rod, twisted and broken, instead of the emblematical instrument belonging to the Muses, held by Genius, inspired by wit, from which all that is pleasing, beautifull and happy can be describ'd to entertain." [35] After reading Jefferson's *Notes on the State of Virginia*, which he had given to her as a present, she wrote passionately: "Oh how I wish My self in those delightful places! Those enchanted Grotto's! Those Magnificent Mountains rivers, &c. &c.! Why am I not a Man that I could sett out immediatly and satisfy My Curiosity, indulge My sight with wonders!" [36]

The question whether or not Jefferson and Maria Cosway became lover and mistress during these weeks has been answered in the negative with extraordinary finality by a good many writers. Nathan Schachner wrote, "There is absolutely no evidence nor reason to believe the relation was anything but platonic." Thomas Fleming insisted, "There was no hope, no future to this infatuation. The lady was married, and too religious to commit adultery." Merrill Peterson, as we have already noted, described it as a pleasant game, with no "ardent desire," and Winthrop Jordan dismissed it as a "superficially frantic flirtation," a mere bagatelle, where the love was "play," and the "affair" was nonexistent. Saul Padover said "the affair was brief and apparently not successful," and Dixon Wecter wrote with contempt, "At forty-three" Jefferson was "older than Franklin at seventy-five."

Only Dumas Malone, of all the male biographers and historians, has been willing to concede that Jefferson "fell deeply in love during that golden September" and to suggest that if ever as a widower he engaged in "illicit love-making . . . this was the time." [37] Helen Bullock, who edited the Maria Cosway–Jefferson letters in 1945 with great discretion, let the correspondence speak for itself, but one of her chapters is called "Peep into Elysium." And Maria Kimball described the romance as "one of the most momentous experiences of Jefferson's life." [38]

The insistence of many of these writers that Jefferson remained continent is a curiosity suggesting that something is at work here that has little to do with scholarship.[39] The nuances and overtones in his letters are richly suggestive, and the writers most certain of Jefferson's continuing chastity minimize or ignore the relevant fact that Maria Cosway returned to Paris for a second autumn without her husband and stayed almost four months. Moreover, Jefferson kept copies of his own letters to Maria, and all of Maria Cosway's to him. His failure to destroy them tells us that he knew that his daughters would one day probably read them, if not a larger audience. This was one love affair he was clearly willing to share with history.

On September 18, 1786, about six weeks after their original meeting, Jefferson and Maria were walking along the Seine westward from the Place Louis XV. In attempting to jump over a fence—whether to retrieve a blowing scarf in the wind or simply in sheer exuberant good spirits one can only guess—he fell very hard and dislocated his right wrist. This at least was the diagnosis of the French surgeons who ineptly treated it, though it would seem from his subsequent agony and failure to recover that he certainly broke a bone, as his daughter Martha believed. "How the right hand became disabled," Jefferson wrote cryptically to William Stephens Smith, "would be a long story for the left to tell. It was by one of those follies from which good cannot come but ill may." [40]

Jefferson's daughter described the accident in later years as if her father had been walking with a man:

> He frequently walked as far as seven miles in the country. Returning from one of those rambles, he was joined by some friend, and being earnestly engaged in conversation he fell and fractured his wrist. He said nothing at the moment, but holding his suffering limb with the other hand, he continued the conversation till he arrived near to his own house, when, informing his companion of the accident, he left him to send for the surgeon. The fracture was a compound one, and probably much swollen before the arrival of the surgeon; it was not set, and remained ever after weak and stiff. [41]

Whether Jefferson really deceived Martha, or whether she never really exorcised her jealousy for Mrs. Cosway and deliberately misled Jefferson's biographer is uncertain.

Maria, frantic to see Jefferson after the accident, had a problem getting away from her husband. On the second day she sent him a note: "I meant to have had the pleasure of seeing you Twice, and I have appeared a Monster for not having sent to know how you was, the whole day." She had planned a morning visit, she said, but her husband had "kill'd My project, I had proposed to him, by burying himself among Pictures and forgetting the hours." She had come late at night, she said, too late to do anything but prove "a disturbance to your Neighbours." Whether she was alone or with her husband is not clear—here the letter is mutilated. But she promised to return the following morning. [42]

Marie Kimball, who dismisses Maria Cosway as "a spoiled, egocentric young woman, with a very limited emotional capacity," and even Dumas Malone, who describes her more charitably as "a lovely, talented capricious creature—half woman and half child," mistakenly believe that the fractured wrist brought an end to the "summer idyl." Malone wrote positively that Jefferson did not join the Cosways until October 4, more than two weeks after the accident, when he went to say goodbye to them both. [43] Both biographers seem to have forgotten that the absence of letters is evidence not of their failure to see each other but the contrary. That Jefferson did see her, perhaps often, is evident from a note Maria wrote to him on October 5, which makes clear that he had been begging her to go out in the carriage with him on an excursion of some sort, and that she had feared it would do his wrist some damage. "You repeatedly said it wou'd do you no harm," she remembered.[44] When she did agree to this excursion on October 4 she had to give Jefferson the dreaded but long expected news that her husband was insisting—despite her protestation that "nothing seems redy"—that they leave for London the next day.[45]

The effect on Jefferson was catastrophic. He described it later in a letter to Maria as if he were talking to himself: "Remember the last night. You knew your friends were to leave Paris to-day. This was enough to throw you into agonies. All night you tossed us from one side of the bed to the other. No sleep, no rest. The poor crippled wrist too, never left one moment in the same position, now up, now down, now here, now there; was it to be wondered at if all it's pains returned?" [46] The next morning he sent for the surgeon, who, he said, could not "devine the cause of this extraordinary change." [47] Unable to go for the farewell visit, as he had planned, Jefferson sent off a little note, laboriously written with his left hand, of necessity somewhat formal, since he knew Cosway would be with Maria when she received it.

> I have passed the night in so much pain that I have not closed my eyes. It is with infinite regret therefore that I must relinquish your charming company for that of the Surgeon whom I have sent for to examine into the cause of this change. I am in hopes it is only the having rattled a little too freely over the pavement yesterday. If you do go, god bless you wherever you go. Present me in the most friendly terms to Mr. Cosway, and let me hear of your safe arrival in England. Addio Addio.
> Let me know if you do not go today.[48]

The Cosways did delay their departure one more day, and Jefferson not only left his home to pay a final visit but even traveled with them the first several miles to the Pavillon de St. Denis. D'Hancarville, also saying goodbye, went along as an unhappy fourth in the carriage. What Cosway thought about these two men who insisted on such a prolonged farewell to his pretty wife is not hard to imagine. He was used to a world of amorous intrigue, and had liaisons of his own. Still, he had a keen sense of property if not propriety, and eventually decided firmly if unsuccessfully against permitting his wife to come back to Paris.

After bidding farewell at St. Denis, Jefferson turned on his heel and walked away, as he put it, "more dead than alive." He and d'Hancarville climbed into a crowded carriage to return to Paris, "like recruits for the Bastille, not having soul enough to give orders to the coachman," and proceeded to console each other with "a mutual confession of distress." [49] Once back at his own hearth Jefferson began to write the great love letter known as "My Head and My Heart," what Julian Boyd properly calls "one of the notable love letters in the English language." [50] In a contrived though not unusual eighteenth-century conceit, he wrote in the form of a dialogue, with first his Head speaking, and then his Heart. Though laboriously written with his left hand, the letter covered twelve pages and exceeded four thousand words. The original has never been found, but Jefferson kept a press copy, as he did of almost all of the subsequent letters he sent to Maria, thus making it possible for him to read and reread their total correspondence in a special reliving of their hours together.

"My Head and My Heart" is so important a window into Jefferson's inner life, and has been the subject of such divergent and contradictory interpretations, that it is here reproduced in full in an Appendix so that every reader may have a look at it himself. Jefferson wrote it in great wretchedness of spirit, and also in considerable physical pain. The wrist did not heal properly, his fingers continued to be swollen for over a year, and some of the muscles permanently atrophied so that he carried about with him for the rest of his life a reminder of his infatuation in what was a real disablement. The immediate suffering compounded his sense of loss, but also revived his old conviction that love invariably brings pain and loss. So the letter can be read on several levels.

Many scholars look at the letter as a debate, and insist that the head emerges triumphant over the heart. Julian Boyd sees it as proof that "reason was not only enthroned as the chief disciplinarian of his life, but also . . . a sovereign to whom the Heart yielded a ready and full allegiance." Merrill Peterson writes that "in the end the head (Jefferson) coolly put the heart (Maria) in its place. Reason and sentiment might divide life between them, yet, for him, one was the master, the other the servant." [51] To say this is to ignore all the subsequent letters Jefferson wrote to Maria, and to forget their months together in the autumn of 1787. "My Head and My Heart" was the first of many tender letters; it is the longest and the most complicated. The dialogue is less a debate than a searching examination of himself, a portrait in words laid in the lap of a woman who was herself far more gifted with the brush and with the harpsichord than with the pen. As a self-portrait there is nothing in the Jefferson literature to compare with it. What he pictures is a deeply tormented man—"the divided empire," he calls it—a man who would be controlled by science and reason debating with a man controlled by sentiment and passion.

It is also, taken as a whole, a remarkable declaration of passion. Falling in love again had brought not only an ecstasy of affection but also a kind of ecstasy of self-knowledge he felt compelled to share.

His Head cried out—I have been punished so often by love—"Advance with caution"—"The art of life is the art of avoiding pain"—"Our own share of miseries is sufficient"—"You rack our whole system when you are parted from those you love." Such phrases, attributed to the Head, in their totality became a cry for love, for reassurance, for the promise of renewal. And his Heart spoke with even greater anguish:

> I am indeed the most wretched of all earthly beings. Overwhelmed with grief, every fibre of my frame distended beyond it's natural powers to bear, I would willingly meet whatever catastrophe should leave me no more to feel or to fear. . . .
>
> I feel more fit for death than life. But when I look back on the pleasures of which it is the consequence, I am conscious they were worth the price I am paying. . . . Hope is sweeter than despair, and they were too good to mean to deceive me. In the summer said the gentleman; but in the spring, said the lady: and I should love her forever, were it only for that!

One sees, too, thinly disguised in this letter, Jefferson's fantasy that the Cosways will visit America, that the husband will die and Maria will be left, to be cherished and comforted at "our own dear Monticello" where with majesty "we ride above the storms." "I hope in god no circumstance may ever make either seek asylum from grief," he protests, but who was better equipped to comfort a widow than himself:

> Deeply practised in the school of affliction, the human heart knows no joy which I have not lost, no sorrow of which I have not drank! Fortune can present no grief of unknown form to me! Who then can so softly bind up the wound of another as he who has felt the same wound himself? But Heaven forbid they should ever know a sorrow!

Let the Cosways come to America, he said, they would find not a nation of anarchy, as the mendacious British press contended, but a people "occupied as we are in opening rivers, digging navigable canals, making roads, building public schools, establishing academies, erecting busts and statues to our great men, protecting religious freedom, abolishing sanguinary punishments, reforming and improving our laws in general"—a nation behaving in fact exactly like Thomas Jefferson.

In a burst of scorn he caricatured his own manner of living since his wife's death:

> Let the gloomy Monk, sequestered from the world, seek unsocial pleasures in the bottom of his cell! Let the sublimated philosopher grasp visionary happiness while pursuing phantoms dressed in the garb of truth! Their supreme wisdom is supreme folly: and they mistake for

happiness the mere absence of pain. Had they ever felt the solid pleasure of one generous spasm of the heart, they would exchange for it all the frigid speculations of their lives.

He finished the letter with conventional good wishes for Richard Cosway, adding moodily, "My health is good, except my wrist which mends slowly, and my mind which mends not at all, but broods constantly over your departure." [52]

Jefferson spent several days writing this letter. He had no sooner sealed the envelope than a letter arrived from John Trumbull, who when returning from Germany had unexpectedly come upon the Cosways in Antwerp. When they told him of Jefferson's accident to his wrist, Trumbull at once wrote his sympathy, and took the opportunity to describe his German tour in detail. Maria Cosway, weary and disconsolate after riding almost all night in the rain, had scribbled a small note in Italian as a postscript.

> I am adding a couple of lines to ask you how you are. I hope the trip to St. Dennys did not cause you to remember us painfully, [and that] I shall soon receive news of your complete recovery, which will give infinite pleasure to your always obliged and affectionate Friend, Maria Cosway.—Mr. Cosway adds his compliments to mine. We arrived here Sunday, three hours past midnight.[53]

When Jefferson received Trumbull's letter and glanced at the signature, he thought for one happy moment that the whole letter was from Maria. Discovering quickly that hers was only a four-line postscript, he wrote with a disappointment that came very close to rage:

> Just as I had sealed the inclosed I received a letter of good length, dated Antwerp, with your name at the bottom. I prepared myself for a feast. I read two or three sentences: looked again at the signature to see if I had not mistaken it. It was visibly yours. Read a sentence or two more. Diable! Spelt your name distinctly. There was not a letter of it omitted. Began to read again. In fine after reading a little and examining the signature, alternately, half a dozen times, I found that your name was to four lines only instead of four pages. I thank you for the four lines however because they prove you think of me. Little indeed, but better little than none. To shew how much I think of you I send you the enclosed letter. . . . I will even allow you twelve days to get through it. . . . I send you the song I promised. bring me in return its subject, *Jours heureux!*

The song was from Sacchini's *Dardanus*:
> Jours heureux, espoir enchanteur!
> Prix charmant d'un amour si tendre!

Je vais la voir, je vais l'entendre,
Je vais retrouver le bonheur! [54]

Adding this letter to his twelve-page "dialogue," Jefferson sent them off to London in a packet in care of John Trumbull, with specific instructions to "deliver it personally." He and Maria had worked out a plan which they hoped would circumvent interception either by her husband or by the spies in the post office, who Jefferson believed regularly read all his mail. Maria was to deliver her letters to Trumbull, who would either find a trusted friend to carry them, or send them to Paris by way of Jefferson's banker, "Mr. Grand," on the rue Neuve des Capucins.[55] Trumbull, who had lived through a scandal in America, with a child born out of wedlock, could be counted on to be compassionate. Jefferson trusted him totally. "Lay all my affections at her feet," he wrote in one letter, and in another, "Kneel to Mrs. Cosway for me, and lay my soul in her lap." [56] On the occasions when Trumbull was not available he used the regular mail service, disguising his seal and omitting his signature. Trumbull was a willing accomplice, and discretion itself. Even fifty years later, when about to publish his autobiography and diary of the period, he reported that the pages of his diary which covered the dates of the Jefferson-Cosway meetings in Paris were torn out and lost.[57]

Back in London Maria fell into melancholy. The delay between Jefferson's letters, she wrote, meant "the punishment of Tantalus." To the twelve-page letter she replied in English and Italian:

> My heart is . . . full or ready to burst. . . . Your letter could employ me for some time, an hour to Consider every word, to every sentence I could write a volume . . .
> Amid the fog and smoke, sadness seems (to reign) in every heart. . . . I must return as soon as possible to my occupations in order not to feel the rigor of the Melancholy which is inspired by this unpleasant climate. . . . Everything is tranquil, quiet and gloomy, there are no Bells ringing. . . . (your letters) will never be long enough.[58]

Cosway's biographer, who knew nothing of the Jefferson affair, would write later of Maria's "depression, dullness of spirits, and nervous agitation," which were "alleviated only by her trips to Paris." [59]

On November 17, 1786, having heard nothing from Jefferson for several weeks, Maria sent him a book of songs and duets she had herself composed, and wrote, impatiently:

> But what does this silence mean. . . . I have awaited the post with so much anxiety and lo each time it arrives without bringing any letters

from Paris, I am really worried. . . . After the pain of separation is past, one lives in continual anxiety. . . . The weather here is very bad, melancholy, sad. . . . Night Thoughts, before the fire, and when the imagination is well warmed up, one could go cool off in a river.[60]

On November 19, Jefferson was writing for the first time with his right hand.

I write with pain and must be short. This is good news for you; for were the hand able to follow the effusions of the heart, that would cease to write only when this shall cease to beat. . . . When sins are dear to us we are but too prone to slide into them again. The act of repentance itself is often sweetened with the thought that it clears our account for a repetition of the same sin.[61]

Ten days later he wrote, "I am determined when you come next not to admit the idea that we are ever to part again. But are you to come again? I dread the answer to this question, and that my poor heart has been duped by the fondness of its wishes. . . . Say many kind things, and say them without reserve. They will be food for my soul." [62]

Evidence of Jefferson's despair escaped in letters to others than Maria. To Eliza House Trist he wrote on December 15, 1786, "I am burning the candle of life without present pleasure, or future object. A dozen or twenty years ago this scene would have amused me. But I am past the age for changing habits. I take all the fault on myself, as it is impossible to be among a people who wish more to make one happy." [63]

Fully expecting that Maria would return to Paris in the spring, he made no effort to find an excuse to go to England. Though he had been enchanted by the English gardens on his visit in the spring of 1786, he detested the court and the people and had vowed never to return. Impatient and teasing, though it was still midwinter, he wrote on December 24, "It is time therefore you should be making your arrangements, packing your baggage."

I was so unlucky when very young, as to read the history of Fortunatus. He had a cap of such virtues that when he put it on his head, and wished himself anywhere, he was there. I have been all my life sighing for this cap. Yet if I had it, I question if I should use it but once. I should wish myself with you, and not wish myself away again. . . . I am always thinking of you. . . . I will believe you intend to go to America, to draw the Natural bridge . . . that I shall meet you there, and visit with you all those grand scenes. . . . I had rather be deceived, than live without hope.[64]

But Cosway resorted to delay and postponement, and when Maria wrote that their trip would not take place until summer Jefferson decided to take a spring trip to Italy. He promised himself a tour of the Roman antiquities in southern France, and wanted to see something of Maria's birthplace in Italy. He did not get as far south as Florence, but did tour northern Italy as well as southern France, and got a very respectful opinion of the Alps, which made him less chauvinistic though no less affectionate toward his Virginia mountains. Even on this trip his letters to others reflected the state of his heart. To Madame de Tessé he wrote from Nîmes, "Here I am, Madam, gazing whole hours at the Maison quarrée, like a lover at his mistress." [65] Upon his return he wrote to Maria Cosway beseeching:

But I am born to lose everything I love. Why were you not with me? So many enchanting scenes which only wanted your pencil to consecrate them to fame. . . . Come then, my dear Madam, and we will breakfast every day à l'Angloise, hie away to the Desert, dine under the bowers of Marly, and forget that we are ever to part again.[66]

Maria meanwhile was in despair lest her husband cancel his summer plans.

I do not know that we shall come to Paris this year. I fear not. My husband begins to doubt it. . . . Why lead me to hope? It seems a dream to have been there and I now wish it to be real.[67]

At some time during the summer, when Cosway decided absolutely against a return to Paris, she found the courage to come by herself. There surely was a letter to Jefferson telling him of this decision, but if so he destroyed it. In fact, in none of the letters Jefferson wrote to Maria, and in none of those he kept of hers, is there evidence that she came to Paris alone in the second autumn. Thus Jefferson demonstrated that he could be as discreet as Trumbull. But come alone she did, as we learn from other sources, and she stayed over three months.

CHAPTER XVI

The Second Interlude

I love those most whom I loved first.

Jefferson to his sister, Mary Jefferson Bolling, July 23, 1787 [1]

When Abigail Adams on June 26, 1787, met the sea captain who had brought Jefferson's eight-year-old Polly across the Atlantic, she discovered with consternation that the slave accompanying the child was not a middle-aged woman, as she had expected, but an adolescent girl of considerable beauty. Sally Hemings, known at Monticello as "Dashing Sally," was described by one slave who knew her as "mighty near white," "very handsome," with "long straight hair down her back." [2] Jefferson's eldest grandson, who could have known her only as a middle-aged and old woman, told Henry Randall she was "light colored and decidedly good looking." [3] Jefferson had asked Francis Eppes to send Polly in care of a responsible friend, with "a careful negro woman, Isabel, for instance, if she has had the small pox." She need not, he said, "come farther than Havre, l'Orient, Nantes, or whatever port she should land at, because I could go there for the child myself, and the person could return to Virginia directly." [4]

Francis and Elizabeth Eppes, who had fought with pleas and procrastination against Polly's going, who had even encouraged their fourteen-year-old son Jack (whom Polly later married) to write telling Jefferson that she would not come without being forced,[5] had capitulated in the spring of 1787, arranging to put her on a British vessel sailing from Norfolk to London in the care of the captain, John Ramsay. But since the slave woman Jefferson had specified was about to "lie in," Polly's kin, instead of finding a substitute of similar age who had had the smallpox, sent the fourteen-year-old quadroon—or "quarteron," as Jefferson would have called her—who had not.[6] Francis Eppes had written, "Isabel or Sally will come with her"; Jefferson did not have to be told who "Sally" was.

The child carried a letter written by her aunt:

> This will, I hope, be handed you by my dear Polly, who I most ardently wish may reach you in the health she is in at present. I shall be truly wretched till I hear of her being safely landed with you. The children will spend a day or two on board the ship with her, which I hope will reconcile her to it. For God's sake give us the earliest intelligence of her arrival.[7]

Polly, who had become almost hysterical whenever separation from her aunt was mentioned,[8] had been lured aboard the ship with her cousins. Once she fell asleep they left the ship, which was quietly cut loose from its moorings, and she awoke to find herself on the Atlantic. There was no one to comfort her but Sally Hemings, who had doubtless taken part in the deception, and who could not have been easily forgiven save that she, too, faced the perils of the voyage ahead. As it turned out, the five weeks had been more of a romp than an ordeal. There were no other females on the ship; they must certainly have been treated like special pets, for Polly came to adore the captain. She clung desperately to him upon arrival and had to be decoyed away in order to effect a separation.[9]

During Polly's first two days in London Abigail Adams was in despair, finding the child alternately in tears and acting "rough as a little sailor." When promised a visit to Sadler's Wells for entertainment, Polly had replied with what Abigail described as an honest simplicity, "I had rather see Captain Ramsay one moment, than all the fun in the world."[10] With Sally Hemings Abigail was even more dismayed. She described her to Jefferson as "a Girl about 15 or 16 . . . the Sister of the Servant you have with you." She is "quite a child," Abigail wrote bluntly, "and Captain Ramsay is of opinion will be of so little Service that he had better carry her back with him. But of this you will be a judge. She seems fond of the child and appears good naturd."[11] It takes no special imagination to see why, for quite different reasons, Abigail Adams and the captain agreed it would be wise if Sally Hemings went back to America.

Both John and Abigail Adams fully expected Jefferson to come to London for his daughter, who quickly became an adored favorite. "Her temper, her disposition, her sensibility are all formed to delight," Abigail wrote. "I never felt so attached to a child in my Life on so short an acquaintance."[12] But Jefferson sent his French servant Petit instead, pleading the pressures of business.[13] A better reason was that he was daily expecting the arrival of Maria Cosway. Actually her departure had been delayed, though Jefferson did not yet know this. So he did not suggest that she meet his daughter in London. Nor did he, in fact, make any effort for her to become acquainted with the Adams family. This stung Maria. After writing to Jefferson on July 9 that her husband doubted if they could come to Paris at all, she continued delicately: "I am sorry I have not had occasion to see your daughter who they say is presently here. I do not know Mrs. Adams, and I flatter myself that if you had believed that I might have been useful to her in any way at all, you would have gratified my desire to show you on every occasion how grateful I am for your friendship." [14] But by the time Jefferson received her letter it was too late. Petit had arrived in London July 5.

Polly was indignant, as were the Adamses, that her father had not come to fetch her himself. Abigail described it tartly:

> Upon Petit's arrival [Polly] was thrown into all her former distresses, and bursting into Tears, told me it would be as hard to leave me as it was her Aunt Epps. She has been so often deceived that she will not quit me a moment least she should be carried away. Though she says she does not remember you, yet she has been taught to consider you with affection and fondness, and depended upon your coming for her. She told me this morning, that as she had left all her Friends in virginia to come over the ocean to see you, she did think you would have taken the pains to come here for her, and not have sent a man whom she cannot understand. I express her own words. . . .
>
> I have not the Heart to force her into a Carriage against her will and send her from me almost in a Frenzy, as I know will be the case, unless I can reconcile her to the thoughts of going and I have given her my word that Petit shall stay untill I can hear again from you.

Even John Adams wrote reproachfully, "I am extreamly sorry, that you could not come for your Daughter in Person." [15]

Three weeks after coming to London, Polly was persuaded to get into a carriage with Petit and Sally Hemings, and they started off for the Channel voyage. Jefferson had not seen his daughter since she was five; she was now nearly nine. She "had totally forgotten her sister," he wrote to Abigail Adams after their meeting, "but thought, on seeing me, that she had recollected something of me." Yet he wrote to Elizabeth Eppes, "She neither knew us, nor should we have known her had we met her unexpectedly." [16]

Jefferson did not mention Sally Hemings in any of the letters to his kin that have been preserved,[17] but the arrival of his daughter and the half sister of his dead wife brought back a flood of nostalgia for Monticello. Polly was small-boned, fragile, and beautiful—as the slave Isaac said later, "low like her mother and longways the handsomest, pretty lady jist like her mother." [18] If Jefferson had regarded Sally in her childhood with any special curiosity one cannot know, though his affection for the whole Hemings family was well known. If it was true, as the slaves said, that Sally had been one of those who heard Jefferson promise his wife on her deathbed that he would never marry again, this memory may have come surging back to both of them on their meeting in Paris. Sally, though only fourteen, was now almost as mature in person as Jefferson's fifteen-year-old Patsy; Abigail Adams had mistaken her age as fifteen or sixteen. If she resembled Martha Wayles in any fashion, there is no record of it. But certainly she brought with her to Paris the fresh, untainted aura of Jefferson's past, the whole untrammeled childhood, the memories of quantities of slave children, the easy, apparently relaxed and guiltless miscegenation of his father-in-law, the many-faceted realities of black and white in Virginia.

Importantly, Sally could bridge the memory gap where Polly could not, bringing news of all of Jefferson's kin, descriptions of what had happened in the slave families, details of the trees and flowers at Monticello, all the small and private happenings that Jefferson hungered for. He wrote back shortly to Nicholas Lewis in Virginia asking for an ear of "small rare white corn" from Monticello, better than what he was cultivating in his Paris garden, also watermelon, cantaloupe, and sweet potato seeds, and a dozen Virginia hams.[19] A few days after Polly's arrival he wrote of her safecoming to his older sister Mary, after whom Polly had been named. "We often write seldomest to those whom we love the most. The distance to which I am removed has given a new value to all I valued before in my own country, and the day of my return will be the happiest I expect to see in this life. . . . I find as I grow older that I love those most whom I loved first." [20] Since this was the only letter he wrote to his sister in five years in Paris, it seems likely that the tender sentiment may not have been directed to her at all.

To his old physician friend, Dr. Gilmer, he now wrote of going home: "I am happy no where else and in no other society, and all my wishes end, where I hope my days will end, at Monticello. Too many scenes of happiness mingle themselves with all the recollections of my native woods and feilds, to suffer them to be supplanted in my affection by any other. I consider myself to be as a traveller only, and not a resident." [21]

Sally Hemings' arrival brought, too, a sudden urgency about the fate of his own slaves. Before her coming, save for the presence of her brother James, he had little personal reminder of the festering problem he had left behind. But his numerous attempts as minister to free white American sailors captured and enslaved by Barbary pirates had served as an insistent reminder that his own countrymen and he himself were no less guilty than the marauders of North Africa. To Edward Rutledge, who had written him that Virginia had suspended the slave trade, he wrote in congratulation, adding, "This abomination must have an end, and there is a superior bench reserved in heaven for those who hasten it." [22] This was written the day before Sally Hemings arrived with Polly in Paris.

Her coming coincided with news from his brother-in-law that he was £1,200 more in debt than he had thought, and he was faced with the decision whether to sell land, or slaves, or to rent out his slaves for a fee. He decided on the last as the least of the three evils, though with a fearfully troubled conscience, knowing that rented slaves were often abused. He asked Eppes to make sure that the rental contract provided that the death of a slave would not mean a diminution in the rent. "Otherwise," he said, "it would be their interest to kill all the old and infirm by hard usage." He continued:

> I am decided against selling my lands. They are the only sure pro-
> vision for my children, and I have sold too much of them already. I
> am also unwilling to sell negroes, if the debts can be paid without. This
> unwillingness is for their sake, not my own; because my debts once
> cleared off, I shall try some plan of making their situation happier,
> determined to content myself with a small portion of their liberty
> labour.[23]

The curious slip of the pen in the last line, where he wrote "liberty" where he meant "labor," is further evidence of his real ambivalence over his continuing ownership in men and women. He described his decision to rent out his slaves "as a man does that of being cut for the stone, with a view to relief." [24] Later he wrote that Great George, Ursula, and Betty Hemings were not to be hired out at all, nor the Hemings youths, Martin and Bob, "otherwise than as they are now." [25] Jefferson had sent word indirectly to Betty Hemings in February 1786 about her son—"James is well. He has forgot how to speak English, and has not learnt to speak French"—this in a letter to his Monticello gardener.[26] Betty had sent back her "compliments" to her son, also through the gardener, for she had apparently never learned to write. She sent also the sad news that her daughter Lucy had died.[27] If Jefferson replied with a personal note of sympathy about the death of still another Lucy, it was in a letter that has since disappeared. Perhaps the news brought back so much pain with the memory of his own Lucy's death that the thought never occurred to him at all.

Exactly when in the late summer of 1787 Jefferson learned that Maria Cosway would come to Paris without her husband is not certain. That he had troubled feelings about the prospect is suggested in a letter of fatherly advice he wrote to his nephew Peter Carr on August 10. Here he wrote of "the moral sense, or conscience" as being "as much a part of a man as his leg or arm." His advice to Peter—to be grateful, generous, charitable, humane, true, just, firm, orderly, and courageous—did not include the specific injunction to be chaste, though he did write, "Health is the first requisite after morality." But in his observations about the value of traveling he wrote out of his own recent experience: "This makes men wiser, but less happy. When men of sober age travel, they gather knowledge which they may apply usefully for their country, but they are subject ever after to recollections mixed with regret, their affections are weakened by being extended over more objects, and they learn new habits which cannot be gratified when they return home." [28]

Jefferson shortly had an object lesson in the disparity between the French and American sexual and social codes, which could only have served to reinforce his realization that to escort Maria Cosway about Paris was one thing, and to travel about with her in America without her husband quite another. The new French minister to the United States, the Comte de Moustier, had embarked for the New World with the beautiful Madame de Brehan, who was his sister-in-law and also his mistress. Jefferson had written warm letters of introduction on her behalf to both Madison and John Jay, describing her as "goodness itself," as "modest and amiable," adding that her husband, as an officer, was "obliged by the times to remain with the army." [29] He was shortly chilled and saddened to learn that Americans treated the couple frostily. Madison wrote stiffly that Moustier "suffers also from his illicit connection with Madame de Brehan which is universally known and offensive to American manners. . . . On their journeys it is said they often neglect the most obvious precautions for veiling their intimacy." [30]

When Mrs. Cosway arrived on August 28, 1787, apprehensive of both her husband's rage and the censure of her priest, she moved into the villa of the Princess Lubomirski, who lived a considerable distance from Jefferson's Hôtel de Langeac. The Princess, who was a cousin of the King of Poland, kept a fashionable salon; word went out that Maria was in Paris to further her painting career, and she was soon seen with an entourage visiting galleries and holding a court of her own, "like the fair Aspasia of old." [31] On the surface it was all very discreet.

After her return to London in December Jefferson complained that he had seen her far too little, only "by scraps." "The time before," he wrote, "we were half days, and whole days together." [32] This letter has been enough to convince many Jefferson scholars that whatever may have happened during the first autumn, nothing whatever happened during the second. Nathan Schachner wrote, "It was not quite like the old times. Perhaps the absence of the essential husband compelled them both to be more circumspect." Merrill Peterson believes it was Jefferson's passion that cooled; Fleming that it was Maria's. Malone writes that "they did not recapture their first fine careless rapture, and it looked as though neither of them really wanted to." Jefferson, he contends, "did not embark upon another adventure with her, but he embarked on no romantic adventure with anybody else." [33]

Actually the autumn brought wretchedness instead of either fulfillment or boredom, and they saw a great deal more of each other than has been heretofore recognized. During the first three weeks Maria was in Paris she sent no letters whatever back to London, and Jefferson's account book shows return visits to the parks and gardens of the previous visit, and sums to Petit, who as before arranged for discreet dinners.[34] John Trumbull, Jefferson's ally back in London, wrote him delicately of her husband's rage:

> You of course see Mrs. Cosway. Pray tell her that *three* posts have pass'd in which no one of her friends has received a single line from her, that Lady Lyttleton, Mr. C., her sister and all the world are not only angry at her for not writing, but suffer all the distress of anxiety least illness or accident should have occasioned her silence. I am commissioned to scold her heartily.[35]

Jefferson replied in a cheerful letter, "I showed Mrs. Cosway the part of your letter respecting her, and begged her to consider the scold as hanging over her head till I could get a machine for scolding invented, because it is a business not fit for any human heart, and especially when to be directed on such a subject as her." Still, his anxiety over the spreading gossip crept in a most curious fashion into the first line of this letter, which began, "So many infidelities in the post office are complained of since the rumors of war have arisen that I have waited a safer opportunity of enclosing you a bill of exchange." Here, it would seem, he came very close to saying what was really bothering him—*So many complaints of our infidelities are coming through the post office.*[36]

That Maria was afraid of her husband is evident in her later letters to Jefferson; [37] she was totally dependent upon Cosway for funds, except for an occasional sale of one of her pictures. Once the secret was out in London that she had taken a lover in Paris, Cosway was certain to be taunted for being a cuckold. As the weeks passed, it became evident that Maria was increasingly unsure of herself in the role of a runaway wife. She was faced with possible loss of income, and must certainly have been racked by fears of pregnancy, to say nothing of God's wrath, for she was a very devout Catholic. The sight of Jefferson's right hand, the fingers still crooked, the muscles noticeably withering, [38] so that he had been forced to give up the violin, must have filled her with horror. Fright over Cosway's reaction did not diminish with passing weeks. Jefferson wrote to Trumbull on November 13, 1787, "Her friends are in continual agitation between the hopes of her stay and the fear of her recall." [39] More and more she behaved with confusion of action to match her confusion of heart. "I left a bad impression in the atmosphier," she apologized later, "I was worse than myself, and realy so bad that Sometimes I hardly knew Myself." [40]

Eleven weeks after her coming Jefferson was thoroughly bewildered. He wrote to Trumbull on November 13, "A fatality has attended my wishes, and her and my endeavors to see one another more since she has been here. From the meer effect of chance, she has happened to be from home several times when I have called her, and I, when she has called on me. I hope for better luck hereafter." [41]

That Maria had in truth begun to put obstacles in the way of their meeting alone is suggested by the first letter Jefferson wrote after her return to London:

> It was not my fault, unless it be a fault to love my friends so dearly as to wish to enjoy their company in the only way it yeilds enjoiment, that is, en petit comité. You make everyone love you. You are sought and surrounded therefore by all. Your mere domestic cortège was so numerous, et si imposante, that one could not approach you quite at their ease. Nor could you so unpremeditately mount into the Phaeton and hie away to the bois de Boulogne, St. Cloud, Marly, St. Germains &c.[42]

That he wanted to be with her alone, and would not be content to be merely one of numerous admirers in her salon, is obvious. That they were actually often alone in Jefferson's home is evident from a cryptic postscript she added to one of her notes to him in Paris, this on December 1, 1787: "I hope Mr. Short will not be out as his usual when I have the pleasure to come to you." [43]

William Short, the discreet secretary, was now surreptitiously courting Rosalie, the very young second wife of the Duc de la Rochefoucauld. Jefferson's daughters were in the convent school every day save Sunday. They had met Mrs. Cosway, and the sensitive and jealous Martha may well have understood the seriousness of her father's affection. Jefferson in early September had rented an apartment in the hermitage of Mont Calvaire, beyond the Bois de Boulogne, where the monks raised grapes, knitted stockings, and maintained apartments for guests who wished to find solitude and meditation. "The sky is clearing, and I shall away to my hermitage," he wrote to Madame de Corny on October 18, 1787,[44] thus giving the impression to his Paris friends that he was the austere hermit his biographers later made him out to be.

That he went to the hermitage is true enough, and he may well have meditated there on the struggle between the continent and incontinent life. But it is possible also that he used the excuse of visiting the hermitage to explain his absences to his friends, and especially his daughters, whenever he had an opportunity for a rendezvous with Maria Cosway somewhere else. That Jefferson saw Mrs. Cosway less rather than more often through the month of November is, however, evident in the note she wrote to him on December 1. Knowing that she must return to London shortly, Jefferson had arranged for dinner with several friends, and Maria had personally invited d'Hancarville, Count Potoki, Julian Niemcewicz, a Polish writer, and her patroness, the Princess Lubomirski. After reporting their acceptances, Maria had written, "If my inclination had been your law I should have had the pleasure of seeing you More than I have. I have felt the *loss* with displeasure. . . . Addieu My dear friend, let me beg of you to preserve Me that name, I shall endeavour to deserve it: & all the Gods will bless us." [45]

Jefferson was with her on her last evening in Paris, December 6, and promised to breakfast with her the final morning and to accompany her on the first leg of her journey. Something happened during their last hours together—Maria later described herself as "Confus'd and distracted" [46]—so that during the night she decided to leave very early, without saying goodbye to anyone. She wrote Jefferson a chilling little note, which he found when he came to the Princess's house:

> I cannot breakfast with you tomorrow; to bid you adieu once is sufficiently painful, for I leave you with very melancholy ideas. You have given my dear Sir all your commissions to Mr. Trumbull, and I have the reflection that I cannot be useful to you; who have rendered me so many civilities.[47]

Jefferson was so wounded by whatever had gone wrong during the last weeks of her stay, and so angered and embittered by the final broken promise, that he wrote no letters to anyone for five days and none to Maria Cosway for seven weeks. Two anguished letters arrived from her before he put pen to paper, and then his letter, compared with the tender communications of the past, was frostiness itself.

What had gone wrong? One cannot be certain, but several phrases in her distracted letters, especially when examined in the light of what we know about the rest of her melancholy life—her utter repudiation of motherhood and marriage, the abandonment of her child, and her eventual return to the convent life of her childhood—suggest that there had been some kind of crucial failure for Maria in the act of love. The farewell note said, "I cannot be useful to you." In the first letter from London she cried out, "Why is it My fortune to find Amiable people where I go, and why am I to be obliged to part with them! . . . You are happy you can follow so Much your inclinations. I wish I could do the same. I do all I can, but with little success, perhaps I dont know how to go about it." In the second letter she continued tormenting herself, "I cannot have even the Satisfaction to unburden My displeasure of [it] by loading you with reproches. . . . I am perfectly sure t'was My fault but my Misfortune." Later, in begging Jefferson to come to London, she promised, ". . . we shall not have a Numerous Cortege, I promise to Make Myself and my Society according to your own wishes. At home we may do it better." [48]

What Maria Cosway seems to have wanted was a rescuing father, not a lover, a role Jefferson refused to play. Such a role was more readily accepted by the aging d'Hancarville, or the *castrato* singer, Luigi Marchesi, with whom she traveled about Europe for a few months in 1790.[49] Cosway is said to have kept a diary, now lost, during a "sketching tour" with the artist Mary Moser, in which he made "lascivious statements about Miss Moser, and invidious comparisons between her and Mrs. Cosway." [50] So wrote Cosway's biographer, Williamson, who claimed to have seen the diary.

Maria, as one may see in her farewell note to Jefferson in Paris, was indignant that Jefferson had commissioned Trumbull rather than herself to paint pictures for him. Her father had pampered her into thinking that she had great talent, but Jefferson wanted her and not her art. Needing his admiration and love, but apparently failing as a mistress, she was further crushed when he looked upon her art as irrelevant. Once back in London, however, she continued to fight with anger, cajolery, and tenderness to recover the adoration she had enjoyed in Jefferson's previous letters. This was no mere coquetry. She teased Trumbull to make a portrait of Jefferson for her, which he finally did, and she preserved it to her death in the convent school for girls which she founded in Lodi, Italy.[51] There too she preserved an envelope Jefferson had addressed to her husband, on the inside of

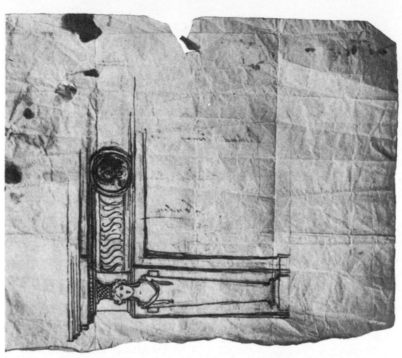
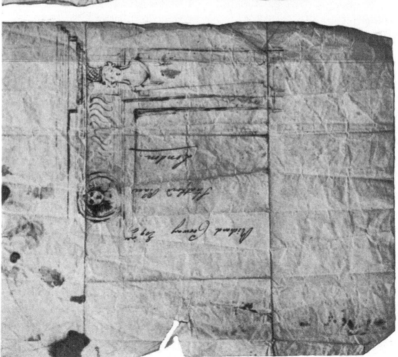

Envelope inscribed by Jefferson, preserved by Maria Cosway, with superimposed sketches in her hand.

which she sketched two small unhappy female faces. One is imprisoned inside a pillar, very like a caryatid, except that the total impression is one not of support but of sad incarceration.[52]

That Maria Cosway knew the love affair with Jefferson was decisively over is evident in her reproachful little note written on Christmas Day 1787. One of her friends in London was the extraordinarily beautiful Angelica Schuyler Church, wife of a British member of Parliament and sister-in-law of Alexander Hamilton. Knowing that Angelica was going to Paris and would certainly seek out Jefferson, Maria wrote, "Have you seen yet the lovely Mrs. Church? . . . If I did not love her so Much I should fear her rivalship, but no I give you free permission to love her with all your heart, and I shall feel happy if I think you keep me in a little corner of it, when you admit her even to reing Queen.—I have not receivd any letter from you. I feel the loss of it." [53]

Jefferson finally replied on January 31, 1788: "I went to breakfast with you according to promise, and you had gone off at 5 oclock in the morning. This spared me indeed the pain of parting, but it deprives me of the comfort of recollecting that pain." He explained his seven-week failure to write with the callously flimsy excuse that he could find no one to carry the letter personally, and distrusted the "infidelity" of the post office. He had seen and approved of Mrs. Church, he said, adding cruelly, "I find in her all the good the world has given her credit for. I do not wonder at your fondness for each other. I have seen too little of her, as I did of you." [54] He did not write to Maria again for almost three months.

But it was not the delicately modeled Angelica Church who replaced Maria Cosway in Jefferson's affections. That the fragile Maria had noticed Sally Hemings in the Hôtel de Langeac is not unlikely; her own Schomberg House had had a celebrated black mistress and model when the house had been rented by an earlier artist tenant, Nathaniel Hone.[55] But Maria's letters showed only a lively jealousy of Angelica Church. The evidence that the real rival was the comely little slave from Monticello, and that their affection began to bloom early in 1788, is complicated and subtle. Some of it is to be found in Jefferson's subsequent letters to Maria Cosway, as gently, with great tenderness and an occasional resurgence of his old affection, he widened the gap between them and finally put an end altogether to her hopes of ever seeing him again.

CHAPTER XVII

Sally Hemings

The earth belongs to the living, and not to the dead.

Jefferson to Madison, September 6, 1789 [1]

Sally Hemings' third son, Madison, born at Monticello in 1805, wrote explicitly of the beginnings of his mother's relationship with Jefferson:

> Their stay (my mother and Maria's) was about eighteen months. But during that time my mother became Mr Jefferson's concubine, and when he was called home she was *enciente* by him. He desired to bring my mother back to Virginia with him but she demurred. She was just beginning to understand the French language well, and in France she was free, while if she returned to Virginia she would be re-enslaved. So she refused to return with him. To induce her to do so he promised her extraordinary privileges, and made a solemn pledge that her children should be freed at the age of twenty-one years. In consequence of his promises, on which she implicitly relied, she returned with him to Virginia. Soon after their arrival, she gave birth to a child, of whom Thomas Jefferson was the father.[2]

Actually Sally Hemings was in Paris not eighteen but almost twenty-six months. Born in 1773, she was between fourteen and fifteen when she arrived, and between sixteen and seventeen when she went back to Virginia. She was certainly lonely in Paris, as well as supremely ready for the first great love of her life, and she was living daily in the presence of a man who was by nature tender and gallant with all women. For any slave child at Monticello Jefferson was a kind of deity. Since her own father John Wayles had died in the year of her

228

birth, Jefferson was perhaps as close to being a parental figure as anyone she had ever known.[3]

In December of 1787 he had said goodbye to a woman he adored, but who had turned out to be guilt-ridden and ill equipped for adultery. He was bewildered, angered, and somewhat disenchanted, but he did not at once cease loving her, or needing her. Now, living under his roof, was a swiftly maturing young woman who represented all that had been alluring and forbidden in the world of his childhood. In his *Notes on the State of Virginia* he had described blacks as more "ardent" than whites, a preconception that could have served only to heighten his dilemma of the moment. He had an important model in the person of his father-in-law, who had turned to a slave woman after the death of the last of his three white wives. And Sally Hemings, too, had a model in her own mother, that same Betty Hemings who had apparently dominated the private life and passions of John Wayles until his death.

The first evidence that Sally Hemings had become for Jefferson a special preoccupation may be seen in one of the most subtly illuminating of all his writings, the daily journal he kept on a seven-week trip through eastern France, Germany, and Holland in March and April of 1788. He went to Amsterdam, where with John Adams he completed negotiations for a Dutch loan to the United States, and arranged for a further loan in the years 1789 and 1790. Then he took off as a tourist. He visited Strasbourg, Metz, Saarbrücken, Mannheim, Heidelberg, Frankfurt, Cologne, and Düsseldorf. Not normally a diary keeper, he did write an almost daily account of his travels. Anyone who reads with care these twenty-five pages must find it singular that in describing the countryside between these cities he used the word "mulatto" eight times.

The road goes thro' the plains of the Maine, which are mulatto and very fine. . . .

It has a good Southern aspect, the soil a barren mulatto clay. . . .

It is of South Western aspect, very poor, sometimes gray, sometimes mulatto. . . .

These plains are sometimes black, sometimes mulatto, always rich. . . .

. . . the plains are generally mulatto. . . .

. . . the valley of the Rhine . . . varies in quality, sometimes a rich mulatto loam, sometimes a poor sand. . . .

. . . the hills are mulatto but also whitish. . . .

Meagre mulatto clay mixt with small broken stones. . . .[4]

In marked contrast is the journal Jefferson had kept while touring southern France in the spring of 1787, just before Sally Hemings' disturbing mulatto presence had come to trouble him. In that account, covering forty-eight printed pages, he used the word "mulatto" only twice, otherwise describing the hills, plains, and earth as dark, reddish-brown, gray, dark brown, and black.[5]

Another quotation in Jefferson's Holland journal is also illuminating. It follows ruminations about the proper shape of a plow, stimulated by the sight of the badly designed moldboard plows he saw in the fields of eastern France. In his travel journal he drew a design and wrote details of the exact construction of a superior model—later developed at Monticello into his famous "plough of least resistance." Considering the ancient symbolism of the plow, it is not surprising, perhaps, that writing about the ideal shape of this ancient and basic agricultural tool led him immediately to observations about the women he had seen in the fields who followed close behind it.

> The women here . . . do all sorts of work. While one considers them as useful and rational companions, one cannot forget that they are also objects of our pleasures. Nor can they ever forget it. While employed in dirt and drudgery some tag of ribbon, some ring or bit of bracelet, earbob or necklace, or something of that kind will shew that the desire of pleasing is never suspended in them. . . . They are formed by nature for attentions and not for hard labour.[6]

This is all very tender, and suggests that he was thinking not at all about the splendidly dressed Maria Cosway when he wrote it.

Jefferson later was extremely proud of his moldboard plow, which was awarded a prize by the Agricultural Society of the Seine. "The plough," he would write, "is to the farmer what the wand is to the Sorcerer, its effect is really like sorcery." [7] He told Robert Fulton his own model was "the finest plough which has ever been constructed in America," and kept a model on display at Monticello. He designed improvements on his original model, writing in 1798, ". . . if the plough be in truth the most useful of all instruments known to man, it's perfection cannot be an idle speculation." [8]

Upon his return to Paris on April 23, 1788, Jefferson found a letter from Maria Cosway reproaching him in mixed rage and anguish for not writing to her for three months. "Your long silence is impardonable. . . . My war against you is of such a Nature that I cannot even find terms to express it. . . . my intention was only to say, *nothing*, send a blank paper; as a Lady in a Passion is not fit for Any thing." [9] Jefferson's reply is a great curiosity. He described briefly his trip to Germany, with a glowing description of the art gallery at Düsseldorf. Here, in describing the painting that excited him above all others, he betrayed, inadvertently as a man often does to an old love, that he had been captured by a new one.

At Dusseldorp I wished for you much. I surely never saw so precious a collection of paintings. Above all things those of Van der Werff affected me the most. His picture of Sarah delivering Agar to Abraham is delicious. I would have agreed to have been Abraham though the consequence would have been that I should have been dead five or six thousand years. . . . I am but a son of nature, loving what I see and feel, without being able to give a reason, nor caring much whether there be one.[10]

"Agar"—Hagar the Egyptian—it will be remembered, was Abraham's concubine, given to him by his wife Sarah when she could not bear a child, and destined to become the legendary mother of the Arab peoples. In this painting she is pictured as very young, partly nude, but seductive in a fashion that is innocence itself. She is blond, with long straight hair down her back. Abraham, though bearded, is far from old, with the nude shoulders and chest of a young and vigorous giant. The round "bull's-eye" windows in the conventional Dutch interior are very like those Jefferson later installed in his own bedroom in Monticello, after remodeling it in 1797.[11]

Although Jefferson included tender passages in this letter to Maria Cosway—"At Dusseldorp I wished for you much. . . . At Heidelberg I wished for you too. In fact I led you by the hand thro' the whole garden"—he confessed callously that he had found it impossible to write a letter to her on the whole seven-week journey. "At Strasbourg I sat down to write to you," he admitted. "But for my soul I could think of nothing at Strasbourg but the promontory of noses, of Diego, of Slawkenburgius his historian, and the procession of the Strasburgers to meet the man with the nose. Had I written to you from thence it would have been a continuation of Sterne upon noses." [12]

Anyone not familiar with Sterne's *Tristram Shandy* would find this passage incomprehensible. Maria Cosway was not only baffled but enraged:

How could you led me by the hand all the way, think of me, have Many things to say, and not find One word to write, *but on Noses?* [13]

In *Tristram Shandy* there is a great deal about noses, including a formal discussion on the hierarchy of caste among men based on their length and shape. Jefferson was specifically referring to the ironic tale told by Slawkenburgius about a Spaniard named Diego whose nose was so long he needed a specially large bedroom in the inn. Diego's visit to Strasbourg had set the city atwitter with argument as to its cause, and on the day he was due to return the whole populace trooped outside the walls in a procession to greet him. Whereupon the French troops, who had been waiting to capture the city, moved in and occupied it without firing a shot.

Even if one understands all this, one may well echo Maria Cosway's queston, "Why Noses?" As we have already asked, "Why mulatto?" Jefferson's bemusement with the one may well have been related to the other. If Sally Hemings, though "mighty near white," retained a suggestion of her grandmother's physical heritage in the shape of her nose, it could be that Jefferson, caught up in a new passion, was cursing the world's insistence on caring about such matters. Though his preoccupation with this girl of mixed blood did not cost him a city, as did the preoccupation of the Strasbourgers with a nose, it would eventually threaten to cost him the presidency.

During the succeeding months after his return to Paris, similar otherwise inexplicable curiosities continued to surface in Jefferson's letters. In the severe cold of January 1789, when the Seine was frozen so solid carriages could cross on the ice, and the Parisian poor perished by the hundreds for want of heat and shelter, Jefferson wrote to Maria Cosway, "Surely it was never so cold before. To me who am an animal of a warm climate, a mere Oran-ootan, it has been a severe trial." [14] In 1789 the word "orangutan" meant for most people not one of the great apes but "wild man of the woods," the literal translation of the Malay words from which it is derived. There was much confusion about the relation of the great apes to man; even the gorilla was as yet unknown in Europe and America. Jefferson had doubtless read Buffon's chapter, "The Orang-Outang, or the Pongo, and the Jocko," in his *Histoire naturelle*, where the French naturalist contributed mightily to the mythology that the great apes ravished women, and himself confused the orangutan, which he had never seen, with the chimpanzee of Africa, which he had seen and which he greatly admired for its capacity to learn some of the habits of men. Buffon also insisted that pygmies were apes, and that some apes were intelligent enough to serve as servants in Africa. [15]

We do not know exactly what Jefferson conceived an "Oran-ootan" to be, but we do know that in his *Notes on the State of Virginia*, published only a few months before Sally Hemings' arrival, he had indiscreetly written that blacks preferred whites over their own species, just as "the Oran-ootan" preferred "the black woman over those of his own species." [16] That he may now suddenly have become uneasy about what he had written concerning this mysterious man of nature, or man of the woods, is suggested by the fact that on October 2, 1788, when he sent away to his London bookdealer a list of books for purchase, he included E. Tyson's *Oran-outang; or, An Anatomy of a Pigmy* (1699), one of the earliest scholarly volumes which had tried to clarify the whole classification problem. Jefferson had good reason to be uncomfortable. For when the Federalist press in America later heard rumors about his slave paramour, the editors needled him cruelly on this very passage in his *Notes*.[17]

There is also what one might call hard evidence as well as psychological evidence that Jefferson in Paris treated Sally Hemings with special consideration. On November 6, 1787, he paid 240 francs to a Dr. Sutton for Sally's smallpox inoculation, a very great sum. Shortly after her arrival a French tutor was hired, whose services lasted at least twenty months. A letter from this Monsieur Perrault to Jefferson on January 9, 1789, makes clear that he was tutoring "gimme" (Jimmy), Sally's brother, and one could expect that Sally would likely have been included. Perrault had come to the kitchen to ask for his pay; there had been an altercation, and the tutor complained bitterly to Jefferson of *"mauvais traitemens de gimme"* and *"Sotisses les plus durs,"* which suggests that Jimmy Hemings was quick of temper and anything but the stereotype of the docile slave.[18] By January 1788, Jefferson had begun to pay this slave youth wages, 24 francs a month, with *"étrennes,"* an additional gift of 12 francs for the New Year holiday. Sally received 36 francs in the same month, but did not get regular wages until December 1788. The French servants received 50 to 60 francs per month.[19]

There is a curious item in Jefferson's account book for April 29, 1789:

$$
\begin{array}{llr}
\text{pd Dupre 5 weeks board of Sally} & 105'' & \text{[i.e., francs]} \\
\text{washing \&c} & \underline{41\text{-}9} & \\
& 146\text{-}9 & {}^{20}
\end{array}
$$

This suggests the possibility that when Jefferson went to Holland and Germany he saw to it that Sally was properly chaperoned in a French home and not left as prey to the French servants at the ministry on the Champs Elysées.

Did he write to her when he was away? Was there ever even a brief note, wishing her well in her study of French? The one record that might illuminate this, the letter-index volume recording Jefferson's incoming and outgoing letters for this critical year of 1788, has disappeared. It is the only volume missing in the whole forty-three-year epistolary record. Julian Boyd tells us that "entries once existed but cannot now be found." [21] Also missing are any letters Jefferson may have written to his daughters on this seven-week trip. On his previous trip to southern France in the spring of 1787 Jefferson had written Patsy five letters, and he had taken his small letter-copying press with him so that copies are extant as well as some originals. This letter press he took with him again to Holland,[22] but even the copies of whatever letters he wrote to his daughters have mysteriously vanished. This raises the question whether or not someone at some time went through Jefferson's papers systematically eliminating every possible reference to Sally Hemings. Letters from Jefferson to Sally's brothers, and from her brothers to him, are extant.[23] But no letters or notes exchanged between Sally Hemings and Thomas Jefferson have as yet ever found their way into the public record.

His account books were preserved intact, however, and here occasional references to Sally during the Paris years provide a slight but important illumination of a record that seems to have been kept as secret as possible. In April 1789, for example, Jefferson began to spend a surprising amount of money on Sally Hemings' clothes. There is an item for 96 francs for "clothes for Sally" on April 6, 72 francs on April 16, and an itemized 23 francs on April 26 for "making clothes for servts." May 25 has another item, "pd making clothes for Sally 25# 2." The money Jefferson spent for Patsy's clothes is several times that of her maid during roughly the same period. Still, if one knows that a pair of gloves could be had for two francs, the expenditure of 216 francs for Sally in seven weeks plus her monthly salary of 24 francs would seem to be considerable, especially when compared with the total lack of specific expenditures on her behalf in the earlier months.

Both Sally and James Hemings knew they were free if they chose to make an issue of it,[24] and Jefferson knew from his earliest months in Paris that even his diplomatic status did not give him the right to hold slaves against their will. When another American in Paris wrote asking him the legal status of a slave boy he had brought with him, Jefferson replied, "The laws of France give him freedom if he claims it, and . . . it will be difficult, if not impossible, to interrupt the course of the law." He added cautiously, and apparently without guilt, "Nevertheless I have known an instance where a person bringing in a slave, and saying nothing about it, has not been disturbed in his possession. I think it will be easier in your case to pursue the same plan, as the boy is so young that it is not probable he will think of claiming freedom." [25]

It will be seen that for a man theoretically intent upon emancipation of all slaves, Jefferson was extremely possessive about his own. When he received a letter from Edward Bancroft asking him pointedly his opinion on the value of Quaker experiments in Virginia where owners freed and then hired their own slaves, Jefferson replied with notable lack of enthusiasm, "As far as I can judge from the experiments which have been made, to give liberty to, or rather, to abandon persons whose habits have been formed in slavery is like abandoning children." And he went on to describe in rather vague terms what was essentially a sharecropping experiment he hoped to carry out on his return, dividing his farms into 50 acres each, importing about as many Germans as he had slaves, and settling them together "intermingled," with the same education "in habits of property and foresight"—all this without emancipation.[26]

Still, Jefferson had under his roof in Paris two slaves who were learning to speak French, who counted themselves free, and were thinking of becoming expatriates. James Hemings, who had served as an apprentice under the cook of the Prince de Conde, and also with a *pâtissier*, was now an experienced chef, and could easily command a salary in Paris.[27] Freeing him would hardly have been "abandoning" a child. In using such an argument against emancipation Jefferson was falling back into a pattern of thinking that had already long been a cliché in Virginia. Whence this sudden backing away from his old zeal for emancipation? In these same months he could on the one hand spend hours translating the Marquis de Condorcet's passionate indictment of slavery, and yet refuse to lend his name to a new organization in France agitating for an end simply to the slave trade.[28] So he was locked in a conflict that was in a sense old, and which had been with him from childhood—but which was now new and compellingly personal.

Jefferson's letter to Bancroft marks the first time in all his writings that he moved backward, however slightly, to defend slavery, just as his failure to free James and Sally Hemings in Paris marks a decisive watershed in his zeal for emancipation. To free them was to lose them, and Jefferson was an extraordinarily possessive man. He did free James Hemings. Faced with the threat of his staying in Paris, Jefferson agreed to emancipate him in Virginia once James had taught someone else at Monticello to cook French style. Jefferson kept his word, but not before seven years had passed.[29] The reasons for not freeing Sally Hemings would complicate the rest of his life.

What meanwhile, during these successive interludes of the heart, had been happening to Jefferson's eldest daughter? By April 1789 she had been in the convent school five years, and was now seventeen.

Though the nuns were kind and motherly, they watched her rigorously and forbade her to leave the school for any purpose without her father's written permission.[30] In America, when father and daughter had been separated, it had been Jefferson who begged for letters from her. But when Jefferson spent thirteen weeks in southern France in 1787, it was she who had chided him for not writing every week, as he had promised, adding, as he had so often written to her, "you are never a moment absent from my thoughts." [31] He replied from Aix-en-Provence with his old tenderness: "No body in this world can make me so happy, or so miserable as you. Retirement from public life will ere long become necessary for me. To your sister and yourself I look to render the evening of my life serene and contented. It's morning has been clouded by loss after loss till I have nothing left but you." [32]

Still, his letters indicate that he continued to treat Patsy very much as he had done when she was eleven. He gave her the same repetitious homiletic advice—never be angry—never be idle—"Be good and be industrious, and you will be what I shall most love in this world." [33] He did not respond, at least in his letters, to her attempts to discuss anything other than her schoolwork, ignoring comments on French scandals and politics, and her rampant abolitionism which burst out in a letter of May 3, 1787—"I wish with all my soul the poor negroes were all freed. It grieves my heart." [34] She told him what he most wanted to hear, "Believe me to be for life your most tender and affectionate child," [35] and he seemed largely unaware that she was no longer a child and was tormented with longings the nature of which she did not herself understand.

William Short, more astute than Jefferson in this matter, sensed that Patsy was jealous of both Maria Cosway and Angelica Church. He wrote secretly to John Trumbull, who had painted portraits of Jefferson for both these women, suggesting that to make a third for Martha Jefferson would be a "very clever gallant thing," to do, and exacting secrecy concerning his own role in the matter. Trumbull followed the suggestion, and we thus have three separate miniatures of Jefferson, all based on the portrait made in the larger *Signing of the Declaration of Independence*. The one made for Martha is the most youthful, the most endearing, with an unusual suggestion of a smile.[36]

Sometime in 1788 Jefferson learned to his consternation that Patsy was considering becoming a nun. The papal nuncio in Paris, Comte Dugnani, who knew Jefferson, wrote to John Carroll of Baltimore on July 5, "The eldest seems to have tendencies toward the Catholic religion. She is only sixteen. Her father, without absolutely opposing her vocation, has tried to distract her." [37] Henry Randall, who had access to Jefferson family gossip, wrote by way of explanation that "the daring and flippant infidelity now rife in French society, disgusted the earnest, serious, naturally reverential girl." [38] But the "daring and flippant infidelity" of Paris had caught up her own beloved parent. She could hardly have missed his new *joie de vivre* in the autumn of 1786 when he first fell in love with Maria Cosway and joined what may well have seemed to her the giddy and lascivious turmoil of the artist colony. She had written to her father in April 1787, "There was a gentleman, a few days ago, that killed himself because he thought his wife did not love him. They had been married ten years. I believe that if every husband in Paris was to do as much there would be nothing but widows left." [39] If she was subtly warning her father to beware of married women as they were all wanton, he did not heed the message.

Jefferson was sufficiently alarmed by Patsy's possible conversion that he thought of taking his daughters home in the summer of 1788. But he delayed. "I wished Polly to perfect her French," he explained to Elizabeth Eppes.[40] Still, in September he formally petitioned for a leave of absence the following spring, planning to take his daughters home in April 1789, arrange for their schooling, and return in the autumn. Though Jefferson complained that the prospect of returning without his daughters was indeed dreary, the fact that he could even consider the separation seems to have been for Patsy a shattering knowledge.

For Jefferson Paris in 1788 was becoming an increasingly exciting political experience. The growing threat of revolution delighted him, and he eagerly became a quiet, even secret, participant, consulting with Lafayette on several papers pertinent to the ever deepening crisis between the King and the Estates-General, which was to be convened in May 1789, the first time since 1614. There has been a great deal of astute analysis of Jefferson's somewhat conservative role in the beginnings of the French Revolution. While the stream of his letters back to the United States in 1788, particularly to Madison, reflect what would seem to be an almost total absorption in the beginnings of the potentially momentous social experiment, they also show that he expected it to move with a good deal more rationality and less upheaval than it did.[41] So, indeed, did everyone else.

There are also letters which offer important clues to Jefferson's personal life in this great year of ferment, clues to intimate conflicts which exploded in a small but crucial fashion in the spring of 1789, just as Paris itself exploded into revolutionary violence. To Anne W. Bingham, an American friend who had recently returned home from Paris, he wrote on May 11, 1788:

The gay and thoughtless Paris is now become a furnace of Politics.
All the world is run politically mad. Men, women, children talk nothing
else; and you know that naturally they talk much, loud and warm.
Society is spoilt by it, at least for those who, like myself, are but
lookers on—You too, have had your political fever. But our good
ladies, I trust, have been too wise to wrinkle their foreheads with politics. They are contented to soothe and calm the minds of their husbands returning ruffled from political debate. They have the good sense
to value domestic happiness above all other, and the art to cultivate it
beyond all others. There is no part of the earth where so much of this
is enjoyed as in America.[42]

Thus Jefferson, who in 1785 had delighted in sparring with the
sharp intellect of Abigail Adams, and who in 1786 and 1787 had listened with admiration to Madame Helvétius, Madame Necker, and
Madame de Staël, now sang the virtues of the totally domestic woman
who lived only to soothe and calm her husband. To an old Virginia
friend he wrote on February 7, 1788, "No attachments soothe the
mind so much as those contracted in early life. . . . I had rather be
shut up in a very modest cottage, with my books, my family and a
few old friends, dining on simple bacon, and letting the world roll on
as it liked, than to occupy the most splendid post which any human
power can give." [43] And he, who had devotedly followed Maria Cosway from gallery to gallery, and who had ordered copies of paintings
by the score and the sculptures of busts of notable Europeans and
Americans, now turned even against the artists. In a paper he drew
up in 1788 for the use of American travelers in Europe, *Hints on
European Travel*, he urged his countrymen to study agriculture,
gardens, architecture, and politics. But for "Painting and Statuary" he
wrote, with a trace of contempt, "Too expensive for the state of wealth
among us. It would be useless and therefore preposterous for us to
endeavor to make ourselves connoisseurs in those arts. They are
worth seeing, but not studying." [44]

In his letter to Anne Bingham he had also written, "Recollect the
women of this capital, some on foot, some on horses, and some in
carriages hunting pleasure in the streets, in routs and assemblies, and
forgetting that they have left it behind them in their nurseries; compare them with our countrywomen occupied in the tender and tranquil amusements of domestic life, and confess that it is a comparison
of Amazons and Angels." [45]

If the political woman—the Amazon—remained a threat, and the domestic woman—the Angel—had now triumphed, still the Angel who
was apparently at present providing the "tender and tranquil amusements" in his own domestic life was in the most crucial sense a

fallen angel, and forbidden. It is not surprising that he wrote to Maria Cosway on May 21, 1789, "All is politics in this capital. Even love has lost it's part in conversation. This is not well, for love is always a consolatory thing. I am going to a country where it is felt in its sublimest degree." [46] In 1786 and 1787 Jefferson could talk about his affection for Maria Cosway at least within a limited circle, including Trumbull, d'Hancarville, William Short, and possibly Angelica Church. But in 1788 he could share his delight in his new love with no one, and had to be content with the glowing generalizations about American angels such as we find in his letter to Mrs. Bingham. There was only one advantage for Jefferson in this new attachment without marriage, as against a new marriage to a woman he could love as much, and that advantage may for Jefferson have been preëminent. The slave girl, unlike a wife, could never be a rival to his old and continuing mistress, politics. Nor need she ever become a threat to any decision-making on his part that had to do with his political life.

We know from his account books that Jefferson in September 1788 went to his old haunts—St. Germain and Marly, and that he went back to the "Desert" in May 1789. Was it Sally Hemings who accompanied him? Conceivably it could have been his daughters. We know that he bought a "watch for Patsy" on January 5, 1789, costing 554 francs, and on June 30 a "ring for Patsy" costing 48 francs. Was it for Sally Hemings, on September 30, 1788, that he paid 40 francs for "a locket"? If so, Jefferson even here was too discreet to leave a trace. Still, only the most naïve of men could have believed that he could continue to keep a liaison with the slave girl secret, especially from his daughters. One wonders if it ever occurred to him that Patsy upon coming home from school on Sunday would look upon the spectacle of her maid newly dressed in stylish Parisian clothes with absolute incomprehension. Perhaps it didn't happen that way. But there is the coincidence that it was in early April that Jefferson spent almost two hundred francs on "clothes for Sally," and that on April 18 Jefferson was appalled to get a note from Patsy formally requesting his permission to let her become a nun. However affectionate the pressures may have been by the motherly nuns, or however Martha may have convinced herself that the life of a nun was her true vocation, the act was one of enormous hostility to her father. One has only to read the letters of the papal nuncio to see with what satisfaction he would have looked upon the conversion of the daughter of a man whose suspicion of priestcraft and contempt for organized religion was known all over Europe. [47]

Randall, who learned of Martha's request to join the nunnery from her children, reported what happened afterward:

For a day or two she received no answer. Then his carriage rolled
up to the door of the Abbaye, and poor Martha met her father in a
fever of doubts and fears. Never was his smile more benignant and
gentle. He had a private interview with the Abbess. He then told his
daughters he had come for them. They stepped into his carriage—it
rolled away—and Martha's school life was ended.[48]

Jefferson's account book provides fascinating additional details. On
April 19, the day before he went to the convent school, he recorded a
purchase of "linen for Patsy," costing 274 francs. On the twentieth
Patsy herself was permitted to buy "lawn and cambrick" amounting
to 332 francs. The explosion of clothes buying continued into May,
with 229 francs for silks, 106 francs for shoes, and 84 francs for stays,
and shortly afterward an important symbolic purchase—48 francs for
"a ring for Patsy." The 12 francs he paid for "a whip for Patsy" on
May 7 suggests that he was now taking her horseback riding. And it
may have been at this time that he arranged to have her portrait
painted by Joseph Boze.[49]

That Jefferson's control over his daughters was implicit rather than
explicit, and that he chose what should and should not be discussed,
even in this important crisis, is suggested by Sarah Randolph, Jefferson's great-granddaughter, who added a significant footnote to the whole
story. "No word in allusion to the subject [of Patsy's becoming a nun]
ever passed between father and daughter, and it was not referred to
by either of them until years afterwards, when she spoke of it to her
children."[50] This is the kind of control many parents succeed in imposing who rule exclusively by love. Where annoyance or even hatred
is explicit, the child has the advantage of being able to reply in kind,
and the hatred can often be exorcised in the heated exchange. This
was not permitted to Martha Jefferson. And one suspects that the
same kind of control was employed by Jefferson in the fall of 1789,
when it could no longer be kept a secret that Sally Hemings was
pregnant.[51]

There had been plenty of political crises in Jefferson's life during
the previous months—a serious bread shortage in Paris because of the
bad harvest of 1788, a riot among Paris workmen which took a hundred lives in April, and finally on July 14 the fall of the Bastille,
which astonished and delighted him. He went to watch the demolition of what he called a "fortification of infinite strength . . . which
in other times had stood several sieges, and had never been taken,"[52]
and noted in his account book a contribution of 60 francs on August
21 for the widows of the men who had been slain capturing it. He
wrote to Madison on July 22, 1789, of "this astonishing train of events

as will be forever memorable in history," concluding with a classic understatement, "Indeed this scene is too interesting to be left at present." [53]

The mob violence and decapitations that accompanied the Bastille destruction did not trouble him, and even as an old man he wrote with satisfaction that when the Duc de la Rochefoucauld-Liancourt forced his way into the King's bedchamber and told him the Bastille's Governor, Lieutenant Governor, and *Prévôt des Marchands* had had their heads chopped off and their bodies dragged through the streets of Paris, the King "went to bed fearfully impressed." [54] Even two years earlier Jefferson had written in defense of Shays' Rebellion, a brief armed revolt of Massachusetts farmers against heavier taxes, which had frightened John and Abigail Adams into believing the United States was threatened with anarchy:

> What country before ever existed a century and half without a re-bellion? And what country can preserve it's liberties if their rulers are not warned from time to time that their people preserve the spirit of resistance? Let them take arms. The remedy is to set them right as to facts, pardon and pacify them. What signify a few lives lost in a cen-tury or two? The tree of liberty must be refreshed from time to time with the blood of patriots and tyrants. It is it's natural manure.[55]

With the revolutionary fervor spreading among French intellectuals Jefferson had become, finally, what Franklin had been before him, a kind of hero in Paris. American inventor James Rumsey, writing home on March 20, 1789, described him as "the most popular Embassador at the french Court." "American principles," he said, "are bursting forth in Every quarter: it must give pleasure to the feeling mind, to see millions of his fellow Creatures Emerging from a state not much better than Slavery." [56] Jefferson had gone daily to Versailles to hear the debates of the Estates-General, and had helped Lafayette draft his Declaration of the Rights of Man, which was presented to the National Assembly on July 11.[57] Though almost no one knew of this special collaboration, the indebtedness of Lafayette's famous docu-ment at least to the Declaration of Independence was secret to no one in the French government, and Jefferson could hardly have lived through these weeks without an exciting sense of involvement, a recog-nition that if not a father he was at least one of the patron saints of the new revolution.

He hoped for a peaceful evolution into a constitutional monarchy, with the King giving "freedom of the press, freedom of religion, free-dom of commerce and industry, freedom of persons against arbitrary arrests, and modification if not total prohibition of military agency in civil cases." And with his characteristic optimism he wrote to John Mason on July 17, "I have not a single doubt of the sincerity of the king, and that there will not be another disagreeable act from him." [58]

There is every indication that when Jefferson finally received congressional permission to return to America he was loath to go, and eager to return quickly to Paris. For the first time he seemed willing to be free of his daughters, and he told Trumbull he expected to come back for several years. Whether he planned to take James and Sally Hemings back with him and return with them again to Paris is unknown; that they were agitating to stay in Paris as free citizens at this point is suggested by the reminiscences of Madison Hemings.

Maria Cosway, learning that Jefferson was returning to America, peppered him with letters begging him to visit her in England en route. "Pray write, pray write," she said, "and dont go to America without coming to England." [59] This request he dodged with pleasantries, suggesting that she and Angelica Church come to America on the same boat, but in the same breath warning her how "furiously displeased" was Madame de Brehan with America, a gentle warning that the United States was not Arcadia, like Paris. [60] Late in May he wrote cruelly that he might be traveling across the Atlantic with Angelica Church. "We shall talk a great deal of you. . . . Adieu, my dear friend. Be our affections unchangeable, and if our little history is to last beyond the grave, be the longest chapter in it that which shall record their purity, warmth and duration." [61] Still, he found it difficult to let go even of this dying love, and told Maria in a letter from the Isle of Wight (he embarked for America this close to London), "The ensuing spring might give us a meeting at Paris with the first swallow. . . . remember me and love me." [62]

The knowledge that he might never return to Paris came to Jefferson stealthily in September, six weeks before he left. He had received a letter from Madison on August 6 with an ominous query: "I have been asked whether any appointment at home would be agreeable to you." [63] Jefferson recognized at once that this was a tacit bid to join the government under the new constitution, with Washington as president, and he replied with as firm a no as he could muster: "You ask me if I would accept any appointment on that side of the water? You know the circumstances which led me from retirement, step by step and from one nomination to another, up to the present. My object is a return to the same retirement. Whenever therefore I quit the present, it will not be to engage in any other office, and most especially any one which would require a constant residence from home." [64]

But could he say no directly to Washington? On the first of September he made a final list of what to take with him and what to leave behind in Paris. Patsy's harpsichord and guitar were to go, along with clocks, beds, mattresses, and clothes, boxes of books specially packed for Franklin, Washington, and Madison, as well as wine, cheese, tea, pictures, busts, and his old phaeton. The list included also two cork oaks, four melon apricots, one white fig, five larch trees, four Cresanne pears, three Italian poplars, and numerous other small trees and plants.[65] So the nostalgia for Monticello showed its power, and underlined the fundamental precariousness of his will to return to France. On September 2 he said goodbye to John Trumbull, whom he had asked to become his secretary should William Short decide to return to America.[66] One hour after Trumbull left for London Jefferson was in bed seriously ill. The old migraine was back for the first time since he had set foot on French soil. It lasted six days.[67] Again it was triggered, it would seem, by a sense of loss. He was losing friends, artists, scholars, scientists, Paris—all of Europe—to say nothing of a place in the new French Revolution, possibly for a few months but probably forever.

How Sally Hemings figured in this agonized conflict is simply non-recoverable. We know only what her son later wrote, that she was pregnant and refused to return to America with Jefferson till he promised to free her children at age twenty-one.[68] We know, too, Jefferson waited to a surprisingly late date—September 16, sixteen days after completing the baggage list and eight days after his recovery—before writing to James Maurice in London the exact specifications for cabins on the boat he was taking: "three master births (for himself and two daughters of 17. and 11. years of age) and births [surely an odd misspelling, under the circumstances] for a man and woman servant, the latter convenient to that of my daughters: A use of the cabbin in common with the others, and not exclusive of them which serves only to render me odious to those excluded." [69] So he insisted that on shipboard he be close to all three young females, from whom he would not—and could not—in the end be separated.

During his six-day illness, Jefferson was treated by Dr. Richard Gem, whom he later described as the ablest doctor he ever met.[70] Gem was a seventy-two-year-old Welshman, known to be an atheist and a strong supporter of the French Revolution. He had been separated from his wife for thirty years, and his children had died in infancy, so he and Jefferson had certain personal tragedies as well as intellectual convictions in common. Out of their conversations during these six days came one of the most remarkable of all Jefferson's writings, the elaborate enunciation of a theme he came to live by, "The earth belongs to the living."

"A subject comes into my head," he wrote to Madison on September 6, 1789, ". . . the question Whether one generation of men has the right to bind another." He believed it to be, he wrote, "a question of such consequences as not only to merit decision, but place also, among the fundamental principles of every government. I set out on this ground," he continued, "which I suppose to be self evident, *'that the earth belongs in usufruct to the living'*: that the dead have neither powers nor rights over it." Again and again he amplified the theme with repetition—"the earth belongs to each of these generations, during it's course fully, and in their own right"— "the earth belongs to the living, and not to the dead."

No other of Jefferson's writings save his Declaration of Independence and Virginia Constitution has been subjected to so much exegesis as this letter to Madison. The ideas in it have been traced to Adam Smith, to Dr. Gem, and to Thomas Paine. Julian Boyd, who has noted that this was the second draft of a smaller document intended for Lafayette, believes it was a legislative proposal intended to be written into the new French system of government, and was later amplified in the letter to Madison to include the American government as well. As Jefferson elaborated his central idea, he argued that no nation should have the right to bind a new generation by public debts, and suggested a permanent legislative program providing that no new laws, constitutions, or financial contracts be drawn up that would last more than a generation, which he defined as nineteen years. "This would put the lenders, and the borrowers also, on their guard," he wrote, and "it would bridle the spirit of war." Boyd believes it was intended to be only a "practical, relevant, utilitarian" device for overthrowing the tyranny of the French institutions, ecclesiastical and feudal. Peterson, who believes Jefferson never intended it to become a part of public law in America, but wrote it as a "moral directive to society," counts it "the most original and most radical idea in the whole Jefferson catalogue." [71]

The great letter, like so many others of Jefferson's, can be read on several levels, political, personal, and deeply psychological. His complaints in it of the injustice of a child's inheriting debts from his parents were an obvious personal reference to the debts which his wife had inherited from John Wayles, and the smaller debt he had inherited from his mother, which were still an albatross around his own neck. But there were two sentences in particular in this letter which suggest a repudiation of something far more deeply buried.

> The earth belongs always to the living generation. They may manage it then, and what proceeds from it, as they please, during their

usufruct. They are masters too of their own persons, and consequently may govern them as they please.[72]

Who was denying Jefferson the right to govern his own person as he pleased? Does one here see him struggling to repudiate the bondage in which he had been so long enchained by the memories of his dead wife? Was he battling also the whole tyranny of the past, with its inherited legacy of taboos against the pursuit of happiness? In this connection one notes with curiosity his choice of nineteen years, instead of twenty or twenty-five, to define a generation. Jefferson tells us that he chose this figure after revising some demographic tables developed by Buffon. Why nineteen? Did it mean anything that the year was 1789, exactly nineteen years since he had met and fallen in love with Martha Wayles?

Jefferson described this new truth as "self evident," but it was no more self-evident in 1789 than the great political ideals of the Declaration of Independence, which he had also called "self-evident." The whole of Europe was a living testament to the truth that the world belonged not to the living but to the dead, who continued inexorably to bind the living in the chains of ancient law, religious ritual, social protocol, and sexual prohibition. As if this were not complicating enough in Jefferson's own life, he was about to return to Virginia, where the bondage of white men to the dead was as nothing compared with the bondage of black men and women to the living. Jefferson would feel the menacing strength of the slaveholding society in the first hours of his arrival. After some months he would write back to Lafayette, using a peculiar metaphor that could have sprung from the complications of his intimate life:

"So far it seemed that your revolution had got along with a steady pace: meeting occasional difficulties and dangers, but we are not to expect to be translated from despotism to liberty, in a feather-bed." [73]

CHAPTER XVIII

The Revolutionary
Goes Home

We return like foreigners, and, like them, require a considerable residence here to become Americanized.

Jefferson to William Short [1]

When Jefferson arrived in Virginia, at that moment as much a French
patriot as an American, he had no idea how conservative was the
country to which he had returned. Nor how rural. If he had suffered
from culture shock during his first months in Paris in 1785, there was
a more profound reverse shock upon return. "I was astonished at the
change," he wrote. "No more like the same people; their notions, their
habits and manners, the course of their commerce, so totally changed,
that I, who stood in those of 1784, found myself not at all qualified to
speak their sentiments, or forward their views in 1790." [2] Letters from
Madison had kept him somewhat informed of the conservative trend,
and in letters to Washington he had openly deplored the absence of a
Bill of Rights in the new constitution. He disliked also the fact that an
American president could succeed himself indefinitely, fearing a drift
toward the tradition of a "president for life," and ultimately a monarchy. So sensitive was he on this subject that he saw monarchists
where they did not exist, suspecting even John Adams, and soon was
plunged into a political turmoil he did not court and was tempera-
mentally ill equipped to handle.

What he first faced, however, was the decision whether to return to

246

France or to accept the post of Secretary of State. That it had been offered him he learned in the Norfolk newspapers as soon as he disembarked, and a formal letter from Washington caught up with him at Eppington. His friends knew that his first reaction was negative.[3] The sight of the still primitive Virginia towns, the bad roads, the vast expanses of forest, served only to heighten his nostalgia for the sophisticated city he had left. Even his arrival had been a near disaster. A bad storm off the Virginia capes carried away the topsails of the *Clermont*, and a brig coming out of port very nearly ran it down. Then two hours after landing Jefferson learned that the ship was afire and that all his luggage, including his public accounts, which he had insisted on bringing across the Atlantic in his own stateroom, was still aboard. Martha Jefferson later wrote that the sailors were in the act of scuttling the ship "when some abatement in the flames was discovered and she was finally saved." [4] Much of the ship was gutted, but Jefferson's precious trunks were saved.

Jefferson and his daughters took four weeks to go from Norfolk to Monticello. True, they were visiting relatives and friends, but Jefferson's letter to Short back in Paris, written December 15, 1789, saying that he was about "to plunge into the Forests of Albemarle," [5] suggests a reluctance to return to the home he had left in such wretchedness seven years before. He wrote to Washington frankly that he had "gloomy forebodings" of "criticisms and censures" if he became Secretary of State and that he would prefer to go back to France, unless the President insisted.[6]

An enthusiastic welcome by both houses of the Virginia legislature in Richmond seems to have been a gratifying public gesture, and he examined with pleasure the new state capitol, built more or less to his specifications after the model he had sent home of his favorite Roman building, the *Maison Carrée* of Nîmes. But it was the arrival at Monticello, faced with a mixture of expectation and dread, that Jefferson and his daughters found overwhelming. Jefferson had earlier written that he wanted provision only for a two-month stay, and a skeletal staff—"Great George, Ursula and Betty Hemings will be there, of course, and if Martin and Bob can join us for the time it will suffice." [7] But all his slaves on the various plantations had been alerted and were permitted to gather for Jefferson's coming, two days before Christmas 1789. He was riding in a carriage with his daughters, accompanied by young Jack Eppes. As they started up the "little mountain," the slaves collected in a crowd around the carriage, shouting and cheering. Finally they stopped the horses, unhitched them, and unheeding of Jefferson's protests, dragged the carriage the last few rods to the house. Martha Jefferson described it years later, still betraying her excitement:

Such a scene I never witnessed in my life. . . . When the door of the carriage was opened they received him in their arms and bore him to the house, crowding round and kissing his hands and feet—some blubbering and crying—others laughing. It seemed impossible to satisfy their anxiety to touch and kiss the very earth which bore him.[8]

Not surprisingly, Martha Jefferson's zeal for emancipation, kindled in Paris, did not survive the homecoming. And her father must have been overwhelmed with this outpouring of affection. He was like a medieval prince returning from a crusade.

It seems likely that Sally Hemings was also in the homecoming carriage, and that her brother James was driving it. One can only guess at the feelings of this handsome slave girl, now nearly seventeen and big with child, when she saw the adulation of the hundred-odd blacks and contemplated her own enslavement and her own future. Jefferson freed her older brother Robert after four years, and her brother James, after six.[9] But he did not free her, and there is no evidence that she ever asked him to.

According to Madison Hemings her child was born "soon after" her arrival in America.[10] Twelve years later, when the Virginia press first exposed the "Dusky Sally" story, James T. Callender, who had talked to Jefferson's neighbors, said her oldest child was a son, "ten or twelve years of age," that his name was Tom, and that he bore a "striking" resemblance to Jefferson. At least two other editors, after checking, corroborated the story.[11] Many years later Jefferson's grandson, Thomas Jefferson Randolph, who had grown up with Sally Hemings' children, freely admitted to biographer Henry Randall that one Hemings son looked so much like Jefferson that "at some distance or in the dusk the slave, dressed in the same way, might have been mistaken for Mr. Jefferson," though this youth may have been either Madison or Eston Hemings, who remained at Monticello till Jefferson's death. When Randall asked Randolph, in view of the derogatory publicity, "why on earth Mr. Jefferson did not put these slaves who looked like him out of public sight by sending them to his Bedford estate or elsewhere," he replied that "Mr. Jefferson never betrayed the least consciousness of the resemblance—and although he (Col. Randolph) and he had no doubt his mother, would have been very glad to have them thus removed, that both and all venerated Mr. Jefferson too deeply to broach such a topic to him. What suited him satisfied them." [12] This is an important reminiscence, bearing out what Sarah Randolph wrote about Jefferson, that he never discussed that which he did not really want to discuss.

With the return to America secrecy deepened. Jefferson's casual notations of expenditures for Sally's clothes disappeared altogether from his account books. Instead there were numerous small sums for "charity," always given upon his arrival at Monticello after an absence, and several curious references to leaving "small money in my drawer at Monticello," one of which amounted to the sizable sum of twenty dollars.[13] These take on significance in the light of Madison Hemings' statement that it was his mother's "duty all her life which I can remember, up to the time of father's death, to take care of his chamber and wardrobe, look after us children and do such light work as sewing, &c." [14] Many expenditures in Jefferson's account books were no longer listed separately, but lumped together under the heading "Miscellaneous," which sometimes represented considerable sums.

He sent gifts at Christmas time from Philadelphia in 1791 and 1792, describing them in his letters to Martha Randolph as "the following articles for your three housemaids." They included in 1791 36 yards of callimaneo, 13½ yards of calico, 25 yards of linen, 9 of muslin, 9 pairs of cotton stockings. In 1792 he sent very much the same kind of gifts, with a suit of his own clothes, "which I have scarcely ever worn," for Robert Hemings. For Martha herself he sent a French cookbook, the *Cuisinière bourgeoise*. Whatever special gifts went to Sally Hemings, if any, did not go by way of his daughter, or if so, were not mentioned in his letters. One slave at Monticello reported, however, that the "leading" servants "were sure to receive presents from his hands" each time he returned to Monticello.[15]

Winthrop Jordan, in exploring the openness of miscegenation in the South during this period, has noted that it was possible to debate publicly "Is sex with Negroes right?" only in the sophisticated port city of Charleston. He quotes Josiah Quincy's diary of 1773, where the Massachusetts clergyman, then visiting Charleston, had written, "The enjoyment of a negro or mulatto woman is spoken of as quite a common thing: no reluctance, delicacy or shame is made about the matter." [16] Everywhere else secrecy was pervasive, and often took the form of elaborate structures of denial. Resentment was growing even against the casual white practice of staying in inns run by blacks. When in September 1790 Jefferson, Madison, and Thomas Lee Shippen breakfasted in Bladensburg, Maryland, with what Shippen described as "an old black woman who keeps the best house in the town and calls herself Mrs. Margaret Adams," she complained that the whites so resented the fact that President George Washington had recently lodged at her inn that they tried "every other expedient to distress her" and finally pulled down her privy. "There was the demolished building when we arrived," Shippen said, her "temple of Cloacina . . . a monument at the same time of the envy of her fellow citizens and her own triumph." [17]

We know that Jefferson's daughter Martha in later years was absolutely tight-lipped about the Sally Hemings scandal, mentioning it only once to two of her sons, to deny the relationship and to exact a promise that the youths would defend their grandfather's reputation always.[18] But what happened in 1790, with the birth of Sally Hemings' first son? Is there evidence of anguish and jealousy on the part of Jefferson's daughters? What kind of accommodation was made? We know only that the seventeen-year-old Martha Jefferson, three months after her arrival from Paris, rushed impetuously into marriage with Thomas Mann Randolph, Jr., son of the Randolph whom Jefferson had lived with at Tuckahoe until the age of nine. This could have happened, of course, without any disillusionment and rage at her father, but the haste is suggestive.

Randolph was tall like Jefferson, which was important for Martha, who had inherited her father's height—and that, Jefferson had written, was "inheriting no trifle." He was also a superb horseman, "elastic as steel," Randall reported, "brilliant, versatile, eloquent in conversation when he chose to be." [19] He had spent a year studying at the University of Edinburgh, with some direction in letters from Jefferson. In his *Autobiography* Jefferson loyally described him as "a young gentleman of genius, science, and honorable mind," [20] though he had by then suffered untold difficulties with him. Randall described him as moody and difficult, "impetuous and imperious in temper." Where Jefferson was sandy-haired, freckled, and serene of countenance, his son-in-law was swarthy, with flashing eyes, the result, as family folklore had it, of the influx of Indian blood, for the young man proudly counted Pocahontas among his ancestors.[21]

Martha met Randolph in late November or early December 1789 and they were married February 23, 1790. Jefferson was pleased with the match. "I scrupulously suppressed my wishes," he wrote to Madame de Corny in Paris, "that my daughter might indulge her own sentiments freely," but "his talents, dispositions, connections and fortune were such as would have made him my own first choice." [22] Randolph's father promised them his plantation at Varina, and Jefferson, though heavily in debt and embarrassed for lack of cash, settled on his daughter 1,000 acres of forest land and twenty-five slaves. Thus he slipped back quickly into a conduct of acquiescence in the conventional patterns of the slave system, and his daughter, receiving the gift of twenty-five blacks, must certainly have been persuaded that there would be no open defying on her father's part of either the slave system or its taboos.

A fortnight after the marriage, when Jefferson was on his way to New York to take over the post of Secretary of State, he made a short but memorable speech in Alexandria in which he spoke of "securing the rights of ourselves and our posterity," and expressed his conviction that "the republican is the only form of government which is not eternally at open or secret war with the rights of mankind." [23] That there was a "secret war" over "the rights of mankind" at Monticello is inescapable. But it surfaced in Jefferson's correspondence with his daughter Martha only in innuendoes. In his first letter to her after her marriage Jefferson wrote from New York, "I feel heavily these separations from you. It is a circumstance of consolation to know that you are happier; and to see a prospect of its continuance in the prudence and even temper of both Mr. Randolph and yourself." The suggestion here is clear enough that Martha had been unhappy. But that Jefferson was desperate to keep the affection of his eldest daughter is also evident: "Neither of you can ever have a more faithful friend than myself, nor one on whom you can count on for more sacrifices. . . . Continue to love me as you have done, and to render my life a blessing by the prospect it may hold up to me of seeing you happy." [24]

Martha, who had spent her honeymoon at Monticello, and was still looking after Polly, replied fondly on April 25, 1790: "I hope you have not given over coming to Virginia this fall as I assure you My dear papa my happiness can never be compleat without your company. Mr. Randolph omits nothing that can in the least contribute to it. I have made it my study to please him in every *thing* and do consider all other objects as secondary to that *except* my love for you." [25] So she assured him of what he most wanted to hear, that he was still first in her heart.

Five months after her marriage Martha wrote to him in what was apparently great agitation, reporting that her father-in-law, whose wife was dead, was about to marry a teen-age girl, Gabriella Harvie. The fifty-year-old Randolph, expecting to have children by his new young wife, had been encouraged by her to raise the price of the Edgehill land he owned, a few miles east of Monticello, which Martha and her husband were intending to buy.[26] Jefferson's reply, like so many of his letters to his daughters, is extraordinary for the skill with which he managed to convey a clear if unhappy message relating to that which he could not bring himself to discuss. The parallel between the elder Randolph's marriage to a very young girl and the troubled involvement of his own with Sally Hemings was altogether too close, and Jefferson was defensive: "Colo. Randolph's marriage was to be expected. All his amusements depending on society, he cannot live alone. . . . He is an excellent good man, to whose temper nothing can be objected but too much facility, too much milk." He urged Martha to redouble her efforts "to keep the affections of Colo. Randolph and his lady," not only to lessen the difficulties over property, but also to preserve her own happiness. Any misunderstanding, he warned, "would be a canker-worm corroding eternally on your minds."

The cankerworm is the larva of a moth that eats the leaves from fruit and shade trees, and frequently destroys all the foliage. "Cankerworm corroding eternally" is a powerful metaphor, profoundly appropriate for what was happening at Monticello. Jefferson then went on to prescribe saintly behavior easy enough for Martha with her father-in-law, but under the circumstances virtually impossible in the situation with her father:

> If the lady has any thing difficult in her disposition, avoid what is rough, and attach her good qualities to you. Consider what are otherwise as a bad stop in your harpsichord. Do not touch on it, but make yourself happy with the good ones. Every human being, my dear, must thus be viewed according to what it is good for, for none of us, no not one, is perfect; and were we to love none who had imperfections, this world would be a desart for our love. All we can do is to make the best of our friends: love and cherish what is good in them, and keep out of the way of what is bad: but no more think of rejecting them for it than of throwing away a piece of music for a flat passage or two. . . . Be you, my dear, the link of love, union, and peace for the whole family.[27]

Whether Martha did indeed become "the link of love, union, and peace for the whole family" we cannot be sure, but there is evidence that she tried. The slave Isaac, who spent his entire life at Monticello, and many years under her management, wrote of her reasonableness and calm. She was, he said, "a mighty peaceable woman; never holler for servant"—"made no fuss nor racket." [28] Not surprisingly, she suffered like her father from migraine headaches. But one thing made it easier for Martha than for Sally Hemings; she was in command.

In his first weeks as Secretary of State Jefferson's preoccupation was still with France. He wrote immediately to all his old friends, William Short, Madame de Corny, Madame d'Enville, Lafayette and his wife, Richard Gem, Ferdinand Grand, the Abbés Arnaud and Chalut, and Philip Mazzei. To Madame d'Houdetot he described his visit to Benjamin Franklin, but did not tell the amiable Frenchwoman that Franklin was dying. "I found our friend Doctor Franklin in his bed, cheerful, and free from pain, but still in his bed. He took a lively interest in the details I gave him of your revolution. I observed his face often flushed in the course of it. He is much emaciated." [29]

A letter from Lucy Paradise in London arrived on April 27, 1790, telling him Maria Cosway was pregnant. "This Lady is with child for the first time. She has been extremely ill, but is Now perfectly recovered and expects in a few Months to Ly in." [30] Four days later, perhaps as the finality of his separation from everything and everyone that he had loved in Europe was borne in upon him and the magnitude of his new duties became ever more apparent, he was seized with another attack of migraine. It lasted almost six weeks. He drove himself furiously and managed despite the pain to finish what became a famous study, "Report on Weights and Measures." [31] The paper, he wrote later, "was composed under a severe attack of periodical head ach which came on every day at Sunrise, and never left me till sunset. What had been ruminated in the day under a paroxysm of the most excruciating pain was committed to paper by candlelight and then the calculations were made." [32]

The headache was still with him on June 11, when a letter came from Maria Cosway herself, again reproachful: "I fear My Dear friend has forgot me: Not One line ever Since your Departure from this part of the world!" [33] Though she would later write to a woman friend, "No one but God himself can know all I suffered when with child," [34] she said not a word about her pregnancy to Jefferson, which must have amused and flattered him a little. He replied congratulating her upon her coming motherhood, not telling her how he had learned of it, and continuing his wistful, half-playful begging that she come to America, "You may make children there, but this is the country to transplant them to." Then he went on, lest she should take him too seriously, to assure her of his own present domestic happiness: "There is no comparison between the sum of happiness enjoyed here and there. All the distractions of your great Cities are but feathers in the scale against the domestic enjoiments and rural occupations, and neighborly societies we live amidst here." He concluded with the familiar teasing "come, but don't come": "I summon you then as a mother to come and join us. You must tell me you will, whether you mean it, or no. En attendant je vous aimerai toujours. Adieu, My Dear Maria." [35] Thus he slipped into French for his declaration of eternal love, as though to put it into English had become too serious and too binding.

This was the real, if not the final goodbye. Maria bore a daughter in June 1790, abandoned her three months later, and took off for the Continent with the celebrated Italian singer Luigi Marchesi, one of the last of the eighteenth-century *castrati*. She did not write to Jefferson for another three and one-half years. It is doubtful if he ever heard of the caustic comment of Horace Walpole, "Surely it is odd to drop a child and her husband and country all in a breath." [36] But since Jefferson was befriending her young architect brother, George Hadfield, who had come to America, he might have learned from him of Maria's desperate attempts in 1793 to get into a convent, and of her pleas to her husband to raise their daughter a Catholic. "May it please the Almighty to enlighten you," she wrote to Cosway, "and show you the blind errors in which you are not only unhappily fallen into but more unfortunately persist in them." [37] Surprisingly, Cosway continued to send his wife money, and when he became ill in 1794 she returned to care for him and her daughter. In two brief notes to Jefferson she then reported her husband's recovery, and described her daughter. "I have found a pretty little girl . . . she shows natural talent & a good soft disposition." [38]

When the child died at age six, Cosway began to show the first signs of psychosis that later enveloped him. He kept the embalmed body of his daughter in their living room in a marble sarcophagus elaborately decorated by his sculptor friend Nollekens, dabbled in animal magnetism, and talked of his powers to raise the dead.[39] Maria, after finally getting the body decently interred in Bunhill Fields, went back to Paris, where she tried briefly to reëstablish herself as a painter.[40] Failing in this, she entered a convent school at Lyons, and later moved on to Lodi, Italy, where she raised enough money among influential Italians to start her convent school for girls. She returned to London only briefly to nurse Cosway in his final illness. By then he was hopelessly psychotic, talking wildly of having conversations with Dante and Praxiteles, and of painting the Virgin Mary posing as his model.[41] In succeeding years Maria now and then timidly wrote a short note to Jefferson. Once he took as long as two years to reply.

In the winter of 1790–91, Jefferson's migraine for the first time in his life became chronic, though it was less incapacitating than the intense, savage onslaughts recorded earlier in several of his letters. It disappeared in the summer of 1791 when he made a vacation trip to Lake George with Madison, and this convinced him that it was related to the pressures and anxieties attendant upon being Secretary of State. The migraine did not return in the autumn of 1791, perhaps because he took up regular horseback riding as daily exercise and relaxation, perhaps too because he had brought Polly back to Philadelphia with him. Though she was in a boarding school, he saw her frequently, and the presence of this thirteen-year-old girl, whose maturing fragile beauty was every day more like that of her mother, seems to have brought him a measure of serenity and happiness.

Polly had always been an indifferent letter writer, but her coming to Philadelphia meant a temporary end to Jefferson's letters to her. This is a loss to history, for these letters had had a special quality of whimsey reserved, it would seem, only for this daughter. On June 13, 1790, he had written, "We had not peas nor strawberries here till the 8th. day of this month. On the same day I heard the first Whip-poor-will whistle. Swallows and martins appeared here on the 21st. of April. When did they appear with you? And when had you peas, strawberries, and whip-poor-wills in Virginia? Take notice hereafter whether the whip-poor-wills always come with the strawberries and peas." [42]

Jefferson returned to Monticello at periodic intervals: for seven weeks in the autumn of 1790, one month in the autumn of 1791, and two months in the summer of 1792. It was a long journey from Philadelphia, and when in January of 1793 he watched a balloon ascent carrying the celebrated Frenchman Blanchard, he wrote wistfully to Martha, "The security of the thing appeared so great that every body is wishing for a baloon to travel in. I wish for one sincerely, as instead of 10. days, I should be within 5 hours of home." [43]

Many expected to see him marry again. Madame de Corny had written from Paris, "*Je vais vous predire votre sort, vous vous remarirez, oui, c'est sûr. Votre femme sera heureuse et vous aussi, je l'espère bien . . .*" [44] However, he settled into the same kind of bachelor existence in Philadelphia as in the months before going to France, going to small dinner parties which began at three in the afternoon, and seeing almost no one in the evenings. He maintained this austere regimen even through his presidency. His own dinners, however, were far more elegant than before; he offered better French wines and excellent French menus. He had furnished his large brick house on High (Market) Street in Philadelphia with the expensive furniture he had shipped home at great cost from Paris. There had been eighty-six packing cases, including "six sofas with gold leaf," fifty-nine chairs, variously upholstered in blue and crimson damask, "velours d'Utrecht," and red morocco, as well as his scientific instruments, clocks, and draperies which alone had cost him over 5,000 francs.[45] He had remodeled the rented house to include a long gallery for books and a large dining room. As always, he spent more than he earned from his salary, and hoped to make up the difference from the sale of Monticello tobacco. But these dinners furnished scant occasion for meeting attractive young women whom he might choose to court.

Though he seemed deliberately to try to avoid new complications of the heart, he did not hesitate to offer advice to younger men and women, especially in cases where love had brought difficulties or tragedy. When Monroe's younger brother made a hasty and ill-advised marriage, Jefferson wrote to the very proper and puritanical James advising forgiveness. "A step of this kind," he urged, "indicates no vice, nor other foible but that of following too hastily the movements of a warm heart." [46]

Later, when he learned of a scandal that rocked the Virginia gentry, where his son-in-law's sister, Anne Cary Randolph, was brought to trial with her lover and cousin, Richard Randolph of Bizarre, for infanticide, he wrote a remarkable letter to his daughter telling her how he would like her to behave toward the unfortunate girl. Richard Randolph had been married to his cousin Judith Randolph, who, in a state of depression after the death of a child, had become addicted to opium. The younger sister, Anne Cary, became involved as a third in the triangle. Her illegitimate child was found dead, and there was some evidence that Richard Randolph had earlier purchased an abortifacient. Patrick Henry and John Marshall took over the defense, and secured an acquittal.

Realizing that his own Martha would feel sullied by the family scandal, Jefferson wrote to her as follows: "Whatever the case may be, the world is become too rational to extend to one person the acts of another. Every one at present stands on the merit or demerit of their own conduct. I am in hopes therefore that neither of you feel any uneasiness but for the pitiable victim, whether it be of error or slander. In either case I see guilt but in one person, and not in her. . . . I shall be made very happy if you are the instruments not only of supporting the spirits of your afflicted friend under the weight bearing on them, but of preserving her in the peace, and love of her friends." [47]

Throwing the whole guilt in this case upon the seducer, as Jefferson did, may tell us something about how he viewed his own role in the lesser and still largely unknown scandal at Monticello. Martha wrote back that she was following "the very conduct you advised me to," adding, however, comments which by their aptness to his own situation could have served only as a stinging reproach to Jefferson: "It is painful to an excess to be obliged to blush for so near a connection. I know it by fatal experience. As for the poor deluded victim I believe all feel much more for her than she does for herself. The villain having been no less successful in corrupting her mind than he has in destroying her reputation. Amidst the distress of her family she alone is tranquil and seems proof against every other misfortune on earth but that of a separation from her vile seducer. . . . I have continued to behave with affection to her which her errors have not been able to eradicate from my heart and could I suppose her penitent I would redouble my attentions to her though I am one of the few who have allways *doubted* the truth of the report." Martha here was consciously writing about her sister-in-law and not Sally Hemings, and this letter was not in any sense a conscious reproach. She signed her letter in the language of her heart—"We are all impatient to see you. . . . believe me ever yours." [48]

CHAPTER XIX

The Satellite Sons

Hamilton and myself were daily pitted in the Cabinet like two cocks.

Jefferson to Dr. Walter Jones, March 5, 1810 [1]

Adams, Jefferson, Hamilton, and Madison all rotated like satellites around Washington. Jefferson, isolated for five years in Paris and only peripherally involved in the making of the new constitution, moved into close proximity in March 1790. But it was too late for him to become the favorite. That place had been gained by Hamilton, who had replaced Madison as Washington's confidant and writing aide, though neither of these younger men ever held the special place of Lafayette. As Flexner writes, Washington "had wept unashamedly at his dinner table when describing his affection for Lafayette. One cannot imagine him doing the same in relation to Jefferson or Hamilton or even Madison." [2]

By virtue of his election as vice-president Adams revolved as the obvious successor, and frankly described his role as "the first prince of the country, and the heir apparent to the sovereign authority." [3] But he never had Washington's intimate friendship, and Hamilton was eager to supersede him politically as well as personally. Both Adams and Hamilton believed that Jefferson also had fantasies of succeeding Washington, which in view of his later political actions seems likely, though he kept evidence of his ambition deeply buried. Madison, who had played a stellar role in writing the Constitution, had become more radical and had moved into Jefferson's orbit, continuing not only as his confidential adviser, a role he was already playing in 1791, but also as an ardent defender and his closest friend. Burr, who had already as a young officer broken with Washington, revolved far out like a dark planet, in an orbit that had not yet crossed that of the more obvious of Washington's heirs.

The diverging political and economic theories of Adams, Jefferson, and Hamilton have been dissected and analyzed by many able historians; there is scarcely a contradiction or confrontation that has not been examined in half a dozen monographs as well as in the numerous biographies of these gifted men.[4] They did quarrel over theories of the ideal government and the nation's economy; they did have diverging attitudes toward the essential nature of man. All had united during the Revolution to dethrone George III, but now this monarch, once so formidable, was merely surly and distant. With the external threat reduced, Washington's princes began to quarrel among themselves, their unity disintegrating, as in most families with father and sons, cracking into fragments over matters of affection as well as power.

The near death of Washington from pneumonia in May 1790 brought a mushrooming of fantasies about the succession. Jefferson, already suffering with migraine when he learned of the gravity of the illness, wrote his daughter a letter which showed he was following every clinical detail with concentration as well as dread. "Yesterday he was thought by the physicians to be dying. However about 4. oclock in the evening a copious sweat came on, his expectoration which had been thin and ichorous, began to assume a well digested form, his articulation became distinct, and in the course of two hours it was evident he had gone thro' a favorable crisis. He continues mending to-day, and from total despair we are now in good hopes of him." Jefferson's despair was real enough. Fond as he had become of Adams in Europe, he could not visualize him replacing the aging giant. In a letter to Madison he had already confided Benjamin Franklin's barbed description of Adams, "Always an honest man, often a great one, but sometimes absolutely mad." [5]

Abigail Adams, horrified at the thought of Washington's dying, and by no means sanguine at the thought of her husband's succeeding him, wrote her sister a frank letter that would surely have dismayed her beloved John.

> I dreaded his death from a cause that few persons, and only those who knew me best, would believe. It appears to me that the union of the states, and concequently the permanancy of the Government depend under Providence upon his Life. At this early day when neither our Finances are arranged nor our Government sufficiently cemented

to produce duration, His death would I fear have had most disasterous concequences. I feared a thousand things which I pray I never may be called to experience. Most assuredly I do not wish for the highest Post . . . thanks to Providence he is again restored.[6]

Hamilton during the crisis of the illness looked not on Adams but upon Jefferson with corroding suspicion. In a manuscript passage crossed out and never published during his lifetime, he wrote that Washington's pneumonia "excited the ambitious ardor of his secretary [Jefferson] to remove out of his way every dangerous opponent [including] . . . the more popular Secretary of the Treasury."[7] Hamilton's view of human nature, despite his aura of cheerfulness, was grimly foreboding. He had proclaimed gloomily in the constitutional debates, "Take mankind in general, they are vicious, their passions may be operated upon. . . . There may be in every government a few choice spirits, who may act from more worthy motives. One great error is that we suppose mankind more honest than they are. Our prevailing passions are ambition and interest; and it will ever be the duty of a wise government to avail itself of the passions, in order to make them subservient to the public good."[8] Adams, looking at Hamilton, saw there the very self-interest Hamilton himself deplored. He described Hamilton's ambition as "transcendant," and said he had "an irresponsible" disposition to intrigue.[9]

Though a stout revolutionist, Adams was greatly attracted by some of the trappings of royalty. He thought Washington should have a more prestigious title than merely "president." "What will the common people of foreign countries, what will the sailors and soldiers say," he asked, " 'George Washington, President of the United States'? They will despise him to *all eternity*."[10] And he speculated to Jefferson that his own daughters might be sought by European aristocrats, and that if Washington had a daughter, "she would be demanded in Marriage by one of the Royal Families of France or England."[11]

That the succession would be a decisive testing of the nation's stability Washington and everyone else in politics recognized. He was not eager for a second term, and frankly described himself to Jefferson on February 29, 1792, as "growing old, his bodily health less firm, his memory, always bad, becoming worse, and perhaps the other faculties of his mind showing a decay to others of which he was insensible himself."[12] But each of the young princes preferred to see Washington live through a second term rather than to have the office captured by someone other than himself. They looked upon the old warrior as a rock, an elemental force, solid as Peter the Apostle. By the autumn of 1792 the snarling among the potential heirs had become so public that Washington himself came to fear that to relinquish the presidency to their internecine warfare might shake the foundations of the young government.

The first break came between Jefferson and Adams. Adams had been so fond of Jefferson in London that he felt free to end one letter, "I am with an affection that can never die, your Friend and Servant, John Adams." [13] But within fifteen months after Jefferson became Secretary of State the two men were beginning to be seriously estranged. Bored by the vice-presidential office, which he described as "the most insignificant . . . that ever the invention of man contrived or the imagination conceived," Adams wrote a series of essays, "Papers on Political History," anonymously published in the *Gazette of the United States* in 1790 as *Discourses on Davila*. It was part Calvinism, part personal cynicism based on his observations of his fellows and of himself. Man, he wrote, is motivated primarily by "a *passion for distinction* . . . a desire to be observed, considered, esteemed, praised, beloved and admired . . . no appetite of human nature is more universal than that for honor," and "love of knowledge and desire of fame, are very often nothing more than various modifications of that desire. . . ." Deploring the efforts of the French Revolution to impose equality, Adams said bluntly, "every man should know his place, and be made to keep it."

What alarmed Jefferson, who recognized the authorship of *Davila* at once, was Adams' insistence that there should be no rival for the presidency. "Where there are rivals for the first place, the national attention and passions are divided . . . they produce slanders and libels first, mons and seditions second, and civil war with all her hissing snakes, burning torches, and haggard horrors at last." [14] To Jefferson it seemed that Adams here was advocating that his own bid for the presidency be made by acclamation, as it had been with Washington, and he found the suggestion outrageous.

Most of the men who had helped found the young republic feared the destructiveness of factions, and had in the beginning hoped that the country could somehow be governed without political parties. Jefferson himself had written from France, "If I could not go to heaven but with a party, I would not go at all." [15] But where he and Madison quickly came to see that party divisions were essential to the electoral system, Washington, Adams, and Hamilton, though themselves Federalist partisans, clung to the fiction that liberty could be preserved without resort to party alliances. Adams in 1812, looking back on his political innocence of 1790, wrote of his *Davila* that "no man in America then believed him," that the "dull heavy volume was urged as full proof, that he was an advocate for monarchy," and that it wrecked his popularity.[16] Adams was never a monarchist, but it is easy to see how the *Davila* speculations, derided as the work of the "Duke of Braintree" and "His Rotundity," could be so interpreted by his political rivals.

The issue upon which the friendship of Jefferson and Adams foundered, however, was Adams' continued denunciation of the French Revolution. Wherever Jefferson went in New York society he unhappily heard France denounced.[17] He counted as an almost personal attack Edmund Burke's speeches in Parliament blistering the French Revolution, republished in May 1790 in the *Gazette of the United States.* Burke called Lafayette's Declaration of the Rights of Man, which Jefferson considered to be in part a child of his own fathering, "a sort of institute or digest of Anarchy . . . a pedantic abuse of elementary principles as would disgrace the imbecility of schoolboys." France, Burke said, was "lying in a sort of trance—an epileptic fit— exposed to the pity or derision of mankind . . . an irrational, unprincipled, proscribing, confiscating, plundering ferocious bloody and tyrannical democracy." [18]

Jefferson, who hoped that "so beautiful a revolution" would "spread through the whole world," [19] knew that it would be impolitic for him to defend openly what was happening in France, but he encouraged pro-French articles in the anti-Federalist press. When Madison sent him a copy of Thomas Paine's volcanic reply to Burke, *The Rights of Man,* Jefferson was exultant. He sent it off at once to the printer who was to make the American edition, writing in an accompanying note that he was glad "something is at length to be publicly said against the political heresies which have sprung up among us." The printer, without Jefferson's permission, used the letter in the Foreword, and soon the press was buzzing with the rumor that the Secretary of State had publicly attacked the Vice-President.

Jefferson, painfully embarrassed, wrote an explanation to Washington, deploring the printer's indiscretion, and describing Adams as "one of the most honest and disinterested men alive." He had for him "a cordial esteem," he said, but then added tartly, "even since his apostasy to hereditary monarchy and nobility, though we differ, we differ as friends should do." [20]

Adams found *The Rights of Man* appalling especially for its militant deism, for he was genuinely pious and God-fearing. But instead of indulging in further anonymous journalism, he let his son take up the cudgels on his behalf. John Quincy Adams, now twenty-four, defended his father and savagely attacked Paine under the pen name of Publicola. Jefferson, believing Publicola was actually John Adams, now tried to calm the whirlwind of faction in Washington's official family by a discreet apology to Adams, explaining the printer's indiscretion. But he underlined his contempt for the tactic of the anonymous article. "I never did in my life either by myself or by any other, have a sentence of mine inserted in a newspaper without putting my name to it; and I believe I never shall," he wrote.[21] Adams for his part denied that he was Publicola, without admitting that the articles were really penned by his son. He also hotly denied that he believed monarchy to be the best form of government, adding with studied contempt, "I know not what your idea is of the best form of government. You and I have never had a serious conversation together that I can recollect concerning the nature of government." [22]

Though Adams went on to protest that their friendship of fifteen years "still is very dear to my heart," the damage done to it was virtually irreparable. They papered over the breach for a time, but Adams continued to defend the "monarchical principle in a republican government," equating political dissent with lawlessness and anarchy. Later when as president he approved the Alien Acts and ruthlessly exploited the Sedition Acts, which made a mockery of the First Amendment, Jefferson came to look upon him as a betrayer of the Revolution.

In December 1792 Adams, who had hoped to see Jefferson warmly endorse him as Washington's obvious heir and ease his way into the presidency without a party battle, wrote sadly to his wife, "I am really astonished at the blind spirit of party which has seized on the soul of this Jefferson. There is not a Jacobin in France more devoted to faction." [23] The break was especially painful to Abigail, who had written to her sister on April 3, 1790, "Mr. Jefferson is here, and adds much to the social circle." [24] The disaffection also tore at Jefferson, who could not really dislodge what he called "a solid affection" for Adams.[25]

Jefferson's first impulse, as the difficulties with Adams became insoluble, had been to resign from Washington's family altogether. Believing that the President would step down in 1792, he hinted to him on February 28, 1792, that he would go out of office at the same time and retire from government service. The very next day, Washington, speaking in what Jefferson described as "an affectionate tone"— and Jefferson was markedly sensitive to the nuances of the President's inflections—begged him to stay on in office, saying what Jefferson most wanted to hear, that he was needed. He would "consider it unfortunate," Washington told him, should his own retirement "bring on the retirement of the great officers of the government . . . this might produce a shock on the public mind of dangerous consequence." [26]

When Jefferson finally did retire, in December 1793, Adams thought the gesture a mere political trick. "Jefferson thinks by this step to get a reputation as an humble, modest, meek man, wholly without ambition or vanity. He may even have deceived himself into this belief. But if the prospect opens, the world will see and he will feel that he is as ambitious as Oliver Cromwell." [27] That Jefferson's desire for retirement was real, and at times overpowering, is, however, beyond doubt. One sees it abundantly in his letters during this period to his daughter Martha.

By January 1792 Martha had borne a daughter, Anne, and was preparing to leave Monticello for a home of her own at nearby Edgehill. Jefferson in January 1792 wrote begging her to make only "leisurely preparations" for their departure and promising on his return to "relieve you from *desagremens* to which I have been sensible you were exposed, without the power in myself to prevent it, but by my own presence." What the disagreements were, he did not say, but he did write of his retirement as being "not very distant" and of his desire "of being home once more . . . where I may once more be happy with you, with Mr. Randolph, and dear little Anne, with whom even Socrates might ride on a stick without being ridiculous." [28]

Replying with what was even for her an unusual display of affection, Martha wrote, "The anxiety you express to be at home makes me infinitely happy. I acknowledge I was under some apprehension that you would be prevailed upon to stay Longer than you intended and I feel more and more every day how necessary your company is to my happiness by the continual and ardent desire I have of seeing you." [29] To which Jefferson replied with as much yearning as if he were writing to a mistress, "The ensuing year will be the longest of my life, and the last of such hateful labours. The next we will sow our cabbages together." [30]

Later when he told Martha he must stay on into Washington's second term, she called it a "cruel disappointment." "Having never in my life been more intent upon any thing I never bore a disappointment with so little patience." [31] To Madison's importunities that he stay on throughout the whole of Washington's second term, Jefferson replied in a remarkable letter on February 27, 1793: "The motion of my blood no longer keeps time with the tumult of the world. It leads me to seek for happiness in the lap and love of my family, in the society of my neighbors and my books, in the wholesome occupations of my farm and my affairs, in an interest or affection in every bud that opens, in every breath that blows around me." He described himself as "worn down with labors from morning to night, and day to day, knowing them as fruitless to others as they are vexations to myself . . . cut off from my family and friends, my affairs abandoned to chaos and derangement, in short, giving everything I love in exchange for everything I hate." [32]

Jefferson was then only fifty. One daughter was with him in Philadelphia, and Martha, her husband, and now two children were no longer at Monticello. His best friends, including Madison, were in Philadelphia. This is not the letter of an embittered or weary old man ready for retirement. One has only to repeat the warm phrases—motion of my blood, in the lap and love of my family, affection in every breath that blows around me, cut off from everything I love—to see that these are the longings of a man truly deprived of love, and that this special deprivation had only incidentally to do with his daughter.

Still, he stayed on in Philadelphia until January 5, 1794. The reasons had to do not only with Washington's genuine need of him, but more particularly his rivalry with Alexander Hamilton. This was a very different phenomenon from his rivalry with Adams, which was always tempered by Jefferson's original respect and affection, and by the fact that Adams was eight years older. Hamilton, the Little Lion, was thirty-six, fourteen years younger than Jefferson, not too distant in age from his own younger brother. Randolph had never in any sense been a rival to Jefferson, and could not as an adult even be a companion, since he was less than mediocre in talent and native intelligence. But Hamilton was bursting with natural talent. Until he moved into Washington's circle Jefferson had never known what it was to be eclipsed by a rival younger than himself. Hamilton had a fine military record, a brilliant intellect, and great political promise. Though he could be overbearing and arrogant to men of a different political complexion, he was graceful and debonair in the kind of company where Jefferson found himself taciturn and hostile. Hamilton had the friendship of the rich and wellborn. He moved among the wealthy merchants of New York and Philadelphia as if he had eaten off silver plates from childhood; he loved to talk about money and finance, and he did it brilliantly. He was listened to with great respect in any case because as Secretary of the Treasury he had more power than any man in the United States save Washington. Jefferson preferred the company of scientists and republicans, despising the merchants and bankers for their greed, and counting them secret monarchists and potential subverters of the republic.

Hamilton was married to Elizabeth Schuyler, daughter of one of the genuine aristocrats of New York—if in a definition of aristocracy one needed four generations of Dutch patroons along the Mohawk, plus political power. Though mistakenly described in some histories as a swarthy Creole, Hamilton according to surviving portraits was fair and rosy-cheeked—with hair almost as reddish as Jefferson's—and had deep-set blue eyes. Where women found Jefferson gentle, gallant, but somehow remote, they saw in Hamilton the potentially seductive lover. Whether it was justified or not, he had the reputation of being a rake, and his openly paraded affection for his wife's exquisite sister, Angelica Church, caused scandalized whispers in New York and Philadelphia. At her lavish balls in New York, where the Churches had moved from London, Angelica betrayed her boredom with her husband and flaunted her delight in her *petit Fripon* with an abandon that embarrassed everyone, it seems, but her sister. John Adams would later write maliciously to Benjamin Rush of Hamilton's "fornications, adulteries, and his incests." [33] Jefferson, who had counted himself Angelica's favorite in Paris, found himself quite superseded.

The two men were forced to see a great deal of each other, and after only a few months Jefferson was treating the vivacious Hamilton with only glacial courtesy. Hamilton, who knew that the Secretary of State had a capacity for warm friendship, and who saw his friendship with Madison deepening, found Jefferson's icy reserve toward himself intolerable. One hears the overtones of his resentment and contempt of the Jefferson-Madison friendship in a derisive metaphor written in a letter to Edward Carrington on May 26, 1792. Theirs, he said, was "*a womanish attachment to France and a womanish resentment against Great Britain. They would draw us into the closest embrace of the former, and involve us in all the consequences of her politics.*" [34] Jefferson was attacked by one of Hamilton's best friends as being "cautious and shy, wrapped up in impenetrable silence and mystery," [35] a description Madison and Monroe would have found preposterous.

Both Jefferson and Hamilton had lost their fathers before becoming adults, the former by death, and the latter by abandonment. It was not surprising then that they looked to the childless Washington as a father and were treated by him as sons. Hamilton, however, had a special need. For all his precocity and brazen display of talent, he lacked one vital asset, legitimacy. The specter of his bastardy haunted him. He seems to have told his wife's family that his mother, Rachel Faucette, (or Fawcett), descendant of a French Huguenot who had fled to the West Indies, had been married to one John Michael Levine (also spelled Lawein) and later divorced. But he did not at first tell them that his own father, James Hamilton, fourth son of a Scottish laird, had never married his mother.[36] By the time the rumors of his bastardy trickled out of the West Indies, however, he was so entrenched in the affections of the whole Schuyler family that nothing could shake the marriage. The private malice of his rivals who spread the information—Adams called him "the bastard brat of a Scotch pedlar" [37]—never seriously upset his national reputation.

James Hamilton had come to the West Indies from Scotland; whether he was responsible for Rachel Levine's abandonment of her husband and small son Peter is not clear. Levine, who in 1759 filed suit for divorce, declared brutally that she "absented herself and went whoring in the Barbados," and the court with traditional cruelty gave him but not her permission to remarry. Meanwhile she had gone to live with James Hamilton and had borne him two sons. He abandoned her when Alexander was ten and they suffered greatly from poverty.[38] When the boy was thirteen his mother died, leaving him as her only legacy three female slaves bequeathed to her by her own mother. At this point her former husband, in a signal act of malevolence—doubtless a clue as to why his wife left him in the first place—sued successfully to take even these slaves away from the illegitimate sons, charging that they belonged to her "only lawfully begotten heir Peter Lawein." So it can be seen that Hamilton in his earliest years learned the penalties of bastardy and the rewards of legitimacy.[39]

He made pathetic attempts later to buy the affection of the father who abandoned him. When the old man learned that there was money to be had from his successful son in America, he did write to him, and Alexander sent him and his brother several thousand dollars he could ill afford. But it was all painfully one-sided. Hamilton never did erase the stain of his bastardy. Instead the rumor spread that Washington, who had spent some time in Barbados in 1751, when Hamilton's mother was there, was in fact his real father. This Hamilton must have found a great curiosity, and perhaps not at all unwelcome.[40]

That he did cherish a fantasy of seeing the childless Washington installed as king, with himself eventually crowned as heir—the supreme act of legitimacy—is evidenced by his extraordinary behavior in the Constitutional Convention, where he had shocked his colleagues by advocating a monarchy and had then stalked out of the convention. He had returned at the last moment, to vote for the Constitution, and later his contributions to the *Federalist Papers* had contributed mightily to its acceptance, especially in his own crucial state of New York. Later, in 1792, he would write to a friend, "I am affectionately attached to the republican theory. . . . This is the real language of my heart." [41] But both Adams and Jefferson believed always that his fatal gesture in the convention was the real key to his political affections, and gave him small credit for his services to the country. Hamilton acted toward Washington very like a son, taking liberties the President would have tolerated in no one else, chafing under his authority but nevertheless holding him in awe, and finally, like Jefferson, climbing out from under the presidential shield after numerous threats to resign from the cabinet. Though he left with relief, as did Jefferson, he nevertheless wrote of Washington when he died, "He was an Aegis very essential to me." [42]

Jefferson was jealous of Hamilton, and carried to Washington stories of his attacks on the Constitution and republican government, telling him that Hamilton had called the Constitution "a shilly-shally thing, of mere milk and water, which could not last, and was only good as a step to something better." [43] Once when Hamilton visited Jefferson's quarters and saw three portraits on the wall, he asked their identity. "They are my trinity of the three greatest men the world has ever produced," Jefferson replied, "Sir Francis Bacon, Sir Isaac Newton, and John Locke." Hamilton stared at them a moment and then said, "The greatest man that ever lived was Julius Caesar." Jefferson, chilled by this choice of hero, took pains to repeat the story for history.[44]

When Jefferson took office, he found Hamilton acting very like a prime minister, directing, commanding, and interfering without apology in every aspect of government, including foreign affairs. Hamilton had over a hundred men working for him in New York, and additional excisemen all over the nation. Jefferson began with a staff of five, all mere copyists. It is small wonder that he described Hamilton as a "colossus" and complained to Washington that the Treasury "possessed already such an influence as to swallow up the whole executive powers." [45] No doubt Jefferson also feared Hamilton would swallow up the whole of Washington's affection.

Jefferson distrusted Hamilton's funding system for restoring the nation's credit, counting it a device to fatten speculators and rob the poor and financially innocent. He feared the power of his Bank of the United States, which suffered very little control by government, but which had enormous potential control over government. He came to believe that Hamilton was giving away Treasury secrets to his friends. The spectacle of Hamilton's onetime Assistant Secretary of the Treasury, William Duer, cousin to Hamilton's wife, leaving the Treasury in 1789 with a shortage of $238,000 on his books, and thereafter being permitted to build up and lose a fortune before finally in 1792 going to jail for his peculations, convinced not only Jefferson but a great many other men who were beginning to call themselves anti-Federalists, or Republicans, that Hamilton was himself guilty of speculating with Treasury funds. To his son-in-law Jefferson wrote that "the credit and fate of the nation seem to hang on the desperate throws and plunges of gambling scoundrels." [46] To Jefferson's profound suspicion that Hamilton was a cheat and embezzler was added a growing conviction that he was responsible also for the nation's "galloping fast into monarchy." [47] It could well have been Jefferson's hatred and jealousy of Hamilton, and his fear for the damage he might do to the republic, more than any other single force, that kept him in government and away from the blissful retirement for which he so often pined.

Convinced that there was no real opposition press in the nation to tell the truth about his rival, Jefferson encouraged a talented young poet friend, Philip Freneau, whom he had given a job as translator in his department, to set up a Republican newspaper. Freneau's *National Gazette* shortly began a series of attacks on Hamilton, describing him as little better than a Tory, and praising Jefferson as a "Colossus of Liberty" who was preventing a return to kingship and aristocracy. Hamilton, enraged, began to write under various pseudonyms in the Federalist sheet, *Gazette of the United States*. He denounced the connection between Jefferson and Freneau as "*indelicate* and *unfit*." Freneau, he said, was "free to defame, but never free to praise," and the situation reminded him "of the Fable of the Viper which stung to death the Countryman, the genial warmth of whose bosom had reanimated its frozen carcase." [48]

So began the venomous newspaper war of 1792–93. Writing under the pseudonyms T. L., An American, Crito, Detector, Catullus, Fact, and Civis, aided by his friend William Loughton Smith as Scourge, Hamilton vilified the Secretary of State not only as a frozen carcass and poisonous snake, but also as an intriguing and ambitious revolutionary, a man of violent passions, "the *promoter* of *national disunion, national insignificance, public disorder and discredit*." [49] Determined to drive Jefferson from the cabinet, he presented a formal list of complaints to Washington. Jefferson for his part disdained to write under a pseudonym but had no hesitation about enlisting the services of Madison and Monroe, who collaborated in writing six unsigned essays, "Vindication of Mr. Jefferson," published in the *American Daily Advertiser*, beginning September 22, 1793. Edmund Randolph, similarly stimulated, attacked Hamilton under the name Aristides.

Washington, appalled to see the two ablest men in his cabinet engaging in a thinly disguised public feud, demanded an end to the quarreling, begging in a letter to Hamilton for "mutual forebearances and temporising yieldings *on all sides*." [50] To Jefferson he pleaded, "If instead of laying our shoulders to the machine, after measures are decided on, one pulls this way and another that, before the utility of the thing is fairly tried, it must inevitably be torn asunder; and in my opinion the fairest prospect of happiness and prosperity that was ever presented to man, will be lost, perhaps forever." [51] Hamilton replied contritely, but with a curious slip of the pen, choosing a verb with a double meaning and thus betraying inadvertently the intensity of his inner hostility, "I will not directly or indirectly say or do a thing that shall endanger a feud." [52] He did not indeed "endanger" the feud; instead his newspaper attacks feeding it grew ever more malevolent. Jefferson, for his part, wrote a hot and anguished letter to Washington from Monticello, accusing Hamilton of meddling in the affairs of the Department of State, of attacking him in the press, of "dealing out treasury secrets among his friends," and of preferring a hereditary over a republican government.

Jefferson's unspoken fear that Hamilton might indeed one day rule as hereditary monarch surfaced in a remarkable line, "I hold it to be one of the distinguishing excellences of elective over hereditary successions, that talents which nature has provided in sufficient proportion, should be selected by the society for the government of their affairs, rather than that this should be transmitted through the loins of knaves and fools, passing from the debauches of the table to those of the bed." He called Hamilton's history "a tissue of machinations against the liberty of the country." Insisting that he would resign in March 1793, Jefferson wrote that he looked forward to it "with the longing of a wave-worn mariner, who has at length land in view, and shall count the days and hours which shall lie between me and it." [53]

On his return to Philadelphia, shortly after sending this letter, Jefferson stopped at Mount Vernon. There, in a difficult confrontation that took place before breakfast, the two statesmen discussed Alexander Hamilton. Washington defended his favorite's financial genius, saying he had seen the credit of the country, once in desperate straits, restored "in a sudden & extraordinary degree." He ridiculed Jefferson's fears of a return to monarchy, saying there were not ten influential men in the United States "who entertained such a thought." When Jefferson begged him to stay on for the second term, for the nation's sake, Washington noted tartly that he was as eager to retire as Jefferson, and turned the argument back upon him. They parted amicably, however, and later Washington wrote, "I believe the views of both of you to be pure and well meant. . . . I have a great, a sincere esteem and regard for you both, and ardently wish that some line may be marked out by which both of you could walk." [54]

Jefferson's arguments and threat of retirement had, however, shaken Washington, for he could think of no competent replacement for his Secretary of State. Adams, whom he did not especially like, would be president in any case, but he knew the Vice-President's relations with

Hamilton to be at least as difficult as those of Adams with Jefferson. In early October Washington decided it was better to run for a second term than to turn the country over to his quarreling surrogate sons.

Hamilton, who believed with Adams that Jefferson's threat to resign was a mere political trick, continued to attack him anonymously, calling him "a Caesar coyely refusing the proffered diadem . . . *rejecting* the trappings, but tenaciously grasping the substance of imperial domination," and "the most intriguing man in the United States." [55] Jefferson could hardly have missed the irony of the fact that these accusations were written by the man whose special hero was Julius Caesar and whose intriguing outdid all others. But one of Hamilton's anonymous charges must have roused in Jefferson a special anxiety. On September 29, 1792, writing under the pseudonym Catullus, Hamilton accused Jefferson of being "a concealed voluptuary," hiding under "the plain garb of Quaker simplicity." [56] He could not know at the time that Hamilton was referring only to his ancient affair—or attempted affair— with Betsey Walker; this he would learn in the open quarreling with Hamilton in 1796.[57] But the fear that his relationship with Sally Hemings had already become public knowledge, and could serve as an extra humiliation for his daughters as well as a political liability, must have been with Jefferson from 1792 forward. This was the first warning signal and he must have known that worse could surface at any moment.

On November 8 he wrote to diplomat David Humphreys in Europe that he was leaving his office in March. "That moment," he said, ". . . is to me as land was to Columbus in his first American voyage." [58] To his landlord Thomas Leiper he wrote on December 9, 1792, that he would give up his Philadelphia house in three months. When Washington suggested that he go back to France for two years he turned down the offer, saying, "I could never again cross the Atlantic." [59]

Before going out of office Jefferson did make one desperate effort to get Hamilton out of the cabinet, which he thought, briefly, in the early months of 1793, might succeed. On February 7 he told the recently reëlected President he would stay on until summer, perhaps until autumn. Washington, greatly pleased, expressed his hope that he would make his peace with Hamilton. In replying Jefferson was honest, up to a point. Conciliation with Hamilton, he said, was impossible —"if by that was meant either was to sacrifice his general system to the other. . . . My wish was, to see both Houses of Congress cleansed of all persons interested in the bank or public stocks—cleansed that is of all corruption." [60] What he did not tell Washington was that he believed Hamilton to be a sink of corruption, and that he himself was already coaching Congressman William Branch Giles of Virginia in a series of resolutions leading toward a congressional investigation which he fully hoped would result in Hamilton's being disgraced before the entire nation.

What had galvanized Jefferson into this secret activity was the electrifying secret news from James Monroe in November 1792 that Hamilton was deeply involved in a Treasury scandal, and that he was being blackmailed for this and for indiscretions in his personal life by one James Reynolds.

No one can know with what convoluted feelings Thomas Jefferson faced the discovery that his detested rival in the cabinet was, like himself, extraordinarily vulnerable in an affair of the heart. He moved with extreme discretion, and during what was a major crisis for Hamilton in December 1792 took no part whatsoever in this aspect of the exposure, keeping the details as he knew them inviolate from the press. He did, however, expect the Maria Reynolds scandal to lead eventually to important disclosures about Hamilton's alleged speculation with Treasury funds. Therefore he let himself become more than peripherally involved.

The Reynolds-Hamilton story has been told in numerous histories, with portraits of Maria varying over the years from the artless victim first painted by James Thomson Callender in 1798 to the "skillful actress and born adventuress" that John C. Miller made her out to be.[61] There has long been agreement that James Reynolds was a cheap swindler who made a living by buying veterans' claims to government land and money at a fraction of their value. He even forged papers of soldiers who had actually died during the Revolution. Those who believe he planned the blackmailing of Hamilton from the beginning and acted as pimp for his wife miss the fact that he had actually abandoned her for another woman for six months, and that it was only when he returned and accidentally discovered her liaison with Hamilton that he saw he had stumbled upon a cache of gold.

But why did Hamilton, darling of the richest and most sophisticated women in New York and Philadelphia, married to a gentle, feminine woman who adored him, become entangled with a woman who was uneducated and desperate, and who let him know in her first interview that she would go to bed with him for money? As Hamilton himself described it, "With a seeming air of affliction she informed me . . . that her husband, who had for a long time treated her very cruelly, had lately left her, to live with another woman, and in so destitute a condition. . . . she had taken the liberty to apply to my humanity for assistance." [62]

It was a beguiling snare, perhaps especially so to Hamilton since it brought echoes of the sad story of his own mother. We know little about Rachel "Hamilton," though she has been widely described as beautiful and high-spirited. But we do know something significant about Hamilton's divided affections and loyalties—how he was attracted in one direction by the virtuous woman, and in the other by the artful prostitute. There is a clue in his very first publication, this a two-stanza poem which appeared in the *Royal Danish American Gazette* in the West Indies when he was sixteen. Here he described two kinds of love, the one idyllic, with love, marriage, and eternal happiness with a virginal shepherdess, the second carnal, with love for Coelia whom he calls "an artful little slut." He ended the second stanza, "Good faith she has you fast." [63]

Certainly when he married Elizabeth Schuyler he married a shepherdess who would never go "whoring in the Barbados." But Hamilton during his courtship of Elizabeth Schuyler had also been seeing another woman right up to the announcement of his engagement,[64] and later, when he was trapped by Maria Reynolds, he was surely lured by the scent of Coelia. How badly he was trapped Hamilton learned on December 15, 1791, when he received two letters. Maria wrote hysterically that her husband was threatening to tell Mrs. Hamilton. "Oh my God I feel more for you than myself and wish I had never been born to give you so mutch unhappiness do not rite to him no not a line but come here soon . . ." Reynolds wrote in pious indignation, ". . . you took the advantage a poor Broken harted woman. . . . I would Sacrefise almost my life to make her Happy. but now I am determined to have satisfaction." And he vowed to take their daughter away so that "She shant see her poor mother." [65] The threatened loss of her child seems to have been enough to cow Maria into the blackmailing imbroglio that followed, though let it be said to her credit that when it was all over she divorced Reynolds. Hamilton, in an initial attempt to buy Reynolds' silence, agreed to pay him a thousand dollars in return for his promise to leave the city. The blackmailer did not leave, but instead turned pimp and gave Hamilton formal permission to continue to visit his wife: When Hamilton stayed away, Maria threatened suicide: "Ease a heart which is ready Burst with Greef I can neither Eate or sleep I have Ben on the point of doing the moast horrid acts." [66] Hamilton's visits then continued, and so did Reynolds' insistent demands for money. It tells something about Hamilton's capacity for projection that it was during this period of clandestine meetings and continuing threats of blackmail that he accused Jefferson anonymously in the press of being "a concealed voluptuary." [67]

Reynolds was content with the arrangement till November 1792, when one of his cheap forgeries caught up with him, and he was jailed for making a claim against the government for a soldier supposedly dead who had turned out to be very much alive. When Hamilton refused to help him get out of jail, Reynolds sent word to Republican leaders of Congress promising revelations, and saying he had it in his power "to hang the Secretary of the Treasury." James Monroe now eagerly joined Congressmen Frederick Muhlenberg and Abraham Venable in exploring a potential scandal that they hoped would prove Hamilton to be the Great Embezzler they had long thought him to be.[68]

After interviewing Reynolds in prison and his wife in her house on Market Street, the three exultant congressmen moved on to Hamilton's office on December 15, 1792, with some damaging letters in Hamilton's own but somewhat disguised hand which they fully expected to take eventually to Washington. Faced with a scandal that could wreck his public career and his marriage, Hamilton admitted the adultery, but denied any financial indiscretion. He counted on the innate decency of the men who were accusing him to keep his private foolishness secret, and so they agreed. Monroe, however, could not resist sending copies of all the papers that had fallen into his hands to Jefferson, and Hamilton later learned of this.[69] None of these men knew that John Beckley, Clerk of the House, had also made copies of the whole Reynolds correspondence, and later, when Beckley leaked everything to journalist James Thomson Callender, it was not he but Monroe and Jefferson who were blamed.[70]

Jefferson recoiled from an open, dirty fight in Congress. And he must have known, after seeing the Reynolds-Hamilton letters, that none of it was of value in proving Hamilton guilty of speculation with Treasury funds. But he was so convinced at this point of Hamilton's financial guilt that he abandoned his plans for retirement and decided to go along with Madison, Monroe, and other Republicans in a congressional investigation of the specific aspects of Hamilton's public activities that had made him most vulnerable. Jefferson hoped in this fashion to give the lie to those who were hinting that he himself was resigning because of some indiscretion or ineptness in office. Resign he would under any circumstances, but he would drag out the scurrilous Hamilton with him. So he fulfilled the vow he had expressed openly to Washington in his impassioned letter of September 9, 1792: "I will not suffer my retirement to be clouded by the slanders of a man whose history, from the moment at which history can stoop to notice

him, is a tissue of machinations against the liberty of the country
which has not only received and given him bread, but heaped its
honors on his head." [71]

Jefferson's agitation over this decision is reflected in a revealing letter
to his daughter Martha, January 26, 1793:

> I have for some time past been under an agitation of mind which I
> scarcely ever experienced before, produced by a check on my purpose of
> returning home at the close of this session of Congress. . . . my mind
> was fixed on it with a fondness which was extreme, the purpose firmly
> declared to the President, when I became assailed from all quarters
> with a variety of objections. Among these it was urged that my re-
> tiring just when I had been attacked in the public papers, would injure
> me in the eyes of the public. . . . These representations have for some
> weeks passed, shaken a determination which I had thought the whole
> world could not have shaken . . .[72]

And it was shortly afterward that he wrote to Washington, as we have
noted, promising to stay on until the autumn of 1793.

Jefferson now secretly drew up a series of resolutions which he
hoped would end in Hamilton's resignation. He accused him of alter-
ing the disposition of funds raised in Europe without telling Congress,
of negotiating a loan at the Bank of the United States against the
public interest, and of arrogance toward the House of Representatives. He also accused Hamilton of manipulating the market for the
benefit of speculators, and implied that there were shortages in the
Treasury accounts, but these charges were eliminated by Congressman William Branch Giles of Virginia for lack of evidence. Giles himself introduced the nine resolutions on February 27, 1793, and Jefferson
never admitted authorship.[73]

Giles made his speech in the House three days before Congress
was to adjourn, assuming that Hamilton would have no time for a
reply and that the scandals could fester over the summer. But Hamilton, in a prodigious burst of labor, prepared replies to all the charges
in two days, and answered them with such brilliance and forensic
skill that he was acquitted on every point by a healthy congressional
majority. Jefferson now felt himself worsted in a peculiarly personal
contest. As he put it graphically to Madison, he was descending
"daily into the arena like a gladiator to suffer martyrdom in every
conflict." [74]

In April, five weeks after this defeat, Jefferson turned fifty. He
celebrated by shipping most of his books and furniture home to
Monticello, and shortly wrote the letter to Madison we have already
quoted, in which he wrote, "The motion of my blood no longer

keeps time with the tumult of the world." In reply to Madison's plea that he stay on in office, he said bluntly, "Inclination cuts off all argument, and so never let there be more between you and me on this subject." [75] He did stay on until the end of December 1793, partly because of the importunities of Washington, partly because he was intent on leaving a clean desk, with no major tasks undone.[76] But he did not stay because of lingering hopes of toppling his younger rival. Hamilton, he was now sure, was impregnable. His departure for Monticello, as James Flexner tells us in his final volume on Washington, "was for the President a tragedy." [77]

CHAPTER XX

Disillusionment in Eden

These mountains are the Eden of the United States. . . .

Jefferson to the Comte de Volney, April 9, 1797 [1]

The most mysterious of all periods in Jefferson's life was his three-year retirement at Monticello, from his arrival in early January 1794 to his departure for Philadelphia as vice-president-elect in February 1797. Henry Randall wrote long ago that many believed his declarations on his retirement "were pure pretences—unfelt—and only designed to play off a stale game to deceive the public, while he was busy as a spider secretly weaving his political webs; setting on foot political machinations to favor his own progress to the Presidency . . . dictating all the secret arrangements of his party." [2] This faithful biographer denied it all, holding that zeal for office was not characteristic of the time, and that Washington himself had no affection even for the presidency. The old suspicion has come down to us, however, especially in the biography of Nathan Schachner, who described Jefferson's renunciation of politics as largely "pretense." [3]

There can be no question that Jefferson really believed in the finality of his retirement, as the barrage of letters he sent to his friends trumpeting this finality attests, though the very thoroughness with which he burned his bridges is evidence of his own recognition of the seductive power of politics which had so often in the past enticed him back. He abandoned newspaper subscriptions, and let his letters, which normally poured out in a daily stream, shrink to a mere trickle. To the new Secretary of State, his friend Edmund Randolph, he wrote wryly and with just a hint of shame on February 3, 1794, "I think it is Montaigne who has said, that ignorance is the softest pillow on which a man can rest his head. I am sure it is true as to everything political, and shall endeavor to estrange myself to everything of that character." But to Madison, to whom he wrote three months after leaving Philadelphia, there was no hint of apology or frustration. "I have never seen a Philadelphia paper since I left . . . have never had a wish to see one, and believe that I never shall take another newspaper of any sort. I find my mind totally absorbed in my rural occupations." [4]

To John Adams, who had sent him a book and wished him well in his retirement, he replied that it "had been postponed for years too long." "I return to farming with an ardor which I scarcely knew in my youth, and which has got the better entirely of my love of study." After a year at Monticello he wrote to a French friend, François d'Ivernois, "I have returned, with infinite appetite, to the enjoyment of my farm, my family and my books." [5] Infinitely the happier, totally absorbed, ardor, infinite appetite—these are strong words with the unmistakable flavor of sexuality. They suggest that satisfactions of the body at Monticello were real. But if this was true, so too were the satisfactions of power. At home he was a monarch without rivals. The outpouring of love and admiration from his family and slaves was continuous; whatever covert resentment and hatred existed at Monticello was either disguised or repressed altogether.

Sally Hemings bore two daughters during Jefferson's retirement, the first, named Harriet, on October 5, 1795.[6] Seven weeks afterward Jefferson wrote to Edward Rutledge, "Your son . . . found me in a retirement I doat on, living like an Antediluvian patriarch among my children & grandchildren, and tilling my soil." [7] So the appropriate though oblique reference to Abraham, seen earlier in his letters to Maria Cosway, surfaced again. Another daughter, Edy, was born to Sally in 1796. Apparently she died in infancy, for her name appears only twice on the bread and fish distribution lists, and then disappears.[8]

During the early part of his retirement, Martha and her husband were away for long periods; relatives and friends visited only in the summer. During most of the year Jefferson lived virtually isolated in a community inhabited almost entirely by a hundred-odd black slaves. In this respect his retirement was very like a return to his childhood in Tuckahoe. And the regression, which infected every aspect of his life, had unexpected consequences.

For the first year one sees in his letters an almost monotonous insistence on his delight in his new tranquillity. To Washington he wrote on May 14, 1794, "I cherish tranquillity too much to suffer political things to enter my mind at all," and he turned down Washington's offer of a post as special envoy to Spain in August with the curt denial, "No circumstances, my dear sir, will ever tempt me to engage in anything public." [9] To Harry Remson he wrote, "Politics are entirely banished from my mind"; to John Adams, "Tranquillity becomes daily more and more the object of my life"; to Archibald Stuart, "My philosophy [is] to encourage the tranquillizing passion." [10] To Madison, who never gave up hope that Jefferson's slumbering political genius would reawaken and who continually fed him political material, Jefferson wrote defiantly on December 28, 1794, that he would not give up his life at Monticello "for the empire of the universe." [11]

Madison meanwhile had found a new and unexpected personal happiness of his own. In 1791, about a year after his return from Paris, Jefferson had urged Madison to move into his own suite. "Come and take a bed and plate with me. I have four rooms of which any one is at your service. . . . To me it will be a relief from the solitude of which I have too much." [12] But Madison had not come, and though they had taken a four-week vacation trip to upper New York and New England together, and had visited at each other's houses on many occasions, there seems to have been a line of intimacy neither would cross. Their affection for each other, and dependence upon each other, was rigorously controlled, and mostly, it would seem, went unmentioned. A grave reserve, a studied formality, dominated the letters they exchanged, and it seems likely that an important aspect of this formality was resolutely carried over into their private association. This may have been one reason their collaboration was so long-lived, and so marvelously profitable for American political development.

It was shortly after Jefferson's departure from Philadelphia that Madison fell in love with Dolley Payne Todd. Frightened away from courtship back in 1782, when he had been turned down by the fifteen-year-old Catherine Floyd, he had remained a bachelor until 1794 when he first saw the vivacious twenty-six-year-old widow. The terrible yellow fever epidemic of 1793 had killed her husband, parents-in-law, and newborn baby. But by April of 1794 she was being seen in the company of Aaron Burr, and though Burr was still married gossip linked their names together in a romance, especially after Dolley appointed him guardian of her two-year-old son. Her letters of the time indicate, however, that she was far more excited by the most eligible bachelor in Philadelphia, "the great little Madison" she called him, than by the flirtatious young lawyer from New York.[13]

Madison, usually the soul of precision, wrote of his marriage to Dolley Todd in a letter to Jefferson that was strikingly awkward and circuitous, describing the ceremony as "the epoch at which I had the happiness to accomplish the alliance which I intimated to you I have been sometime soliciting." [14] He took his new bride to Monticello in the spring of 1795. One can only wonder how Jefferson, seeing the unmistakable happiness of his old friend, felt about his own twelve-year failure to seek out a similarly marriageable woman. Whether he confided in Madison his affection for Sally Hemings, or instead went to great lengths to preserve his façade of secrecy and evasion, one cannot know for certain, though the latter seems the much more likely. Later, when the press first broke the story of the liaison, Madison called it "incredible." [15]

During Jefferson's first year of retirement he worked furiously at farming, trying to repair his eroded fields, and planned an elaborate crop-rotation system to restore the fertility of the soil. He established a small nail factory, where young slaves made up to 10,000 nails a day, bringing in a much needed cash income, until a deluge of cheap nails from England virtually destroyed his market. The *Garden Book*, neglected for years, was now burgeoning with planting notations. He listed vegetables, currants, berries, and herbs enough to delight the palate of a French prince—sage, balm, mint, thyme, lavender, marjoram, camomile, tansy, rue, wormwood, southernwood, rosemary, and hyssop. There were listings of Indian peas, corn, buckwheat, Irish potatoes, and dry rice. His slaves planted 1,157 peach trees, which were arranged in divided rows with a road between. To anyone reading his letters having to do with planting at Monticello in these years it is apparent that he hoped to transform his 10,000 rugged acres eventually into a well-manicured English country landscape. "These mountains," he wrote to his French philosopher friend, the Comte de Volney, "are the Eden of the United States for soil, climate, navigation and health." [16]

In 1795, probably to his astonishment, Jefferson received two letters from Maria Cosway. There was nothing in them about her long abandonment of her husband and child, or even an indication that she had been away from London at all save the single line, "I am come home to England," and her reference to her daughter, "I have found a pretty little girl . . ." [17] Jefferson took over six months to reply. He began then gallantly enough, "I am eating the peaches, grapes and figs of my own garden & I only wish I could eat them in your native country, gathered on the spot & in your good company." He suggested a trip with her to Italy, a safe enough gesture for he indicated he would invite also Mrs. Church and Madame de Corny. Then he came back abruptly to reality:

> We will leave the rest of the journey to imagination, & return to what is real. I am become, for instance, a real farmer, measuring fields,

following my ploughs, helping the haymakers. . . . How better this, than to be shut up in the four walls of an office, the sun ever excluded . . . the morning opening with the fable repeated of the Augean stable, a new load of labours in place of the old. . . . From such a life, good Lord, deliver me!

He went on to suggest that his present life had something of the quality of Eden. "I am permitted from the innocence of the scenes around me to learn to practice innocence toward all, hurt to none, help to as many as I am able." [18]

It was all very idyllic, this garden of retirement. But nothing happened quite as Jefferson described it. The rains continued to erode his fields, which he had not yet learned to protect by contour plowing. The olive and orange trees he had brought from Italy sickened, as did the sugar maples from New England. Two years after leaving politics he wrote to George Washington, "Never had any reformer so barbarous a state of things to encounter as I have. It will be the work of years before the eye will find satisfaction in my fields." [19] To Francis Willis he complained—and here one who remembers his tender descriptions of the "mulatto hills . . . also whitish" in Germany may also wonder whether the complaint screened a more subtle sorrow— "My hills are too rough ever to please the eye, and as yet unreclaimed from the barbarous state in which the slovenly business of tobacco making has left them." [20]

The erosion of his fields was as nothing compared with the erosion in his family of the love and peace he had come home to enjoy. In the first seven months of his retirement both his daughters, Martha's husband, and her two small children lived with him at Monticello. Randolph was given to sudden rages which Martha, accustomed to a father who was serenity itself in her presence, could have found only incomprehensible. Henry Randall wrote of the son-in-law, "If his father-in-law was a bold rider, he was a desperate one. Darkness, the swollen ford, the rushing river, the wildly beating storm, stopped not his journey when his horse's head was pointed homeward. The tall spare figure wrapped in a horseman's cloak, the blazing but abstracted eye, the powerful blood-horse, splashed with mud and foam, and dashing swiftly onward, are yet familiar objects in the recollections of many." [21]

By August 1794 Randolph had developed a mysterious health problem. He began traveling from one doctor to another, first as far as Boston, later from spa to spa in Virginia. Jefferson was far too protective of his daughter to intimate anything about mental illness in any letter, but others who knew young Randolph described him as "an eccentric man of genius," "a wild visionary, and a victim to the delusions of a vivid imagination." His later breakdowns [22] leave no doubt that he suffered from some kind of mental ailment, and one suspects that living with his prestigious and inordinately possessive father-in-law served greatly to exacerbate it. Randolph would once write plaintively to Jefferson that when living at Monticello he felt like "the proverbially silly bird" who could not "feel at . . . ease among swans." [23] Martha, by continuing to rate her father first in the hierarchy of her affections, served only to remind her husband of his manifest deficiencies. Even eight years after her marriage she could write to her father that no "*new* ties can weaken the first and best of nature." [24]

If Jefferson was inept at handling family finances, Randolph was infinitely worse. Though he had been given a great deal of land by his father and father-in-law, as well as slaves, there never seemed to be enough cash for Martha. Jefferson's account book shows that in addition to many small sums for her, on October 7, 1795, he loaned his son-in-law £1,248.[25] Randolph's health problem was so critical in the summer of 1795—Jefferson described it to Madison as "nearly hopeless." [26]—that it was decided the two small Randolph children, Anne, who was four, and Thomas Jefferson, almost two, would come to Monticello and live with their grandfather. Polly, called Maria since the days of her schooling in France, would help in their care. Randolph's self-esteem, already badly damaged, could hardly have been bolstered by the fact that Jefferson had taken over the raising of his two children. During the next two years Martha and her husband either lived alone at their Varina plantation on the James River, or traveled about in a desperate search for the tranquillity Jefferson was himself constantly writing about.

Jefferson treasured his grandchildren, but the small Jefferson missed his mother, and was broken-hearted when she returned on one visit and took Anne away but left him behind at Monticello. She promised to return for him but did not. Jefferson hinted at the boy's distress in a letter to his daughter later. "We are all well here, my dear daughter, and Jefferson particularly so. He often repeats that you told a story, 'that you did,' when you got into the carriage and said you would come back for him. His cheeks swell with emphasis as he asseverates this." And he wrote delicately to his son-in-law to avoid medicines, to exercise, and by "the force of reason" endeavor "to counteract the mechanical effects of the disease on your spirits." [27]

Meanwhile Jefferson himself, for all his cheerful descriptions about his life in retirement, was actually suffering severe health problems of his own. He confided in Madison, writing on April 27, 1795, "My health is entirely broken down within the last eight months." [28] We would know nothing about the nature of this "breaking down" were it not that seven years later, when with great foreboding he saw in his daughter Maria symptoms of withdrawal and alienation from society, he wrote her a letter remarkable for its candor and self-revelation, in which he reported what had happened to him during this period of presumed tranquillity and happiness in his special Eden.

> I think I discover in you a willingness to withdraw from society more than is prudent. I am convinced our own happiness requires that we should continue to mix with the world, and to keep pace with it as it goes; and that every person who retires from free communication with it is severely punished afterwards by the state of mind into which they get, and which can only be prevented by feeding our sociable principles.
>
> I can speak from experience on this subject. From 1793. to 1797. I remained closely at home, saw none but those who came there, and at length became very sensible of the ill effect it had upon my own mind, and of it's direct and irresistible tendency to render me unfit for society, and uneasy when necessarily engaged in it. I felt enough of the effect of withdrawing from the world then, to see that it led to an antisocial and misanthropic state of mind, which severely punishes him who gives in to it: and it will be a lesson I never shall forget as to myself.[29]

The summertime, normally the happiest period at Monticello, was spoiled in 1795 by the illnesses of his daughter Maria, his two visiting sisters, and their slaves. The house, he wrote to Martha, "has been a mere hospital." [30] His depression deepened when he learned that the burden of his debts, already more than £7,500, was to be even heavier when another £1,000 was added in 1795 by a new judgment against the property formerly belonging to his father-in-law John Wayles. This was a direct result of the treaty John Jay had negotiated with the British, which Jefferson had denounced privately as "a monument of folly or venality . . . universally execrated." [31] The Jay Treaty provisions permitted new hope to British merchants who had brought suit to get payment of private American debts, and this included debts Jefferson thought properly paid off when he sold property during the Revolution and paid the money into the Virginia Land Office. His own British creditors, who refused the depreciated currency from the Land Office, brought two suits against Jefferson, and he lost them both. It is small wonder that Jefferson wrote bitterly to his good friend Mann Page on August 30, 1795: "I do not believe with the Rochefoucaults and Montaignes, that fourteen out of fifteen men are rogues. . . . But I have always found that rogues would be uppermost." [32] The final blow fell when Justice Samuel Chase of the Supreme Court on March 19, 1796, ruled that whatever debts had been paid into the Virginia Land Office must be repaid. This cost the citizens of Virginia £272,000, sent many a destitute landowner across the Appalachians, and made Chase's name anathema in the state.

Aside from Jay's Treaty, the only certain stimulant to any kind of serious political comment from Jefferson during these years was the activity of Alexander Hamilton. In October 1794, when a few angry farmers in Pennsylvania refused to pay the tax on whiskey, and Washington sent a force of 12,000 militiamen under Hamilton to bring them to heel, Jefferson responded to the fiasco with little more than an ironic comment. The militia, he wrote to Madison, were "objects of their laughter, not of their fear." [33] But when John Beckley sent him a box of newspapers containing Hamilton's vigorous defense of Jay's Treaty, written under the pseudonyms Curtius and Camillus, Jefferson sent them along to Madison begging him to strike back. "Hamilton is really a colossus to the anti-republican party," he wrote. "Without numbers, he is an host within himself. . . . For God's sake take up your pen, and give a fundamental reply." [34]

Jefferson himself would not lift a pen of his own to write to any newspaper against what he considered a Federalist betrayal of America to the British crown. Though he denounced Jay as "a rogue of a pilot" who had run the country "into an enemy's port," he described himself in the same letter as but "a passenger, leaving the world and its government to those who are likely to live longer in it." And in an importantly revealing metaphor he likened his whole earlier career to that of Don Quixote: "I have laid up my Rosinante in his stall, before his unfitness for the road shall expose him faultering to the world." [35]

When Madison reminded Jefferson that his name would assuredly be brought up by the Republican party as a successor to Washington, Jefferson replied with a long and serious letter saying that Madison himself should be the candidate. "The little spice of ambition which I had in my younger days," he added, "has long since evaporated, and I set still less store by a posthumous than present name. . . . The question is forever closed with me. . . ." [36] He had no reluctance to convey this conviction to the more likely heir apparent, writing bluntly to John Adams, who had sent him a book from a French friend, ". . . it is on politics, a subject I never loved, and now hate. I will not promise therefore to read it thoroughly." [37] Still, there are letters written during the retirement period where the metaphorical language suggests that Jefferson had always loved, and still loved, politics, all the while he hated it. In the deepest recesses of his consciousness Jefferson felt himself to be not the liberated, unfettered, supremely tranquil man of his conscious writing but instead a giant chained, or Ulysses drugged by the singing of the Sirens. To Horatio Gates he wrote on February 3,

1794, "The length of my tether is now fixed for life between Monticello and Richmond." [38] To William Branch Giles he wrote on December 17, 1794, "Hold on then like a good & faithful seaman till our brother sailors can rouse from their intoxication & right the vessel." [39]

In January 1796, appalled at the sight of boxes of rotting manuscripts and disintegrating printed documents in his library, he wrote to George Wythe that he was "wrapping and sewing them up in oil cloth, so that neither air nor moisture can have access to [these] precious monuments of our property, and our history." And he offered to act as archivist of Virginia legal material. It was all poignantly symbolic, a struggle against the obvious rotting of his own talents and genius. Still, he specified that he would undertake the copying and preservation only "if it can be done in the neighboring towns of Charlottesville or Milton, farther than which I could not undertake to go from home." So the "tether" still held. During the whole of his thirty-seven-month period of retirement he never stirred more than seven miles from Monticello.

The first important evidence that Jefferson was emerging from the "slough of despond" into which he had fallen came in February 1796. After years of talk and desultory planning, of postponement after postponement, Jefferson finally began to remodel his Monticello house. Broken stone had been brought up the mountain for the new foundation as early as January 1793. Slaves made bricks through the summer of 1794, so many that Jefferson wrote to George Wythe in October 1799, "We are now living in a brick kiln." [40] But almost two years passed before he ordered the beginning of the actual demolition. He planned to tear down the front façade and part of the second story, widening the house, and expanding the front into an impressive foyer with a balcony, topped by an octagonal roof. This new dome, he later admitted to a friend, was built on the same principle as the dome of the Halle aux Bleds.[41]

The possibility can be suggested that since buildings often symbolize in dreams the body of a woman, Jefferson, in tearing down and rebuilding Monticello after the pattern of the place where he first met Maria Cosway, may have been unconsciously defining and redefining the ideal woman, which he had clearly not yet found in his own life. The very act of tearing down and reconstructing suggests also, and perhaps more importantly, a preoccupation with his own somewhat damaged psyche, his own "unfitness for the road," and a conscious effort to remake, if not himself, at least the dwelling place of his body and the delight of his intellect and whole aesthetic consciousness. Dumas Malone has written that Monticello was "his home, his body, the center of his personal universe."

It can be argued also that there was a wholly practical reason for remodeling the Monticello house, that Jefferson expected his daughter Martha and her family to move in with him each summer and needed new bedrooms, and that the architect in Jefferson would never be content with less than perfection in his own villa. But the remodeling of Monticello was no mere working out of a practical plan to add extra bedrooms and achieve aesthetic perfection. The timing of the demolition and the beginnings of the rebuilding had a great deal to do with Jefferson's emergence from his long period of depression. The reconstruction was obviously therapeutic. His letters now take on a whole new quality of vitality and exuberance, and one may safely insist that whatever the nature of the unconscious healing process, the rebuilding of Monticello symbolized for Jefferson something of very great psychic significance. It was no accident that this coincided with a revival of his interest in politics and his reëntry into political life.

Still, the recovery was uneven, as can be expected with prolonged depression. In late April 1796 Jefferson was seriously ill again, so much so that he despaired of his life. Though he was only fifty-three, he may have had morbid recollections at this time about his father's dying. Peter Jefferson had been carried off at forty-nine. To his old friend Philip Mazzei, now back in Florence, he wrote on April 24, "I begin to feel the effects of age. My health has suddenly broken down, with symptoms which give me to believe I shall not have much to encounter of the *tedium vitae.*" Still, he was well enough in this same letter to write a lively description of the state of American politics, which he found deplorable. Since his own departure from the government, he said, it had been taken over by "timid men who prefer the calm of despotism to the boisterous sea of liberty," by leaders who were assimilating "the rotten as well as the sound parts of the British model." In a line later made famous by publication, he continued, "It would give you a fever were I to name to you the apostates who have gone over to these heresies, men who were Samsons in the field and Solomons in the council, but who have had their heads shorn by the harlot England." Though this was obviously an attack on Washington and Hamilton, the metaphorical language is most curious, and it may well be that on a less obvious level Jefferson was describing himself—that it was he who preferred the "calm of despotism" as slaveholder at peaceful Monticello rather than the turbulent sea of liberty in Philadelphia, that it was he who had been shorn of his God-given strength by an alien Delilah from a people who, at least when surly and threatening in their bondage, could not but be the enemy.

In this same letter to Mazzei Jefferson also wrote, "We have only to awake and snap the Lilliputian cords with which they have been entangling us during the first sleep which succeeded our labors." [42] Like

Gulliver, Jefferson himself was a giant being held by a thousand small cords. The fact that his own major entanglement, his tethering, his "intoxication," stimulated in Jefferson fantasies of Ulysses, Gulliver, and Samson tells us something significant about one of the ingredients essential to his special illness. There can be no depression without hatred. And the nuances in these letters tell us that though being tethered at Monticello had brought love and tranquillity, capitulation to the tethering had also awakened deeply repressed rage. Perhaps this explains why Jefferson found it possible in 1796, in order to raise money to pay for the rebuilding of Monticello, to mortgage all his slaves.[43]

CHAPTER XXI

Triangles at Monticello

It is easier to concieve than express the sensations which the sight of the preparations for your return inspires us. I look forward to Thursday with raptures and palpitations not to be described; that day which will once more reunite me to those most dear to me in the world.

Martha Jefferson Randolph to Jefferson, July 1, 1798 [1]

When the celebrated French republican savant and refugee, the Comte de Volney, visited Monticello in June 1796, he noted in his journal astonishment at seeing slave children as white as himself. *"Mais je fus étonné de voir appeler noirs et traiter comme tels des enfants aussi blanc que moi."* [2] Volney, who had known both Jefferson and Franklin in Paris, had joyfully joined the revolutionary intellectuals only to end up in prison during the Terror of 1793, and had barely escaped the guillotine. Jefferson was delighted to see him, and despite the demolition work at Monticello persuaded him to stay three weeks. Volney had an estate in Corsica to rival that of Jefferson and was equally excited about plants and planting. He had brought his book, *Les Ruines; ou, Meditations sur les révolutions des empires*, a vitriolic attack on the French clergy, which so gratified Jefferson he promised to translate it for the American market. Volney brought also a firsthand account of the debasement of the revolution to which he and Jefferson had helped give birth.

If Jefferson was saddened by Volney's account of how the Revolution was murdering its own sons, Volney for his part was appalled by the sight of his celebrated libertarian friend acting the role of *maître*, and still more appalled by the *"demi-nudité misérable et hideuse"* of his

287

field-hand slaves. Volney wrote in his journal of "*ces figures hagardes, cet air inquiet, cachotier* (sic), *ces regards craintifs et haineux,*" adding, "*tout cet ensemble me saisit d'un premier sentiment de tristesse et de terreur que je dus voiler.*" When they visited the fields, he wrote, Jefferson carried "*un fouet,*" a small whip, which he shook at the obviously indolent. There followed "*une scène comique,*" with the slaves working furiously under their master's menacing gestures, only to relapse into lassitude as soon as his back was turned.[3]

The spectacle of Jefferson shaking a whip runs counter to the idyllic image of the gentle master which has been transmitted by American historians for almost two centuries. We know that as president he wrote to his son-in-law specifically forbidding his overseers to use the whip "but in extremities," because it served to "degrade" the slaves "in their own eyes."[4] But the comic aspect—Volney likened the scene to troops of trained monkeys and dogs dancing to the baton of a master on the Paris streets—suggests that Jefferson's growling and threatening was a piece of expected theater, and that the slaves recognized it as such. Still, the scene is a troubling one, and helps to explain why Jefferson would write morosely, as he did to Stephens T. Mason on October 27, 1799, "I find I am not fit to be a farmer with the kind of labor we have."[5]

Another distinguished French refugee, the Duc de la Rochefoucauld-Liancourt, who followed Volney to Monticello in June 1796 and stayed a week, painted a quite different picture. "His negroes are nourished, clothed, and treated as well as white servants could be," he wrote, and said Jefferson "animates them by rewards and distinctions; in fine, his superior mind directs the management of his domestic concerns with the same abilities, activity, and regularity which he evinced in the conduct of public affairs."[6] And he made no reference to "white" slave children whose presence had so shocked Volney. Volney would naturally not have asked Jefferson who had fathered these children. But he did write in his journal that miscegenation was common among the mulatto slave women and the white workmen, many of them foreigners, and indentured servants.[7]

If Jefferson needed a warning about keeping his liaison with a slave woman hidden, which is unlikely, his secrecy could only have been reinforced by the spectacle of what had recently happened to another famous French exile, Talleyrand, who after fleeing to the United States in 1794 had scandalized the citizens of Philadelphia by openly escorting a handsome mulatto woman about the streets. The result, as one biographer of Talleyrand put it, was that he "signed his own social death warrant."[8] Washington had refused to see him from the beginning for political reasons, but once the news of this indiscretion was bruited about, the doors of fashionable Philadelphia closed tight against him. Paris had tolerated and protected Talleyrand even though, as a priest, he had a reputation for being a libertine. He had mistaken the New World for Jamaica, where, as Edward Long wrote in 1774, "He who would presume to shew any displeasure against such a thing as simple fornication, would for his pains be accounted a simple blockhead; since not one in twenty can be persuaded, that there is either sin; or shame in cohabiting with his slave." [9]

Virginia was far more parochial than either Paris or Jamaica. Trapped in a system which permitted interracial sex as long as it was kept secret, and which continued to encourage the open sale of men, women, and children as if it were a God-given right, Jefferson was pulled first in the direction of his revolutionary idealism and then in its opposite. This we see particularly in 1794. His account book for November 19, 1794, contains the following entry:

> The draught on Maury is by order of James Monroe in part of his debit for Thenia & her children, valued at £173. currency exchange was then 40 pct. which makes it £125–11–5 ster.

Thenia was Sally Hemings' twenty-seven-year-old sister.[10] Perhaps Monroe, who lived on a plantation nearby, owned the father of her children, and Jefferson sold her to unite a family. This he did on other occasions. However, the evidence that Jefferson would sell any Hemings family slave indicates how far he had slipped backward from the emancipation zeal of his earlier years. He could have freed her, as her father, John Wayles, could have freed her years earlier. Neither of them chose this course. Later, in 1806, the Virginia legislature passed a law saying that all slaves emancipated after May 1, 1806, must be banished within twelve months "or sold for the benefit of the literary fund." [11] But this peculiarly barbarous law was not in force in 1794. At this point emancipation was relatively easy in Virginia.

Jefferson did free Sally's brother Robert Hemings, this in the same year he sold her sister Thenia. Robert had fallen in love with a slave woman belonging to George Frederick Strauss in Richmond, and had had a child by her. Strauss advanced £60 to Robert to pay for his freedom, and Jefferson signed the manumission papers on Christmas Eve 1794. However happy this emancipation celebration may have been, Jefferson made it apparent he regretted losing this slave, writing to Thomas Mann Randolph with the curious phrase that Strauss had "debauched him from me." [12] His extraordinary possessiveness regarding the Hemings slaves, and their reciprocal affection, is illuminated in a letter his daughter wrote to him on January 15, 1795, describing a visit with the newly freed Robert:

I saw Bob frequently while in Richmond. He expressed great uneasiness at having quitted you in the manner he did and repeatedly declared that he would never have left you to live with any person but his wife. He appeared to be so much affected at having deserved your anger that I could not refuse my intercession when so warmly solicited towards obtaining your forgiveness. The poor creature seems so deeply impressed with a sense of his ingratitude as to be rendered quite unhappy by it but he could not prevail upon himself to give up his wife and child.[13]

This letter illuminates also Martha's feelings toward at least one of the Hemings family, who was after all in a very real sense her uncle. She saw him "frequently," which suggests familiarity and friendship, but she also described him patronizingly as a "poor creature." Thus she defined the distance between them.

Jefferson had promised to free James Hemings when they were in Paris, but he was not eager to lose one so highly trained in French cookery. He had persuaded James to come back to Monticello from Philadelphia by giving him a promise in writing on September 15, 1793, that he would free him as soon as he taught a successor, and the emancipation celebration took place, again on a Christmas Eve, in 1795, though he was not technically free till February 5, 1796. Jefferson, on February 26 gave him $30 for his expenses to Philadelphia, and he took off happily, apparently making his way back to Paris. When he later returned, Jefferson reported to Martha with mixed fondness and exasperation, "James is returned to this place, and is not given up to drink as I had been informed. He tells me his next trip will be to Spain. I am afraid his journeys will end in the moon. I have endeavored to persuade him to stay where he is, and lay up money." [14]

In Virginia the limited enthusiasm for emancipation roused by the Revolution was largely dissipated by 1797, and whatever lingered was destroyed by news of the massacres on Santo Domingo. An uprising of blacks seeking freedom under the Jamaican voodoo priest, Boukman, beginning in 1791, had started a race war, with whites murdering blacks, with blacks murdering whites, and the mulattoes—a distinct caste group—the victims of both. When the 6,000 French soldiers on the island dwindled almost to zero, the civilian whites, who had kept control of the cities and towns, invited in British soldiers for protection. But the charismatic black commander, Toussaint L'Ouverture, fired by the egalitarian idealism of the French Revolution, built up a formidable army of blacks and mulattoes and began to drive the British out of the island. Word of his phenomenal success filtered into Virginia in the summer of 1797, and a hysteria of terror concerning slave insurrection spread through the whole South.[15]

St. George Tucker, one of the few whites in Virginia who looked upon the black liberation of Santo Domingo as good reason for emancipation in Virginia rather than as an excuse for further slave repression, wrote to Jefferson in the summer of 1797 and sent him his antislavery pamphlets,[16] warning that unless emancipation measures were immediately begun there could be a costly holocaust.. Jefferson agreed with him. "The day which begins our combustion must be near at hand; and only a single spark is wanting to make that day to-morrow. . . . every delay lessens the time we may take for emancipation." He brought up his old question, "Whither shall the colored emigrants go?" Then he added a line of peculiar poignancy as it reflected his own secret dilemma: "But if something is not done, and done soon, we shall be the murderers of our own children." [17]

The necessity for secrecy concerning Jefferson's liaison with Sally Hemings pervaded every aspect of their relationship. Even in his *Farm Book* she remained surprisingly anonymous. Though he wrote Sally's name many times, on the slave inventories, the distribution lists for fish, beef, blankets, and linen, he never included her last name, as he did that of her mother and several of her brothers. He listed her often just below that of her sister Critta, and there is no indication in the *Farm Book* that she was singled out for special treatment. Jefferson noted the date of the birth of her daughter Harriet, October 5, 1795, but he did not anywhere indicate the date that this daughter died, and were it not for a letter from his daughter Martha reporting her death in late 1797 we would not know why she disappeared from the *Farm Book* listings.[18]

Jefferson listed Sally's daughter Edy twice in 1796, on bread and fish distribution lists.[19] Then she too disappears from the *Farm Book*. There is, however, a haphazard quality to all his early *Farm Book* listings. Sometimes children were listed with their mothers, often not at all, and sometimes separately, especially as the children grew older. Occasionally Jefferson noted deaths on old lists; many times he crossed out names and there is no clue as to the reason. He made slave inventories so seldom it would seem to have been an unpleasant chore. When he was vice-president his distribution lists became sporadic; when he became president they ceased altogether. Only after his retirement did the *Farm Book* reflect truly meticulous attention. Before 1810 it is a record as much of the disorder as of the order in Jefferson's life.

Jefferson delayed making a new slave inventory after his return from Paris until 1794. Then he listed Sally Hemings but not the son who had been born shortly after their return. This absence has been cited as evidence that Tom did not exist, that he was a mere creature of the poisonous imagination of James Thomson Callender. It may also be evidence that Jefferson chose to consider him free from birth, either because he had been conceived on the free soil of France, or because Jefferson had so promised his mother. On the slave inventories of 1798 and 1810 Jefferson listed Sally with subsequent children born to her— Beverly, the second Harriet, Madison, and Eston. A "Tom" shows up consistently on the food and clothing distribution lists from 1794 to 1801, but it can be persuasively argued that in every case the name stood for Tom Shackleford, an old slave wagoner and foreman of slaves whom Jefferson greatly trusted, and whom in his letters he sometimes called Shackleford and sometimes Tom. He died in 1801.

From 1773 to 1826 Jefferson owned or hired five or six different slaves named Tom. They can, with patience, be sorted out. A mysterious Tom, who cannot be easily identified, appears on an important listing in 1810, his name included in a curious manner so that he could be counted as slave or free. He appears again on a summer clothing distribution list in 1811, and then disappears. In 1811 "Tom Hemings" would have been twenty-one, the age of freedom promised to his mother in Paris. So, perhaps inadvertently, Jefferson named and counted him in this important record.[20] One must note, however, that Madison Hemings, born in 1805, makes no mention of an older brother Tom in his reminiscences, nor does his former slave friend Israel, who was born in 1800. Jefferson's granddaughter, Ellen Randolph Coolidge, in discussing what happened to the "yellow children" at Monticello in a detailed letter of great significance in this matter, wrote that she knew of her "own knowledge" that Jefferson permitted each of his slaves as were sufficiently light to pass for white to withdraw quietly from the plantation; it was called running away, but they were never reclaimed. "I remember," she wrote, "four instances of this, three young men and a girl, who walked away and staid away—their whereabouts was perfectly known but they were left to themselves—for they were white enough to pass for white." [21]

Since Jefferson mentioned three "runaways" in his *Farm Book*, two of whom, Beverly and Harriet Hemings, were Sally Hemings' children, it seems likely that the fourth was Tom Hemings, and that he left Monticello at a relatively early age, probably shortly after the story of his mother's relationship with Jefferson broke into the press in 1802. Perhaps his mother chose not to discuss this son with anyone after his departure and made every effort to protect his identity in the white society by a mantle of silence. Such behavior is common even today among relatives of a black who "passes."

The name of Sally, as we have noted, virtually disappeared from

Jefferson's account books after his return from Paris, though there are a great many expenditures for "charity" on the days of his return to and departure from Monticello, and there are those special references to his leaving sums in his "small drawer" at Monticello—$16.30 on June 4, 1806; $17.43 on May 3, 1807—and numerous notations such as "small debts 20 D." and "small expenses, 20 D." which could represent gifts he did not care to identify further. There is a single reference to Sally on September 27, 1801, when Jefferson wrote, "left . . . for Mrs. Sneed for Sally 3 D." Polly Sneed was a teacher who tutored Thomas Jefferson Randolph in 1799, and whose name appears irregularly in the account books from 1792 to 1802. It is not absolutely clear that her "services to the negro women" had to do only with the schooling, but since she charged only $6 for "6 months schooling of Thos Jefferson," Martha's eldest son, it would appear that her services to Sally Hemings had been substantial.[22]

The extent to which Jefferson kept Sally Hemings and her children relatively anonymous in his *Farm Book* would seem to be symbolic of his entire relationship with her. It was a kind of automatic denial, in the written record, that this slave woman and her children were important to him. Such denial was routine in the South, the accepted way of life. The denial was accepted too, though in a different fashion, by the slave who was genuinely loved. Here the slave was peculiarly deprived of the right to, and even the desire for, emancipation, because freedom meant loss of the love relationship. If Jefferson had freed Sally Hemings it would have been to lose her, and it meant also that she would lose him. For although a master could carry on a liaison with a slave in relative secrecy without public censure, it was very much more difficult and socially dangerous with a free Negro. And the very act of manumission had to be a matter of public record.

For Sally Hemings to have demanded freedom would have meant two things: either that she meant to leave him, as her brother James did, or that she was prepared to see his reputation damaged. As long as she remained a slave she was no threat to him of any kind. His control was total, for he retained the right to sell her if he chose. She could be of damage to him only if he freed her; by that act too he would do great social damage to himself, unless he abandoned her. But the innate decency of Jefferson, as well as his whole libertarian philosophy, must have cried out against this terrible anomaly, and the conflict over it must certainly have contributed to his depression. The injustice of it all was underlined in an especially poignant fashion for both of them in 1795–96, when Martha Randolph lost a baby daughter and then Sally Hemings lost one.

Martha was visiting a health spa with her husband when her child Eleanor was born, August 30, 1795. The infant died almost immediately. When Jefferson learned of the tragedy, he sent for the tiny body and had it interred in his family burial plot.[23] But in 1796, when Sally's child Edy died, she was buried, one must presume, in the slave cemetery at Monticello. Anything else would have been unthinkable.* So the unbridgeable gap in status between daughter and mistress was underlined and perpetuated.

The effect on Jefferson's daughters of the continuing intimacy between Sally Hemings and Jefferson, as evidenced by the births of her children, is not as irrecoverable as one might suppose. All three young women knew who was in command when Jefferson was away. Jefferson made it explicit in a letter to Maria after her marriage, when she was expected to spend some time at Monticello in his absence. "The servants will be here under your commands," he wrote, "and such supplies as the house affords." [24] Maria, however, had responded with great delicacy. "The servants we shall carry up will be more than sufficient for ourselves and you would perhaps prefer yours being employed in some way or other." [25] Still, no one could have lived long at Monticello without knowing that Sally Hemings was in charge of Jefferson's "chamber and wardrobe." [26] Martha's own son related that his mother never sat in her father's bedroom-sitting room. It was, he wrote, Jefferson's *sanctum sanctorum.*" [27] Something of the nature of the accommodation Jefferson's daughters made is revealed in the nuances of their correspondence with their father. Two surprises emerge from their letters, one that Jefferson was in a continuing agony of apprehension lest he lose his daughters' love, and second, that Martha at least, instead of showing revulsion and indignation, engaged in a heightened and almost palpable seduction of her father in her letters, a seduction that was as innocent as it was unconscious.

The political story of Jefferson's abandonment of his Eden for the maelstrom of politics—which meant that letters to his daughters became frequent—will be recounted in the following chapter. The personal story as it related to his daughters is not entirely independent of the political happenings, but can be examined quite by itself. When Jefferson was elected vice-president, he went off alone to the inauguration ceremony. Neither of his daughters accompanied him. He stayed in Philadelphia only eleven days, March 2 through March 12, 1797. During his absence Maria went to stay with Martha at the Varina

* The slave cemetery at Monticello has long since disappeared, but one grave marker was recently unearthed. It reads in part, "My dear affectionate wife Priscilla Hemmings, departed this life on Friday, the 7th of May 1830, age 54."

plantation. Jefferson wrote to Maria and to Thomas Mann Randolph on March 11; astonishingly he wrote not a single detail in his letter about the ceremony, and no hint of his exhilaration at being back on the political scene. There is a little gossip in his letter to Maria about her Philadelphia friends, and a suggestion that she stay longer with her sister. Then followed an almost desperate affirmation of his affection:

> On my part, my love to your sister and yourself knows no bounds, and as I scarcely see any other object in life, so would I quit it with desire whenever my continuance in it shall become useless to you.[28]

"I live only to love and be loved by you"; this was Jefferson's unceasing cry. But he did not honor either of his daughters by real communication on any other level.

Maria followed his admonition and stayed with her sister, so when Jefferson returned to Monticello from the inauguration ceremonies he had no one save his slaves to whom he could describe the excitement of his becoming the vice-president of the United States. They were not enough. Desolate, he wrote to Martha on March 27, 1797, "The bloom of Monticello is chilled by my solitude. It makes me wish the more that yourself and your sister were here to enjoy it. I value the enjoiments of this life only in proportion as you participate them with me. All other attachments are weakening, and I approach the state of mind when nothing will hold me here but my love for yourself and sister and the tender connections you have added to me. I hope you will write to me as nothing is so pleasing during your absence as these proofs of your love. Be assured my dear daughter that you possess mine in it's utmost limits." [29]

Again, there was no description of the inauguration, no mention even of the new President, John Adams, whom Martha had known in Paris. There was, however, an important communication, which Martha —the seducer and the seduced—could not have missed: *All other attachments are weakening; nothing will keep me in Monticello but my love for you and your sister.* Though Martha was distressed to the point of morbidity by the dangers involved in the imminent inoculation of her children against smallpox, she nevertheless replied immediately: "The anxiety I feel on their account my Dear Father does not prevent my feeling most sensibly for the solitude and gloom of your present situation. I never take a view of your solitary fire side but my heart swells. However as nothing detains us now but the children I hope soon [to] be restored to your paternal embraces." [30]

Here one sees an elaborate fiction being maintained between Jefferson and Martha concerning his relations with Sally Hemings. Martha would insist always that Jefferson's fireside was "solitary" unless she was there to share it. Her son, Thomas Jefferson Randolph, related many years later that only once in all his memory did his mother refer to the stories that Jefferson had fathered Sally Hemings' children, and then she made a stiff-lipped denial. This he related to Henry Randall, who reported the conversation:

> Mr. Jefferson's oldest daughter, Mrs. Gov. Randolph, took the Dusky Sally stories much to heart. But she never spoke to her sons but once on the subject. Not long before her death she called two of them—the Colonel and George Wythe Randolph—to her. She asked the Colonel if he remembered when "—— Henings (the slave who most resembled Mr. Jefferson) was born." He said he could answer by referring to the book containing the list of slaves. He turned to the book and found that the slave was born at the time supposed by Mrs. Randolph. She then directed her sons attention to the fact that Mr. Jefferson and Sally Henings could not have met—were far distant from each other—for fifteen months prior to such birth. She bade her sons (to) remember this fact, and always to defend the character of their grandfather.[31]

The *Farm Book*, plus the elaborate chronologies made by Jefferson scholars which document almost every day of his life, demonstrate that contrary to what Martha Randolph told her sons, Jefferson was not only not "distant" from Sally Hemings but in the same house nine months before the births of each of her seven children, and that she conceived no children when he was not there. This Martha must have known, but in the fashion of children who repress what they cannot bear to know, manufactured a denial that came to be for her a kind of truth. The fact that Jefferson's nephew, Peter Carr, was in Monticello numerous summers up to 1796, and that he and his brother Samuel seem to have had an easy camaraderie with slave women, made the denial easier. Sometime, exactly when one cannot know, Martha Randolph convinced herself that it was the Carr brothers who fathered Sally Hemings' children, and in one fashion or another communicated this to her children.[32] The fact that Sally's oldest son had been conceived in France seems to have been conveniently forgotten.

Maria, who had never been as trapped as Martha in her father's inordinately possessive affection, was by 1797 deeply in love with her cousin, Jack Eppes, and trying to find the courage to tell her father. La Rochefoucauld-Liancourt, who saw her in June 1796, when she was seventeen, called her "remarkably handsome," adding that "she will, doubtless, soon find that there are duties which it is still sweeter to perform than those of a daughter."[33] Eppes had not been Maria's only suitor. Jefferson's good friend and advocate in Congress, William Branch Giles, had courted her, and Jefferson may even have preferred Giles as a potential son-in-law over his nephew. The Monticello slave Isaac, who was more sensitive than Jefferson about his daughter's passions, watched Giles being repudiated, and commiserated with his desolation.[34] Maria, for her part, was so afraid to tell her father of her true love that she left it to her sister to communicate her intention to marry.

When Jefferson received the letter, he hid his hurt that Maria had not written to him directly, and replied—to Martha, not Maria—a gallant acquiescence on her choice: "She could not have been more so to my wishes, if I had had the whole earth free to have chosen a partner for her." There followed, as so often in Jefferson's letters to Martha, a passage of important innuendo:

> I now see our fireside formed into a groupe, no member of which has a fibre in their composition which can ever produce any jarring or jealousies among us. No irregular passions, no dangerous bias, which may render problematical the future fortunes and happiness of our descendants. We are quieted as to their condition for at least one generation more.[35]

The order was clear: there must be no jarring or jealousies. These Jefferson would exclude by a simple act of will. This was Jefferson's way with his daughters. But along with the order was the reference to the "irregular passion," the "dangerous bias." Who but himself was guilty? So the faint hint of apology, regret, and shame surfaced again.

Maria was married to Jack Eppes in a quiet ceremony at Monticello on October 13, 1797, midst all the demolition chaos. Jefferson gave the couple "26 slaves, with certain stock of horses, cattle and hogs," along with 819½ acres as close to Monticello as Martha's acreage at Edgehill, and begged that if they chose to live away from Monticello at all, "it must be at Pantops." [36] Fortunately for their marriage, there was no house at Pantops, and Maria and her husband settled near his parents in Eppington. Jefferson found the distance intolerable.

When he went back to Philadelphia on December 4, 1797, Sally Hemings was again pregnant, and her children were ill. A few days after his departure the two-year-old Harriet died. Martha Randolph, living at nearby Varina, waited six weeks before informing her father:

> Pleurisies, rheumatism and every disorder proceeding from cold have been so frequent that we have scarcely had at any one time *well* enough to tend the sick. Our intercourse with Monticello has been allmost

daily. They have been generally well there except Tom and Goliah who are both *about* again and poor little Harriot who died a few days after you left us.[37]

Goliah was a small slave child, age six. Sally Hemings' son Tom in December 1797 would have been about seven. There were two old slaves—Goliah, and Tom Shackleford—but Martha made no effort to distinguish which of the slaves she was writing about, and took for granted that her father knew. If the "pleurisy" she mentioned was the great killer of children, diphtheria, it would have ravaged the small children and left untouched the old slaves, who had long since developed an immunity through exposure. If this is so, then this letter is of special significance on more than one count; it is evidence from Martha herself that there was a child named Tom whom Jefferson cared enough about that she felt an obligation to report on his recovery.[38] The letter also tells us, by implication, that Martha acted as if no letters were ever exchanged between her father and Sally Hemings.

When Martha wrote this letter reporting Harriet Hemings' death, she must have known that Sally Hemings was again pregnant, and that the child had been conceived during her father's five-month stay at Monticello—July 11 to December 4, 1797.[39] What we see in this letter, following the death announcement, is a very special outpouring of affection:

> I look forward with great impatience to March. I am afraid to flatter my self with the hope of seeing you sooner and I feel every day more strongly the impossibility of becoming habituated to your absence. Separated in my infancy from every other friend, and accustomed to look up to you alone, every sentiment of tenderness my nature was susceptible of was for many years centered in you, and no connexion formed since that could weaken a sentiment interwoven with my very existence.[40]

If Jefferson wrote to Sally Hemings about the death of little Harriet, as seems likely, there is no record of it. He did write immediately to Martha. It is an altogether extraordinary letter. He made no mention of the bad news in her letter, denying by omission the importance of what she had written to him, expressing instead relief at her reassurances of love, and begging her to move back to Monticello. The letter began, "I ought oftener, my dear Martha, to receive your letters, for the very great pleasure they give me, and especially when they express your affections for me. For though I cannot doubt them, yet they are among the truths which tho' not doubted we love to hear repeated." Still, the heart of the letter was heavy with melancholy and laced with desire: "Indeed I feel myself detaching very fast, perhaps too fast, from every thing but yourself, your sister, and those who are identified with you. These form the last hold the world will have on me, the cords which will be cut only when I am loosened from this state of being. I am looking forward to the spring with all the fondness of desire to meet you all once more." [41] Martha might well have misinterpreted the letter to read what she fondly hoped, that the death of this child had had no special impact on her father. For we can be sure she was very intent on one thing, that her father love her own children beyond all others. In this, as we shall see, she may well have succeeded.

Sally Hemings bore a son, whom she named Beverly, on April 1, 1798.[42] Jefferson, who was in Philadelphia at the time, noted in his account book on April 2, "Gave Laurence Allwine ord on Barnes for 26 D. for a stick sopha and mattras." Allwine was a Philadelphia furniture maker. It is possible that the sofa and mattress were ordered for Sally Hemings in anticipation of the birth. In the same week that he purchased them, he wrote to Martha of buying "an excellent harpsichord for Maria," which he ordered sent to Monticello. Martha, who dined at Monticello on April 28, inspected the harpsichord, which she described as "a charming one I think tho certainly inferior to mine." She did not mention the birth of Sally Hemings' new son.[43]

Jefferson, before receiving this letter, had written to Martha "to express all my love to you, and my wishes once more to find myself in the only scene where, for me, the sweeter affections of life have any exercise." [44] And when he reported definite plans for a visit to Monticello in July she responded with the letter quoted at the beginning of this chapter, in which she wrote of her "raptures and palpitations not to be described." [45]

Jefferson's correspondence with Maria lacked the special fervor of his exchanges with Martha, though he continued his pressure upon her to return to live near Monticello. Maria refused, at least in the beginning of her marriage, to let herself be drawn into her father's web. She wrote to him infrequently when he was vice-president; in one letter she inadvertently referred to her father-in-law as "my father," [46] which must have caused Jefferson special pain.

Maria, moreover, could needle her father a little. After a visit to Petersburg in May 1798 in which she had met John and Betsey Walker, she felt free to hint at the ancient scandal, though this was long before it broke into the newspapers: "We there met with Mr. John Walker and his lady, the latter seem'd pleas'd to see me and press'd me to visit her at her house, but I was not sorry that her husband did not think proper to invite me, for it would have been disagreeable to be forced to invent excuses where there was one so evident and so insurmountable." [47] But there is no hint in any letter of Maria's that has been preserved that she even knew a slave called Sally Hemings.

Though Martha and her family visited Monticello often during Jefferson's vice-presidency, there were many months when he was home without either daughter; so light were his duties that from the time of his election in December 1796 until his election as president (finally settled February 17, 1801) he spent only twenty-one months in Philadelphia and the remaining twenty-seven in Monticello. In letters to his friends he often confided his delight in leaving the duties of office to return to his children. He wrote to Edward Rutledge on June 24, 1797, "Tranquillity is an old man's milk. I go to enjoy it in a few days, and to exchange the roar and tumult of bulls and bears, for the prattle of my grandchildren and senile rest." [48] But Jefferson was as yet only fifty-four, and would not be "senile" at eighty-three. His metaphor of "old man's milk" could distantly suggest a young breast on which to lay his head.

CHAPTER XXII

Candidate à Contre Coeur

Let those come to the helm who think they can steer clear of the difficulties. I have no confidence in myself for the undertaking.

Jefferson to Madison, December 17, 1796 [1]

James Madison was the nation's first president-maker. Unlike the later
political catalysts who played this role—Van Buren for Jackson, Mark
Hanna for McKinley, Colonel House for Wilson, and Louis Howe for
Franklin Roosevelt—Madison already had real political stature. In
1796, he was as deserving of the high office as Jefferson simply by
virtue of his service to the republic as the essential father of the Constitution, to say nothing of his zealous role in vote-getting and direction
of the Republican party in Congress. This Jefferson himself recognized,
and told Madison that it was he who should succeed Washington. Such
a prospect, he wrote, is "the first wish of my heart." [2]

As presidential timber, however, Madison was never Jefferson's match,
as he recognized from the beginning. Even in his physical presence
Jefferson dominated like a benign deity. Though Madison never went
out without his high conical hat, nothing served really to enhance the
physical stature of this small tense man, and it is not surprising that
Washington Irving should shrivel his image among American school
children with the contemptuous epithet "withered little applejohn."
The lively Margaret Bayard Smith, who adored Jefferson, found Madison only moderately impressive. He was "entertaining, interesting and
communicative" in private, she wrote, but once a stranger came into
the gathering he became "mute, cold and repulsive." [3] Benjamin
Rush remembered that Jefferson in 1790 described Madison as "the

greatest man in the world," [4] homage one need not take too seriously. Surely it was a superlative tossed off in affectionate banter. But there was enormous respect here; in describing Madison to a friend in 1812 he wrote with something of the earlier hyperbole, "I do not know in the world a man of purer integrity, more dispassionate, disinterested, and devoted to genuine Republicanism; nor could I in the whole scope of America and Europe point out an abler head." [5] And in his *Autobiography* Jefferson wrote of "the rich resources of his luminous and discriminating mind."

Once Washington announced that he would under no circumstances serve a third term, it was, however, Madison and not Jefferson who began to agitate quietly that his best friend be first choice of the Republican party for president. Fearing that Jefferson would forbid any party effort on his behalf, Madison now shrewdly stopped communicating with him altogether. There were as yet no formal procedures for the selection of presidential candidates, and this election saw the choices emerge through party caucuses. Importantly, once Jefferson discovered what was happening he did not withdraw his name. But he took no part in the election, and as Malone put it, "in a fatalistic mood he silently acquiesced in a judgment which the leaders of his party regarded as inevitable." [6] Under the Constitution, as yet unrevised by the Twelfth Amendment, it was altogether likely for men of different parties to be elected president and vice-president, since the first honor went to the man with the highest delegate votes, and the vice-presidency to the second highest. The Federalists united on John Adams and Thomas Pinckney, the latter chosen largely because he was a Southerner who might take votes away from Jefferson. Hamilton, who was in a frenzy lest his old cabinet rival win a surprise victory, wrote, "It is all-important to our country that Washington's successor shall be a safe man. But it is far less important who of many men that may be named shall be the person than that it shall not be Jefferson." [7]

The thought of Jefferson winning even second place as vice-president troubled John Adams. Such "opposite boxes," he wrote to Abigail, would mean "a dangerous crisis in public affairs." In any case Adams was determined never to serve under Jefferson. "I am the heir apparent," he said, ". . . but the French and the demagogues intend to set aside the descent. . . . I have no very ardent desire to be the butt of party malevolence. Having tasted that cup, I find it bitter, nauseous, and unwholesome." [8] A letter to his son during the campaign reflected the nausea. "Kings and princes will be kings and princes, in spite of experience, and demagogues will be demagogues, and people will be people . . . and mankind are condemned to such a state of humiliation that the best they can do is to set one fool, knave, and madman to watch and bind another fool, knave, and madman." [9] Still, Adams' old ebullience saved him. He was confident of victory, and of his right to be victor. He was honest and could even be self-critical, writing candidly to his wife after the election, "I have looked into myself and see no meanness or dishonesty there. I see weakness enough but no timidity." [10]

Jefferson, the most silent presidential candidate in American election history, wrote during the entire campaign not a single letter mentioning politics. Newspapers and handbills found their way to his hilltop, however, and he saw the polarization and simplification, the lofty exaggeration, the dirty innuendo. It is not clear if he knew that Hamilton secretly connived against Adams in favor of Pinckney. He would have been pleased to know that Abigail Adams preferred him to Pinckney for vice-president. This she had written privately to her husband, adding, "You know my friendship for that gentleman has lived through all his faults and errors—to which I have not been blind." [11] Jefferson had seen the Republican press praise his own "unsullied integrity" and his "zeal for human happiness," and the Federalist press attack him as inept, whimsical, indecisive, and cowardly. He had read a pamphlet by a South Carolina congressman describing him as an atheist, puppet of France, and foe of Washington and of the Union itself.[12] Jefferson complained later that he had been "a fair mark for every man's dirt." To Edward Rutledge he wrote, "I did not know myself under the pens either of my friends or foes. It is unfortunate for our peace, that unmerited abuse wounds, while unmerited praise has not the power to heal." [13]

Though Jefferson wrote privately to his son-in-law Randolph on November 28 that he sincerely wished "to be second on that vote rather than the first," [14] it is evident that he was watching the votes with fascination. Though the official tally was 71 votes for Adams, with 68 for himself, 59 for Pinckney, and 30 for Aaron Burr, he always believed that the real vote was 69 to 70, noting to Volney that "one real elector in Pennsylvania was excluded from the voting by the miscarriage of the votes, and one who was not an elector was admitted to vote." [15] The near victory astonished, exhilarated, but also frightened him. When it seemed for a time that there might be a tie vote, he wrote in consternation to Madison: "There is nothing I so anxiously hope, as that my name may come out either second or third. . . . the last would leave me at home the whole year, and the other two-thirds of it. . . . I pray you and authorize you fully, to solicit on my behalf that Mr. Adams may be preferred. He has always been my senior, from the commencement of our public life, and the expression of the public will being equal, this circumstance ought to give him the preference. . . . Let those come to the helm who think they can steer clear of the difficulties. I have no confidence in myself for the undertaking." [16]

Once his place as second was established he wrote to Edward Rutledge: "I protest before my God, that I shall from the bottom of my heart, rejoice at escaping. I know well that no man will ever bring out of that office the reputation which he carries him into it. The honeymoon would be as short in that case as in any other, and its moments of extasy would be ransomed by years of torment and hatred. . . . I have no ambition to govern men; no passion which would lead me to delight to ride in a storm." Still, there was in this letter a hint of malice against the victor. "Our eastern friend will be struggling with the storm which is gathering over us; perhaps he will be shipwrecked in it." [17]

Nevertheless, severing the tether that had kept him for over three years within a radius of seven miles of Monticello turned out to be difficult. He toyed with the idea of being sworn in as vice-president in Virginia rather than Philadelphia, but dropped the idea as socially offensive. "I shall escape into the city as covertly as possible," he wrote Madison.[18] His approach was reported, however, and he was greeted by a crowd carrying a banner, "Jefferson the Friend of the People," and by a company of artillery that fired sixteen rounds from two twelve-pounders, all of which he may have found less troublesome than he expected.

In the inaugural ceremony on March 4, 1797, Washington was dressed in black, Adams in "light drab," wearing also a sword and a cockade. Jefferson, whose hair was tied in a queue and slightly powdered, wore a long blue single-breasted frock coat. He was sworn in first in the Senate Chamber, where he paid brief tribute to the "eminent character" of Adams, and prayed for "the Government, the happiness and prosperity of our common country." Then he led the Senate to the House, where Adams was inaugurated. The crowd cheered Washington like men possessed. Adams later wrote to his wife, "Everybody talks of the tears, the full eyes, the streaming eyes, the trickling eyes." During the ceremony, Washington, who was genuinely pleased with the election results, radiated such serenity that Adams fancied him saying to himself, "Ay, I am fairly out and you fairly in! See which of us will be happiest." [19]

The new President, inordinately tense, had written to Abigail he feared he would faint in the sight of the world. But he gave a fine bipartisan speech urging unity and peace, denying the falsities of the campaign and insisting on his loyalty to the Constitution and to republican government. As the three founding fathers left the hall, there was a mutually deferential little exchange over the problem of who should precede the other two. Washington, in a symbolic gesture that had far more meaning than implicit good manners, insisted that first Adams and then Jefferson lead the way before him. So the nation passed its first test, the transference of power, without bloodshed or violence and with exquisite courtesy.

Always the compulsive historian, Adams wrote the full details to his wife, calling the ceremony "the sublimest thing ever exhibited in America." Later, as if embarrassed by what he had written, he described it more precisely as "the sight of the sun setting full-orbed, and another rising (though less splendid)." [20] All of which was in decisive contrast with Jefferson, who described nothing to either his daughters or his friends, save for a wry note to Volney in which he dismissed the whole inauguration celebration as "a thousand visits of ceremony and some of sincerity." [21] Whence this reluctance to record what was after all a major triumph? Was he hiding a vexation at being second, which he could admit to no one, least of all himself? One cannot know, though, as we shall see, when he became president in 1801 he could not hide his excitement and gratification.

While Jefferson moved back into politics, Madison did the reverse, deliberately retiring to his plantation in Virginia in what would seem to be a curious modeling of his life on the pattern of the friend he had just succeeded in pushing into the vice-presidency. His marriage to Dolley Todd had resulted in no children. Aaron Burr wrote cryptically to James Monroe eighteen months after the marriage, "Madison is still childless, and I fear like to continue so." Jefferson was troubled by this failure, so obviously blamed on Madison, since Dolley had had children by her first husband, and wrote sadly to a friend in 1801 that Madison was "not yet a father." [22] Though Madison and Jefferson saw each other frequently in Virginia from 1797 to 1800, Jefferson missed his friend's talents in Congress, which was still dominated by increasingly hostile Federalists. But Madison did not emerge from retirement, save for a brief stint in the Virginia legislature in 1799, until Jefferson as president asked him to be his Secretary of State, a post Madison had refused when offered it by Washington in 1793.

Whatever hopes Jefferson had in 1797 for a restoration of his damaged friendship with John Adams were frozen in their first conversation. Jefferson called on him the day before the inauguration to pay his respects. Afterward he wrote down the details of what had turned out to be a painful confrontation. The new President's first gesture on greeting him was to suggest that he go to France. The fabric of diplomatic relations between the French Directory and the United States was indeed badly torn; French frigates were seizing American ships in the West Indies, and Federalists were clamoring for a declaration of war against the "government by guillotine" that had destroyed the once fair prospects for liberty and peace. Had Jefferson been anything but vice-president, the offer would have been an act of statesmanship. But Adams, disarmingly tactless as only he could be, betrayed his real feelings in a single sentence. Jefferson reported him as saying "that it would have been the first wish of his heart to have got me to go there, but that he supposed it was out of the question, as it did not seem justifiable for him to send away the person destined to take his place in case of accident to himself, nor decent to remove from competition one who was a rival in the public favor."

Having lived for eight years as vice-president, knowing well the death wishes that inevitably accompany the office, Adams was now very aware that this tall Virginian who had come so close to edging him out of the presidency might well himself be thinking of just such "accidents" as could thrust him fortuitously into the top post. However cogent the diplomatic reasons, Adams also simply wished to see his major rival three thousand miles away, and could not keep from saying so. But he felt uneasy about the suggestion and unjustified in pressing it. Jefferson, always sensitive to nuances in the statements of his rivals, dug in his heels. "My inclination," he told Adams, "would never permit me to cross the Atlantic again." [23]

Three days later, at a farewell dinner given by Washington, Jefferson and Adams left the party at the same moment and walked down the street together. They talked about the possibility of Madison's going to France, and the hostility of Adams' own cabinet to the idea. "When we came to Fifth street," Jefferson wrote, "where our road separated, his being down Market street, mine off along fifth . . . we took leave; and he never after that said one word to me on the subject, or ever consulted me as to any measures of the government." [24] It was a total separation, as Jefferson recognized in retrospect. As their roads separated so did their politics—and their lives. They would never again join in friendship except in letters, and this only when both were very old men.

That Jefferson would be totally shut out of the executive arm of the government he guessed in the first week in office. That he was virtually without power he learned shortly afterward. Adams was quickly captured by the High Federalists in his cabinet, though he did not know for a long time, nor did Jefferson, that three men in the cabinet—Timothy Pickering, Oliver Wolcott, and James McHenry, all Francophobes —were the willing tools of Alexander Hamilton. Though Jefferson had never expected to be overwhelmed by duties—confiding to Benjamin Rush on January 22, 1797, "a more tranquil and unoffending station could not have been found for me. . . . It will give me philosophic evenings in the winter, and rural days in the summer" [25]—still he counted himself a friend to Adams and a government officer with invaluable diplomatic experience. He found the new idleness humiliating.

"It gives me great regret to be passing my time so uselessly," he wrote to Martha on December 27, 1797, "when it could have been so importantly employed at home. I cannot but believe that we shall become ashamed of staying here." [26] He compiled a manual of rules for the Senate, designed to regularize and tighten lax procedures, of such excellence in definition that it remains in use today. He complained to his daughters of the "dreary scene where envy, hatred, malice, revenge, and all the worse passions of men are marshalled to make one another as miserable as possible." To Martha he wrote on June 8, 1797, "I have seen enough of political honors to know that they are but splendid torments." [27] The disintegration of old friendships Jefferson found especially painful. "Men who have been intimate all their lives," he wrote, "cross the street to avoid meeting . . ." [28] Adams, who may well have been the only one dodging chance encounters with Jefferson, for his part came to believe that Jefferson had "a mind soured, yet seeking for popularity, and eaten to a honeycomb with ambition, yet weak, confused, uninformed, and ignorant." [29] Not surprisingly, Jefferson rushed back to Monticello at every opportunity, and when he was in Philadelphia he sought out Republican friends only, or spent his time with scientists. As new President of the American Philosophical Society, he spoke and wrote happily on his Indian excavations—he had years before cut through a burial mound in Virginia with something of the precision of a modern archaeologist—on the giant fossil bones found in Kentucky, on the superiority of its moldboard plow.

Had there been only domestic problems dividing Jefferson and Adams, their friendship need not have been totally corroded. But England and France were still locked in a war embrace which, intensified by the coming of Napoleon to power, was to continue with only the briefest interruptions until 1815. The French Directory insolently refused to accept Adams' envoy, and French privateers during two months in the spring of 1798 captured half a million dollars' worth of American shipping. Adams sent to Paris new envoys, John Marshall, Charles C. Pinckney, and Elbridge Gerry, who were conspicuously insulted by Talleyrand, now Minister of Foreign Affairs, who no doubt sourly remembered his social ostracism in Philadelphia. Talleyrand coolly demanded among other things a bribe of $250,000 as an advance payment for smoothing negotiations between France and the United States. Such bribes, successfully extracted from Europeans, had already fattened his pockets. But Marshall, Pinckney, and Gerry asked for their passports and exposed the whole story in the American press.

The episode helped to generate a xenophobia in the United States that would not be matched till the Bolshevik hysteria of the 1920s. Though the Directory massed troops on the coast of France for an invasion not of America but of England (an action that was prudently discouraged as impossible by the young general Bonaparte, who in 1798 diverted the French armed effort into an invasion of Egypt instead), many Americans believed the rumor that a French invasion of the United States was imminent. Even the levelheaded Washington was convinced that a small force of Frenchmen, landed on the American coast, would be supported by enough American "Jacobins," to occasion a revolt for the purpose of overthrowing the Federalist government, and he was now privately calling the Republicans "the curse of the country." [30] Jefferson, who had no idea of the extent to which Washington participated in the general hysteria, years later read these statements with horror when Washington's letters were published, calling them "monuments of mortal decay" over which "we must forever weep." [31]

The Congress of 1798 became a war Congress. Adams made a fiery speech against France which Jefferson privately branded as "insane," and he recorded soberly for history that Adams in a private party had told him "anarchy in France had done more harm in one night than all the despotism of their Kings had ever done in twenty or thirty years." [32] Jefferson could only watch helplessly as the Federalist majority passed twenty war measures, suspending commerce with France, authorizing seizure of French naval vessels, declaring the treaty alliance of 1778 suspended, ordering the building of naval frigates, and the immediate enlistment of 10,000 men, with plans for a provisional army of 50,000. Washington, called out of retirement to head the forces, insisted that Alexander Hamilton be put in command, a step that fortunately appalled Adams as much as Jefferson and quenched some of his enthusiasm for heavy enlistments. For his part Hamilton, his fantasies inspired by Bonaparte, now began to dream of taking an army overland to conquer New Orleans and Mexico and then jointly with the British to divide up the whole of Spanish America.

French refugees, once welcomed, were now looked upon as potential spies, and singers of the "Marseillaise" were hissed off the Philadelphia stage. Congress passed alien laws requiring fourteen years instead of five for naturalization, and providing stiff penalties for violation of new and repressive alien residence rules. Jefferson was convinced that this measure, "worthy of the eighth or ninth century," he wrote, was aimed at his own friends, especially Volney, Albert Gallatin, and the Polish patriot Thaddeus Kosciusko. He watched in sorrow as resident Frenchmen, fearing imprisonment, signed up in droves for passage back to Europe.[33]

Having a decent regard for political amenities, Jefferson felt that as vice-president he could not attack Adams, however "insane" his foreign policy. Nor could he publicly deplore French actions lest this be construed as Republican agreement in the declaration of war against France that he feared might come at any moment. Yet his total public silence lent wing to surreptitious Federalist aspersions that he was a Jacobin conspirator. The Fourth of July brought an immense Federalist rally, where a toast was proposed that became immortal in the anti-Jefferson literature: "To Adams, may he like Samson, slay thousands of Frenchmen with the *jawbone* of Jefferson."

The Vice-President's response to the hysterical internal crisis of the United States tells us much about his growing political maturity, but also something about the special technique he was forging as a defense against his impulse to flee under personal attack. He wrote masses of letters. They poured out in a quiet but continuing stream, models of good sense and reasonableness in a time of national paranoia. He acknowledged that America was treated with contempt by both belligerents, and deplored the French attacks on American shipping equally with the British. But he suggested prudently a toleration of the depredations "as the Danes & Swedes do, curtailing our commerce and waiting for the moment of peace." Instead of the folly of alliance with Britain in a war against France, he urged a divorce from both. "Commerce with all nations, alliance with none." Many Federalists would have been astonished to know that Jefferson could write at this time, "The subjugation of England would be a general calamity." [34] He warned Republicans against secession talk: "Who can say what would be the evils of a scission, and when and where they would end." He encouraged faith: "A little patience, and we shall see the reign of witches pass over, their spells dissolve, and the people, recovering their true sight, restore their government to its true principles." [35]

Jefferson was forced by his very position as presiding officer of the Senate to sign the war bills and the repressive civil bills he so detested. This he did with much discomfort. But with the first reading in Congress of the Sedition Act, designed to punish "domestic traitors," he found his position absolutely insupportable. The bill as finally passed was bad enough, providing heavy fines and imprisonment for anyone found guilty of writing, publishing, or speaking anything of "a false, scandalous and malicious" nature against the government, Congress, or the President. The office of vice-president, as Jefferson was quick to see, was not specifically mentioned as protected from attack. The bill as originally written had declared France and the French to be enemies of the United States, and had called for the death penalty for anyone found guilty of giving them aid and comfort. This would have meant that Jefferson himself would be liable to hanging for making a speech defending France.

Later, looking back on "the reign of witches," Jefferson wrote, "No man who did not witness it can form an idea of their unbridled madness and the terrorism with which they surrounded themselves." [36] At the time he was in despair. After hearing the first reading of the Sedition Act he abruptly abandoned Congress, which would not adjourn for six weeks, and went home to Monticello. Again, as in the past, instead of blasting the opposition publicly in times of great rage and conflict, he fled. His masses of letters had served to strengthen his own defenses, but had been little better than straws against the public hurricane of frenzy against France. Jefferson remained at Monticello four and one-half months. During the first seven weeks, from June 24 to August 22, 1798, he wrote almost no political letters. But he emerged from these weeks with steel in his spine, determined to take over formally the reins of his party and to fight for the presidency.

During the remaining months at Monticello, where he remained through most of December 1798, he wrote and planned, connived and plotted. His five months of rumination resulted in two remarkably disparate documents, both of them fascinating evidences of his new response to political and personal attack. In a curious way the two were related.

The first was a long essay on the usefulness of the study of Anglo-Saxon, written in response to a document sent him from London by Herbert Croft, who was compiling an English-German dictionary. It tells us about the nature of the fantasy world Jefferson escaped into for a time in the summer of 1798. Playing with languages was a relaxing game for Jefferson, as mathematics had been in his youth. He returned now to what he pointed out had been the language of Britain for seven centuries. Charmed by his discovery that in Anglo-Saxon the Biblical line "the earth was without form and void" was rendered as "the earth was *idle* and empty," [37] he went on to make comparative columns of Anglo-Saxon, Middle English, and modern English for the whole first chapter of Genesis. So we have the spectacle of the radical politician—denounced as a blasphemer even on his return to Monticello because he had held a reception en route on the Sabbath—now playing in three dialects with the story of God's creation of a new world. Something decidedly had gone wrong with his own New World. And he may have found some solace in reviewing the Lord's problems.

The second document born of these five months of rumination was Jefferson's famous Kentucky Resolutions, introduced into the legislature of that state in 1799. The fact that he wrote these Resolutions, but even more the use to which he put this document, demonstrates that there had been a major revolution in Jefferson's response to attack. The writing was a joint secret effort with Madison, whose own version, introduced into the Virginia legislature, took a milder form. Both constituted a blast against the detested Alien and Sedition Acts. Since the Supreme Court had not yet assumed the right of judicial review of any act of Congress, there was no way these acts could be declared unconstitutional and void save by state action. That writing the Resolutions was an act of political desperation is reflected in Jefferson's letter to John Taylor on November 26, 1798. "Our General Government," he wrote, "has, swallowed more of the public liberty than even that of England." And he was frankly fearful that the next Congress would declare the Senate and the President to be in office for life.[38]

Unfortunately the Resolutions, in defining the right of states in the federal union to nullify acts of Congress, also implicitly affirmed the right of secession. The federal union, Jefferson wrote, was a compact among several states; these states were "not united on the principle of unlimited submission to their general government," and "every State has a Natural right in cases not within the compact . . . to nullify of their own authority all assumptions of powers by others." [39] Whether Jefferson guessed when he wrote these resolutions of their potential for destructive mischief is unlikely. He went to great pains to keep his authorship secret, and it was not discovered for many years. Certainly giving to the states—to his own state of Virginia which in 1799 he was still calling "a nation"—even the right of nullification was an act of political regression. In doing it he gave to the pro-slavery secessionists of the future a formidable weapon, and none of his letters over the years deploring the idea of secession were of much use in counteracting it. In this case the written fruits of his five-month return to Monticello turned out in the end to be poisonous.

But in 1799 the legislatures of Kentucky and Virginia used the Resolutions with discretion, primarily as a weapon of protest. Five thousand copies of the Virginia Resolutions were distributed as campaign literature in the election of 1800.[40] By January 6, 1799, Jefferson was already poised for his assault on Adams. This we see in a letter to Elbridge Gerry where he wrote what was essentially the Republican party platform. Jefferson was opposed to "monarchising" the Constitution, and in favor of the preservation of all states' rights "not yielded by them to the Union." He was for "a government rigorously frugal and simple," and for "free commerce with all nations, political connection with none." He would have no standing army in time of peace, and only such naval forces as were essential to protect coasts and harbors. "I am not," he wrote passionately, "for linking ourselves by new treaties with the quarrels of Europe, entering that field of slaughter to preserve their balance. . . . The first object of my heart is my own country." [41] It was a platform that would make him president.

Certain fortuitous events in Europe helped Jefferson, notably Nelson's defeat of the French fleet in Aboukir Bay at the mouth of the Nile, which resulted in the bottling up of Bonaparte's army in North Africa for three years. This happened in August 1798, but months had to pass before the strategic consequences affected United States politics. Finally even the most hysterical Federalists were convinced that the French invasion of America was a phantom. Adams' own fears quieted; his essential good sense reasserted itself. In February 1799 he dealt Hamilton's grandiose military fantasies a fatal blow, and he delighted the Republicans by making a decisive gesture for peace with France; he appointed an envoy to reopen negotiations. In June 1798 Jefferson had thought war with France "almost inevitable." By August 1799 he could write even about Federalist encroachments against civil liberties with a light hand. "But great heavens!" he wrote to Edmund Randolph on August 18. "Who could have conceived in 1789, that within ten years we should have to combat such windmills!" [42] So the Alien and Sedition Acts had proved to be windmills and not giants after all. But Jefferson, firmly astride the Rosinante he had been so reluctant to take out of his stall in 1795, was now riding furiously forward, determined to knock them down in any case as political monstrosities. Only John Yankee was in his way.

Jefferson's final break with Adams was made public in 1799. In the same year his long cherished friendship with Washington came to an abrupt end. Unlike the tie with Adams, the severing of which had been made easy by Adams' political folly, the collapse of all relationship with Washington gave Jefferson great anguish. It began with an unfortunate accident, when the letter Jefferson had written to Philip Mazzei complaining of "Samsons in the field and Solomons in the council . . . who have had their heads shorn by the harlot England" unexpectedly appeared in the *New York Minerva*. Mazzei had foolishly translated the letter into Italian and had given it to an editor in Florence; the

Paris *Moniteur* turned the Italian into French, and the *Minerva* translated the letter back into English. In the process some key words were changed, and Jefferson's "harlot" became "whore."

The Mazzei letter was reproduced everywhere in the Federalist press, and read on the floor of the House. Though criticizing Washington had now become common enough in the Republican press, the catching of Jefferson playing this forbidden game gave enormous satisfaction to his enemies. John Marshall later wrote self-righteously to Hamilton, "The morals of the author of the letter to Mazzei cannot be pure."[43] Jefferson, after much embarrassed consultation with his friends, decided to remain silent, and the old lion in retirement at Mount Vernon never commented on the letter. The only comfort to Jefferson was his knowledge that Adams too had lost the friendship of Washington. When the gossiping Dr. Rush reported to Jefferson on April 5, 1798, that Abigail Adams had told him "not a scrip of a pen has passed between the late and present President since he came into office," Jefferson made a note of it, and chose to preserve the note for history.[44]

Whatever may have been retrievable in the friendship between Washington and Jefferson was finally demolished by 1799 by an ill-conceived intrigue played by Jefferson's nephew Peter Carr. Hoping apparently to trap Washington into a private attack on Jefferson, to be used against him as the Mazzei letter was being used against Jefferson, Carr wrote a fulsome letter to Washington deploring the "unmerited calumny" heaped upon him, which he signed with the pseudonym John Langhorne. Washington wrote only a routine letter in reply. But John Nicholas, a busybody post-office clerk, noting that a letter from Washington to an unknown Langhorne was picked up by Jefferson's nephew, wrote at once to Mount Vernon and hinted of conspiracy. Washington, already wounded by the Mazzei letter, and long suspicious of Jefferson's Francophile tendencies, swallowed the Nicholas suggestions intact. By the time Jefferson had unraveled the mystery of his nephew's folly, it was too late to repair anything.[45]

When Washington died unexpectedly of a throat infection on December 14, 1799, Jefferson was at Monticello. Congress declared December 26 a day of official mourning, but Jefferson was not asked to speak in the ceremonies. Moreover, the man chosen to make the official eulogy was Light-Horse Harry Lee, his avowed enemy, who Jefferson was convinced had helped poison the mind of the late president against him. The affront must have been like a blow in the face. Not surprisingly, he delayed his return to Philadelphia by two days, in order to miss the ceremonies of mourning altogether.

Though later in his first inaugural address Jefferson paid fleeting tribute to Washington as "our first and great revolutionary character," destined for "the fairest page in the volume of faithful history," it was not until 1814, when Walter Jones sent him a manuscript history of the Revolution and asked for his comments that the old barriers of humiliation gave way. What he then wrote, fifteen years after Washington's death, was not an obituary so much as a seasoned judgment with traces of pain.

> I think I knew General Washington intimately and thoroughly, . . . His mind was great and powerful, without being of the very first order; his penetration strong, though not so acute as that of a Newton, Bacon, or Locke; and so far as he saw, no judgment was ever sounder. It was slow in operation, being little aided by invention or imagination, but sure in conclusion. . . .
>
> He was incapable of fear. . . . Perhaps the strongest feature in his character was prudence . . . but, when once decided, going through with his purpose, whatever obstacles opposed. His integrity was most pure, his justice the most inflexible I have ever known. . . . He was, indeed, in every sense of the words, a wise, a good, and a great man.
>
> His temper was naturally irritable and high toned; but reflection and resolution had obtained a firm and habitual ascendency over it. If ever, however, it broke its bonds, he was most tremendous in his wrath.

Jefferson continued with a note of poignancy: "His heart was not warm in its affections; but he calculated every man's value, and gave him a solid esteem proportioned to it." "A solid esteem" was all he had been able to wrest from the nation's father, while Hamilton and Lafayette had basked in a special warmth Jefferson had seen but never himself felt. He described his own relationship with him when he was Secretary of State as "confidential and cordial," but admitted that before his death Washington had come to distrust him as a French "theorist," holding "principles of government, which would lead infallibly to licentiousness and anarchy." Could he have seen him again, Jefferson suggested wistfully, "these malignant insinuations should have been dissipated before his just judgment, as mists before the sun." Then Jefferson wrote what he might well have said about Washington had he been given the chance to speak alongside Henry Lee:

"I felt on his death, with my countrymen, that 'verily a great man hath fallen this day in Israel.' " [46]

CHAPTER XXIII

Callender

I write truth, and am not a commonplace railer.

Callender to Jefferson, October 26, 1798 [1]

James Thomson Callender has come down in history as the most spiteful, malignant, and poisonous of all Jefferson's enemies. For Jefferson disciples he is the Antichrist, and in character the antipode of Jefferson himself. He was primarily and obsessively a defamer of the great. Since the Vice-President went out of his way to befriend this journalist in the beginning, his betrayal is made out to be all the more reprehensible; Callender was the vicious dog that bit the hand that fed him. Certainly of all Jefferson's enemies none had so devastating an impact on his private and public reputation.

Callender moved into Jefferson's orbit in 1797 as a young Republican disciple, a journalist praising his hero with unparalleled ardor. Six years later he was dead of drowning in the James River in Richmond, accused of drunkenness and sodomy, detested by Republican and Federalist alike. In the interim he caused more mischief than any newspaperman of his age, and left the reputations of both Alexander Hamilton and Thomas Jefferson badly charred. Though his attack on Jefferson was malicious and personal there was also great cunning in it.

Like many destructive men he had a talent for smelling out weakness in others, and he made himself out to be a meticulous reporter with abundant documentation to prove his charges. Readers of his exposés had the impression that his files were bulging with letters and affidavits. Some he published, others he did not, but since some of

315

the charges which were most derided as lies turned out to be true, he cannot be dismissed as a wholesale inventor of slander. There seemed to be some special necessity in him to destroy not only men of eminence but also his own benefactors.

Callender had begun his career of defamation in England with anonymous attacks on Samuel Johnson. Soon after he made life dangerous for himself by attacking George III. Charged with sedition, he fled to the United States in 1793 and managed to get his seditious pamphlet, *Political Progress of Britain*, published serially in the *New York Bee*. Jefferson, ever alert to the necessity of encouraging talented Republican journalists, wrote his approval of the pamphlet to a friend, and Callender used the phrase from his letter—"the most astonishing concentration of abuses . . . in any government"—in the Foreword to the American edition published in Philadelphia in 1795. Thus launched, Callender plunged into pamphleteering for the Republican party, writing at first for Franklin's grandson, Benjamin Franklin Bache, on the staff of the *Aurora*. Jefferson, then going into retirement, for a period took no further notice of him.

In 1797 Callender published a series of tracts, *History of the United States for the Year 1796*, one of which praised Jefferson's *Notes on the State of Virginia* as a volume uniting "the sweetness of Xenophon and the force of Polybius, information without parade, and eloquence without effort." No one much noticed his praise, but the whole nation was titillated when in Nos. V and VI he exposed the embarrassing alliance of Alexander Hamilton and Mrs. Reynolds. John Beckley, annoyed when the Federalists fired him as Clerk of the House, had given him the material.[2] During the interval since Monroe, Venable, and Muhlenberg had first confronted Hamilton with Reynolds' letters in 1792, the blackmailer had disappeared, and his wife had begun to live with her co-partner in conspiracy and fraud, Jacob Clingman, whom she was shortly to marry.[3] Clingman insisted to Callender that Maria Reynolds had never been the blackmailing whore she appeared to be, and swore that Hamilton and Reynolds had together forged her love letters in an affort to throw the Republican congressmen off the scent of Hamilton's Treasury speculations, which Clingman intimated involved $30,000. Happy to believe the worst of Hamilton, Callender accepted Clingman's word, and in his exposé Maria Reynolds emerged as an only slightly besmirched woman of virtue, while Hamilton was made out to be an infamous villain, guilty not only of Treasury fraud but also of perjury, forgery, and defamation of female character. "So much correspondence could not refer exclusively to wenching," Callender wrote. "No man of common sense will believe that it did. . . . The solicitude of Mr. Hamilton to get these people out of the way is quite contradictory to an amorous attachment for Mrs. Reynolds, and bespeaks her innocence in the clearest stile." [4]

Hamilton, after checking with Venable and Muhlenberg, believed Monroe to be the man who had leaked the story, and rushed to his lodgings. Monroe indignantly maintained his innocence, saying his own copies of the incriminating correspondence were "yet . . . sealed with his friend in Virginia." Hamilton called his denial "totally false," and Monroe called Hamilton a scoundrel. By this time the ritual of the *code duello* had taken over; there was nothing left for Hamilton but to say, "I will meet you like a gentleman," and for Monroe but to reply, "I am ready. Get your pistols." [5] As it turned out, the duel was prevented by the politic intercession of Aaron Burr, who thus ironically spared Hamilton to meet his own bullet seven years later.

Monroe's "friend in Virginia" was obviously Thomas Jefferson, and Hamilton now suspected him of turning over the Reynolds correspondence to Callender. Actually Jefferson had learned of the Callender exposé even before publication and had tried to prevent it. He "advised that the papers should be suppressed," Callender later wrote, ". . . but his interposition came too late. Mr. Hamilton knew that Mr. Jefferson was master of his secret but had kept it." [6] Exactly when Hamilton confronted Jefferson with the charge that he had leaked the material is unknown, but Jefferson's secretary William Burwell later wrote that it was at this time that Hamilton "threatened him with a public disclosure" of the Betsey Walker story. [7] Gossip that Jefferson had indeed been guilty of exposing Hamilton through Callender eventually became so widespread that Jefferson took pains to see that it was officially denied in two leading Republican newspapers, the *Aurora* and the *Richmond Examiner*. [8]

Hamilton delayed telling the press about Betsey Walker, perhaps because he was convinced of Jefferson's innocence concerning his own scandal. Instead he published in John Fenno's *Gazette of the United States* a confession astonishing in its political naïveté and in the wealth of its detail. "The charge against me," he said, "is a connection with one James Reynolds for purposes of improper pecuniary speculation. My real crime is an amorous connection with his wife. . . . This confession is not made without a blush." [9] What this confession did to Hamilton's marriage, and to what he called his "unoffending and amiable wife," now in the late stages of a pregnancy, can only be imagined. He tried to involve Jefferson obliquely, and blasted at "the spirit of jacobinism" which "seems to threaten the political and moral world with a complete overthrow."

This publication was a supreme act of folly. After reading the pathetic letters of Maria Reynolds no one believed Hamilton innocent of adultery,[10] and many were unconvinced of his innocence in Treasury speculations. John Adams privately described him as a man whose fierce ambitions sprang from "a superabundance of secretions" that he "could not find whores enough to draw off." [11] Jefferson wrote harshly to John Taylor that Hamilton's willingness to plead guilty to adultery seemed "rather to have strengthened than weakened the suspicions that he was in truth guilty of the speculations." [12]   And after the Republican press had finished "taking pot shots at the 'Colossus of Monocrats,' " as John C. Miller notes, "it was improbable that Hamilton could have been elected to any high office in the United States." [13]

One lesson Jefferson learned from Hamilton's political idiocy was the usefulness of silence. To answer calumny in the press, he was now certain, served only to reinforce and exaggerate it. He would not make the same mistake when Callender exposed his own amours in September 1802. But what did Jefferson really feel about Hamilton's tawdry affair? And about Hamilton's threats to expose his own indiscretion? There is no answer to these questions save in the subdued and somewhat compassionate retrospection he put on paper in 1818. Hamilton by then had been dead from Burr's bullet for fourteen years. Jefferson at the time was organizing the "ragged, rubbed and scribbled" scraps of paper he had kept which described his conversations with Hamilton and Washington, later to be published as his *Anas*. "I have given to the whole a calm revisal," Jefferson wrote, "when the passions of the time are passed away." [14] But his intense jealousy of Hamilton was even then far from extinguished.

In a beguiling summation of Hamilton's character he did absolve him of personal corruption, and very nearly absolved him of private corruption with Mrs. Reynolds:

> He was, indeed, a singular character. Of acute understanding, disinterested, honest, and honorable in all private transactions, amiable in society, and duly valuing virtue in private life [how carefully the words were chosen!]—yet so bewitched and perverted by the British example—as to be under thorough conviction that corruption was essential to the government of a nation.

Nevertheless he attacked Hamilton's financial system as "a puzzle to exclude popular understanding and inquiry," and "a machine for corruption of the legislature." "Immense sums," he said, "were filched from the poor and ignorant, and fortunes accumulated by those who had themselves been poor enough before. . . . Men thus enriched by the dexterity of a leader, would of course follow the chief who was leading them to fortune." Then he blasted Hamilton with the libel that became instantly famous with the publication of the *Anas*. Hamilton, he said, "was not only a monarchist, but for a monarchy bottomed on corruption."[15] So Jefferson insured that posterity would know his own judgment, and biographers and historians have been lining up ever since on the side of one man or the other.

Jefferson's account book tells us that on June 20, 1797, he paid Callender $15.14 for copies of his *History*. This may have been the date of their first meeting,[16] when he tried to persuade Callender to abandon the idea of exposing Hamilton's adultery. It was on this date in any case that Jefferson began to subsidize with small sums this small, misshapen man, whose head always seemed slightly twisted, and who could do that which Jefferson found it impossible to do, lose himself utterly in vitriolic attack. Later Jefferson wrote that in the beginning he considered Callender "a man of genius," and "a man of science fled from persecution," and he had no hesitation in sending copies of his volumes to his daughter Martha and her husband.[17] Callender's praise had an intellectual quality that Jefferson must particularly have enjoyed when it was directed toward himself, but his vituperation had a kind of demonic brilliance that may have attracted Jefferson even more. So rigorous was his own self-discipline, he probably found in Callender's explosions of hate vicarious relief from the rages he could not himself express. Callender printed about his enemies that which he could not himself say even in private and which he may not have permitted himself even to think.

In the beginning Jefferson knew nothing of Callender's alcoholism or the degradation of his private life. Thomas Leiper, Jefferson's old landlord, befriended Callender and his wife and four children. That Jefferson may have had something to do with this is suggested by a detail in his account book, which shows that he gave $25 to Leiper "in charity" January 19, 1798. Otherwise the charities to Callender proper seem to be rigorously identified. This was a more careful accounting than one sees in his recording of the friendly lending and borrowing among Madison, Monroe, Short, and himself, or of the charities freely doled out to his improvident younger brother Randolph, and to persons he didn't bother even to name. Perhaps something warned Jefferson from the beginning that here his record should be meticulous.[18]

Callender's wife died in 1798. Later a venomous journalist said her death was hastened by Callender's "barbarity and brutality," that he had left her "to wallow in filth, ignorance and misery, while he was indulging in intoxication," and that he suffered her in the end "to perish in her own filth until maggots were engendered beneath her and along her spine!"[19] Accused of a petty theft, Callender fled to

Virginia, leaving his four children to the charity of Thomas Leiper. Describing himself as a fugitive from the Sedition Law, he won the sympathy of Stephens T. Mason, who took him into his home and promised to aid him till he had finished a new anti-Federalist book. Callender hoped to make enough money to buy some acreage near Monticello. Like many other men attracted by Jefferson's magnetism he nourished fantasies of living close to him. He may indeed have known that Jefferson had encouraged good friends like Mazzei, Madison, Monroe, and Short to purchase acreages near his own. On September 26, 1799, he wrote to Jefferson saying he wanted to "come up James River . . . and try to find 50 acres of clear land, and a hearty Virginia female, that knows how to fatten pigs, and boil hommony, and hold her tongue; and then adieu to the rascally society of mankind." [20]

By now Jefferson may have heard rumors of Callender's snarling quarrels and drinking. Perhaps the crudity with which he wrote about remarriage so soon after his wife's death was offensive. Jefferson later told James Monroe, "I discouraged his coming into my neighborhood." Still, he continued to correspond with Callender in a friendly fashion, leaving his letters unsigned, because of "the curiosity of the post office." [21] In Richmond Callender was given a post on the *Examiner* by Jefferson's good friend, Meriwether Jones, and was shortly contributing to five Republican journals.[22] Though the circulation of the *Examiner* soared, Callender made enemies instantly, as was his fashion. By August 1799 the Federalists were threatening to ride him out of town on a rail, and he wrote to Jefferson in apparent terror that he was "in danger of being murthered." [23] Jefferson wrote him a sympathetic note, and on September 23 sent word to George Jefferson, who handled some of his accounts in Richmond, to send Callender another fifty dollars.

Jefferson freely contributed information on foreign affairs of the past for Callender's book, information not of a secret nature but of a kind which was known only to congressmen and which he wanted to see publicized generally. "If it could be understood to come to you through some such channel," he wrote Callender, "it would save the public from reading all the blackguardism which would be vented on me were I quoted." [24] When Callender sent him the proof sheets of the first score or more pages of his new volume, *The Prospect before Us*, Jefferson wrote, "Such papers cannot fail to produce the best effect. They inform the thinking part of the nation." [25] But the volume itself turned out to be a compound of such spleen and scurrility that Jefferson was disturbed, fearing it would do more mischief than good for the Republican party. Though directed largely against John Adams,

Callender's vituperation smudged even the shining armor of Washington, derided as "the grand lama of Federal adoration, the immaculate divinity of Mt. Vernon." Callender described Adams as "that strange compound of ignorance and ferocity, of deceit and weakness," a "hideous hermaphroditical character which has neither the force and firmness of a man, nor the gentleness and sensibility of a woman." "Take your chance," he said, "between Adams, war, and beggary, and Jefferson, peace and competency." [26]

With the publication of *The Prospect before Us*, Abigail Adams counted Callender worthy of hanging. And once she found out that Jefferson had been subsidizing him, her cordial and affectionate friendship, already greatly strained, froze into glacial silence.[27]

In the mounting hysteria of the election campaign of 1800 the Federalists declared the Republicans to be Jacobin traitors, conspirators, and anarchists—in Noah Webster's words, "the refuse, the sweepings of the most depraved part of mankind." Republican journalists other than Callender denounced Washington as a secret traitor and Adams as "a ruffian deserving the curses of mankind." [28] A major difference between the two parties, however, was that where the Republicans simply ranted, the Federalists put the Republicans in jail. The testy, hypersensitive Adams, aided by his punitive Secretary of State, Timothy Pickering, and the shockingly partisan Supreme Court justice, Samuel Chase, now proceeded to make a mockery of the First Amendment. Congressman Matthew Lyon of Vermont was sentenced to jail for four months and fined $1,000 because he had protested Adams' "unbounded thirst for ridiculous pomp, foolish adulation and selfish avarice." Jefferson's good friend Thomas Cooper, refugee from England, was convicted of tending to incite "insurrection against the government" because he attacked Adams for enlarging the army and navy, and because, in Justice Chase's words, "he intended to mislead the ignorant, and inflame their minds against the President, and . . . influence their votes in the next election." Cooper went to jail protesting bitterly, "Is it a crime to doubt the capacity of the president?" His wife died before he was released. Benjamin Franklin Bache, editor of the Republican *Aurora*, was charged with sedition but died of yellow fever before the trial. His successor, William Duane, managed to keep out of jail for his anti-Federalist attacks by a series of legal maneuverings but was finally indicted on October 17, 1800.[29]

Callender was brought to trial in June 1800, with Samuel Chase, who served as federal court judge as well as Supreme Court justice, presiding as the single magistrate. He interrupted Callender's three defense lawyers so often and with such palpable contempt that they angrily withdrew from the case. The jury, packed with eager Federalists, found Callender guilty after only two hours in retirement, this despite the fact that he had no counsel for his defense. His trial had lasted a single day.[30] Jefferson was outraged, as were many other Virginians, who had seen their own legislature twice denounce the Alien and Sedition Acts as unconstitutional and who were appalled at the jailings for simple political dissent. When the minutes of Callender's trial were published and circulated as a campaign document in the election, the trial became a national sensation, and did much to help Jefferson's election.

Callender, buried in the Richmond jail, found himself for a brief period, and for the only time in his life, a popular partisan hero. Meriwether Jones in the *Richmond Examiner* called him a "heroic Martyr of liberty—the Admiration of Goochland—the Delight of Manchester—the Glory of Fredericksburg—the Pride of Amelia—the Boast of Albemarle—the Champion of Republicanism—and the favourite son of Democracy." The Federalist press, on the other hand, denounced him as "a Luciferian combination of avarice and anarchy." [31] In the Richmond jail, furiously writing a second volume of *The Prospect before Us*, Callender demonstrated that prison had not sweetened his temper and that martyrdom had not dulled his pen. He called Adams "a repulsive pedant, a gross hypocrite, and an unprincipled oppressor . . . in private life, one of the most egregious fools on the continent," and "a ruffian supereminently entitled not only to laughter, but likewise to the curses of mankind." [32]

Writing to Jefferson on October 27, 1800, he described the jail as "a den of wretchedness and horror."

> Chase has sent me a letter that he will beat me; and I have advertised that, in case of an attack, I'll shoot him. . . . Your goodness will forgive the loquacity of joy; but my heart is sick with the pain of gladness at the anticipation of the time when the herd of federal robbers shall be hunted from their den; when oppression shall feel the pang she has inflicted; and rapine regorge a portion of their prey.[33]

Although Jefferson wrote him a note of sympathy, he had become increasingly alarmed by Callender's venom. As he wrote later to Monroe, "His first writings here had fallen far short of his original Political Progress, and the scurrilities of his subsequent ones began evidently to do mischief. As to myself, no man wished more to see his pen stopped; but I considered him still a proper object of benevolence." [34] After winning the election, Jefferson promised upon his inauguration to pardon Callender and remit his fine, as he did the others sentenced under the hated sedition law.

While scribbling maledictions in the cell at the Richmond jail, Callender was permitted to read the Virginia newspapers. It may have been here, scrutinizing W. A. Rind's attacks on Jefferson in the *Virginia Federalist*, that he first saw hints that Jefferson had a slave mistress. As early as June 23, 1800, Rind had written that he had "damning proofs" of Jefferson's "depravity." Callender later wrote that he believed Rind's surmise "to be absolute calumny." [35] But the rumor was enough to kindle his curiosity, and his chronic compulsion to ferret out secrets could not be long restrained. He may also have seen the charge in the *New York Commercial Advertiser* of October 9, 1800, that Jefferson was "a spendthrift, a libertine, . . . and an Atheist," whose private life was far from spotless. After his release from jail he was annoyed because of a delay in the repayment of the fine, but still more embittered by what seemed a growing hostility of Jefferson toward him. He would complain to Madison that Jefferson "had on various occasions, treated me with such ostentatious coolness and indifference, that I could hardly say that I was able to love or trust him." [36] If his hero had feet of clay he must know it at all costs. Sometime before April 1801 he set out for Charlottesville to question Jefferson's neighbors, and it was here that he learned in surprisingly accurate detail a great deal about Sally Hemings.[37]

CHAPTER XXIV

Jason

The storm we have passed through proves our vessel indestructible.

Jefferson to Lafayette, March 1, 1801 [1]

Jefferson's emergence during the campaign of 1800 as a resolute, determined, and wily candidate for president can be charted, though with some difficulty, in his letters, where he shows himself to be politic, shrewd, restrained, and often secretive. He sent his most confidential letters by special messenger, often with instructions that the missives be burned. Only in his letters to his daughters did he express what he hid from everyone else, the complexity of his commitment to the capture of the presidency and his reaction to the unexpected crisis that threatened to deprive him of his victory. There was no more fretting about not challenging the man who "has always been my senior." Adams had now become a threat to the republic.

Unlike the campaign which made him vice-president, this one saw Jefferson's total participation. His letters show a constantly mounting exhilaration at the evidences of affection pouring in from his countrymen. A campaign biography, the first in American political history, was written and 5,000 copies distributed. Republicans at rallies sang the campaign song, a copy of which Jefferson clipped and pasted in his Monticello scrapbook:

> Rejoice, Columbia's sons rejoice
> To tyrants never bend the knee
> But join with heart and soul and voice
> For Jefferson and Liberty

324

From Georgia up to Lake Champlain
From seas to Mississippi's shore
Ye sons of freedom loud proclaim
THE REIGN OF TERROR IS NO MORE

Jefferson's exhilaration in the election was not shared by his daughters, and Martha in particular seems to have been one of the unhappiest women in America when her father was elected president. Jefferson had conducted the campaign from Monticello, where he remained from May 10 to the end of November. The house had been crowded with visitors, which Martha found intolerable. "I suffered much more seeing you allways at a distance," she wrote later, "than if you had still been in Philadelphia, for then at least I should have enjoyed in anticipation those pleasures which we were deprived of by the concourse of strangers which continually crowded the house when you were with us." [2]

Though the Federalist attack against Jefferson took much the same form as in 1796, there were new charges, new denigrations. Rind's *Virginia Federalist*, in an effort to lessen the glowing image of Jefferson as author of the Declaration of Independence, said that his writing it was "an accidental honor in the arrangement of committees." [3] The *New York Commercial Advertiser* ran a series of articles by one who signed himself Burleigh, which topped every previous diatribe in vituperation and hysteria. Burleigh predicted that a Jefferson victory would mean civil war, that thousands of Frenchmen and Irishmen, "the refuse of Europe who have fled from the pillory and the gallows, and are here stirring up revolution, watching for plunder, and rioting in the thoughts of dividing up the property of the honest," would "rush from their lurking places, whet their daggers, and plunge them into the hearts of all who love order, peace, virtue, and religion." In the South, Burleigh predicted, the slaves, "tools with which Jacobinism delights to work," would revolt and "lay waste the fair fields of our southern brethren," [4] implying that Jefferson himself would lead the slave insurrections. The propaganda poisoned the already somewhat hostile Martha Washington to such a degree that she confided to the visiting clergyman Manasseh Cutler her opinion that Jefferson was "one of the most detestable of mankind." [5]

In late June a rumor spread through the Federalist press that Jefferson had died. The *Aurora* scolded later, "When lions fall, asses bray. . . . the asses of aristocracy, fearing the paws of the republican lion, reported his death—because they wished him so!" [6] A public charge by the Reverend Cotton Mather Smith that Jefferson had defrauded and robbed a widow and fatherless children of an estate to which he had been executor, to the amount of £10,000 sterling, stung him sufficiently to write to Uriah McGregory asking him to deny the story. "Every tittle of it is fable," he said.[7]

Clergymen told their parishioners that a vote for Jefferson was a vote against Christianity, and warned that if he won they would have to hide their Bibles in their wells. Jefferson was urged by friends to make his religious position clear, but he was far too wily to lay himself open on that score. Having only recently written to the distinguished scientist-preacher Joseph Priestley, "You have sinned against church and king, and can therefore never be forgiven," [8] he was not likely to invite the kind of abuse Priestley had suffered as a result of his heretical sermons. Priestley's house, laboratory, and church had been burned in England, and now he was threatened with deportation under Adams' Alien Act.

In dodging Benjamin Rush's appeal for "a letter on Christianity," Jefferson wrote, tactfully at first, that he had no time, and that it would do no good. What he was finally moved to write, however, was that he would never court the clergy by offers of compromise. The Episcopalian and Congregationalist churches in particular, he noted, still hoped to be named as the established church of the United States. Each church knew that his success in the election "threatens abortion to their hopes." Then he went on, with that elegant and eloquent fierceness that bursts forth so rarely in his letters, to write one of the most famous of all his lines: "And they believe rightly: for I have sworn upon the altar of God, eternal hostility against every form of tyranny over the mind of man." [9]

Jefferson's daughters were both increasingly jealous of his ever mounting delight in politics; Martha in particular clung to him all the more passionately as he seemed to turn away from her. Her husband's mental health had improved when Jefferson left Virginia for Philadelphia as vice-president, and in March 1797 he had even entered the contest for delegate to the Virginia legislature from Albemarle County. But he seems to have deliberately killed his own chances by failing to appear on election day. Jefferson, who felt personally humiliated, reproached him by letter, and sent a circular letter of apology "to every militia captain . . . which I hope," he wrote, "will set the thing to rights. I am more anxious you should possess the affections of the people than you should make use of them. Their esteem will contribute much to your happiness: whether the office they might confer would do so is another question." [10] Randolph's excuse, that he had stayed home to help nurse his children, who had just been inoculated for smallpox, did not improve his masculine image in Virginia.

Martha, who could hardly have failed to make increasingly invidious comparisons between her husband and her celebrated father, was further humiliated in the spring of 1800 when Randolph importuned Jefferson for a new loan and was turned down. Jefferson had just discovered some financial errors he had made in the handling of the estate of William Short, from whom he had borrowed money, and had had to mortgage an additional 1,000 acres of his own property to meet the new drain. He wrote a regretful letter to his son-in-law explaining his embarrassment.[11] Martha, writing to her father the following week, concluded her letter with an explicit expression of preference: "Adieu Dear and respected Father. Hasten I entreat you, the blest moment which will reunite me to all my heart holds dear in the world." [12]

Jefferson was in Washington, the new seat of the government, when the news came in December of his victory over Adams. He had left Monticello on November 24, 1800, visiting Martha at Edgehill en route. She waited two full months before writing to him. "I should not have waited for your letter my Dearest Father," she began, "had it been in my power to have written sooner but incredible as it may appear, that in a period of 2 months not one day could have been found to discharge so sacred and pleasing a duty." The letter continued in a morose fashion, filled with complaints about the political throngs at Monticello during the previous summer, with details of numerous small illnesses, and with distress over the failure of her attempts to educate her children up to her exacting standards. She concluded, "Adieu again dearest beloved Father. 2 long months still before we shall see you. In the meantime rest assured of the first Place in the heart of your affectionate child." [13] Not a word about his election to the presidency of the United States! Nor did she mention his election in subsequent letters. When Jefferson after an unexpected and bitter contest with Burr—who though slated to be vice-president had through an accident emerged with the identical number of votes as Jefferson—wrote in February of his final victory,[14] still she did not write. Jefferson, cruelly hurt, finally exploded in protest: "It is a terrible thing that people will not write unless they have materials to make a long letter: when three words would be so acceptable." [15]

Maria, on the other hand, had written frankly of her excitement about the election, though she made it clear that she would consider her father's increasing absences a personal loss. "We are still in anxious suspense about the election," she wrote on December 28, 1800. "If the event should be as it is expected I shall endeavor to be satisfied in the happiness I know it will give to so many tho I must confess mine would have been greater Could I be forever with you and see you happy." [16] Maria seems to have been much more content in her marriage than Martha, and happy in the environs of Eppington, where she had spent five years with Francis, Elizabeth, and Jack Eppes as a child. Unfortunately she had inherited her mother's body as well as her beauty, and had the same calamitous problems with childbearing. Her first child, a daughter, born apparently prematurely on New Year's Eve 1799, lived less than a month. Jefferson, remembering the sad deaths of his own infants, had written her a letter of ineffable tenderness:

> How deeply I feel it in all it's bearings, I shall not say, nor attempt consolation where I know that time and silence are the only medicines. . . . I know no happiness but when we are together. . . . My attachments to the world and whatever it can offer are daily wearing off, but you are one of the links which hold to my existence, and can only break off with that. You have never by a word or deed given me one moment's uneasiness; on the contrary I have felt perpetual gratitude to heaven for having given me, in you, a source of so much pure and unmixed happiness. . . . I cannot find expressions for my love.[17]

Maria suffered from ill health increasingly after the death of her daughter; breast infections were followed by back pains that made her a semi-invalid for two years.[18] She became bored by her life in Bermuda Hundred—"Nothing can be more retired than the life we lead here"—increasingly envious of her sister's proximity to Monticello. Always jealous of what she considered her sister's superior intellect, she must now have envied also her sturdy body, for Martha continued successfully to bear a healthy child every year or two. According to one of Martha's daughters, Maria "undervalued and disregarded her own beauty . . . saying that people only praised her for that because they could not praise her for better things." She "sometimes mourned over the fear that her father *must* prefer her sister's society, and *could* not take the same pleasure in hers." [19]

During the election crisis of February 1801, when it was by no means certain that Jefferson would be able to surmount the intrigue to make Burr president, Maria chose this moment to write a plaintive letter, complaining of her father's preference for Martha. "Sensible of the distance which Nature has placed between my sister and myself . . . I rejoice that you have in her a source of comfort and one who is in every way worthy of you, satisfied if my dear papa is only assured that in the most tender love to him I yield to no one." [20]

Jefferson, who had always in his letters subtly advertised his preference for Martha, now for the first time realizing the nature of Maria's grievance, took time out from the exasperating battle in Washington to reply gently: "No, never imagine that there can be a difference with me between yourself and your sister. You have both such dispositions as engross my whole love, and each so much entirely that there can be no greater degree of it than each possess. Whatever absences I may be led into for a while, I look for happiness to the moment when we can all be settled together, no more to separate." [21]

But when he had survived the political crisis and was inaugurated, Maria denied him a letter of congratulation, as had Martha. So she, too, by an act of omission repaid him for accumulated subtle grievances. Important negative communication among them continued to be implicit, not explicit. This was the Jefferson way of life. Astonishingly, it was the daughters who put their father on the defensive. It was he who, instead of expecting and indeed demanding their enthusiastic collaboration in his political life, found himself instead explaining and apologizing. To Maria he wrote:

> I feel no impulse from personal ambition to the office now proposed to me, but on account of yourself and your sister, and those dear to you. I feel a sincere wish to see our government brought back to its republican principles, to see that kind of government firmly fixed, to which my whole life has been devoted. I hope we shall now see it so established, as that when I retire it may be under full security that we are to continue free and happy.[22]

Jefferson's hunger for domestic tranquillity at Monticello had now also become intertwined with his ambitions for social harmony for the republic. "If we can once more get social intercourse restored to its pristine harmony," he wrote to Thomas Lomax on February 25, 1801, "I shall believe we have not lived in vain." [23]

It had never occurred to the makers of the Constitution that in case of a tie between the two major contestants the losing parties could play the role of president-maker. The slight danger of this had occurred to both Jefferson and Burr, but each thought it had been obviated in advance. Burr had been brought in as second on the party ticket because of his earlier resourceful work in New York, where by card-indexing of voters, ward by ward canvassing, and enlisting the support of Tammany Hall he had captured the New York legislature for the Republicans. To prevent his ending up with the exact number of votes as Jefferson it had presumably been arranged that Burr would get one less vote than Jefferson in Rhode Island, and also one less in either South Carolina or Georgia. By accident none of these plans was realized. Jefferson and Burr were tied with 73 votes each; Adams had 65, Pinckney 64, and John Jay one. The election was thus thrown into the House of Representatives, and a lame-duck Federalist House at that, most of whose members would be out of office in March 1801. Immediately the Federalists seized upon the idea of making Burr president. Burr was "unprincipled," as Hamilton described him; he could therefore be manipulated. This they knew in advance was not true of Jefferson.

At first Jefferson took it for granted that Burr would decline gracefully. During the initial vote-counting, when it seemed likely that Burr would be second, he had written letters indicating Jefferson was the first choice of both party and country.[24] Jefferson wrote to his daughter Maria from Washington on January 4, 1801, "The Federalists were confident at first they could debauch Colo. B. from his good faith by offering him their vote to be President, and have seriously proposed it to him. His conduct has been honorable and decisive, and greatly embarrasses them." [25] By this date, however, Burr had learned of the tie vote and was blandly telling Jefferson's friends, Samuel Smith and Colonel Benjamin Hitchburn, that he saw no reason, if the House chose, why he should not be president and Jefferson vice-president.[26] Jefferson thus learned belatedly that he had a rival even more intriguing and deadly than Hamilton. To worsen matters, Federalists in the House were planning, should there be a tie vote between Jefferson and Burr on the floor, to declare an interim president, preferably the newly appointed Chief Justice, John Marshall. Adams himself did not oppose the idea: "I know no more danger of a political convulsion, if a President *pro tempore* . . . should be made President by Congress, than if Mr. Jefferson or Mr. Burr is declared as such. . . . This, however, must be followed by another election, and Mr. Jefferson would be chosen." [27]

Actually Adams greatly preferred Jefferson to Burr, whom he described as a "dexterous gentleman" rising "like a balloon filled with inflammable air" over the heads of "all the old patriots, all the splendid talents, the long experience, both of federalists and antifederalists. . . . an encouragement to party intrigue and corruption!" [28] But he could not bring himself to say this to Jefferson. Hostile, and deeply wounded by defeat, he is said to have greeted Jefferson, when the latter called on him after the election, with a bitter cry, "You have turned me out! You have turned me out!" [29] He had taken special pleasure in appointing Jefferson's enemy, John Marshall, to the Supreme Court, and was now encouraging Congress to pass the last-minute Judiciary Act, creating twenty-three new federal judgeships, which he intended to fill with Federalists before leaving office.

When Jefferson formally called upon him to ask him if the rumors were true that Marshall or some other Federalist might be made an

interim president, Adams was cold and cagey. He seemed to think the
office of the presidency was at this point negotiable, observing, as
Jefferson later wrote, that "it was in my power to fix the election by a
word . . . by declaring I would not turn out the federal officers, not
put down the navy, nor spunge the national debt." [30] Jefferson kept
his temper. The stakes were high, and the situation delicate. He
"turned the conversation to something else," he said, and thus saved
his rage for his *Anas*.

At this point in the crisis his letters to his daughters reflected a
brief return of his old compelling desire to flee back to Monticello.
To Martha he wrote on February 5, in language astonishing for the
sensuousness of its imagery:

> Worn down here with pursuits in which I take no delight, sur-
> rounded by enemies and spies, catching and perverting every word
> which falls from my lips or flows from my pen, and inventing where
> facts fail them, I pant for that society were all is peace and harmony,
> where we love and are loved by every object we see. And to have that
> intercourse of soft affections hushed and supported by the eternal
> presence of strangers goes very hard indeed, and the harder as we see
> that the candle of life [is] burning out, so that the pleasures we lose
> are lost forever.

To Maria he wrote on February 15, "The scene passing here makes me
pant to be away from it: to fly from the circle of cabal, intrigue and
hatred, to one where all is love and peace." [31]

But this time, toughened by the knowledge that the election was
rightfully his and that the people had demonstrated their affection in
the total vote, he acted for the first time like a true sovereign. Like
Washington before him and Jackson after, he stood his ground, and he
successfully used the threat of military power to resolve an internal
crisis. The House began balloting on February 11. Eight states stood
for Jefferson, six for Burr, with Maryland and Vermont evenly divided
and thus unable to carry the election for Jefferson. As the deadlock
held, the rumors of an interim Federalist president increased. Jefferson,
believing that "that precedent once set would be artificially reproduced, and end soon in a dictator," [32] now met privately with the
Federalist leaders. Here, as he described it in a letter to James Monroe,
he let it be known "openly and firmly . . . that the day such an act
passed, the Middle States would arm, and that no such usurpation,
even for a day, should be submitted to." "This first shook them,"
Jefferson reported. And his additional threat to call a new constitutional convention "to reorganize the government, and to amend it"—
which meant a more radical Constitution—shook them still more. [33]

Word filtered north that the Virginia militia was arming for a march on Washington, and the Federalist press now accused Jefferson of agitating for civil war.

During all this imbroglio Jefferson had an unexpected ally in Alexander Hamilton. Even during the campaign Hamilton had inadvertently aided Jefferson when, in an effort to replace Adams as a candidate by the militaristic Pinckney, he had privately printed a splenetic attack on Adams as a man of "disgusting egotism, distempered jealousy, and ungovernable indiscretion." [34] Thanks to Burr, this pamphlet had been gleefully reprinted in the Republican press, and had helped to shatter the Federalist party. Now, to the astonishment of many, Hamilton threw his support to Jefferson. In a justly celebrated letter to James A. Bayard, of Delaware, whose vote in the end determined the election, Hamilton wrote of Jefferson: "I admit that his politics are tinctured with fanaticism; that he is too much in earnest in his democracy; that he has been a mischievous enemy to the principal measures of our past administration; that he is crafty and persevering in his objects; that he is not scrupulous about the means of success, nor very mindful of truth, and that he is a contemptible hypocrite." But this was high praise, compared with what Hamilton wrote to Bayard and others of Burr: "He is in every sense a profligate; a voluptuary in the extreme, with uncommon habits of expense. . . . He is artful and intriguing to an inconceivable degree . . . bankrupt beyond redemption except by the plunder of his country. . . . he will certainly attempt to reform the government à la Bonaparte . . . as unprincipled and dangerous a man as any country can boast—as true a Catiline as ever met in midnight conclave—" [35]

One of the reasons that Hamilton so exactly comprehended the true nature of Burr's intriguing, conspiratorial character was that they had so much in common. Burr was Hamilton in excess, Hamilton in caricature. Where Hamilton was selective in his extramarital adventures, bedding only with women who he thought cared for him, Burr was totally profligate. Where Hamilton was careless of the monetary peculations of his relatives and business associates, but scrupulous about his own financial integrity, Burr was as corrupt with money as with women. Only his daughter Theodosia, the child of the one woman in his life who had meant something to him but who was now dead, aroused the best in him. Hamilton had fantasied glory like that of Napoleon—"that unequaled conqueror," he wrote, "from whom it is painful to detract" [36]—but he wanted such glory legitimately under the aegis of Washington. Burr was to demonstrate that nothing could curb his ambition, not even the idea of splitting the United States.

The balloting lasted five days. One all-night session saw the delegates sleeping uncomfortably in their greatcoats, slumped on chairs or stretched out on the floor. Jefferson's friend, Joseph Nicholson of Maryland, though ill with a high fever, was carried through the snow to ballot, and lay on the cot in the chilly anteroom. "It is a chance that this kills him," Federalist Harrison Gray Otis wrote to his wife in wonder. "I would not thus expose myself for any President on Earth." [37] Jefferson, who must have been deeply shaken by such evidence of friendship, remained outwardly imperturbable as he presided in the Senate Chamber during the tense six-day crisis. "Calm and self-possessed," wrote one fascinated woman observer, "he retained his seat in the midst of the angry and stormy, though half smothered passions that were struggling around him, and by this dignified tranquillity repressed any open violence—though insufficient to prevent whispered menaces and insults, to these however he turned a deaf ear, and resolutely maintained a placidity which baffled the designs of his enemies." [38]

Jefferson always insisted he did not go into the presidency with his hands tied, though Samuel Smith of Maryland after a conversation with him quietly let it be known that Jefferson would be reasonable on such matters as the reduction of the navy and support of public credit. Whether Jefferson authorized Smith to speak on his behalf will probably always be matter of dispute. But the possibility must have been lurking in the back of Jefferson's mind that corrupted delegates could at any moment take the presidency away from him. As James A. Bayard later expressed it, "By deceiving one man (a great blockhead), and tempting two (not incorruptible)" Burr might have made himself president.[39] As it turned out, Jefferson predicted that a break would come on the sixth day, and it did. Bayard, who rather liked the idea of being president-maker, announced that he would cast a blank ballot and thus broke the impasse.

Jefferson's combination of toughness and fairness, his refusal to resort to bludgeoning and violence, his control both of his own rage and the rage of his party members, paid handsomely. The Federalists by contrast emerged as the tricksters and manipulators, the men who had demonstrated by their deeds that they held the Constitution in contempt. "A little more prudence and moderation" on their part, Jefferson wrote, "and it would have been long and difficult to unhorse them. Their madness had done in three years what reason alone, acting against them, would not have effected in many." [40] Letters of congratulations now poured in from everyone Jefferson cared about—everyone, as we have seen, save his own daughters. The old revolutionist, Sam Adams, crippled with palsy, had turned against his cousin in the election. "The Storm is over," he wrote to Jefferson, "and we are in port." [41] No letter, apparently, gave Jefferson as much satisfaction as that of the aging Quaker John Dickinson, who in the first flush of the Revolution could not bring himself to sign the Declaration of Independence, but who had nevertheless joined the revolutionary militia and had fought for the Constitution. Jefferson replied with a letter in which the overtones suggest that he felt almost as if he had been congratulated by his own father.

> No pleasure can exceed that which I received from reading your letter of the 21st ultimo. It was like the joy we expect in the mansions of the blessed, when received with the embraces of our forefathers, we shall be welcomed with their blessing as having done our part not unworthily of them.

In this letter he returned again to the metaphor he preferred above all others, that of Jason, commander of the *Argo*, who brought back successfully the sacred Golden Fleece to Greece.

> The storm through which we have passed, has been tremendous indeed. The tough sides of our Argosy have been thoroughly tried. Her strength has stood the waves into which she was steered, with a view to sink her. We shall put her on her republican tack, and she will now show by the beauty of her motion the skill of her builders.[42]

After the victory Jefferson went to what was called the President's House to say goodbye to Abigail Adams, who was to leave Washington a fortnight before the inauguration. Whether he saw John Adams then we do not know. Abigail had been deeply troubled by Jefferson's irreligion. "Can the placing at the head of the nation two characters known to be Deists be productive of order, peace, and happiness?" she wrote to her son Thomas, and then, for reasons known only to her, crossed out the paragraph.[43] She was no less bitter than her husband over the election loss. But the Adamses were suffering, too, from a special and largely unpublicized sorrow, the death the previous November of their son Charles. Jefferson had known him as a boy in Paris, and no doubt offered his sympathy. Charles had been a witty, singing, flute-playing youth of much charm and promise, but had died as a dissolute alcoholic of a liver infection and dropsy. He had squandered his own money, and that of his friends and brothers, and had brought little but suffering to his attractive wife. When Adams had learned in detail of his son's debaucheries, he had sloughed him off in a rage. "I renounce him," he had written to his wife. "King David's Absalom had some ambition and some enterprise. Mine is a mere rake, buck, blood and beast."[44]

His last hours in office Adams spent writing in the names of Federalist judges, so that Jefferson could not appoint Republican ones under the new Judiciary Act.[45] Then in an incredible display of pettiness, he scurried away from Washington at 4 A.M. on inauguration day, as Page Smith has written, "toothless, palsied, and bruised in spirit." To his son Thomas he wrote, "If I were to go over my life again, I would be a shoemaker rather than a statesman." [46]

Adams could flagellate himself openly, however, as Jefferson never could, and was capable of astute self-criticism. In a letter showing as much contrition as spleen, he confessed to Federalist William Tudor what he could never admit to the new President, that his own party had "vainly overrated its own influence and popularity," misunderstood the causes of its own power, "and so wantonly destroyed them." With a little common sense, he said, "we should not have been overthrown by Philip Freneau, Duane, Callender, Cooper and Lion, or their great patron and protector." [47] Out of pique, vanity, and fear he had jailed or tried to jail these editors and political dissenters. And it was they, aided by the "great" Jefferson, who had succeeded instead in throwing him out of office. Thus he admitted what a wretched blunder the Sedition Act had been.

Whether Adams similarly admitted having blundered within his own family we do not know. When Jefferson took over Adams' desk, he found a letter which had been delivered too late to reach the latter before his hasty dawn departure, and he forwarded it on with a formal little note. Adams replied with a poignant letter that was surely meant to be, at least in part, an explanation for his recent incivility:

> Had you read the Papers inclosed they might have given you a moment of Melancholly or at least of Sympathy with a mourning Father. They relate wholly to the Funeral of a Son who was once the delight of my Eyes and a darling of my heart, cutt off in the flower of his days, amidst very flattering Prospects by causes which have been the greatest Grief of my heart and the deepest affliction of my Life.[48]

Jefferson, angered at what he called the "indecent conduct" [49] of Adams' midnight appointments, did not reply. This was the last letter either man would send to the other for eleven years.

On his inauguration day Jefferson, plainly dressed, walked from his lodging at Conrad and McMunn's to the Capitol with a group of friends. A company of artillery from the new City of Washington and riflemen from Alexandria paraded before the boarding house, and cannon roared when he entered the north wing of the Capitol. Almost everything in Washington was unfinished, including the Capitol, described by Henry Adams as "two wings without a body." The city was in part Jefferson's; he had planned it with George Washington, and his draftsman's pen had touched many a blueprint. Gouverneur Morris had written ironically to a French friend, "We only need here houses, cellars, kitchens, scholarly men, amiable women, and a few other such trifles, to possess a perfect city." But Jefferson in looking out over the raw and sprawling village, its clumps of hastily built houses divided by swamps and forest, saw instead a beautiful semi-rural landscape that would not stifle him. "We find this a very agreeable country residence," he would write to Thomas Mann Randolph, "good society and enough of it, and free from the heat, the stench, and the bustle of a close built town." [50]

Inside the Senate Chamber the absence of John Adams was instantly noted. And there were few in the audience who, looking up at Jefferson, flanked by Aaron Burr on his right hand and John Marshall on his left, could not have known, as Henry Adams described it later, that here were "three men who profoundly disliked and distrusted each other." Jefferson was bland, informal, and amiable, by his manner an aristocrat as well as a democrat. When he spoke his voice carried to only the first few rows of the crowded Chamber; most of those who strained to hear his address had to read it in the Washington papers the next day. He had come, as Henry Adams said, "to claim the place of an equal between Pitt and Bonaparte," and there is every evidence in the inaugural address that he understood perfectly the nature of his role in the history of his nation, and his new political position in the western world.[51]

His address, one of the great seminal papers in American political history, was to have an almost Biblical impact. Tactically it was a speech of healing and conciliation. "We are all republicans; we are all federalists," he said, and those among the most frenetic of his enemies in the audience relaxed in surprise. He even reached out to define the rights of these enemies—the monarchical Federalists whom he counted privately as "incurables, to be taken care of in a mad house, if necessary, and on motives of charity." [52] With great precision of expression and Miltonian beauty of style, he made one of the supreme definitions of minority rights in the American political record: "If there be any among us who would wish to dissolve this Union or to change its republican form, let them stand undisturbed as monuments of the safety with which error of opinion may be tolerated where reason is left free to combat it."

His speech was not only a political but also a personal testament, reflecting his concept of the ideal man as well as the ideal government. Though he spoke modestly of the "weakness" of his own powers, and his "anxious and awful presentiments," still when he spoke of the government itself, the bark he had helped to build, he radiated confidence. "I know, indeed, that some honest men fear that a republican government cannot be strong. . . . I believe this, on the contrary, the strongest government on earth." And he went on to define "the sum of good government" in terms that could apply as equally to a man as to a state—"a wise and frugal government, which shall restrain men from injuring one another, which shall leave them otherwise free to regulate their own pursuits of industry and improvement, and shall not take from the mouth of labor the bread it has earned." Here, as in his Declaration of Independence when he wrote that all men were created equal and entitled to life, liberty, and the pursuit of happiness, he was enunciating an ideal as if it were a reality. This was one of Jefferson's special qualities as a revolutionary statesman, that he could define the visionary future as if it were the living present, and this without any sense of contradiction.

It has been endlessly debated if Jefferson, in writing these lines, intended them to be universally applied. It would seem to be inconceivable that he did not think guiltily about his own slaves when he wrote of taking "from the mouth of labor the bread it has earned," and of "the minority . . . which equal laws must protect, and to violate which would be oppression." But perhaps the contradiction has always been in the mind of the listener and reader rather than in Jefferson. Perhaps he was never confused when he said "It is so," and meant "It will be so." When he said also in the inaugural address, "Let us restore to social intercourse that harmony and affection without which liberty and even life itself are but dreary things," he was reflecting the impact upon himself of the Monticello way of life, the place where "we love and are loved by every object that we see." [53] Harmony and affection—the twin ideals he insisted upon and imposed upon his family and slaves without any conscious understanding that this was despotism however benevolent—these he believed he had found at Monticello. Nothing, not the selfishness or melancholy of his daughters, the burdens of his debts, nor the inescapable oppressions of slavery on his own plantations could shake this conviction. In this respect it can be said that Jefferson dwelt in a fantasy world. Like all great leaders who have brought a juster government to men, his fantasy of the just world was so intertwined with the real world that it blurred the contradictions in his own behavior, a total consciousness of which might have served to destroy his faith in his own destiny.

Adams believed men everywhere corrupt. "We have no Americans in America," he lamented. "The Federalists have been no more Americans than the Antis." [54] But Jefferson at this same time would write, "The steady character of our countrymen is a rock to which we may safely moor." [55] This was no mere expression of the difference between the elected and the defeated. It reflected the profound difference in their respective attitudes toward the human race and toward themselves. When it came to political reality, the honest self-flagellating Adams saw too clearly; he believed that because men are by nature corrupt so will the republic be corrupt and thus certain to be repudiated in the end. Jefferson saw political reality through the blur of his fond hopes. This is one of the reasons the populace turned toward Jefferson and away from Adams.

Jefferson wrote to Lafayette with satisfaction on March 1, 1801, "The storm we have passed through proves our vessel indestructible." To John Dickinson he wrote that "our revolution and its consequences, will ameliorate the condition of man over a great portion of the globe." [56] What the nation had weathered was not revolution but counterrevolution. Nothing else would have roused Jefferson from the lethargy into which he had slipped, nothing but the threatened destruction of his *Argo* would have turned this Jason into a man of steel.

CHAPTER XXV

Betrayal

I laid it down as a law to myself, to take no notice of the thousand calumnies issued against me, but to trust my character to my own conduct, and the good sense and candor of my fellow citizens. . . .

Jefferson to Wilson C. Nicholas, June 13, 1809 [1]

Jefferson's presidency has been called anticlimactic, as if all the drama of his life had been played out in advance. Once the prize was won and the best of him written into the first inaugural address, little is supposed to have remained to call forth superlatives. His Louisiana Purchase has been described as a fortuitous accident, owing "more to the, vagaries of Bonaparte's ambition than to Jefferson's cautious diplomacy." [2] It is true that the good fortune of the Peace of Amiens in 1802 gave him a temporary respite from what he called "the exterminating havoc" of western Europe, enabling him to carry out his cherished plan to reduce the army to 3,000 men and the navy to a handful of frigates. Though a war with Tripoli broke out almost as soon as he became president, he counted it a minor matter of state, handled it with firmness, and did not let it escalate. His major repairs to the damaged republic, his restoration of freedom of the press and of speech, and his aborting of the Hamiltonian trend toward militarism, were all carried out without fanfare. Jefferson was not one to advertise his own virtues.

One of his first acts as president was the freeing of David Brown, who had gone to jail for eighteen months for raising a liberty pole in Dedham, Massachusetts, with the sign:

No Stamp Act, No Sedition, No Alien Bills, No Land Tax;
Downfall to the Tyrants of America,
Peace and retirement to the President,
Love Live the Vice-President and the Minority;
May moral virtue be the basis of civil government

Brown had served out his sentence, but was still imprisoned because he had no money to pay his fine. The hated Sedition Act was permitted to expire by the new Republican Congress; the fears engendered by the Alien Acts subsided, and the country once more threw open its doors "to fugitives from the oppressions of other countries." Jefferson took into his cabinet as Secretary of the Treasury Swiss-born Albert Gallatin, one of the men intended for deportation by the militant Federalists. With the aid of this canny financier he was able to reduce the $10 million public debt and at the same time reduce taxes. He abolished altogether the hated federal tax on whiskey, thereby, as Samuel Eliot Morison has written, making himself "immortal in the mountains." As his popularity mounted, the Federalist party virtually disappeared as an organized political force, though several strong Federalist papers remained active, as Jefferson noted, "to keep up a solitary and ineffectual barking." [3]

Among the Federalists dismissed was young John Quincy Adams, who held a minor post. Jefferson later explained to Abigail that he had not known her son was among the wholesale dismissals, but she could not forgive him for turning out of office both her husband and her favorite offspring. The son forgave Jefferson long before his mother did, and like so many young Federalists of his generation was eventually captured by the seemingly effortless Jefferson magic. "You can never be an hour in this man's company," he wrote, "without something of the marvellous." [4] Among the younger enthusiastic Republicans was Samuel Harrison Smith, publisher of the Washington *National Intelligencer*, and his attractive wife Margaret, who had been raised a Federalist. Shortly after election day Jefferson had called on Smith at his home and the young woman, not knowing who the visitor was, talked to him alone for a few moments. "The chilled feeling" she felt at first was only momentary, she wrote later. "I know not how it was, but there was something in his manner, his countenance and voice that at once unlocked my heart." When her husband entered and introduced him, she said, "I felt my cheeks burn and my heart throb, and not a word more could I speak while he remained." Afterward she reflected:

> And is this the violent democrat, the vulgar demagogue, the bold atheist and the profligate man I have so often heard denounced by the

federalists? Can this man so meek and mild, yet dignified in his manners, with a voice so soft and low, with a countenance so benignant and intelligent, can he be that daring leader of a faction, that disturber of the peace, that enemy of all rank and order?

It was she who reported the story that became a part of the imperishable legend of Jefferson's inauguration day, that when he returned from the ceremonies to have dinner at his usual boarding house, Conrad and McMunn's, he was permitted to take his usual seat far from the fire, at the coldest end of the table.[5]

Jefferson proved to be not only an unlocker of hearts but also a superb administrator. "The leadership he sought," Henry Adams wrote, "was one of sympathy and love, not of command." [6] Those who loved and served him so admired his amiability and control that they did him the further honor of imitating him. James Madison, his new Secretary of State, became in this regard a smaller edition of Jefferson himself. Though in the past Jefferson had professed to detest power for its own sake, he now used it adroitly, with an underplayed but nevertheless exuberant self-confidence. When he wrote to William Short on October 3, 1801, "We feel ourselves strong, & daily growing stronger," [7] it was both a personal statement and a description of the United States.

Those who would minimize his role in the purchase of Louisiana need only reflect on how Burr or Hamilton would have managed in his place. So accustomed are Americans to the seeming inevitability of the thing that they forget how rare was the very idea of purchase of territory to avoid war over it. It had been done: Louis XIV had purchased Dunkirk from the British. But the accepted procedure among nations was to win glory by capturing territories with blood, and when in December 1801 the Spanish government ordered the closing of the port of New Orleans, Federalists clamored almost automatically for the forcible seizure of the city. Jefferson privately called them "maniacs," saying they would bring on a true blockade by a superior naval force instead of the relatively innocuous "paper blockade from New Orleans" which permitted the Mississippi River to remain open. To seize the city, he said, would mean "seven years war, the loss of one hundred thousand lives, an hundred millions of additional debt . . . and that demoralization which war superinduces on the human mind." Even if his plans for purchase should fail, he wrote, it would be better to wait "till we have planted a population on the Mississippi itself sufficient to do its own work without marching men fifteen hundred miles from the Atlantic shores to perish by fatigue and unfriendly climates." [8] Such was the eminent sanity of the former war governor of Virginia.

When Jefferson wrote to Sir John Sinclair on June 30, 1803, "Peace is our passion," [9] he was expressing no mere political slogan but a dominating theme in his life. Liberation, once his compelling hunger, had long since given way to his need for tranquillity. This personal need influenced many aspects of his foreign policy, as well as numerous domestic decisions, all the while continuing to dominate his private life. Even to his grandchildren Jefferson would write in 1802, "It is a charming thing to be loved by everybody; and the way to obtain it is, never to quarrel or be angry with anybody." [10] While this special formula for behavior resulted in a remarkably tranquil first term, it resulted also in a major failure of omission, the gravest in Jefferson's political life. This was his failure to do anything of consequence to destroy slavery.

The revolutionary fervor of the 1770s and 1780s had galvanized many states into legislating for emancipation. By 1804 every state north of Maryland had abolished slavery, though in several states, like New York and New Jersey, the plan for gradual emancipation permitted remnants of slavery to linger for a generation. One sees, for example, the anomaly of Alexander Hamilton's holding slaves until his death, but nevertheless belonging to the New York emancipation society. In Virginia, the Carolinas, and Georgia, however, emancipation efforts had been only sporadic, and with the invention of the cotton gin in 1793 were largely doomed. Few Virginians followed the example of Washington, whose conscience rested easy with the knowledge that his slaves would be freed with the death of his widow.

Two domestic events as well as the continuing crises in Santo Domingo contributed to Jefferson's inertia about emancipation, an inertia that for a time became absolute paralysis. One was the Gabriel conspiracy of 1800, the other the exposé of his own private life by James Thomson Callender. Gabriel was a free black, twenty-four years old, who reportedly planned to arm a thousand slaves with crude swords, guns, and bayonets and lead a slave insurrection in Richmond on the night of August 30, 1800. Many slaves were actually assembling when betrayed by one of their own members. A hysteria of fear convulsed the whites; Governor James Monroe had cannon set up at strategic points in Richmond, and 650 militiamen were assembled to protect the city. Scores of slaves and free blacks were arrested, and twenty-five were hanged.[11] Jefferson, vacationing at Monticello during the bloody reprisals, was appalled at the carnage. He wrote to Monroe on September 20, "There is a strong sentiment that there has been hanging enough. The other states and the world at large will forever condemn us if we indulge in a principle of revenge, or go one step beyond absolute necessity." And he strongly urged deportation of the suspected slaves instead of execution.[12]

Virginia Federalists blamed the "Jacobin Jefferson" for the Gabriel conspiracy, saying it had been planned by his henchman James Thomson Callender. Actually Callender, who was then serving his sentence for sedition in the Richmond jail, was as much a Negrophobe as any man in the South. He wrote to Jefferson details of the conspiracy as it was being described in Richmond during the hangings: "The plan was to massacre all the whites, of all ages, and sexes; and all the blacks who would not join them; and then march off to the mountains, with the plunder of the City. Those wives who should refuse to accompany their husbands were to have been butchered along with the rest, an idea truly worthy of an African heart." Five blacks had been hanged that day, he reported, and he later wrote to Jefferson of the hanging of fifteen more.[13]

The Gabriel hysteria resulted in a flurry of legislative activity in Richmond to tighten slave controls. After another insurrection scare in 1802 there was increasing talk of banishment from the state of all newly freed slaves, which became a law in 1806. When Jefferson became president, the Virginia legislature requested him to negotiate with an African state to permit deportation of any suspected slave conspirator. Jefferson wrote to Rufus King, his minister to Great Britain, asking him to make inquiries in the British-held colony of Sierra Leone. His letter showed a compassion for the would-be insurrectionists rare among his Virginia friends: "They are not felons, or common malefactors, but persons guilty of what the safety of society, under actual circumstances, obliges us to treat as a crime, but which their feelings may represent in a far different shape. They are such as will be a valuable acquisition to the settlement already existing there." [14] But he did not, and felt he could not, show his feelings publicly.

Similarly he hid his feelings about Toussaint L'Ouverture, now ruler of Santo Domingo, whose example he believed had sparked the bloody fantasies of Gabriel. When the French chargé d'affaires in Washington, L. A. Pichon, told Jefferson in 1801 that Napoleon was intent on recapturing the island from "the Bonaparte of the Antilles," he did not apparently also say that Napoleon intended to restore slavery. Pichon reported back to Talleyrand, whether correctly or not, that Jefferson said it would be easy, if the United States furnished the French fleet with supplies, to "reduce Toussaint to starvation," and further that "his example menaced every slaveholding state." When in 1802 General Victor Leclerc landed 10,000 French troops on Santo Domingo and asked for American aid in supplies, Jefferson flatly refused, saying it would make an enemy of Toussaint. By this time Jefferson had the alarming news that Napoleon had forced the retrocession of Louisiana from Spain to France, and knew that every French soldier pinned down by Toussaint in Santo Domingo would mean one less bound for New Orleans. When Toussaint was betrayed by treachery into French hands early in 1802, to die miserably in a cold French prison in the Jura Mountains, Jefferson predicted correctly that "another black leader will arise, and a war of extermination will ensue; for no second capitulation will ever be trusted by the blacks." [15]

The French forces Napoleon intended using to consolidate an American empire, sent first to subdue Santo Domingo, disappeared in that terrible quagmire. Leclerc lost 24,000 men in nine months to disease and to black arms. He was wildly calling for extermination of all blacks on the island when he himself fell victim to disease. Jefferson doubtless realized, what his historian Henry Adams wrote later, that the successful purchase of Louisiana at this point was in large measure due to "the desperate courage of 500,000 Haitian Negroes who would not be enslaved." [16] But he did not say so, publicly or privately. Instead he followed with growing horror the career of the new black hero, Jean Jacques Dessalines, who after leading a successful revolt against the French had himself elected governor of Haiti for life in 1804, and then ordered a massacre of all the French remaining in the country. The horror was universal among whites in the United States, and served to dampen Jefferson's enthusiasm for emancipation. It also reinforced his conviction that in the southern states it must be accompanied by deportation.

Deportation, however, meant for Jefferson the end of the Monticello way of life. So the private as well as the public complexities seemed increasingly insoluble. He remained silent on his Rosinante, and detoured around this potent menace, which was neither windmill nor chimera but a true giant, becoming ever more bloated with each passing year.

Jefferson had ample warning during the election of 1800 that his private life could be a lively subject for political exploitation, as Hamilton's had been. Still, he hastened back to Monticello at every opportunity. During his first twenty-two months in office he made three trips home, and spent altogether eight months. Though neither daughter was living at Monticello, he returned for the first time less than four weeks after his inauguration and stayed a month. He went back to Washington on April 26, 1801. Sometime in May, Sally Hemings bore another daughter, and named her Harriet after the small daughter who had died in 1797.[17]

The first warning of trouble from Callender came in late April, shortly after Jefferson began to work at the serious business of being president. Callender got out of jail before the inauguration, having served his full nine-month term, but had been forced to pay his fine of

$200 before being released. Jefferson now gave Callender an official pardon on March 16 and had his Attorney General Levi Lincoln send off a letter to the federal marshal in Richmond, David Randolph, ordering him to repay the sum. Randolph, whose wife was a sister to Jefferson's son-in-law, detested Jefferson. Not only was he a hard-nosed Federalist, but also he stood to lose money from his own pocket in the repayment, so he balked. By this time Callender had collected enough information in the Charlottesville area about Jefferson's slave family to give him a tool for blackmail. Further angered when Jefferson failed to answer a letter he wrote on April 12, he complained to James Madison of Jefferson's "ostentatious coolness and indifference," and asked that he be made postmaster at Richmond, nastily implying a threat if the appointment were not forthcoming. "Mr. Jefferson has not returned one shilling of my fine. I now begin to know what Ingratitude is. . . . I am not a man who is either to be oppressed or plundered with impunity." [18]

Jefferson, alerted by Madison, wrote to James Monroe suggesting that Callender be paid with private monies, and enclosed an order that $50 be paid from his own funds. Meanwhile, back in Richmond, Randolph had finally agreed to pay Callender, but told him he must come to his own house to collect the $200, and the wary journalist, suspecting that he would be beaten up, refused to go and demanded instead that the money be sent by mail.[19] By this time, however, he was far more intent on the Richmond postmaster job than the $200, and in late May set out for Washington intent on blackmail. Lacking the courage to threaten Jefferson himself, he went to Madison.

"The money was refused with cold disdain," Callender wrote later, "which is quite as provoking as direct insolence. Little Madison . . . exerted a great deal of eloquence to shew that it would be improper to repay the money at Washington. . . . (Black Sally was fluttering at my tongue's end; but with difficulty I kept it down.)" [20] Madison, who may or may not have known the President's danger, discouraged Callender's request for the Richmond post, but did tell Jefferson of Callender's presence and his demand. Jefferson now did a foolish thing. He gave his secretary Meriwether Lewis $50 to give to Callender immediately, noting the gift in his account book on May 28, 1801, as charity, and described the whole disagreeable episode to Monroe in a letter the following day:

> Since mine of the 26th Callender is arrived here. He did not call on me; but understanding he was in distress I sent Capt Lewis to him with 50 D. to inform him we were making some inquiries as to his fine which would take a little time, and lest he should suffer in the meantime I sent him &c. His language to Capt Lewis was very high

toned. He intimated that he was in possession of things which he could and would use of in a certain case: that he received the 50 D not as charity but a due, in fact as hush money; that I knew what he expected, viz, a certain office, and more to this effect. Such a misconstruction of my charities puts an end to them forever. You will therefore be so good as to make no use of the order I enclosed to you. He knows nothing of me which I am not willing to declare to the world myself.[21]

Monroe, greatly alarmed, wrote back to Jefferson suggesting that he get "all letters however unimportant" from Callender, and that he communicate word of the blackmail threat to Meriwether Jones. "He has that ascendancy over the wretch to make him do what is right." [22] We do not know if Jefferson confided in Meriwether Jones, but the Virginia editor certainly did not stop Callender's mouth. Nor did he succeed in getting him to return any of Jefferson's correspondence. Callender returned to Richmond, where David Randolph paid him his $200 on June 20, 1801.[23] But irreparable damage had been done. Callender knew that the President and his key men now looked upon him as a common blackmailer, and that he was finished with the Republican party. He did not, however, attack Jefferson for more than a year.

In August 1801 the President returned to Monticello for a two-month vacation. It was not a tranquil summer. His nephew Dabney Carr was involved in a duel, and bound over to the local court to keep the peace. Carr, who lunched at Monticello in mid-August, later wrote of the occasion to a friend. He described his opponent as "a recreant coward," and his own pistols as "excellent," but did not describe his conversation with his celebrated uncle.[24] Visitors and workmen swarmed in and out of the still unfinished house. Jefferson's two daughters, both pregnant, came home to Monticello to bear their children. Virginia Randolph was born on August 22 and Francis Eppes on September 20. Together with Sally Hemings' small Harriet, they added up to three infants in the house, which was still short of bedrooms. Jefferson later wrote sadly to Martha, "I set down this as a year of my life lost to myself, having been crowded out of the enjoiment of the family during the only recess I can take in a year. I believe I must hereafter not let it be known when I intend to be home, and make my visits by stealth." [25]

When an epidemic of the dreaded whooping cough swept through the children on the hill, Martha and Maria stayed on a month after Jefferson left for Washington. Martha wrote to her father, "Ellen and Cornelia were particularly ill both delirious one singing and laughing the other (Ellen) gloomy and terrified equally unconscious of the objects around them. My God what a moment for a Parent. The agonies of Mr. Randolph's mind seemed to call forth every energy of mine. I had to act in the double capacity of nurse to my children and comforter to their Father." [26] Maria's infant son, who was extremely frail, also contracted the disease, and when she left she took Sally Hemings' older sister Critta with her back to Bermuda Hundred as a nurse. That there had been some kind of trouble at Monticello in addition to the sickness and overcrowding was hinted at in letters Maria wrote to her father.

"With how much regret have I look'd back on the last two months that I was with you," she wrote on January 24, 1802, "more as I fear it will allways be the case now in your summer visits to have a crowd." In April she said, "I shall write again by Crity when she goes up. I hope you had no objection to her spending the winter with me. She was willing to leave home for a time after the fracas which happen'd there and is now anxious to return." [27] The nature of the "fracas" is unknown.

The summer of 1802 brought renewed hints to Jefferson that the curtain of his private life was shortly to be destroyed. On July 10, 1802, the *Port Folio*, a Federalist literary sheet in Philadelphia, published an anonymous ballad hinting that the President preferred black women. It said in part:

> Our massa Jefferson he say
> Dat all men free alike are born;
> Den tell me, why should Quashee stay,
> To tend de cow and hoe de corn?
> Huzza for massa Jefferson:
>
> And why should one hab de white wife,
> And me hab only Quangeroo?
> Me no see reason for me life!
> No! Quashee hab de white wife too,
> Huzza, &c.
>
> For make all like, let blackee hab
> De white womans . . . dat be de track!
> Den Quashee de white wife will hab
> And massa *Jefferson shall hab de black.*
>
> Huzza for us den! we de boys
> To rob, and steal, and burn, and kill;
> Huzza! me say, and make de noise!
> Huzza for Quashee! Quashee will
> Huzza for massa Jefferson! [28]

Callender meanwhile had joined the staff of the *Richmond Recorder*, a Federalist sheet begun by Henry Pace the previous summer. He began to attack Jefferson early in July with what was for him a low-keyed political polemic, pointing out importantly, however, that Jefferson had favored him with gifts of money and praise, quoting Jefferson's letters as proof. For the first time the public learned that Jefferson as vice-president had subsidized and encouraged the reporter who had exposed Hamilton's love intrigue, and who had defamed Washington and Adams. Hamilton's new newspaper, the *New York Evening Post*, in October republished Callender's articles and specifically accused Jefferson of inciting the vitriolic journalist to expose Hamilton and Mrs. Reynolds.

Jefferson was enraged and baffled by the betrayal. According to one report, he went into "a violent passion," called Callender "a damn'd rascal, and a damned eternal mendicant." The phrases were exact enough, but Jefferson's defense, as reported to Callender himself, was ingenuous. "I did give the dam'd rascal the hundred dollars, but it was mere charity." [29] He used the same defense in a letter to James Monroe.

> I am really mortified at the base ingratitude of Callender. It presents human nature in a hideous form. It gives me concern, because I perceive that relief, which was afforded him on mere motives of charity, may be viewed under the aspect of employing him as a writer.[30]

After reading Callender's articles Abigail Adams believed the worst. Eventually she wrote to Jefferson:

> Until I read Callenders seventh Letter containing your compliment to him as a writer and your reward of 50 dollars, I could not be made to believe, that such measures could have been resorted to: to stab the fair fame and upright intentions of one, who to use your own Language "was acting from an honest conviction in his own mind that he was right." This Sir I considered a personal injury. This was the Sword that cut asunder the Gordian knot, which could not be untied by all the efforts of party Spirit, by rivalship by Jealousy or any other malignant fiend.[31]

Republican editors, enraged at Callender's apostasy, now proceeded to cut him to pieces. They dredged up material from his life in Scotland to show that he had threatened his old patron, Lord Gardenstone, "with a prosecution for the aid he gave him," thus demonstrating that he had stabbed a benefactor in the back before." [32] Meriwether Jones lashed out at Callender in the *Richmond Examiner* of August 14, 1802:

The facts, the damning facts of your apostacy, ingratitude, cowardice, lies, venality and constitutional malignancy, glare you in the face Callender with the petrifying lividness of an imp of the infernal regions. One is tempted to explain in the language of General Charles Lee, "I wish I was a dog, that I might not call man my brother."

This was all Callender needed. On September 1, 1802, he printed the material he had been keeping in reserve for many months:

It is well known that the man, *whom it delighteth the people to honor*, keeps and for many years has kept, as his concubine, one of his slaves. Her name is SALLY. The name of her eldest son is Tom. His features are said to bear a striking though sable resemblance to those of the president himself. The boy is ten or twelve years of age. His mother went to France in the same vessel with Mr. Jefferson and his two daughters. The delicacy of this arrangement must strike every portion of common sensibility. What a sublime pattern for an American ambassador to place before the eyes of two young ladies! . . .

Some years ago, the story had once or twice been hinted at in *Rind's Federalist*. At that time, we believed the surmise to be an absolute calumny. . . .

By this wench Sally, our president has had several children. There is not an individual in the neighbourhood of Charlottesville who does not believe the story, and not a few who know it. . . . Mute! Mute! Mute! Yes very Mute! will all those republican printers of biographical information be upon this point.

On September 22 Callender corrected a factual error. "The negro wench did *not* go to France in the same vessel with the president. Mr. Jefferson sailed first, with his elder daughter. The younger Miss Jefferson went afterwards, in another vessel, with the black wench, as her waiting maid." [33]

The articles released a tornado of abuse. The *Aurora* editor described the squalor and horror at the death of Callender's wife. Meriwether Jones republished this account in his *Richmond Examiner*, and denounced the Callender exposé as filth, blasphemy, lies, and pollution. "Come forth thou hideous and fateful mortal," he cried. "Thou clot hearted Scot . . . thou art a thief." [34] Jones realized, however, that to hurl insults at Callender would not stop the spread of the Sally Hemings story. He proceeded to answer it with some care:

That this servant woman has a child is true. But that it is Mr. Jefferson's or that the connection exists, which Callender mentions, is *false*. I call upon him for evidence. . . . Is it strange therefore, that a servant of Mr. Jefferson's at a house where so many strangers resort, who is daily engaged in the ordinary vocations of the family, like thousands of others, should have a mulatto child? Certainly not. . . . Mr. Jefferson has been a Bachelor for more than twenty years. . . . not a spot tarnished his widowed character until this frightful sea calf in his wild frenzy, thought proper to throw his phlegm at him. Are you not afraid, Callender, that some avenging fire will consume your body as well as your soul? Stand aghast thou brute, thy deserts will yet o'ertake thee.[35]

So began the defense, one later adopted by Jefferson's heirs, that someone else was responsible for fathering Sally Hemings' children. No one seems to have protested Meriwether Jones' admission—astonishing in any southern editor—that mulatto children were being born by the "thousands," casually fathered by strangers. Meanwhile Callender was threatened, as he himself reported it, with "cropping of ears, and tar and feathers, and horsewhipping, and murder." [36] No one challenged him to a duel; this would have dignified him with the rank of gentleman. None of the threats kept him from publishing additional details. On September 15, 1802, he noted that Sally had all together "five mulatto children," a correct figure for this date, though he seems not to have been told that two of them had died in infancy.[37] He reported that Sally had "fifteen or thirty gallants *of all colours*," a canard that may have sprung from gossip about her mother. Of the latter we have already noted Madison Hemings' later report that she had fourteen children by four fathers, two white and two black.[38]

"If eighty thousand white men in Virginia followed Jefferson's example," Callender wrote on September 22, "you would have FOUR HUNDRED THOUSAND MULATTOES in addition to the present swarm. The country would no longer be habitable, till after a civil war, and a series of massacres. We all know with absolute certainty that the contest would end in the utter extirpation of both blacks and mulattoes." Warning Republicans that if they did not cast Jefferson overboard, like the prophet Jonah, Callender predicted the party would be "gone forever." Had he waited till just before the election of 1804, he said, "every store would have been decorated with prints of president Tom, and his mother, who is a slut as common as the pavement." [39]

Many Federalist editors reprinted the Callender material, some with glee, some with caution. Bronfon, editor of the *Gazette of the United States*, used the opportunity to publish for the first time the ancient story of Jefferson's attempted seduction of Betsey Walker, which he had learned from Alexander Hamilton.[40] He pretended to treat the Sally Hemings material circumspectly, saying it was old gossip, and he wanted proof:

In the last Recorder we find an article respecting Mr. Jefferson, a certain black Sally, who went with him to France, and her yellow son named Tom. . . . We have heard the same subject freely spoken of in Virginia, and by Virginian Gentlemen; but as we possess no positive vouchers for the truth of the narrative, we do not choose to admit it into the Gazette, while there remains a possibility of it being a calumny. If it is not true, it will doubtless be contradicted by proper authority, and Callender will be punished, as he ought, for so enormous a libel.[41]

The *Boston Gazette* editor wrote piously, ". . . we feel for the honour of our country. . . . we do most honestly and sincerely wish to see the stain upon the nation wiped away by the appearance on it at least of some colorable reason for believing in the purity of its highest character," and he begged for "evidence of his innocence." [42]

He waited in vain. Long ago Jefferson had written that he would never "answer the calumnies of the newspapers. . . . For while I should be answering one, twenty new ones would be invented." [43] Since then he had been subjected to the chastening spectacle of Hamilton's calamitous defense on his own behalf. Still, Jefferson did violate his own practice of silence by writing one letter under the pseudonym Timoleon, which appeared on June 25, 1803, in the *Richmond Examiner*, though the fact that it was his own did not come to light till 1963. Here he answered one of Callender's charges, but it was an obscure and unimportant one, having nothing to do with Sally Hemings but with a complaint that he had paid a debt of £50 to one Gabriel Jones in depreciated currency.[44] Later he delegated his presidential secretary William Burwell to answer various repetitive attacks on his character, but Burwell, also writing under a pseudonym, said of the slave-paramour charge only that it was "below the dignity of a man of understanding." [45]

Jefferson's silence seemed to his friends and enemies to be total. Inevitably it was used as evidence of his guilt. Callender, in a seeming attempt at fairness, reported that James Madison found the miscegenation story "incredible," that David Humphreys, who had been in France with Jefferson, called it a falsehood, and also Henry Lee. And he reported that the Republican *Watch Tower* denounced it as a damnable lie.[46] Jefferson's friends in Richmond, he reported,

. . . set out with a sturdy denial of Sally's existence. They had been in this country their whole lives. They had never heard a word of her. *How then could Callender get hold of the story?* Depend upon it, sir, the whole thing must be a lie. It cannot possibly be true, a thing so brutal, so disgraceful! A thing so foreign to Mr. Jefferson's character! The scoundrel has been disappointed and affronted, you know, and this way he seeks revenge.[47]

Callender had not known about Betsey Walker. This story he now happily reprinted from the *Gazette of the United States*, and dredged up anew the hackneyed charges of Jefferson's cowardice as war governor of Virginia. With increasing vulgarity he struck at Jefferson through his daughters. "Jefferson before the eyes of his two daughters," he wrote, "sent to his kitchen, or perhaps to his pigstye, for this Mahogany coloured charmer," and he declared himself prepared to meet the President in a court of justice with a dozen witnesses "as to the black wench and her mulatto litter." [48]

Other Federalist editors, less crude but still gleeful, made sly references to Jefferson's past reputation as a man without passion, and quoted his unfortunate comments in his *Notes on the State of Virginia* about "the preferences of the Oran-ootan for the black woman over those of his own species." On this point the editor of the *Frederick-Town Herald* was merciless:

. . . at first sight it does appear somewhat odd, that "the solemn, the grave, and the didactic" Mr. Jefferson, a philosopher and metaphysician whom the world might take to be

a man whose blood
Is very snow-broth; one who never feels
The wanton stings and motions of the female,
But doth rebuke and blunt his natural edge
With profits of the mind, study and fast.

that such a man should have lived in the habitual violation of the seventh commandment with one of his own slaves!

After quoting from the *Notes on the State of Virginia*, the editor added, "By the same criterion he might be making himself out to be an 'Oran-ootan.' . . . there is merriment in the subject which we should be graceless enough to pursue at the President's expence, were it less offensive to serious and decent contemplation." [49]

This same editor said subsequently that he waited three months for a denial from Jefferson and finally did some inquiring on his own. He then wrote positively, "Our belief in it is fixed," and added details which matched the description later published by Sally Hemings' son Madison:

Other information assures us that Mr. Jefferson's Sally and their children are real persons, and that the woman herself has a room to herself at Monticello in the character of semstress to the family, if not as house-keeper, that she is an industrious and orderly creature in her behaviour, but that her intimacy with her master is well known, and that on this account she is treated by the rest of his house as one much above the level of his other servants. Her son, whom Callender calls president Tom, we are assured, bears a strong likeness to Mr. Jefferson.[50]

Similarly the editor of the Lynchburg *Virginia Gazette*, who said he waited two months for a denial of the Callender stories, sought out his own sources of information and said he found "nothing but proofs of their authenticity." Troubled by the humiliation for Jefferson's daughters, he scolded the President like an indignant parish vicar for not having married a nice white girl:

> These daughters, who should have been the principal object of his domestic concern, had the mortification to see illegitimate mulatto sisters, and brothers, enjoying the same privileges of parental affection with themselves. Alas! Mr. Jefferson did not your philosophy teach you the impropriety of such proceedings? Did not the holy scriptures shew you the sin, which you were thus heaping upon your own soul, against the day of wrath? . . . Why have you not married some worthy woman of your own complexion. . . .[51]

John Adams was one of the few Federalists of the time who might have had an answer to this last question, for he could speak authoritatively about Sally Hemings' beauty, having seen her in London. Adams believed in the truth of Callender's account, saying it was "a natural and almost unavoidable consequence of that foul contagion in the human character—Negro slavery." [52] Deeply Puritan, he had long ago written to his wife, "I have no confidence in any Man who is not exact in his Morals." [53] Now he found circulation of the story not only saddening but frightening. Almost at once he retired to his study in what was clearly a mild state of panic, and began writing his autobiography. He wrote only a few pages, and then abandoned the manuscript for over two years. But in these pages, written he said not for posterity but for his children, he put the record straight for all history to see about the women in his own life:

> I was of an amorous disposition and very early from ten or eleven Years of Age, was very fond of the Society of females. . . . This I will say—they were all modest and virtuous Girls and always maintained this Character through Life. No Virgin or Matron ever had cause to blush at the sight of me, or to regret her Acquaintance with me. No Father, Brother, Son or Friend ever had cause of Grief or Resentment for an Intercourse between me and any Daughter, Sister, Mother, or any other Relation of the female Sex. My children may be

assured that no illegitimate Brother or Sister exists or ever existed. These Reflections, to me consolatory beyond all expression, I am able to make with truth and sincerity.[54]

Adams had more compassion than his peppery wife, who wrote to Jefferson, when an opportunity presented itself in 1804, with a cruelty that was no less severe because of her uncompromising honesty, "The serpent you cherished and warmed, bit the hand that nourished it, and gave you sufficient specimens of his talents, his gratitude, his justice, and his truth." [55] Jefferson replied defensively that he had at first considered Callender "a man of genius, unjustly persecuted," and knew "nothing of his private character." His charities to him, he said, "were no more meant as encouragements to his scurrilities, than those I give to the beggar at my door are meant as rewards for the vices of his life." And he pointed out with justice that he did not hold her husband responsible for the calumny hurled in his own direction by the Federalist press.[56]

Young John Quincy Adams joined the ballad makers who were lampooning Jefferson, but his own anonymous verses, tasteful and delicate by comparison with the others, did not appear until March 1807.[57] Most of these ballads disappeared quickly into oblivion, but it seems likely that Jefferson, an omnivorous newspaper reader, saw most of them, including the following, which appeared first in the Boston Gazette and then in the Philadelphia Port Folio of October 2, 1802. There was some envy in it.

Tune *Yankee Doodle*

Of all the damsels on the green,
    On mountain, or in valley,
A lass so luscious ne'er was seen,
    As Monticellian Sally.

Yankee doodle, who's the noodle?
    What wife were half so handy?
To breed a flock of slaves for stock,
    A blackamoor's the dandy.

Search every town and city through,
    Search market, street and alley;
No dame at dusk shall meet your view,
    So yielding as my Sally.
        Yankee doodle, etc.

When press'd by loads of state affairs
    I seek to sport and dally

The sweetest solace of my cares
Is in the lap of Sally.
Yankee doodle, etc.

Yet Yankee parsons preach their worst—
Let Tory Wittling's rally!
You men of morals! and be curst,
You would snap like sharks for Sally.
Yankee doodle, etc.

She's *black* you tell me—grant she be—
Must colour always tally?
Black is love's proper hue for me—
And white's the hue for Sally.

What though she by the glands secretes;
Must I stand shil-I shall-I?
Tuck'd up between a pair of sheets
There's no perfume like Sally.[58]

You call her slave—and pray were slaves
Made only for the galley?
Try for yourselves, ye witless knaves—
Take each to bed your Sally.

Yankee doodle, whose the noodle?
Wine's vapid, tope me brandy—
For still I find to breed my kind
A negro-wench the dandy!

Chief Justice John Marshall, enjoying the humiliation of the President, made the mistake of telling Callender how much he approved of the *Richmond Recorder.* "Mr. Marshall says," the *Recorder* promptly trumpeted, "that this is the best conducted paper in America, that such an editor must be supported, and that he never before saw such a variety of subjects so correctly handled." [59] Whereupon Meriwether Jones in the *Richmond Examiner* proceeded to hurl an inkpot of his own at the Chief Justice, intimating that he tampered with his own slave women. "We should like to know what part of the Recorder is so palatable to the General. Perhaps it is the story of Sally. . . . The General knows that upon this point his character is not *invulnerable.*" [60]

Thus the country had the spectacle of the Federalists accusing Jefferson of exposing Hamilton's affair with Mrs. Reynolds, the Republicans accusing Hamilton of exposing Jefferson's affair with Betsey Walker,[61] and both parties respectively accusing Jefferson and John

Marshall of having slave mistresses. It is small wonder that the non-presidential election campaign of 1802 has been called the most slanderous in American history. Callender's attacks set the standard.

Still, it can be seen that Callender used the *Recorder* not only as an instrument for attacking the man he had once loved, but also as a mirror for exposing himself. In a staccato of self-flagellation he continued to reprint the anti-Callender assaults of other editors, including those stimulated by his earlier attacks on Adams and Washington. He seems to have taken as much pleasure in this self-mortification as in his abuse of the great men of his time. Like the criminal who exults in the newspaper accounts of his own crime, Callender reported that the Federalist *New York Evening Post* had denounced him as "a reptile, "treacherous and deceitful," who with brazen impudence had published "blasphemous slanders against the character of Washington." [62] With this same obsessional dedication to his own degraded image he reproduced a violent Republican attack upon himself from the *Richmond Examiner* of August 11, 1802:

> He has no character, no honor, no sensibility, and his squalid impotence shields him from the dread of personal chastisement. . . . If you refute one fib or calumny, he picks up or invents another, in endless succession. . . . His appearance is certainly calculated to impress one with the belief that the author of his being, like Æsop and Phaedrus, had fancifully endowed an Ourang-Outang with a few of the attributes of humanity.[63]

Meriwether Jones had once written perceptively that Callender "acts the very part he so eloquently describes." [64] By now Jones was too enraged to be analytical. In an open letter to Callender on November 3, 1802, he frankly wished him in Hell. "The James river you tell us, has suffered to cleanse your body; is there any menstruum capable of cleansing your mind. . . . Oh! could a dose of James river, like Lethe, have blessed you with forgetfulness, for once you would have neglected your whiskey." No one could have guessed at this point that Callender's body within nine months would be found drowned in three feet of water, the James River proving indeed to be his Lethe in the end.

CHAPTER XXVI

Jefferson under Attack

When the accident of situation is to give us a place in history, for which nature has not prepared us by corersponding endowments, it is the duty of those about us carefully to veil from the public eye the weaknesses, and still more, the vices of our character.

Jefferson on George III, January 1776 [1]

When Callender's first article exploded in Richmond in September 1802, Jefferson was vacationing at Monticello with his daughters. No editor had the temerity to send a reporter there, but many freely indulged in editorial fantasy about the interplay of affection and jealousy among the women who loved Jefferson. Boston and Philadelphia papers depicted his daughters as "weeping to see a *negress* installed in the place of their mother." [2] The *Virginia Gazette* reproached Jefferson for treating Sally Hemings "in the same manner as he formerly treated their mother." [3] Callender freely painted Sally as a common slut "from which the debauchee, that prowls for prey in the purlieus of St. Giles, would have shrunk with horror." [4]

None seemed to understand that some kind of accommodation had been made long ago. Sally Hemings had been at Monticello since childhood; Martha and Sally, virtually the same age, had grown up together. Maria had been at Monticello when Sally bore three of her five children, and both Maria and Martha may have genuinely grieved for her when her two infant daughters died. Whatever the accommodation, long-standing but probably always fragile, it had now, however, been shattered by the publicity. For only secrecy and denial could have made bearable whatever Jefferson's daughters had long known, or assumed, or feared, or buried, about the relationship between "Dashing Sally" and their father.

How much Sally Hemings herself learned of her sudden, nation-
wide publicity, whether through Jefferson or through the slave grape-
vine, and with what mixture of regret and secret pride she reacted to
it, are simply nonrecoverable. Hers, after all, was the total accommodation. Even her third son, Madison, who eventually felt compelled
to tell his mother's story, could communicate nothing of this special
crisis. When he was born, January 19, 1805, Sally Hemings' name was
still bubbling up occasionally in the Federalist press. But by the time
he was old enough to understand even dimly the incredible complexities of his own identity, the famous man Sally Hemings told him was
his father was out of politics and living in relatively quiet retirement.
By then Madison's oldest brother Tom had disappeared from Monticello, and his mother apparently chose not to talk about him. Tom had
become for Madison Hemings a nonperson, or at least a nonbrother.[5]

At what age Madison Hemings was told that Jefferson was his father
we do not know. Neither can we know whether Jefferson ever indicated their relationship by word or deed, or even by special nuances of
behavior.* Nor can we know if Jefferson treated Sally's older children,
Tom, Beverly, and Harriet, differently from Madison. All that Madison
himself wrote, and this with implicit bitterness, was the following: "He
was uniformly kind to all about him. He was not in the habit of showing partiality or fatherly affection to us children. We were the only
children of his by a slave woman. He was affectionate toward his white
grandchildren, of whom he had fourteen, twelve of whom lived to
manhood and womanhood." [6] That Sally Hemings knew from the

---

* It is possible that Jefferson in a covert fashion acknowledged the paternity of
Sally Hemings' sons Tom and Beverly in his account book for August 23, 1800. Following a visit of the census taker, he wrote:

August 23, 1800		Census of My Family		
Males free whites under 10	2	Females	2	4
10 under 16	1		0	1
16 under 26	3		1	4
26 under 45	1		0	1
45 upwards	1		0	1
slaves				93
				104

The "family" seems to have included Thomas and Martha Randolph (though
actually Martha was twenty-seven), their son Thomas Jefferson, age 7, and two
daughters, Ellen and Anne, age 4 and 8. Can the two other white males, one under
the age of 10 and the other age 10 to 16, be identified as Sally Hemings' sons Tom,
then 10, and Beverly, age 2? By Jefferson's own definition of what constituted a
mulatto, and by Virginia law at that time, both were white, though technically
slaves since their mother was a slave. The white man aged "45 upwards" is clearly
Jefferson. The three white males age 16 to 26 seem to have been white workmen
living at Monticello, since none of Jefferson's nephews, Peter, Samuel, and Dabney
Carr, had lived at Monticello since 1796. (See Appendix III.)

beginning that this essential rejection was to be expected seems likely. This was the traditional code of miscegenation in the plantation South, of which she herself was a product. If she had any romantic fantasies of a different situation, stimulated perhaps by the taste of freedom in France, they must have been cruelly dispelled long before the crisis of 1802. As recently as July 1802, when an epidemic of measles was sweeping Virginia, and Jefferson was fearful that Maria's new son—who was extremely delicate and had suffered from convulsive fits—might be exposed, he ordered all the slave children at Monticello who were ill with the disease removed from the area before their arrival, save for "Bet's or Sally's children," who he suggested be moved into the cabin of Betty Hemings.[7]

Importantly, however, Jefferson did not send Sally and her children away to another plantation, though Martha, according to one of her sons, "would have been very happy to have them thus removed." [8] If ever there was an opportunity to abandon his slave family, this was the time. But Sally Hemings remained at Monticello and bore two more sons there. Both were conceived when Jefferson was vacationing at home. Jefferson apparently would not send Sally Hemings away either to please his daughters or to insure a second term in office. When her son Tom left Monticello is unknown. It is likely, as we have said, that he was one of the four "yellow children" at Monticello, described by Jefferson's granddaughter Ellen Randolph Coolidge as "white enough to pass for white," who were permitted to leave under the euphemism of "running away." [9]

Having made his dangerous decision of the heart in 1802, Jefferson now had to face two problems, how to keep the affection of his daughters, and how to find some way to dampen the publicity as fast as possible so that it would not ruin his chances for a second term.

Jefferson had been trying since his inauguration to persuade his daughters to visit him for long periods in Washington, but they had resisted all his importunities with denial and postponement, usually because of the illnesses of their children. The rift between Jefferson and his son-in-law Randolph was widening, and it had been with some difficulty in 1802 that he persuaded him to abandon a plan to move to Mississippi and raise cotton.[10] Now, suddenly, both his daughters capitulated. It was agreed that Jefferson would go back to Washington first, and that Maria would follow shortly, leaving at home her year-old son. Martha planned to take her son Jefferson and six-year-old daughter Ellen, leaving the others behind with their father. For these women to abandon their husbands and several very young children for a period extending well into midwinter suggests that the daughters were responding to what was for their father a desperate need.

Perhaps Jefferson deluded himself into thinking that he could insulate his daughters from the Virginia press and gossip, which was now leaping from plantation to plantation. In the President's House he could at least prevent their seeing the *Richmond Recorder*, with its pornographic ballads, and its speculation about whether or not he had tried to seduce Betsey Walker after as well as before his marriage. By this device Jefferson could protect them through the worst period, and, more important, see for himself how they stood with him. Their presence in Washington would also serve, obviously, to dampen the gossip of a rift between them resulting from the scandal.

When Jefferson arrived in Washington in early October 1802, he wrote back to his daughters complaining of "excessive soreness all over and a deafness and ringing in the head." [11] Though he blamed it on having ridden for two days through fog, it seems likely that his body, as in the past, was responding to loss, and that his old headache was back. In this case it was the loss of his reputation as a man of impeccable morality, a philosopher who lived by reason rather than by passion; in brief, a man "whose blood is very snow-broth"—a reputation in which, despite his occasional descriptions of himself in private letters as a "savage" and an "Oran-ootan," he must nevertheless have taken some pride. A fortnight later he reported to his daughters that he still felt "rheumatic," and complained with an almost frantic urgency about the repeated delays in their departure.[12]

Meanwhile he was moving diffidently among his cabinet members and other friends, watching with some anxiety but increasing relief the slow returns from the October elections. He wrote of Callender on October 10, 1802, to Robert Livingston, in a letter that betrayed his anxiety about the effect of the charges on his own political future. "You will have seen by our newspapers, that with the aid of a lying renegade from republicanism, the federalists have opened all their sluices of calumny. Every decent man among them revolts at his filth. There cannot be a doubt, that were a Presidential election to come this day, they would certainly have but three New England States, and about half a dozen votes from Maryland and North Carolina. . . ." [13] To Levi Lincoln he wrote, "Federalist bitterness increases with their desperation. They are trying slanders now which nothing could prompt but a gall which blinds their judgments as well as their consciences. I shall take no other revenge, than, by a steady pursuit of economy and peace, and by the establishment of republican principles in substance and form, to sink federalism into an abyss from which there shall be no resurrection for it." [14] So Jefferson intimated that Callender was a liar, worthy only of a hell from which there could be no resurrection. That Callender's descriptions of Sally Hemings were "filth" seems true enough. Beyond these generalized protests at Callender's slander Jefferson would not go. He would make no specific denials about Sally Hemings in public or in private.

Martha and Maria arrived in Washington in late November and stayed six weeks. They could hardly have been kept wholly insulated from Callender's writings since there were reprintings, explosions of rage in Republican papers, and insistent demands for presidential denials in the Federalist press. Bawdy ballads continued to appear. The Philadelphia *Port Folio* printed the following on January 22, 1803:

> Cease, cease old man, for soon you must,
> Your faithless cunning, pride, and lust,
> Which Death shall quickly level:
> Thy cobweb'd Bible ope again;
> Quit thy blaspheming crony, Paine,
> And think upon the Devil.

> Resume thy shells and butterflies,
> Thy beetle's heads, and lizard's thighs,
> The state no more controul:
> Thy tricks, with *sooty Sal* give o'er:
> Indulge thy body, Tom, no more;
> But try to save thy *soul*.

Thomas Paine, newly returned from France, was visiting at the President's House during the worst of this crisis and stayed two weeks. He was impressed by the warm affection of Jefferson's daughters for their father, and was totally convinced that Callender's charges were false. Later he published an article calling them "the blackest effusions of the blackest calumny that ever escaped the envenomed pen of a villain." [15] Paine's recently published *Age of Reason*, which seemed to most Americans a blueprint for atheism, had added to his reputation for Jacobinism and cost him what little popularity he still had in the New World. The *New York Evening Post* on November 3, 1802, called its contents "too blasphemous to meet the public eye." Paine, it said, called Christ "an *impostor*, the Apostles '*quibblers and mountebanks*,' the Bible '*a book of riddles*,' and the New Testament, '*the reverse of Truth*.'" During Paine's stay at the President's House the *Port Folio* denounced him as "*the greatest infidel on earth*." "Is he," the editor asked, "a fit companion for Thomas Jefferson, the president of the United States?" [16] Paine's very presence was a political liability, and the fact that he stayed two weeks showed how stubborn Jefferson could be about his friends.

Paine and Jefferson were both lampooned in an extraordinary ballad called "Black and White" that appeared in Boston and Philadelphia in April 1803. It began as follows:

> A statesman so great, and a damsel so neat,
> Convers'd about things where they were;
> They ogl'd and chatted, and made it quite late,
> *Tall Tom* was the name of the statesman so great,
> And *Sally* the name of the *fair*.

> And now says *Tall Tom*, since to-morrow I start,
> With a message for Washington city,
> I cannot help saying before I depart,
> I fear that *Tom Paine*, with his air and his art,
> Has made, or will make, an attack on your heart
> And enter it even to pity.

> Do you mean to affront me, the *fair Sally* said,
> I ne'er heard the like in my life.
> For if you be living, or if you be dead,
> I swear I will never love *one* in your stead;
> I'll be constant and true as a wife.

As the ballad continued, Paine arrives after Jefferson leaves and is successfully seducing Sally when they are interrupted by an apparition:

> His hair seem'd on fire! he utter'd no sound,
> He spoke not, he mov'd not, he look'd not around. . . .

> His hat was *full-cock'd*, and of beaver the best,
> He had on one boot and one shoe,
> A little *pedometer* hung from his neck,
> A large pair of compasses went from his back,
> O'er a coat that seem'd not very new. . . .

> His *silver hook'd* cloak he unclos'd;
> But what artist can paint her dismay and surprise,
> When a large roll of brimstone shone full in her eyes,
> And the ghost of *Tall Tom* stood expos'd.

Paine calls for help and slaves attack the specter, beating at him with their shovels. When they realize they cannot hit him and stop, he speaks:

> Behold me, *false Ethiop*, behold me he cried,
> Learn the *cause* and *effect* of this evil,

"God grants, that to punish your falsehood and pride,
"My ghost, with a message from hell cut and dried,
"Should come at this moment, stand close by your side,
"Then carry you off to the devil."

Thus saying, his arms around poor *Sally* he grip'd,
Tho's she screech'd to the *people* around,
Her throat from one ear to the other he rip'd,
He pull'd out her tongue, through the floor then he slipp'd,
And never since that has been found.

Paine flees; the ballad ends, as a proper ballad should, with the myth of eternal renewal of the crime:

Twelve times in the year when the moon is at full,
And mortals are snoring in bed,
Her sprite haunts that place all cover'd with wool,
And patiently waits for her *Thomas* to pull,
The tongue by its roots from her head.

Two hundred new slaves with a leap and a pride,
All dance round a high blazing fire,
And when to the end of the circle they come,
They drink out of warming pans full of hot rum,
And this is their toast, "here's success to *Tall Tom*,
"And the devil take *Sal* for a liar." [17]

This ballad, radiating hatred for Paine and Sally, is surprising in its implicit sympathy for Jefferson. He is betrayed by a fair and wanton woman, and betrayed also by a friend, the hated foreigner and atheist. Sally is justly punished by having her throat cut and tongue pulled out, but Jefferson's success in the end is toasted by his slaves, as the lying and seducing woman is carried off to Hell. Many likewise cursed not the President but his paramour. Others felt the long widowed Jefferson was entitled to his own private life; they were revolted not by the miscegenation but only by the publicity. Many men may have in fantasy joined happily with him, believing, like the earlier ballad maker we have quoted, that the black woman was more "luscious" and "yielding" than the white, and approving this new evidence that their philosopher president was neither effete nor impotent.[18]

The counterreaction against Callender's prurient articles was greatly aided by the presence in Washington during December and January of Jefferson's two daughters and his grandchildren. Margaret Bayard Smith found Martha Randolph, though "rather homely," nevertheless "a delicate likeness of her father," and called her "one of the most lovely women I have ever met with, her countenance beaming with intelligence, benevolence and sensibility." She described her daughter Ellen as "one of the finest and most intelligent children I have ever met." [19] To his first formal dinner of the season Jefferson invited only Federalists. Among the guests was the Reverend Manasseh Cutler, who though a clergyman and outspoken Federalist was not sufficiently troubled by the scandal to turn down the invitation. He looked at Maria and Martha with great curiosity. "They appeared well-accomplished women," he wrote in his diary, "very delicate and tolerably handsome. The president was very social." Cutler noted also in his diary with some irony, what the *Port Folio* called "one of the most remarkable events of the present time," that Jefferson had begun going to church:

> He and his family have constantly attended public worship in the Hall. . . . On the third Sabbath, it was very rainy, but his ardent zeal brought him through the rain on horseback to the Hall. Although this is no kind of evidence of any regard to religion, it goes far to prove that the tide of bearing down and overturning our religious institutions, which, I believe, has been a favorite object, is now given up.[20]

Cutler wrote that Jefferson's dress "has been quite decent," tacitly acknowledging that the press accounts of his careless, threadbare clothes were exaggerated, though it was true that the man who had been fastidious about his dress while in Paris now affected a style of almost ostentatious simplicity. Senator William Plumer, seeing Jefferson for the first time at the President's House, dressed in "an old brown coat, red waistcoat, old corduroy small clothes, much soild—woolen hose—& slippers without heels," thought at first he was a servant.[21] Such informality had served from the beginning of his presidency to endear him with the Republicans, who counted it an appropriate gesture against the glitter of foreign courts.

Jefferson did not stint, however, on food and wine, the quality of which made his dinners attractive to Federalist and Republican alike. His daughters, knowing the precarious nature of his finances and the frightening escalation of his debts, must have been appalled at the cost of the daily presidential hospitality, for Jefferson never dined alone. There were always eight or nine people, and often as many as eighteen. Maria in particular was distressed at the cost of her own stay in Washington, which her father insisted on paying in full, including the cost of new clothes.

When his daughters started back for Virginia, Jefferson accompanied them a short distance. Maria wrote back a tender letter describing her "depression of spirits" at the parting. "The pain of seeing you turn back alone after having experienc'd so many happy hours with you My dear Papa in the little room to us endear'd by your sitting in it allways, and the recollection of the heavy expense this journey has been to you for indeed it must be in all immense, made my heart ache." Then most obliquely she referred to his celibate life and hinted that she would like to see him respectably married. "How much do I think of you at the hours which we have been accustom'd to be with you alone My dear Papa and how much pain it gives me to think of the unsafe and solitary manner in which you sleep upstairs." Unsafe indeed had Jefferson's bedroom proved to be at Monticello! She finished by telling her father what he most wanted to hear, that he was still loved and revered: "Adieu dearest and Most beloved of fathers. I feel my inability to express how much I love and revere you. But you are the first and dearest to my heart." [22]

So the unconscious seduction back and forth continued. For this brief holiday Jefferson, it would seem, had had two adoring children, with both husbands banished and both girls caught up in their father's orbit, with Black Sally and Mrs. Walker either explained, or ignored, or temporarily buried, and with Jefferson in any case forgiven.

During the months following the Callender exposure Jefferson in public was imperturbability itself, successfully pretending to a serenity he certainly did not feel. His message to Congress, read on December 15, 1802, was a masterly study in nonexacerbation. It was not surprising that Alexander Hamilton described it contemptuously as a lullaby. Jefferson outraged no one; all was optimism, gentleness, and satisfaction. Just as his private mask hid his own turbulent emotions, so the public mask hid the gravest problems that were facing the nation. The opening lines of his speech set the tone:

> Another year has come around and finds us still blessed with peace and friendship abroad; law, order, and religion, at home, good affection and harmony with our Indian neighbors; our burdens lightened, yet our income sufficient for the public wants, and the produce of the year great beyond example.[23]

The frightening specter of Napoleon's troops arriving at the Mississippi and grabbing the vast potential empire beyond its western banks was so camouflaged that most Americans had no notion whatever of the possibility of the threat. Jefferson also minimized the undeclared war with Tripoli. And he pointed out with satisfaction new settlements of boundaries with Indians, an impressive reduction of the public debt, and a surplus in the Treasury.

With great adroitness he managed to get Congress secretly to pass a bill giving him free use of $2 million for negotiating with Napoleon, and he set in motion the diplomatic procedures that led to the successful Louisiana Purchase. With the same kind of delicate manipulation he won congressional support for the expedition to the Pacific. Camouflaging his real intent, which was a highroad across the continent, he then won passports for his explorers into British, Spanish, and French territory with vague proposals of "literary and scientific" endeavors. So Jefferson during the most harassed hours of his private life laid the groundwork for his two greatest triumphs as president, the Louisiana Purchase and the road to the Pacific.

As usual, when he could, he kept important posts "in the family," choosing as head of the expedition to the Pacific his disciple and private secretary, Meriwether Lewis, whom he had long ago instructed in surveying in Albemarle County. Back home to Albemarle County Jefferson also sent for a replacement for Lewis, choosing Lewis Harvie for his new secretary, a young man who in his fierce loyalty to Jefferson had already threatened to kill editors Callender and Pace.[24] Jefferson's secretaries were all lively, unconventional, and irreverent youths. Lewis Harvie and his successor William Burwell, as one dour clergyman noted, were "the men that broke up William and Mary's College, and were afterward expelled from New Jersey College for Atheism and infidelity." [25]

Meanwhile Callender's assaults continued. Like a hound dog on the scent of an old trail he sought out John Walker, and in a series of articles from October 13, 1802, through March 9, 1803, he amplified the original disclosures Bronfon had published in the *Gazette of the United States*. Callender described Betsey Walker as he had Maria Reynolds, a paragon of innocence. She had repulsed Jefferson's first seduction attempt, he said, "with the contempt it deserved." In describing the second attempt, Callender sneered at the President's virility. "We did not suspect that the great personage had possessed that *ardor of constitution*, which was necessary for the renewal of so detestable, and so desperate a scheme." [26] John Walker, who had known for many years about Jefferson's attempts to seduce his wife and had long since made his peace with the memory, now found himself the nation's most celebrated putative cuckold, an object of widespread sniggering and derision. Though he was being used as a dupe for political purposes, he seems to have cared little about destroying the President politically. He did care a great deal about his honor in Virginia. He refused to let Callender publish a letter Jefferson had sent him, which was apparently a confession of his guilt; instead he challenged the President to a duel. Henry Lee was the bearer of the message.[27]

Not content with attacking Jefferson, Callender began throwing brickbats at other benefactors, notably George Hay, who had been one of his defense lawyers in his own sedition trial. When he accused Hay of suppressing evidence in a local court case, this lawyer, who was the son-in-law of James Monroe and very much a part of Jefferson's "inner family," armed himself with a cudgel and followed Callender down a Richmond street and into a store, where he beat him about the head and shoulders. Hay said later that he came upon Callender accidentally, but there seems to have been nothing accidental about the club he carried, and Callender insisted Hay struck the first blow from the rear. He flattened the editor's high hat and left many bruises along with a deep gash across his forehead. Later in court Callender said the hat had saved his life. He had lost "four pounds of blood," had fainted several times, and was blind in one eye for a fortnight thereafter.[28]

Beating up editors was already commonplace in the young United States, and the practice had not been notably penalized. Abel Humphreys, who had administered a beating to Benjamin Franklin Bache, editor of the Republican *Aurora*, had afterward been given a diplomatic mission by John Adams.[29] Hay was given a vote of thanks by fifteen members of the Virginia legislature, and when he was summoned to the courthouse to give an account of the assault, Peter Carr, Jefferson's approving nephew, walked at his side.[30] Jack Eppes, Jefferson's son-in-law, who was in Richmond to attend Hay's trial, wrote to the President that the courthouse was so crowded he could not get inside to hear the arguments.[31] Hay was bound over to keep the peace. Later, in 1805, Jefferson employed him as his private attorney, and he would act as one of the prosecution against Aaron Burr.[32]

Callender denounced Hay in the *Recorder* as an "assassin and murderer," and Hay in return took both Callender and Pace to court, where he demanded that the *Recorder's* "torrent of calumny and abuse" be stopped altogether. The judge obliged by ordering both editors to give $500 each as security against future offensive writing. Pace did, but Callender vowed he would go to jail five million times before paying the sum. And to jail he went. At which point the *Washington Federalist* noted ironically that the very Republicans who had screamed loudest against the Sedition Act were now guilty of the same kind of attack against freedom of the press.[33]

In the Richmond jail, Callender continued to write for the *Recorder*, still the same demonic machine of fury and invective. In ranting against Hay, and a kindred enemy named Sawney McRae, he showed increasing evidence of his own morbidity:

> The Recorder swears that his [Hay's] name, with that of McRae, shall soar on the Eagle wings of infamy, along the four winds of heaven,

till room is not left for an additional stroke, till their whole characters shall become one common indistinguishable wound, till the agonies of rage and madness, as they sometimes have done, may possibly extinguish those sensibilities by which disgrace is felt.[34]

Faced with the increasingly poisonous situation in Richmond, the challenge to a duel by John Walker, and the threat of publication of his letter or letters to Walker, Jefferson made a discreet fortnight visit to Monticello from March 11 to March 31, 1803. He arrived in time to discover that Callender had extended his charges to include the Langhorne letter scandal involving Peter Carr and George Washington.[35] Moreover, Callender had charged Jefferson with atheism, using a copy of an old letter Jefferson had sent to Peter Carr from Paris, which had said, "Question with boldness even the existence of a god; because, if there be one, he must more approve of the homage of reason than of blindfold fear." [36]

Depressed and desperate, Jefferson now wrote to his old friend John Page, "We are now both drawing towards the end of the career of life as well as of honour," he said. "We began together, & probably shall end nearly together." He invited Page and his wife to vacation with him at Monticello, hinting delicately at the Walker difficulty as if he were soliciting his help—for Page was still Walker's friend—but did not dare do so openly. "You have another old friend too in the neighborhood to attract you: and tho' he & I have unhappily fallen out by the way, yet both cherish your friendship, and neither says with Achilles 'my friend must hate the man who injures me.' " [37] Page wrote back of his reverence and affection for Jefferson, whom he called "the most exalted & most deserved exalted character . . . upon earth." "Curses on the Tongue of Slander!" he said. "Perdition seize the wretches who would open the scars of wounded Friendship, to gratify private resentment & party spirit." [38]

The prospect of fighting a duel with John Walker over shadows of a past thirty-five years dead must have seemed to Jefferson in March 1803 an improbable nightmare. Someone arranged a discreet meeting at the home of James Madison. Here Jefferson talked with Walker, Henry Lee, and John Randolph. There was no duel. Madison on April 20 wrote partly in code to James Monroe, who had left for France on March 9, 1803. "The affair between *the President* and J. Walker has had a happy *éclaircissement*. Even this general communication is for your *own bosom* as already *privy to the affair*." [39] And except for the single reference to the aborted duel in the *Richmond Recorder* of May 28, 1803, there was no newspaper publicity whatever.

We know something of the technique Jefferson used to heal Walker's bruised honor, because the letter he wrote to Walker just after their meeting was copied and the copy preserved. It was certified to be exact by none other than Chief Justice John Marshall, who like a good many other Federalists was now privately meddling in Jefferson's private life. In this letter Jefferson promised to do what he could to end the offensive publicity at least in the Republican press, if corresponding efforts were made to stop Callender and other Federalist editors.

> If Callender & Coleman & Caldwell can be silenced, the others are but copyers. . . . these people slander for their bread, & as long as customers can be found who will read and relish and pay for their lies, they will fabricate them for the market. . . .
>
> With respect to the Bee which you particularly mention I know not the editor I scarcely ever see his paper. But through a friend who knows him I can have a total silence recommended to him, probably with effect. Through the same channel the Aurora and American Citizen may probably be induced to silence. . . . my best endeavors shall be used by these & all other means to consign this unfortunate matter to all the oblivion of which it is susceptible.
>
> I certainly could have no objection to your shewing my letter to W. Nicholas and to the ladies of your family. My greatest anxieties are for their tranquillity.[40]

So Walker was persuaded to back down, and Callender wrote with regret that "the publication of the documents has for some time been suspended." [41] For a time the story did largely disappear from the nation's press.

One letter written by Jefferson to his son-in-law Randolph that might have illuminated Jefferson's relations with Martha during this whole ordeal has curiously disappeared. All we have is Randolph's reply of May 22, 1803: "I received it on my return from Amhurst and did with it, in regard to Martha, as you directed. With respect to others, no act [?] or of any kind has occurred since, for me to do anything, or perhaps never may, that subject having ceased I believe to afford discourse to the malignant, as well as the idle and inquisitive. Should it again arise I shall with the weight [?] my zeal inspires represent to those disposed to agitate it the danger they incur of being charged with baseness or folly for reviving or propagating a story engendered itself by hatred and agitating the misery of individuals who are never heard of in good or in evil." [42]

There is an important but oblique reminiscence in the memoirs of Jefferson's granddaughter, Ellen Randolph Coolidge. She describes her mother's anger at the attack of the British poet, Thomas Moore, who had met Jefferson and later—in Ellen's words—had written "an outpouring of wrath and venom seldom equalled." What Moore had actually done was to write a poem mentioning the President's black mistress:

> The patriot, fresh from Freedom's councils come,
> Now pleased retires to lash his slaves at home;
> Or woo, perhaps some black Aspasia's charms,
> And dream of freedom in his bondsmaid's arms.

"My mother, as she has often told me," Ellen wrote, "was indignant, even exasperated. So was the excellent and honest Mr. William Burwell, who had been my grandfather's private secretary. . . . But the injured individual only smiled at their charge and was not himself in the smallest degree annoyed." [43]

Though he kept his travail remarkably secret, these months were for Jefferson a period of profound crisis of the spirit. Evidence of his torment can be seen best in a paper he wrote just after his return to Washington in April 1803, which he distributed only to his daughters and a close friend, with instructions to keep it strictly confidential. The decision to write it, he told Benjamin Rush, came when he was jogging along on his horse returning to the capital. During his stay at Monticello, he said, he had received a pamphlet from Joseph Priestley, *Socrates and Jesus Compared*, and it inspired him to put his "religious creed on paper." [44] Ever since Priestley's flight from England to America, and his first meeting with Jefferson in Philadelphia in 1797, Priestley had been a kind of mentor. The two men had exchanged many letters, and Jefferson had adopted totally the concept of a "reasonable Christianity," as expounded in Priestley's two-volume *History of the Corruptions of Christianity*, where he had ruthlessly stripped away all dogmas accumulated by Christians over the centuries, including the concept of the godhood of Jesus. "Yours is one of the few lives precious to mankind," Jefferson had written to him on March 21, 1801, "and for the continuance of which every thinking man is solicitous." [45]

Priestley's new pamphlet, *Socrates and Jesus Compared*, coming as it did when Jefferson was full of despair, had an extraordinary impact. Here were compared the virtues of the two most influential figures in western history, both of whom had been executed for political sin. Socrates, Priestley wrote, was a man without vice who devoted himself to promoting virtue in others. Nevertheless, along with other Greeks of his day he thought nothing of fornication; he condoned the profession of courtesans, and he even availed himself of the services of the celebrated courtesan Aspasia. On the other hand the morality of Jesus, who had never married, Priestley insisted, was truly pure. He quoted with favor the admonition of St. Paul, who counted fornicators and adulterers no better than thieves and extortioners, and warned that none of them "shall inherit the kingdom of God." [46]

It was all too close, too disturbing, and Jefferson may well have wondered, since the pamphlet had been so recently written, if Priestley when he wrote it had had the indiscretions of Jefferson in mind as well as those of Socrates. Was he deliberately prodding the presidential conscience? In any case, within a fortnight after his return to Washington, Jefferson wrote a remarkable document, the nature of which has never been fully understood because its connection with this special crisis has been entirely overlooked. Jefferson's *Syllabus of an Estimate of the Doctrines of Jesus, Compared with Those of Others* is generally described simply as a defense against the continuing public libel that he was an atheist. It was much more an attempt at a resolution of a shattering personal dilemma. The *Syllabus* said in brief, I am a good Christian, a man who reveres Jesus, though I cannot accept his godhood. Still, I accept his moral system as being better than either that of the ancient philosophers or that of the ancient Jews. But in Jefferson's use of metaphors, in his repetitions, in the very choice of subject—the great and innocent man cut down by "the altar and the throne"—one sees him wrestling with his own sense of betrayal and crucifixion.

Jesus' "parentage was obscure," Jefferson wrote, "his condition poor; his education null; his natural endowments great; his life correct and innocent; he was meek, benevolent, patient, firm, disinterested, and of the sublimest eloquence." But his doctrines had been "mutilated, misstated," "disfigured by the corruptions of schismatizing followers," "frittered into subtleties and obscured with jargon"—as indeed had Jefferson's own writings. The moral system of Jesus, Jefferson wrote, "if filled up in the style and spirit of the rich fragments he left us, would be the most perfect and sublime that has ever been taught by man." But the greatest contribution of Jesus was this: "He pushed his scrutinies into the heart of man; erected his tribunal in the region of his thoughts, and purified the waters at the fountain head." [47]

Jefferson, too, was pushing his "scrutinies into the heart of man." He had never in all his life been so betrayed, first by Callender, who was called "Judas" by the Republican press, and second by the Walkers, who for all their protestations about how damaged they were by the publicity, had nevertheless freely permitted what was either an ancient flirtation or an ancient folly to be resurrected for purposes of political destruction. Now, too, his affection for Sally Hemings, and hers for him, long a private and inoffensive secret, had been turned into political pornography. Still, there was guilt. Jefferson was pushing his "scrutinies into the heart of man"—most deeply into his own.

He began his *Syllabus* with a curious sentence: "In a comparative view of the Ethics of the enlightened nations of antiquity, of the Jews and of Jesus, no notice should be taken of the corruptions of reason among the ancients, to wit, the idolatry and superstition of the vulgar, nor of the corruptions of Christianity by the learned among its professors." [48] Could the repetition of the word "corruption" suggest that he was not so much contemplating the "corruptions of Christianity" or the "corruptions of reason" as the corruptions of Thomas Jefferson? That he was defensive and anxious shows not only in the document itself but also in the letters accompanying it, which he sent to his daughters and to Benjamin Rush. To Martha he wrote, "A promise made to a friend some years ago, but executed only lately, has placed my religious creed on paper. I have thought it just that my family, by possessing this, should be enabled to estimate the libels published against me on this, as on every other possible subject." [49]

To Benjamin Rush he wrote a careful letter saying that this religious creed was the fruit of "a life of enquiry & reflection." He could not, however, escape making some reference to his current difficulties. "And in confiding it to you, I know it will not be exposed to the malignant perversions of those who make every word from me a text for new misrepresentations and calumnies." He felt no obligation, he said, to any "inquisition over the rights of conscience"; questions of faith were a private matter "between God and himself." [50] So too, he seems to have been saying, were questions of the heart.

During the writing of this *Syllabus*, Jefferson conceived the idea of making his own private, expurgated New Testament. He would strip away its "corruptions," leaving out all references to the supernatural— the Virgin Birth, the miracles, the Resurrection, and the complexities of the crucifixion, including only, as he put it later, "the matter which is evidently his, and which is as easily distinguishable as diamonds in a dunghill." [51] This project he began to carry out in the winter of 1804–5.

By the time he had finished his forty-six-page pamphlet he had found a pragmatic excuse for the whole project, envisioning it as a useful tool for enlightening the Indians about Christianity without troubling them with conversion. To make the title palatable to the clergy he devised the following: "The Philosophy of Jesus of Nazareth, extracted from the account of his life and teachings as given by Matthew, Mark, Luke and John. Being an abridgement of the New

Testament for the use of the Indians, unembarrassed with matters of fact or faith beyond their comprehension." The scholar emerged totally from the man of anguish as he conceived the idea of putting his expurgated New Testament in parallel columns with matching texts in Greek, Latin, and French. He sent away for Greek texts in January 1804, and for French texts in January 1805, but had to abandon the project as the duties of the presidency became more onerous. He completed his compilation finally in 1816, and had it bound in red morocco with gilt edging, with the title "Morals of Jesus" stamped upon the spine in gold. In the end he kept the whole matter secret, recognizing that the clergy would consider such sophisticated excision and comparative textual criticism certain proof of his atheism.[52] It was published after his death as *The Jefferson Bible*. Privately he maintained that this "Life and Morals of Jesus of Nazareth" was "a document in proof that I am a *real Christian*, that is to say, a disciple of the doctrines of Jesus," a far truer Christian than those clergymen who "have compounded from the heathen mysteries a system beyond the comprehension of man, and of which Jesus "were he to return to earth, would not recognize one feature." [53]

His old hatred of clergymen, stiffened by their attacks on his personal morality during his presidency, never really lessened. As late as 1816 one can see that despite all his brave attempts at denial no other group in America could fill him with so much rage: "I am not afraid of the priests," he wrote. "They have tried upon me all their various batteries, of pious whining, hypocritical canting, lying and slandering, without being able to give me one moment of pain." [54]

Jefferson emerged scarred from the crisis of the Callender betrayal but fortified in his conviction that in matters of conscience man should suffer no inquisition save that self-imposed in a private dialogue with God. Callender, however, sank ever more inextricably into a swamp of pollution and despair. As his crescendo of attacks increased so did his drunkenness, and he began to talk of suicide. Meriwether Jones, who reported this, said his four children, newly arrived in Richmond, refused to see "their distracted father, continually and excessively intoxicated . . . nearly putrid in his own filth." [55] In early July 1803, Callender began to quarrel with his co-editor, Pace, calling him "an infatuated wretch whom the Almighty seems to have forsaken, and who is now raving in the agonies of desperate guilt." Pace replied with an Extra vilifying Callender, accusing him of sodomy, and suing him for $2,000 damages.

The following week Pace himself was beaten by several men, including Meriwether Jones, who, reporting everything in his own paper, wrote that if "the divorced catamite" intruded himself again into decent company "he shall be kicked from it." [56] The next day, July 17, Callender was found dead in the James River. The coroner's jury ruled that he had gone there "with intent to bathe, but being in a state of intoxication . . . came to his death by an accidental drowning, and not otherwise." The water in the river, it was reported, was three feet deep. Meriwether Jones wrote bluntly, "Our own opinion is that Callender's drowning was not 'accidental' but *voluntary* . . . putting a miserable end to a miserable life." [57]

Three weeks later Jones published a letter signed Censor, an appraisal of Callender that was surprisingly perceptive and compassionate. Callender, he said, had been the "scorn of women," and had "never probably been the object of tenderness and love." Callender's body was buried in some haste, the night of the same day he drowned.[58]

The publicity Jefferson hoped was buried surfaced again in 1805, when the *New England Palladium* dragged up all the old charges, saying that Jefferson was "a coward, a calumniator, a plagiarist, a tame, spiritless animal," a man who had "taken to his bosom a sable damsel," and had "assaulted the domestic happiness of Mrs. W____." Jefferson's friends in the Massachusetts legislature tried to punish the editors, Young and Minns, by revoking the printing contract they had with the state. The legislative hearings turned instead into a trial of the President. What New England Federalists wanted was a confession to be used for the purposes of his political destruction. "God will bring every secret thing unto Judgment," one legislator said. Jefferson might think, he argued, that "even adultery, when known, was a small crime, when unknown, not at all." And he held that since Virginia forbade marriages of whites with Indians, Negroes, or mulattoes, Jefferson was at least a breaker of the law.

The *Palladium* editors won their fight, and the hearings were published as an anti-Jefferson tract.[59] A Virginian named Thomas Turner added to the fires by restating all the old charges in the *Boston Repertory* of May 31, 1805. Meanwhile John Walker, enraged at the revival of stories of his alleged cuckoldry, began renewed demands for satisfaction, and Henry Lee began harrying Jefferson with threats.[60] Apparently an agreement was worked out whereby Jefferson would write two letters to friends acknowledging his own guilt and attesting to Betsey Walker's innocence. On July 5, 1805, Jefferson wrote the required letter to his Attorney General Levi Lincoln, with a copy to his Secretary of the Navy Robert Smith. To Smith he sent the following explanatory covering note, which afterward became famous, as the original letters disappeared:

The enclosed copy of a letter to Mr. Lincoln will so fully explain its own object, that I need say nothing in that way. I communicate it to particular friends because I wish to stand with them on the ground of truth, neither better nor worse than that makes me. You will perceive that I plead guilty to one of their charges, that when young and single I offered love to a handsome lady. I acknolege its incorrectness. It is the only one founded in truth among all their allegations against me.[61]

But Walker was still unhappy. When Lee called on Jefferson at Monticello in September 1806, Jefferson insisted that the satisfaction Walker was still demanding must take a form "least derogatory" to what was due his situation and his character. Lee then wrote to Jefferson on September 8 that he had passed on this message, and that Walker would be satisfied with "a written paper from you going only to his lady's entire exculpation without the mixture of any exulpation of yourself. This paper he desires should be acknowledged before any two of yr friends in the world, to prevent at any future day the intimition of its being a forgery." [62] Thus he demanded that Jefferson acknowledge his own guilt but clarify absolutely his wife's innocence. Jefferson apparently met this last demand. As Malone put it, "As a gentleman he could do no less." [63]

CHAPTER XXVII

Death, Hatred, and the Uses of Silence

When you and I look back on the country over which we have passed, what a field of slaughter does it exhibit! Where are all the friends who entered it with us. . . . As if pursued by the havoc of war, they are strewed by the way, some earlier, some later, and scarce a few stragglers remain to count the numbers fallen.

Jefferson to John Page, June 24, 1804 [1]

Jefferson's presidency was punctuated by deaths. Callender's could have brought only relief, though his disclosures continued to cause trouble. But old friends like Sam Adams, Edmund Pendleton, Stephens T. Mason, and Mann Page died, and Jefferson now began to keep track with a kind of morbid fascination of the deaths of the signers of his Declaration of Independence. Several months before his election his slave Jupiter, exactly his own age, who had attended him like a shadow at William and Mary, and who had for years served as his coachman, died after nine days of suffering. Martha blamed it on medicine prescribed by a black doctor; Jefferson, however, wrote his son-in-law that he feared it came from Jupiter's insistence on accompanying him part way to Philadelphia. Knowing he was ailing, Jefferson said, he had "engaged Davy Bowles," but "Jupiter was so much disturbed at this that I yielded." His death, Jefferson continued sadly, "leaves a void in my administration which I cannot fill up." James Hemings died in 1801. All we know is that Jefferson wrote to Thomas Mann Randolph of his "tragical end." [2]

For a time in 1801, when Jefferson was stricken with dysentery, he thought himself doomed to an early dying but kept the illness secret save from his doctor, and found a cure finally in riding horseback two hours a day, which suggests that the cause may have lain in the tensions created by his office.[3] During 1804 Jefferson's older sister Mary died in January, and his beloved daughter Maria in April. In July Aaron Burr slew Alexander Hamilton with a single shot at the Weehawken dueling ground. In 1806 a villainous grandnephew poisoned George Wythe by putting arsenic in his coffee. Later, in 1809, Meriwether Lewis, who had become a hero as a result of his memorable trip to the Pacific, died in a fashion that strongly suggested suicide.[4] All these people in one fashion or another had had a special impact on Jefferson, and with the exceptions of Callender and Hamilton, their deaths left him to a greater or lesser degree bereft. Since with Callender's drowning Jefferson lost the most vitriolic of all his foes, and the Burr-Hamilton duel in a single shattering moment eliminated two major political rivals, he could not have looked upon death as wholly an evil, and in 1803 and 1804 more than any other years of his life he must have specially pondered the ways of fate.

Increasing age had not increased Jefferson's faith in the idea of a heaven. "When I was young I was fond of speculations which seemed to promise some insight into that hidden country," he observed to a clergyman on December 5, 1801, "but . . . I have for very many years ceased to read or to think concerning them, and have reposed my head on that pillow of ignorance which a benevolent Creator has made so soft for us. . . . I have thought it better, by nourishing good passions and controlling the bad, to merit an inheritance in a state of being of which I can know so little, and to trust for the future to Him who has been so good for the past." [5] The childhood idea of heaven had receded, as had the religious notion that illness was punishment for private sin. But the primitive fears about "good passions" and "bad passions" clung to him, and when he was struck with personal tragedy, the ancient punishing fears returned.

Jefferson was not overfond of his older sister Mary Bolling. Her husband John Bolling was an alcoholic—in Maria's words "in a state of constant intemperance allmost . . . happy only with a glass in his hand"—and the couple had at one time been separated. Jefferson wrote tartly of his sister's "constant string of little checks and obstacles," her disposition "to criticize and question" her husband, especially in company. "I wish my sister could bear his misconduct with more patience," he wrote frankly to Maria. "It might lessen his attachment to the bottle, and at any rate would make her own time more tolerable." [6] She had been ill and perhaps her death was not unexpected. But when she died Maria was pregnant again, and Jefferson was in a state of intense anxiety concerning his daughter's general debility. When Maria wrote to him of Mary Bolling's death, Jefferson, full of foreboding and reluctant to talk of death at all, made no mention of his sister in his reply. Instead he bombarded his daughter with advice, begging her to secure a midwife, and to have the means to call a physician "on the first alarm." He tried rather clumsily at the same time to lighten her fears. "I am anxious on your account. You are prepared to meet it with courage I hope. Some female friend of your Mamma's (I forget whom) used to say it was no more than a knock on the elbow." [7]

Maria, approaching confinement, admitted to being "low in spirits and health." Knowing that it would please her father, she reported that the eight small acacia trees he had given her, which she kept in pots in her bedroom, were all flourishing. She begged, in what would be her last request, that he order the emigré engraver Saint-Mémin, who specialized in making expert likenesses with a physiognotrace, to make a portrait of Jefferson for herself and Martha. "If you did but know what a source of pleasure it would be to us while so much separated from you to have so excellent a likeness of you you would not I think refuse us. It is what we have allways most wanted all our lives." [8] Remembering no doubt that Trumbull had made a portrait of Jefferson for Martha in Paris, she asked for two engravings, and thus tactfully avoided reproving him for what she seems always to have felt, that he favored Martha over herself.

Maria's depressed spirits were deepened by the frailty of her son Francis, who had suffered from birth from convulsive fits. When she went to stay with Martha at Edgehill, the older sister wrote in alarm to her father of "the noise in the head, and the foaming at the mouth and the drawing back of the head." Knowing the shame and fear that came with having an epileptic child, she promised to keep her suspicions secret.[9]

Both Maria and Martha's husbands had been elected to Congress in 1802 and Jefferson insisted on their living with him in the President's House. Eppes had succeeded William Branch Giles, his former rival for Maria's hand, who had retired for reasons of ill health. But Randolph, not to be outdone by his younger brother-in-law, whom he felt Jefferson preferred in any case, ran for office in Albemarle County without consulting his father-in-law. He barely defeated his rival, Jefferson's staunch friend, Samuel J. Cabell, who promptly contested the honesty of the election proceedings. A congressional committee took five months before it permitted Randolph to take his seat; meanwhile Jefferson tried both to make peace with the embittered Cabell and to keep his son-in-law in good spirits through the difficult period of waiting. Jefferson would rather have had his daughters than his sons-in-law with him in Washington, but being now almost as involved with these two young men as if they had been his sons, he was as intent on preserving their affection for him as that of his daughters. He did his best to help them in their careers, not an easy task with a Congress suspicious of the President's nepotism. Jefferson's letters to Randolph and Eppes show that he treated them very much as adults, with circumspection and tact, and that he wrote constantly to them of political matters he would never have dreamed of discussing with his daughters. But he could not help preferring Eppes, with his unfailing good humor, to the morose Randolph, with his periodic depressions and fits of rage. Even Randolph's daughter Ellen described her Uncle Jack as "a gay, good-natured laughing man," and her own father as "cold and austere." [10]

As Maria's confinement approached in February 1804, Jefferson urged Eppes to return home without waiting for Congress to adjourn. The young husband left in time, but a violent winter storm prevented his being ferried across the Potomac in the usual place, and when he sought out an upper crossing and started home on unfamiliar roads he became lost. Ice on the road hampered him further, and he had to walk his horse much of the dreary distance to Charlottesville. When he arrived at Edgehill, Maria had already given birth to a daughter on February 15. "A thousand joys to you, My dear Maria," Jefferson wrote when he heard the news,[11] exultant that she had survived the hazards of birth. Though the little girl, who was named Martha, flourished, her mother, like her mother before her, was ill almost from the beginning, and the ever healthy Martha, who also had an infant daughter, took the baby to her own breast to suck.

Remembering the terrible lingering illness of his wife and her gradual loss of the will to live, Jefferson, seized with what he described as "a terrible anxiety," alternated between prayer—"God bless you my ever dear daughter and preserve you safe to be the blessing of us all"—and virtual commands to her to "resolve to get strong to make us all happy." [12] When he learned of Maria's breast abscess and continual nausea, he begged her husband to bring "old and genuine" sherry from Monticello, and urged that he take Maria there for the whole summer.[13] The slaves made a litter, and carried the young mother with infinite gentleness the four miles to the top of the little mountain.

Once Congress adjourned, Jefferson hastened home, arriving April 4, 1804. Though the clinical details he described to Madison on April 9 were alarming, he was optimistic that his own presence would call her back from death.

> I found my daughter Eppes at Monticello, whither she had been brought on a litter by hand, so weak as barely to be able to stand, her stomach so disordered as to reject almost every thing she took into it,

a constant small fever, & an imposthume [abscess] rising in her breast. . . . Her spirits and confidence are favorably affected by my being with her, and aid the effects of regimen.[14]

On April 13, his sixty-first birthday, Jefferson wrote to Madison again, "Our spring is remarkably uncheary. A North West wind has been blowing three days. . . . My daughter exhibits little change. No new imposthume has come on, but she rather weakens. Her fever is small & constant." [15]

On April 17 he wrote in his account book, "This morning between 8 & 9 o'clock my dear daughter Maria Eppes died." She was twenty-five. Four days later, writing to Madison, he was utterly unable to express his grief; there was nothing but a kind of strangled understatement, "On the 17th instant our hopes and fears here took their ultimate form. . . . a desire to see my family in a state of more composure before we separate will keep me somewhat longer." [16] It was not until two months had passed that Jefferson, replying to a letter of condolence from his old friend John Page, could write openly of his anguish: "Others may lose of their abundance, but I, of my want, have lost even the half of all I had. My evening prospects now hang on the slender thread of a single life." Fearful that even the rugged Martha might die he said, "Perhaps I may be destined to see even this last cord of parental affection broken," and he went on to write of the "field of slaughter" death had wrought among their friends, as if pursued "by the havoc of war." He took refuge, as after his wife's death, in fantasies about a hereafter. "We have however the traveller's consolation. Every step shortens the distance we have to go; the end of our journey is in sight, the bed wherein we are to rest, and to rise in the midst of the friends we have lost." And he concluded the letter to Page wistfully, "We have not many summers to live. While fortune places us then within striking distance, let us avail ourselves of it, to meet and talk over the tales of other times." [17]

The phrase in this letter stating that Maria was "half of all I had" might be thought to be an explicit repudiation of his slave children. The day before her death Jefferson had written to Gideon Granger a largely political letter which had ended on a somber, and uncharacteristic, religious note: "He alone who walks strict and upright, and who, in matters of opinion, will be contented that others should be as free as himself, and acquiesce when his opinion is fairly overruled, will attain his object in the end. And that this may be the conduct of us all, I offer my sincere prayers, as well as for your health and happiness." [18] In this moment of impending tragedy he was certainly reflecting on the "man who walks strict and upright," and in the succeeding days of inexpressible sorrow he may have even further divided his "good passions" from his "bad passions" and taken refuge in denial and rejection of the children conceived by his dark and secret mistress.

Social protocol had always demanded public rejection in all cases of miscegenation with blacks. Many white men went further, and denied to themselves the reality of their paternity of their mulatto children by an unexpressed syllogism that was also a fantasy—often an unconscious one. "It is lust that results in children born out of wedlock. It is the black woman who lusts, and who has seduced me against my will. Therefore the children are hers, not mine." [19] Jefferson very likely did not take refuge in this common defense against guilt. In the same letter to John Page in which he wrote of losing "half of all I had," he also said, "But whatever is to be our destiny, wisdom, as well as duty, dictates that we should acquiesce in the will of Him whose it is to give and take away, and be contented in the enjoyment of those who are still permitted to be with us." [20] And there is important evidence that in this great crisis of bereavement he turned for solace to "those still with us," to the young black mother, the source of continuing life.

Sometime during Jefferson's visit home for Maria's illness—April 4 to May 11, 1804—Sally Hemings conceived another child. A son, whom she named Madison, was born on January 19, 1805. But Sally's son could have been no substitute for the Maria whom Jefferson had loved for twenty-five years, and it may well be that his very presence in later years served to bring back the memory of her death, and thereby further widened the already unbridgeable gap between them. Madison Hemings later wrote that he was named at the suggestion of Dolley Madison, who "happened to be at Monticello at the time of my birth, and begged the privilege of naming me, promising my mother a fine present for the honor. She consented, and Mrs. Madison dubbed me by the name I now acknowledge, but like many promises of white folks to the slaves she never gave my mother anything." [21]

We do not know whether Dolley Madison truly suggested the name, or simply promised a present when she learned that the baby had been named Madison.[22] Forgetting a promise is often an act of hostility as ancient as gift-giving, and this failure, along with countless other such slights, must certainly have been related to Madison Hemings by his mother. White women, as Mary Boykin Chesnut's diary later demonstrated, in matters of miscegenation had weapons of their own. When Martha Randolph bore her second son, January 17, 1806, she named him James Madison.[23] It could have been a symbolic erasure.

Among the many letters of condolence that poured in with Maria's death was one from Abigail Adams. "The powerfull feelings of my heart," she wrote, "burst through the restraint, and called upon me to shed the tear of sorrow over the departed remains, of your beloved and deserving daughter." She reminded him of the weeks Maria had spent with her in London when a child of eight. "The tender scene of her separation from me, rose to my recollection, when she clung around my neck and wet my Bosom with her tears, saying, 'O! now I have learnt to Love you, why will they tear me from you.' " [24]

Deeply sensitive to the overtones, and forgetting that friendship often encompasses a measure of hate along with love, Jefferson now chose to believe that Abigail had never shared John's hostility to him. He sent the letter on to Maria's husband, writing in a covering note, "The sentiments expressed in it are sincere. Her attachment was constant . . . expressing them to me is a proof that our friendship is unbroken on her part. . . . I retain it strongly both for herself and Mr. Adams. . . . I am happy that this letter gives me an opportunity of expressing it to both of them." [25] There followed a brief, increasingly painful and altogether extraordinary correspondence between Jefferson and Abigail Adams, with Jefferson at first writing under the illusion that both husband and wife were reading his letters, and afterward not really believing her when she assured him she was writing in confidence, and that "No eye but my own has seen what has passed." [26] Jefferson's first letter was a restrained but certain gesture toward destroying what he called the "line of separation" between their "valued and fully reciprocated" friendship. But he made a mistake near the end of it by bringing up old politics, complaining that "one act of Mr. Adams's life, and one only" gave him "personal displeasure," his midnight appointments of district judges, some of whom had been chosen from among his most "ardent political enemies." [27]

Even this slight attack loosened a torrent, demonstrating that Maria's death had not only stimulated sorrow and compassion in Abigail, but had also released—as death often does—a long accumulated concentration of resentment. She chose this time of suffering to hurl back at him all her old fury about Jefferson's support and defense of Callender, "a wretch who was suffering a just punishment of the Law due to his crimes for writing and publishing the basest libel, the lowest and vilest Slander which malice could invent, or calumny exhibit against the Character and reputation of your predecessor." [28]

Jefferson, who would have written very differently had he believed that theirs was the secret correspondence she said it was, not surprisingly responded aggressively, as if he were writing to Adams himself. Though he expressed regret at Callender's scurrilities, he pointed out that he never blamed Adams for the libels of the Federalist editors against himself. Then he launched into an assault on the Sedition

Act, with the remarkably tactless pronouncement: "I considered and now consider that law to be a nullity as absolute and as palpable as if Congress had ordered us to fall down and worship a golden image." [29]

Abigail, no doubt taking enormous secret delight in carrying on a political debate with the President of the United States without her husband's censorship, now hurled back not only a passionate defense of the Sedition Act, but also a denunciation of Jefferson's assumption of the right to annul it. "If a Chief Majestrate can by his will annul a law, where is the difference between a republican, and a despotic Government? That some restraint should be laid upon the assassin, who stabs reputation, all civilized Nations have assented to." And with great dexterity she needled him about his "honour, and independence of Character," and his failure to consider "Characters as it respects their Moral worth and integrity." Although she wrote piously, "Faithfull are the wounds of a Friend. . . . I bear no malice I cherish no enmity," [30] in her fourth and last letter, with which she vehemently closed the correspondence, she finally opened her heart:

> Having once entertained for you a respect and esteem, founded upon the Character of an affectionate parent, a kind Master, a candid and benevolent Friend, I could not suffer different political opinions to obliterate them from my mind, and I felt the truth of the observation, that the Heart is long, very long in receiving the conviction that is forced upon it by reason. Affection still lingers in the Bosom, even after esteem has taken its flight.[31]

Callender, it seems, had opened to her the terrible truth—Jefferson was not an affectionate parent nor a kind master nor a candid and benevolent friend. What she feared when she first saw Sally Hemings in London had come to pass; Jefferson had betrayed his slave, his daughters, and his friend, Abigail Adams, who had genuinely loved him. Thus she cried out in protest, not only for herself and for white women generally, but also for every married woman to whom this gentle, gallant widower had managed to communicate the feeling that she was peculiarly important in his life.

The only good that came out of this exchange of seven letters was clarification of the fact that Jefferson had not fired young John Quincy Adams out of malice, but inadvertently, without his even knowing that Adams' name was on a list of Federalist offices to be given over to Republicans. Otherwise the correspondence was a disaster, Jefferson himself admitting later it was "highly disgraceful to us both." [32] Abigail, overcome with guilt, showed it all to her husband on November 19, 1804. What John Adams said to her is not, alas, a matter of record. That after all these years of their marriage she could surprise

him into speechlessness is possible, for he took the letters and filed
them away with a little note:

> The whole of this Correspondence was begun and conducted without
> my Knowledge or Suspicion. Last Evening and this Morning at the
> desire of Mrs. Adams I read the whole. I have no remarks to make upon
> it at this time and in this place.[33]

Jefferson for his part was so wounded by Abigail's scalpel that even
eight years later, when Benjamin Rush finally succeeded in getting
him to begin a correspondence with John Adams, he agreed to the
"fusion of mutual affections" only if Abigail was not to be included.
"It will only be necessary," he said, "that I never name her." [34] She
had not only committed the inexcusable offense for a woman, she
had meddled in politics, but also she had done something far more
blameworthy. She had passed judgment, without any compassion for
his special agonies, on the morality of his private life.

Jefferson was in Washington on July 11, 1804, when his Vice-President met Alexander Hamilton on the Jersey Palisades overlooking the
Hudson River and put a bullet into his liver and spine. The news of
Hamilton's death after thirty hours of agony came like a thunderbolt
to the nation. Dueling was against the law in New York; to give or
receive a challenge was a misdemeanor, and conviction brought dis-
qualification from any "Office of honor, profit or confidence in the
state" for twenty years. Hamilton himself had helped in the effort to
pass this civilizing statute.[35] The institution of the duel had long
offered dubious public sanction for the murderous impulses of men
who hated; what was not recognized was that it offered also suicidal
opportunities for men who turned their hate inward. Undoubtedly
there were many men caught up unwillingly in the primitive ritual,
who secretly rowed across the Hudson to the Jersey shore and blasted
away at each other in what was widely accepted as the ultimate test of
masculinity simply because they did not know how to refuse. But the
practice was increasingly criticized as legitimized murder.

Hamilton's eldest son Philip had been killed in November 1801 in
what seemed to many to be a senseless futile gesture. Actually his
death had special complications, the nature of which contributed to
the extraordinary replay of the duel by Hamilton himself two and
one-half years later. Hamilton's political fortunes had plummeted with
the publication of his admission of adultery with Mrs. Reynolds;
how his image as a father plummeted with his five sons and two
daughters cannot be measured. After Jefferson's inauguration, Hamilton
had campaigned in the gubernatorial election in New York, working

for the Federalist candidate Stephen Van Rensselaer against the Republican George Clinton. He had been appalled to find hostile crowds jeering at him as *"thief, rascal, villain, scoundrel."* [36] According to family tradition, the Hamilton sons adored their father and were enraged at the brickbats hurled in his direction.

Philip, who was a youth very much like Hamilton—witty, handsome, and intelligent, with the reputation of being a debonair young rake—had taken particular note of the maledictions of Republican George Eacker, who in a Fourth of July speech in 1801 had accused Hamilton of wanting to lead an army to destroy the Republican party. In late November Philip Hamilton and a friend found themselves seated in a theater box next to that of Eacker and began baiting him. Eacker collared the youths in the hall outside and called them rascals and blackguards. The next day both challenged him to a duel. Despite desperate efforts by Philip's uncle, John Church, the duels took place. Hamilton's friend exchanged shots with Eacker without mishap to either, but when the testy lawyer faced young Hamilton he shot to kill. Philip, who had made clear to his second that he would not fire, fell to the ground fatally wounded, his gun discharging harmlessly in the air.[37]

Philip had gone out of his way to invite a duel, had gone into the duel with no intention of firing, thus inviting a wound or death, all this to defend the honor of his father, a father who had by a humiliating public confession recently brought agonies to his family and made himself the butt of national ridicule. Philip could have chosen no way to die that would have brought his parent greater agony and guilt.

Hamilton called the event "beyond comparison the most afflicting of my life," saying, "the brightest, as well as the ablest, hope of my family has been taken from me." Few knew that the duel cost him also his eldest daughter, Angelica, who was unable to cope with her brother's death and went mad. She would remain mad until her death at seventy-three.[38] The double tragedy changed the whole quality of Hamilton's life. Mrs. Hamilton, pregnant with her eighth child, found some small solace when she bore a son, and named him Philip after the eldest. But Hamilton mourned his son in a fashion that suggested he had turned to dreaming of death himself. He rejoiced, he said, that the dead youth was "out of the reach of the seductions and calamities of a world full of folly, full of vice, full of danger, and of least value in proportion as it is best known." [39] Looking back on his political career, he saw himself cursed by the Republicans for his betrayal of the Constitution, and by the Federalists for his betrayal of his party. "Perhaps no man in the United States," he said defensively in 1802, "has sacrificed or done more for the present Constitution than myself; and contrary to all my anticipations of its fate . . . I am still laboring to prop the frail and worthless fabric. Yet I have the murmurs of its friends no less than the curses of its foes for my reward. . . . Every day proves to me more and more, that this American world was not made for me."

He became an ardent Bible reader, and in 1802 proposed the establishment of a "Christian Constitutional Society," a network of political clubs over the nation dedicated to teaching the tenets of both Christianity and Federalism against the atheistic tendencies of Jefferson. He lost all taste for a military career.[40] None of this new enthusiasm prevented his speculating madly in land, or in spending enormous sums on a pretentious country house, the Grange, whose noble prospect over the Hudson River in upper Manhattan was almost as impressive as Jefferson's at Monticello.

Though he continued to attack Jefferson through his mouthpiece, William Coleman, editor of the New York Evening Post, frequently dictating articles that appeared under Coleman's name, the old shrillness was gone. Jefferson to Hamilton's astonishment had proved to be a stout nationalist and a tough, energetic executive who had destroyed neither his funding system nor his Bank of the United States. The nation had not collapsed in anarchy. Hamilton applauded the Louisiana Purchase where other Federalists denounced it as unconstitutional and a monumental extravagance. He approved passage of the Twelfth Amendment, and in what was for him a rare deference to the great unwashed, urged that presidential electors be chosen by the people, and urged his party members to take a leaf out of Jefferson's book and woo the masses.[41]

Though Hamilton had originally approved the Sedition Act, he somersaulted when Federalist editor Harry Croswell, editor of the New York Wasp, was brought to trial for libeling Jefferson.[42] He joined in Croswell's defense, and made one of the great speeches in American history in defense of the freedom of the press. Without the right to attack the president, Hamilton said, "good men would become silent, corruption and tyranny would go on, step by step in usurpation." But something more than deprivation of office figured in the conversion of Alexander Hamilton. The appeal for Harry Croswell revolved around the question of whether or not a man accused of libeling another has the right to use the truth of the libel as a defense. This had touched Hamilton on an old unhealed sore.

No prominent American political figure had paid so inordinate a price for telling the truth about himself, and in his speech of February 13, 1804, Hamilton argued that every man does have the right to use the truth of a libel in his defense. The real crime, he argued, is not the act of telling the truth, but the maliciousness of the intent. And whether or not the intent was to defame is the problem for the jury to decide. Hamilton's defense of Harry Croswell was in a most poignant sense a defense also of himself. "I never did think the truth was a crime," he said. "I am glad the day is come in which it is to be decided." Had telling the truth about his own adultery been a crime against his family? This seems to have been the question gnawing at him. His only answer could be, as with Croswell, there had been no malicious intent.[43]

In the end, it was Hamilton's telling the truth about Aaron Burr that cost him his life. Despite all his fleeting dreams about being a Caesar in the New World, Hamilton had an abiding affection for the Constitution and the republic, and he had come to believe that Burr despised both. When in the spring of 1804 a group of New England senators entered a conspiracy to split off New England and New York from the United States and form a northern confederacy, and asked Hamilton to be their military leader, he denounced them with contempt. But he was greatly troubled to learn that they had since turned to Burr. He remembered that Burr had said to him in 1800, "General, you are now at the head of the Army. . . . Our Constitution is a miserable paper machine. You have it in your powers to demolish it, and give us a proper one, and you owe it to your friends and the country to do it." Hamilton had replied that he could not effect a *coup d'état* if he wanted to, and that he was "too much troubled with that thing called morality to make the attempt." To which Burr had replied in French, "General, all things are moral to great souls." [44]

For Hamilton the Constitution was not "a miserable paper machine," but "a frail and worthless fabric" which he had been propping up to his own surprise for fifteen years. Secession for Hamilton meant separation and abandonment. But Burr, rejected by Jefferson as a candidate for vice-president in 1804,[45] running for the governorship of New York on the Federalist ticket, knew that if he was ever to be president at all, it could only be as president of a truncated nation, sheared away from the area where the "paper machine" added up votes for Thomas Jefferson.

Fearful that Burr would win the governorship and carry out the secession conspiracy, Hamilton once more began his barrage of private denunciation. "Go to Boston," he begged John Adams' son-in-law. "Tell them . . . for God's sake to cease these threatenings about the dissolution of the Union. It must be made to hang together as long as it can be made to." [46] Though Burr suffered a humiliating defeat—22,139 to 30,829 for Morgan Lewis—and would have lost even without

Hamilton's intercession, Burr nevertheless put the full blame on what seemed to him his endlessly intriguing personal demon. When by accident one of Hamilton's countless private slurs was printed in an Albany newspaper, Burr flung it like a gauntlet at Hamilton's feet and demanded satisfaction.

A great many acts of Hamilton in the ensuing days suggest that Henry Adams was right when he wrote that Hamilton "allowed himself to be drawn into a duel, but instead of killing Burr he invited Burr to kill him." [47] He could have avoided the duel but instead wrote his apology only when it was patently too late for it to be accepted. In a farewell letter he frankly admitted that he had wounded Burr politically, stated that he deplored dueling, and also that he would reserve his first fire and perhaps even his second. When both Hamilton and Burr attended a Fourth of July party at the Society of Cincinnatus, Hamilton in a display of pathetic bravado leaped up on the table and sang an old military ballad, "The Drum," as if he had no cares in the world, while Burr watched grimly from a distance.

No man invites death in this fashion, with an advance decision not to fire, without knowing that his own death will serve also as a weapon to maim his opponent. But Hamilton's death, as he also knew in advance, would be a catastrophe for his wife. In the first of his three final letters he spoke of "the considerations which constitute what men of the world denominate honor." The last two letters, addressed specifically to his wife, suggested that conventional matters of honor may well have been secondary to a more anguishing conflict concerning his deeply religious, long-suffering, and presumably always forgiving Elizabeth. Here, for all his conventionally pathetic language about love and farewell to "my darling, darling wife," the "best of wives and best of women," he nevertheless put the terrible burden of his death squarely upon her shoulders. On July 10, he wrote: "You had rather I should die innocent than live guilty." [48]

Hamilton would pay for his "sins," for the crime of telling the truth about Burr, and, more important, the crime of telling the truth about himself, thereby absolving himself of "malicious intent." And in going down in blood on the "altar of honor," on the same spot as had his son, and carrying the same pistols, he would also take with him—not in death but in political destruction—the hated Burr, in Hamilton's eyes the true conspirator, the true Catiline, the epitome of all the evils which had at one time or another been attributed to himself.

Jefferson, brought up since childhood in the tradition that silence was better than attack, could have looked upon Hamilton's senseless manner of taking himself out of the world only as corroboration of the value of silence over speech, or at least the value of silence over vituperative speech. Of the duel he wrote nothing, and apparently said nothing that could be reported as significant to posterity, whereas the irrepressible Adams would write eventually to Jefferson himself, "His most determined Ennemies did not like to get rid of him that Way." [49]

Had Jefferson failed to recognize instantly that Burr now was politically dead, the remarkable outpouring of grief and demonstrated horror in the nation's press would have shortly enlightened him. Though indictments for murder in both New York and New Jersey hung over Burr's head, he continued to preside over the United States Senate, even in the impeachment trial of Supreme Court Justice Samuel Chase, whom Jefferson and his friends, in a concerted attack on the power of the Federalist-minded judiciary, were trying unsuccessfully to get out of office. Senator Plumer, watching Burr carefully, thought his "easy, graceful manners" gone, and found him "uneasy, discontented, and hurried." [50] Jefferson, however embarrassed by having as his vice-president a man denounced as a murderer, continued to observe party protocol, inviting Burr to dinner, and even granting several appointments in the West which Burr favored. But he took care to see that the party caucuses that selected Governor George Clinton as his running mate for his second term gave Burr not a single vote. Thus the President went into the election of 1804 without this albatross about his neck.

The new running mate was a proven Republican of consistent vote-getting capacity. He was also too old and too ailing to be in any sense a rival to Jefferson himself. Nor would he be a rival to Madison, who Jefferson intended should be his successor. In the election of 1804 Jefferson received 162 out of 176 electoral votes; to Charles C. Pinckney he lost only Connecticut and Delaware, and two electoral votes in Maryland. As Henry Adams put it, "Rarely was a Presidential election better calculated to turn the head of a President, and never was a President elected who felt more keenly the pleasure of his personal triumph. . . . the idol of four fifths of the nation. . . . he had annihilated opposition." [51]

No death during Jefferson's presidency brought him the peculiar kind of agony that came with the murder of his old law teacher George Wythe. On June 4, 1806, he received a letter from William Duval in Richmond saying that Wythe was dying of poisoning, that his free mulatto boy named Michael Brown was already dead, and that arsenic had been found in the bedroom of Wythe's grandnephew, George Sweney. Duval, who had first been told that Wythe was ill of cholera, wrote in horror, "We had no idea that Sweney had poisoned the whole family." [52] The "whole family" consisted of Wythe, a widower since the death of his second wife in 1787, a mulatto housekeeper named Lydia Broadnax, and her son Michael Brown. All had been poisoned when they ate strawberries and drank coffee which had been liberally dosed with arsenic.

Wythe, who had no children of his own by his two wives, but had befriended his grandnephew "like a son," had written a will on April 20, 1803, in which he left his house and a good deal of his property to Lydia Broadnax and another former slave named Benjamin. He had left half his bank stock to the young mulatto Michael, with instructions that Thomas Jefferson be the executor in charge of his "maintenance, education & other benefit." The remainder of his bank stock he willed to Sweney, with the provision that he would get it all should Michael Brown die before him. The boy died of the poison; his mother survived. Wythe lived long enough to assert that he had been murdered, and to cut Sweney out of his will altogether. By the time Jefferson was told all these details, Sweney was in jail not only charged with murder but also with having forged several checks in Wythe's name.

Duval described Lydia Broadnax to Jefferson as follows: "Never had a man a more faithful servant, her attention to Mr. Wythe was incessant and always studied to please him." "Michael Brown," he said, "was humble and good—he had caught the suavity of his Master's manners." When the dying Wythe heard of Michael's death, Duval said, "he made a long Breath—and pathetically said—Poor Boy." [53] Duval sent Jefferson a copy of Wythe's will, which as it turned out included not only a request that he serve as executor for Michael Brown's education, but also a bequest to Jefferson of his two silver cups, his gold-headed cane, and his entire superb library.

The distraught Jefferson wrote back, "Such an instance of depravity had been hitherto known to us only in the fables of the poets. . . . He was my antient master, my earliest & best friend. . . . I had reserved with fondness for the day of my retirement, the hope of inducing him to pass much of his time with me." [54] Whether Jefferson noted with more than passing interest the date of Wythe's will one cannot know. April 20, 1803, was relatively recent; it represented that period in Jefferson's life when he had weathered the worst of the Callender publicity but had not repudiated his slave mistress or her children either by public pronouncement or by private deed, such as sending them away from Monticello. Jefferson must have surmised, with many others in Virginia once the details of the will were circulated, that Lydia Broadnax was almost certainly Wythe's concubine and Michael

Brown his son. That the President believed that Wythe had waited in writing his will till he was certain he could count on Jefferson's support for his son seems likely. Jefferson wrote with regret of the boy's death to Duval, ". . . not only for the affliction it must have cost Mr. Wythe, but also it has deprived me of an object for the attentions which would have gratified me unceasingly with the constant recollection & execution of the wishes of my friend." [55] He asked Duval for a portrait of Wythe, and when told that Lydia Broadnax had a profile engraving he asked for a copy. The housekeeper, as it turned out, kept the copy, and insisted that Jefferson be given the original.[56]

Sweney's trial was the sensation of Richmond. For a white man to leave a house and grounds to his mulatto housekeeper, and bank stock to her yellow son, and to ask none other than the President of the United States to be responsible for the boy's education seemed such an obvious advertisement of the boy's paternity that it left many of the citizens of Richmond aghast. Edmund Randolph and William Wirt rushed to defend Sweney, and since under Virginia law no black could testify against a white man, he was acquitted. He was found guilty of forging checks in his uncle's name, but even this charge was dropped on appeal. The indictment against Sweney for poisoning Michael Brown "was quashed without a trial." [57] Thus the whole legal paraphernalia of Virginia law was perverted to absolve the forger and murderer and to dramatize the legal sanction of the murder of a man who would so advertise his miscegenation. The fact that Wythe was one of Virginia's most distinguished sons, and a signer of the Declaration of Independence, only served to make it more imperative that his gesture be repudiated and buried in the most expeditious fashion possible.

The legal exoneration of George Wythe Sweney was also a public warning to Thomas Jefferson. Nothing could have furnished more dramatic evidence of the hatred of Virginia whites for the man who conveyed by public or legal gesture his acceptance of a yellow child. If Jefferson periodically cherished fantasies that in time there might be some kind of equality for Sally Hemings' children, this again would have jolted him back to reality. It is clear enough that there was only one possible solution for these children if they were to have a free and even decent life; they must be somehow schooled and permitted to pass into white society. That this had already happened to Sally's eldest son has been suggested in an earlier chapter. In 1806 when Wythe was poisoned, Sally Hemings was thirty-three, Jefferson sixty-three. That he was forced ever more certainly into the conflicts and ambiguities of silence concerning his slave family is increasingly obvious. Still, there are faint echoes and footprints in the records.

Jefferson was at Monticello from August 5 to September 30, 1807. Sally Hemings bore her last child, a son named Eston,* on May 21, 1808.[58] Jefferson was also in Monticello on the day this boy was born,[59] and his account book reads as follows: May 22, "Gave the children 1 D." On May 27 he noted, "pd for whiskey @ 2/6 15.83." Not himself a whiskey drinker, Jefferson purchased this kind of liquor usually for celebrations, such as New Year's, which included slaves.

* Mr. Wilson Randolph Gathings informs me that Eston, the unusual name Sally Hemings gave her last son, was the name of the birthplace in Yorkshire, England, of Jefferson's maternal ancestor, William Randolph. It was also the middle name of one of Jefferson's favorite Randolph relatives, Thomas Eston Randolph, who had married Jane Cary Randolph, sister of Jefferson's son-in-law, Thomas Mann Randolph, Jr.

CHAPTER XXVIII

Jefferson and Burr

Burr's conspiracy had been one of the most flagitious of which history will ever furnish an example. . . . But he who could expect to effect such objects by the aid of American citizens, must be perfectly ripe for Bedlam.

Jefferson to Du Pont de Nemours, July 14, 1807 [1]

When Aaron Burr was tried for treason in Richmond in 1807, the language of the indictment smelled of the Inquisition: ". . . not having the fear of God before his eyes . . . being moved and seduced by the instigation of the devil, wickedly devising and intending the peace and tranquillity of the United States to disturb, and to stir, move, excite insurrection, rebellion and war . . ." [2] The odor of brimstone for a time followed Burr into the history books; even the urbane Henry Adams called him "the Mephistopheles of politics." [3] Jefferson, while believing Burr's conspiracy to be "daring and dangerous," [4] nevertheless discounted personal devils as a force in any man's life. He perceived dimly, what many Burr biographers since have not, that where there is so much grandiose lying there must be delusion and madness. John Adams after Burr's capture wrote to Dr. Benjamin Rush that he had never believed Burr a fool, but if he really planned that which he was accused of he "must be an Idiot or a Lunatick." [5] Yet both Rush and Adams were so captivated by Burr's performance at the trial that they were willing to speculate that if he were acquitted he might still become president of the United States. [6] Many were totally baffled, like Senator William Plumer, who said, "Burr is capable of much wickedness, but not so much folly." [7]

Jefferson knew more about mental derangement than has been generally realized, not only having grown up with a sister who was retarded but also having suffered through the serious two-year illness of his son-in-law in 1794–95 that was clearly mental in nature. When the grieving Dr. Benjamin Rush wrote to him in 1811 that one of his sons had killed a friend in a duel and had become insane as a result, Jefferson wrote back with sympathy and optimism, "I have myself known so many cases of recovery from confirmed insanity, as to reckon it ever among the recoverable diseases." [8] By then he could speak with even more authority on the subject, for his son-in-law had weathered a second breakdown.

The Burr conspiracy has been told countless times, but no one has pointed out that in the same weeks that Jefferson was trying to evaluate dispatches from the West indicating that his former vice-president was planning to assassinate him and split the United States, his son-in-law was threatening suicide. Both had fantasies of murder; Burr wanted to hang Jefferson, and Randolph seemingly wanted to kill only himself, but his hatred fanned out, as with many would-be suicides, to embrace his whole family. Randolph was described by Senator William Plumer as "a bashful timid man . . . a pleasant agreeable companion . . . much devoted to books." As congressman he had made only one speech in the House, and was on no important committees. In June 1806, however, he had quarreled violently with his distinguished and erratic congressional kinsman, John Randolph of Roanoke, denouncing him on the floor of the House as "bankrupt forever as a popular statesman." When the newspapers began predicting a duel, Jefferson was distraught. He wrote to his son-in-law:

> How different is the stake which you two would bring into the field! On his side, unentangled in the affections of the world, a single life, of no value to himself or others, on yours, yourself, a wife, and a family of children, all depending for their happiness and protection in this world on you alone. Should they lose you, my care for them, a poor substitute at my time, could continue, by the course of nature, but for a short time. Seven children, all under the age of discretion and down to infancy could then be left without guide or guardian but a poor broken-hearted woman, doomed herself to misery the rest of her life. And should her frail frame sink under it, what is then to become of them? Is it possible that your duties to these dear objects can weigh more lightly than those to a gladiator? [9]

The duel was avoided, but afterward Randolph began to quarrel with his brother-in-law Jack Eppes, presumably over the disposition of Maria's property. Chief among his grievances was that he believed Jefferson preferred Eppes to himself.

Jefferson, sheltering both sons-in-law in the President's House even after Maria's death, was as intent on domestic tranquillity there as in Monticello. As Henry Adams noted, though "not despotic in temper," Jefferson could be "within certain limits, very tenacious of his purpose, and he had to a certain degree the habits of a paternal despot." [10] On February 16, 1807, there was an explosion of some kind between the two young men, and Randolph, after writing a bitter letter to Jefferson, moved into a boarding house. The published family letters from Jefferson to his daughter and his own unpublished letters to Randolph indicate only that the aggrieved son-in-law at once became gravely ill. That he was actually threatening suicide we learned from unpublished letters of William Burwell, who helped Jefferson in the crisis.

To Randolph's bitter farewell letter Jefferson wrote an immediate reply: "I had for some days perceived in you a gloom which gave me uneasiness. I knew there was a difference between Mr. Eppes and yourself, but had no idea it was as deep seated as your letter shews it to be. I never knew the cause, nor ever wished to know it. My affections for you both were warm. . . . What acts of mine can have induced you to suppose that I felt or manifested a preference of him, I cannot conceive. . . . I well recollect the invitation which dropped from me to Mr. Eppes the other day in your presence. It was unpremeditated, I felt my error the moment I had uttered it. . . . You speak of other acts indicating a preference. I know not what they were, and am conscious they have been misconstrued." [11]

It is not from this letter but from Burwell's cryptic notes to Jefferson during this week that we learn the true gravity of Randolph's condition. Burwell wrote, ". . . with some difficulty . . . I have succeeded in quieting Mr. R's mind. . . . I will not for a moment lose sight of the subject. . . . I will effectually avert that calamity. . . . He feels the same love and respect for you he always did. . . . Mr. R . . . observed he was indifferent to live . . . inspired with shame for having left you." [12] Senator William Plumer, living in the same boarding house, reported rumors that Randolph had quarreled with Eppes, noted with surprise that though "not a military man—yet he has a pair of pistols & sword laying on the mantle piece in his chamber." [13] Jefferson on February 19 wrote gently to Randolph, "I have been guilty of an error for which I take just blame to myself, really loving you as I would a son (for I protest I know no difference) I took it too much for granted you were as sensible of it as myself." He protested that "not a word or thought" of criticism "ever escaped from me to any mortal." Later he begged Randolph to return to the President's House, promising him privacy, and sent him a bank draft.[14]

But the son-in-law refused to return. He was bled by his doctors into desperate weakness; on March 4 Senator Plumer wrote in his diary that Randolph was so ill he feared his sickness "will terminate fatally." [15] Jefferson communicated nothing of the gravity of the illness to Martha, though in reading his barrage of letters she could hardly have failed to guess its nature. Sometime during this desperate crisis Randolph was persuaded by his doctors that he must abandon politics altogether and return to his farm and family. The agony of the experience for Jefferson brought on a new attack of his migraine, which lasted from March 14 to mid-April 1807. It could only have been exacerbated by the forthcoming trial of Aaron Burr. Apparently it was during these weeks that Jefferson became determined that when he himself would retire to Monticello in 1809 Martha and her family must move under his own roof. He could count on his own presence to quiet Randolph's storms, or he could at least protect his daughter and her children from them. By June 29, 1807, he could write cheerfully to his granddaughter Ellen, "Hope is so much pleasanter than despair, that I always prefer looking into futurity through her glass." [16]

But hope and cheerfulness, and even real affection and tenderness, could not prevent the deadly erosion to Randolph's self-esteem which resulted from Jefferson's continuing control over his whole family, particularly the affections of Randolph's wife. When Martha learned of her father's migraine attack, she wrote to him longingly of his forthcoming retirement when "the *first* and most important object with me will be the dear and sacred duty of nursing and chearing your old age, by every endearment of filial tenderness. My fancy dwells with rapture upon your image seated by your *own* fireside surrounded by your grand children contending for the pleasure of waiting upon you." [17]

The pathology of Aaron Burr, which Jefferson had to confront in the same months, had a wholly different dimension. Here was a major political conspiracy of breathtaking audacity, conceived by a man with an already formidable record of betrayal, generated and mixed in a caldron of personal hatred of which the ingredients were not comprehended in Jefferson's time and are not wholly understood in our own. That he himself was a prime object of Burr's hatred Jefferson sensed only partially at first, and when he realized the staggering proportions of this hatred, he responded with as much wonder as counter-hatred. His wonder was not so much that Burr hated him, or even that he had planned his assassination and talked about it freely, but that he could have become so divorced from reality as to misread the heart of the American people by believing that large numbers of them would support him in his plan to split the United States. This was the proof for Jefferson that Burr was "ripe for Bedlam," and indeed in our own time Burr's would be regarded as a fairly unambiguous case of paranoia. "The designs of our Catiline are as real as they are romantic," Jefferson wrote of Burr in December 1806. But the model of the Roman conspirator was not appropriate for the American people, who, Jefferson said, were not "the scourings of Rome." [18]

What appalled Jefferson most in the end was not the posturing, the lying, the grandiose fantasies, or even the skill Burr demonstrated in feigning innocence at his trial, but the degree to which the whole conspiracy was turned into a political attack upon himself with the active collusion of the Chief Justice of the Supreme Court. This he felt was the real threat to the integrity of the republic. For if the most prestigious man in the judiciary, the independent third arm of the government, could for the purposes of a cheap attack on the president blithely free a man who had actively planned to subvert the Constitution and break the Union in two, then the republic itself was in grave danger.

The documentary proofs of Burr's treasonous activities were not complete in the spring of 1807; it would take Henry Adams' assiduous digging in the archives of London, Paris, and Madrid to establish conclusively what Jefferson suspected, that Burr even as vice-president had been actively conniving with the ministers of England and Spain to sever the United States along the ridge of the Allegheny Mountains. Nevertheless the Burr co-conspirators who turned state's evidence did have enough details of this and complementary plans to hang Burr had their evidence been permitted to come before the jury. That he was not convicted was chiefly due to John Marshall's eagerness to embarrass the President; it was also to a lesser degree due to the great difficulty Jefferson had in punishing anyone.

Burr's life before 1805 had already shown patterns of betrayal and conspiracy. The pervading theme of his life had been lack of trust. He seemed always to be expecting hostility, even inviting it, especially from men in authority, and he had learned very early to take precautionary measures by advance betrayal. Burr had been born into a distinguished family, his father the president of New Jersey (later Princeton) College and his mother the daughter of the stormy genius of American Calvinism, Jonathan Edwards. Both parents died before he was two, and his grandmother Edwards, who took him into her home, died after six months. He was befriended briefly by a Dr. William Shippen and his wife. Then at three, together with his five-year-old sister Sally, he became the ward of a twenty-one-year-old bachelor uncle who was already caring for six children under the age of fifteen, orphaned by the smallpox and dysentery epidemics that carried off Burr's family.[19]

Timothy Edwards was by all accounts a harsh and bigoted young Puritan who beat the children put into his care. Sally Burr became asthmatic, and Aaron began running away. At four, when he first escaped, he was not found for several days. At ten, when he tried to run away to sea, and his uncle tracked him to the ship, he climbed to the top of the mainmast and refused to come home without promise of amnesty from punishment. Such was the measure of his desperation. His only solace was his sister, whom he wrote to later in cipher, a conspiratorial device he may have adopted early, along with others, to circumvent his uncle's tyranny.

Gifted with a fine intellect, he entered New Jersey College at thirteen. At first he toyed with the ministry as a possible profession and then decisively rejected it, becoming preoccupied instead with political and military fantasy. His commencement address, "Castles in the Air," [20] and his early essay "On Passions" demonstrate in the very piousness of his rejection of great military heroes a fatal fascination for them that foreshadowed his own future. "Lo Alexander and Cesar," he wrote, "the fabled heroes of antiquity, to what lengths did passion hurry them? Ambition, with look sublime, bade them on, bade them grasp at universal dominion, and wade to empire through seas of blood!" [21] Thirty-four years later he would write the famous cipher letter to General James Wilkinson that almost brought him to the gallows, "I guarantee the result with my life and honor; with the lives the honor and the fortunes of hundreds of the best blood of our country." [22]

Like Napoleon, whom he greatly admired, Burr was small in stature, five foot six and small-boned as well. Called "Little Burr" when he entered the revolutionary army, he wrote to his sister with satisfaction of his high fox-tailed hat which helped, he said, to make up "my Deficiency in point of size." [23] He joined the expedition to Canada under Benedict Arnold—whose later treachery he must have pondered with special curiosity—seeking out intelligence work, which included going into disguise as a Catholic priest. His only distinguished act as a soldier came through an incident of insubordination. When serving under General Henry Knox in the New York area he saw that his company was trapped and about to be annihilated by the British and defied Knox, who stubbornly insisted on staying in the trap. Pleading with the men to disobey their commander, he led them to safety, winning their gratitude and affection and the annoyance of the discomfited general. The act set a dangerous precedent for his active fantasy life.

Washington took the gifted young officer into his "family." One day, however, upon entering his own office he surprised Burr at his desk reading a confidential manuscript. He blasted him with a "terrific reproof," and Burr responded by asking for a transfer. Never thereafter did Burr speak of Washington with anything but hatred. Matthew Davis, Burr's first biographer and friend of forty years, wrote, "His prejudices against General Washington, were immoveable." [24] Later, when Burr was a senator from New York, he persuaded Jefferson, then Secretary of State, to let him copy documents in his office, upon which Washington, discovering what was happening, instantly forbade the privilege. In 1793, when Madison and Monroe suggested that Burr be considered as envoy to England in place of Chief Justice John Jay, Washington said icily that "he had made it a rule of life never to recommend or nominate any person for a high office and responsible situation in whose integrity he had not confidence; that, wanting confidence in Colonel Burr, he could not nominate him . . ." [25] The odor of intrigue, the whispers of bribery, the charge of opportunism—as Jefferson put it, "He was always at market, if they had wanted him" [26] —followed Burr through every aspect of his life, as lawyer, party organizer, land speculator, and senator. But so obvious were his political talents and so persuasive his personal charm that he surmounted the suspicions in one fashion or another—even a duel with Hamilton's brother-in-law John Church, who had accused him of bribery in 1799— until his blatant betrayal of Jefferson in 1801.

It is Burr's relations with women, however, that most illuminate his incapacity to trust, his inordinate capacity for betrayal, and his ceaseless searching for what he had been cheated of as a child. Burr could have consciously remembered nothing of his mother, who died when he was two, but he did possess a letter his mother had written just after the death of her husband and shortly before her own. Aaron, as an infant of one year, had just recovered from a serious illness when Esther Edwards Burr wrote to her father as follows:

> God showed me that the child was not my own, but his, and that he had a right to recall what he had lost. . . . But how good is God! He hath not only kept me from complaining, but comforted me, by enabling me to offer up the child by faith. . . . one evening, in talking of the glorious state my dear departed must be in, my soul was carried out in such longing desires after this glorious state, that I was forced to retire from the family to conceal my joy. . . . God is certainly fitting me for himself; and when I think it will be soon that I shall be called hence, the thought is transporting.[27]

However Burr chose to read this letter, as a searching son or a cynical, irreligious adult, he could hardly have missed his mother's ecstatic search for death.

As a young man Burr early gained the reputation of a libertine.

"His intrigues were without number," Matthew Davis wrote. "His conduct most licentious. The sacred bonds of friendship were unhesitatingly violated when they operated as barriers to the indulgence of his passions. For a long period of time he seemed to be gathering, and carefully preserving, every line written to him by any female, with or without reputation; and, when obtained, they were cast into one common receptacle—the profligate and corrupt, by the side of the thoughtless and betrayed victim. All were held as trophies of victory—all esteemed alike valuable." [28]

Davis, assembling Burr's papers for a biography, read these missives with mounting fascination and horror, but Burr forbade the destruction of a single page. Yet after Burr's death the biographer, in an act of benighted piety, burned them all. Later biographers gathered evidence from other sources to document at least in part the lifelong record of seduction. For a time, after he married Theodosia Prevost, widow of a British officer, mother of five children, and ten years older than himself, Burr seems to have found the essential mothering he had missed. Theodosia Burr was not only an educated and uncommonly intelligent woman but also a warm and passionate wife. "My Aaron," she would write, "dark is the hour that separates my soul from itself." [29] Burr wrote to her that she was the first to prove to him that woman had a soul instead of a mere instinct for coquetry. But naturally he betrayed her too. There seems always to have been gnawing at him a special hunger. "Why," he once asked his wife, "is man alone . . . discontented, anxious—sacrificing the present to idle expectations. . . . Never enjoying, always hoping?" [30]

Burr's beautiful daughter, named Theodosia after her mother, was as close to her father as Martha Jefferson to her father. Each of these fathers demanded a rigorous dedication to a reading program destined to make his daughter a fit companion for himself. The letters between Theodosia Burr and her father are justly famous. Like Jefferson, Burr corrected his daughter's spelling, and he also took pains with her literary style. There was, however, an easy camaraderie between Burr and Theodosia that one does not see in the tense, controlled, but nevertheless passionate interchanges between Jefferson and Martha. Burr called Theodosia a hussy while she called him an idiot. Burr was openly seductive. "I amuse and torment myself fancying your occupations, your thoughts, your attitudes at different hours in the day and night," he wrote, and she would write in turn, even after her marriage, "I kiss you with all my heart." [31]

Burr's wife died of cancer in 1794, and he began again his ceaseless and almost ritualized wooing of other women, much of it described to his daughter. Theodosia's marriage to the son of a millionaire planter in South Carolina came in February 1801. That his election betrayal of Jefferson in the same month had something to do with the loss of his daughter is a possibility, inasmuch as one detects a pattern in his later betrayals, each of which seemed to follow some loss, as though he were seeking a compensation in destruction. A year after Theodosia's marriage Burr was heavily in debt, "ruined in politics as well as fortune," one observer wrote.[32] At this time he sent his daughter an ominous letter, hinting at a scheme the nature of which is unknown but which may have had something to do with his new friendship with General James Wilkinson, spy in the pay of Spain, master intriguer and double agent: [33]

> I project . . . a journey southward at some time, yet nameless, during the current year (or century). Now, if my evil stars, or good ones should, against my will and my judgment, take me through Norfolk I am ruined and done; and there my journey will most infallibly end. That I had better be hanged or drowned, you will readily agree. The antidote or preventative is in your hands, or, if you please, head.[34]

If Burr believed it was an evil star or a good one that sent him to the Weehawken dueling ground two years later we do not know. By then he was a prisoner of his own hatreds. The press was full of stories that on returning from the duel with Hamilton he greeted his neighbor cheerily, and breakfasted with his cousin in perfect composure, all of which seemed to suggest a malignant satisfaction in the shooting. That there was actually great conflict in him over the killing, especially as the public outrage against it reached fever pitch, is suggested by a letter to Theodosia on August 2, 1804, in which he wrote, "Don't let me have the idea that you are dissatisfied with me a moment. I cant just now endure it." Still, he wrote to her on the following day a note that showed a certain grim gratification: "You will find the papers filled with all manner of nonsense and lies. Among other things, accounts of attempts to assassinate me. These, I assure you are mere fables. Those who wish me dead prefer to keep me at a very respectful distance." [35] Theodosia forgave him this act, as she forgave all his follies, but the woman Burr had been courting for some time, unknown save for her name—Burr called her *la pauvre Celeste*—abandoned him.[36]

Having cut down Hamilton only to discover that he had ruined himself politically, Burr found that his hatreds, instead of being dissipated, were only compounded, and the full concentration of them he now directed against Thomas Jefferson. The maturing of his grandiose conspiracy came within weeks after the killing. Its pathological nature is suggested not alone by the timing, but also by the unrealistic nature of the planning, as well as by the fact that Burr babbled about his intentions to so many. It was as if from the beginning he was crying out to be caught and punished.

Hamilton was slain on July 11, 1804; on August 6 Anthony Merry, British minister to the United States, sent word to London that Burr was offering his services to the British crown to help "effect a separation of the western part of the United States from that which lies between the Atlantic and the mountains, in its whole extent." The British foreign office considered the matter with interest, if some astonishment, and kept the negotiations open through Burr's agent in London, Charles Williamson. By March 29, 1805, Burr had offered a matured plan for conquering New Orleans; all he needed, he said, was a loan of half a million dollars and a British squadron at the mouth of the Mississippi.[37] By this time the scheme was well known to the French minister in Washington, who wrote to Talleyrand that Burr "would rather sacrifice the interests of his country than renounce celebrity and fortune." [38] Thus Burr was seen by the foreign diplomats not as a madman but as a freebooter, filibuster, and adventurer who would be the Napoleon of the West.

Burr had confided in "General" William Eaton, who had led a courageous but abortive expedition against the ruler of Tripoli and who had since become disenchanted with Jefferson. Eaton hinted at the conspiracy to Jefferson, but the President refused to take him seriously. He then told Burr's plans in detail to two congressmen, John Cotton Smith and Samuel Dana. They agreed Burr should be hanged but scoffed at the plan as "chimerical." As Eaton unfolded the details they did indeed seem to smack of lunacy. Burr planned to raise a force of men, invade Washington, and assassinate Jefferson ("Hang him!—throw him into the Potomac!—send him to Carter's Mountain," he said), then seize the ships in the Washington Navy Yard, rob the mint, and sail to New Orleans. There, joined by a British naval force and supported by General James Wilkinson, whom Jefferson had appointed as governor of Louisiana territory, he would capture the city and set up a rival confederacy. The story was not invented by Eaton, as some of Burr's admirers have suggested. Jonathan Dayton, ex-senator from New Jersey who had joined Burr in the conspiracy, revealed virtually the same plan to the Spanish minister Don Carlos Martinez Yrujo, as Henry Adams discovered years later in the archives in Madrid.[39] That Burr and Yrujo were spending time together was well known to Jefferson before the *Aurora* published the fact on November 5, 1806.

What Burr kept from Yrujo was the second step in his planned conspiracy. Having once set up a western confederacy, he planned to take an expedition to Mexico, free the inhabitants from the hated

Spaniards, and make himself emperor with his daughter as empress. This he confided in full to Harman Blennerhassett, a congenial Irish adventurer who had become his ally in Ohio and who babbled the details rather freely on his own. In his preliminary planning trip in the West in 1805 Burr even succeeded in enlisting the support of Andrew Jackson and Henry Clay, but only because he told them that his sole design was to drive the Spaniards off the continent and because he hinted that he had the secret support of Jefferson. To others, however, in his incredibly loosemouthed fashion, Burr talked wildly of driving the President and Congress into the Potomac and with four or five hundred men taking possession of New York. This he said to one George Morgan, who promptly wrote the story to Jefferson.[40]

As the details filtered in, from first one source and then another,[41] Jefferson found it increasingly difficult to dismiss them, especially since he had been long suspicious of Burr and knew of his involvement in the New England secession conspiracy of 1803–4.[42] But Jefferson and everyone else in government remembered Burr's farewell speech to the Senate which had brought tears to the eyes of old patriots. The Senate, he had said, was "a sanctuary, a citadel of law, of order, of liberty," an "exalted refuge where, if anywhere, resistance will be made to the storms of political phrensy and the silent arts of corruption." If the Constitution was destined to perish, he had concluded dramatically, "by the sacrilegious hands of the demagogue or the usurper, which God avert, its expiring agonies will be witnessed on this floor." [43] Who in 1805 could be made to believe that Burr, in making this speech, was a cool and diabolical liar, plotting that very act of usurpation and demagoguery against which he warned the Senate?

Burr was no ordinary liar but a man beset by devouring inner conflicts. On the one hand he was truly planning assassination and usurpation, and on the other, in the manner of many paranoid personalities, he was at the same time warning his friends against himself. He even warned Jefferson in an extraordinary confrontation in May 1806. Burr began the interview by complaining that Jefferson treated him coldly, then insolently demanded a foreign post, and finally threatened Jefferson, saying that he could do him "much harm." Jefferson, on guard, kept his replies cautious, telling Burr he recognized his talents but was also sensitive that "the public had withdrawn their confidence from him." He indicated he could not be threatened, but ended the conference on a friendly note,[44] and later Burr came to the President's House to dinner. With Burr dining at the same table drinking his own wine, Jefferson could watch him further, meanwhile masking his own profound suspicions.

William Eaton during this period was telling more and more men in government that Burr was planning to set up a confederacy of western states and then "turn Congress out of doors and hang Tom Jefferson." When Gideon Granger wrote the details of Eaton's story to Jefferson on October 16, 1806,[45] and dispatches came from the West reporting that Burr was now actively recruiting men along the Ohio for an army, Jefferson finally called in his cabinet and reported all the details of the conspiracy. On October 22 letters went out to the governors of the western states and territories alerting them to arrest Burr the moment he made an overt move.[46]

Nothing better illuminates Burr's capacity for the "big lie"—a technique used with success by many delusional personalities in politics—than his famous cipher letter to General James Wilkinson on July 29, 1806. Though he had been turned down coldly now by both England and Spain, he wrote that "naval protection of England is secure," that a British squadron was promised for outside New Orleans, and that he himself would rendezvous with Wilkinson at Natchez with the first five hundred or thousand men by December 15. "The govt invite us to glory and fortune," he concluded. "It remains to be seen whether we deserve the boon." [47] Actually Burr had nothing except $8,000 he had borrowed from his son-in-law, the promise of Blennerhassett's island home on the Ohio as a hidden center for gathering men and supplies, the festering discontent of a handful of New Orleans Creole leaders who disliked American rule, and the dubious promise of General Wilkinson that he could carry the allegiance of the three thousand men under him to support an uprising against Jefferson and the Union. When he started off down the Mississippi from Blennerhassett's, Burr had managed to recruit fewer than fifty men, and most of these came only for promises of acreages on the Wichita River and of glory in Mexico. His tongue had wagged so indiscreetly that Ohio newspapers were already alerted that something dubious and possibly dangerous was being organized by the former vice-president of the United States. The suspicious federal prosecutor of Kentucky haled him before a grand jury in Frankfort, but with the help of his lawyer, young Henry Clay, Burr turned the investigation into a triumph. So skillful was his acting the role of the persecuted man that after his acquittal the whole town turned out to a ball in his honor.[48]

Jefferson meanwhile had decided that should Burr succeed in his coup he would order 20,000 militia in the West to retake New Orleans,[49] and had General Wilkinson chosen to stay in the conspiracy, the President could well have had a bloody revolt on his hands, however desperate and short.[50] But Wilkinson, alerted by Jonathan Dayton that Jefferson was about to replace him,[51] now decided to betray

Burr rather than risk a halter about his own neck. On October 21, 1806, he wrote to Jefferson such details as would implicate Burr and, as he perhaps hoped, elevate himself into the role of savior of the United States. Then he arrested five of Burr's agents in New Orleans and sent them off to Washington. Jefferson, on receiving this dispatch, at once issued a proclamation on November 27, 1806, describing the conspiracy in general terms and calling upon the people to aid in putting down any insurrection.

It was said at Burr's trial that when he learned at Bayou Pierre on January 10 that Wilkinson had betrayed him and that the Governor of Mississippi Territory had ordered his arrest, he said to his men, "Fly for your lives or the Philistines will be upon you."[52] This was a revealing metaphor. Henceforth Burr shifted in fantasy to the role of Samson, a modern giant betrayed by treachery but determined that if he were brought to trial he would bring down the two pillars of the temple, Wilkinson and Jefferson, in a crashing ruin that would destroy them both. Wilkinson wrote later to Jefferson that he felt himself to be "between Scylla and Charybdis. The jury would dishonor me for failing in my duty, and Burr and his conspirators for performing it."[53] He could hardly tell the whole truth about Burr without hanging himself. And as it turned out seven members of the grand jury voted to indict him along with Burr. Jefferson could not hang the most important witness, who had turned state's evidence, but could he continue to keep such an obvious scoundrel in office as United States general?[54] Should he fire him he might fail to coöperate as a witness, and without his evidence Burr could turn the trial into a farce. There was no real alternative for Jefferson save to swallow his disgust and support Wilkinson as best he could. Burr, recognizing Jefferson's dilemma, made the most of it at the trial. But Burr, unlike Samson, had no Jehovah on his side.

With Burr in custody Jefferson lost all interest in prosecuting his dupes. "Their crimes are defeated," he wrote to a friend, and their punishment "is not the subject of even a wish on my part."[55] He believed Burr guilty; he also believed him mad, and was enormously relieved that the conspiracy had collapsed without the necessity of calling out a single regiment. "The hand of the people," he wrote to the Governor of Ohio on February 2, 1807, "has given the mortal blow to a conspiracy which, in other countries, would have called for an appeal to armies, and has proved that government to be the strongest of which every man feels himself a part."[56] In the beginning he took for granted that Burr would be indicted and found guilty. In laying the details of the conspiracy before Congress, on January 22, 1807, Jefferson unfortunately said publicly that Burr's guilt was "beyond question." John Adams fingered the blunder instantly, writing to Benjamin Rush that if Burr's guilt were as "clear as the Noon day Sun the first Magistrate ought not to have pronounced it so before a Jury had tryed him." [57]

Burr, however, thanks again to his remarkable histrionic talents, was absolved by the grand jury in Mississippi Territory. Upon learning that he was not totally free, but had to report daily, he fled. After he had spent almost a month in the wilderness disguised as a river boatman, a sharp-eyed observer spotted him near the Spanish border. Burr had donned an old blanket coat and broken-down white hat, but could not hide his aristocratic mien; more important perhaps, there was no audience in the wilderness. In Richmond, where he was brought to trial before a federal court on March 30, 1807, he had as his audience the whole nation. Crowds poured into the city as to a great public fair, and they were rewarded with superb theater.

As Samuel Johnson once wrote, "When a man knows he is to be hanged in a fortnight, it concentrates his mind wonderfully." Burr served as his own lawyer, along with several others, in the grand-jury investigation, helping select the jurymen, cross-examining with great skill. Though everyone in Richmond who could read a newspaper had seen the depositions of William Eaton and General James Wilkinson and had heard that Burr had threatened to assassinate Jefferson, the spectacle of Burr himself in court, cool and courteous, insisting that the witnesses were perjured and that Jefferson was persecuting him for political purposes, confused even some of the President's friends. The very excesses of Burr's conspiratorial fantasies now served as a boon. Most people associated lunacy with wildly bizarre behavior. Listening to Burr's calm, measured defenses and protestations of innocence and affection for the United States, many found him incapable of the secession folly. That he had been trying to raise an expedition against the hated Spaniards troubled few; many counted it an act of patriotism, an honorable and inexpensive way of liberating the southern territories and annexing them to the United States without waiting for the dubious expedient of purchase, as Jefferson wanted, at least with Spanish Florida. It was this seeming reasonableness that had temporarily persuaded Andrew Jackson and Henry Clay. And as Burr argued the case in court and before his friends and walked about the city with his beautiful daughter, he may have come to believe in the role himself. For unlike the role of the actor on the stage, that played by the paranoid can come very close to being reality itself, serving often as a defense to keep the deluded man from slipping into the more terrifying reality of overt psychosis. Burr could write passionately to his daughter,

"I may be immured in dungeons, chained, murdered in legal form, but I cannot be humiliated or disgraced." [58]

By early March 1807 Jefferson had ominous warnings that the trial would be complicated and a danger to himself. It was his misfortune that Chief Justice John Marshall, acting also as federal court judge in Richmond, was the chief presiding judge. The origins of the difficulties between Marshall and Jefferson are still obscure; apparently they went back to the days of the Revolution in Virginia.[59] In 1795 Jefferson had complained privately to Madison about Marshall's "profound hypocrisy," [60] which suggests that their mutual hostility was by then more venomous than could be explained by mere party differences. When Adams appointed Marshall to the Supreme Court, he knew that he was choosing an enemy of Jefferson's, and the old hostility had since been exacerbated by mutual jockeying for power. Now each served at the top of an independent arm of the government, and Marshall had already incurred Jefferson's wrath by insisting, in his astutely written *Marbury v. Madison* decision, that the Supreme Court had the right to review the constitutionality of acts of Congress, a decision that Jefferson felt arrogated far too much power to the courts. In what Merrill Peterson calls the "duel between executive and the judiciary," [61] certainly a prolonged contest between expert political swordsmen, Marshall by that decision had made "a palpable hit," and in the Burr trial he made another.

After three days of initial hearings in Richmond in late March 1807, Marshall decided that Burr should be committed only on the charge of "high misdemeanor"—for launching an expedition against Spain in time of peace—leaving the treason charge to be decided by the grand jury. Then he freed two of Burr's associates for lack of evidence. Burr was shortly free on bail and being feted in Richmond by Jefferson's enemies. John Wickham, one of Burr's lawyers, gave a fashionable party, inviting both Burr and Marshall. Incredibly, Marshall went to it. The *Richmond Enquirer* on April 10, 1807, described the occasion as "the treason rejoicing dinner," a shocking violation of judicial propriety. Thus Jefferson had early warning that the total resources of Marshall's talents would be utilized on Burr's behalf. At this point the trial took on for Jefferson a wholly new dimension; the judiciary had once more become, as in Adams' time, a tool of politics.

Jefferson had already struggled with the problem of how a republic could rid itself of the judge who was corrupt, or insane, or who rendered verdicts for political purposes. He had had only mixed success. In England, and indeed also in Massachusetts, judges could be dismissed by joint action of the legislative and executive arms of government.[62] But the only way Jefferson had been able to rid the country of the unfortunate ministrations of Federal Judge John Pickering, who was obviously insane, was by an impeachment trial in the United States Senate, where thanks to the rigidities of the Constitution he had to be charged with "high crimes and misdemeanors." The device, though successful, had in this instance been an embarrassment to all compassionate men. When the same device in 1805 was used against Justice Samuel Chase, whose verdicts had been flagrantly political, it failed. Jefferson knew that in John Marshall he had a far tougher, more resourceful and intelligent opponent than Chase—a man virtually impossible to unseat however often he dined with the defendant and his lawyer in a trial over which he was presiding. Jefferson did not know what was divulged later with the publication of Harman Blennerhassett's secret journal, that Marshall had continued to play chess with Burr's lawyer Wickham. He had even been heard to say, "Don't you think you will be able to check-mate these fellows, and relieve us from being kept here three weeks more?" [63]

In any case Jefferson had come to believe impeachment "a farce which will not be tried again." This he wrote to William Branch Giles in an important letter on April 20, 1807, a whole month before the grand-jury investigation began. Here too he revealed the sensitivity and flexibility with which he was meeting the new turn in the Burr imbroglio. "Against Burr, personally," Jefferson wrote, "I never had one hostile sentiment. I never indeed thought him an honest, frank-dealing man, but considered him as a crooked gun, or other perverted machine, whose aim or shot you could never be sure of." This was an exact phrase, "a crooked gun," arguing deformity in the original making rather than a deformity in Burr's morality. That he thought Burr mad he would write to both Du Pont de Nemours and Lafayette, and there is some evidence in his letter to Giles that he would take no more pleasure in hanging a madman than in impeaching poor lunatic Judge John Pickering. If Burr were acquitted, he said, the act would demonstrate to "the common sense of the nation," that the nation's judiciary could proclaim immunity to that very "class of offenders which endeavors to over turn the Constitution." The solution, he said, must be a constitutional amendment preventing the federal courts from being "independent of the nation." "If their protection of Burr produces this amendment," he said, "it will do more good than his condemnation would have done. . . . I shall rejoice in it." [64] Thus even before Burr's trial, Jefferson had already channeled much of his rage away from him, and into constructive planning for improving the stability of the republic. Later, he would see to it that an amendment to the Constitution was introduced in Congress in 1807 and 1808 making it possible for judges to be removed by a joint action of the president and both houses of Congress. In both instances it failed, and the Supreme Court under Marshall became a formidable veto power to which Jefferson was never reconciled, and its members remained virtually invulnerable to removal.

That Jefferson was not vindictively bent on hanging Burr, as some biographers have charged, showed also in the fashion in which, from behind the scenes, he directed the prosecution. He had selected as chief lawyer for the prosecution George Hay, his loyal but quick-tempered Richmond friend who had physically bludgeoned James Callender. Hay was not greatly gifted, and Jefferson's letters of instruction to him during the trial paid far more attention to the accumulation of evidence than to the tactics of a tough, aggressive attack. Neither Hay nor the two lawyers who assisted him, William Wirt and Alexander MacRae, were a match for the chief lawyer for the defense, the crafty and pugnacious Luther Martin, who, though coarse, vituperative, and frequently drunk—he sipped constantly from a flask of brandy throughout the trial—nevertheless seized the initiative and never let it go. Martin was the son-in-law of Michael Cresap, whom Jefferson had long ago denounced as a slayer of innocent Indian women and children. The lawyer now turned the tables, insinuating that Jefferson was a tyrant thirsting for Burr's innocent blood. The President, he said, "has let slip the dogs of war, the hell hounds of persecution to hunt down my friend."

It was Burr, however, who attracted crowds to the trial; he was cool and confident, low-keyed, ironic, and deadly. In replying to the charge that he had tried to raise an army against the United States, he said, "Our president is a lawyer, and a great one too. He certainly ought to know what it is that constitutes a war. Six months ago, he proclaimed that there was a civil war. And yet for six months have they been hunting for it, and still can not find one spot where it existed. There was, to be sure, a most terrible war in the newspapers; but nowhere else." [65]

At one point he electrified the audience by demanding that Jefferson himself be subpoenaed and forced to bring a letter to Wilkinson, in which he hinted falsely that the President had issued an order to kill Burr on the Mississippi, and to seize his property.[66] This was the crowning evidence of Burr's audacity, that he could visualize himself cross-examining the President of the United States at his own trial for treason. Had Jefferson been less intelligent he might have fallen into this lethal trap. He drily refused to come. As so often in his life, he resolved a personal dilemma by moving into the abstraction of political theory. The president could not be independent of the judiciary as provided under the Constitution, he pointed out patiently, if he let himself be subject to the beck and call of every federal judge over the nation. He would send papers * to the trial, he said, but the prerogative of choice among them must be his own.[67] So he set an important precedent, and scored a point over John Marshall, who did not dare subject him to the penalty of contempt of court.

After the grand jury decided that Burr and five of the conspirators who had gathered at Blennerhassett's Island must stand trial, the former vice-president was incarcerated in the Richmond penitentiary. Here he was treated with uncommon courtesy. Gifts of butter, fruit, and ice poured into his cell. He was permitted to greet friends and acquaintances of both sexes, who were neither screened nor searched. As during his trial in Mississippi, he managed to seek out a woman to solace his bed. Harman Blennerhassett, who found Burr's multiple conquests dismaying, marveled that the woman was able to pass his guards. "Jupiter might invisibly elude the guards of Danae," he wrote ironically in his prison journal, "but the *bonne amie* of the Col. does not I suppose occasionally pass his keepers with the same address." [68]

The trial was short. George Hay confessed before it was half over, "I shan't be able to hang Burr." In truth he could not. John Marshall was determined to free him, and this was done by a piece of legal trickery which did little for his reputation and which prevented important material, such as Burr's contracts with the Spanish minister, from ever coming before the court. Earlier in the summer Marshall had ruled in regard to two of Burr's associates, "If a body of men be assembled, for the purpose of effecting by force a treasonable purpose, all those who perform any part, however minute, or *however remote from the scene of action* . . . are to be considered traitors. But there must be an actual assembling of men, for the treasonable purpose to constitute a levying of war." [69] Now with Burr's case up for a ruling, he somersaulted from his previous one, stating that since Burr was not actually present on Blennerhassett's Island when the men assembled he could not be found guilty. Later, on the treason charge, he ruled that since the object of the Burr expedition had been the invasion and capture of Mexico, Burr was innocent of treason against the United States. Jefferson later privately attacked Marshall's "gloomy malignity," and "garblings of evidence." [70] In our own time Samuel Eliot Morison has noted ironically that Marshall held that "the mere gathering of force with intent to promote secession was not treason if the expedition collapsed." [71]

* He would send all papers "in furtherance of justice," he said, reserving the right to keep those where publication would endanger "the public welfare." And he did send all the documents Marshall requested.

In the end the verdict was a victory for Jefferson. Burr had complained at the trial that he was being treated as if he were under a European despotism.[72] Jefferson in the same period had written to Lafayette, "Altho' there is not a man in the United States who doubts his guilt, such are the jealous provisions of our laws in favor of the accused against the accuser, that I question if he is convicted." [73] Jefferson would not relax the "jealous provisions of our laws" even if they were distorted by the Chief Justice.[74] Burr's charge that Jefferson was a despot was reduced to an absurdity by the trial itself, and it was Marshall and not Jefferson who was hanged in effigy in Richmond along with Burr and Luther Martin.

Burr shortly thereafter sneaked aboard a vessel bound for Europe—disguised in a sailor's habit, Jefferson said [75]—finally enjoying, after fifty-one years, the sea voyage he had hoped for when he ran away from his uncle at age ten. If any further proof is necessary that Burr was a compulsive conspirator, one needs only to look at the plots he hatched during his five years abroad, each one more divorced from reality than the last. He schemed to have Napoleon invade the United States, and he also plotted a joint Franco-British conquest of the American continent. His grandiose fantasies continued to unfold even as he left Europe to return to America. "I hope never to visit this country again," he wrote on departing from England on March 26, 1812, "unless at the head of fifty thousand men." [76]

When he arrived in New York, again in disguise, he discovered perhaps to his astonishment that no one cared whether he came back or not save his daughter, who was then living in South Carolina. Shattered by the death of her only child, she boarded a ship for New York, hoping to find comfort in a reunion with her father, but the ship disappeared in a storm off Cape Hatteras. Thus Burr's very homecoming, in this tragically accidental fashion, cost him the one woman he had most loved during his life. He resumed his law practice, and even dispensed small kindnesses, including financial aid for his old lawyer, Luther Martin, who had become an impoverished alcoholic. At seventy-six Burr married an eccentric heiress of mixed reputation, Elizabeth Jumel, and promptly began losing her money in Texas real estate. She filed for divorce in 1834, charging infidelities, and employing as her lawyer a man named Alexander Hamilton. As Burr lay dying a Dutch clergyman visited him. When he asked Burr if he expected salvation, the eighty-year-old man, facing in death the ultimate conspirator, replied with a certain wry honesty, "On that subject I am coy." [77]

CHAPTER XXIX

A Genius for Peace

I think one war enough for the life of one man.

Jefferson to John Langdon, August 2, 1808 [1]

Jefferson's passion for peace affected every aspect of his presidency. With a skill so dexterous as to be largely invisible to his own compatriots he kept the peace in his own party—except for the small rebellion led by John Randolph, who could keep peace with nobody. He prevented a dangerous rift between Madison and Monroe from widening into an enmity that might have split the Republicans in two. Although Monroe in 1806 disregarded his orders and initiated a treaty with England so unacceptable that Jefferson would not even permit its publication, he treated the humiliated diplomat with great gentleness and suggested that he might take the post of the governorship of Louisiana Territory. Monroe, however, was determined to run against Madison for president. Jefferson wrote with dismay, "I see with infinite regret a contest between yourself and another, who have been very dear to each other, and equally so to me. . . . I have ever viewed Mr. Madison and yourself as two principal pillars of my happiness. Were either to be withdrawn, I should consider it as among the greatest calamities which could assail my future peace of mind." Though the rift persisted for two years, Jefferson maintained his friendship separately with each man, and continued in overtures which aided in the final reconciliation in 1810.[2]

It must not be thought, however, that Jefferson was incapable of handing out harsh criticism or even calculated insult. Almost everyone in Washington knew that he had greeted the British minister Anthony Merry in their first official meeting "not merely in undress, but actually standing in slippers down at the heels (as Merry described it indignantly to his King) and both pantaloons, coat, and underclothes indicative of utter slovenliness and indifference to appearances." Jefferson had compounded the insult later when Merry took his ostentatiously dressed wife to the President's House, only to see Jefferson ignore protocol and take into the dining room instead the woman he most enjoyed talking to—Dolley Madison. The whispered ejaculation of the Spanish minister, Yrujo, "This will be the cause of war," helped to make this one of the best remembered dinners in American diplomatic history.

That Anthony Merry remembered that George III had ostentatiously turned his back on Thomas Jefferson in London in 1786, and reflected that the President might have been paying off a personal as well as a national affront, is most unlikely; no diplomat in Washington had less comprehension of the subtleties of Thomas Jefferson than Merry. He was not mollified by a perusal of Jefferson's "Rules of Etiquette," drawn up for the use of diplomats in Washington City. It said in part:

> In social circles all are equal, whether in, or out, of office, foreign or domestic; & the same equality exists among ladies and among gentlemen . . . "pell-mell–and–next the door" form the basis of etiquette in the societies of this country.[3]

Mrs. Merry too remained unmollified when Jefferson, in a gentle gesture of apology that would have been understood perfectly in the French salons, sent her as a gift some packets of seeds.

Throughout his presidency Jefferson pursued a policy of peaceful purchase and of negotiation to avoid war with the Indians. In 1791 he had written, "The most economical as well as the most humane conduct towards them is to bribe them into peace, and to retain them in peace by eternal bribes," pointing out that military expeditions against them in that year alone would "have served for presents on the most liberal scale for one hundred years." When there was serious trouble with the Osages in 1808, he wrote to Meriwether Lewis, then governor of Louisiana Territory, recommending economic sanctions: "Commerce is the great engine by which we are to coerce them, and not war." [4] Always he hoped to see the Indians adopt agriculture and abandon their nomadic life. And though it may be argued that his system of peaceful purchase resulted in prodigious cheating of the Indians in terms of the true value of their birthright, and also that there was some wanton killing, Jefferson nevertheless avoided the indiscriminate slaughter permitted and sometimes even encouraged by his successors, preserving to the end the friendliness and respect for the red men which he had seen as a boy in the actions of his own father.

It was in his negotiations with European powers, however, that Jefferson's equanimity and control—what Max Beloff has called the tension between "his instinctive view that an enlightened democracy has no need of war and the facts of his own age" [5]—were most severely tested. That he would avoid being drawn into the slaughter in Europe during Napoleon's pursuit of hegemony was predictable. That he would be derided as a coward for maintaining neutrality in the face of repeated humiliations to the nation was also predictable. Josiah Quincy in a letter to John Adams called him "a dish of skim-milk curdling at the head of our nation." "Fear of responsibility and love of popularity are now master passions, and regulate all the movements. . . ." Quincy said, "The Presidential term will have expired, and then—away to Monticello, and let the devil take the hindmost." But Jefferson had lived with the taunt of cowardice over many years, and while he did not like it he was no longer afraid of it. He had untraditional notions about honor, whether his own or that of his country. "The unfailing mark of a primitive society," Henry Adams would write, "was to regard war as the most natural pursuit of man," and he described with some awe how Jefferson distinguished himself from other leaders of his time not only by his dislike of war as a profession but also by his obstinate pursuit of other means to obtain political ends. The President, Adams said, "had a genius for peace." [6]

The necessity for peace dominated his public life, as the necessity for tranquillity ruled his private life. He would not let himself be drawn into a private duel with John Walker, or into a public duel with Great Britain, however insolent her demands and degrading her depredations. During his last two years in office the provocation to war against England was intense and persistent, but in these years, more than any other in his life, reason was truly his guide, and the volatile impulses of resentment and anger, as well as anxieties about "honor" which in effect project images of masculinity into the international sphere, were contained and stifled for the public good. None of this would have been possible had Jefferson not been at peace with himself both as president and as a man.

In his second term, however, simultaneous with the Burr conspiracy, Jefferson faced the worst war crisis of his presidency. To this crisis he brought the bitter memories of his war experiences in Virginia in 1780, which had already served to stiffen his determination to stay neutral in the international hostilities between Napoleon and Great Britain that followed the collapse of the Peace of Amiens in 1802.

Importantly, too, his old sympathies for France had decisively altered.[7]

Jefferson detested Napoleon from that moment in 1804 when he crowned himself emperor. Though he had predicted that once the Corsican set up a monarchy "a million of Brutuses" would "devote themselves to destroy him,"[8] he found himself instead watching in incomprehension and disbelief as Bonaparte, to the acclaim of France, marched across Europe, overwhelming everything in his path. During his presidency Jefferson was too discreet to put his hatred into letters, though in one to John Langdon on August 2, 1808, he did describe England as "the whale of the ocean" and Napoleon as "his brother robber on the land." And to Colonel John Taylor he wrote of his mortification "that we should be forced to wish success to Bonaparte, and look to his victories as our salvation."[9] He repeatedly told the French minister to the United States how much he loved France, but the shrewd Turreau could hardly have missed Jefferson's failure to praise his master.[10] After his own retirement Jefferson freely called Napoleon an unprincipled tyrant who was deluging the earth with blood—a cold-blooded, calculating, unprincipled usurper without a virtue—a great scoundrel—the Attila of the age—the ruthless destroyer of ten millions of the human race—a man who saw nothing in this world but himself, and looked on the people under him as his cattle, beasts for burden and slaughter.[11]

Still, it was England that Jefferson always looked upon as the major threat to America, that England which by Nelson's brilliant victory at Trafalgar in October 1805 was now able to dispose its warships off every major port, impress American seamen at will, and threaten hanging to those who would not serve on British decks. "The death of Bonaparte," he wrote in 1810, "would, to be sure, remove the first and chiefest apostle of the desolation of men and morals. . . . The death of George III? Not at all. He is only stupid. . . . But his nation is permanent, and it is that which is the tyrant of the ocean."[12]

On June 23, 1807, when the U.S. frigate *Chesapeake*, bound for the Mediterranean, was intercepted off Hampton Roads by the British *Leopard* and the captain demanded the right to search for British sailors aboard, the American captain refused. The two frigates were not badly matched; the *Leopard* had fifty-two guns to the *Chesapeake*'s forty, but the latter were twenty-four-pounders as against the British eighteen-pounders. But the American commander was so unprepared for action—hot coals had to be brought up from the galley to light the matches—that his warship suffered three withering broadsides and the loss of three dead and eighteen wounded, without his being able to fire a single shot in return. The *Chesapeake* struck her colors, and the British captain took off one British deserter and three native Americans. The first was hanged and the others threatened with hanging unless they agreed to enter British service.

The *Chesapeake* affair, Henry Adams wrote, "seethed and hissed like the glowing olive-stake of Ulysses in the Cyclops' eye, until the whole American people, like Cyclops, roared with pain and stood frantic on shore, hurling abuse at their enemy, who taunted them from safe ships." [13] Had Jefferson chosen to declare war at that moment, he would have had the whole nation behind him. "Never since the battle of Lexington," he wrote on July 14, 1807, "have I seen this country in such a state of exasperation." [14] He ordered British ships out of American waters, alerted the state governors to ready their militiamen, ordered supplies for the building of more gunboats—small, defensive craft for use in harbors—and called Congress into session. To his son-in-law Randolph he wrote on July 13, "We are making every preparation for war." [15] But the war hawks noted with dismay that his date for convening Congress was a full three months distant, October 26, 1807. Turreau, who reported to Talleyrand a conversation with Jefferson on July 18, 1807, wrote that while the President talked of taking Canada and the Floridas, "if the English do not give us the satisfaction we demand," he seemed to be "lashing himself to take a warlike attitude." Turreau was convinced Jefferson and Madison would do "everything that is possible to avoid it," having nothing to gain and everything to lose by war." [16] And at the end of July Jefferson set off blithely for Monticello.

Jefferson's long and frequent vacations at home had already brought him some abuse. During his first four years in office he had spent altogether thirteen months at Monticello. John Adams' record, however, was roughly the same; he had spent 385 days out of his four years away from the seat of government, most of them at Braintree. Jefferson insisted defensively that he worked even harder at Monticello than in Washington because so much had to be done in writing. But the departure southward so soon after the *Chesapeake* killings was an open advertisement to the country that its president was content—as Jefferson wrote to Du Pont de Nemours on July 14, 1807—to seek "reparation for the past, and security for the future," rather than the glory of conquest in Canada and the Floridas. Moreover, in August 1807 the Burr trial was under way in Richmond, and Jefferson may well have counted on that to deflect attention from the *Chesapeake* matter. To declare war was to invite the British navy to the American coast. And Jefferson was no more anxious to lose New Orleans to the British than to Aaron Burr.

Still, it was not easy for him to maintain neutrality in the face of growing British depredations. "England had never learned to strike soft in battle," Henry Adams wrote. "She expected her antagonists to fight; and if they would not fight, she took them to be cowardly or mean. Jefferson and his government had shown over and over again that no provocation would make them fight; and from the moment that this attitude was understood America became fair prey." [17] Britain not only tightened her control over shipping to France, but also extended it to America. The Orders in Council of November 11, 1806, declared that any American ships which did not first sail to England for licensing would be a fair prize at sea. These Orders applied even to ships bound for the West Indies, thus grossly outraging American sovereignty. At the same time England cut American profits by imposing an exorbitant duty on cotton. American ships whose officers refused to obey the Orders were taken as prizes to enrich the coffers of the British navy, and American seamen went into British dungeons. Napoleon meanwhile, in his Berlin and Milan decrees, declared a reverse blockade of British ports, which he eventually extended to America, making United States vessels prey to French privateers. So Jefferson's seamen were now threatened by British and French alike, though the latter naturally had the lesser power to do mischief at sea.

As Jefferson saw it, he now had three choices: war, submission and tribute, or a self-imposed embargo which would deny the British their important American market. Though he was determined not to be shamed into an impetuous declaration of war by young war hawks like Henry Clay and John C. Calhoun, who talked openly of capturing Canada and the Spanish Floridas, he was not entirely immune to the collective national emotion that would later be labeled "manifest destiny." In Madison's presidency, he would discuss frankly with him the possibility of acquiring Cuba from Napoleon and of acquiring Canada through a war with Britain. We should then, he wrote, "have such an empire for liberty as she has never surveyed since the creation; and I am persuaded no constitution was ever before so well calculated as ours for extensive empire and self-government." [18] And though in 1808 he wrote to John Langdon, "I think one war enough for the life of one man," he recognized that he was not entirely powerful enough to prevent it, adding, "Still, if it becomes necessary, we must meet it like men, old men indeed, but yet good for something." [19]

At this moment Jefferson was sixty-five. He was not yet old either in body or in political acumen. Unlike many old men in politics who seem to need power to survive as men as well as politicians, Jefferson had no desire to exploit the explosive international scene either to keep himself longer in office or to prove his essential virility.

With great dexterity he persuaded Congress in November 1806 to pass an embargo instead of declaring war. By this device he hoped first to bring home the 20,000 to 30,000 American seamen on the high seas, thus protecting them from European jails, as well as their 2,000 ships and $80 million in cargo. Second, he planned to test the effectiveness of economic sanctions in place of war, hoping to pinch the British economy with sufficient severity to coerce the government into repealing the Orders in Council. In this fashion he would keep his people from becoming involved in what he called "the present paroxysm of the insanity in Europe." [20]

The Embargo was not only an economic weapon of presumably great potential; it was also an extraordinary experiment in withdrawal and isolation. Some 30,000 seamen were immediately unemployed, and merchants who benefited by their connections with the shipping industry quickly suffered. This Jefferson had anticipated, as he did the suffering of his own Virginians, whose cotton and tobacco shipments abroad represented for many citizens almost their only cash income. Jefferson expected local manufactures to spring up, replacing those goods made in England, and they quickly did. So he shifted importantly from his old ideal of the agrarian state selling its products abroad to the ideal of the self-sufficient state. "I trust the good sense of our country will see," he said, "that its greatest prosperity depends on a due balance between agriculture, manufactures and commerce, and not in this protuberant navigation which has kept us in hot water from the commencement of our government." [21]

In a very real sense Jefferson was asking the nation to retire from its enemies—and its large maritime commerce—as he himself expected shortly to retire to Monticello. As his slaves wove cloth and made nails, so the nation would turn to small factories; there would be independence; there would be no entangling alliances, and Europe could go on with its self-immolation while America survived in economic as well as geographical isolation. The blending between the personal man and the political man at this point in Jefferson's career was long ago recognized by Henry Adams. "The idea of ceasing intercourse with obnoxious nations reflected his own personality in the mirror of statesmanship," Adams wrote.[22] He quoted as evidence a portion of a letter Jefferson had written on November 24, 1808, to his sixteen-year-old grandson:

> Be a listener only, keep within yourself, and endeavor to establish with yourself the habit of silence, especially on politics. In the fevered state of our country no good can ever result from any attempt to set one of these fiery zealots to rights, either in fact or in principle. They are determined as to the fact they will believe and the opinions on which they will act. Get by them, therefore, as you would by an angry

bull; it is not for a man of sense to dispute the road with such an animal.[23]

The advice was good for social life, Adams held, "but could not be made to suit the arena of politics." Indeed the British bull was "not only angry, but mad with pain and blind with rage; his throat and flanks were torn and raw where the Corsican wolf had set his teeth . . . his blood-shot eyes no longer knew friend from foe, and he rushed with a roar of stupid rage directly upon the President. . . . To fly was the only resource." [24] But Jefferson never looked upon his course as flight, even though the establishment of the Embargo was followed hard upon by his announcement in December 1807 that he would retire at the end of his second term as president. He still had fifteen months left in office. He had no expectation of bringing the British bull to its knees, but hoped simply to deflect his course. "The embargo," he wrote to Levi Lincoln on March 23, 1808, "is the last card we have to play, short of war." He hoped it would last no more than a year, and hoped too that by then there would be peace in Europe. If peace did not come, and the Orders in Council were not revoked, then Congress "would have to consider at what point of time the embargo, continued, becomes a greater evil than war." [25]

This was a temperate, sane, and imaginative approach to the increasingly desperate problem of American shipping. Jefferson never expected the Embargo to be without cost, counting it "a temporary evil to save us from a greater." [26] But the war in Europe continued on its frenzied course, and the Embargo was slower in hurting the British than the Bostonians. Even the textile manufacturers in English cities did not begin to go bankrupt as quickly as the cotton raisers in Georgia. Though many new factories sprang up in America, and clever young entrepreneurs made fortunes, commerce generally languished. Thirteen-year-old William Cullen Bryant, prodded by his Jefferson-hating father, began what would be a distinguished career as a poet with an attack on the Embargo. It even included a slur on Jefferson's "sable" mistress:

> When shall this land, some courteous angel say,
> Throw off a weak, and erring ruler's sway? . . .
> Oh wrest, sole refuge of a sinking land,
> The sceptre from the slave's imbecile hand! . . .
> Go, wretch, resign the presidential chair,
> Disclose thy secret measures foul or fair . . .
> Or where Ohio rolls his turbid stream,
> Dig for huge bones, thy glory and thy theme;
> Go scan, Philosophist; thy —— charms,
> And sink supinely in her sable arms. . . .[27]

Despite supplementary congressional acts which tried to close the land traffic to Canada and to prevent misuse of the coastal traffic, frauds multiplied and smuggling became a national scandal. New England became so hostile to the Embargo—Jefferson later described her as four dead states hanging on the body politic—secession talk flourished, and young John Quincy Adams brought word secretly to Jefferson in great alarm that influential Federalists were secretly negotiating with British agents to effect a separation.[28] As Jefferson neared the end of his term, and it became clear to the British that his hand-picked successor, who had served for eight years as Secretary of State mirroring Jefferson's foreign policy, would easily be elected president, significant pressures were brought to bear in London to relax the Orders in Council. By now there was suffering also in Manchester, and Jefferson was promised by the British minister that the Orders would be revoked by June 10, 1809.[29] This would be five weeks after he left office; it was promise enough to make him believe for a brief and happy time that his experiment in economic sanctions in lieu of war had truly succeeded.

To his great mortification, however, what he described as a "panic" swept through Congress in March 1809; the Embargo was repealed just before he went out of office, and a substitute nonintercourse measure passed to replace it. All trade was opened save with England and France, but this meant that the economic pressure of the Embargo was curtailed because it was easy for the great European belligerents to get whatever goods they wanted from America through indirect channels. The end of the Embargo cost the new Madison administration most of its bargaining power; the Orders in Council were not revoked; what Jefferson called the "insulting, tyrannical and malicious" conduct of Great Britain continued.[30] By the time Madison declared war in 1812, over 6,000 men had been impressed and almost a thousand ships taken.[31]

Jefferson counseled against war right up to the final disastrous declaration. To William Wirt he wrote on May 3, 1811:

War against Bedlam would be just as rational as against Europe, in its present condition of total demoralization. When peace becomes more losing than war, we may prefer the latter on principles of pecuniary calculation. But for us to attempt, by war, to reform all Europe, and bring them back to principles of morality, and a respect for the equal rights of nations, would show us to be only maniacs of another character. We should, indeed, have the merit of the good intentions as well as the folly of the hero of La Mancha.[32]

Don Quixote often appeared in Jefferson's value judgments. There were times, as we have seen, when he wryly spoke of his own Rosinante in his stall and counted himself a well-intentioned madman for believing he could influence the course of history. But he would not be caught up in the apocalyptic destruction of the Napoleonic wars, and he counted on population increase and on purchase to extend the strategic borders of the United States.

What Madison did not know, when finally, white-faced and trembling, he gave in to the war hawks in Congress and asked the legislators for a declaration of war, was that the British government had finally capitulated to the economic weapon—blunted though it was—and had revoked the Orders in Council. By the time that word came to him via the slow Atlantic ships, it was too late. When Jefferson learned that the declaration of war had coincided in time with the British conciliatory repeal "then going on one thousand leagues distant," he wrote of it privately to William Short with his characteristic understatement as "certainly a misfortune." [33] Had there been an Atlantic cable to carry the news there would have been no war, and Jefferson's policy of economic coercion would have been accorded by history the respect it deserves. As it is, there was never any question in his own mind about the power of the economic weapon, especially for a nation which neither possessed nor needed significant military power. He wrote to Thomas Leiper on June 11, 1815, that the "continuance of the Embargo for two months longer would have prevented our war." [34]

When the outbreak of war became certain, Jefferson knew he must be loyal to his successor and keep his sorrow and regret hidden. We see evidence of his regret in a letter he wrote on April 25, 1812, to his old boyhood school friend James Maury in England, to whom he wrote fitfully through his lifetime and whom he could trust with discretion:

> But if ever I was gratified with the possession of power, and of the confidence of those who had entrusted me with it, it was on that occasion when I was enabled to use both for the prevention of war, towards which the torrent of passion here was directed almost irresistibly, and when not another person in the United States, less supported by authority and favor, could have resisted it.[35]

So in this quiet letter, which apotheosizes rationality in politics, Jefferson registered his discreet satisfaction that he had kept the peace. And as an old man of seventy-eight he wrote to John Adams: "I hope we shall prove how much happier for man the Quaker policy is, and that the life of the feeder is better than that of the fighter." [36]

CHAPTER XXX

Like a Patriarch of Old

There is a tranquillity about him, which an inward peace could alone
bestow.

Margaret Bayard Smith, describing Jefferson
at Monticello, August 1, 1809 [1]

Jefferson would return to Virginia in March 1809 to live out his days
in a world that was far more repressive to blacks than the one he
had left for the presidency in 1801. After 1805 anyone helping a slave
to run away was liable to a fine of $100 to $500 and two or four
years in prison. All slaves freed after 1806 were subject to immediate
banishment from Virginia unless the owner secured a special dispensa-
tion from the legislature. Under the old liberal manumission law,
which Jefferson had helped to write, the free black population in the
state had risen from 3,000 to 30,000. However, during the same period
the number of slaves had grown from 250,000 to almost 400,000, and
emancipation sentiment lessened in direct proportion to the increase.
Breeding slaves for sale to the Deep South had become profitable,
and many free blacks were kidnaped and carried to South Carolina
for transshipment to Georgia and Mississippi Territory.

Since the Gabriel conspiracy, free Negroes in Virginia had become
objects of suspicion and hatred. Though there were as yet no laws
prohibiting slaves to read, some schools for free black children had
been forced to close, and many in this unfortunate caste were forced
into vagrancy and thievery.[2] The insistence of the leading Virginia
statesmen on the impossible, that emancipation must be accompanied

422

by colonization, had proved worse than useless, though it is unlikely that Jefferson himself recognized this. His ambivalence concerning slavery deepened even during his presidency, as he continued to live with slavery and off it, and to do this with a resignation that was for the most part cheerful and contented. He bought at least eight slaves while president. His account books show the purchase of "2 Negro men, Isaac & Charles from William T. Colston of Alexa. for 400 D. paiable at 30 days . . . and 500 D. paiable at 60 days," May 6, 1805, and "a negro woman Lucretia, her 2 sons John & Randall & the child of which she is pregnant when born, for £ 180," August 21, 1805. On May 11, 1807, he bought from Randolph Lewis "a woman Mary 27 y old, and her two sons (6 and 4) . . . wife and children of Moses" for £ 150. The last purchase seems to have been to unite a family.

Jefferson shifted constantly in what he wrote and said about blacks, depending on his feelings at the moment. Back in 1791, when the Negro mathematician, inventor, and astronomer Benjamin Banneker had written to him protesting the general sentiment that blacks were "considered rather as brutish than human, and scarcely capable of mental endowments," and had sent him his own *Almanac* as proof to the contrary, Jefferson had replied cordially, and had even helped Banneker to gain a position in laying out plans for Washington City. Later, while acknowledging Banneker's mathematical talent, Jefferson belittled his literary capacity, calling his letters "childish and trivial." This he said to a young British diplomat, Augustus John Foster, visiting at Monticello in 1807. Foster greatly irritated Jefferson during his stay by his emphasis on British moral superiority over Americans on the slavery issue. Emancipation, Jefferson finally said to Foster, "was an English hobby, and . . . the English are apt to ride their hobbies to death." He shocked Foster by saying he considered blacks "to be as far inferior to the rest of mankind as the mule is to the horse, and as made to carry burthens." And "he appeared to think," Foster said, "that we should only render the Negroes' fate more miserable by our perseverance in endeavouring to abolish the [slave] trade."[3]

Foster may have been a bad reporter; in any case he stimulated Jefferson's old spleen against the British. Actually Jefferson had already asked Congress in his message of December 1806 to end the Atlantic slave trade, and aided by his son-in-law Randolph in the House he vigorously supported the legislation in its difficult passage through Congress. The fight was acrimonious, with portentous talk of secession. Peter Early of Georgia said bluntly on the floor of the House, "A large majority of people in the Southern states do not consider slavery as even an evil"; young Andrew Jackson went on record opposing emancipation because it would make land values in Kentucky drop 75 percent; and John Randolph of Roanoke argued that "possession of slaves was essential to the formation of a perfect gentleman." [4] So Jefferson had warning of the temper of the younger generation from whom he had hoped so much.

The antislave trade bill did pass, providing a fine of $20,000 and forfeiture of the ship for anyone equipping a slave ship, and a fine of $1,000 to $10,000 with imprisonment from five to ten years for anyone transporting and selling blacks on the Atlantic. But the fate of the wretched slaves who might in the future survive the Atlantic passage, and the punishment of the slavers, was left to the individual states, which meant that smuggling in subsequent decades would make a mockery of the ban. South Carolina, the only state which still permitted the slave trade in 1807, saw 15,000 slaves shipped in to Charleston to meet the expected deadline. Some ten to twenty thousand a year would be smuggled into the South before the Civil War.[5]

Though Jefferson as president had forbidden the slave trade in Louisiana Territory, thereby incurring the wrath of many New Orleans citizens, he had not encouraged the passage of a bill in Congress to make up for the defeat of his great Ordinance of 1784, which would have banned slavery in all new states beyond the original thirteen. Had he fought for such a ban in the territory of the Louisiana Purchase it would have supplemented the Ordinance of 1787, which had successfully blocked the spread of slavery into Ohio, Indiana, and Illinois. But the evil was permitted to spread anywhere in Louisiana Territory without Jefferson's lifting a finger to block it. Shortly after taking office he had written to a friend, "We see the wisdom of Solon's remark, that no more good must be attempted than the nation can bear." [6] This had been his recipe for handling the slavery problem. Though Jefferson would acknowledge that emancipation would not come in his own time, he was certain that it would come eventually, as he wrote to Edward Coles in 1814, whether "by the generous energy of our own minds; or by the bloody process of St. Domingo." [7] How much his acquiescence in the dangerous postponement of emancipation had to do with the satisfactions of his personal life at Monticello one can only speculate.

By 1807 he was already impatient for retirement, and beginning to send things home from Washington. To Elizabeth Trist he wrote on December 27, 1807, "The ensuing year will be the longest year of my life." [8] During his final packing he wrote to Charles Willson Peale on February 6, 1809 of his satisfaction in departing "to those scenes of rural retirement after which my soul is panting." [9] To Alexander von Humboldt, the great German naturalist who had visited him in

Washington, he wrote on March 6, 1809, "Within a few days I shall bury myself in the groves of Monticello." [10]

No newspaperman captured the special quality of Jefferson's pleasure in the inauguration of James Madison so well as Margaret Bayard Smith in letters to her sister. Madison shook her hand at the ceremony, she reported, "but it was when I saw our dear and venerable Mr. Jefferson that my heart beat." When he saw her, she wrote, "he advanced from the crowd, took my hand affectionately and held it five or six minutes." While she paid some attention to Dolley Madison's "plain cambrick dress with a very long train," and "bonnet of purple velvet and white satin with plumes," she was far more intent on watching the departing president and the president-elect. Madison was "extremely pale and trembled excessively when he first began to speak, but soon gained confidence and spoke audibly." She watched Jefferson, graceful and relaxed, obviously happy in his successor. "I do believe father never loved son more than he loves Mr. Madison," she wrote.

After the ceremony, when she insisted on following the crowd of friends to the President's House and her husband teased her openly, saying to Jefferson that "the ladies *would* follow him," Jefferson replied with a wistful reminiscence: "That is right, since I am too old to follow them. I remember in France when his friends were taking leave of Dr. Franklin, the ladies smothered him with embraces and on his introducing me to them as his successor, I told him I wished he would transfer these privileges to me, but he answered, 'You are too young a man.'"

Margaret looked up at him. "Did this not imply," she said to her sister, "that now this objection was removed? I had a great inclination to tell him so." But she did not dare, and Jefferson missed being "smothered with embraces," for which he so obviously hungered. Perhaps this was one reason that he violated a taboo that had begun with the death of his wife and that night went to the inaugural ball.

"Am I too early?" he asked a friend upon arriving. "You must tell me how to behave for it is more than forty years since I have been to a ball." And when the guests, seeing Jefferson dancing happily, contrasted his gaiety with Madison's pale and worried face, Jefferson explained it, smiling, "I have got this burthen off my shoulders, while he has now got it on his." [11]

During his years in Washington Jefferson had kept a mockingbird in his study, which he let fly freely about when he was alone and which he had taught to sit on his shoulder and even eat from his own lips.

"How he loved this bird!" Margaret Smith wrote. "How he loved his flowers! He could not live without something to love."[12] Now, in March 1809, he was out of his own cage, released from what he called "the shackles of power."[13] He refused to wait for good weather, taking off in a storm, and he grew so impatient when his carriage became repeatedly mired down in the wretched roads that he took to his horse and rode eight hours through the blinding snow.[14] This was a retirement totally unlike his departure from the bitter gladiatorial contest with Hamilton in 1794. He left now in elation and fulfillment; like Washington he had weathered eight years in office. He had doubled the size of his country and prevented its cracking apart; in the face of insolent provocations from England and France he had kept his temper and the temper of his people; they had remained united behind him in keeping the peace.

The contradiction, however, between Jefferson's attitude toward power over the American people and power over his own slaves cries out for explanation. We have seen that Jefferson never needed power in government as a bulwark either to his masculinity or to his self-esteem. However gratified he was by the affection of his people, as expressed in the vote, the exercise of power he found to be a burden and an enchainment. "Never," he wrote in 1811, "have I ever been able to conceive how any rational being could propose happiness to himself from the exercise of power over others."[15] Still, he clung to the absolute power of the master of the plantation without any seeming awareness that he was in truth a despot in his own realm. In ruling at Monticello he held on to the past, preserving the world of his childhood, with all its secret pleasures—the ancient world of his parents in which he now lived as master and adult. In acquiescing in the postponement of the end of slavery—by his own apathy, indifference, and hesitation—he postponed also his own aging, and in a sense his own death, and indeed the death of Monticello.

The significance of Monticello as a fountain of youth and source of love we see in Jefferson's short but revealing speech to his neighbors of Albemarle County, who had met and written an address formally welcoming him home. For his neighbors, as for many of his relatives, Jefferson had mixed sentiments. Some were openly hostile to him; some had gossiped freely of his slave mistress to James Callender; and when Jefferson learned that they planned a formal welcome he deliberately circumvented it by saying that he could not predict the exact day of his arrival.[16] Still, their written letter of welcome he found affecting, and replied to it a fortnight after his arrival home. "I receive, fellow citizens," he wrote, "with inexpressible pleasure, the cordial welcome you are so good as to give me." The "pomp, the turmoil, the bustle and splendor of office, have drawn but deeper sighs for the tranquil and irresponsible occupations of private life, for the enjoyment of an affectionate intercourse with you, my neighbors and friends, and the endearments of family love, which nature has given us all, as the sweetener of every hour. For these I gladly lay down the distressing burdens of power."

The tender phrases bubbled up—irresponsible occupations, affectionate intercourse, endearments of family love, the sweetener of every hour. So this sixty-six-year-old statesman communicated his domestic contentment. It poured out despite himself, for he had no social license to discuss with anyone his secret happiness. He was especially pleased, he said, to receive evidences of approbation from "individuals who have known me in private life." Then, suddenly defensive, Jefferson finished by quoting from the Bible, to which he so rarely turned: "Of you then, my neighbors," he said, "I may ask, in the face of the world, whose ox have I taken, or whom have I defrauded? Whom have I oppressed, or of whose hand have I received a bribe to blind mine eyes therewith?" [17] It was as if, once more, he felt himself under attack.

Margaret Bayard Smith and her husband visited Jefferson at Monticello on August 1, 1809, when he had been in retirement about five months. He showed them about his library with obvious pleasure, taking down from the shelf an edition of *Piers Plowman* two hundred and fifty years old, and a volume containing the letters of Cortez to the King of Spain. He opened his small closet with garden seeds hung in little phials, "labeled and hung on little hooks . . . in the neatest order." And he talked with seeming freedom about himself. "The whole of my life has been a war with my natural taste, feelings and wishes. Domestic life and literary pursuits, were my first and my latest inclinations. . . . And like a bow though long bent, which when unstrung flies back to its natural state, I resumed with delight the character and pursuits for which nature designed me." He was indeed unstrung, relaxed, and happy in the presence of this adoring young woman whom he had so often seated next to himself at dinner in the President's House. That she reminded him fondly of the bride he had brought to Monticello in a snowstorm thirty-seven years before seems evident, for though it was August he began to talk to her of what it was like to stand at the door to the west, to see a snowstorm "rising over the distant Allegheny, come sweeping and roaring on, mountain after mountain, till it reaches us, and then when its blast is felt, to turn to our fire side, and while we hear it pelting against the windows to enjoy the cheering blaze."

Though she wrote fervently, "I have seen, I have listened to, one of the greatest and best of men. . . . truly a philosopher, and a truly good man, and eminently a great one," having "a tranquillity about him, which an inward peace could alone bestow," still she was deeply disturbed by his slaveholding. The slave cabins, she reported, "though much better than I have seen on any other plantation, appear poor and form most unpleasant contrast with the palace that rises so near them." One wonders what questions this sharp-eyed young woman asked of the house slaves, and of the fair slave children who ran errands for the guests. Did she dare question them at all? Did she single out Sally Hemings, now thirty-six, even to learn the names of her children? Beverly was now eleven, Harriet eight, Madison four, and Eston one. Did Margaret Smith wonder about the whereabouts of the son whom Callender had called President Tom? She wrote with evident anger about the "clouds of calumny" which had threatened Jefferson "with a wreck of happiness and fame." And she noted with special interest his study-bedroom, "the door of which is never opened but by himself, and his retirement seems so sacred that I told him it was his sanctum sanctorum." [18] But she protected him, as did almost everyone else.

Jefferson suffered briefly from retirement shock, writing to Dr. Benjamin Rush on September 22, 1809, "A retired politician is like a broken down courser, unfit [for the] turf, and good for little else."[19] A year after his retirement began he wrote to John Langdon, "Now, take any race of animals, confine them in idleness and inaction, whether in a stye, a stable or a state-room, pamper them with high diet, gratify all their sexual appetites, immerse them in sensualities, nourish their passions, let everything bend before them, and banish whatever might lead them to think, and in a few generations they become all body and no mind. . . . Such is the regimen in raising Kings." The kings who had reigned while he was in Europe he disparaged. Louis XVI, the kings of Spain and of Naples were "fools"; the King of Denmark, Gustavus of Sweden, and Joseph of Austria were "really crazy"; and the King of Prussia, successor to Frederick the Great, was "a mere hog in body as well as in mind." [20]

There could have been certain discomforting similarities between this "regimen in raising Kings" and his own. That Jefferson had more than a passing interest in the debaucheries of monarchs is suggested by George Ticknor, who visited Monticello and noted a privately bound six-volume edition of scandalous memoirs of the courts of France and England. "These documents of regal scandal seemed to me to be favorites with the philosopher," Ticknor wrote, "who pointed them out to me with a satisfaction somewhat inconsistent with the measured gravity he claims in relation to such subjects generally.[21]

But with Jefferson now there was no descent into the swamp of depression as in 1795. During whatever year one samples out of the years of his retirement up to the beginning of real debility at seventy-six there is evidence of tranquillity and lightness of spirit. To the artist Charles Willson Peale he wrote on May 5, 1809, "I am . . . enjoying a species of happiness I never before knew, that of doing whatever hits the humour of the moment without responsibility or injury to any one." In 1811 he wrote again to Peale, "I have often thought that if heaven had given me a choice of my position and calling, it should have been a rich spot of earth, well watered, and near a good market for the productions of the garden. . . . though an old man, I am but a young gardener." [22] His slave Isaac later said that whenever Jefferson walked or rode about his acreage he was always singing. ". . . hardly see him anywhar out doors but what he was singin: had a fine clear voice, sung minnits [minuets] & sich: fiddled in the parlor." [23] His granddaughter Ellen, who now slept in the room above him at Monticello, described him humming old tunes, "generally Scotch songs but sometimes Italian airs or hymns." [24] Again and again in his letters he returned to the old theme he had first enunciated in Paris, "The earth belongs to the living." [25] To John Armstrong he wrote in 1813, "The happiness of the domestic fireside is the first boon of heaven." [26] In 1817 he insisted to Dr. John Manners that the "King of Kings" had "made it a law in the nature of man to pursue his own happiness. . . . there is not another nation, civilized or savage, which has ever denied this natural right. . . . How it is among our savage neighbors, who have no law but that of Nature, we all know." [27] It was as close as he dared come to admitting his continuing satisfaction with the "savage neighbor" he could talk of to no one at all.

Lest one assume that it was Jefferson's daughter Martha who was largely responsible for his domestic happiness in retirement, let us look hard at what her moving to Monticello with her whole family in 1809 actually meant. Though she was now queen of Monticello, and no doubt happier than she had been for many years, still she was almost constantly pregnant, bearing a child every year or eighteen months until 1818, by which time she had had twelve, of whom eleven grew to maturity. She suffered constantly from the humiliating knowledge that her husband was contributing almost nothing financially for their upkeep. Though Randolph had recovered from his mental breakdown in Washington, and had become in many respects a superior farmer to most of his neighbors, particularly in his introduction of horizontal, or contour, plowing to prevent erosion of the Virginia hillsides, he was nevertheless sinking into debt at a faster rate than

Jefferson. He had a brief period of success, when elected governor of Virginia in 1819, but his third year ended in failure and near disgrace. Even in this period, instead of providing for his children he was constantly giving money to his impecunious younger brothers and sisters and to improvident friends.

"He could not say No to importunate pleaders," his daughter Ellen wrote, "to distressed gentlemen relatives or neighbors, or old school fellows. . . . He was always crippled by debts not of his own contracting, and lived a life of painful frugality and self-denial only to enable others to keep above water for a short time their foolish heads." [28] To deny one's own family money which one cheerfully supplies to wastrels argues enormous hostility toward that family. If one reads the frank unpublished memoir of Randolph's daughter, the biography of him by William H. Gaines, Jr., and the reminiscences of overseer Edmund Bacon, one sees that Jefferson's picture of this Eden of affection and tranquillity had a darker face.

"As my father advanced in life," Ellen Randolph wrote, "and his pecuniary difficulties increased, he became more morose, more irritable, more suspicious. My own belief is that nothing but the mingled dignity, forbearance and kindness of my grandfather prevented some outbreak which might forever have alienated two men bound by the strongest ties." Randolph frequently gave way to "paroxysms of rage" in front of his wife, and while he treated his daughters with affection he was unjust and ungenerous to his sons, particularly his eldest, Jefferson's namesake, whom Randolph often tried to cane even after the son had become an adult. Jefferson, to counter the smoldering hatred of his son-in-law, "adopted the wise plan of seeming ignorance," Ellen wrote, "and his unalterable calm, his affectionate politeness made it entirely impossible to begin an unpleasant discussion. The angry spirit was subdued. . . . Thus my mother was spared the heaviest of misfortunes, a positive disunion between her father and her husband." [29] Not surprisingly, Martha suffered seriously from migraine like her father, whose headaches had now disappeared altogether.

The gravest burden for Jefferson at Monticello, aside from difficulties with his son-in-law, was his increasing debt. He had been forced to borrow $8,000 just to liquidate his Washington debts when he left the presidency. In April 1815, after agonizing over the British destruction of the Library of Congress in the War of 1812, he arranged to sell his library of 6,000 volumes for $23,950, less than half its auction value, as the nucleus of a new library for the American people. But most of this money went to pay debts to William Short and Thaddeus Kosciusko. [30] Jefferson found the empty bookshelves intolerable. "I cannot live without books," he wrote, [31] and though he could ill afford the luxury, he began building a new library. The British diplomat Augustus John Foster was incensed that Congress did not vote him the money and refuse to accept the books till after his death, calling it "another great slur upon the character of Congress." In 1816–17 Jefferson's account book shows that he spent during that year almost as much on books as upon clothing for his slaves, $480.80, as against $525.28, though this figure may be misleading, since a good deal of wool and cotton cloth was woven on the estate.

As visitors and relatives continued to come to Monticello in droves, sometimes staying for weeks (which caused great resentment among the grandchildren), the expenses of feeding them became an additional drain on Jefferson's resources. Young Jefferson Randolph, seeing the impending bankruptcy of both his father and his grandfather, tried to persuade his father to turn the Edgehill plantation over exclusively to the raising of tobacco and of slaves for sale. Both men were appalled. Jefferson had written to his son-in-law in 1809, "I consider it much better to sell this property than my slaves. . . . I have raised many of them myself and know them all well." [32] Still, he was trapped in the system that insisted on putting a cash value on a human being, and was capable of writing to John Eppes on June 30, 1820, "I consider a woman who brings a child every two years as more profitable than the best man of the farm, what she produces is an addition to the capital, while his labors disappear in mere consumption . . ." [33] In the end both the Edgehill and Varina plantations belonging to Randolph had to be sold, and Jefferson suffered in the knowledge that the slaves he had given to his daughter as her dowry, and the slave children born to them since that date, must be put up for auction.

The Monticello slaves were not sold during Jefferson's lifetime. He managed to pay off the mortgage on these slaves which he had incurred for the remodeling of Monticello, and he planned to leave them as capital for his daughter and her children, knowing that Randolph would leave nothing. All through his retirement years his slave problems continued to be entangled with other family problems—finances, deference, honor, reputation, and sex. That he suffered from guilt there is ample evidence; it seems not to have been a continuing, gnawing anxiety but rather a tormenting surge of anguish when something specific forced recognition upon him of the enormous difference between his theoretical ideal society and his daily life.

One such incident came in 1811, when Lilburn and Isham Lewis, nephews of Jefferson, "literally chopped a Negro slave to pieces." It was a hideous story that abolitionists later retold and that Robert Penn Warren made the subject of a moving poetic volume, *Brother* to *Dragons*, in 1953.[34] One can only guess Jefferson's response to the tragedy. We do know his response, however, to a different kind of reminder of the enormity of slavery. This was thrust upon him in 1814, when he received a remarkable letter from young Edward Coles, a neighbor and brother of his onetime secretary Isaac Coles. The Coles family was very wealthy; Edward himself had scores of slaves, but unlike his family he found slavery detestable beyond endurance. He decided to take all his slaves to Illinois, where he planned to free them and set up each family on 160 acres of land. Though his own family thought him mad, he persisted in the planning and wrote to Jefferson soliciting his public aid. Seeing in Coles' quixotic plan the kind of dramatic public gesture he might himself have made as a spur to antislavery activity, Jefferson was deeply shaken. He admitted to his young neighbor his regret that most Southerners thought slaves "were as legitimate subjects of property as their horses and cattle," but then drifted into evasion. Slavery, he said, rendered the slave himself "incapable as children of taking care of themselves." His own slaves gave the lie to this; there were blacksmiths, carpenters, spinners, gardeners, and farmers on his plantations; many could support themselves economically even though illiterate, and several of his slaves could read and write. In holding that his own slaves were children, Jefferson was denying them the dignity of maturity and the right of decision-making, the same rights for which he had long ago urged separating from George III.

He begged Coles to abandon his plan, and instead to "come forward in the public councils, become the missionary of this doctrine truly christian; insinuate & inculcate it softly but steadily." To "insinuate and inculcate softly" was Jefferson's way of life. But against the ever accelerating evil of slavery, pleading and insinuation were beginning to look like political imbecility. Still, for Coles to expect the seventy-one-year-old Jefferson to mount his Rosinante and sound the clarion call for emancipation was asking the impossible. "This, my dear sir," Jefferson wrote, "is like bidding old Priam to buckle the armour of Hector. . . . This enterprise is for the young. . . . It shall have all my prayers, & these are the only weapons of an old man." [35] For a man who believed so little in the efficacy of prayer, this was really an admission that he had no weapons at all.

Perhaps the most remarkable line in Jefferson's letter to Edward Coles is his reference to miscegenation. "The amalgamation of whites with blacks," he wrote, "produces a degradation to which no lover of his country, no lover of excellence in the human character, can innocently consent." One must note especially his inclusion of the word "innocently." Jefferson had been responsible for miscegenation—but innocently—with love and without debauchery of the slave woman. But his octoroon children had been subjected by Virginia society to the same degradation as the blackest African, and he had been pilloried for siring them. Amalgamation for Jefferson truly did not raise the black; it only degraded the white.

Coles, who was secretary for a time to James Madison, finally did take his slaves to Illinois, and carried out his emancipation plans. Eventually he became governor of Illinois, a living demonstration that the saintly gesture need not be political suicide.[36] But Jefferson was trapped not only by his debts but also by his passionate affection for Monticello. He could not have followed Coles even if he had been young. Nevertheless, the mathematics of miscegenation continued to preoccupy him. When in 1815 the brash Francis C. Gray asked him indiscreetly at what point does a black man become white, Jefferson replied, "You asked me in conversation, what constituted a mulatto by our law. . . . Our canon considers two crosses with the pure white, and a third with any degree of mixture, however small, as clearing the issue of negro blood." Then he went on to write a complicated chart of mathematical possibilities.[37]

. . . Let us express the pure blood of the white in the capital letters of the printed alphabet, the pure blood of the negro in the small letters of the printed alphabet, and any given mixture of either, by way of abridgment in MS. letters.

Let the first crossing be of a, pure negro, with A, pure white. The unit of blood of the issue being composed of the half of that of each parent will be $\frac{a}{2} + \frac{A}{2}$. Call it, for abbreviation, h (half blood).

Let the second crossing be of h and B, the blood of the issue will be $\frac{h}{2} + \frac{B}{2}$, or substituting for $\frac{h}{2}$ its equivalent, it will be $\frac{a}{4} + \frac{A}{4} + \frac{B}{2}$, call it q (quarteroon) being $\frac{1}{4}$ negro blood.

Let the third crossing be of q and C, their offspring will be $\frac{q}{2} + \frac{C}{2} = \frac{a}{8} + \frac{A}{8} + \frac{B}{4} + \frac{C}{2}$, call this e (eighth), who having less than $\frac{1}{4}$ of a, or of pure negro blood, to wit $\frac{1}{8}$ only, is no longer a mulatto, so that a third cross clears the blood.

From these elements let us examine their compounds. For example, let h and q cohabit, their issue will be $\frac{h}{2} + \frac{q}{2} = \frac{a}{4} + \frac{A}{4} + \frac{a}{8} + \frac{A}{8} + \frac{B}{4} = \frac{3a}{8} + \frac{3A}{8} + \frac{B}{4}$, wherein we find $\frac{3}{8}$ of a, or negro blood.

Let h and e cohabit, their issue will be $\frac{h}{2} + \frac{e}{2} = \frac{a}{4} + \frac{A}{4} + \frac{a}{16} +$

$$\frac{A}{16} + \frac{B}{8} + \frac{c}{4} = \frac{5a}{16} + \frac{5A}{16} + \frac{B}{8} + \frac{c}{4} \text{ , wherein } \tfrac{5}{16} \text{ } a \text{ makes still a mulatto.}$$

Let q and e cohabit, the half of the blood of each will be $\frac{q}{2} + \frac{e}{2} =$

$$\frac{a}{8} + \frac{A}{8} + \frac{B}{4} + \frac{a}{16} + \frac{A}{16} + \frac{B}{8} + \frac{C}{4} = \frac{3a}{16} + \frac{3A}{16} + \frac{3B}{8} + \frac{C}{4} \text{ , wherein } \tfrac{3}{16}$$

of a is no longer a mulatto, and thus may every compound be noted and summed, the sum of the fractions composing the blood of the issue being always equal to unit. . . .

The closest that Jefferson dared come to defending miscegenation was his open championship of amalgamation with Indians. Though Virginia law forbade intermarriage with Indians as well as blacks and mulattoes, Jefferson as president had had no hesitation in saying to a group of Delawares, Mohicans, and Munries on December 21, 1808, "You will mix with us by marriage, your blood will run in our veins, and will spread with us over this great island." [38] He did not have the bulldog courage the nation would see later in Richard Johnson, vice-president under Martin Van Buren, who openly admitted that he had two daughters by a mulatto slave named Julia Chinn, and educated them. Whites ostentatiously snubbed the daughters when Johnson tried to introduce them into society, but he saw that they married white men and willed them his property. It was widely rumored that he had gone through a marriage ceremony with their mother. The circumstances shocked whites in North and South, but this scandal did not keep him from becoming vice-president.[39]

That Jefferson persisted in his secrecy was inevitable; that he was not wholly tranquil in spirit living "like a patriarch of old"—as he described himself again in 1820 to Maria Cosway [40]—was also inevitable. In 1816 he wrote to Amos J. Cooke, "And if the Wise be the happy man . . . he must be virtuous too; for, without virtue happiness cannot be." And he quoted significantly from Ecclesiastes:

I sought in my heart to give myself unto wine; I made me great works; I builded me houses; I planted me vineyards; I made me gardens and orchards, and pools to water them; I got me servants and maidens, and great possessions of cattle; I gathered me also silver and gold, and men singers and women singers, and the delights of the sons of men, and musical instruments of all sorts; and whatsoever mine eyes desired I kept not from them; I withheld not my heart from any joy. Then I looked on all the works that my hands had wrought, and behold! all was vanity and vexation of spirit! I saw that wisdom excelleth folly, as light excelleth darkness.[41]

When Jefferson wrote this letter, Beverly Hemings was eighteen, Harriet fifteen, Madison eleven, and Eston eight. Madison Hemings tells us, "My brothers, sister Harriet and myself, were used alike. They were put to some mechanical trade at the age of fourteen. Till then we were permitted to stay about the 'great house,' and only required to do such light work as going on errands." [42] In the reminiscences of the slave Isaac there is a reference to "the baloon that Beverly sent off," [43] which suggests that something of Jefferson's fascination had carried over to this youth, and that this one of Sally's sons had experimental and scientific interests. On July 20, 1820, overseer Edmund Bacon sent Jefferson a note, "Do you no that Beverly has been absent from the carpenters for about a week." [44] Beverly was then twenty-two. Jefferson wrote "run away 22" after Beverly's name in his *Farm Book* on page 130; the definite date of the notation cannot be established.

Madison Hemings wrote that "Beverly left Monticello and went to Washington as a white man. He married a white woman in Maryland, and their only child, a daughter, was not known by the white folks to have any colored blood coursing in her veins. Beverly's wife's family were people in good circumstances." [45] All of which suggests that Beverly had schooling along with Jefferson's white grandchildren as well as training as a carpenter, and that he may also have had financial aid.

Monticello overseer Edmund Bacon wrote of Harriet Hemings that Jefferson "freed one girl some years before he died, and there was a great deal of talk about it. She was nearly as white as anybody and very beautiful. People said he freed her because she was his own daughter. . . . When she was nearly grown, by Mr. Jefferson's direction I paid her stage fare to Philadelphia and gave her fifty dollars. I have never seen her since and don't know what became of her. From the time she was large enough, she always worked in the cotton factory. She never did any hard work." Loyally supporting the "family denial," Bacon insisted that Harriet was not Jefferson's daughter. "She was ——'s daughter," he said. "I know that. I have seen him come out of her mother's room many a morning when I went up to Monticello very early." [46] But Harriet was born in 1801, and Bacon did not come to Monticello until 1806. He never lived in the "big house." There is no listing in Jefferson's account book of a special sum of $50 given to Edmund Bacon in 1822, which may be further evidence that Jefferson did give a good deal of money away of which he kept no record whatsoever. That $50 was no trifling sum is evident if one looks at Bacon's first contract; he agreed to serve as overseer for Jefferson for one

Roll of the negroes according to their ages.
Albemarle.

1727. Squire
31. Goliah
43.
Will   8. Sep. 1810.
1820
Maddox 8. Apr. 21. 1811
52. John
55. Davy
56. Amy
57. Doll
Betty Brown   8. 1809.
59.
60. Ned
Lewis
61. Nance
62. Jenny Ned's
68. Isaac
Bagwell
Jenny Lewis's
69. Critta
70. Peter Hemings
Minerva
73. Sally
75. John Hemings
76. James

1793. Edwin
Virginia Bagwell's
94. Scilla Ned's
Dolly Ned's
95.
James Lewis
Esther
96. Phillip
Zena
Isaac Ned's
Scilla Jenny's
97. Sanco
Ambrose
Evelina
Ursula
Doe.
98.
Will Ned's
1800. Nancy Bagwell
Isabel Ned's
Thrimston Ned's
Israel Ned's
01. William Ned's
Flora Scilla's
Mary Bob's

1811. Aggey Ursula's
Syp. Jenny Scilla's.
Dec. Jenny Tammy's
Oct. Matilda Minerva's
Dec. 24. Robert Virginia's
1812. Oct. 27. Zacharian Minerva's
Dec. 6. Betty Ann Edy's
1813. Tammy Lindsay Esther's
Mar. Edmund Rachael B.
Fanny Scilla's
Squire Henry Cretia's
Oct. 1. Thomas Ursula's
May. Marshall Moria's [Exelavina's]

1814.
Jane
1815. Jean S. Peter Edy's
July. James Bant. Cretia's
Aug. Patsy Moria's
Syp. Amanda Virginia's
1816. Jan. 21. Louisa Ursula's
April. 15. Agester Moria's
July

1817. John

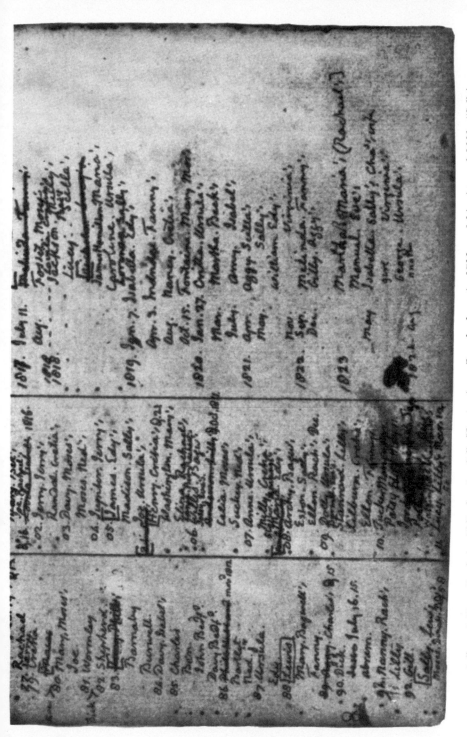

Jefferson's Farm Book (p. 130) showing Sally Hemings' son Beverly, born in 1798, and his sister of 1801, "Sally's Harriet," as runaways in 1822. (The two halves of the reproduction are overlapped for clarity)

year; his pay was $100 and 600 pounds of pork. Jefferson himself put a cryptic "run 22" after Harriet's name in his *Farm Book* on the same page [130] that noted Beverly's departure.

Madison Hemings wrote of his sister Harriet with a touch of irony. "[She] married a white man in good standing in Washington City, whose name I could give, but will not, for prudential reasons. She raised a family of children, and so far as I know they were never suspected of being tainted with African blood in the community where she lived or lives. I have not heard from her for ten years, and do not know whether she is dead or alive. She thought it to her interest, on going to Washington, to assume the role of a white woman, and by her dress and conduct as such I am not aware that her identity as Harriet Hemings of Monticello has ever been discovered." [47]

Sally Hemings' two youngest sons, Madison and Eston, assisted in the gardening. Jefferson apparently gave them some land to themselves; his account book on December 11, 1824, states, "Pd Madison and Eston for 100 cabbages," a certain indication of special treatment. At fourteen Madison was apprenticed to his uncle, John Hemings, master carpenter and furniture craftsman at Monticello. The slave Isaac reported that Madison Hemings "learned to be a great fiddler." [48] Who but Jefferson would or could have provided the instrument and the training? But Madison did not vouchsafe this information, or if he did it was not published. He gives the impression that his education had been neglected. "I learned to read by inducing the white children to teach me the letters and something more," he wrote; "what else I know of books I have picked up here and there till now I can read and write." We do not know if the writing of the memoir is wholly his, but if it is it indicates a competence far superior to that of the average white carpenter of his time. It also argues a reluctance to give thanks to Jefferson, who clearly deprived him of the affection he must have felt was due him.

The reminiscences of Israel Jefferson, another Monticello slave, who had settled in Ohio near Madison Hemings, which were published shortly after his, are written in so similar a style as to suggest that both memoirs were written by the same newspaperman after interviews with these ex-slaves. But the details of the latter importantly support Madison Hemings' story. Israel, who said his father's name was Edward Gillett, described how for fourteen years he had made the fire in Jefferson's bedroom and private chamber, cleaned his office, dusted his books, and run errands. Sally Hemings, he said, "was employed as his chamber-maid, and . . . was his concubine. This I know from my intimacy with both parties, and when Madison Hemings declares that he is a natural son of Thomas Jefferson, the author of the Declaration of Independence, and that his brothers Beverly and Eston and sister Harriet are of the same parentage, I can as conscientiously confirm his statement as any other fact which I believe from circumstances but do not positively know." [49]

Did it trouble Jefferson that he could not acknowledge any of the four sons of Sally Hemings as his own? That he felt the deprivation keenly of not having a single legitimate son in whom he could feel pride is suggested by a letter he wrote to Charles Willson Peale shortly before his death. Peale, by then a distinguished portrait painter, had written to Jefferson proudly of the success of his own sons, whom he had named Rembrandt, Reubens, Titian, and Franklin, boasting that his son Rembrandt's equestrian portrait of Washington had been hung in Independence Hall. Jefferson wrote back wistfully, "Among your greatest happiness must be the possession of such sons, so devoted to the arts of taste, as well as of use, and so successful in them." [50]

Ellen Coolidge wrote that all of Sally Hemings' children were fair, and that they were either freed in Jefferson's will or allowed to leave voluntarily. Her brother, Thomas Jefferson Randolph, had told her they had been fathered by either Peter or Samuel Carr, and this she stoutly believed. They were altogether four yellow children, she said, "slaves as were sufficiently white to pass for white, . . . three young men and the girl, who walked away and staid away—their whereabouts was perfectly known but they were left to themselves." [51] One is reminded in reading her letter (the owner, a Jefferson heir, did not permit publication in full until May 18, 1974) of what Mrs. Frances Trollope wrote of Jefferson in her *Domestic Manners of the Americans* in 1832. "I once heard it stated by a democratical adorer of this great man, that when, as it sometimes happened, his children by Quadroon slaves were white enough to escape suspicion of their origin, he did not pursue them if they attempted to escape, saying laughingly: 'Let the rogues get off, if they can; I will not hinder them.' This was stated in a large party, as proof of his kind and noble nature, and was received by all with approving smiles." [52]

We do not know if it was Tom or Madison or Eston Hemings that Jefferson's grandson was describing when he talked to Henry Randall, who reported the conversation as follows:

> Walking about mouldering Monticello one day with Col. T. J. Randolph (Mr. Jefferson's oldest grandson) he showed me a smoke blackened and sooty room in one of the collonades, and informed me it was Sally Henings' room. He asked me if I knew how the story of Mr. Jefferson's connection with her originated. I told him I did not. "There was a better excuse for it, said he, than you might think: she had children which resembled Mr. Jefferson so closely that it was plain

that they had his blood in their veins." He said in one case the resemblance was so close, that at some distance or in the dusk the slave,
dressed in the same way, might have been mistaken for Mr. Jefferson.—
He said in one instance, a gentleman dining with Mr. Jefferson looked
so startled as he raised his eyes from the latter to the servant behind
him, that his discovery of the resemblance was so perfectly obvious to
all. Sally Hening was a house servant and her children were brought up
house servants—so that the likeness between master and slave was
blazoned to all the multitudes who visited this political mecca.

Randolph then went on to assure Randall that Peter and Samuel
Carr were the actual fathers of Sally Hemings' children but forbade
him to use the information.

"When I rather pressed him on the point," Randall wrote, Randolph pointed to the family graveyard and said, "You are not bound
to prove a negation. If I should allow you to take Peter Carr's corpse
into Court and plead guilty over it to shelter Mr. Jefferson, I should
not dare again to walk by his grave: he would rise and spurn me." So
the grandson by unconscious innuendo suggested the truth of that
which he had just vehemently denied.[53]

Jefferson noted in his *Farm Book* only three runaways, Beverly,
Harriet, and Critta Hemings' son Jamy, born in 1787, when Jefferson
was in Paris. It is possible that either Peter or Samuel Carr was Jamy's
father, and that this circumstance gave rise to the "family denial" in
regard to the children of Sally Hemings. Jamy, according to the *Farm
Book* [60], ran away in 1804, at age seventeen. Presumably the fourth
slave, "white enough to pass for white," was, as we have already indicated, "Tom Hemings," celebrated in the newspaper publicity of
1802 to 1805. Against the possibility that Sally Hemings took also the
nephews as lovers we must consider Jefferson's fierce possessiveness and
the fact that Sally's children were all conceived during, and only during,
periods when he was at home. Besides, by 1800 the Carr brothers had
plantations and slaves of their own.[54]

Let us remember that Sally Hemings and her children did not have
to share Monticello with the whole Randolph family—save in the summertime—until 1809. By then Tom had long since gone, Beverly was
eleven and Harriet nine. The younger Madison and Eston, however,
would have remembered no years without Martha Randolph in total
charge. They watched Beverly and Harriet escape into the white world,
but also saw their mother trapped permanently in the status of a
house slave, however favored, with Martha Randolph continuing as
the ruling mistress, even handing out her clothing. That this was
done by Jefferson's order is evident from a memorandum from Jefferson to Edmund Bacon, which said in part, "Mrs. Randolph always

chooses the clothing for the house servants; that is to say, for Peter Hemings, Burwell, Edwin, Critta, and Sally." [55] That Jefferson's white grandchildren were brought up under the elaborate pretense of non-relationship with the Hemings children seems clear enough. Thus it is not surprising that Madison and Eston Hemings, though freed by the provisions of Jefferson's will and counted legally white, and so listed on the Albemarle County census of 1830, still chose to remain in the black community and marry colored women like their mother.[56]

The peace and serenity of Monticello was enforced by Jefferson's remarkable will, by his capacity for ordering a general happiness, by his denial of the suffering, the humiliation, and the ugliness. "We were free from the dread of having to be slaves all our lives long," Madison wrote, "and were measurably happy." This was an exact phrase. At Monticello, when contrasting his lot with those of other slaves, Madison Hemings counted himself lucky. It was only later, as a free adult in Ohio, that he came to sense the importance of the story of his mother and her children. How long the desire to tell the story festered in him one cannot know; it may have begun very early. But it was not until 1873 that he found a newspaperman willing to believe, and to publish what he had written.

Perhaps it was the necessity of continuing to deny so many natural rights to Sally Hemings, and the necessity also of rejecting and separating himself from her children, demanded by the whole white community and no doubt demanded most of all in silence by his own daughter, that reinforced Jefferson's lifelong conviction that there could be no emancipation of slaves without deportation. If the hatred and tyranny and sadism of the whites would result, as he feared, in threatened slave insurrection and a war of races, loving brought no real solution either, only secrecy, denial, humiliation, guilt, and loss. So it may have seemed to him. All we know, however, was that in 1820 at seventy-seven, when in his *Autobiography* he penned the magnificent line now appearing in the interior of his memorial in Washington, "Nothing is more certainly written in the book of fate, than that these people are to be free," he did not end the sentence there, as it is ended in his memorial. Instead he added the following: "nor is it less certain that the two races, equally free, cannot live in the same government. Nature, habit, opinion, have drawn indelible lines of distinction between them."

We know, too, that when in 1820 he learned of the savage battle in Congress over the admission of Missouri into the Union as a slave state, he roused from his torpor like an old lion who has long been asleep. When northern Congressmen demanded gradual emancipation as the price of admission and Southerners threatened secession he was horrified. "This momentous question," he wrote, "awakened and filled me with terror. I considered it at once as the knell of the Union." Even the final compromise, which extended the Mason-Dixon Line into the west, with slave states to the south and free states to the north, he counted "a reprieve only, not a final sentence." Such a geographical line, he insisted, "coinciding with a marked principle, moral and political, once conceived and held up to the angry passions of men, will never be obliterated; and every new irritation will mark it deeper and deeper."

Then in a terrible reversal of the great precedent he had set in 1784, when he had fought for the exclusion of every slave from every territory of the West, he now argued feebly that "their diffusion over a greater surface would make them individually happier, and proportionally facilitate the accomplishment of their emancipation, by dividing the burden on a greater number. . . ." He had, it is true, seen slavery disappear in the states of the North, where the number of blacks was small. But he had also seen its terrifying acceleration in the South, and must surely have known how fatuous was such a hope. "Gradually, with due sacrifices," he insisted, "a general emancipation and *expatriation* could be effected." "But as it is, we have the wolf by the ears, and we can neither hold him, nor safely let him go. Justice is in one scale, and self-preservation the other." As for the secession threat, he called it an "act of suicide on themselves, and of treason against the hopes of the world." [57] But he bowed to the threat, as did countless statesmen in the decades that followed, till Thaddeus Stevens would say in 1859, "We have saved the Union so long I think we will save it to death." [58]

To Lafayette Jefferson wrote defensively in 1820 that diffusion of slavery would "dilute the evil everywhere, and facilitate the means of getting finally rid of it." He added:

> The boisterous sea of liberty indeed is never without a wave, and that from Missouri is now rolling towards us, but we shall ride over it as we have over all others. It is not a moral question, but one merely of power. Its object is to raise a geographical principle for the choice of a President, and the noise will be kept up till that is effected.[59]

As Henry Adams pointed out, Jefferson was a bad sailor; the ocean frightened him. He had written many times of guiding his Argosy over the sea of revolution and the sea of politics. Now the analogy had sadly changed. His tumultuous sea of the moment was the "sea of liberty." For Jefferson in 1821 the sea of liberty for blacks had become the most terrifying of all.

CHAPTER XXXI

Writer of Letters

You and I ought not to die before We have explained ourselves to each other.

John Adams to Jefferson, September 10, 1816 [1]

There were times during his retirement when Jefferson thought wistfully of Paris. "Were it not for my family and possessions," he wrote to William Short on March 25, 1815, "I should prefer that residence to any other. Paris is the only place where a man who is not obliged to do anything will always find something amusing to do. Here the man who has nothing to do is the prey of ennui. . . . a family for leisure moments, and a farm for profession for those of employment are indispensable for happiness. These mixed with books, a little letter writing, and neighborly and friendly society constitute a plenum of occupation and of happiness which leaves no wish for the noisy & barren amusements and distractions of a city." [2] To fight the ennui Jefferson responded not with a little letter writing, and relaxation in a friendly society, but with a fantastic outpouring of letters and with years of intense involvement in a new creation, the University of Virginia.

The several thousand letters he wrote from 1809 to 1826, constituted his continuing legacy to the American people; they also appeased his insatiable appetite for communication, and for proof that he was still revered and loved. He counted all the letters coming to him in the single year of 1821—they numbered 1,267—and complained bitterly about the necessity of answering them. His life, he said, was that of a mill horse who sees no end to his circle but in

443

death. "To such a life that of a cabbage is paradise." But he did answer the letters all the same, with patience, courtesy, and elegance in the writing. He could not bear to be thought churlish by even the most outrageously demanding correspondent. In his letters to Madison as president he continued to discuss political matters, though he did his best, as a matter of principle, to offer no advice unless it was specifically requested.

He made it a general principle, too, not to solicit public office for any of his friends or acquaintances. He violated this only twice when James Monroe was president, asking office for Bernard Peyton, a young protégé from Richmond, and for William Duane, his stout old defender on the staff of the *Aurora*. When he was turned down coldly in both instances, he was aghast at the new President's ingratitude. "I am indeed sorely and deeply wounded," he wrote to Peyton. "I supposed that 60. years of faithful service would weight with them as much as a broken leg. . . . It was the first opportunity I had ever given of obliging me. I have miscalculated, and shall better understand my place hereafter." [3] Still, he remained on friendly terms with Monroe, and Charlottesville admirers on several occasions gathered in excitement when they saw the three presidents, Jefferson, Madison, and Monroe, sitting in a tavern together. "We adore Mr. Jefferson," the Virginian Francis Gilmer wrote, "we admire Mr. Madison, and we esteem Mr. Monroe." [4]

Unlike most aging men, Jefferson in an important sense remained a revolutionist to the end, far more so than either of his successors in the presidency. Only on slavery did he remain prey to ancient fears. Impatient of property requirements for voters, he called for "general suffrage" and "equal representation in the legislature." On the national scene he wanted to see the electoral college abolished and the executive "chosen by the people." Increasingly alarmed by what he called the "imbecilities of dotage" of federal and Supreme Court judges, he advocated "judges elective or amovable." [5] To his old antagonist Henry Lee he wrote in a friendly letter at age eighty-one, "Men by their constitutions are naturally divided into two parties: 1. Those who fear and distrust the people, and wish to draw all powers from them into the hands of the higher classes. 2. Those who identify themselves with the people, have confidence in them, cherish and consider them as the most honest and safe, although not the most wise depository of the public interests." [6]

Jefferson never lost faith in the people or in the democratic process which he believed would result in the surfacing of a "natural aristocracy of virtue and talents." The wealthy, however, he continued to distrust up to his death. In 1795, as we have seen, he had written to Mann

Page, "I do not believe . . . that fourteen out of fifteen men are rogues. . . . But I have always found that rogues would be uppermost." [7] The rogues in politics Jefferson had generally found among the very rich. He continued to believe that no special laws were necessary to protect the wealthy. "Enough of these," he wrote, "will find their way into every branch of the legislation to protect themselves." [8]

When he first retired, his friends expected him to begin immediately the writing of his memoirs. Repeatedly he refused. "To become my own biographer is the last thing in the world I would undertake," he wrote in 1816.[9] And in 1817, at age seventy-four, he wrote to a friend, "You say I must go to writing history. While in public life I had not time, and now that I am retired, I am past the time. To write history requires a whole life of observation, of inquiry, of labor and correction. Its materials are not to be found among the ruins of a decayed memory." [10] Adams too found the idea of writing memoirs burdensome. To Benjamin Rush he wrote, "To rummage trunks, letter books, bits of journals, and great heaps and bundles of old papers is a dreadful bondage to old age and an extinguisher of old eyes." Later he wrote again to Rush, "I have made several attempts, but it is so dull an employment that I cannot endure it. I look so much like a small boy in my own eyes that with all my vanity I cannot endure the sight of the picture." [11]

Jefferson finally yielded at age seventy-seven, and began an autobiography, "for my own more ready reference," he said, "and for the information of my family." But his habits of control were by then frozen into a kind of glacial rigidity; he could not give himself up to reminiscence. He had a deep antipathy to the idea of telling anything about his personal life, and the bare recording of the facts of his career quickly became a sterile enterprise. After sixty-odd pages he wrote, "I am already tired of talking about myself." Once he had described his farewell to Paris in 1789, he abandoned the memoir altogether, possibly because the most pressing secret of his life became in this year of overpowering importance. It is possible, too, that he came to see the whole enterprise of writing even the simple facts of his political life as too complicated and hazardous for his multitudinous friendships.

Most important of all, Jefferson could not dwell on the past for very long except to search for models with which to improve the future. Augustus John Foster, after a visit to Monticello, noted that in conversation Jefferson "was visionary and loved to dream, eyes open, or, as the Germans say, 'zu schwärmen.'" The whole of America, Foster said, "is the paradise for 'Schwärmers,' futurity there offering a wide frame for all that imagination can put into it." [12] At seventy-seven

Jefferson was still dreaming with his eyes open, his creative impulses almost as vigorous as at twenty-seven. He was now deeply involved in the building of the University of Virginia, a project which he had long dreamed of and which wholly captured him at seventy-five. It occupied his seemingly inexhaustible architectural energies up to his death. He surveyed the site in Charlottesville himself, and laid out the stakes. With the help of architects William Thornton and Benjamin Latrobe he drew up blueprints for most of the buildings. He planned the curriculum and selected most of the faculty, the majority of them scholars from Europe. His famous Rockfish Gap report, written for the state commission that adopted plans for the university in August 1818, included not only the general scheme for the university but also plans for free public education in Virginia, still in a scandalously primitive and neglected state compared with education in New York and New England. The necessity of education for the prosperity, power, and happiness of the nation was an old theme with Jefferson, first elaborated in his *Notes on the State of Virginia*. He had returned to it as governor of Virginia when fighting to reform the curriculum of William and Mary, and again in his unsuccessful efforts when president to create a national university. "Enlighten the people generally," he wrote in 1816, "and oppressions of body and mind will vanish like evil spirits at the dawn of day." [13] The theme in his old age became a "holy cause," an antidote to mental vegetation, and a factor in the prolongation of his life.

Since his retirement Jefferson had built a second house at his Poplar Forest plantation, a refuge from the unasked and offensively curious visitors who flocked to Monticello. He had also designed several houses for his friends. For the University of Virginia Jefferson went back again to Palladio, designing the campus as "an extended Villa Meledo," but modified and transmuted for the practical purposes of university life. For the Rotunda he chose as a model the Roman Pantheon, though in smaller size, and designated it for the library. He planned also for it to be a kind of planetarium, with stars in their positions in the firmament controlled by an operator in an ingeniously designed movable seat. Though the college as finally finished differed somewhat from his original designs, it nevertheless emerged as one of the most extraordinary architectural creations in American civilization. Kenneth Clark has described this classic "academical village," with its "low open lines, covered ways between the buildings, and the great trees in each small garden," as having "something of the character of a Japanese temple." [14]

Jefferson's curriculum for his university was no less an achievement in the history of American education. He planned for courses in modern as well as ancient languages, in pure mathematics, military and naval architecture, mechanics, optics, astronomy, pneumatics, geography, anatomy, physical chemistry, mineralogy, philosophy, natural history, law, belles-lettres, and fine arts. Still deeply suspicious of any religious sect save those of the Quakers and the Unitarians, he omitted religious instruction except as a branch of ethics, in effect / outlawing the establishment of a divinity school. He also confined medical studies to theory only, so suspicious was he of general medical practice, which he called "the charlatanism of the body," as he called religion "the charlatanism of the mind." Priests, he said, "dread the advance of science as witches do the approach of daylight." [15] The university, he wrote, "will be based on the illimitable freedom of the human mind. For here we are not afraid to follow truth wherever it may lead, nor to tolerate error so long as reason is left free to combat it." [16]

When the exasperating difficulties with financing were finally solved, the university opened in May 1824 with ten pavilions and 109 dormitory rooms for 218 students. Jefferson at first was in favor of self-government for the students and a minimum of discipline, but a student riot, which he himself at eighty-two helped to quell, and which resulted in three expulsions (one his own nephew) and eleven severe reprimands, convinced him that severer regulations were essential. His pride in the university was reflected in the epitaph he wrote for his own grave marker. The stone should be engraved to read, he said, "Author of the Declaration of Independence, and of the Statute of Virginia for Religious Freedom, and Father of the University of Virginia," because by these testimonials "I wish most to be remembered."

Though he had taken pains with the education of his white daughters, Jefferson made no provision, either in his university plans or in his plans for general education, for systematized schooling for women. Here he differed little from most American men, who believed that women should be kept at home, and as domestic as possible. Moreover he approved the French rule that "no lady dances after marriage." [17] Even in a pure democracy, he wrote bluntly to Samuel Kercheval on September 5, 1816, women "could not mix promiscuously in the public meetings with men." To permit it would mean "depravation of morals and ambiguity of issue." He deplored the increasing participation of women in the night meetings of the Presbyterian evangelists in Richmond, where the women, he said, "attended by their priests, and sometimes henpecked husband, pour forth the effusions of their love to Jesus, in terms as amatory and carnal, as their modesty would permit them to use to a mere earthly lover." [18]

The non-domestic woman, the promiscuous woman, the political woman, the religious hysteric—all were deplorable, perhaps in an important sense threatening.

Jefferson compartmentalized his radicalism. He would widen the suffrage, but not for women or blacks; he would liberate the human mind as long as it was male; he would follow truth "wherever it may lead." One should not blame Jefferson for falling short of perfection as a liberator of the human spirit. He continued by default rather than by purpose to follow traditions concerning women that were in his time practically universal. After his death, his institutional and intellectual legacy served to aid the liberation of both women and blacks. Without it, their respective kinds of enslavement might have been prolonged indefinitely in America.

On New Year's Day 1812, John Adams wrote a letter to Thomas Jefferson breaking the silence between them that had lasted eleven years. Adams was then seventy-six, Jefferson sixty-eight. Benjamin Rush, who had been writing to both men, had been teasing them to end their long estrangement. With guile, flattery, and delicate entreaty he slowly broke down their barriers. Jefferson, insisting at first that a mending of the old friendship was impossible, nevertheless sent Rush copies of his exchange with Abigail Adams in 1804, and Rush pointed out the affection in her letters, and minimized the hostility. In the summer of 1811 Jefferson's young abolitionist friend, Edward Coles, paid Adams a visit, at which time he spoke warmly of Jefferson's respect and affection for the aging ex-president. Upon hearing this Adams burst out, "I have always loved Jefferson and still love him."

When Coles returned to Monticello with this story, all the ice in Jefferson's memories melted. He wrote immediately to Rush, repeating Adams' affectionate words. "This is enough for me," he added. "I only needed this knowledge to revive towards him all the affections of the most cordial moments of our lives." [19] By now Adams could not wait to begin. He sent Jefferson proudly what he described as "two Pieces of Homespun," two volumes his son John Quincy had published called *Letters on Rhetoric and Oratory*, prepared when he was teaching at Harvard College. Jefferson replied with a letter that began stiffly but quickly mellowed into warm reminiscence:

> A letter from you calls up recollections very dear to my mind. It carries me back to the times when, beset with difficulties and dangers, we were fellow laborers in the same cause, struggling for what is most valuable to man, his right of self-government. Laboring always at the same oar, with some wave ever ahead threatening to overwhelm us

and yet passing harmless under our bark, we knew not how, we rode through the storm with heart and hand, and made a happy port.[20]

Rush, delighted at his success, wrote to Adams, "I rejoice in the correspondence. . . . I consider you and him as the North and South Poles of the American Revolution. Some talked, some wrote, and some fought to promote and establish it, but you and Mr. Jefferson *thought* for us all." [21] There were 158 letters in all, 109 from Adams, 49 from Jefferson. Adams, more aggressive, eager, and hungry, wrote always with a sense of urgency. "The Seconds of Life, that remain to me, are so few and so short; (and they seem to me shorter and shorter every minute) that I cannot stand upon Epistolary Ettiquette; and though I have written two Letters, yet unnoticed I must write a third." Again he wrote, "Never mind it, my dear Sir, if I write four letters to your one; your one is worth more than my four. . . . You and I ought not to die, before We have explained ourselves to each other." [22]

At first, as we have seen, Jefferson could not forgive the peppery Abigail, and indicated to Rush rather frostily that "from this fusion of mutual affections, Mrs. Adams is of course separated. It will only be necessary that I never name her." [23] But name her he did, almost at once, in postscripts, and they even exchanged altogether six rather formal letters. The correspondence had barely resumed when Adams' only daughter, Nabby Adams Smith, age 49, died of breast cancer. Dr. Rush had urged an immediate operation when Adams first wrote to him about her condition. "This remedy is the knife. . . . Should she wait till it supperates or even inflames much, it may be too late. The pain of the operation is much less than her fears represent it to be." [24] Abigail wrote in anguish to Jefferson of their hopes that the operation had cured her, and of her suffering when the cancer "communicated itself through the whole mass of the Blood." "You called me to talk of myself," she concluded, and answered with lines from Shakespeare:

> Greif has changed me since you saw me last,
> And carefull hours, with times deformed hand
> Hath written strange defections o'er my face.

The despairing Adams wrote that before her illness Nabby had been "the healthiest and firmest of us all." [25]

Jefferson, who had known Nabby as a young flower in Paris, relived again the death of his own daughter Maria, struck down also by a disease of the breast. He could not bring himself to reply for several weeks. Then he wrote, "I know the depth of the affliction it has caused, and can sympathise with it the more sensibly, inasmuch as there is no degree of affliction, produced by the loss of those dear to us, which experience has not taught me to estimate. I have ever found time and silence the only medicine, and these but assuage, they never can suppress, the deep-drawn sighs which recollection for ever brings up, until recollection and life are extinguished together." [26]

The letters that continued over the years are a marvelous outpouring, livened by an affection both men were determined should not again be jeopardized. The Adams letters are volatile, ebullient, ranging from comedy and fantasy to spleen and rage. His more somber view that man's nature was essentially evil often seems more realistic than Jefferson's more cheerful assessment, but his pessimism was only spasmodic. At one moment he would write, "I am weary of Philosophers, Theologians, Politicians, and Historians. They are immense Masses of Absurdities, Vices and Lies." And at another he could say, "I am not weary of Living. Whatever a peevish Patriarch might say, I have never yet seen the day in which I could say I have had no Pleasure; or that I have had more Pain than Pleasure." [27] They discussed subjects as varied as the origin of the American Indians, the character of Napoleon, the nature of aristocracy, the future of science, the nature of the rational man, the uses of grief, and inevitably the coming of death, for which neither man was eager. Though Adams was willing to discuss politics, Jefferson veered away, fearing a resurgence of the old acrimony. "Shall we, at our age . . ." he said, "exhibit ourselves, as gladiators?" [28]

When books were published that included letters from Adams criticizing Jefferson, and letters from Jefferson criticizing Adams—appearing without permission of either author—the two friends brushed aside the embarrassments as of no consequence. In a gentle fashion they continued to compete with each other, comparing numbers of grandchildren and great-grandchildren, and notes as to how far each could walk or ride horseback without fatigue. Adams pitied Madison his childlessness. Children, he wrote, "have cost us Grief, Anxiety, often Vexation and some times humiliation; Yet it has been cheering to have them about Us; and I verily believe they have contributed largely to keeping Us alive." [29] When Jefferson congratulated Adams on his son's winning the presidency in 1824, the proud father called the letter "the most consolatory" he ever received in his life.[30] Jefferson took special pleasure in sending his grandchildren, Ellen and Thomas Jefferson Randolph, to Massachusetts to visit Adams. In his letter introducing his namesake, he wrote, "Like other young people he wishes to be able, in the winter nights of old age, to recount to those around him what he has heard and learnt of the Heroic age preceding his birth, and which of the Argonauts particularly he was in time to have seen." [31]

Adams was frankly jealous of Jefferson's enormous popularity. "My Reputation has been so much the Sport of the public for fifty Years," he said, "and will be with Posterity, that I hold it, a bubble, a Gossameur, that idles in the wanton Summers Air." He lamented that there would be no monuments erected to his memory. "Your Administration," he said, "will be quoted by Philosophers as a model, of profound Wisdom; by Politicians, as weak, superficial and short sighted. Mine, like Pope's Woman, will have no character at all." [32]

Though Jefferson wrote that "an hour of conversation would be worth a volume of letters," history would have been the loser had this been possible. Each man took great pains with his letters, which were meant to be reread and savored on lonely winter nights. Both recognized that in time the correspondence would find its way into print; Adams was importuned by a printer as soon as word was out that the friendship between the two ex-presidents had been mended. As one by one their friends died, the two men became increasingly dependent upon each other. "While you live," Adams wrote, "I seem to have a Bank at Montecello on which I can draw for a Letter of Friendship and entertainment when I please." [33] And Jefferson wrote not long afterward, "Take care of your health and be assured that you are most dear to me." [34]

Inevitably, in this eager interchange of feeling and ideas, Adams' curiosity led him into forbidden country. In a letter that skirted dangerously close to the mysteries of Jefferson's intimate life, Adams began a discussion of selective breeding. He translated a quotation from Theognis, stating that whereas a man setting out to purchase horses, asses, or rams would "inquire for the Wellborn," and choose from the good breeds, yet the same man would be perfectly willing in choosing a wife to marry a shrew if enough money came with her.[35] Jefferson somewhat surprisingly let himself be drawn into the subject, and wrote about it as if he had seriously reflected on the problem. "The selecting the best male for a Haram of well chosen females . . ." he admitted, "would doubtless improve the human, as it does the brute animal, and produce a race of veritable *aristocrats*. For experience proves that the moral and physical qualities of man, whether good or evil, are transmissible in a certain degree from father to son. But I suspect that the equal rights of men will rise up against this privileged Solomon and oblige us to continue acquiescence under *the degeneration of the race of men*,* which Theognis complains of, and to content

* In the original the italicized words are in Greek.

ourselves with the accidental aristoi produced by the fortuitous concourse of breeders. For I agree with you that there is a natural aristocracy among men. The grounds of this are virtue and talents. . . . The natural aristocracy I consider as the most precious gift of nature for the instruction, the trusts, and government of society." [36]

Adams, replying in a lively letter—which had so much talk of sex (what he called "generation") that he dared not submit it to his wife or daughters-in-law for copying and sent it along in his own palsied hand with the request that it be returned—moved on into a discussion of the impact of beauty upon history. Among the non-aristocratic women who had profoundly influenced history he listed Eve, Judith, Ruth, Madame de Maintenon, and Mrs. Fitzherbert. He dwelt particularly on Lady Emma Hamilton, Admiral Nelson's mistress, whom he described as the "daughter of a green Grocer" who had caused "the tryumphs of the Nile, of Copinhagen and Trafalgar." But of American women, he wrote, "For mercy's sake do not compell me to look to our chaste States and Territories, to find Women, one of whom lett go, would, in the words of Holophernes' Guards 'deceive the whole earth.' " [37] This was as close as Adams dared come in tempting Jefferson to confidences about the impact of non-aristocratic beauty on his own life. Jefferson, apparently sensing the drift of Adams' seemingly lighthearted speculation, let several letters go by without answering; he had no more to say about selective breeding, and nothing whatever to say about women.

In October 1818, Adams, who had been discussing with Jefferson "the uses of grief," wrote to him that his wife was dying. "Now Sir for my Griefs! The dear Partner of my Life for fifty four Years as a Wife and for many Years more as a Lover, now lyes in extremis, forbidden to speak or be spoken to. If human Life is a Bubble, no matter how soon it breaks. If it is as I firmly believe an immortal Existence We ought patiently to wait the instructions of the great Teacher. I am, Sir, your deeply afflicted Friend." [38] Later Jefferson replied sadly, "The public papers, my dear friend, announce the fatal event of which your letter of Oct. 20 had given me ominous foreboding. . . . I know well, and feel what you have lost, what you have suffered, are suffering, and what you have to endure." He went on to comfort Adams with fantasies of Heaven, about which he himself had many doubts, writing of "an ecstatic meeting with the friends we have loved and lost and whom we shall still love and never lose again." [39] With Adams the idea of a hereafter was essential to his happiness, and he fled from any new scientific discovery that threatened his religious orthodoxy. There "never was but one being who can Understand the

Universe," he had written to Jefferson in 1813, and "it is not only vain but wicked for insects to pretend to comprehend it." [40]

Though Jefferson paid due reference to the idea of Heaven in a crisis of death, he was alert to every scientific advance that cast doubt on it, and was increasingly tough-minded in his skepticism. "The Almighty himself could not construct a machine of perpetual motion," he wrote to Dr. Robert Peterson in 1812, "while the laws exist which He has prescribed for the government of matter in our system." [41] He had no hesitation at age eighty-one in calling the Revelation of St. John "the ravings of a maniac, no more worthy nor capable of explanation than the incoherences of our own nightly dreams." [42] In the same month he wrote to Adams in excitement describing new surgical experiments on animals where sections of the brain were removed, and specific motor and sensory functions disappeared—"will, intelligence, memory"—yet the animal continued to live. "I wish to see what the spiritualists will say to this," Jefferson wrote. "Whether, in this state, the soul remains in the body deprived of it's essence of thought, or whether it leaves it as in death, and where it goes?" [43] Earlier he had written, "Say nothing of my religion. It is known to my god and myself alone." And to Ezra Stiles he wrote, "I am of a sect by myself." [44]

In 1816 Adams asked Jefferson, "Would you go back to your Cradle and live over again your 70 years?" and they bounced the idea back and forth in an inventive and revealing interchange. Jefferson replied, "I say Yea. I think with you that it is a good world on the whole, that it has been framed on a principle of benevolence, and more pleasure than pain dealt out to us. . . . I steer my bark with Hope in the head, leaving Fear astern." [45] Adams, pursuing the question further, asked Jefferson if he would live his life over again forever, saying that he for one would not. Eternal succession, he wrote, "would terrify me, almost as much as Annihilation." [46] Jefferson, however, found the idea agreeable, provided he did not have to repeat his childhood and youth, or his extreme old age. From twenty-five to sixty, he said, "I would say Yes; and might go further back, but not come lower down." [47]

Very late in life they returned to the same theme again. Adams, recalling the deaths of his parents, wife, children, and friends, now declared he would not live his life over again even once. "Instead of suffering these griefs again, I had rather go forward and meet my destiny." [48] Jefferson, perhaps because he had so little of Adams' religious faith, felt differently. "I should not be unwilling, without however wishing it. And why not? I have enjoyed a greater share of health than falls to the lot of most men; my spirits have never failed me except under those paroxysms of grief which you, as well as myself, have experienced in every form: and with good health and good spirits the pleasures surely outweigh the pains of life. Why not taste them again, fat and lean together. Were I indeed permitted to cut off from the train the last 7. years, the balance would be much in favor of treading the ground over again." [49] So he underlined his personal testimony that through most of his adult life he had been in truth a happy man.

CHAPTER XXXII

The Monticello Tragedy

There is a ripeness of time for death.

Jefferson to Adams, August 1, 1816 [1]

Jefferson's last years brought ill health and grinding anxieties. The panic of 1819 and a series of crop failures destroyed his ever-elusive hopes that he could climb out of the morass of debt into which he had been steadily sinking for many years. His failure to face his own increasing indebtedness, his chronic optimism about next year's bumper crop, unexpected disasters such as the flood that destroyed his mill dam, all contributed to the inexorable slippage toward bankruptcy. There were certain expenditures Jefferson would not reduce, especially the costs of hospitality. Even in Paris, when he had written diffidently to Madison about asking Congress to provide him more money so that he could properly meet the social duties of a minister, he would not let Madison press the matter to the point of angering the congressmen. "I had rather be ruined in fortune," he wrote, "than in their esteem." [2]

Jefferson could not stomach the thought that anyone would believe him niggardly. Though he himself dined abstemiously, forgoing the quantities of meat thought normal for men of taste, drinking wine instead of spirits, his menus were always superb samples of French cooking, and his wine was of exceptional quality. Even at eighty-two he was ordering Muscat de Riversalle in 150-bottle lots.[3] Though his leechlike relatives and the hordes of visitors to Monticello were a constant drain, he could not think of sending them away other than well wined and dined.

Edmund Morgan has said that "Jefferson's concern with the perniciousness of debt was almost obsessive." [4] The very obsessional quality of his concern suggests great inner conflict, not only over the fear of being thought stingy, but also over reluctance to repay the money he himself owed. Why should he have managed with such remarkable success when president to reduce the national debt, while ever increasing his own? The debt his mother had incurred to British bankers in 1770 was still unpaid by Jefferson in 1808. His debts to his good friends William Short and Thaddeus Kosciusko, dragging on for years, could not have been paid at all had he not sold his books to the Library of Congress. But in the end he counted their friendship ahead of his affection for his books. Inherited debts he counted monstrously unfair, as we see in his oft-stated proposal that all debts be canceled every nineteen years.

There were many debts Jefferson did not want to pay, some he felt he did not even owe. There were some he deferred paying out of necessity, and some he was intent on paying quickly, like the small sums he borrowed frequently from Madison. Certainly there was some aggression here. But Jefferson was no petty complainer who feels undervalued and underpaid for his services to his country. On the contrary, he indulged himself like a prince, confident that such was his right as an aristocrat of the spirit and valued servant to the state. It is likely that this habit of indulgence began as a child in his relations with one or both of his parents, most certainly his father, who looked upon him as the heir apparent and as his most talented child. Jefferson could not himself bear the thought of being held an ungenerous parent, either in love or in money. So he poured out sums continually for the members of his family, which included his improvident brother and son-in-law, the three sons of his sister, Martha Carr, and even the drunken Charles Bankhead, who married his granddaughter Anne.

In the end it was this sense of obligation to the larger family that led him into the most disastrous financial blunder of his life. His favorite grandson, Thomas Jefferson Randolph, had married the daughter of Wilson Cary Nicholas, an old friend. In 1818 Nicholas was governor of Virginia, director of a Richmond bank, and thought to be worth $300,000. Why he needed the signature of Jefferson on a loan of $20,000, and why Jefferson, with misgivings, signed the note, remain mysterious. This was the kind of cavalier endorsement many Virginia gentlemen gave for one another; it is unlikely, however, that the debt-ridden Jefferson would ever have done it had not Nicholas in a sense become a member of his "family."

When the panic of 1819 closed banks all over Virginia, Nicholas was among those dragged into ruin, and he shortly afterward died.

Jefferson was now responsible for the total $20,000 loan, the interest payment on which alone amounted to $1,200 a year.[5] When he first learned of his friend's bankruptcy, Jefferson suffered an attack of indigestion and stoppage of bowels that nearly cost him his life.[6] In increasingly apprehensive letters to his son-in-law Randolph he described the desolation in his area brought about by the bank failures, and predicted that should he be held responsible for the whole "calamitous engagement for Col. Nicholas," he could not "foresee the issue." [7] He was forced to sell a large number of slaves to his grandson, Francis Eppes, for $3,500, consoling himself by the thought that they would be kept in the family. But this sum was only a piece of driftwood in the flood. Even the sale of Poplar Forest did not alleviate the threat of ruin and possible loss of Monticello. By now Jefferson owed well over $100,000.[8]

At this point Thomas Jefferson Randolph offered to take over the management of all of Jefferson's property. His grandfather agreed with relief, and the young man labored heroically to save Monticello. "I served my grandfather, mother and her children," he later wrote, "with as much fidelity as I could have served my God." [9] For a time it seemed as if he might succeed. Even the wretched fortunes of Thomas Mann Randolph took a temporary upward swing. With Virginia banks closed and many of her citizens bankrupt, there was enormous public hostility to the whole institution of banking. Jefferson's ancient distrust of banks was now remembered, and several politicians turned to his son-in-law as a fitting representative of the anti-banking tradition, suggesting that he run for governor of the state. Since the governor was not elected by popular vote at this time, Randolph needed to win only a majority vote in the legislature.

Jefferson fed him ideological ammunition. "There seemed to be so general a sickening at the effect of the banks," he wrote on August 9, 1819, "that I hope the country is ripe for suppressing them by degrees, but entirely in the end." [10] Randolph's mental illnesses had been so successfully kept a secret from the public that he was able to win in 1819, and by small majorities in 1820 and 1821. As governor he reflected the enlightened republicanism of his father-in-law. He advocated gradual emancipation but also deportation of the slaves, and worked strenuously for the building of the University of Virginia. His wife, however, refused to join him at Richmond, save for a few weeks in his second term, and he began to drink heavily. By the end of his third term he had acquired a reputation for acrimonious public quarreling and was counted a failure even among his friends. He wrote feverishly to Jefferson on November 21, 1822, hinting again of suicide: "I could flee to the grave with determined mind, to escape from such hateful sophistry and such unprincipled conduct and opinion as I have been compelled so long to witness and to hear." [11]

Meanwhile Randolph's debts had steadily accumulated; when he left office he owed $33,000.[12] Slipping again into the old quagmire of illness, he turned the deeds to all of his property over to his son Jefferson. But once bereft of both title and property he became ever more depressed, refusing to visit Monticello save at night, and finally breaking off all communication with both his father-in-law and his son. His friend Francis Gilmer described him at this point as "broke to atoms, in mind, body, and estate." [13] When the son was forced to sell both the Edgehill and Varina estates, Randolph became locked in paranoia, accusing both Jefferson and his son of being leaders in a plot against him. "I am the victim of the avarice of one," he wrote Jefferson, "encouraged . . . by the vengeance of many." [14]

Jefferson apologized for not coming to Randolph's aid financially, and said he did not hold him personally responsible for his bankruptcy, which he blamed on "the gambling operations of money brokers." He begged Randolph to return to Monticello. "Restore yourself to the bosom of your family and friends. They will cherish your happiness as warmly as they ever did, and more so perhaps, as more needing the soothing balm of their affections, with your varied education and resources of books, you can never want employment of mind, and some excitement to bodily exercise may perhaps be found in experiments of agriculture. . . . relieve the grief of the family with which your absence afflicts them and resume the place in society which is still yours." [15] But the gentle therapy Jefferson had found useful for himself in periods of melancholy was no balm for the blinding rages of the son-in-law, who, unlike Jefferson, was now loved by virtually no one. He did not return to Monticello during Jefferson's last years, and in his own will Jefferson cut him out of all rights in handling the property he left to Martha.

In 1823 Jefferson was saddened by the death of his son-in-law John Eppes, and in 1826 shattered by the death of his granddaughter Anne, whose death it was widely believed had been hastened by the brutality of her husband. The young couple had lived at Monticello for a period, and the whole family had come to detest young Bankhead. Though a handsome man with a distinguished lineage, he had proved to be, in Ellen Randolph's bitter words, "a worthless . . . malignant drunkard." [16] Overseer Edmund Bacon reported that he beat his wife, once in front of her mother. "I have seen him ride his horse into the barroom at Charlottesville and get a drink of liquor. I have seen his wife run from him when he was drunk and hide in a potato hole to get out of danger." When Thomas Jefferson Randolph met Bankhead on the Charlottesville courthouse steps in 1819 and accused him of abusing his sister, Bankhead stabbed him several times with a long knife. "I think he would have killed him," Bacon said, "if I had not interfered and separated them." [17]

When Jefferson heard the news of the stabbing, it was nightfall. He mounted his horse and galloped him down the hill through the dark the several miles to Charlottesville. "I had been laid on a bale of blankets in the crating Room of a store," the grandson wrote later, "and had borne myself with proper fortitude; but when he entered and knelt at my head and wept aloud I was unnerved." [18] Bankhead was arrested and posted bond, but was never brought to trial. He was even permitted to return on occasion to Monticello. Once, when spending the night there, he kept demanding more brandy, but Burwell, now Jefferson's most trusted slave, who kept the keys to the liquor cellar, finally refused to refill his glass. Bankhead, already very drunk, went into such a rage that Martha Randolph, reluctant to call her husband or father, sent for the overseer, who lived nearby. Thomas Mann Randolph was roused by the shouting, however, and made his way to the dining room just as Bacon came in. In the candlelight the drunken Bankhead mistook Randolph for the slave Burwell and began to curse him. At this point Randolph seized an iron poker and knocked his son-in-law down—as Bacon put it, "as quick as I ever saw a bullock fall. The blow peeled the skin off one side of his forehead and face, and he bled terribly. If it had been a square blow, instead of glancing off as it did, it must have killed him." [19]

When Anne Bankhead died on February 11, 1826, Jefferson wrote in sorrow to her brother, "Heaven seems to be overwhelming us with every form of misfortune." [20] Ellen Randolph later wrote bitterly that her sister's death came "happily for herself." [21]

At age seventy-eight Jefferson fell from a broken step leading down from a terrace at Monticello and broke his left wrist and arm. As the bones healed this wrist swelled and stiffened, as had his right wrist thirty-four years before. "Crippled wrists and fingers make writing slow and laborious," he wrote to Adams on October 12, 1823. "But, while writing to you, I lose the sense of these things, in the recollection of antient times, when youth and health made happiness out of every thing. I forget for a while the hoary winter of age, when we can think of nothing but how to keep ourselves warm, and how to get rid of our heavy hours until the friendly hand of death shall rid us of all at once." Though he had installed Franklin stoves at Monticello, and found them far more efficient than fireplaces, he still hated the cold, telling Adams, "I shudder at the approach of winter, and wish I could sleep through it with the Dormouse, and only wake with him in spring, if ever." [22]

An enlarged prostate gland and swelling in his legs made walking increasingly difficult, but he continued to ride with pleasure, and the riding may indeed have served to ease the problem. "I am too weak to walk further than my garden without suffering," he wrote to Charles Willson Peale in 1822, "altho' I ride without fatigue 6. or 8. miles every day and sometimes 20." [23] Once his horse stumbled in a torrent and fell. Jefferson's crippled wrists were caught in the reins and he barely escaped drowning. But he passed off the incident as of no consequence. When George Ticknor visited him in December 1824, he found Jefferson, in his eighty-second year, still riding ten to fifteen miles a day. "Mr. Jefferson seems to enjoy life highly, and very rationally," Ticknor reported, "but he said well of himself the other evening, 'When I can neither read nor ride, I shall desire very much to make my bow.'" [24] More than anything else Jefferson feared senility. He reported to Adams that Charles Thomson, one of the signers of the Declaration of Independence, at ninety-three, was "chearful, slender as a grasshopper, and so much without memory that he scarcely recognises the members of his household." "Is this life?" Jefferson asked. "It is at most but the life of a cabbage; surely not worth a wish." [25]

When Lafayette at age sixty-seven was invited by President James Monroe to visit America, he was 100,000 francs in debt. Nevertheless he borrowed money for his passage, and planned an elaborate itinerary in the New World. Although he spent only one day in Quincy, Massachusetts, with John Adams, he stayed almost six weeks with Jefferson, and later on his way home returned again to see him. In November 1824 a great crowd assembled at Monticello to witness the first meeting of Lafayette and Jefferson, who had not seen each other since 1789, shortly after the fall of the Bastille. Jefferson Randolph, who helped with the celebration, described how his grandfather, feeble with age, walked down from his terrace as Lafayette descended from his carriage. Jefferson, he said, "got into a shuffling quickened gait until they threw themselves with tears into each others arms—of the 3 or 400 persons present not a sound escaped except an occasional supprest sob, there was not a dry eye in the crowd—altho invited into the house none would enter." [26] Later there was a formal dinner in the still unfinished Rotunda of the University of Virginia, with *champignons farcis* and *tournedos*, and the best French wine from the Monticello cellar.[27]

Lafayette was accompanied by one of his sons, whom he had named George Washington, and also by a twenty-nine-year-old Scotswoman,

Frances Wright, who together with her sister had been following him on his triumphant journey, generally at a discreet distance. She was a rich young orphan of singular intelligence and courage, who had fallen in love with America at age eighteen. Her first trip to the New World had resulted in an affectionate book, Views of Society and Manners in America, copies of which she had sent to both Jefferson and Lafayette. The latter had promptly invited her to La Grange, his summer home outside Paris, and she had stayed on. Lafayette had her portrait painted and hung it in his study, and she spent long periods with him in Paris as well as at La Grange. A remarkable letter remains in which she begged Lafayette either to marry her or to adopt her. He did neither. But he did permit her to be seen with him on numerous occasions on his American tour, despite vehement protests from his daughters against her being permitted to accompany him at all.

Frances Wright had written to Lafayette shortly before his departure: "No one will believe that Frances and Camilla will go to America at this time merely to go there. Our intimate connection is too well and universally known in both hemispheres. . . . You must be our father not in a doubtful and covert way but in an open and manly one. . . . we will assume together the place of your children—we will call you father—we will be with you as children, and despising and confronting slanders which thus met in the face will slink away. If not this, honest friend . . . we must part." [28] Lafayette acceded to her demand at least in one important instance, writing to Jefferson delicately in advance expressing the wish that Frances and her sister be entertained at Monticello on a visit coinciding with his own. "You and I are the two persons in the world whose esteem she values most," he said. "I wish, my dear friend, to present these two adopted daughters of mine to Mrs. Randolph and you." [29]

How long Frances Wright and her sister stayed at Monticello is unknown. The important but hitherto overlooked memoir of the young slave Israel, who waited on table during the visit, and also served as carriage driver, makes no mention of the sisters but does contain a fascinating reminiscence of a conversation in the carriage between Jefferson and Lafayette, which he overheard:

> Lafayette spoke English indifferently; sometimes I could scarcely understand him. But on this occasion my ears were eagerly taking in every sound that proceeded from the venerable patriot's mouth.
> Lafayette remarked that he thought that the slaves ought to be free; that no man could rightfully hold ownership in his brother man; that he gave his best services to and spent his money in behalf of the Americans freely because he felt that they were fighting for a great and noble principle—the freedom of mankind; that instead of all being free a

portion were held in bondage (which seemed to grieve his noble heart); that it would be mutually beneficial to masters and slaves if the latter were educated, and so on. Mr. Jefferson replied that he thought the time would come when the slaves would be free, but did not indicate when or in what manner they would get their freedom. He seemed to think that the time had not then arrived. To the latter proposition of Gen. Lafayette, Mr. Jefferson in part assented. He was in favor of teaching the slaves to learn to read print; that to teach them to write would enable them to forge papers, when they could no longer be kept in subjugation.

This conversation was very gratifying to me, and I treasured it up in my heart." [30]

That Jefferson was on the defensive is apparent. That he was being jolted out of his apathy about Negro education and emancipation by Frances Wright as well as by Lafayette one can also be certain. Greatly excited by the socialist community being set up in America by Robert Owen and the community already established by George Rapp in Pennsylvania, she was formulating plans for using part of her substantial fortune for setting up her own small utopia in the South, where whites and slaves would live together on terms of equality, where the slaves would be educated and freed, their emancipation paid for out of the corporate profits of the community. Her breathtaking new radicalism included opposition to racial taboos in sex relations, integrated schools for blacks and whites, and universal education.[31] With what sharpness of insight she speculated about Jefferson's own patriarchal habits on the basis of firsthand observation of Sally Hemings and the white slave children at Monticello one cannot know, though one suspects from her later activity and writing that she must have looked upon Jefferson's liaison—bearing certain obvious similarities to her own with Lafayette—with great compassion.

Frances Wright was six feet tall, the same height as Jefferson's own daughter. Like Martha she was not especially beautiful, though curls softened the lines of her strong and lively face. There could, however, have been no greater contrast than the lives of these two intelligent and educated women. Frances had been liberated by the death of her parents, by her great wealth, by the quality of her imagination and courage, though she was as intent on winning the affection of Lafayette as Martha Jefferson was on holding that of her father. But Martha was burdened with a husband who moved in and out of madness, was so plagued with debt that she was not certain that she could even properly educate her twelve children, and was trapped in a social milieu that looked aghast at the public acknowledgment of any kind of sexual impropriety. It is likely that Martha found Frances Wright far more threatening than exciting.

There is good evidence, however, that though Jefferson saw much in Frances that he normally detested in women, he was nevertheless captivated by her, as Lafayette had been. And he could hardly have failed to see in the whole arrangement—especially if Lafayette confided in him about the fury of his own daughters—a ménage remarkably similar to his own. Shortly after visiting Monticello, Frances sent Jefferson a detailed plan of her projected community [32] and begged for his public support. His reply to this "new woman," certainly the first he had known since his days in the salons of Paris, and far more daring, is an important letter. Though he had been ill for three months, often suffering excruciating pain, so much so, he told her, that he was often unable to think or write, he read her plan with care and replied as follows:

> At the age of eighty-two, with one foot in the grave, and the other uplifted to follow it, I do not permit myself to take part in any new enterprises, even for bettering the condition of man, not even in the great one which is the subject of your letter, and which has been through life that of my greatest anxieties. The march of events has not been such as to render its completion practicable within the limits of time allotted to me; and I leave its accomplishment as the work of another generation. . . . The abolition of the evil is not impossible; it ought never therefore to be despaired of. Every plan should be adopted, every experiment tried, which may do something towards its ultimate object. That which you propose is well worthy of trial. It has succeeded with certain portions of our white brethren, under the care of a Rapp and an Owen; and why may it not succeed with the man of color? . . . You are young, dear Madam, and have powers of mind which may do much in exciting others in this arduous task. I am confident they will be so exerted, and I pray to Heaven for their success, and that you may be rewarded with the blessings which such efforts merit.[33]

Here was no talk of deportation—no stricture against miscegenation. *Every plan should be adopted, every experiment tried.* That Jefferson could write this at eighty-two tells us not only the measure of the extraordinary impact of Lafayette and Frances Wright, but also something about his increasing anxiety concerning slavery as he approached death.

Jefferson did not live long enough to learn of the failure of the black and white community Frances Wright set up in Nashoba, Tennessee, the first interracial community in America which truly experimented with equality. It would fail financially, as all such experiments failed in the nineteenth century, and would suffer even more from stories that filtered out of Nashoba about miscegenation and free love. Frances Wright would be denounced as "the Great Red Harlot of Infidelity," and her name become a byword for fanaticism and radicalism. Even James Madison would write to Lafayette disapprovingly of her "universally obnoxious" views "of amalgamating the white and black population." [34]

In these days of increasing illness Jefferson answered only those letters he cared about. A letter from Maria Cosway had arrived in 1823, telling him of her success in founding a convent school for girls in Lodi, Italy. Her ambition, she said, was "to see these children I have had the care of turn out good wives, excellent Mothers *et bonnes femmes des ménages* which was not understood in these countries and which is the primary object of Society and the only usefull." He had not replied. A new letter came on February 21, 1825, not long after the visit of Frances Wright. Maria made a poignant little request:

> I have had my saloon painted, with the representation of the 4 parts of the World, & the most distinguished objects in them. I have at a loss for America. . . . Washington town is mark'd and the Seminary: if you favor me with some description, that I might have it introduced, you would oblige me much.[35]

Again Jefferson did not reply. Perhaps he felt that a painting of Monticello and his new university (certainly no seminary!) did not belong in a Catholic convent school for girls turning out *bonnes femmes de ménage*—any more than he belonged to Maria Cosway.

After Lafayette left Monticello for the West, Jefferson, mindful of the fact that the "hero of two continents" had spent a portion of his own fortune aiding the American Revolution and was now in perilous financial straits, quietly urged that Congress make an appropriate gesture of gratitude. The old general was cheerfully voted $200,000 and a township of land.[36] No such gesture was ever made by Congress for the bankrupt Jefferson, or ever initiated by his friend and protégé President James Monroe. On the contrary, the creditors holding Jefferson's notes became ever more menacing, and it seemed in 1826 as if he would be forced into bankruptcy and Monticello would be lost. Jefferson, seeing the spectacle of his own son-in-law living in a small house and so bereft of property that he could not even vote, was now so desperate he authorized his grandson to try to get the consent of the Virginia legislature to organize a lottery for the sale of all his land. He hoped by this device to get enough money to pay the mortgages and debts, and still leave a comfortable sum for Martha and the education of her younger children. The winners of the lottery would get the land and slaves, but Monticello would be saved.

"Should the application for the lottery fail," Jefferson wrote to Joseph Cabell, "I must sell house and all here and carry my family to Bedford where I have not even a log hut to put my head into." [37] The lottery would cost the state nothing, he said, and in a sad gesture of abasement that should have been forced on no president, least of all this one, he carefully enumerated his services to the nation. To Madison he also wrote of his fear that he would not have even "ground for burial." He concluded this, one of the saddest of all his letters, "To myself you have been a pillar of support through life. Take care of me when dead, and be assured that I shall leave you with my last affections." [38]

Despite the vigorous efforts of Jefferson Randolph, the tickets to the lottery sold slowly. But as word of Jefferson's straits spread north, private subscriptions began to be raised in other states, and on the basis of these promises—many of them never to be fulfilled—the lottery was abandoned. Jefferson, however, was permitted to live out the last two months of his life happy in the belief that at least Monticello would be saved and that the Negroes would "all remain." [39]

Meanwhile he continued to suffer periods of devastating pain. He had for many years distrusted doctors, detesting their methods of bleeding and purging, and was fond of telling the story that whenever he saw three physicians together he looked up "to discover whether there was not a turkey buzzard in the neighborhood." Now, however, he was driven by pain to seek out a Dr. Robley Dunglison, of Philadelphia, whose memoirs afford invaluable details of Jefferson's last illness.[40] Dunglison diagnosed a severe constriction in the urethra due to the enlarged prostate gland, and prescribed gum catheters which brought him some relief. Still, when Lafayette came back for his brief farewell visit in 1825, he found Jefferson semi-reclined on a couch in great pain, unable either to lie down, walk, or stand. Assuring him that there were better quality catheters made in Paris, Lafayette promised to send him some. One hundred arrived after Jefferson's death.

During his last months nightly doses of laudanum made it possible for him to sleep. How much he took of this opium derivative is not known; a letter from Martha of October 13, 1825, tells us only that she had been forced by "the fatigue of last week" to increase the dose "by 100 drops." Still, so resilient was his body, and so tough his constitution, that he recovered enough to resume his horseback riding. Martha described his health on November 26, 1825, as "wonderfully improved," writing that he had ridden five miles "without inconvenience."[41]

The necessity of making out his will reminded Jefferson, if indeed any single day passed in his life without some reminder, of his failure to bring about an end to slavery even at Monticello. He had tried in the past to solace himself that he had done as much as he could, writing to Adams in 1820, "We have willingly done injury to no man; and have done for our country the good which has fallen our way, so far as commensurate with the faculties given us. That we have not done more than we could cannot be imputed to us as a crime before any tribunal."[42] But his use of the words "crime" and "tribunal" tells us that he had by no means rid himself of guilt for not having done more to eradicate this, his "greatest anxiety." What were the alternatives open to him in 1826 when he made out his will? One cannot know. His overseer Bacon tells us that he wanted devoutly to free all his slaves but could not.[43] Jefferson did not know how much money the private subscriptions would amount to; they could hardly have been expected to reach his total indebtedness of $107,000. All might be lost in the end—as it was after his death—but at least his slaves constituted liquid capital. Most of his hill-country land once worth $50 to $100 an acre was now valued at only $10 to $20.[44]

There were some slaves who had to be freed. How could he select among them? In the end he chose five. All were members of the Hemings family. The first he listed was Burwell, his personal valet for many years, to whom he promised freedom and left a bequest of $300 to aid him in his trade of painter and glazier. Burwell was the forty-three-year-old son of Sally Hemings' older half sister Bett. Jefferson next listed Sally Hemings' half brother John Hemings, Monticello's expert cabinetmaker. The two sons of Sally Hemings who had not yet "run away," Madison, age twenty-one, and Eston, age eighteen, were added to the list. The fifth to be freed was the iron craftsman and blacksmith Joe Fossett, son of Sally Hemings' older half sister Mary Hemings, and this action gave rise in later years to the legend that he, too, was Jefferson's son.[45]

Why did Jefferson fail to free Sally Hemings, leaving her emancipation to be discreetly arranged by his daughter within two years after his death? Freeing a slave meant automatic banishment from Virginia, unless special permission was granted by the legislature. Thus, freeing her would have meant driving her out of the state unless a formal petition went to Richmond. Jefferson provided for this petition with the five slaves freed in his will. But such a gesture for his celebrated concubine would have meant instant publicity, such as had been so humiliating during his presidency. This Jefferson seems to have been determined to avoid, for his daughter's sake if not for Sally's as well. Though not freeing her was a risk, he seems clearly to have trusted Martha to make the gesture for freedom that he could not.

Israel, the Monticello slave who later emigrated to Ohio and lived near Madison Hemings, wrote that Jefferson had freed Sally Hemings along with her children.[46] But she was not mentioned in Jefferson's will, and after his death she appeared on the official slave inventory of 1827 as worth $50. She was then fifty-four. Importantly, however, Israel Jefferson's memoir suggests that the emancipation gesture for Sally Hemings was indeed Jefferson's, and not a mere afterthought by his daughter. The reminiscence of this former Monticello house servant would seem, therefore, to underline Jefferson's continuing concern for Sally Hemings right up to his death.

How Sally Hemings mourned the death of Thomas Jefferson must remain unknown. And unless material hitherto lost or suppressed comes to light, we must remain forever baffled about the feelings of Sally Hemings during the whole of her life.

C. Vann Woodward has written of Jefferson, "It fell to the lot of one Virginian to define America." [47] It was in his private life that Jefferson defined the relationship between blacks and whites in America, acting out in the most specific sense the psychosexual dilemma of the whole nation. Other great men in history have loved unlettered women, among them Rousseau and Goethe, each of whom lived for years with virtually illiterate mistresses and then in the end married them. But Jefferson's dilemma was peculiarly American. So savage were the penalties of this kind of love in the New World that he could neither admit it nor defend it without fear of social ostracism, and he had to keep up an elaborate pretense that it did not exist. He could not openly, and perhaps even privately admit his paternity of Sally's children. He could not give them the kind of education he cherished, and he had to reconcile himself in the end to the knowledge that the only way he could save them was to banish them from his presence. This, then, would seem to have been the ultimate tragedy at Monticello, the unwritten and unadmitted tragedy in Jefferson's life.

That he continued to suffer anxiety and guilt we see in the last letter of his life. In June 1826 Jefferson received a request to speak at the fiftieth anniversary celebration of the signing of the Declaration of Independence. Too feeble even to leave his house, he had to write a letter declining the invitation. So grave was his continuing debility, worsened by a severe diarrhea, that he must have known that this letter would be his last public statement. Inasmuch as the first draft of this letter still exists, we know that he worked over it with care, amending and cutting to improve its precision and beauty. One thing he did not hide in this letter: he wanted terribly to be in Washington. "It adds sensibly to the sufferings of sickness," he wrote, "to be deprived by it of a personal participation in the rejoicings of that day. . . . I should, indeed, with peculiar delight, have met and exchanged there congratulations personally with the small band, the remnant of that host of worthies, who joined with us on that day, in the bold and doubtful election we were to make for our country, between submission or the sword; and to have enjoyed with them the consolatory fact, that our fellow citizens, after half a century of experience and prosperity, continue to approve the choice we made."

Then he wrote a final judgment of his Declaration of Independence that showed a recognition of its prodigious and continuing impact. He included in this judgment what would seem to be a last and ringing indictment of slavery. The Declaration, he said, "will be (to some parts sooner, to others later, but finally to all), the signal of arousing men to burst the chains under which monkish ignorance and superstition had persuaded them to bind themselves, and to assume the blessings and security of self-government. That form which we have substituted, restores the free right to the unbounded exercise of reason and freedom of opinion. All eyes were opened, or opening, to the rights of man. The general spread of the light of science has already laid open to view the palpable truth, that the mass of mankind has not been born with saddles on their backs, nor a favored few booted and spurred, ready to ride them legitimately, by the grace of God." [48]

If ever two men in history chose and controlled the moment of their dying, they were John Adams and Thomas Jefferson. Each was determined to reach the fiftieth anniversary of the signing of the Declaration of Independence, and neither knew that their gentle competition for this great milepost would end in victory and death for both. Shortly before midnight on the third of July Jefferson asked Nicholas Trist—son of his old admirer Eliza and husband to his granddaughter Virginia—"This is the Fourth?" The following morning Trist wrote to his brother, "He has been dying since yesterday morning, and till twelve o clock last night, we were in momentary fear that he would not live, as he desired, to see his own glorious Fourth." He had stopped taking medicine, Trist reported, and had said in a tone of impatience when pressed to swallow it, "Oh God!" and then more placidly, "No! nothing more!" [49]

John Adams' last words, uttered on the same day, were "Thomas Jefferson still survives." Only one other signer of the Declaration of Independence, Charles Carroll, was left.

With Jefferson's death, life at Monticello as he had known it collapsed. Martha, bereft and wretched, went for a time to live in Boston with her daughter, Ellen Coolidge, taking her eight-year-old son George Wythe and twelve-year-old daughter Septimia, leaving Nicholas Trist in charge at Monticello. Randolph, apparently liberated by Jefferson's death and his wife's departure, almost at once recovered his reason, found a job, and did excellent mapping along the Florida border. Once the task was finished, however, he slipped back into alienation and despair. He returned to Monticello for a reconciliation with his wife in March 1828, but insisted on living separately in the north pavilion. There he died within three months, June 20, 1828, age sixty.[50] Shortly afterward Monticello was sold, and many of the slaves went on the auction block.

By this time Sally Hemings had been freed and was living with her sons Madison and Eston in a small rented house near Monticello. When the terrible tearing asunder—the sale and slave auction of 1829 —came to the great house in which she had spent almost the whole of her life, she was fifty-six. In 1830 the U.S. Census of Albemarle County, Virginia, listed Eston Hemings as head of a family, and as a white man. The other members of this family were listed under his name by age and sex only, as was traditional at the time. There is a listing of a woman—fifty to sixty years of age—described as white. This was Sally Hemings. If the census taker, knowing something of her history, took it upon himself in making this small descriptive decision to absolve Jefferson of the so-called sin of miscegenation, he served only to underline further the irony and tragedy in her life.[51]

She died in 1835, age sixty-two, and her two sons then moved on into Ohio, with Eston migrating further into Wisconsin. One of Sally's grandsons, Thomas Eston Hemings, fought as a Union soldier in the Civil War, dying in the prison pen at Andersonville. Martha Jefferson Randolph died in 1836, age sixty-four. One of her sons, George Wythe Randolph, became the first Secretary of War in the Confederate government, serving under Jefferson Davis, who had been christened in 1808 with the name of the third president of the United States.

The former slave Israel returned to Monticello in 1866. "Near there," he wrote, "I found the same Jefferson Randolph. . . . He had grown old, and was outwardly surrounded by the evidences of former ease and opulence gone to decay. . . . Except his real estate, the rebellion stripped him of everything, save one old, blind mule. He said that if he had taken the advice of his sister, Mrs. Colleridge [Coolidge], gone to New York, and remained there during the war, he could have saved the bulk of his property. But he was a rebel at heart, and chose to go with his people. . . . I went back to Virginia to find the proud and haughty Randolph in poverty, at Edgehill, within four miles of Monticello, where he was bred and born. Indeed, I then realized, more than ever before, the great changes which time brings about in the affairs and circumstances of life." [52]

Monticello itself fell into appalling decay, to be rescued and in part restored by Jefferson M. Levy, who not surprisingly became as tenacious about his ownership as had been Jefferson himself. Virginia ladies arranged for the purchase of Monticello and dedicated it as a national shrine on July 4, 1926, the 150th anniversary of the signing of the Declaration of Independence, and the one hundredth anniversary of Jefferson's death. Artists and restorers then proceeded to transform it into the manicured jewel sought out today by countless pilgrims, the "Mecca of Democracy."

As Merrill Peterson has written, Monticello is now "a fascinating museum, a shrine to Jefferson's memory," commemorating his services to the nation, "above all his political philosophy." [53] The modern Monticello is indeed like "the Jefferson image in the American mind," ascetic, cerebral, cool, and elegant. One misses the snorting horses Jefferson loved, the smell of manure, the clinking of wine glasses, the shouting of children. There are no jealous adoring women, no drunken or surly relatives, no signs of madness or violence. The little mountain is shorn of its slave cabins, shorn too of its essential humanity.

But it was the humanity of Jefferson that fired his genius. The humanity was comprised of more than his loves and his hatreds; there was his fear of enslavement clashing with his habits of benevolent despotism, his affection for power tempered by his extraordinary guilt over its abuse, his normal need for sexual fulfillment coupled with his attraction for the forbidden, his hunger for affection and esteem assuaged not only by his multiple friendships and several loves but also by his fanatical obedience to his larger fantasies of what constituted his duty to the state. His passion, guilt, indignation, and despair, even his weakness, were all tempered by his intellect. They also served to mold and direct it.

His ambivalences, instead of corroding his principles, corrupting his essential decency, and incapacitating him for work, were in the most extraordinary fashion harnessed to creative endeavor—to the perfect constitution, the nondespotic state, the ideal home and garden, the enlightened university. Only his conflict over the just treatment of the black people in his life, whose voices, certainly articulate at the time but silent in the documents that have come down to us, remained unresolved, troubling, and corrosive. The Jefferson legacy, then, may be looked at as a fountain of dazzling complexity, its beauty compounded by the sunlight of his rare intelligence, but its sources of power—including the rewarding but intermittently tragic secret loves—hidden and deep in the earth.

Appendices

Reminiscences of Madison Hemings

I never knew of but one white man who bore the name of Hemings. He was an Englishman and my great grandfather. He was captain of an English whaling vessel which sailed between England and Williamsburg, Va., then quite a port. My [great-]grandmother was a fullblooded African, and possibly a native of that country. She was the property of John Wales, a Welchman. Capt. Hemings happened to be in the port of Williamsburg at the time my grandmother was born, and acknowledging her fatherhood he tried to purchase her of Mr. Wales who would not part with the child, though he was offered an extraordinarily large price for her. She was named Elizabeth Hemings. Being thwarted in the purchase, and determined to own his own flesh and blood he resolved to take the child by force or stealth, but the knowledge of his intention coming to John Wales' ears, through leaky fellow servants of the mother, she and the child were taken into the "great house" under their master's immediate care. I have been informed that it was not the extra value of that child over other slave children that induced Mr. Wales to refuse to sell it, for slave masters then, as in later days, had no compunctions of conscience which restrained them from parting mother and child of however tender age, but he was restrained by the fact that just about that time amalgamation began, and the child was so great a curiosity that its owner desired to raise it himself that he might see its outcome. Capt. Hemings soon afterwards

* "Life Among the Lowly, No. 1," *Pike County (Ohio) Republican*, March 13, 1873.

sailed from Williamsburg, never to return. Such is the story that comes down to me.

Elizabeth Hemings grew to womanhood in the family of John Wales, whose wife dying she (Elizabeth) was taken by the widower Wales as his concubine, by whom she had six children—three sons and three daughters, viz: Robert, James, Peter, Critty, Sally and Thena. These children went by the name of Hemings.

Williamsburg was the capital of Virginia, and of course it was an aristocratic place, where the "bloods" of the Colony and the new State most did congregate. Thomas Jefferson, the author of the Declaration of Independence, was educated at William and Mary College, which had its seat at Williamsburg. He afterwards studied law with Geo. Wythe, and practiced law at the bar of the general court of the Colony. He was afterwards elected a member of the provincial legislature from Albemarle county. Thos. Jefferson was a visitor at the "great house" of John Wales, who had children about his own age. He formed the acquaintance of his daughter Martha (I believe that was her name, though I am not positively sure,) and an intimacy sprang up between them which ripened into love, and they were married. They afterwards went to live at his country seat Monticello, and in course of time had born to them a daughter whom they named Martha. About the time she was born my mother, the second daughter of John Wales and Elizabeth Hemings was born. On the death of John Wales, my grandmother, his concubine, and her children by him fell to Martha, Thomas Jefferson's wife, and consequently became the property of Thomas Jefferson, who in the course of time became famous, and was appointed minister to France during our revolutionary troubles, or soon after independence was gained. About the time of the appointment and before he was ready to leave the country his wife died, and as soon after her interment as he could attend to and arrange his domestic affairs in accordance with the changed circumstances of his family in consequence of this misfortune (I think not more than three weeks thereafter) he left for France, taking his eldest daughter with him. He had had sons born to him, but they died in early infancy, so he then had but two children—Martha and Maria. The latter was left at home, but was afterwards ordered to follow him to France. She was three years or so younger than Martha. My mother accompanied her as her body servant. When Mr. Jefferson went to France Martha was a young woman grown, my mother was about her age, and Maria was just budding into womanhood. Their stay (my mother's and Maria's) was about eighteen months. But during that time my mother became Mr. Jefferson's concubine, and when he was called back home she was *enciente* by him. He desired to bring my mother back to Virginia with him but she demurred. She was just beginning to understand the French language well, and in France she was free, while if she returned to Virginia she would be re-enslaved. So she refused to return with him. To induce her to do so he promised her extraordinary privileges, and made a solemn pledge that her children should be freed at the age of twenty-one years. In consequence of his promises, on which she implicitly replied, she returned with him to Virginia. Soon after their arrival, she gave birth to a child, of whom Thomas Jefferson was the father. It lived but a short time. She gave birth to four others, and Jefferson was the father of all of them. Their names were Beverly, Harriet, Madison (myself), and Eston—three sons and one daughter. We all became free agreeably to the treaty entered into by our parents before we were born. We all married and have raised families.

Beverly left Monticello and went to Washington as a white man. He married a white woman in Maryland, and their only child, a daughter, was not known by the white folks to have any colored blood coursing in her veins. Beverly's wife's family were people in good circumstances.

Harriet married a white man in good standing in Washington City, whose name I could give, but will not, for prudential reasons. She raised a family of children, and so far as I know they were never suspected of being tainted with African blood in the community where she lived or lives. I have not heard from her for ten years, and do not know whether she is dead or alive. She thought it to her interest, on going to Washington, to assume the role of a white woman, and by her dress and conduct as such I am not aware that her identity as Harriet Hemings of Monticello has ever been discovered.

Eston married a colored woman in Virginia, and moved from there to Ohio, and lived in Chillicothe several years. In the fall of 1852 he removed to Wisconsin, where he died a year or two afterwards. He left three children.

As to myself, I was named Madison by the wife of James Madison, who was afterwards President of the United States. Mrs. Madison happened to be at Monticello at the time of my birth, and begged the privilege of naming me, promising my mother a fine present for the honor. She consented, and Mrs. Madison dubbed me by the name I now acknowledge, but like many promises of white folks to the slaves she never gave my mother anything. I was born at my father's seat of Monticello, in Albemarle county, Va., near Charlottesville, on the 19th day of January, 1805. My very earliest recollections are of my grandmother Elizabeth Hemings. That was when I was about three years old. She was sick and upon her death bed. I was eating a piece of bread and asked her if she would have some. She replied: "No; granny don't want bread any more." She shortly afterwards breathed her last. I have only a faint recollection of her.

Of my father, Thomas Jefferson, I knew more of his domestic than his public life during his life time. It is only since his death that I have learned much of the latter, except that he was considered as a foremost man in the land, and held many important trusts, including that of President. I learned to read by inducing the white children to teach me the letters and something more; what else I know of books I have picked up here and there till now I can read and write. I was almost 21 years of age when my father died on the 4th of July, 1826.

About his own home he was the quietest of men. He was hardly ever known to get angry, though sometimes he was irritated when matters went wrong, but even then he hardly ever allowed himself to be made unhappy any great length of time. Unlike Washington he had but little taste or care for agricultural pursuits. He left matters pertaining to his plantations mostly with his stewards and overseers. He always had mechanics at work for him, such as carpenters, blacksmiths, shoemakers, coopers, &c. It was his mechanics he seemed mostly to direct, and in their operations he took great interest. Almost every day of his later years he might have been seen among them. He occupied much of the time in his office engaged in correspondence and reading and writing. His general temperament was smooth and even; he was very undemonstrative. He was uniformly kind to all about him. He was not in the habit of showing partiality or fatherly affection to us children. We were the only children of his by a slave woman. He was affectionate toward his white grandchildren, of whom he had fourteen, twelve of whom lived to manhood and womanhood. His daughter Martha married Thomas Mann Randolph by whom she had thirteen children. Two died in infancy. The names of the living were Ann, Thomas Jefferson, Ellen, Cornelia, Virginia, Mary, James,[1] Benj. Franklin, Lewis Madison,[2] Septemia and Geo. Wythe. Thos. Jefferson Randolph was Chairman of the Democratic National Convention in Baltimore last spring which nominated Horace Greeley for the Presidency, and Geo. Wythe Randolph was Jeff. Davis' first Secretary of War in the late "unpleasantness."

Maria married John Eppes, and raised one son—Francis.

My father generally enjoyed excellent health. I never knew him to have but one spell of sickness, and that was caused by a visit to the Warm Springs in 1818. Till within three weeks of his death he was hale and hearty, and at the age of 83 years he walked erect and with

1. James Madison
2. Meriwether Lewis

stately tread. I am now 68, and I well remember that he was a much smarter man physically, even at that age, than I am.

When I was fourteen years old I was put to the carpenter trade under the charge of John Hemings, the youngest son of my grandmother. His father's name was Nelson, who was an Englishman. She had seven children by white men and seven by colored men—fourteen in all. My brothers, sister Harriet and myself, were used alike. They were put to some mechanical trade at the age of fourteen. Till then we were permitted to stay about the "great house," and only required to do such light work as going on errands. Harriet learned to spin and to weave in a little factory on the home plantation. We were free from the dread of having to be slaves all our lives long, and were measurably happy. We were always permitted to be with our mother, who was well used. It was her duty, all her life which I can remember, up to the time of our father's death, to take care of his chamber and wardrobe, look after us children and do such light work as sewing, &c. Provision was made in the will of our father that we should be free when we arrived at the age of 21 years. We had all passed that period when he died but Eston, and he was given the remainder of his time shortly after. He and I rented a house and took mother to live with us, till her death, which event occurred in 1835.

In 1834 I married Mary McCoy. Her grandmother was a slave, and lived with her master, Stephen Hughes, near Charlottesville, as his wife. She was manumitted by him, which made their children free born. Mary McCoy's mother was his daughter. I was about 28 and she 22 years of age when we married. We lived and labored together in Virginia till 1836, when we voluntarily left and came to Ohio. We settled in Pebble township, Pike county. We lived there four or five years and during my stay in that county I worked at my trade on and off for about four years. Joseph Sewell was my first employer. I built for him what is now known as Rizzleport No. 2 in Waverly. I afterwards worked for George Wolf Senior. and I did the carpenter work of the brick building now owned by John J. Kellison in which the Pike County Republican is printed. I worked for and with Micajab [?] Hinson. I found him to be a very clever man. I also reconstructed the building on the corner of Market and Water streets from a store to a hotel for the late Judge Jacob Row.

When we came from Virginia we brought one daughter (Sarah) with us, leaving the dust of a son in the soil near Monticello. We have born to us in this State nine children. Two are dead. The names of the living, besides Sarah, are Harriet, Mary Ann, Catharine Jane, William Beverly, James Madison and Ellen Wales. Thomas Eston died in the Andersonville prison pen, and Julia died at home. William,

James and Ellen are unmarried and live at home, in Huntington township, Ross county. All the others are married and raising families. My post-office address is Pee Pee, Pike county Ohio.

[The U.S. Federal Census of Huntington Township, Ross County, Ohio, for 1870 lists Madison Hemings, mulatto, age 65, born in Virginia. Written below this name is the following: "This man is the son of Thos. Jefferson." His real estate is listed as worth $1,500, and his personal belongings as worth $300. Hemings died of consumption on November 28, 1877, age 72 years. His death notice in the Probate Court records of Ross County, Ohio, II, 15, lists him as "colored, male," born in Virginia, widowed, with the occupation of farmer. His personal goods, sold at public auction for $221.59, included a bedstead, a mare, wagon, and carpenter's tools. His real estate was sold for $685; his debts were listed as $963.93. Property records in Chillicothe, Ohio, show seven transactions involving Madison Hemings, and two involving Eston Hemings. Madison bought 25 acres for $150 on July 25, 1856, and sold them for $250 on December 30, 1859. On September 25, 1865, he bought 66 acres for $660; these were sold after his death for $682. Eston Hemings and his wife Julia Anne sold a lot for $590 on August 10, 1850, and another lot on August 18, 1852, for $1,000.

Madison's granddaughter, Mrs. Nellie E. Jones, of Watseka, Illinois, wrote to Stuart G. Gibboney, at the Thomas Jefferson Memorial Foundation, Monticello, on August 10, 1938, stating that she had a pair of spectacles, silver buckle, and an inkwell that had belonged to Jefferson. Her great-grandmother, Sally Hemings, had given them to her son Madison, she said, and at his death they were inherited by her mother. Mrs. Jones was the daughter of Mary A. Hemings, who, according to the Ross County Courthouse records, Chillicothe, Ohio, was married on April 25, 1864, to David Johnson.]

Reminiscences of Israel Jefferson

I was born at Monticello, the seat of Thos. Jefferson, third President of the United States, December 25—Christmas day in the morning. The year, I suppose, was 1797. My earliest recollections are the exciting events attending the preparations of Mr. Jefferson and other members of his family on their removal to Washington, D.C., where he was to take upon himself the responsibilities of the Executive of the United States for four years.

My mother's name was Jane. She was a slave of Thomas Jefferson's, and was born and always resided at Monticello till about five years after the death of Mr. Jefferson. She was sold, after his death, by the administrator, to a Mr. Joel Brown, and was taken to Charlottesville, where she died in 1837. She was the mother of thirteen children, all by one father, whose name was Edward Gillett. The children's names were Barnaby, Edward, Priscilla, Agnes, Richard, James, Fanny, Lucy, Gilly, Israel, Moses, Susan, and Jane—seven sons and six daughters. All these children, except myself, bore the surname of Gillett. The reason for my name being called Jefferson will appear in the proper place.

After Mr. Jefferson had left his home to assume the duties of the office of President, all became quiet again in Monticello. But as he was esteemed by both whites and blacks as a very great man, his return home, for a brief period, was a great event. His visits were frequent, and attended with considerable ceremony. It was a time looked forward to with great interest by his servants, for when he came home many of

* "Life Among the Lowly, No. 3," *Pike County (Ohio) Republican,* December 25, 1873.

them, especially the leading ones, were sure to receive presents from his hands. He was re-elected President in 1804, and took his seat for the second term in 1805. Of course, his final term closed in March, 1809, when he was succeeded by James Madison. At that time I was upwards of twelve years of age.

About the time Mr. Jefferson took his seat as President for the second term, I began the labors of life as a waiter at the family table, and till Mr. J. died was retained in Monticello and very near his person. When about ten years of age, I was employed as postillion. Mr. Jefferson rode in a splendid carriage drawn by four horses. He called the carriage the landau. It was a sort of double chaise. When the weather was pleasant the occupants could enjoy the open air; when it was rainy, they were protected from it by the closing of the covering, which fell back from the middle. It was splendidly ornamented with silver trimmings, and, taken altogether, was the nicest affair in those aristocratic regions. The harness was made in Paris, France, silver mounted, and quite in keeping with the elegant carriage. The horses were well matched, and of a bay color. I am now speaking of the years of my boyhood and early manhood. My brother Gilly, being older than I was, rode the near wheel horse, while I was mounted on the near leader. In course of time Mr. Jefferson rode less ostentatiously, and the leaders were left off. Then but one rider was needed. Sometimes brother Gilly acted as postillion; at other times I was employed. We were both retained about the person of our master as long as he lived. Mr. Jefferson died on the 4th day of July, 1826, when I was upwards of 29 years of age. His death was an affair of great moment and uncertainty to us slaves, for Mr. Jefferson provided for the freedom of 7 servants only: Sally, his chambermaid, who took the name of Hemmings, her four children—Beverly, Harriet, Madison and Eston—John Hemmings, brother to Sally, and Burrell [Burwell] Colburn, an old and faithful body servant. Madison Hemmings is now a resident of Ross county, Ohio, whose history you gave in the Republican of March 13, 1873. All the rest of us were sold from the auctioneer's block, by order of Jefferson Randolph, his grandson and administrator. The sale took place in 1829, three years after Mr. Jefferson's death.

I was purchased by Thomas Walker Gilmer, I married Mary Ann Colter, a slave, by whom I had four children—Taliola (a daughter), Banobo (a son), Susan and John. As they were born slaves they took the usual course of most others in the same condition in life. I do not know where they now are, if living; but the last I heard of them they were in Florida and Virginia. My wife died, and while a servant of Mr. Gilmer, I married my present wife, widow Elizabeth Randolph, who was then mother to ten children. Her maiden name was Elizabeth Farrow. Her mother was a white woman named Martha Thackey. Consequently, Elizabeth, (my present wife) was free-born. She supposes that she was born about 1793 or '94. Of her ten children, only two are living—Julia, her first born, and wife of Charles Barnett, who live on an adjoining farm, and Elizabeth, wife of Henry Lewis, who reside within one mile of us.

My wife and I have lived together about thirty-five years. We came to Cincinnati, Ohio, where we were again married in conformity to the laws of this State. At the time we were first married I was in bondage; my wife was free. When my first wife died I made up my mind I would never live with another slave woman. When Governor Gilmer was elected a representative to Congress, he desired to have me go on to Washington with him. But I demurred, I did not refuse, of course, but I laid before him my objections with such earnestness that he looked me in the face with his piercing eye, as if balancing in his mind whether to be soft or severe, and said:

"Israel, you have served me well; you are a faithful servant; now what will you give me for your freedom?"

"I reckon I will give you what you paid years ago—$500," I replied.

"How much will you give to bind the bargain?" he asked.

"Three hundred dollars," was my ready answer.

"When will you pay the remainder?"

"In one and two years."

And on these terms the bargain was concluded, and I was, for the first time, my own man, and almost free, but not quite, for it was against the laws of Virginia for a freed slave to remain in the State beyond a year and a day. Nor were the colored people not in slavery free; they were nominally so. When I came to Ohio I considered myself wholly free, and not till then.

And here let me say, that my good master, Governor Gilmer, was killed by the explosion of the gun Peacemaker, on board the Princeton, in 1842 or 1843, and had I gone to Washington with him it would have been my duty to keep very close to his person, and probably I would have been killed also, as others were.

I was bought in the name of my wife. We remained in Virginia several years on sufferance. At last we made up our minds to leave the confines of slavery and emigrate to a free State. We went to Charlottesville Court House, in Albemarle county, for my free papers. When there, the clerk, Mr. Garrett, asked me what surname I would take, I hesitated, and he suggested that it should be Jefferson, because I was born at Monticello and had been a good and faithful servant to

Thomas Jefferson. Besides, he said, it would give me more dignity to be called after so eminent a man. So I consented to adopt the surname of Jefferson, and have been known by it ever since.

When I came to Cincinnati, I was employed as a waiter in a private house, at ten dollars a month for the first month. From that time on I received $20, till I went on board a steamboat, where I got higher wages still. In time, I found myself in receipt of $50 per month, regularly, and sometimes even more. I resided in Cincinnati about fourteen years, and from thence came on to the farm I am now on, in Pebble township, on Brushy Fork of Pee Pee creek. Have been here about sixteen years.

Since my residence in Ohio I have several times visited Monticello. My last visit was in the fall of 1866. Near there I found the same Jefferson Randolph, whose service as administrator I left more than forty years ago, at Monticello. He had grown old, and was outwardly surrounded by the evidences of former ease and opulence gone to decay. He was in poverty. He had lost, he told me, $80,000 in money by joining the South in rebellion against the government. Except his real estate, the rebellion stripped him of everything, save one old, blind mule. He said that if he had taken the advice of his sister, Mrs. Cooleridge [Coolidge], gone to New York, and remained there during the war, he could have saved the bulk of his property. But he was a rebel at heart, and chose to go with his people. Consequently, he was served as others had been—he had lost all his servants and nearly all his personal property of every kind. I went back to Virginia to find the proud and haughty Randolph in poverty, at Edge Hill, within four miles of Monticello, where he was bred and born. Indeed, I then realized more than ever before, the great changes which time brings about in the affairs and circumstances of life.

Since I have been in Ohio I have learned to read and write, but my duties as a laborer would not permit me to acquire much of an education. But such as I possess I am truly thankful, and consider what education I have as a legitimate fruit of freedom.

The private life of Thomas Jefferson, from my earliest remembrance, in 1804, till the day of his death, was very familiar to me. For fourteen years I made the fire in his bedroom and private chamber, cleaned his office, dusted his books, run of errands, and attended him about home. He used to ride out to his plantations almost every fair day, when at home, but unlike most other Southern gentlemen in similar circumstances, unaccompanied by any servant. Frequently gentlemen would call upon him on business of great importance, whom I used to usher into his presence, and sometimes I would be employed in burnishing or doing some other work in the room where they were. On such occasions I used to remain; otherwise I retired and left the gentlemen to confer together alone. In those times I minded but little concerning the conversations which took place between Mr. Jefferson and his visitors. But I well recollect a conversation he had with the great and good Lafayette, when he visited this country in 1824 or 1825, as it was of personal interest to me and mine. General Lafayette and his son George Washington, remained with Mr. Jefferson six weeks, and almost every day I took them out to a drive.

On the occasion I am now about to speak of, Gen. Lafayette and George were seated in the carriage with him. The conversation turned upon the condition of the colored people—the slaves. Lafayette spoke indifferently; sometimes I could scarcely understand him. But on this occasion my ears were eagerly taking in every sound that proceeded from the venerable patriot's mouth.

Lafayette remarked that he thought that the slaves ought to be free; that no man could rightly hold ownership in his brother man; that he gave his best services to and spent his money in behalf of the Americans freely because he felt that they were fighting for a great and noble principle—the freedom of mankind; that instead of all being free a portion were held in bondage (which seemed to grieve his noble heart); that it would be mutually beneficial to masters and slaves if the latter were educated, and so on. Mr. Jefferson replied that he thought the time would come when the slaves would be free, but did not indicate when or in what manner they would get their freedom. He seemed to think that the time had not then arrived. To the latter proposition of Gen. Lafayette, Mr. Jefferson in part assented. He was in favor of teaching the slaves to learn to read print; that to teach them to write would enable them to forge papers, when they could no longer be kept in subjugation.

This conversation was very gratifying to me, and I treasured it up in my heart.

I know that it was a general statement among the older servants at Monticello, that Mr. Jefferson promised his wife, on her death bed, that he would not again marry. I also know that his servant, Sally Hemmings, (mother to my old friend and former companion at Monticello, Madison Hemmings,) was employed as his chamber-maid, and that Mr. Jefferson was on the most intimate terms with her; that, in fact, she was his concubine. This I know from my intimacy with both parties, and when Madison Hemmings declares that he is a natural son of Thomas Jefferson, the author of the Declaration of Independence, and that his brothers Beverly and Eston and sister Harriet are of the same parentage, I can as conscientiously confirm his statement as any other fact which I believe from circumstances but do not positively know.

I think that Mr. Jefferson was 84 years of age when he died. He was hardly ever sick, and till within two weeks of his death he walked erect without a staff or cane. He moved with the seeming alertness and sprightliness of youth.

[According to Jefferson's *Farm Book* (130), Israel, described as "Ned's Israel," was born in 1800, not 1797. His brothers and sisters— Moses, Barnaby, "Scilla, Ned's" for Priscilla, "Aggy, Ned's" for Agnes, etc.—can for the most part be identified on the same page.]

"My Head and My Heart"

Jefferson to Maria Cosway, Paris, October 12, 1786
(*Papers*, Boyd, X, 443–53)

[MY DEAR] MADAM

Having performed the last sad office of handing you into your carriage at the Pavillon de St. Denis, and seen the wheels get actually into motion, I turned on my heel and walked, more dead than alive, to the opposite door, where my own was awaiting me. Mr. Danquerville was missing. He was sought for, found, and dragged down stairs. [We] were crammed into the carriage, like recruits for the Bastille, and not having [sou]l enough to give orders to the coachman, he presumed Paris our destination, [and] drove off. After a considerable interval, silence was broke with a "je suis vraiment affligé du depart de ces bons gens." This was the signal for a mutual confession [of dist]ress. We began immediately to talk of Mr. and Mrs. Cosway, of their goodness, their [talents], their amability, and tho we spoke of nothing else, we seemed hardly to have entered into matter when the coachman announced the rue St. Denis, and that we were opposite Mr. Danquerville's. He insisted on descending there and traversing a short passage to his lodgings. I was carried home. Seated by my fire side, solitary and sad, the following dialogue took place between my Head and my Heart.

Head. Well, friend, you seem to be in a pretty trim.

Heart. I am indeed the most wretched of all earthly beings. Overwhelmed with grief, every fibre of my frame distended beyond it's natural powers to bear, I would willingly meet whatever catastrophe should leave me no more to feel or to fear.

Head. These are the eternal consequences of your warmth and precipitation. This is one of the scrapes into which you are ever leading us. You confess your follies indeed: but still you hug and cherish them, and no reformation can be hoped, where there is no repentance.

Heart. Oh my friend! This is no moment to upbraid my foibles. I am rent into fragments by the force of my grief! If you have any balm, pour it into my wounds: if none, do not harrow them by new torments. Spare me in this awful moment! At any other I will attend with patience to your admonitions.

Head. On the contrary I never found that the moment of triumph with you was the moment of attention to my admonitions. While suffering under your follies you may perhaps be made sensible of them, but, the paroxysm over, you fancy it can never return. Harsh therefore as the medecine may be, it is my office to administer it. You will be pleased to remember that when our friend Trumbull used to be telling us of the merits and talents of these good people, I never ceased whispering to you that we had no occasion for new acquaintance; that the greater their merit and talents, the more dangerous their friendship to our tranquillity, because the regret at parting would be greater.

Heart. Accordingly, Sir, this acquaintance was not the consequence of my doings. It was one of your projects which threw us in the way of it. It was you, remember, and not I, who desired the meeting, at Legrand & Molinos. I never trouble myself with domes nor arches. The Halle aux bleds might have rotted down before I should have gone to see it. But you, forsooth, who are eternally getting us to sleep with your diagrams and crotchets, must go and examine this wonderful piece of architecture. And when you had seen it, oh! it was the most superb thing on earth! What you had seen there was worth all you had yet seen in Paris! I thought so too. But I meant it of the lady and gentleman to whom we had been presented, and not of a parcel of sticks and chips put together in pens. You then, Sir, and not I, have been the cause of the present distress.

Head. It would have been happy for you if my diagrams and crotchets had gotten you to sleep on that day, as you are pleased to say they eternally do. My visit to Legrand & Molinos had publick utility for it's object. A market is to be built in Richmond. What a commodious plan is that of Legrand & Molinos: especially if we put on it the noble dome of the Halle aux bleds. If such a bridge as they shewed us can be thrown across the Schuylkill at Philadelphia, the floating bridges taken up, and the navigation of that river opened, what a copious resource will be added, of wood and provisions, to warm and feed the poor of that city. While I was occupied with these objects, you were dilating with your new acquaintances, and contriving how to prevent a separation from them. Every soul of you had an engagement for the day. Yet all these were to be sacrificed, that you might dine together. Lying messengers were to be dispatched into every quarter of the city with apologies for your breach of engagement. You particularly had the effrontery [to] send word to the Dutchess Danville that, in the moment we were setting out to d[ine] with her, dispatches came to hand which required immediate attention. You [wanted] me to invent a more ingenious excuse; but I knew you were getting into a scrape, and I would have nothing to do with it. Well, after dinner to St. Cloud, from St. Cloud to Ruggieri's, from Ruggieri to Krumfoltz, and if the day had been as long as a Lapland summer day, you would still have contrived means, among you, to have filled it.

Heart. Oh! my dear friend, how you have revived me by recalling to my mind the transactions of that day! How well I remember them all, and that when I came home at night and looked back to the morning, it seemed to have been a month agone. Go on then, like a kind comforter, and paint to me the day we went to St. Germains. How beautiful was every object! the Port de Neuilly, the hills along the Seine, the rainbows of the machine of Marly, the terras of St. Germains, the chateaux, the gardens, the [statues] of Marly, the pavillon of Lucienne. Recollect too Madrid, Bagatelle, the King's garden, the Dessert. How grand the idea excited by the remains of such a column! The spiral staircase too was beautiful. Every moment was filled with something agreeable. The wheels of time moved on with a rapidity of which those of our carriage gave but a faint idea, and yet in the evening, when one took a retrospect of the day, what a mass of happiness had we travelled over! Retrace all those scenes to me, my good companion, and I will forgive the unkindness with which you were chiding me. The day we went to St. Germains was a little too warm, I think, was not it?

Head. Thou art the most incorrigible of all the beings that ever sinned! I reminded you of the follies of the first day, intending to deduce from thence some useful lessons for you, but instead of listening to these, you kindle at the recollection, you retrace the whole series with a fondness which shews you want nothing but the opportunity to act it over again. I often told you during it's course that you were imprudently engaging your affections under circumstances that must cost you a great deal of pain: that the persons indeed were of the greatest merit, possessing good sense, good humour, honest hearts, honest manners, and eminence in a lovely art: that the lady had moreover qualities and accomplishments, belonging to her sex, which might form a chapter apart for her: such as music, modesty, beauty, and that softness of disposition which is the ornament of her sex and charm of ours. But that all these considerations would increase the pang of separation: that their stay here was to be short: that you rack our whole system when you are parted from those you love, complaining that such a separation is worse than death, inasmuch as this ends our sufferings, whereas that only begins them: and that the separation would in this instance be the more severe as you would probably never see them again.

Heart. But they told me they would come back again the next year.

Head. But in the mean time see what you suffer: and their return too depends on so many circumstances that if you had a grain of prudence you would not count upon it. Upon the whole it is improbable and therefore you should abandon the idea of ever seeing them again.

Heart. May heaven abandon me if I do!

Head. Very well. Suppose then they come back. They are to stay here two months, and when these are expired, what is to follow? Perhaps you flatter yourself they may come to America?

Heart. God only knows what is to happen. I see nothing impossible in that supposition, and I see things wonderfully contrived sometimes to make us happy. Where could they find such objects as in America for the exercise of their enchanting art? especially the lady, who paints landscape so inimitably. She wants only subjects worthy of immortality to render her pencil immortal. The Falling spring, the Cascade of Niagara, the Passage of the Potowmac thro the Blue mountains, the Natural bridge. It is worth a voiage across the Atlantic to see these objects; much more to paint, and make them, and thereby ourselves, known to all ages. And our own dear Monticello, where has nature spread so rich a mantle under the eye? mountains, forests, rocks, rivers. With what majesty do we there ride above the storms! How sublime to look down into the workhouse of nature, to see her clouds, hail, snow, rain, thunder, all fabricated at our feet! And the glorious Sun, when rising as if out of a distant water, just gilding the tops of the mountains, and giving life to all nature!—I hope in god no circumstance may ever make either seek an asylum from grief! With what sincere sympathy I would open every cell of my composition to receive the effusion of their woes! I would pour my tears into their wounds: and if a drop of balm could be found at the top of the Cordilleras, or at the remotest sources of the Missouri, I would go thither myself to seek and to bring it. Deeply practised in the school of affliction, the human heart knows no joy which I have not lost, no sorrow of which I have not drank! Fortune can present no grief of unknown form to me! Who then can so softly bind up the wound of another as he who has felt the same wound himself? But Heaven forbid they should ever know a sorrow!—Let us turn over another leaf, for this has distracted me.

Head. Well. Let us put this possibility to trial then on another point. When you consider the character which is given of our country by the lying newspapers of London, and their credulous copyers in other countries; when you reflect that all Europe is made to believe we are a lawless banditti, in a state of absolute anarchy, cutting one another's throats, and plundering without distinction, how can you expect that any reasonable creature would venture among us?

Heart. But you and I know that all this is false: that there is not a country on earth where there is greater tranquillity, where the laws are milder, or better obeyed: where every one is more attentive to his own business, or meddles less with that of others: where strangers are better received, more hospitably treated, and with a more sacred respect.

Head. True, you and I know this, but your friends do not know it.

Heart. But they are sensible people who think for themselves. They will ask of impartial foreigners who have been among us, whether they saw or heard on the spot any instances of anarchy. They will judge too that a people occupied as we are in opening rivers, digging navigable canals, making roads, building public schools, establishing academies, erecting busts and statues to our great men, protecting religious freedom, abolishing sanguinary punishments, reforming and improving our laws in general, they will judge I say for themselves whether these are not the occupations of a people at their ease, whether this is not better evidence of our true state than a London newspaper, hired to lie, and from which no truth can ever be extracted but by reversing everything it says.

Head. I did not begin this lecture my friend with a view to learn from you what America is doing. Let us return then to our point. I wished to make you sensible how imprudent it is to place your affections, without reserve, on objects you must so soon lose, and whose loss when it comes must cost you such severe pangs. Remember the last night. You knew your friends were to leave Paris to-day. This was enough to throw you into agonies. All night you tossed us from one side of the bed to the other. No sleep, no rest. The poor crippled wrist too, never left one moment in the same position, now up, now down, now here, now there; was it to be wondered at if all it's pains returned? The Surgeon then was to be called, and to be rated as an ignoramus because he could not devine the cause of this extraordinary change.—In fine, my friend, you must mend your manners. This is not a world to live at random in as you do. To avoid these eternal distresses, to which you are for ever exposing us, you must learn to look forward before you take a step which may interest our peace.

Everything in this world is matter of calculation. Advance then with caution, the balance in your hand. Put into one scale the pleasures which any object may offer; but put fairly into the other the pains which are to follow, and see which preponderates. The making an acquaintance is not a matter of indifference. When a new one is proposed to you, view it all round. Consider what advantages it presents, and to what inconveniences it may expose you. Do not bite at the bait of pleasure till you know there is no hook beneath it. The art of life is the art of avoiding pain: and he is the best pilot who steers clearest of the rocks and shoals with which it is beset. Pleasure is always before us; but misfortune is at our side: while running after that, this arrests us. The most effectual means of being secure against pain is to retire within ourselves, and to suffice for our own happiness. Those, which depend on ourselves, are the only pleasures a wise man will count on: for nothing is ours which another may deprive us of. Hence the inestimable value of intellectual pleasures. Ever in our power, always leading us to something new, never cloying, we ride, serene and sublime, above the concerns of this mortal world, contemplating truth and nature, matter and motion, the laws which bind up their existence, and that eternal being who made and bound them up by these laws. Let this be our employ. Leave the bustle and tumult of society to those who have not talents to occupy themselves without them. Friendship is but another name for an alliance with the follies and the misfortunes of others. Our own share of miseries is sufficient: why enter then as volunteers in those of another? Is there so little gall poured into our own cup that we must needs help to drink that of our neighbor? A friend dies or leaves us: we feel as if a limb was cut off. He is sick: we must watch over him, and participate of his pains. His fortune is shipwrecked: ours must be laid under contribution. He loses a child, a parent or a partner: we must mourn the loss as if it was our own.

Heart. And what more sublime delight than to mingle tears with one whom the hand of heaven hath smitten! To watch over the bed of sickness, and to beguile it's tedious and it's painful moments! To share our bread with one to whom misfortune has left none! This world abounds indeed with misery: to lighten it's burthen we must divide it with one another. But let us now try the virtues of your mathematical balance, and as you have put into one scale the burthens of friendship, let me put it's comforts into the other. When languishing then under disease, how grateful is the solace of our friends! How are we penetrated with their assiduities and attentions! How much are we supported by their encouragements and kind offices! When Heaven has taken from us some object of our love, how sweet is it to have a

bosom whereon to recline our heads, and into which we may pour the
torrent of our tears! Grief, with such a comfort, is almost a luxury! In
a life where we are perpetually exposed to want and accident, yours is
a wonderful proposition, to insulate ourselves, to retire from all aid,
and to wrap ourselves in the mantle of self-sufficiency! For assuredly
nobody will care for him who cares for nobody. But friendship is precious not only in the shade but in the sunshine of life: and thanks to
a benevolent arrangement of things, the greater part of life is sunshine.
I will recur for proof to the days we have lately passed. On these
indeed the sun shone brightly! How gay did the face of nature appear!
Hills, vallies, chateaux, gardens, rivers, every object wore it's liveliest
hue! Whence did they borrow it? From the presence of our charming
companion. They were pleasing, because she seemed pleased. Alone,
the scene would have been dull and insipid: the participation of it
with her gave it relish. Let the gloomy Monk, sequestered from the
world, seek unsocial pleasures in the bottom of his cell! Let the sub-
limated philosopher grasp visionary happiness while pursuing phan-
toms dressed in the garb of truth! Their supreme wisdom is supreme
folly: and they mistake for happiness the mere absence of pain. Had
they ever felt the solid pleasure of one generous spasm of the heart,
they would exchange for it all the frigid speculations of their lives,
which you have been vaunting in such elevated terms. Believe me then,
my friend, that that is a miserable arithmetic which would estimate
friendship at nothing, or at less than nothing. Respect for you has
induced me to enter into this discussion, and to hear principles uttered
which I detest and abjure. Respect for myself now obliges me to
recall you into the proper limits of your office. When nature assigned
us the same habitation, she gave us over it a divided empire. To you
she allotted the field of science, to me that of morals. When the
circle is to be squared, or the orbit of a comet to be traced: when
the arch of greatest strength, or the solid of least resistance is to be
investigated, take you the problem: it is yours: nature has given me
no cognisance of it. In like manner in denying to you the feelings of
sympathy, of benevolence, of gratitude, of justice, of love, of friendship, she has excluded you from their controul. To these she has
adapted the mechanism of the heart. Morals were too essential to the
happiness of man to be risked on the incertain combinations of the
head. She laid their foundation therefore in sentiment, not in science.
That she gave to all, as necessary to all: this to a few only, as sufficing
with a few. I know indeed that you pretend authority to the sovereign
controul of our conduct in all it's parts: and a respect for your grave
saws and maxims, a desire to do what is right, has sometimes induced
me to conform to your counsels. A few facts however which I can

readily recall to your memory, will suffice to prove to you that nature has not organised you for our moral direction. When the poor wearied souldier, whom we overtook at Chickahominy with his pack on his back, begged us to let him get up behind our chariot, you began to calculate that the road was full of souldiers, and that if all should be taken up our horses would fail in their journey. We drove on therefore. But soon becoming sensible you had made me do wrong, that tho we cannot relieve all the distressed we should relieve as many as we can, I turned about to take up the souldier; but he had entered a bye path, and was no more to be found: and from that moment to this I could never find him out to ask his forgiveness. Again, when the poor woman came to ask a charity in Philadelphia, you whispered that she looked like a drunkard, and that half a dollar was enough to give her for the ale-house. Those who want the dispositions to give, easily find reasons why they ought not to give. When I sought her out afterwards, and did what I should have done at first, you know that she employed the money immediately towards placing her child at school. If our country, when pressed with wrongs at the point of the bayonet, had been governed by it's heads instead of it's hearts, where should we have been now? hanging on a gallows as high as Haman's. You began to calculate and to compare wealth and numbers: we threw up a few pulsations of our warmest blood: we supplied enthusiasm against wealth and numbers: we put our existence to the hazard, when the hazard seemed against us, and we saved our country: justifying at the same time the ways of Providence, whose precept is to do always what is right, and leave the issue to him. In short, my friend, as far as my recollection serves me, I do not know that I ever did a good thing on your suggestion, or a dirty one without it. I do for ever then disclaim your interference in my province. Fill paper as you please with triangles and squares: try how many ways you can hang and combine them together. I shall never envy nor controul your sublime delights. But leave me to decide when and where friendships are to be contracted. You say I contract them at random, so you said the woman at Philadelphia was a drunkard. I receive no one into my esteem till I know they are worthy of it. Wealth, title, office, are no recommendations to my friendship. On the contrary great good qualities are requisite to make amends for their having wealth, title and office. You confess that in the present case I could not have made a worthier choice. You only object that I was so soon to lose them. We are not immortal ourselves, my friend; how can we expect our enjoiments to be so? We have no rose without it's thorn; no pleasure without alloy. It is the law of our existence; and we must acquiesce. It is the condition annexed to all our pleasures, not by us who receive, but by him who gives them. True, this condition is pressing cruelly on me at this moment. I feel. more fit for death than life. But when I look back on the pleasures of which it is the consequence, I am conscious they were worth the price I am paying. Notwithstanding your endeavors too to damp my hopes, I comfort myself with expectations of their promised return. Hope is sweeter than despair, and they were too good to mean to deceive me. In the summer, said the gentleman; but in the spring, said the lady: and I should love her forever, were it only for that! Know then, my friend, that I have taken these good people into my bosom: that I have lodged them in the warmest cell I could find: that I love them, and will continue to love them thro life: that if misfortune should dispose them on one side of the globe, and me on the other, my affections shall pervade it's whole mass to reach them. Knowing then my determination, attempt not to disturb it. If you can at any time furnish matter for their amusement, it will be the office of a good neighbor to do it. I will in like manner seize any occasion which may offer to do the like good turn for you with Condorcet, Rittenhouse, Madison, La Cretelle, or any other of those worthy sons of science whom you so justly prize.

I thought this a favorable proposition whereon to rest the issue of the dialogue. So I put an end to it by calling for my nightcap. Methinks I hear you wish to heaven I had called a little sooner, and so spared you the ennui of such a tedious sermon. I did not interrupt them sooner because I was in a mood for hearing sermons. You too were the subject; and on such a thesis I never think the theme long; not even if I am to write it, and that slowly and awkwardly, as now, with the left hand. But that you may not be discoraged from a correspondence which begins so formidably, I will promise you on my honour that my future letters shall be of a reasonable length. I will even agree to express but half my esteem for you, for fear of cloying you with too full a dose. But, on your part, no curtailing. If your letters are as long as the bible, they will appear short to me. Only let them be brim full of affection. I shall read them with the dispositions with which Arlequin in les deux billets spelt the words "je t'aime" and wished that the whole alphabet had entered into their composition.

We have had incessant rains since your departure. These make me fear for your health, as well as that you have had an uncomfortable journey. The same cause has prevented me from being able to give you any account of your friends here. This voiage to Fontainbleau will probably send the Count de Moutier and the Marquise de Brehan to America. Danquerville promised to visit me, but has not done it as yet. De latude comes sometimes to take family soupe with me, and entertains me with anecdotes of his five and thirty years imprisonment. How fertile is the mind of man which can make the Bastille and Dungeon of Vincennes yeild interesting anecdotes. You know this was for making four verses on Mme. de Pompadour. But I think you told me you did not know the verses. They were these. "Sans esprit, sans sentiment, Sans etre belle, ni neuve, En France on peut avoir le premier amant: Pompadour en est l'epreuve." I have read the memoir of his three escapes. As to myself my health is good, except my wrist which mends slowly, and my mind which mends not at all, but broods constantly on your departure. The lateness of the season obliges me to decline my journey into the South of France. Present me in the most friendly terms to Mr. Cosway, and receive me into your own recollection with a partiality and a warmth, proportioned, not to my own poor merit, but to the sentiments of sincere affection and esteem with which I have the honour to be, my dear Madam, your most obedient humble servant,   TH: JEFFERSON

APPENDIX III

The Family Denial

What one might call the "family denial," begun by Jefferson's grandson, Thomas Jefferson Randolph, holds basically that Jefferson was not at Monticello when Sally Hemings' children were conceived, and that they were fathered instead by one of his nephews, either Peter or Samuel Carr. Apart from the fact that this allegation does not explain the case of the child conceived in Paris, it can easily be demonstrated—by checking Jefferson's *Farm Book* and the chronologies of his life as assembled by Dumas Malone and Paul L. Ford—that Jefferson was indeed at Monticello nine months before the birth of every one of Sally Hemings' children mentioned in the *Farm Book*. I have presented this documentation in full within the pages of this book. Moreover, it takes very little research in the enormous file of family letters at the University of Virginia to demonstrate that both Peter Carr and his brother Samuel were elsewhere, managing plantations with slaves of their own, during most of the years that Sally Hemings was bearing children at Monticello.

Numerous letters between Peter Carr and Jefferson show that in 1791, 1792, and part of 1793 young Carr alternated between Spring Forest, where his mother lived, and Monticello. He then left and began practicing law, returning briefly during the summer of 1796. Jefferson wrote to Thomas Mann Randolph on November 28, 1796, that "P. Carr is on the point of marriage." [1] By 1799 he had a son. Samuel Carr, who corresponded very little with Jefferson, did not live at Monticello save briefly during his youth when his mother's whole

[1] *Writings*, L. and B., XVIII, 201.

493

family stayed there in 1782. He married in 1795. In 1802 he and his wife were living at Dunlora with his mother; afterward he moved to the South Fork of the Rivanna River, a few miles north of Charlottesville. The 1830 census of Albemarle County lists him as having six children and forty-four slaves.

The "family denial" first became public in 1874, when James Parton published his *Life of Thomas Jefferson* and described a conversation between Henry S. Randall and Thomas Jefferson Randolph, in which the latter stated that Peter Carr had fathered Sally Hemings' children.[2] This data came from a letter to Parton from Randall, which was eventually published in full in Milton E. Flower, *James Parton, the Father of Modern Biography* (Duke University Press, 1951, pp. 236–39). The letter reads as follows:

Courtland Village, N.Y.
June 1, 1868

DEAR SIR—

The "Dusky Sally Story"—the story that Mr. Jefferson kept one of his slaves, (Sally Henings) as his mistress and had children by her, was once extensively believed by respectable men, and I believe both John Quincy Adams and our own Bryant sounded their poetical lyres on this very poetical subject!

Walking about mouldering Monticello one day with Col. T. J. Randolph (Mr. Jefferson's oldest grandson) he showed me a smoke blackened and sooty room in one of the collonades, and informed me it was Sally Henings' room. He asked me if I knew how the story of Mr. Jefferson's connection with her originated. I told him I did not. "There was a better excuse for it, said he, than you might think: she had children which resembled Mr. Jefferson so closely that it was plain that they had his blood in their veins." He said in one case the resemblance was so close, that at some distance or in the dusk the slave, dressed in the same way, might have been mistaken for Mr. Jefferson.— He said in one instance, a gentleman dining with Mr. Jefferson looked so startled as he raised his eyes from the latter to the servant behind him, that his discovery of the resemblance was so perfectly obvious to all. Sally Hening was a house servant and her children were brought up house servants—so that the likeness between master and slave was blazoned to all the multitudes who visited this political mecca.

Mr. Jefferson had two nephews, Peter Carr and Samuel Carr whom he brought up in his house. They were the sons of Jefferson's sister and her husband Dabney Carr, that young and brilliant orator described by Wirt, who shone so conspicuously in the dawn of the Revolution, but who died in 17(?). Peter was peculiarly gifted and amiable. Of Samuel I know less. But he became a man of repute and

[2] James Parton, *Life of Thomas Jefferson* (Boston, 1874), 569–70.

sat in the State Senate of Virginia. Col. Randolph informed me that Sally Henings was the mistress of Peter, and her sister Betsey the mistress of Samuel—and from these connections sprang the progeny which resembled Mr. Jefferson.[3] Both the Hening girls were light colored and decidedly good looking. The Colonel said their connection with the Carrs was perfectly notorious at Monticello, and scarcely disguised by the latter—never disavowed by them. Samuel's proceedings were particularly open.

Col. Randolph informed me that there was not the shadow of suspicion that Mr. Jefferson in this or any other instance had commerce with female slaves. At the periods when these Carr children were born, he, Col. Randolph, had charge of Monticello.[4] He gave all the general directions, gave out their clothes to the slaves, etc., etc. He said Sally Hening was treated, dressed, etc., exactly like the rest. He said Mr. Jefferson never locked the door of his room by day: [5] and that he (Col. Randolph) slept within sound of his breathing at night.[6] He said he had never seen a motion, or a look, or a circumstance which led him to suspect for an instant that there was a particle more of familiarity between Mr. Jefferson and Sally Henings than between him and the most repulsive servant in the establishment—and that no person ever living at Monticello dreamed of such a thing.[7] With Betsy Hening, whose children also resembled him, his habitual meeting, was less frequent, and the chance of suspicion still less, and his connection (connexion) with her was never indeed alleged by any of our northern politicians, or *poets*.

Col. Randolph said that he had spent a good share of his life closely about Mr. Jefferson—at home and on journeys—in all sorts of circumstances and he fully believed him chaste and pure—as "immaculate a man as God ever created."

Mr. Jefferson's oldest daughter, Mrs. Gov. Randolph, took the Dusky Sally stories much to heart. But she never spoke to her sons but once on the subject. Not long before her death she called two of them—the

---

[3] Betsey Hemings was the daughter of Betty Hemings, and was Sally Hemings' half sister. She is listed as Betsy Brown in the *Farm Book*, and had eight children: Billy, born in 1777; Wormley in 1781; Burwell in 1783; Brown in 1785; Melinda in 1787; Edwin in 1793; Robert in 1799, and Mary in 1801. There is no indication that Jefferson freed any of these slaves save Burwell, his trusted valet during his last years. The late John Cook Wyllie, University of Virginia expert on the Monticello slaves, has stated that Betsey's first two children were by a different father from those born later, but there is no evidence in his notes at the University of Virginia where this information came from.

[4] Actually Thomas Jefferson Randolph did not assume charge of Monticello until 1819, eleven years after Sally Hemings' last son was born.

[5] In a memoir, *The Last Days of Jefferson* (quoted in *Jefferson at Monticello*, 135), Randolph stated that Jefferson's bedroom was his *sanctum sanctorum*, and that even his own daughters never sat in it.

[6] Jefferson's bedroom was on the first floor at Monticello; the grandchildren slept on the second floor.

[7] Randolph himself contradicted this statement in the same interview.

Colonel and George Wythe Randolph—to her. She asked the Colonel if he remembered when "—— Henings (the slave who most resembled Mr. Jefferson) was born." He said he could answer by referring to the book containing the list of slaves. He turned to the book and found that the slave was born at the time supposed by Mrs. Randolph. She then directed her sons attention to the fact that Mr. Jefferson and Sally Henings could not have met—were far distant from each other—for fifteen months prior to such birth. She bade her sons (to) remember this fact, and always to defend the character of their grandfather. It so happened when I was afterwards examining an old account book of the Jeffersons I came *pop* on the original entry of this slaves birth: and I was then able (to know) from well known circumstances to prove the fifteen months separation—but those circumstances have faded from my memory. I have no doubt I could recover them however did Mr. Jefferson's vindication in the least depend upon them.

Colonel Randolph said that a visitor at Monticello dropped a newspaper from his pocket or accidentally left it. After he was gone, he (Colonel Randolph) opened the paper and found some very insulting remarks about Mr. Jefferson's mulatto children. The Colonel said he felt provoked. Peter and Samuel Carr were lying not far off under a shade tree. He took the paper and put it in Peter's hands, pointing out the article. Peter read it, tears coursing down his cheeks, and then handed it to Samuel. Samuel also shed tears. Peter exclaimed "Ar'nt you and I a couple of —— pretty fellows to bring this disgrace on poor old uncle who has always fed us! We ought to be ——, by ——!"

I could give fifty more facts were there time and were there any need of it, to show Mr. Jefferson's innocence of this and all similar offenses against propriety.

I asked Col. Randolph why on earth Mr. Jefferson did (not) put these slaves who looked like him out of the public sight by sending them to his Befond [Bedford] estate or elsewhere.—He said Mr. Jefferson never betrayed the least consciousness of the resemblance—and although he (Col. Randolph) and he had no doubt his mother, would have been very glad to have them removed, that both and all venerated Mr. Jefferson too deeply to broach such a topic to him. What suited him, satisfied them. Mr. Jefferson was deeply attached to the Carrs—especially to Peter. He was extremely indulgent to them and the idea of watching them for faults or vices probably never occurred to him.

Do you ask why I did not state, or at least hint the above facts in my Life of Jefferson? I wanted to do so, but Colonel Randolph, in this solitary case alone, prohibited me from using at my discretion the information he furnished me with. When I rather pressed him on the point, he said, pointing to the family graveyard, "You are not bound to prove a negation. If I should allow you to take Peter Carr's corpse into Court and plead guilty over it to shelter Mr. Jefferson, I should not dare again to walk by his grave: he would rise and spurn me." I am exceedingly glad Col. Randolph *did* overrule me in this particular. I should have made a *shameful* mistake. If I had *unnecessarily* defended him (and it was purely *unnecessary* to offer any defense) at the expense of a dear nephew—and a noble man—hating (?) a single folly.—

I write this *currente calamo*, and you will not understand that in telling what Col. Randolph and others said, I claim to give their precise language. I give it as I *now* recall it. I believe I hit at least the essential purport and spirit of it in every case.

Do you wonder that the above explanations were not made by Mr. Jefferson's friends when the old Federal Party were hurling their villanies at him for keeping a Congo Harem. Nobody could have furnished a hint of explanation outside the family. The secrets of an old Virginia Manor house were like the secrets of an Old Norman Castle. Dr. Dungleson and Professor Tucker had lived years near Mr. Jefferson in the University and were often at Monticello. They saw what others saw. But Dr. D. told me that neither he nor Prof. T. ever heard the subject named in Virginia. An awe and veneration was felt for Mr. Jefferson among his neighbors which in their view rendered it shameful to even talk about his name in such a connexion. Dr. D. told me that he never heard of Col. Randolph talking with anyone on the subject but me. But he said in his own secret mind he had always believed the matter stood just as Col. Randolph explained it to me.

You ask if I will not write a cheap Life of Jefferson of 600 pages, to go into families who will not purchase a larger work. I some years ago commenced such a condensed biography. I suspended the work when the storm of Civil War burst over the land. I have not again resumed it. I may yet do so hereafter—I have been strongly urged to the work by a prominent publishing house, and if I find time I may again mount my old hobby.

I must again express my regret that I cannot send you a fine autograph letter of Mr. Jefferson on some interesting topic—but I am stripped down to those his family expected me to keep. But I send you some characteristic leaves—one from his draft of his Parliamentary Law.

Very truly yours,
HENRY S. RANDALL

James Parton, Esq.

The second document supporting the "family denial" consists of a letter from Ellen Randolph Coolidge to her husband, Joseph Coolidge, Jr., October 24, 1858, now in the hands of Harold J. Coolidge. A copy is in the University of Virginia library. I had read the entire letter, but Mr. Coolidge permitted me to quote directly only one paragraph, that relating to the four "yellow children" who were "white enough to pass for white." Since publication of this book, Mr. Coolidge permitted Dumas Malone to print the entire letter in the *New York Times* of May 18, 1974. It reads as follows:

Edgehill
24 October 1858

I am just from church, a church originally planned by Grandpapa, where I heard a good sermon from an Episcopalian Clergyman, a young man, the Revd. Mr. Butler.

I have been talking freely with my brother Jefferson on the subject of the "yellow children" and will give you the substance of our conversation, with my subsequent reflections.

It is difficult to prove a negative. It is impossible to prove that Mr. Jefferson never had a coloured mistress or coloured children and that these children were never sold as slaves. The latter part of the charge however is disproved by it's atrocity, and it's utter disagreement with the general character and conduct of Mr. Jefferson, acknowledged to be a humane man and eminently a kind master. Would he who was always most considerate of the feelings and the well-being of his slaves, treat them barbarously only when they happened to be his own children, and leave them to be sold in a distant market when he might have left them free—as you know he did several of his slaves, directing his executor to petition the Legislature of Virginia for leave for them to remain in the State after they were free. Some of them are here to this day.

It was his principle (I know that of my own knowledge) to allow such of his slaves as were sufficiently white to pass for white men, to withdraw quietly from the plantation; it was called running away, but they were never reclaimed. I remember four instances of this, three young men and one girl, who walked away and staid away. Their whereabouts was perfectly known but they were left to themselves—for they were white enough to pass for white. Some of the children currently reported to be Mr. Jefferson's were about the age of his own grandchildren. Of course he must have been carrying on his intrigues in the midst of his daughters family and insulting the sanctity of home by his profligacy. But he had a large family of grandchildren of all ages, older & younger. Young men and young girls. He lived, whenever he was at Monticello, and entirely for the last seventeen years of his life, in the midst of these young people, surrounded by them, his intercourse with them of the freest and most affectionate kind.

How comes it that his immoralities were never suspected by his own family—that his daughter and her children rejected with horror and contempt the charges brought against him? That my brother, then a young man certain to know all that was going on behind the scenes, positively declares his indignant disbelief in the imputations and solemnly affirms that he never saw or heard the smallest thing which could lead him to suspect that his grandfather's life was other than perfectly pure. His apartments had no private entrance not perfectly accessible and visible to all the household. No female domestic ever entered his chambers except at hours when he was known not to be there and none could have entered without being exposed to the public gaze. But again I would put it to any fair mind to decide if a man so admirable in his domestic character as Mr. Jefferson, so devoted to his daughters and their children, so fond of their society, so tender, considerate, refined in his intercourse with them, so watchful over them in all respects, would be likely to rear a race of half-breeds under their eyes and carry on his low amours in the circle of his family.

Now many causes existed which might have given rise to suspicions, setting aside the inveterate rage and malice of Mr. Jefferson's traducers.

The house at Monticello was a long time in building and was principally built by Irish workmen. These men were known to have had children of whom the mothers were black women. But these women were much better pleased to have it supposed that such children were their master's. "Le Czar m'a fait l'honneur de me faire cet enfant." There were dissipated young men in the neighborhood who sought the society of the mulattresses and they in like manner were not anxious to establish any claim of paternity in the results of such associations.

One woman known to Mr. J. Q. Adams and others as "dusky Sally" was pretty notoriously the mistress of a married man, a near relation of Mr. Jefferson's, and there can be small question that her children were his. They were all fair and all set free at my grandfather's death, or had been suffered to absent themselves permanently before he died. The mother, Sally Hemmings, [sic] had accompanied Mr. Jefferson's younger daughter to Paris and was lady's maid to both sisters. Again I ask is it likely that so fond, so anxious a father, whose letters to his daughters are replete with tenderness and with good counsels for their conduct, should (when there were so many other objects upon whom to fix his illicit·attentions) have selected the female attendant of his own pure children to become his paramour! The thing will not bear telling. There are such things, after all, as moral impossibilities.

The habit that the southern slaves have of adopting their master's names is another cause of misrepresentation and misapprehension. There is no doubt that such of Mr. Jefferson's slaves as were sold after his death would call themselves by his name. One very notorious villain who never had been the property of Mr. Jefferson, took his name and proclaimed himself his son. He was as black as a crow, and born either during Mr. Jefferson's absence abroad, or under some other circumstances which rendered the truth of his assertion simply impossible.

I have written thus far thinking you might chuse to communicate my letter to Mr. Bulfinch. Now I will tell you in confidence what Jefferson told me under the like condition. Mr. Southall and himself being young men together, heard Mr. Peter Carr say with a laugh, that "the old gentleman had to bear the blame of his and Sam's (Col. Carr) misdeeds."

There is a general impression that the four children of Sally Hemmings were *all* the children of Col. Carr, the most notorious good-natured Turk that ever was master of a black seraglio kept at other men's expence. His deeds are as well known as his name.—I have written in very great haste for I have very little time to write. We sat down sixteen at my brother's table to-day, and are never less than twelve —Children, grandchildren, visiters, friends—I am in a perfect whirl. Yet this is the way in which I lived during all my girlish days, and then it seemed the easiest and most natural thing imaginable. Now I wonder how any head can bear it long. But Jefferson and Jane are the most affectionate parents and the kindest neighbors that I know.

Mrs. Coolidge, writing thus to her husband in 1858, was clearly troubled over the publicity attending the wide circulation of William Wells Brown's novel, *Clotel; or, The President's Daughter* (1853), which held, erroneously, that a slave mistress of Jefferson and her daughter had been sold at auction in the Deep South. In replying to this, Mrs. Coolidge inadvertently relayed valuable information concerning Sally Hemings' children. She is in error, however, in stating that Jefferson, "whenever he was at Monticello, and entirely for the last seventeen years of his life," lived surrounded by his grandchildren, who never suspected his "immoralities." The scandal became nationally known in 1802. The Randolph children, though they spent summers at Monticello, did not move there permanently until 1809, after all of Sally Hemings' children were born.

Mrs. Coolidge is again in error in writing that Sally had only four children; there were, as we know, seven, two of whom died in infancy. Her statement that four slaves, three young men and a girl, "white enough to pass for white," were permitted to leave Monticello is important. The *Farm Book* lists only three slave runaways, Sally's children Beverly and Harriet, and Critta Hemings' son, Jamy, who ran away in April 1804. He had been born in 1787, when Jefferson was in Paris, and ran away at seventeen. The fourth runaway may have been, as we have suggested, Sally's son, Tom, conceived in Paris, and described in the *Richmond Recorder* September 1, 1802, as being "ten or twelve years of age" and bearing "a striking though sable resemblance" to Jefferson (see p. 349). He may have left Monticello when Ellen Wayles Randolph was a very small girl.

One cannot deny the possibility that the Carr brothers may have found slave mistresses at Monticello in the years before they had plantations and slave women of their own. It is possible that Jamy, son of Critta Hemings, was son to one of them. Importantly, neither Peter nor Samuel Carr ever publicly defended Jefferson's innocence, nor did Jefferson ever blame his nephews in any document that has come down to us.

Notes

CHAPTER I The Semi-Transparent Shadows

1. Henry S. Randall, *The Life of Thomas Jefferson*, 3 vols. (New York, 1858), III, 510.

2. Jefferson to General Thaddeus Kosciusko, June 1812, *Writings of Thomas Jefferson*, Paul L. Ford, ed., 10 vols: (New York, 1892–99), IX, 362.

3. Jefferson to John Langdon, August 2, 1808, and "Address to the Republican Citizens of Washington County, Maryland," March 31, 1809, *Writings of Thomas Jefferson*, Andrew Lipscomb and Albert Bergh, eds., 20 vols. (Washington, D.C., 1903), XVI, 310, 359; hereafter designated as *Writings*, L. and B.

4. Jefferson to Edmund Bacon, December 26, 1808, *Thomas Jefferson's Garden Book, 1766–1824*, Edwin M. Betts, ed. (Philadelphia, 1944), 383; Jefferson to Peter Minor, September 24, 1811, *Thomas Jefferson's Farm Book* (Princeton, 1953) [138]. A photographic record of the *Farm Book* was published by Edwin Morris Betts, with commentary and relevant extracts from Jefferson's other writings, including letters concerning his slaves. The page references in the *Farm Book* are the same as Jefferson's own. Other pagination, by Betts, is indicated in this volume in brackets for purposes of distinguishing it from that of the photographic record.

5. *Autobiography of Thomas Jefferson, with an Introductory Essay by Dumas Malone*, adapted from *Jefferson the Virginian* (Boston, 1948), 62.

6. Jefferson to John Adams, March 25, 1826, *The Adams-Jefferson Letters*, Lester J. Cappon, ed. (Chapel Hill, N.C., 1959), 614.

7. Albert J. Nock, *Jefferson* (New York, 1926), 33; Nathan Schachner, *Thomas Jefferson: A Biography* (New York, 1951), vii.

8. Malone, *Jefferson the Virginian*, vii.

9. Merrill Peterson, *The Jefferson Image in the American Mind* (New York, 1960), vii; *Thomas Jefferson and the New Nation* (New York, 1970), viii.

10. Bernard Bailyn, "Boyd's Jefferson: Notes for a Sketch," *New England Quarterly*, XXXIII (1960), 382.

11. Henry Adams, *History of the United States during the Administrations of Jefferson and Madison*, 9 vols. (New York, 1891–93), I, 277.

12. Jefferson to Skelton Jones, July 28, 1809, *Writings*, L. and B., XII, 302.

13. Quoted in Emanuel Hertz, *The Hidden Lincoln, from the Letters and Papers of William H. Herndon* (New York, 1938), 230.

14. See Erik Erikson, *Gandhi's Truth* (New York, 1969), *Young Man Luther* (New York, 1958); Eugene Victor Wolfenstein, *The Revolutionary Personality: Lenin, Trotsky, Gandhi* (Princeton, 1967). See also Mohandas Gandhi, *An Autobiography: The Story of My Experiments with Truth* (Boston, 1957), 30, 31.

15. Eric McKitrick, "The View from Jefferson's Camp," *New York Review of Books*, December 17, 1970.

16. Quoted in Samuel F. Bemis, *John Quincy Adams and the Foundations of American Foreign Policy* (New York, 1949), 14.

17. *Journal of William Maclay* (New York, 1890), 265-66.

18. Margaret Bayard Smith, *The First Forty Years of Washington Society, Portrayed by the Family Letters of Mrs. Samuel Harrison Smith . . .*, Gaillard Hunt, ed. (New York, 1906), 6.

19. Randall, *Jefferson*, III, 348.

20. Jefferson to James Monroe, May 5, 1811, *Writings*, L. and B., XIII, 59.

21. Gouverneur Morris, *Diary and Letters*, Anne Cary Morris, ed. (New York, 1888), II, 424; *Letters of Joseph Dennie*, Laura G. Peder, ed., Maine University Studies (1936), 179.

22. *The Literary Bible of Thomas Jefferson: His Commonplace Book of Philosophers and Poets*, with an Introduction by Gilbert Chinard (Baltimore, 1928), 31.

23. Winthrop Jordan, *White over Black: American Attitudes toward the Negro 1550-1812* (Chapel Hill, N.C., 1968), 462.

24. First published in the *Virginia Advocate* and reproduced here in Appendix II. See also *The Papers of Thomas Jefferson*, Julian P. Boyd, ed., 18 vols. (Princeton, 1950-72), X, 454n; hereafter referred to as *Papers*, Boyd.

25. Jordan, *White over Black*, 462; Peterson, *Jefferson and the New Nation*, 348.

26. *Frederick-Town (Virginia) Herald*, quoted in the *Richmond Recorder*, September 29, 1802. The "snow-broth" quotation comes from Shakespeare's *Measure for Measure*, I:4, 57-58, referring to Lord Angelo. For McKitrick's statement, see "The View from Jefferson's Camp," *New York Review of Books*, December 17, 1970.

27. Sigmund Freud, *Leonardo da Vinci: A Study in Psychosexuality*, Modern Library edition (1947), 109.

28. Lerone Bennett in "Thomas Jefferson's Negro Grandchildren," *Ebony*, November 1954, published photographs of elderly blacks who traced their ancestry back to Jefferson through Joe Fossett, who was one of the slaves freed in Jefferson's will. For a discussion of the merits of this claim see p. 554. William Edward Farrison has described and traced to its beginnings the story that Jefferson's slave daughters and mistress were sold at auction in New Orleans. He has also traced with great skill how this account grew out of the Sally Hemings story, as described by James T. Callender in the *Richmond Recorder* of 1802, and was gradually combined with other miscegenation stories, resulting finally in William Wells Brown's novel, *Clotel; or, The President's Daughter* (London, 1853). See Farrison's "Origin of Brown's *Clotel*," *Phylon*, XV (December 1954), 347-54.

29. *Richmond Recorder*, September 1, 1802.

30. James Thomas Flexner, *George Washington: The Forge of Experience*, 1732-1775 (Boston, 1965), 157, 39.

31. McKitrick, "The View from Jefferson's Camp."

32. Carl Becker, *The Declaration of Independence* (New York, 1922), 216.

CHAPTER II   The Parents

1. Randall, *Jefferson*, I, 13; Sarah N. Randolph, *The Domestic Life of Thomas Jefferson*, Dumas Malone, ed. (New York, 1958), 19-20.

2. Randall, *Jefferson*, I, 15.

3. "Memoirs of Edmund Bacon" (overseer at Monticello), *Jefferson at Monticello*, James A. Bear, Jr., ed. (Charlottesville, Va., 1967), 71.

4. Randall, *Jefferson*, I, 13, 15. Jefferson's handwriting, according to Randall, also resembled that of his father.

5. *Autobiography*, 19-20.

6. Randall, *Jefferson*, I, 15.

7. Thomas Jefferson Randolph Ms., University of Virginia. See also Malone, *Jefferson the Virginian*, 46.

8. Randall, *Jefferson*, I, 14.
9. Jefferson to Wilson C. Nicholas, April 19, 1816, *Writings*, L. and B., XIV, 482.
10. Thomas Lewis, *The Fairfax Line: Thomas Lewis's Journal of 1746*, J. W. Wayland, ed. (New Market, Va., 1925), 20, 28–29.
11. One of the German officers described this in a Hamburg newspaper. See *Papers*, Boyd, IV, 174; see also William Peden's note in his excellent edition of Jefferson's *Notes on the State of Virginia* (Chapel Hill, N.C., 1955), xviiin.
12. Obituary speech by William Wirt, October, 19, 1826, *Writings*, L. and B., XIII, xiii.
13. *Autobiography*, 22.
14. Jefferson to John Adams, June 11, 1812, *Adams-Jefferson Letters*, 307. Ontasseté was also called Outacity. See also Malone, *Jefferson the Virginian*, 61. Jefferson heard this speech at age nineteen.
15. Randall, *Jefferson*, I, 7; *Papers*, Boyd, I, 9n.
16. Jefferson to Thomas Jefferson Randolph, November 24, 1808, *The Family Letters of Thomas Jefferson*, Edwin M. Betts and James A. Bear, Jr., eds. (Columbia, Mo., 1966), 362–63. The paragraphing does not exist in the original.
17. Jefferson to John Dickinson, March 6, 1801, *Writings*, L. and B., X, 216–17.
18. Flexner, *Washington: The Forge of Experience*, 19–20; *George Washington in the American Revolution, 1775–1783* (Boston, 1967), 337, 417.
19. Carl Van Doren, *Benjamin Franklin* (New York, 1941), 7–8.
20. Lincoln wrote this in a brief autobiography for John L. Scripps. See Lincoln, *Collected Works*, Roy P. Basler, ed., 9 vols. (New Brunswick, N.J., 1953–55), IV, 62.
21. Lincoln to John D. Johnston, November 25, 1851, January 12, 1851, *Collected Works*, Basler, ed., II, 113, 96–97.
22. There are, of course, many references to "my mother's estate" and to "my mother" in Jefferson's account books, having to do with expenditures on her behalf.
23. Randall, *Jefferson*, I, 10, 16–17.
24. Ms. memoir on Jefferson, University of Virginia Library.
25. I have not included the abbreviations in the original, but the complete words as filled out by Julian Boyd. Jefferson to John Page, February 21, 1770, *Papers*, Boyd, I, 34–35. Actually some account books, papers of Peter Jefferson, and the famous *Garden Book*, begun in 1766, which by then may have been at Monticello, were saved.
26. Jefferson to William Randolph, June 1776, *Papers*, Boyd, I, 409–10.
27. *Autobiography*, 19.
28. Peterson, *Jefferson and the New Nation*, 9.
29. Ellen Randolph Coolidge described Jane Rodgers as "a stern strict lady of the old school, much feared and little loved by her children." Ms., University of Virginia.
30. Malone, *Jefferson the Virginian*, 13–17. Malone points out that Randolph "shared a consignment" of 380 Negroes the year of his daughter's marriage to Peter Jefferson, October 1739.
31. Randall, *Jefferson*, I, 7; *Notes on the State of Virginia*, 85.
32. Jefferson to Thomas Adams, February 20, 1771, *Papers*, Boyd, I, 62.
33. Julian Boyd traces the authorship of this inscription to Benjamin Franklin rather than one of the regicides of Charles I. See *Papers*, Boyd, I, 677–79.
34. Jefferson to Martha Randolph, February 20, 1771, *Family Letters*, 51
35. Undated clipping, Jefferson scrapbook, University of Virginia.
36. Jefferson to Angelica Schuyler Church, September 21, 1788, *Papers*, Boyd, XIII, 623.
37. Jefferson to James Madison, June 20, 1787, *Papers*, Boyd, XI, 482.
38. *Autobiography*, 110.
39. Jefferson to C. F. C. de Volney, February 8, 1805, *Writings*, L. and B., XI, 64.

40. Jefferson to John Adams, March 25, 1826, August 1, 1816, *Adams-Jefferson Letters*, 614, 483.
41. Randall, *Jefferson*, I, 3.

CHAPTER III   A Sense of Family

1. Randall, *Jefferson*, I, 11.
2. Jefferson to Thomas Mann Randolph, Jr., then his son-in-law, November 14, 1793, Ms., University of Virginia.
3. Ralph Ketcham, *James Madison: A Biography* (New York, 1971), 12.
4. *Notes on the State of Virginia*, 162.
5. Sarah N. Randolph, *Domestic Life*, 23.
6. *Notes on the State of Virginia*, 138.
7. Benjamin Quarles, *The Negro in the American Revolution* (Chapel Hill, N.C., 1961), 172.
8. Jefferson to Martha Jefferson, November 28, 1783, *Family Letters*, 19–20.
9. Jefferson to Martha Jefferson, March 28, April 7, 1787, *Family Letters*, 34, 36.
10. Abigail Adams to John Quincy Adams, January 17, 1780, Page Smith, *John Adams*, 2 vols. (New York, 1962), I, 469.
11. Jefferson to Martha Jefferson, March 28, 1787, *Family Letters*, 35.
12. Jefferson to Martha Jefferson, April 7, March 28, 1787, *Family Letters*, 36–37.
13. Jefferson to Randolph Lewis, April 23, 1807, "Slaves and Slavery," *Farm Book* [26].
14. Jefferson to Maria Jefferson Eppes, February 15, 1801, *Family Letters*, 196.
15. James Maury, "To Christians of Every Denomination among Us, Especially Those of the Established Church, an Inquiry into the Pretensions of Preachers Called Anabaptists . . . ," a pamphlet published posthumously in 1771. Maury died in 1769.
16. Maury, "To Christians of Every Denomination . . ." See also the James Maury letters in *John Fontaine: Memoirs of a Huguenot Family*, Ann Maury, ed., a reprint of the 1852 edition (New York, 1907), 380, 398, 411, 418–19, 424.
17. Jefferson to Elbridge Gerry, March 29, 1801, *Writings*, L. and B., X, 255.
18. Jefferson to Priestley, January 27, 1800, *Writings*, L. and B., X, 147.
19. Jefferson to John Page, January 20, 1763, *Papers*, Boyd, I, 8.
20. Jefferson to James Monroe, March 20, 1782, *Papers*, Boyd, VI, 184.

CHAPTER IV   A Capacity for Involvement

1. Jefferson to Alexander Donald, July 28, 1787, *Papers*, Boyd, XI, 632.
2. Maury to Elizabeth Jerndon, June 1, 1827, in Anne Fontaine Maury, ed., *Intimate Virginiana*, (Richmond, 1941), 13; quoted in Schachner, *Jefferson*, 23–24; Jefferson to Dabney Carr the younger, January 19, 1816, *Writings*, L. and B., XIV, 401.
3. Sarah Randolph, *Domestic Life*, 23.
4. Randall, *Jefferson*, I, 131, from the Nicholas Trist memoranda.
5. Jefferson to William Wirt, August 5, 1815, *Writings*, L. and B., XIV, 341. See also Daniel Webster, *Private Correspondence*, I, 364ff.
6. Jefferson to Archibald Stuart, April 18, 1795, *Writings*, Ford, VII, 8.
7. The original is missing. A copy was furnished to Randall by Jefferson's grandson. See Randall, *Jefferson*, I, 9, and *Papers*, Boyd, I, 3, 3n.
8. The account book for Peter Jefferson's estate, in the Huntington Library, reveals that Maury charged Jefferson £22 for 1758, and only £16 for 1759, indicating perhaps that the partying had indeed interfered with his schooling, and had cut short the period he boarded with him.

9. "Memoir of John Page," in *Virginia Historical Register*, III, 151.
10. Schachner, *Jefferson*, 29.
11. *Autobiography*, 20.
12. Jefferson to L. H. Girardin, January 15, 1815. *Writings*, L. and B., IV, 231.
13. *Autobiography*, 20–21.
14. Malone, in *Jefferson the Virginian*, 76, tells the story, but doubts its authenticity.
15. L (1758), part 2, 746–47; Malone, *Jefferson the Virginian*, 77.
16. Jefferson to L. H. Girardin, January 15, 1815, *Writings*, L. and B., XIV, 231.
17. Jefferson to William Small, *Papers*, Boyd, I, 165–66.
18. Malone, *Jefferson the Virginian*, 97.
19. Jefferson to John Sanderson, August 31, 1820, Library of Congress, 38932–34, Jefferson to William Duval, June 14, 1806, Library of Congress, 27898.
20. Jefferson to William Wirt, August 5, 1815, *Writings*, L. and B., XIV, 341, Robert D. Meade, *Patrick Henry: Patriot in the Making* (New York, 1957), 95.
21. Jefferson to John Page, *Papers*, Boyd, I, 15.
22. Jefferson to Thomas Cooper, February 10, 1814, *Writings*, L. and B., XIV, 85.
23. Wythe's will in Library of Congress, 159, 27971–72, Schachner, *Jefferson*, 522. See also above, pp. 389–91.
24. *Writings*, L. and B., XIII, 187.
25. As reported in Steve Harvey, Bertrand Russell obituary, *Los Angeles Times*, February 8, 1970.
26. Randall, *Jefferson*, I, 32.
27. The only copy which exists is a revised version made in 1814.
28. Comment of Jefferson to Nicholas P. Trist, after reading Wirt's life of Patrick Henry, reported in Randall, *Jefferson*, I, 40.
29. Jefferson to John Page, January 23, 1764, *Papers*, Boyd, I, 15.
30. George Tucker, *The Life of Thomas Jefferson*, 2 vols. (Philadelphia, 1837), I, 29ff.
31. Schachner, *Jefferson*, 40, citing William Meade, *Old Churches of Virginia* (Philadelphia, 1857), I, 99.
32. Jefferson to John Page, December 25, 1762, *Papers*, Boyd, I, 3–6.
33. Jefferson to John Page, January 20, 1763, with postscripts added February 12 and March 11, *Papers*, Boyd, I, 7–8.
34. Jefferson to John Page, July 15, 1763, quoting Page's letter to him of May 30, *Papers*, Boyd, I, 9.
35. Jefferson to John Page, July 15, 1763, *Papers*, Boyd, I, 10.
36. Jefferson to John Page, October 7, 1763, *Papers*, Boyd, I, 11.
37. Jefferson to John Page, January 19, 1764, *Papers*, Boyd, I, 14.
38. Jefferson to William Fleming, March 20, 1764, *Papers*, Boyd, I, 15–16.
39. Jefferson to John Page, April 9, 1764, *Papers*, Boyd, I, 17.
40. Malone, *Jefferson the Virginian*, 84.
41. Schachner, *Jefferson*, 42; Peterson, *Jefferson and the New Nation*, 19.
42. Tucker, *Life*, I, 29.
43. Jefferson to John Page, July 15, 1763, *Papers*, Boyd, I, 10.
44. Betsey Ambler to Mildred Smith, Richmond, 1781, "Old Virginia Correspondence," *Atlantic Monthly*, LXXXIV (1899), 538.

CHAPTER V   A Problem with the Forbidden

1. Ellen Randolph Coolidge memoirs, Ms. 56, University of Virginia.
2. The Otway verses are copied into the blank pages of Jefferson's *Virginia Almanack* for 1770, Library of Congress. The Spanish lyric is pasted into one of Jefferson's several scrapbooks at the University of Virginia and is impossible to date.
3. Randall, *Jefferson*, I, 28.

4. Jefferson to John Page, February 21, 1770, *Papers*, Boyd, I, 36.
5. Randall, *Jefferson*, I, 41.
6. Randall, *Jefferson*, I, 41.
7. From the account book of 1771, quoted in *Thomas Jefferson's Garden Book*, Betts, ed., 25–26.
8. University of Virginia Library. Sarah Randolph in her *Domestic Life*, 39, described Elizabeth as "rather deficient in intellect." For Jefferson's difficulties in keeping purchases for Elizabeth separate from his own, see *Fee Book*, Huntington Library. Thomas Walker reminded Jefferson of the problem of expenditures for Elizabeth's clothes in a letter on January 19, 1790, *Papers*, Boyd, XVI, 115.
9. As reported in a letter from Thomas Walker to Jefferson, January 19, 1790, *Papers*, Boyd, XVI, 115.
10. Jefferson to John Page, July 15, 1763, *Papers*, Boyd, I, 11.
11. *Garden Book*, 4.
12. *Notes on the State of Virginia*, 164–65.
13. Jefferson to Benjamin Rush, September 23, 1800, *Writings*, L. and B., X, 173.
14. Memo books, 1767–70, Library of Congress, quoted in Schachner, *Jefferson*, 60.
15. Jefferson to James Fishback, September 27, 1809, *Writings*, L. and B., XII, 315.
16. Jefferson to John Page, October 7, 1763, *Papers*, Boyd, I, 12.
17. Walker never permitted publication of this letter during his lifetime, though essential details derived from it, or from earlier verbal accounts, poured out in the anti-Jefferson press after 1802. See pp. 366, 368–69, 374–75. The original of this letter is missing, but a copy written in the hand of Henry Lee found its way eventually into the Jefferson papers in the Library of Congress, 27117–21. Dumas Malone first published it, with obvious distaste, as Appendix III in his *Jefferson the Virginian* in 1948.
18. Library of Congress, 27117–21. Malone included all save a portion of the third paragraph, and the crossed-out "bridegrooms," an interesting slip of Walker's pen. See *Jefferson the Virginian*, 449–50. The amount Jefferson owed was apparently very small. Thomas Walker wrote to Jefferson on January 19, 1790, in answer to an inquiry about this indebtedness, "I know of no debts due from the estate except a little to myself, nor any to it," *Papers*, Boyd, XVI, 114.
19. William Burwell memoir, Ms., Library of Congress.
20. For a detailed discussion of this episode, see pp. 374–75.
21. Schachner, *Jefferson*, 764.
22. Malone, *Jefferson the Virginian*, 155.
23. Peterson, *Jefferson and the New Nation*, 709.
24. Malone, *Jefferson the Virginian*, 450.
25. Jefferson to Maria Cosway, October 12, 1786, *Papers*, Boyd, X, 444. See Appendix II.
26. *American Citizen*, July 24, 1805. Paine noted further that Mrs. Walker must then be "upwards of sixty years of age," and denounced the tale as one "of which the public knows no fact, and is possessed of no evidence." He had not, however, seen Walker's letter to Henry Lee. The Paine article is in *Complete Writings of Thomas Paine*, Philip S. Foner, ed., 2 vols. (New York, 1945), 986.
27. Jefferson apparently never received the original letter from Walker sent on this date. When Walker sent him a copy on April 4, 1803, Jefferson expressed regret that he had never seen the original, saying he would have answered it at once. Jefferson to Walker, April 13, 1803, Virginia Historical Society. See also Chapter 26.
28. William Burwell memoir, Ms., Library of Congress; *New York Evening Post*, April 5, 1805.
29. Flexner, *Washington: The Forge of Experience*, 202, 197, 39, 324, 200.
30. James Monroe to Jefferson, September 4, 1809, Library of Congress, 33464; Hugh Nelson to Jefferson, September 4, 1809, Library of Congress, 33465; Schachner, *Jefferson*, 766.

CHAPTER VI Martha Jefferson

1. Martha Jefferson to Eleanor Conway Madison, August 8, 1780, *Papers*, Boyd, III, 532. This letter was reproduced in Marie Kimball, *Jefferson: The Road to Glory, 1743–1776* (New York, 1943), 170.
2. Sarah Randolph, *Domestic Life*, 44, and "Memoirs of a Monticello Slave," *Jefferson at Monticello*, 5.
3. Randolph, *Domestic Life*, 44.
4. Ellen Randolph Coolidge memoir, Ms. 66, University of Virginia Library. In a discreet letter to James Oglivie February 20, 1771, Jefferson indicated that Martha's family approved of him, *Papers*, Boyd, I, 63.
5. Robert Skipwith to Jefferson, September 20, 1771, *Papers*, Boyd, I, 84.
6. Jefferson to Robert Skipwith, August 3, 1771, *Papers*, Boyd, I, 78.
7. For a photostat of the marriage bond see Sarah Randolph, *Domestic Life*, 42.
8. Jefferson to Robert Skipwith, August 3, 1771, *Papers*, Boyd, I, 78.
9. Malone, *Jefferson the Virginian*, 432.
10. According to her grandson, Madison Hemings. See his reminiscences, Appendix I. See also John Cook Wyllie's genealogy of the Hemings family, as published in *Jefferson at Monticello*, 25.
11. Appendix I.
12. *Jefferson at Monticello*, 4.
13. The twelve surviving children of Betty Hemings were Mary (1753–92+); Martin (1755–1807); Bett (1759–1827+); Nance (1761–1827+); Robert (1762–1819); James (1765–1801); Thenia (1767–95+); Critta (1769–1827+); Peter (1770–1827+); Sally (1773–1835); John (1775–1830+); Lucy (1777–86). Plus signs indicate that no further information was available after the sale of these slaves, or their listing in the slave inventory taken after Jefferson's death. Lucy, it will be seen, died as a child. See *Jefferson at Monticello*, 24–25.
14. *White over Black*, 467.
15. Mary Boykin Chesnut, *A Diary from Dixie*, Ben Ames Williams, ed. (Boston, 1949), 21.
16. *Farm Book*, 15.
17. She is listed as being at Elkhill in 1774, *Farm Book*, 18. A blanket distribution list for 1776 includes Betty Hemings' name along with other slaves normally listed at Elkhill (*Farm Book*, 27), but the account books list payments to Betty Hemings February 5, 1775, April 1, 1776, and July 17, 1783.
18. See Appendix I.
19. Two remain unaccounted for and may have died young. See Appendix I.
20. *Jefferson at Monticello*, 99.
21. This ad appeared October 8, 15, 22, 1772. See *Papers*, Boyd, I, 96n.
22. Randall, *Jefferson*, I, 338–39.
23. Randall wrote that Martha Jefferson Randolph wrote this memoir at the request of Jefferson's earlier biographer, George Tucker.
24. Randall, *Jefferson*, I, 45.
25. *Garden Book*, 35.
26. In a copied memorandum, Jefferson listed the death as June 10, 1771. But the *Fee Book* has an entry on February 26, 1772, for "goods imported for Mrs. Jefferson & J. Skelton from Cary & Co." Had the boy lived in June 1771, one would probably have seen evidence in Jefferson's account book. As Malone points out, Jefferson was at Martha's home, The Forest, on June 9, 1771, and left. He would probably have returned at once had the boy died on June 10. See Malone, *Jefferson the Virginian*, I, 158, 432n. The *Fee Book* has an entry reading, "John Skelton, son of Bathurst, in acct. with Th. Jefferson, his guardian in right of Martha, his wife."

27. As Jefferson described it to his daughter Martha when she was having similar difficulties with her own daughter Anne, October 26, 1792, *Family Letters*, 105. See also Jefferson to Thomas Mann Randolph, October 19, 1792, Library of Congress 13465.

28. Malone, *Jefferson the Virginian*, 443.

29. See James S. Ackerman, *Palladio* (London, 1966); Fiske Kimball, *Thomas Jefferson: Architect* (Boston, 1916).

30. *Travels in North America in the years 1780, 1781, and 1782*, by the Marquis de Chastellux [François-Jean de Beauvoir], introduction and notes by Howard C. Rice, Jr., (Chapel Hill, N.C., 1963), II, 391.

31. *Garden Book*, 69, 81.

32. Jefferson to Thomas Adams, June 1, 1771, *Papers*, Boyd, I, 71.

33. Schachner, *Jefferson*, 61; Malone, *Jefferson the Virginian*, 122; Randall, *Jefferson*, I, 47–48.

34. *Virginia Gazette*, May 20, 1773, *Papers*, Boyd, I, 98.

35. *Literary Bible*, 10, 184; Malone, *Jefferson the Virginian*, 178.

36. Julian Boyd, *Papers*, VII, 586n, quoted the above translation, from the London edition of 1787. For a slightly different version, see the Howard Rice translation in his 1963 edition of Chastellux, *Travels in North America*, II, 392.

CHAPTER VII The Revolutionary

1. *Papers*, Boyd, VI, 60.

2. *Jefferson and the New Nation*, 45, 28.

3. Jefferson to Maria Cosway, October 12, 1786, *Papers*, Boyd, X, 451.

4. *Autobiography*, 21.

5. Jefferson to Edward Coles, August 25, 1814, *Writings*, Ford, IX, 477. One is reminded of the fact that Lincoln's first bill introduced into Congress in 1848 called for the ending of the slave trade and emancipation in the District of Columbia. See also Robert McColley, *Slavery in Jeffersonian Virginia* (Urbana, Ill., 1964), Donald L. Robinson, *Slavery in the Structure of American Politics, 1765–1820* (New York, 1971), 81, and Jordan, *White over Black*, 124.

6. A bill providing the right of manumission as Jefferson desired did not pass the Virginia assembly until 1782. The first abolition society was organized in Pennsylvania in April 1775. *A Summary View of the Rights of British America* (Williamsburg, Va., 1774), *Papers*, Boyd, I, 130.

7. *Papers*, Boyd, I, 33. Sandy had been inherited from Jefferson's father. Jefferson sold him to Colonel Charles Lewis on January 29, 1773.

8. James Hugo Johnston, in examining the court records of the sixty Virginia Negroes condemned for rape between 1789 and 1833, discovered that in twenty-seven of the cases white citizens testified for the Negroes, declaring that the woman in each case "had encouraged and consented to the act," and many whites petitioned the governor for leniency to revoke the sentences of execution. Since Johnston had only the rape record cases to count, one may assume that there were many more than sixty cases of white woman–black slave miscegenation which simply went unreported, and certainly many more cases of sexual relations without the identifying offspring. See his *Race Relations in Virginia, and Miscegenation in the South, 1776–1860* (Amherst, Mass., 1970), 257–58.

9. *Howell v. Netherland*, April, 1770, reproduced in *Writings*, Ford, I, 376, 470–81.

10. This may be seen today in the Huntington Library.

11. Jefferson's 1775 account book is in the Huntington Library. Controversy over whether Michael Cresap had really been responsible for the murders of Logan's family broke out when Jefferson's *Notes* first appeared, and in the 1800 edition he presented a great many affidavits strengthening his original charges. Still the contro-

versy continued. See Jefferson's Appendix 4, *Notes*, 226–54, and Peden's authoritative analysis, *Notes*, 298–301. Peden notes that thanks to Washington Irving's *Sketch Book* and the McGuffey *Readers*, Logan's speech was memorized by generations of American school children.

12. Jefferson to William Wirt, August 14, 1814, *Writings*, L. and B., XIV, 169; William Wirt, *Sketches of the Life and Character of Patrick Henry*, (Hartford, Conn., 1852), 83.

13. Andrew Burnaby, *Travels through North America*, R. R. Wilson, ed. (New York, 1904), quoted by Malone, *Jefferson the Virginian*, 91.

14. Gordon S. Wood, *The Creation of the American Republic* (Chapel Hill, N.C., 1969), 3; Samuel Eliot Morison, *Oxford History of the American People* (New York, 1965), 172. See also Bernard Bailyn, *Ideological Origins of the American Revolution* (Cambridge, Mass., 1967), 19.

15. *The Commonplace Book of Thomas Jefferson: A Repertory of His Ideas on Government*, Gilbert Chinard, ed. (Baltimore, 1926), 175–76, Schachner, *Jefferson*, 75. When Jefferson saw the book advertised for sale, he wrote to John Page on May 17, 1776, asking him to buy it for him, *Papers*, Boyd, I, 294.

16. Edmund Burke, *Speech on Conciliation with America* (New York, 1911), 48.

17. Quoted in Bailyn, *Ideological Origins*, 114.

18. For a copy of the agreement with its 92 signatures, see *Papers*, Boyd, I, 27–31.

19. The apparent American victory had been aided by the death of Townshend, the resignation of William Pitt, and the coming of Lord North, who believed adding to the cost of British products in the colonies would serve only to lessen sales, with adverse affects on the British merchants.

20. Walpole to the Reverend William Mason, February 14, 1774, in Peter Gay, *The Enlightenment*, 2 vols. (New York, 1967–69), II, 409. Burke, *Speech on Conciliation*, March 22, 1775, 23.

21. Dickinson, Quincy, and Washington are thus quoted in Bailyn, *Ideological Origins*, 233, 120. For Jefferson's statement, see *A Summary View . . .* , *Papers*, Boyd, I, 125.

22. Gay, *The Enlightenment*, II, 410.

23. Bailyn, *Ideological Origins*, 20.

24. See the British invoice listing the books, October 2, 1769, in *Papers*, Boyd, I, 33–34.

25. *Commonplace Book*, Chinard, ed., 26.

26. John Adams, *Diary and Autobiography*, Lyman H. Butterfield, ed., 4 vols. (Cambridge, Mass., 1961), I, 72–73.

27. Bailyn, *Ideological Origins*, 55, 19.

28. Adams, *Diary and Autobiography*, December 17, 1773, II, 85–86.

29. *Autobiography*, 25.

30. Max Beloff, *Thomas Jefferson and American Democracy* (New York, 1949), 56–57.

31. *Papers*, Boyd, I, 126. The *Summary View . . .* was published by friends of Jefferson in Williamsburg without his consent in 1774.

32. Erikson, *Young Man Luther*, 226.

33. See Bailyn, *Ideological Origins*, 311, 313; Morison, *Oxford History of the American People*, 121, 200; Peterson, *Jefferson and the New Nation*, 32.

34. Burke, *Speech on Conciliation*, March 22, 1775.

35. Adams, *Diary and Autobiography*, September 24, 1775, II, 181; July 15, 1776, II, 63.

36. Paine, *Common Sense* (New York, 1960), 85; *American Crisis*, no. 6, in *Life and Works*, Van der Weyde ed., III, 86, 94–95. See also Edwin G. Burrows and Michael Wallace, "The American Revolution: The Theology and Psychology of National Liberation," *Perspectives in American History*, VI (1972), 167–306.

37. Benjamin Franklin, *Writings*, Albert H. Smyth, ed., 10 vols. (New York, 1906–7), IX, 261.

38. *Papers*, Boyd, I, 134–37.
39. Malone, *Jefferson the President: First Term, 1801–1805* (Boston, 1970), 186; Peterson, *Jefferson and the New Nation*, 722.
40. *Autobiography*, 26.

CHAPTER VIII   Jefferson and Independence—
The Domestic Problem

1. The physician was Dr. Thomas Hinde. His son's account, and that of Miss Sally Campbell, who described the incarceration in the cellar, were reported in Meade, *Patrick Henry: Patriot in the Making*, 281. Miss Campbell wrote, "I have always heard that Patrick Henry's wife was crazy."
2. Wirt, *Patrick Henry*, 139.
3. James Cheetham, *Life of Thomas Paine* (New York, 1809); Alfred O. Aldridge, *Man of Reason: The Life of Thomas Paine* (Philadelphia, 1959).
4. *Complete Writings of Thomas Paine*, Foner, ed., II, 1119–20.
5. January 6, 1788, *Writings*, Foner, ed., II, 1275; speech in the French National Convention, January 19, 1793, *Writings*, Foner, ed., I, 558–59.
6. Flexner, *Washington in the American Revolution*, 282–83.
7. *Adams Family Correspondence*, Lyman H. Butterfield, ed. (Cambridge, Mass., 1963), I, 324. Abigail Adams to John Adams, November 12, 1775.
8. John C. Miller, *Sam Adams: Pioneer in Propaganda* (Boston, 1936), 327.
9. Page Smith, *John Adams*, I, 205.
10. James T. Flexner, *George Washington and the New Nation, 1783–1793* (Boston, 1969), 193.
11. Flexner, *Washington: The Forge of Experience*, 343.
12. See the collection of songs of the American Revolution, Evert and George L. Duyckinck, eds., *Cyclopedia of American Literature*, 2 vols. (New York, 1856), I, 479.
13. Adams, *Diary and Autobiography*, June 25, 1774, II, 97.
14. Samuel Ward to Henry Ward, quoted in *Papers*, Boyd, I, 676n.
15. *Papers*, Boyd, I, 225–33, 405 n.
16. Adams to Timothy Pickering, August 6, 1822, *John Adams, Life and Works*, Charles Francis Adams, ed., 10 vols. (Boston, 1856), II, 513–14.
17. John Adams to Abigail Adams, August 18, 1776, May 15, 1777, *Adams Family Correspondence*, II, 100, 239.
18. See Jefferson's letter to his brother-in-law Francis Eppes, November 21, 1775, *Papers*, Boyd, I, 264.
19. Jefferson to John Randolph, August 25, 1775, *Papers*, Boyd, I, 241–42. The Jefferson account book for 1775 (Huntington Library) lists payment of £13 for Randolph's violin on August 17.
20. Jefferson to John Randolph, November 29, 1775, *Papers*, Boyd, I, 269–70. Peyton Randolph had died on October 22, 1775.
21. Adams, *Diary and Autobiography*, II, 182.
22. Jefferson to Francis Eppes, November 7, 1775, *Papers*, Boyd, I, 252.
23. John Page to Jefferson, November 24, 1775, *Papers*, Boyd, I, 265–66. For Dunmore's proclamation, see Quarles, *The Negro in the American Revolution*, 19, and for additional details see Quarles, 27–28.
24. Robert C. Nicholas to Jefferson, November 25, 1775, *Papers*, Boyd, I, 267.
25. Jefferson to Francis Eppes, November 21, 1775, *Papers*, Boyd, I, 264.
26. Randall, *Jefferson*, I, 140–41, wrote that Jefferson spent time raising money for troops in Boston, but admits that there was less business than usual recorded in his account book. See also Schachner, *Jefferson*, 116; Malone, *Jefferson the Virginian*, 214; Peterson, *Jefferson and the New Nation*, 84; Chinard, *Thomas Jefferson: The*

Apostle of Americanism (Boston, 1939), 66. Chinard mistakenly says he had "left at Monticello a sick mother (and) . . . wife who had recently lost a child," missing both the fact that Jefferson's mother died after an illness "of one hour," and that Martha Jefferson had spent months with her sister after the death of her small daughter. Schachner notes that Jefferson "did draw up a list of militia volunteers from Albemarle, but this seems to have been about all he did in connection with his duties as County Lieutenant." Schachner, *Jefferson*, 116. For the list, see Library of Congress, 1063.

27. Julian Boyd records not a single letter between December 10, 1775, and May 16, 1776. Nor does he find evidence of missing letters as in the fall of 1775. See *Papers*, Boyd, I, 297n.

28. Thomas Nelson to Jefferson, February 4, 1776, *Papers*, Boyd, I, 286; Jefferson to Nelson, May 16, 1776, *Papers*, Boyd, I, 292.

29. Schachner, *Jefferson*, 168.

30. This paper was not published until 1940. See *Papers*, Boyd, I, 283, 284n.

31. *Common Sense*, 27.

32. Abigail Adams to John Adams, March 2, 16, 31, 1776. *Adams Family Correspondence*, I, 353, 360, 370.

33. John Page to Jefferson, April 6, 1776, *Papers*, Boyd, I, 287.

34. Jefferson to his mother's brother, William Randolph, June 1776, *Papers*, Boyd, I, 409. Jefferson wrote to Nelson, "I arrived here last Tuesday after being detained hence six weeks longer than I intended by a malady of which Gilmer can inform you." May 16, 1776, *Papers*, Boyd, I, 292. Gilmer was Jefferson's physician.

35. Jefferson to Thomas Cooper, October 27, 1808, *Writings*, L. and B., XII, 180; and Jefferson to Dr. Vine Utley, March 21, 1819, Sarah Randolph, *Domestic Life*, 371.

36. Harold G. Wolff, *Headache and Other Pain* (New York, 1948), 257; Paul B. Beeson and Walsh McDermott, *Textbook of Medicine* (Philadelphia, 1963), 1540.

37. *Notes on the State of Virginia*, 24–25.

38. Edmund Pendleton to Jefferson, May 24, 1776, *Papers*, Boyd, I, 296.

39. Jefferson to John Page, May 17, 1776, *Papers*, Boyd, I, 293.

40. *Papers*, Boyd, I, 330n.

41. Jefferson to Thomas Nelson, Jr., May 16, 1776, *Papers*, Boyd, I, 292.

42. The letter to Gilmer is missing, but it is clear from other letters that Gilmer made the request to the Convention with some embarrassment. See Edmund Randolph to Jefferson, June 23, 1776, *Papers*, Boyd, I, 407, 408n.

43. *Autobiography*, 50. See Julian Boyd's admirable detective work on the three Jefferson drafts of the constitution, *Papers*, Boyd, I, 329–37, 337–45, 337n.

44. *Notes on the State of Virginia*, 65.

45. Jefferson to the Comte de Moustier, October 9, 1787, *Papers*, Boyd, XII, 224.

46. Quoted in John C. Miller, *The Federalist Era, 1789–1801* (New York, 1960), 127.

CHAPTER IX   The Flight from Power

1. John Adams to Timothy Pickering, August 22, 1822, Adams, *Life and Works*, II, 512, 514.

2. John Adams to Pickering, August 2, 1822, Adams, *Life and Works*, II, 514.

3. Jefferson to Madison, August 30, 1823, *Writings*, L. and B., XV, 462.

4. *Papers*, Boyd, I, 317–18.

5. *Autobiography*, 35.

6. In a vigorous new defense Donald L. Robinson argues persuasively that Jefferson wrought these lines with great care, trusting they would avoid offense to slaveowners but still "constitute a serious obstacle for those who looked forward to

opening the slave trade after the attainment of independence." Robinson notes that even the ultra-radical Samuel Adams never sought to interfere with slavery for fear he would "jeopardize the unity of the colonies." *Slavery in the Structure of American Politics,* 1765-1820, 82.

7. *Papers,* Boyd, I, 319.
8. Beloff, *Jefferson and American Democracy,* 69.
9. "Anecdotes of Benjamin Franklin," *Writings,* L. and B., XVIII, 168-69.
10. Julian Boyd says the first appearance was in the Boston *Continental Journal Weekly Advertiser,* July 1, 1784, *Papers,* Boyd, VII, 312n.
11. "Familial Politics: The Killing of the King," Ms. For a detailed description of the celebrations in the colonies, see "The Fireworks of 1776," chap. 11, in John H. Hazelton, *The Declaration of Independence: Its History* (New York, 1906), 240-82.
12. As reported by John Adams to William Plumer, March 28, 1813, Edmund C. Burnett, *Letters of Members of the Continental Congress,* 8 vols. (Washington, D.C., 1921), I, 537.
13. John Adams to Abigail Adams, July 3, 1776, *Adams Family Correspondence,* II, 29.
14. Benjamin Rush in a letter to John Adams, July 20, 1811, described this episode as taking place in August, which indicates that the occasion was probably the second signing, on the official parchment copy, which took place August 2, 1776. Benjamin Rush, *Letters,* Lyman H. Butterfield, ed., 2 vols. (Princeton, 1951), II, 1090.
15. For Boyd's definitive discussion of the controversy, see *Papers,* Boyd, I, 299-309. For Jefferson's own account of the proceedings of Congress, see *Papers,* Boyd, I, 309-28, and his *Autobiography.*
16. Account book, July 4, 1776. See also Malone, *Jefferson the Virginian,* 229-30.
17. John Page to Jefferson, July 20, 1776, *Papers,* Boyd, I, 468.
18. Jefferson to Edmund Pendleton, June 30, 1776, *Papers,* Boyd, I, 408.
19. Jefferson to William Fleming, July 1, 1776, *Papers,* Boyd, I, 412-13.
20. Jefferson indicated his prediction that "our trial can be severe" for no longer than three months to William Fleming, July 1, 1776, *Papers,* Boyd, I, 412. For his letter to Pendleton, June 30, 1776, see *Papers,* Boyd, I, 408.
21. Edmund Pendleton to Jefferson, August 10, 1776, *Papers,* Boyd, I, 489.
22. Jefferson to Francis Eppes, July 23, 1776, *Papers,* Boyd, I, 473.
23. Jefferson to Richard Henry Lee, July 29, 1776, *Papers,* Boyd, I, 477.
24. Jefferson to John Page, July 30, 1776, *Papers,* Boyd, I, 483.
25. Jefferson to Francis Eppes, August 9, 1776, *Papers,* Boyd, I, 488.
26. Edmund Pendleton to Jefferson, August 26, 1776, *Papers,* Boyd, I, 508.
27. Richard Henry Lee to Jefferson, September 27, 1776, *Papers,* Boyd, I, 522.
28. That Martha disliked leaving Monticello is clear from a letter Jefferson wrote to John Page after he had become governor of Virginia and had to move his family to Williamsburg. The fact that Mrs. Page was there, Jefferson said, would "help reconcile" his wife to the situation. June 3, 1779, *Papers,* Boyd, II, 279.
29. Jefferson to John Hancock, October 11, 1776, *Papers,* Boyd, I, 524.
30. Richard Henry Lee to Jefferson, November 3, 1776, *Papers,* Boyd, I, 589.
31. *Autobiography of Benjamin Rush: His "Travels through Life"* . . . , George W. Corner ed. (Princeton, 1948), 151.
32. Account book, October 1, 1776.
33. Jefferson to Franklin, August 13, 1777, *Papers,* Boyd, II, 27.
34. John Adams to Jefferson, May 26, 1777, *Papers,* Boyd, II, 21-22.
35. The extraordinary number and variety of bills which bear his imprint can be seen in the meticulous compilation of vol. II of his papers by Julian Boyd, who calls him "a veritable legislative drafting bureau." *Papers,* Boyd, II, 306n.
36. See Jefferson's "Notes on Locke and Shaftesbury," *Papers,* Boyd, I, 544-50, Peterson, *Jefferson and the New Nation,* 139.
37. "A Bill for Establishing Religious Freedom," *Papers,* Boyd, II, 545-46. See

also his voluminous outline and notes for a remarkable speech he made in favor of a preliminary "Resolution for Disestablishing the Church of England and for Repealing Laws Interfering with Freedom of Worship," *Papers*, Boyd, I, 530–39.

38. *Notes on the State of Virginia*, 161.

39. *Autobiography*, 51.

40. Boyd insists that his legislative achievements were "more extensive than biographers have recognized," but it is clear from Boyd's own meticulous examination and compilation of this record that much of the success was due to James Madison's determined follow-up after Jefferson left Virginia, and he could hardly have been elated by the nature of his victories in 1779. See *Papers*, Boyd, II, 307n.

41. Chastellux, *Travels in North America*, II, 389.

42. Martha Carr to Jefferson, February 26, 1787, quoted in *Papers*, Boyd, XV, 635.

43. John Adams to Caroline De Windt, his granddaughter, Abigail Adams Smith, *Journal and Correspondence* (New York, 1841), 242. Adams concluded this fascinating letter, "So questions, and so answers your affectionate grandfather."

44. Lee to Jefferson, August 25, 1777. Lee had complained on April 29, 1777, about Jefferson's failure to answer his letters. *Papers*, Boyd, II, 13, 29.

45. Washington, *Writings*, John C. Fitzpatrick, ed., 39 vols. (Washington, D.C., 1931–44), XIII, 467.

46. Rutledge to Jefferson, February 12, 1779, *Papers*, Boyd, II, 234.

47. Account book, April 29, 1799.

48. Jacob Rubsamen, who had married into the Bland family of Virginia, discovered the newspaper account in the letter of a German officer, translated it, and sent it to Jefferson December 1, 1780. *Papers*, Boyd, IV, 174.

CHAPTER X   Jefferson in the War

1. Jefferson to James Monroe, May 20, 1782, *Papers*, Boyd, VI, 184.

2. *Notes on the State of Virginia*, 155.

3. Jefferson to James Innes, May 2, 1781, *Papers*, Boyd, V, 594.

4. Jefferson to J. P. G. Muhlenberg, January (29), 31, 1781, *Papers*, Boyd, IV, 487. Boyd prints the deleted matter in italics.

5. Pendleton to Jefferson, May 11, 1779, Papers, Boyd, II, 266.

6. Irving Brant, *James Madison*, 5 vols. (Indianapolis, 1941–53), I, 316.

7. The "agreeable circle," the letter makes clear, included the British general and Baron and Baroness von Riedesel. Jefferson to William Phillips, June 25, 1779, *Papers*, Boyd, III, 15.

8. Jefferson to Lafayette, March 10, 1781, *Papers*, Boyd, V, 113. See also Louis Gottschalk, *Lafayette and the Close of the American Revolution* (Chicago, 1942), 150. For Jefferson's difficulties with von Steuben, see *Papers*, Boyd, VI, 619ff. and Friedrich Kapp, *The Life of Frederick William von Steuben* (New York, 1959).

9. See Piers Mackesy, "British Strategy in the War of American Independence," in David L. Jacobson, *Essays on the American Revolution* (New York, 1970), 177–79.

10. See Jefferson to John Skinker and William Garrard, April 14, 1781, *Papers*, Boyd, V, 451–52.

11. See Peterson, *Jefferson and the New Nation*, 217–19, and Malone, *Jefferson the Virginian*, 302–69.

12. Quarles, *The Negro in the American Revolution*, 20, from R. H. Lee, *Memoir of the Life of Richard Henry Lee* (Philadelphia, 1825), II, 9.

13. Dunmore insisted that had it not been for the smallpox he would have had 2,000 Negro followers. He kept agitating for arming the slaves to the end of the war, but the British officers in general had little enthusiasm for the idea of black soldiers, and most of the blacks who came under British influence were treated like booty

rather than as slaves to be emancipated. Still, thousands of slaves fled to the British side, especially after the surrender of Cornwallis. Quarles estimates that 4,000 were evacuated from Savannah, 6,000 from Charleston, and 4,000 from New York. Thousands more were taken by the French. The overwhelming majority settled in the British Caribbean islands. Many expecting to be free, as Quarles notes, "were seized by those holding no legal title, and sold for rum, coffee, sugar, and fruits." This was not the fate of the several thousand who were settled in Canada. Here, under the leadership of Thomas Peters, about a thousand former slaves were organized and sent to Sierra Leone, where they founded Freetown. See Quarles, *The Negro in the American Revolution*, 158-81.

14. Madison to Joseph Jones, November 28, 1780, Madison, *Writings*, Gaillard Hunt, ed., 9 vols. (New York, 1900-1910), I, 107.

15. Luther P. Jackson, *Negro Soldiers and Seamen in the American Revolution* (Norfolk, Va., 1944), vi. Thomas Nelson, Jr., wrote to Washington November 21, 1777, that the state was drafting free Negroes "as it was thought that they could best be spared." Quarles, *The Negro in the American Revolution*, 74.

16. Quarles, *The Negro in the American Revolution*, 108.

71. *Papers*, Boyd, V, 627.

18. *Farm Book*, 29. This was a fairly large proportion of the 129 slaves he then owned. See his account book for April 15, 1782, which lists "129 slaves. 2 free."

19. "Memoirs of a Monticello Slave," *Jefferson at Monticello*, 9-11.

20. The rumor that the British deliberately infected slaves with smallpox and sent them home may have been true. Quarles quotes a remarkable letter from General Alexander Leslie to Cornwallis, July 13, 1781: "About 700 Negroes are come down the River in the Small Pox. I shall distribute them about the Rebell Plantations." *The Negro in the American Revolution*, 142.

21. Jefferson to William Gordon, July 16, 1788, *Papers*, Boyd, XIII, 363.

22. Jefferson's payment on December 31, 1779, of £125 for five visits to Dr. James McClurg, and £6 for medicine, is further evidence of Mrs. Jefferson's ill health.

23. *Papers*, Boyd, III, 532. An announcement of the drive appeared in the *Virginia Gazette*, August 9, 1780. It is possible Jefferson dictated the letter for his wife, but since there is nothing else in her own hand, one cannot make any kind of stylistic comparisons.

24. Jefferson's letter to von Riedesel is missing, and we have only Jefferson's summary of the Baron's reply, *Papers*, Boyd, IV, 4.

25. Jefferson to Lee, September 13, 1780, *Papers*, Boyd, III, 643.

26. Page to Jefferson, December 9, 1780, *Papers*, Boyd, IV, 192.

27. A battery was under construction only at Hoods, on the James River. Jefferson to Benjamin Harrison, November 30, 1780, *Papers*, Boyd, IV, 168-69.

28. Jefferson to Charles François, Chevalier D'Anmours, November 30, 1780, *Papers*, Boyd, IV, 168.

29. Jefferson's account book shows that he paid the midwife £30 on January 1, 1781. For milk he noted payments of £2 and £3 almost every day. He began giving Mrs. Jefferson money on December 17, with a payment of £200.

30. *Papers*, Boyd, IV, 195.

31. Randall, *Jefferson*, I, 299.

32. See Jefferson to Washington, January 10, 1781, and Washington to Jefferson, February 6, 1781, *Papers*, Boyd, IV, 333-35, 543-44.

33. See especially Gottschalk, *Lafayette and the Close of the American Revolution*, 202-4.

34. Jefferson to Oliver Towles, April 14, 1781; Jefferson to John Skinker and William Garrard, April 14, 1781, *Papers*, Boyd, V, 454, 451.

35. Jefferson to David Jameson, April 16, 1781, *Papers*, Boyd, V, 468.

36. Jefferson to Timothy Matlack, April 18, 1781, *Papers*, Boyd, V, 490.

37. John Floyd to Jefferson, April 16, 1781, *Papers*, Boyd, V, 467.

38. Jefferson to James Monroe, May 20, 1782, *Papers*, Boyd, VI, 186.

39. Malone, *Jefferson the Virginian*, 351.
40. Gottschalk, *Lafayette and the Close of the American Revolution*, 218.
41. Jefferson to Washington, May 28, 1781, *Papers*, Boyd, VI, 32–33.
42. Washington to Jefferson, June 8, 1781, *Papers*, Boyd, VI, 82–83.
43. *Papers*, Boyd, VI, 30–31. Kapp, *Life of von Steuben*, 439, has a bitter letter from von Steuben to Lafayette, June 3, 1781, "Here I am with five hundred and fifty men in a desert, without shoes, shirts, and what is still worse, without cartridge-boxes," etc.
44. Lafayette to Jefferson, May 31, 1781, *Papers*, Boyd, VI, 52, 53n.
45. Another of Rebecca Burwell's daughters. See her letter to Mildred Smith, 1781, in "Old Virginia Correspondence," *Atlantic Monthly*, LXXXIV (1899), 538.
46. Henry Lee, *Memoirs of the War in the Southern Department of the United States*, 2 vols. (Philadelphia, 1812), II, 234.
47. See Boyd's comprehensive compilation, "Notes and Documents Relating to the British Invasions in 1781," which includes everything Jefferson ever wrote about the Arnold and Tarleton raids. *Papers*, IV, 256–77. This includes Jefferson's 1816 version of a diary and notes he kept in 1781. For the above, see IV, 265.
48. See Thomas Jefferson Randolph's memoirs, Ms., University of Virginia, 18, reporting what must have been an exaggeration, since the dragoons left after eighteen hours, that Caesar remained three days and nights under the portico without food. George Tucker in his 1837 life of Jefferson related this story in detail, as did Randall.
49. Jefferson to William Gordon, July 16, 1788, *Papers*, Boyd, XIII, 363–64.
50. Lafayette to Jefferson, May 31, 1781, *Papers*, Boyd, VI, 52. This was the letter intercepted by the British.
51. Randall, *Jefferson*, I, 279; Henry Lee, *Memoirs of the War . . .* , II, 252–71.
52. For the charges advanced by Nicholas with Jefferson's answers, see *Papers*, Boyd, VI, 106–7. They were written after July 31, 1781.
53. Randall, *Jefferson*, I, 363.
54. Thomas McKean, thinking Jefferson had not received the official notification, sent him a duplicate on August 20, 1781, *Papers*, Boyd, VI, 116.
55. Jefferson to Lafayette, August 4, 1781, *Papers*, Boyd, VI, 112.
56. Jefferson to Lafayette, August 4, 1781, *Papers*, Boyd, VI, 112. For his explanatory and self-deprecatory letter to Thomas McKean, August 4, 1781, carried by Lafayette, see *Papers*, Boyd, VI, 112.
57. Lafayette to Jefferson, July 1, 1781, *Papers*, Boyd, VI, 104; Lafayette to Washington, September 8, 1781, Gottschalk, *Letters of Lafayette to Washington*. 135, quoted in Malone, *Jefferson the Virginian*, 364.
58. Franklin to Jefferson, July 5, 1782, *Papers*, Boyd, VI, 194.
59. Jefferson to Edmund Randolph, September 26, 1781, *Papers*, Boyd, VI, 118.
60. Jefferson to Washington, October 28, 1781, *Papers*, Boyd, VI, 129.

CHAPTER XI   Jefferson Writes a Book

1. Jefferson to Charles Thomson, June 21, 1785, *Papers*, Boyd, VIII, 245.
2. *Notes on the State of Virginia*, 125.
3. Monroe to Jefferson, October 1, 1781, *Papers*, Boyd, VI, 124; Jefferson to Monroe, October 5, 1781, *Papers*, Boyd, VI, 127.
4. "Diary of Arnold's Invasion and Notes on Subsequent Events in 1781," *Papers*, Boyd, IV, 260.
5. Four of these had to do with the proposed assignment in Paris. Boyd lists six, *Papers*, VI, xxiii–xxiv, and on page 104n he notes that a letter was written to Lafayette June 14, 1781, which is missing.
6. Jefferson to Monroe, October 5, 1781, *Papers*, Boyd, VI, 127.
7. Jefferson to Marbois, December 20, 1781, *Papers*, Boyd, VI, 142.

8. Jefferson to Madison, May 11, 1785, *Papers*, Boyd, VIII, 147–48.
9. Adams to Jefferson, May 22, 1785, Jefferson to Adams, May 25, 1785, *Papers*, Boyd, VIII, 160, 164.
10. Madison to Jefferson, May 12, 1786, *Papers*, Boyd, IX, 517.
11. Jefferson to Alexander Donald, September 17, 1787, *Papers*, Boyd, XII, 133.
12. *Notes on the State of Virginia*, 127–28.
13. *Ibid.*, 19–20.
14. *Ibid.*, 55–56.
15. *Ibid.*, 64–65.
16. *Ibid.*, 59–60.
17. *Ibid.*, 164–65.
18. Jefferson to Monroe, May 20, 1782, *Papers*, Boyd, VI, 184.
19. *Notes on the State of Virginia*, 159–60.
20. *Ibid.*, 161.
21. Among the many new studies on the problem of slavery in the eighteenth century, see especially Winthrop Jordan, *White over Black: American Attitudes toward the Negro, 1550–1812*, and David Brion Davis, *The Problem of Slavery in Western Culture* (Ithaca, N.Y., 1966). See also Peter Gay, *The Enlightenment*, II, 410–23, and Eugene D. Genovese, *The World the Slaveholders Made* (New York, 1969), 21–113.
22. *Garden Book*, 1782, 95.
23. Letters of John Hemings are extant, and there is evidence that both Robert and James Hemings were literate. Jefferson hired a French tutor for James Hemings during his stay in Paris. See the letter from the French tutor complaining about difficulties collecting his pay, *Papers*, Boyd, XIV, 426.
24. *Notes on the State of Virginia*, 140. See also Jordan, *White over Black*, 283–85.
25. See Robert McColley, *Slavery in Jeffersonian Virginia*.
26. *Notes on the State of Virginia*, 138–43; Jefferson to Chastellux, June 7, 1785, "I beleive the Indian to be in body and mind equal to the whiteman. I have supposed the blackman, in his present state, might not be so. But it would be hazardous to affirm that, equally cultivated for a few generations, he would not become so." *Papers*, Boyd, VIII, 186.
27. Jordan, *White over Black*, 238, 495–96.
28. Peterson, *The Jefferson Image in the American Mind*, 175–80; Jordan, *White over Black*, 481.
29. *Notes on the State of Virginia*, 142.
30. *Ibid.*, 141.
31. *Ibid.*, 138.
32. Quarles, *The Negro in the American Revolution*, 172.
33. *Notes on the State of Virginia*, 163.
34. George Wythe wrote to Jefferson from Williamsburg on December 31, 1781: "I desired Martin to take the roan horse then in good plight to assist him in carrying home the servant he recovered in my neighbourhood. Send me a description of the other servants belonging to you, whom you suspect to be in the lower part of the country. I have heard of several lurking there, supposed to be slaves." *Papers*, Boyd, VI, 144.
35. See Quarles, *The Negro in the American Revolution*, 167–74.
36. *Notes on the State of Virginia*, 163.

CHAPTER XII   The Two Marthas

1. Jefferson to Maria Cosway, July 1, 1787, *Papers*, Boyd, XI, 520.
2. Jefferson to James Monroe, May 20, 1782, *Papers*, Boyd, VI, 185.
3. Jefferson to Isaac Zane, December 24, 1781, *Papers*, Boyd, VI, 143.

4. Jefferson to George Nicholas, July 28, 1781, *Papers*, Boyd, VI, 105.
5. Report of October 1781, read December 12, 1781, *Papers*, Boyd, VI, 136n.
6. "Charges Advanced by George Nicholas, with Jefferson's Answers," *Papers*, Boyd, VI, 107.
7. For the original resolution, before the deletions, see *Papers*, Boyd, VI, 135–36. The resolution was printed in the *Virginia Gazette*, December 22, 1781.
8. *Papers*, Boyd, VI, 137n.
9. Randolph to James Madison, June 1, 1782, May 10, 1782, quoted in *Papers*, Boyd, VI, 187n, 651n.
10. Jefferson to Madison, December 8, 1784, *Papers*, Boyd, VII, 558. The damaging comments were written in code. For the mention of his former affection, see Jefferson to Archibald Stuart, April 18, 1795, *Writings*, Ford, VIII, 8.
11. *Garden Book*, 94.
12. Jefferson to Thomas Stone, March 16, 1782, *Papers*, Boyd, VI, 167.
13. Jefferson to Madison, March 24, 1782, *Papers*, Boyd, VI, 171.
14. Chastellux, *Travels in North America*, II, 40–51.
15. Jefferson to Monroe, May 20, 1782, *Papers*, Boyd, VI, 186.
16. Account book, April 30, 1779, shows Jefferson's payment of £6.
17. John Tyler to Jefferson, May 16, 1782, *Papers*, Boyd, VI, 183–84. For Tyler's letter of resignation, see *Papers*, Boyd, V, 316.
18. Jefferson to Monroe, May 20, 1782, *Papers*, Boyd, VI, 184–86.
19. "Reminiscences of Th. Jefferson," by Martha Randolph, from a Ms. copy made by Mary and Anne Cary Randolph, written in answer to questions from George Tucker for his biography. See his *Life of Thomas Jefferson*, I, 158, and *Papers*, Boyd, VI, 200n.
20. Monroe reported the false report to Jefferson June 28, 1782, *Papers*, Boyd, VI, 192.
21. Randolph to Madison, Madison Papers, Library of Congress, *Papers*, Boyd, VI, 652.
22. *Garden Book*, 94.
23. Martha Jefferson Randolph, finding it later, endorsed the packet, "A Lock of my Dear Mamma's Hair inclosed in a verse which she wrote." That the lines came from *Tristram Shandy* and were not written by Martha Jefferson was established by Professor Edward L. Hubler. See *Papers*, Boyd, VI, 196–97n.
24. *Jefferson at Monticello*, 99–100. See Appendix I, part 2, for the memoir of Israel Jefferson.
25. For the birth dates of these women, see *Farm Book*, 128. Bacon may have confused the slave Ursula, who was alive, age 45, in 1782, but dead by 1806, with another Ursula, born in 1787. See *Farm Book*, 15, 128. Betty Hemings lived until 1807. See *Farm Book*, 30, 60.
26. First published in Tucker, *Life*, I, 158. There are no entries in Jefferson's account book for eight days after Martha's death. On September 14 he accepted a payment from "Richd Gaines" of £29 for tobacco.
27. Randolph to Madison, September 20, 1782; Madison to Randolph, September 30, 1782, *Papers*, Boyd, VI, 199n.
28. *Garden Book*, 95. Hornsby was one of Jefferson's neighbors.
29. Jefferson to Elizabeth Eppes, October 3 (?), 1782, *Papers*, Boyd, VI, 198–99.
30. Jefferson to Chastellux, November 26, 1782, *Papers*, Boyd, VI, 203.
31. Jefferson to Elizabeth Eppes, October 3 (?), 1782, *Papers*, Boyd, VI, 198.
32. Martha Wolfenstein, "How is Mourning Possible?," *Psychoanalytic Study of the Child*, XXI (1966), 93–123.
33. Jefferson to Martha Jefferson, November 28, 1783, *Family Letters*, 19–20. Julian Boyd points out that this letter later became a gift to Queen Victoria, *Papers*, VI, 360n.

CHAPTER XIII   The Return to Politics

1. Translated and quoted by Julian Boyd, *Papers*, VII, 82n.
2. So he told Margaret Bayard Smith. See her *First Forty Years of Washington Society*, 412. He did invite the Adams family in Paris to attend a masked ball, February 7, 1785, but in the end they did not go. See Abigail Adams Smith, *Journal and Correspondence*, 46–47.
3. Jefferson to Maria Cosway, October 12, 1786, *Papers*, Boyd, X, 448–49.
4. Jefferson to Madison, February 14, 1783, *Papers*, Boyd, VI, 242–43.
5. Jefferson to Madison, May 7, 1783, *Papers*, Boyd, VI, 266.
6. For a detailed description, see *Papers*, Boyd, VI, vii-x; see also *Papers*, Boyd, VII, 464.
7. Jefferson to Madison, August 31, 1783, *Papers*, Boyd, VI, 335–36.
8. *Garden Book*, 101; Randall, *Jefferson*, I, 388.
9. Jefferson to Marbois, December 5, 1783, *Papers*, Boyd, VI, 374.
10. *Ibid.*
11. Jefferson's orders as described by Francis Hopkinson to Robert Bremner, November 28, 1783, *Papers*, Boyd, VI, 359.
12. Jefferson to Martha Jefferson, December 11, 1783, *Family Letters*, 21.
13. Francis Hopkinson to Jefferson, January 4, 1784, reporting on the tutor, Pierre du Simitiere, *Papers*, Boyd, VI, 444.
14. Jefferson to Martha Jefferson, December 22, 1783, *Family Letters*, 22.
15. Jefferson to Peter Carr, December 11, 1783, *Papers*, Boyd, VI, 379–80.
16. Eliza House Trist to Jefferson, April 13, 1784, *Papers*, Boyd, VII, 97.
17. Jefferson to Eliza Trist, August 18, 1785, *Papers*, Boyd, VIII, 403.
18. Jefferson to John Trumbull, December 18, 1786, *Papers*, Boyd, X, 611.
19. See Ralph Ketcham, James Madison, 36. Benjamin Rush reported the Witherspoon statement in his *Autobiography*. See the George W. Corner edition, 181.
20. Brant, *James Madison*, I, 107, 134. See also Ketcham, *James Madison*, 51.
21. For the list, see *Papers*, Boyd, VII, 240.
22. Brant, *James Madison*, 277.
23. Harry Ammon, *James Monroe: The Quest for National Identity* (New York, 1971), 29, Boyd, *Papers*, III, 622.
24. Jefferson to Madison, January 30, 1787, Jefferson to William Temple, May 7, 1786, *Papers*, Boyd, XI, 97, IX, 466.
25. From William Wirt, *Letters of a British Spy* (1803), quoted in Ammon, *James Monroe*, 369.
26. Abigail Adams Smith, *Journal and Correspondence*, 45.
27. Philip Mazzei, *Memoirs of the Life and Peregrinations of the Florentine, Philip Mazzei, 1730–1816*, Howard R. Marraro, trans. (New York, 1942), 192. See also Malone, *Jefferson and the Ordeal of Liberty* (Boston, 1962), 267.
28. Jefferson to Martha Jefferson, February 18, 1784, *Family Letters*, 24. Jefferson to William Short, March 1, 1784, *Papers*, Boyd, VI, 570. There is no reference to headaches in the fortnight following Mrs. Jefferson's death, but it is possible that he suffered migraine attacks then, and that his daughter simply did not mention them.
29. Translated and quoted by Julian Boyd, *Papers*, Boyd, VII, 82n.
30. G. K. van Hogendorp to Jefferson, April 6, 1784, *Papers*, Boyd, VII, 81.
31. Jefferson to G. K. van Hogendorp, May 4, 1784, *Papers*, Boyd, VII, 208–9.
32. Dr. James Tilton to Gunning Bedford, *Papers*, Boyd, VI, 407n.
33. *Papers*, Boyd, VI, 413.
34. Flexner, *Washington in the American Revolution*, 550.
35. *Autobiography*, 70.
36. *Writings*, Ford, III, 447.
37. *Papers*, Boyd, VI, 574.

38. Jefferson to Madison, April 25, 1784, *Papers*, Boyd, VII, 118.
39. Jefferson to Jean Nicolas Démeunier, "Observations on Démeunier's Manuscript," *Papers*, Boyd, X, 58.
40. Jefferson to Jean Nicolas Démeunier, June 26, 1786, *Papers*, Boyd, X, 63.

CHAPTER XIV   Restlessness and Torment

1. Jefferson to Eliza House Trist, August 15, 1785, *Papers*, Boyd, VIII, 404.
2. Jefferson to James Monroe, March 18, 1785, *Papers*, Boyd, VIII, 42.
3. Jefferson to Eliza House Trist, August 15, 1785, *Papers*, Boyd, VIII, 404.
4. See Jefferson's letter to Madison, September 6, 1789, *Papers*, Boyd, XV, 396.
5. Martha Jefferson to Eliza House Trist, after August 24, 1785, *Papers*, Boyd, VIII, 436.
6. November 23, 1804, John Quincy Adams, *Memoirs*, I, 317.
7. Martha Jefferson to Eliza House Trist, after August 24, 1785, *Papers*, Boyd, VIII, 437.
8. Account book, August 3, 1784.
9. Martha Jefferson to Eliza House Trist, after August 24, 1785, *Papers*, Boyd, VIII, 437.
10. For the most detailed account of Jefferson in Paris, see Marie Kimball, *Jefferson: The Scene of Europe, 1784 to 1789* (New York, 1950).
11. Martha Jefferson to Eliza House Trist, *Papers*, Boyd, VIII, 437.
12. Jefferson to G. K. van Hogendorp, November 20, 1784, *Papers*, Boyd, VII, 545.
13. Jefferson's account book for August 26, 1784, reads, "paid at the Abbaie de Panthemont for Patsy 1500 f." James Maury reported his mother's unhappiness over Patsy's school in a letter to Jefferson, September 17, 1786, *Papers*, Boyd, X, 389. Jefferson replied tactfully December 24, 1786, *Papers*, Boyd, X, 628.
14. Ms. reminiscences of Martha Jefferson Randolph, University of Virginia.
15. Martha Jefferson to Eliza House Trist, *Papers*, Boyd, VIII, 437.
16. Abigail Adams Smith, *Journal and Correspondence*, 16.
17. John Adams to Jefferson, January 22, 1825, *Adams-Jefferson Letters*, 606–7. Jefferson lived for a short period at No. 5 cul-de-sac Taitbout.
18. *Letters of Mrs. Adams, the Wife of John Adams*, Charles Francis Adams ed., 2 vols. (Boston, 1848), I, 193.
19. Page Smith, *John Adams*, II, 604, 608.
20. Abigail Adams Smith, *Journal and Correspondence*, 21–26, Page Smith, *John Adams*, II, 609, 612.
21. Adams to Arthur Lee, January 31, 1785, Page Smith, *John Adams*, II, 616.
22. Adams to Eldridge Gerry, December 12, 1784, *Papers*, Boyd, VII, 382n.
23. Jefferson to Madison, January 30, 1787, *Papers*, Boyd, XI, 94–95.
24. Jefferson to Abigail Adams, September 25, 1785, *Papers*, Boyd, VIII, 548.
25. Abigail Adams Smith, *Journal and Correspondence*, 45.
26. James Currie to Jefferson, November 20, 1784, *Papers*, Boyd, VII, 538–39.
27. Jefferson to Francis Eppes, February 5, 1785, *Papers*, Boyd, VII, 635–36.
28. Elizabeth Eppes to Jefferson, October 13, 1784, *Papers*, Boyd, VII, 441.
29. Jefferson to Francis Eppes, January 13, 1785, *Papers*, Boyd, VII, 601. From an entry in the SJL.
30. Jefferson to Elizabeth Eppes, December 14, 1786, *Papers*, Boyd, X, 594.
31. Maria Jefferson to Jefferson, September 13, 1785 (?), *Family Letters*, 29.
32. Jefferson to Maria Jefferson, September 20, 1785, *Family Letters*, 29–30.
33. May 8, 1785, *Letters of Mrs. Adams*, II, 93.
34. Jefferson to William Short, May 3, 1785, *Papers*, Boyd, VIII, 134.
35. Jefferson to Elizabeth Eppes, September 22, 1785, *Papers*, Boyd, VIII, 540.
36. Jefferson to James Currie, September 27, 1785, *Papers*, Boyd, VIII, 558.

37. Jefferson to James Monroe, June 17, 1785, *Papers*, Boyd, VIII, 233.

38. Jefferson to John Adams, May 25, 1785, *Papers*, Boyd, VIII, 164; Jefferson to Samuel Smith, August 28, 1798, *Writings*, L. and B., X, 55.

39. Lafayette to Washington, Lafayette *Memoirs*, II, 192; Lafayette to McHenry, Gottschalk, *Lafayette and the Close of the American Revolution*, 258, quoted by Boyd, *Papers*, X, 477n.

40. Jefferson to Charles Bellini, September 30, 1785, *Papers*, Boyd, VIII, 569.

41. Jefferson to Madison, January 30, 1787, *Papers*, Boyd, XI, 95.

42. David Humphreys, *Life and Times*, 2 vols. (New York, 1917), I, 31⁻.

43. Jefferson to Madison, January 30, 1787, *Papers*, Boyd, XI, 95–96.

44. See Bernard Bailyn, "Boyd's Jefferson: Notes for a Sketch," *New England Quarterly*, XXXIII (1960), 380–401; Samuel F. Bemis, *American Secretaries of State and Their Diplomacy* (New York, 1927), II; Dumas Malone, *Jefferson and the Rights of Man* (Boston, 1951), 1–150; Peterson, *Jefferson and the New Nation*, 298–389.

45. Jefferson to Abigail Adams, June 21, 1785, *Papers*, Boyd, VIII, 239.

46. Jefferson to Eliza House Trist, August 18, 1785, and to Charles Bellini, September 30, 1785, *Papers*, Boyd, VIII, 404, 568.

47. *Autobiography*, 75. For Adams' account, see *Life and Works*, I, 420, and Malone, *Jefferson and the Rights of Man*, 55.

48. Jefferson to William Stephens Smith, September 28, 1787, *Papers*, Boyd, XII, 193.

49. Jefferson to Washington, May 2, 1788, *Papers*, Boyd, XIII, 128.

50. *Papers*, Boyd, XIII, 269.

51. Kimball, *Jefferson: The Scene of Europe*, 86–87.

52. Jefferson to Charles Bellini, September 30, 1785, *Papers*, Boyd, VIII, 589.

53. Jefferson to Madison, August 2, 1787; Jefferson to Angelica Church, September 21, 1788, *Papers*, Boyd, XI, 664; XIII, 623.

54. Jefferson to Eliza House Trist, August 18, 1785, *Papers*, Boyd, VIII, 404.

55. Jefferson to John Banister, Jr., October 15, 1785, *Papers*, Boyd, VIII, 636.

56. Jefferson to Chastellux, September 2, 1785, *Papers*, Boyd, VIII, 468.

57. Jefferson to Geismar, September 7, 1785, *Papers*, Boyd, VIII, 500.

58. Jefferson to Charles Bellini, September 30, 1785, *Papers*, Boyd, VIII, 568–69.

59. Kimball, *Jefferson: The Scene of Europe*, 257.

60. Gottschalk, *Lafayette and the Close of the American Revolution*, 418.

61. Van Doren, *Benjamin Franklin*, 651.

CHAPTER XV My Head and My Heart

1. Jefferson to Maria Cosway, October 12, 1786, *Papers*, Boyd, X, 446; see Appendix II.

2. See Appendix II.

3. See Appendix II. The dome of the Halle aux Bleds was constructed by Legrand and Molinos. The building was torn down in the 1880s to make way for the present Bourse du Commerce. The Medici column is still standing. Boyd (*Papers*, X, 435) reproduces a picture by Maréchal of the Halle aux Bleds just as Jefferson saw it in 1786.

4. Quoted by William Hazlitt, in George C. Williamson, *Richard Cosway, R.A.* (London, 1905), 55.

5. William Hazlitt, *Conversations with James Northcote*, Edmund Gosse, ed. (London, 1894), 99.

6. Allan Cunningham, *The Lives of the Most Eminent British Painters, Sculptors, and Architects*, 6 vols. (London, 1829–33), VI, 6.

7. Ellen C. Clayton, *English Female Artists*, 2 vols. (London, 1876), I, 316; Williamson, *Richard Cosway*, 20.

8. Maria Cosway to M. Chambers, July 11, 1816, Ms., Collegio di Maria SS. Bambina, Lodi, Italy.

9. Williamson, *Richard Cosway*, 20.

10. Maria Cosway to Richard Cosway, March 22, 1815, Ms., Maria Cosway Letterbook, Lodi, Italy. Maria Cosway also wrote to a Mrs. Chambers, May 29, 1816, ". . . the moment he gave himself to Hammersmith, began to lead him from me and from his home. . . . Hammersmith was drop'd for another acquaintance which kept him farther from me. peevish, cross, we were not happy." Ms., Letterbook, Lodi, Italy.

11. Cunningham, *Lives of the Most Eminent British Painters*, VI, 10.

12. Helen D. Bullock, *My Head and My Heart: A Little Chronicle of Thomas Jefferson and Maria Cosway* (New York, 1945), 20.

13. Hazlitt, *Conversations with James Northcote*, 62.

14. January 1784, reproduced in Horace Walpole, *Anecdotes of Painting in England, 1760–1795, with Some Account of the Principal Artists . . .* , F. W. Hilles and P. B. Daghlian, eds., 5 vols. (New Haven, 1937), V, 127–28.

15. Quoted in Williamson, *Richard Cosway*, 43. Wolcott called Cosway "The Tiny Cosmetic," and caricaturist Mat Darley made an etching of him with the title "The Macaroni Miniature Painter." The title stuck to him for life. Williamson, *Richard Cosway*, 31.

16. Williamson, *Richard Cosway*, 52.

17. See Marguerite Steen, *The Lost One: A Biography of Mary (Perdita) Robinson* (London, 1937), 190–91. Jefferson mentioned the volume, *Progress of Female Virtue and Female Dissipation*, which contained a set of aquatint engravings by Maria Cosway, in a letter to his daughter Martha Jefferson Randolph, October 7, 1804. *Family Letters*, 262. He had seen a magazine account.

18. This gossip was reported in Williamson, *Richard Cosway*, 28, 49.

19. Jefferson to Abigail Adams, August 9, 1786, *Papers*, Boyd, X, 202.

20. Jefferson to John Jay, January 11, 1789, *Papers*, Boyd, XIV, 430.

21. Jefferson to Maria Cosway, October 12, 1786. See Appendix II.

22. Maria Cosway to Allan Cunningham, Lodi, Italy, May 24, 1830, Williamson, *Richard Cosway*, 17.

23. Maria Cosway to Allan Cunningham, Williamson, *Richard Cosway*, and Maria Cosway to M. Chambers, July 11, 1816, Maria Cosway Papers, Lodi, Italy.

24. Williamson, *Richard Cosway*, 18.

25. Jefferson to Maria Cosway, October 12, 1786. See Appendix II.

26. Jefferson's visits can be reconstructed by a careful checking of his account book, his October 12, 1786, letter to Maria Cosway, and *Autobiography of Colonel John Trumbull, Patriot-Artist, 1756–1843*, Theodore Sizer, ed. (New Haven, 1953). The Cosway friendships in Paris were detailed in Williamson, *Richard Cosway*. D'Hancarville, whom Jefferson referred to as Mr. Danquerville, was a classical archaeologist and antiquarian who in 1785 had published a book on Greek art, notable for its sophistication in relating art to ancient religious phallic worship. *Recherches sur l'origine, l'esprit et les progrès des arts de la Grèce; sur leurs connections avec les arts et la religion des plus anciens peuple connus . . .* (London, 1785). His letters to Maria Cosway may be seen in the Museo Circo, Lodi, Italy. Only one of Jefferson's original letters to Maria Cosway was preserved. See *Papers*, Boyd, X, 432n. The others published by Julian Boyd and Helen Bullock are taken from Jefferson's own press copies, preserved by his heirs. The envelope addressed to Richard Cosway, Stratford Place, London, in Jefferson's hand, along with Trumbull's portrait of Jefferson, are in the Collegio di Maria SS. Bambina, Lodi, Italy. See *Papers*, Boyd, X, xxxix, 466.

27. Jefferson's account book includes the following: September 7, "pd seeing Machine of Marly 6 f the chateau 6 f Pd Petit towards dinner at Marly 12f pd at Lowechienne f"; September 8, "pd at Concert Spiritual 6 f"; September 9, "pd. seeing Gardes marbles 12f"; September 14, "pd seeing machine 3 f"; September 16, "pd seeing Desert 12 f."

28. Jefferson to Maria Cosway, October 12, 1786. See Appendix II.
29. Jefferson to Abigail Adams, August 9, 1786, *Papers*, Boyd, X, 203.
30. Jefferson to William Stephens Smith, August 9, 1786, *Papers*, Boyd, X, 213.
31. Jefferson to George Wythe, August 13, 1786, *Papers*, Boyd, X, 244.
32. *Writings*, L. and B., XVIII, 438. In 1785 Jefferson had purchased a twenty-two-volume set of Bell's English poets (account book, October 13, 1785). His "Thoughts on English Prosody," mistakenly dated by editors Lipscomb and Bergh as having been written in 1789, was actually written between August and September 18, 1786, as Julian Boyd has pointed out. Some of the revisions were written with Jefferson's left hand, after the dislocation or breaking of his wrist September 18, 1786. See *Papers*, Boyd, X, 498n. See also Jefferson to Chastellux, October 1786, *Papers*, Boyd, X, 498.
33. *Writings*, L. and B., XVIII, 426, 430, 434.
34. *Writings*, L. and B., XVIII, 443.
35. Maria Cosway to Jefferson, February 15, 1787, *Papers*, Boyd, XI, 148–49. The letter was delivered to Jefferson personally by d'Hancarville, *Papers*, Boyd, XI, 150n.
36. Maria Cosway to Jefferson, February 15, 1787, *Papers*, Boyd, XI, 149.
37. Schachner, *Jefferson*, 317; Thomas Fleming, *The Man from Monticello: An Intimate Life of Thomas Jefferson* (New York, 1969), 136; Peterson, *Jefferson and the New Nation*, 348; Jordan, *White over Black*, 462; Saul Padover, *Jefferson* (New York, 1942), 140; Dixon Wecter, *The Hero in America* (New York, 1945), 154; Malone, *Jefferson and the Rights of Man*, 72.
38. Kimball, *Jefferson: The Scene of Europe*, 159.
39. See Fawn M. Brodie, "Jefferson Biographers and the Psychology of Canonization," *Journal of Interdisciplinary History*, II (1971), 155–71.
40. Jefferson to William Stephens Smith, October 22, 1786, *Papers*, Boyd, X, 478. Lyman Butterfield discovered a letter among the papers of William Temple Franklin which established the date and place of the accident. Le Veillard wrote to Franklin September 20, 1786, "Day before yesterday Mr. Jefferson dislocated his right wrist when attempting to jump over a fence in the 'Petit Cours.' " See Lyman Butterfield and Howard C. Rice, "Jefferson's Earliest Note to Maria Cosway with Some New Facts and Conjectures on His Broken Wrist," *William and Mary Quarterly*, 3rd series, V (1948), 26–33, 620–21. *Papers*, Boyd, X, 432n.
41. Quoted in Randall, *Jefferson*, I, 456.
42. Maria Cosway to Jefferson, September 20, 1786, *Papers*, Boyd, X, 393.
43. Kimball, *Jefferson: The Scene of Europe*, 168–69; Malone, *Jefferson and the Rights of Man*, 72, 74.
44. Maria Cosway to Jefferson, October 5, 1786, *Papers*, Boyd, X, 433.
45. *Ibid.*
46. Jefferson to Maria Cosway, October 12, 1786. See Appendix II.
47. *Ibid.*
48. Jefferson to Maria Cosway, October 5, 1786, *Papers*, Boyd, X, 431–32.
49. Jefferson to Maria Cosway, October 12, 1786. See Appendix II.
50. *Papers*, Boyd, X, 453n. Balzac also left copies of his love letters.
51. *Papers*, Boyd, X, 453n; Peterson, *Jefferson and the New Nation*, 349.
52. Jefferson to Maria Cosway, October 12, 1786. See Appendix II.
53. Maria Cosway to Jefferson, October 9, 1786, *Papers*, Boyd, X, 441. This note is in Italian, appended to a letter by John Trumbull. Boyd gives the original and a translation. Several scholars have mistakenly believed that this four-line note was Maria Cosway's reply to the twelve-page letter from Jefferson, "My Head and My Heart."
54. Jefferson to Maria Cosway, October 13, 1786, *Papers*, Boyd, X, 458–59.
55. Jefferson to John Trumbull, October 13, 1786, *Papers*, Boyd, X, 460.
56. Jefferson to John Trumbull, February 23, 1787, August 26, 1788, *Papers*, Boyd, XI, 181, XIII, 546.
57. "I very much regret the loss of these twenty days," Trumbull wrote, ". . . I

distinctly recollect, however . . . that Mr. Jefferson joined our party almost daily; and here commenced his acquaintance with Mrs. Cosway, of whom very respectful mention is made in his published correspondence." Trumbull, *Autobiography*, 120.
    58. Maria Cosway to Jefferson, October 30, 1786, *Papers*, Boyd, X, 494–96. Julian Boyd filled in what he believed might have been the original words, in the holes gnawed by mice or rats, and he translated the Italian.
    59. Williamson, *Richard Cosway*, 44, 49.
    60. Maria Cosway to Jefferson, November 17, 1786, translated from the Italian, *Papers*, Boyd, X, 538–39.
    61. Jefferson to Maria Cosway, November 19, 1786, *Papers*, Boyd, X, 542.
    62. Jefferson to Maria Cosway, November 29, 1786, *Papers*, Boyd, X, 555.
    63. Jefferson to Eliza House Trist, December 15, 1786, *Papers*, Boyd, X, 600.
    64. Jefferson to Maria Cosway, December 24, 1786, *Papers*, Boyd, X, 627.
    65. Jefferson to Madame de Tessé, March 20, 1787, *Papers*, Boyd, XI, 226.
    66. Jefferson to Maria Cosway, July 1, 1787, *Papers*, Boyd, XI, 520.
    67. Maria Cosway to Jefferson, July 9, 1787, *Papers*, Boyd, XI, 569.

CHAPTER XVI   The Second Interlude

    1. Jefferson to Mary Jefferson Bolling, July 23, 1787, *Papers*, Boyd, XI, 612.
    2. Reminiscences of Isaac, in *Jefferson at Monticello*, 4.
    3. Randall to James Parton, June 1, 1868, in Milton E. Flower, *James Parton: The Father of Modern Biography* (Durham, N.C., 1951), 236–42.
    4. Jefferson to Francis Eppes, August 30, 1785, *Papers*, Boyd, VIII, 451.
    5. John Wayles Eppes to Jefferson, May 22, 1786, *Papers*, Boyd, IX, 560.
    6. Martha Jefferson Carr mentioned the pregnancy of Isabel in a letter to Jefferson, January 2, 1787, *Papers*, Boyd, XV, 633. Francis Eppes to Jefferson, April 14, 1787, *Papers*, Boyd, XV, 636. (Supplementary Documents.) Jefferson used the word "quarteron" in a letter of December 23, 1793, *Writings*, L. and B., IX, 276.
    7. Elizabeth Eppes to Jefferson, May 7, 1787, *Papers*, Boyd, XV, 637.
    8. Francis Eppes to Jefferson, April 11, 1786, *Papers*, Boyd, XV, 625.
    9. As Jefferson described it to his sister, Mary Jefferson Bolling, July 23, 1787, *Papers*, Boyd, XI, 612.
    10. Abigail Adams to Jefferson, June 27, July 6, 1787, *Papers*, Boyd, XI, 502, 551.
    11. Abigail Adams to Jefferson, June 27, 1787, *Papers*, Boyd, XI, 503.
    12. Abigail Adams to Jefferson, July 10, September 10, 1787, *Papers*, Boyd, XI, 573, XII, 112.
    13. Jefferson to Abigail Adams, July 1, 1787, *Papers*, Boyd, XI, 515.
    14. Maria Cosway to Jefferson, July 9, 1787, *Papers*, Boyd, XI, 569.
    15. Abigail Adams to Jefferson, July 6, 1787, *Papers*, Boyd, XI, 551–52; John Adams to Jefferson, July 10, 1787, *Papers*, Boyd, XI, 575.
    16. Jefferson to Abigail Adams, July 16, 1787, *Papers*, Boyd, XI, 592; Jefferson to Elizabeth Eppes, July 28, 1787, *Papers*, Boyd, XI, 634.
    17. The SJL indicates that several letters to his sisters and sister-in-law have not been found.
    18. *Jefferson at Monticello*, 5.
    19. Jefferson to Nicholas Lewis, September 17, 1787, *Papers*, Boyd, XII, 135.
    20. Jefferson to Mary Jefferson Bolling, July 23, 1787, *Papers*, Boyd, XI, 612.
    21. Jefferson to George Gilmer, August 12, 1787, *Papers*, Boyd, XII, 26.
    22. Jefferson to Edward Rutledge, July 14, 1787, *Papers*, Boyd, XI, 559.
    23. Jefferson to Francis Eppes, July 30, 1787, *Papers*, Boyd, XI, 652–53.
    24. *Ibid.*, 653.
    25. Jefferson to Nicholas Lewis, July 11, 1788, *Papers*, Boyd, XIII, 343.
    26. Jefferson to Antonio Giannini, February 5, 1786, *Papers*, Boyd, IX, 254.
    27. Antonio Giannini to Jefferson, June 10, 1786, *Papers*, Boyd, IX, 624n.

28. Jefferson to Peter Carr, August 10, 1787, *Papers*, Boyd, XII, 14–18.
29. Jefferson to Madison, October 8, 1787, Jefferson to John Jay, October 8, 1787, *Papers*, Boyd, XII, 219, 217.
30. Madison to Jefferson, December 8, 1788, *Papers*, Boyd, XIV, 340–41.
31. Bullock, *My Head and My Heart*, 78.
32. Jefferson to Maria Cosway, April 24, 1788, XIII, 104.
33. Schachner, *Jefferson*, 352; Peterson, *Jefferson and the New Nation*, 349; Fleming, *The Man from Monticello*, 142; Malone, *Jefferson and the Rights of Man*, 138–39, 81.
34. September 12, "pd expences at St. Germain 4/4"; September 25, "pd Petit 6 f."; September 28, "pd Petit 27 f."; September 29, "pd Petit 24 charity 6"; September 30, "pd at Kings Garden 18f."
35. Trumbull to Jefferson, September 17, 1787, *Papers*, Boyd, XII, 139.
36. Jefferson to Trumbull, October 4, 1787, *Papers*, Boyd, XII, 206–7.
37. "I am afraid to question my Lord and Master on this subject," she would write concerning a third visit to Paris, April 29, 1788, *Papers*, Boyd, XIII, 115.
38. Jefferson described the muscles as "losing rather than gaining in point of suppleness," in a letter to Dr. George Gilmer, August 12, 1787, *Papers*, Boyd, XII, 26.
39. Jefferson to Trumbull, November 13, 1787, *Papers*, Boyd, XII, 358.
40. Maria Cosway to Jefferson, April 29, 1788, *Papers*, Boyd, XIII, 115.
41. Jefferson to Trumbull, November 13, 1787, *Papers*, Boyd, XII, 358.
42. Jefferson to Maria Cosway, January 31, 1788, *Papers*, Boyd, XII, 540.
43. Maria Cosway to Jefferson, December 1, 1787, *Papers*, Boyd, XII, 387. It is undated and unsigned, endorsed by Jefferson, "Cosway Maria."
44. Jefferson to Madame de Corny, October 18, 1787, *Papers*, Boyd, XII, 246. Jefferson arranged to rent the apartment on September 5, 1787, and paid 60 francs on October 12, 1787.
45. Maria Cosway to Jefferson, December 1, 1787, *Papers*, Boyd, XII, 387. This was followed by the postscript concerning William Short, already quoted.
46. Maria Cosway to Jefferson, December 10, 1787, *Papers*, Boyd, XII, 415.
47. Maria Cosway to Jefferson, December 7, 1787, *Papers*, Boyd, XII, 403.
48. Maria Cosway to Jefferson, December 10, 1787, *Papers*, Dec. 25, 1787, April 29, 1788, *Papers*, Boyd, XII, 415, 459, XIII, 115.
49. Julian Boyd states that she went off with Marchesi in September 1790, *Papers*, XVI, 551. Maria Cosway wrote of her admiration for Marchesi, "the Most wonderfull Singer I ever heard," in a letter to Jefferson on April 29, 1788, *Papers*, Boyd, XIII, 115. See also Horace Walpole, *Works*, W. S. Lewis, ed., XI, 285n; and *Grove's Dictionary of Music and Musicians*, H. C. Colles, ed., III, 318.
50. Williamson, *Richard Cosway*, 50–51.
51. The Trumbull portrait, which remained unknown to Jefferson scholars until 1952, is reproduced in Boyd's edition of the Jefferson Papers, X, 466, along with a similar portrait Trumbull made at the same time for Angelica Church. See Elizabeth Cometti, "Maria Cosway's Rediscovered Miniature of Jefferson," *William and Mary Quarterly*, 3rd series, IX (1952), 152–55.
52. The envelope is addressed to Stratford Place, to which the Cosways had been forced to move from the expensive Shomberg House after Cosway fell into disfavor in the eyes of the Prince of Wales, who disapproved of his sympathy with the French Revolution. The original is in Lodi. The originals of Jefferson's letters to Maria have disappeared, but Jefferson scholars are hopeful they may surface in Ireland, where Maria's sister finally settled.
53. Maria Cosway to Jefferson, December 25, 1787, *Papers*, Boyd, XII, 459–60. One-third of the last leaf of the letter is missing.
54. Jefferson to Maria Cosway, January 31, 1788, *Papers*, Boyd, XII, 539–40.
55. Williamson, *Richard Cosway*, 30.

CHAPTER XVII   Sally Hemings

1. Jefferson to Madison, September 6, 1789, *Papers*, Boyd, XV, 396.
2. *Pike County Republican*, March 13, 1873. See Appendix I.
3. Her father, John Wayles, had died May 28, 1773, as recorded in Jefferson's account book on May 31. Born the year of his death, Sally had lived for a time at the Elkhill plantation (*Farm Book*, 18), and had come with her mother to Monticello before 1776. The *Farm Book* frequently lists Sally's name with the year of her birth, '73, after it.
4. "Notes of a Tour through Holland and the Rhine Valley," *Papers*, Boyd, XIII, 8–33. See especially 17, 19–20, 22, 24–25, 28–29.
5. "Notes of a Tour into the Southern Parts of France, &c," *Papers*, Boyd, XI, 415–63. Freud noted that many landscapes in dreams, especially wooded hills, were often symbols for the female body. *Complete Psychological V Works*, (1900–1901), part 2, 356.
6. "Notes of a Tour through Holland and the Rhine Valley, *Papers*, Boyd, XIII, 27. Freud noted the phallic symbolism, in dreams, of "ploughs, hammers, rifles, revolvers, daggers, etc." *Complete Psychological Works*, V, part 2, 356.
7. Jefferson to Charles Willson Peale, April 17, 1813 (film, University of Virginia, Case M, Reel 50 B).
8. Jefferson to Robert Fulton, April 16, 1810, *Writings*, L. and B., XIX, 173. Jefferson to St. John Sinclair, March 23, 1798, *Garden Book*, 653.
9. Maria Cosway to Jefferson, March 6, 1788, *Papers*, Boyd, XII, 645.
10. Jefferson to Maria Cosway, April 24, 1788, *Papers*, Boyd, XIII, 103–4. Trumbull had urged Jefferson to visit the Düsseldorf gallery, though he held Adriaen van der Werff's paintings in contempt, describing them as "mere monuments of labor, patience, and want of genius." Trumbull, *Autobiography*, 137. A copy of the Düsseldorf museum catalogue may be seen today among Maria Cosway's papers in the library of the Collegio di Maria SS. Bambina, Lodi, Italy.
11. When I first pointed out the relationship between "Agar" and Sally Hemings in "The Great Jefferson Taboo," *American Heritage*, XXIII (June 1972), 53–54, John Maass traced the present location of the Adriaen van der Werff painting to a museum in Franconia, Bavaria. It was he who first pointed out the similarity in hair styles between that of Hagar and Sally Hemings, and the similarity in window styles between those in the painting and those at Monticello. See Maass, "Postscripts to History," *American Heritage*, XXIV (December, 1972), 111.
12. Jefferson to Maria Cosway, April 24, 1788, *Papers*, Boyd, XIII, 104.
13. Maria Cosway to Jefferson, April 29, 1788, *Papers*, Boyd, XIII, 115.
14. Jefferson to Maria Cosway, January 14, 1789, *Papers*, Boyd, XIV, 446.
15. Buffon, *Natural History*, 10 vols. in 5 (London, 1792), IX, 149–77. Buffon described the confusion of scholars such as Linnaeus, M. Noel, M. de la Broff, and Edward Tyson as to whether the orangutan was a great ape or a wild man, but himself added to the wild inaccuracies of the period.
16. *Notes on the State of Virginia*, 138.
17. *Frederick-Town Herald*, reprinted in the *Richmond Recorder*, September 29, 1802. See p. 352.
18. Julian Boyd summarized the letter and reproduced most of it in the original French, *Papers*, XIV, 426. The Missouri Historical Society kindly furnished me a copy.
19. Account book, 1788–89.
20. James A. Bear, Jr., who transcribed the account books at the University of Virginia, describes Madame Dupré in his index as "Sally Hemings's Paris landlady." The delay of a year in making the payment was not unusual for Jefferson.
21. *Papers*, Boyd, VI, viii.

22. *Papers*, Boyd, XII, 655n. One example of a letter to Patsy which exists in the original and in the press copy, May 21, 1787, may be seen in *Papers*, Boyd, XI, 370.
23. There are eleven letters from John Hemings to Jefferson presently in the University of Virginia Library.
24. According to Madison Hemings. See Appendix I.
25. Jefferson to Paul Bentalou, August 25, 1786, *Papers*, Boyd, X, 296.
26. Jefferson to Edward Bancroft, January 26, 1789, *Papers*, Boyd, XIV, 492-93, mistakenly dated 1788. It is a reply to Bancroft's letter of September 16, 1788.
27. *Papers*, Boyd, XI, 98n, 99n, 297-98.
28. See "Jefferson's Notes from Condorcet on Slavery," January 1789, *Papers*, Boyd, XIV, 494-98; Jefferson to Brissot de Warville, February 11, 1788, *Papers*, Boyd, XII, 577-78.
29. See p. 290.
30. See Martha Jefferson to Jefferson, April 9, 1787, *Family Letters*, 37.
31. Martha Jefferson to Jefferson, March 25, 1787, *Family Letters*, 34.
32. Jefferson to Martha Jefferson, March 28, 1787, *Family Letters*, 35.
33. Jefferson to Martha Jefferson, May 21, 1787, *Family Letters*, 41-42.
34. Martha Jefferson to Jefferson, May 3, 1787, *Family Letters*, 39.
35. *Ibid.*
36. *Papers*, Boyd, XIV, xxxvi. Boyd reproduces the portrait made for Martha Jefferson in XIV, 328. The portraits made for Maria Cosway and Angelica Church are reproduced in X, 467.
37. The original source, Melville, *John Carroll of Baltimore*, gives the date of the Dugnani letter as July 5, 1787. But since he speaks of Jefferson's planning to take both daughters home, and gives Patsy's age as sixteen, the letter could have been written only in 1788. Polly did not arrive in Paris until July 15, 1787. See *Papers*, Boyd, XIV, 356n, who gives a portion of the original letter.
38. Randall, *Jefferson*, I, 538.
39. Martha Jefferson to Jefferson, April 9, 1787, *Family Letters*, 37-38. Martha may have been especially impressed by this story because her own father had been married just ten years.
40. Jefferson to Elizabeth Eppes, December 15, 1788, *Papers*, Boyd, XIV, 355.
41. See especially Peterson, *Jefferson and the New Nation*, 370-89, Malone, *Jefferson and the Rights of Man*, 180-237.
42. Jefferson to Anne Willing Bingham, May 11, 1788, *Papers*, Boyd, XIII, 151.
43. Jefferson to A. Donald, February 7, 1788, *Papers*, Boyd, XII, 572.
44. *Papers*, Boyd, XIII, 269.
45. Jefferson to Anne Willing Bingham, May 11, 1788, *Papers*, Boyd, XIII, 152.
46. Jefferson to Maria Cosway, May 21, 1789, *Papers*, Boyd, XV, 142-43.
47. See *Papers*, Boyd, XIV, 356n.
48. Randall, *Jefferson*, I, 538. Jefferson's account book for April 20, 1789, reads, "paid at Panthemont in full 625-15-2."
49. Julian Boyd dates this charming portrait, which shows Martha Jefferson at seventeen, with reddish hair, blue eyes, and cream-colored dress, as having been made in the spring of 1789. There are no letters to Boze, and the account book indicates no payment to him. The portrait is reproduced by Boyd in *Papers*, XIV, 361. See also XIV, xli.
50. Sarah Randolph, *Domestic Life*, 146.
51. See Appendix I.
52. *Autobiography*, 108.
53. Jefferson to Madison, July 22, 1789, *Papers*, Boyd, XV, 299-300.
54. *Autobiography*, 108.
55. Jefferson to William Stephens Smith, Adams' son-in-law, November 13, 1787, *Papers*, Boyd, XII, 356.
56. Rumsey to Benjamin West, March 20, 1789, Rumsey to Charles Morrow, March 27, 1789, quoted in *Papers*, Boyd, XV, 81n, 82n.

57. See Jefferson to Lafayette, June 3, 1789, and his "Draft of a Charter of Rights," *Papers*, Boyd, XV, 165–68.

58. Jefferson to Willliam Carmichael, August 9, 1789; Jefferson to John Mason, July 17, 1789, *Papers*, Boyd, XV, 338, 278.

59. Maria Cosway to Jefferson, December 23, 1788, *Papers*, Boyd, XIV, 372.

60. Jefferson to Maria Cosway, January 14, 1789, *Papers*, Boyd, XIV, 446.

61. Jefferson to Maria Cosway, May 21, 1789, *Papers*, Boyd, XV, 143.

62. Jefferson to Maria Cosway, October 14, 1789, *Papers*, Boyd, XV, 521.

63. Madison to Jefferson, May 27, 1789, *Papers*, Boyd, XV, 153.

64. Jefferson to Madison, August 29, 1789, *Papers*, Boyd, XV, 369.

65. "List of Baggage Shipped by Jefferson from France," *Papers*, Boyd, XV, 375.

66. Jefferson to Trumbull, May 21, 1789, *Papers*, Boyd, XV, 143–44.

67. Jefferson to Trumbull, September 9, 1789, *Papers*, Boyd, XV, 407.

68. See Appendix I.

69. Jefferson to James Maurice, September 16, 1789, *Papers*, Boyd, XV, 433.

70. Jefferson to Madison, January 13, 1821, *Papers*, Boyd, XIV, 359n. Mazzei, who had known Dr. Gem for thirty-two years, described him as *"un des meilleurs hommes du monde et veritable philosophe," Papers*, Boyd, XV, 385n.

71. Peterson, *Jefferson and the New Nation*, 383–84.

72. Jefferson to Madison, September 6, 1789, *Papers*, Boyd, XV, 392–97. Actually Jefferson delayed sending it to Madison until January 9, 1790, at which time he made numerous small changes.

73. Jefferson to Lafayette, April 2, 1790, *Papers*, Boyd, XVI, 293.

CHAPTER XVIII   The Revolutionary Goes Home

1. Jefferson to William Short, October 3, 1801, *Writings*, L. and B., X, 286.

2. *Ibid.*, 284–85.

3. Madison wrote to Washington January 4, 1790, "I was sorry to find him so little biassed in favor of the domestic service allotted to him . . . ," Madison, *Writings*, Hunt, ed., I, 501.

4. Randall, *Jefferson*, I, 551.

5. Jefferson to William Short, December 14, 1789, *Papers*, Boyd, XVI, 28.

6. Jefferson to Washington, December 15, 1789, *Papers*, Boyd, XVI, 34–35.

7. Jefferson to Nicholas Lewis, December 16, 1788, written when he thought he would be home in May of 1789, *Papers*, Boyd, XIV, 362.

8. First published in George Tucker, *Life*, I, 301–2, from a manuscript transcribed by Anne Cary Randolph, dated by Julian Boyd as 1828–29. Wormley, a house slave who saw the homecoming as a boy, supported Martha Jefferson's description. See Randall, *Jefferson*, I, 551–53, and *Papers*, Boyd, XVI, 169n.

9. "Slaves and Slavery," *Farm Book* [15]. Robert was freed December 24, 1794, and James February 5, 1796. Jefferson's account book, February 26, 1796, notes: "gave James Hemings on his emancipation to bear exp. to Phila 30.D."

10. See Appendix I. Madison Hemings, who was not born until 1805, said this child died in infancy. Here he is confusing this child with Sally's two daughters, Edy and the first Harriet, who died in infancy in 1795 and 1796. It seems likely that "Tom Hemings" had either left Monticello by 1805 or shortly after, and that Madison had no knowledge of him because of the secrecy surrounding his possible "passing" into the white society. See pp. 291–92, 531–32 for a fuller account.

11. See pp. 352–53.

12. Randall to James Parton, June 1, 1868, in Flower, *James Parton: The Father of Modern Biography*, 237, reproduced here in Appendix III. Randolph believed, however, that the children of Sally Hemings were fathered by Peter or Samuel Carr.

13. June 8, 1808. June 4, 1806, has the notation, "left in my drawer at Monticello in small money 16.30."

14. See Appendix I.
15. Jefferson to Martha Jefferson Randolph, December 4, 1791, December 13, 1792, *Family Letters*, 91, 107. For Israel Jefferson's account of the gift-giving, see Appendix I, part 2.
16. Winthrop Jordan, *White over Black*, 145-47.
17. Thomas Shippen to William Shippen, September 15, 1790, *Papers*, Boyd, XVII, 464-65.
18. See Randall to James Parton, June 1, 1868, in Flower, *James Parton*, 237. For a discussion of the allegation of Jefferson's grandchildren that Sally Hemings' children were actually fathered by Peter and Samuel Carr see pp. 493-98.
19. Jefferson to Elizabeth Eppes, December 15, 1788, *Papers*, Boyd, XIV, 355; Randall, *Jefferson*, I, 558.
20. Jefferson, *Autobiography*, 117.
21. Randall, *Jefferson*, I, 558.
22. Jefferson to Madame de Corny, April 2, 1790, *Papers*, Boyd, XVI, 290.
23. March 11, 1790, *Papers*, Boyd, XVI, 225.
24. Jefferson to Martha Jefferson Randolph, April 4, 1790, *Family Letters*, 51.
25. Martha Jefferson Randolph to Jefferson, April 25, 1790, *Family Letters*, 53.
26. Ellen Randolph Coolidge later described this as a most unwise second marriage, where the second wife succeeded in alienating Randolph from all his children by his first wife. Because of her Randolph made property settlements which left his five younger children nearly destitute, and the burden of supporting them fell upon Martha's new husband. Ellen Coolidge memoirs, Ms., University of Virginia Library.
27. Jefferson to Martha Jefferson Randolph, July 17, 1790, *Family Letters*, 60-61.
28. *Jefferson at Monticello*, 16.
29. Jefferson to Madame d'Houdetot, April 2, 1790, *Papers*, Boyd, XVI, 292.
30. Lucy Ludwell Paradise to Jefferson, March 2, 1790, *Papers*, Boyd, XVI, 198.
31. *Papers*, Boyd, XVI, 602-17.
32. Jefferson to Thomas Cooper, October 27, 1808, *Writings*, L. and B., XII, 180.
33. Maria Cosway to Jefferson, April 6, 1790, *Papers*, Boyd, XVI, 312.
34. Maria Cosway to M. Chambers, May 29, 1816, Maria Cosway Letterbook, Lodi, Italy.
35. Jefferson to Maria Cosway, June 23, 1790, *Papers*, Boyd, XVI, 550-51.
36. Walpole to Mary Berry, June 1791, Walpole, *Works*, XI, 285. Maria Cosway remembered their estrangement in a letter of March 22, 1815: "You changed more and more daily. No more regard, affection, or consideration you must remember our conversations were always *disputes*. I confess my weakness in not being able to bear it." Maria Cosway Letterbook, Lodi, Italy.
37. Maria Cosway to Richard Cosway, March 1, 1793, Maria Cosway Letterbook, Lodi, Italy. Maria Cosway's brother was an artist and architect. Jefferson helped secure him employment with William Thornton and E. S. Hallet, who helped design the Capitol. Henry Russell Hitchcock, *Architecture, Nineteenth and Twentieth Centuries* (Baltimore, 1958), 6.
38. Maria Cosway to Jefferson, November 13, November 24, 1794, Bullock, *My Head and My Heart*, 140-41.
39. Williamson, *Richard Cosway*, 23, 57.
40. When William Hazlitt was in Paris in 1803, he saw Maria Cosway strolling down a Paris street on the arm of Lucien Bonaparte. Ralph M. Wardle, *Hazlitt* (Lincoln, Nebr., 1971), 74.
41. Williamson, *Richard Cosway*, 53. After Cosway's death of a paralytic stroke in 1821, Maria held an exhibition of his paintings and drawings, taking pains to send several of the best to their former patron and friend, now King George IV. She wrote to Frances Douce on April 21, 1822, "Nobody came, and I have made an expence. . . . The King returned *all* I sent." Douce Mss. XXIV, no. 32, Bodleian Library, Oxford.
42. Jefferson to Maria Jefferson, June 13, 1790, *Family Letters*, 58-59.
43. Jefferson to Martha Jefferson Randolph, January 14, 1793, *Family Letters*, 109.

44. Madame de Corny to Jefferson, July 23, 1790, *Papers*, Boyd, XVII, 259.
45. Kimball, *Jefferson: The Scene of Europe*, 111. In addition he had ordered Petit to send pairs of Angora cats, Angora goats, Bantam fowl, skylarks, and red-legged partridges, quantities of macaroni, Parmesan cheese, and "Vinaigre d'Estragon." Eventually he persuaded Petit himself to join him in the New World. *Papers*, Boyd, XVI, 322.
46. Jefferson to James Monroe, April 17, 1791, *Writings*, Ford, V, 318.
47. Jefferson to Martha Jefferson Randolph, April 28, 1793, *Family Letters*, 116.
48. Martha Jefferson Randolph to Jefferson, May 16, 1793, *Family Letters*, 118.

CHAPTER XIX   The Satellite Sons

1. Jefferson to Dr. Walter Jones, March 5, 1810, *Writings*, L. and B., XII, 371.
2. Flexner, *Washington and the New Nation*, 414.
3. Adams to Henry Knox, March 30, 1797, *Life and Works*, VIII, 536, quoted in Malone, *Jefferson and the Ordeal of Liberty*, 299.
4. See especially Richard Hofstadter, *The Idea of a Party System: The Rise of Legitimate Opposition in the United States, 1780–1840* (Berkeley, Cal., 1969); Joseph Charles, *The Origins of the American Party System* (Williamsburg, Va., 1951); John C. Miller, *The Federalist Era*; Noble E. Cunningham, Jr., *The Jeffersonian Republicans: The Formation of Party Organization, 1789–1801* (Chapel Hill, N.C., 1957).
5. Jefferson to Martha Jefferson Randolph, May 16, 1790, *Family Letters*, 56; Jefferson to Madison, July 29, 1789, *Papers*, Boyd, XV, 316.
6. Abigail Adams to Mary Cranch, *New Letters of Abigail Adams 1788–1801*, Stewart Mitchell, ed. (Boston, 1947), 49.
7. Quoted by Adrienne Koch, "Hamilton and Power," in *Alexander Hamilton: A Profile*, Jacob E. Cooke, ed. (New York, 1967), 225.
8. *Records of the Federal Convention*, Max Ferrand, ed. (New Haven, 1911), I, 388–89.
9. Koch, "Hamilton and Power," in *Alexander Hamilton*, Cooke, ed., 225.
10. Miller, *The Federalist Era*, 8.
11. Adams to Jefferson, October 9, 1787, *Papers*, Boyd, XII, 220–21.
12. *Anas*, *Writings*, L. and B., I, 287.
13. Adams to Jefferson, January 2, 1789, *Papers*, Boyd, XIV, 411.
14. Adams, *Life and Works*, VI, 228–403.
15. Jefferson to Francis Hopkinson, March 13, 1789, *Papers*, Boyd, XIV, 650. See also Hofstadter, *The Idea of a Party System*.
16. Adams' note, dated 1812, published with *Davila*, *Life and Works*, VI, 227.
17. See especially his letter to William Short, January 8, 1825, describing the large dinner parties in New York in 1790, *Writings*, Ford, XII, 395.
18. Reproduced in *Papers*, Boyd, XVI, 261–62.
19. Jefferson to Sir John Sinclair, August 24, 1791, *Writings*, L. and B., VIII, 231.
20. Jefferson to Washington, May 8, 1791, *Writings*, L. and B., VIII, 192–93.
21. Jefferson to Adams, July 17, 1791, *Adams-Jefferson Letters*, 246.
22. Adams to Jefferson, July 29, 1791, *Adams-Jefferson Letters*, 248.
23. John Adams to Abigail Adams, December 26, 1792, Page Smith, *John Adams*, II, 833.
24. Abigail Adams to Mary Cranch, April 3, 1790, *New Letters*, 44.
25. Jefferson to Madison, January 22, 1797, *Writings*, L. and B., IX, 367.
26. *Anas*, *Writings*, L. and B., I, 287–88.
27. Peterson, *Jefferson and the New Nation*, 516.
28. Jefferson to Martha Jefferson Randolph, January 15, 1792, *Family Letters*, 93.
29. Martha Jefferson Randolph to Jefferson, February 20, 1792, *Family Letters*, 94.
30. Jefferson to Martha Jefferson Randolph, March 22, 1792, *Family Letters*, 96.

31. Martha Jefferson Randolph to Jefferson, February 27, 1793, *Family Letters*, 112.

32. Jefferson to Madison, June 9, 1793, *Writings*, L. and B., IX, 118-19.

33. John Adams to Benjamin Rush, September 1807, *The Spur of Fame: Dialogues of John Adams and Benjamin Rush, 1805-1813*, John A. Schultz and Douglass Adair, eds. (San Marino, Calif., 1966), 93.

34. Hamilton, *Papers*, Harold Syrett et al., eds., 17 vols. (New York, 1961-73), XI, 439.

35. William Loughton Smith, under the pseudonym "Scourge," *Gazette of the United States*, September 22, 1792.

36. Nathan Schachner, *Alexander Hamilton* (New York, 1946), 5, 106, 17. The name was variously spelled Levine, Lawein, and Lavien.

37. Adams to Benjamin Rush, January 25, 1806. *Spur of Fame*, 48.

38. At seventeen Hamilton published an article in the *Royal Danish American Gazette* describing the hurricane that devastated St. Croix September 6, 1772. It has autobiographical overtones: "See tender infancy pinched with hunger and hanging on the mother's knee for food! See the unhappy mother's anxiety. Her poverty denies relief, her breast heaves with pangs of maternal pity, her heart is bursting, the tears gush down her cheeks. Oh sights of woe! O distress unspeakable! My heart bleeds, but I have no power to solace." Hamilton, *Papers*, Syrett, ed., I, 34ff.

39. "Protocol of the Dealing Court in Christianstadt, August 3, 1768," quoted in Gertrude Atherton, *A Few of Hamilton's Letters* (New York, 1903), xvi.

40. Schachner, *Alexander Hamilton*, 10-13.

41. Hamilton to Edward Carrington, May 26, 1792, *Papers*, Syrett, ed., XI, 440.

42. Hamilton, *Works*, Henry Cabot Lodge, ed., 12 vols. (New York, 1904), X, 356-57.

43. *Anas*, *Writings*, L. and B., I, 318.

44. *Writings*, Ford, IX, 296.

45. Conversation with Washington, February 28, 1792, *Anas*, *Writings*, L. and B., I, 286.

46. Jefferson to Thomas Mann Randolph, March 16, 1792, Library of Congress, 12478; see also John C. Miller, *Alexander Hamilton and the Growth of the New Nation* (New York, 1959), 305.

47. *Anas*, *Writings*, L. and B., I, 353.

48. July 25, August 11, 1792, Hamilton, *Papers*, Syrett, ed., XII, 124, 189, 194.

49. See Miller, *Hamilton and the Growth of the New Nation*, 349-50.

50. Washington to Hamilton, August 26, 1792, Hamilton, *Papers*, Syrett, ed., XII, 277.

51. Washington to Jefferson, August 23, 1792, quoted in Randall, *Jefferson*, II, 77.

52. Hamilton to Washington, September 9, 1792; Hamilton, *Papers*, Syrett, ed., XII, 348.

53. Jefferson to Washington, September 9, 1792, *Writings*, L. and B., VIII, 395-407.

54. *Anas*, October 1, 1792, *Writings*, L. and B., I, 315-19; Washington to Jefferson, October 18, 1782, quoted in Randall, *Jefferson*, II, 92.

55. Hamilton, *Papers*, Syrett, ed., September 29, October 17, 1792, XII, 500-504.

56. *Ibid.*, September 29, 1792, XII, 504.

57. William Burwell memoir, Ms., Library of Congress.

58. Jefferson to David Humphreys, November 8, 1792, *Writings*, L. and B., VIII, 438.

59. *Anas*, February 20, 1793, *Writings*, L. and B., I, 336.

60. *Anas*, February 7, 1793, *Writings*, L. and B., I, 332.

61. James T. Callender, *Sketches of the History of America* (Philadelphia, 1798), chap. 5; Miller, *Hamilton and the Growth of the New Nation*, 333.

62. Reynolds pamphlet, August 31, 1797, Hamilton, *Papers*, Syrett, ed., X, 377n.

63. April, 1771, Hamilton, *Papers*, Syrett, ed., I, 6-7. Coelia comes from the Greek word meaning "belly" or "abdomen."

64. Schachner, *Alexander Hamilton*, 108.
65. Hamilton, *Papers*, Syrett, ed., X, 376, 379.
66. Maria Reynolds to Hamilton, written sometime between January 23 and March 18, 1792, Hamilton, *Papers*, Syrett, ed., X, 557.
67. For an account of Hamilton's visits and Reynolds' insistent demands for money, see *Papers*, Syrett, ed., X–XIII, up to August 30, 1792.
68. For an excellent account, see Miller, *Hamilton and the Growth of the New Nation*, 333–42.
69. Callender, *Sketches of the History of America*, 101–2. Callender wrote, "Mr. Jefferson had received a copy of these documents, and He never shewed them, nor ever spoke of them, to any person."
70. See pp. 535–36 for a discussion of Julian Boyd's new interpretation of the Maria Reynolds–Hamilton correspondence. Hamilton could not resist an oblique reference to his troubles when he wrote John Jay in December 1792 of "the malicious intrigues to stab me in the dark . . . [which] render my situation scarcely tolerable." *Papers*, Syrett, ed., XIII, 338.
71. Jefferson to Washington, September 9, 1792, *Writings*, L. and B., VIII, 407.
72. Jefferson to Martha Jefferson Randolph, January 26, 1793, *Family Letters*, 110.
73. Miller, *Hamilton and the Growth of the New Nation*, 331; Peterson, *Jefferson and the New Nation*, 476–79. Dumas Malone, *Jefferson and the Ordeal of Liberty*, 15–36, denies that Jefferson wrote the resolutions, but admits that he supported the inquiry.
74. Jefferson to Madison, January 22, 1797, recalling 1793, *Writings*, L. and B., IX, 368.
75. Jefferson to Madison, June 9, 1793, *Writings*, L. and B., IX, 119–20.
76. Samuel F. Bemis noted that when he resigned "the problems of American neutrality were mostly settled, aside from the question of neutral rights at sea." *American Secretaries of State*, II, 88.
77. James T. Flexner, *George Washington: Anguish and Farewell*, 1793–1799 (Boston, 1972), 110.

CHAPTER XX   Disillusionment in Eden

1. Jefferson to Volney, describing the Virginia mountains, April 9, 1797, quoted in *Volney et l'Amérique*, Chinard, ed. (Baltimore, 1923), 80.
2. Randall, *Jefferson*, II, 234.
3. Schachner, *Jefferson*, 577.
4. Jefferson to Edmund Randolph, February 3, 1794, Jefferson to Madison, April 3, 1794, *Writings*, L. and B., IX, 280, 283.
5. Jefferson to John Adams, April 25, 1794, Jefferson to François d'Ivernois, February 6, 1795, *Writings*, L. and B., IX, 283–84, 297. The letter to Adams is mistakenly described by the editors as a letter to Washington, despite the definite reference within it to Mrs. Adams.
6. *Farm Book*, 31 (obscurely inscribed at the bottom of the page).
7. Jefferson to Edward Rutledge, November 30, 1795, *Writings*, L. and B., IX, 313.
8. *Farm Book*, 50–51. Harriet, the first of Sally's two daughters with this name, is listed with her mother on pages 31, 52–53, in the *Farm Book*.
9. Jefferson to Washington, May 14, 1794, Jefferson to the Secretary of State, Edmund Randolph, September 7, 1794, *Writings*, L. and B., IX, 288, 290.
10. Jefferson to Harry Remson, October 30, 1794, *Garden Book*, 219; Jefferson to John Adams, February 6, 1795, *Adams-Jefferson Letters*, 257; Jefferson to Archibald Stuart, April 18, 1795, *Writings*, Ford, VII, 8.
11. Jefferson to Madison, December 28, 1794, *Writings*, L. and B., IX, 297.
12. Jefferson to Madison, March 13, 1791, Jefferson Papers, Library of Congress,

quoted in Adrienne Koch, *Jefferson and Madison: The Great Collaboration* (New York, 1950), 114.

13. Ketcham, *James Madison*, 376–80.
14. Madison to Jefferson, October 5, 1794, Koch, *Jefferson and Madison*, 162–63.
15. As reported by Callender in the *Richmond Recorder*, September 29, 1802.
16. Jefferson to Volney, April 9, 1797, *Volney et l'Amérique*, Chinard, ed., 80. The letters referring to gardening were collected in the Betts edition of his *Garden Book*.
17. The letters came through John Trumbull, and had been written in London on November 13 and 24, 1794. Bullock, *My Head and My Heart*, 140–41.
18. Jefferson to Maria Cosway, September 8, 1795, Bullock, *My Head and My Heart*, 142–43.
19. Jefferson to Washington, September 12, 1795, Library of Congress, quoted in part in the *Garden Book*, 238.
20. Jefferson to Francis Willis, July 15, 1796, Library of Congress, quoted in part in the *Farm Book*, 266.
21. Randall, *Jefferson*, II, 225.
22. William H. Gaines, Jr., *Thomas Mann Randolph: Jefferson's Son-in-Law* (Baton Rouge, La., 1966), 38–39, 80, 157.
23. Randolph to Jefferson, October 29, 1802, quoted in Gaines, *Thomas Mann Randolph*, 48.
24. Martha Jefferson Randolph to Jefferson, July 1, 1798, *Family Letters*, 166.
25. Account book, October 7, 1795.
26. Jefferson to Madison, July 15, 1795, Library of Congress, 16888, quoted in Malone, *Jefferson and the Ordeal of Liberty*, 235.
27. Jefferson to Martha Jefferson Randolph, February 14, 1796, *Family Letters*, 136; Jefferson to Thomas Mann Randolph, January 18, 1796, Library of Congress, 17028.
28. Jefferson to Madison, April 27, 1795, *Writings*, L. and B., IX, 302–3.
29. Jefferson to Maria Jefferson Eppes, March 3, 1802, *Family Letters*, 219.
30. Jefferson to Martha Jefferson Randolph, July 31, 1795, *Family Letters*, 134.
31. Jefferson to Thomas Mann Randolph, Jr., August 11, 1795, Library of Congress, 15702.
32. Jefferson to Mann Page, August 30, 1795, *Writings*, L. and B., IX, 306–7. See also Isaac S. Harrell, *Loyalism in Virginia: Chapters in the Economic History of the Revolution* (Durham, N.C., 1926), 162–77.
33. Jefferson to Madison, December 28, 1794, *Writings*, Ford, VI, 518.
34. Jefferson to Madison, September 21, 1795, *Writings*, L. and B., IX, 309–11.
35. Jefferson to Mann Page, August 30, 1795, *Writings*, L. and B., IX, 306–7.
36. Jefferson to Madison, April 27, 1795, *Writings*, L. and B., IX, 303.
37. Jefferson to John Adams, February 28, 1796, *Adams-Jefferson Letters*, 259. The book was François d'Ivernois, *Des Révolutions de France et de Genève* (London, 1795).
38. Jefferson to Horatio Gates, February 3, 1794, Library of Congress, 16571.
39. Jefferson to William Branch Giles, December 17, 1794, *Writings*, Ford, IV, 515.
40. Jefferson to George Wythe, October 24, 1794, Library of Congress, 16749, quoted in Malone, *Jefferson and the Ordeal of Liberty*, 233.
41. Jefferson to Thomas Munro, March 4, 1815, Malone, *Jefferson and the Ordeal of Liberty*, 228.
42. Jefferson to Philip Mazzei, April 24, 1796, *Writings*, L. and B., IX, 336–37.
43. Malone, *Jefferson and the Ordeal of Liberty*, 234. The note was not paid off till June 7, 1818. He mortgaged 150 slaves. See Malone's "Long Note on Jefferson's Debts," *ibid.*, 529.

CHAPTER XXI Triangles at Monticello

1. Martha Jefferson Randolph to Jefferson, July 1, 1798, *Family Letters*, 166.
2. Jean Gaulmier, *Un Grand Témoin de la révolution et de l'empire* (Paris, 1959), 211.
3. *"Leur indolence à remuer leurs houes était extrême. Le maître prit un fouet pour les effrayer, et bientôt, ce fut une scène comique; placé au milieu de leur troupeau, il s'agitait, grondait, menacait, et se turnait de tous côtés. Or, à mesure qu'il tournait le visage, les noirs changeaint d'attitude: ceux qu'il regardait en face travaillaient mieux; ceux qu'il ne voyait pas du tout cessaient tout travail; et s'il faisait volte-face, la houe se levait à sa vue, et dormait derrière son dos. Ce tableau me rappela ces troupes de singes et de petits chiens habillés que nous voyons dans let rues de Paris danser au geste d'un batôn. . . ."* Gaulmier, *Un Grand Témoin de la révolution et de l'empire*, 210–11.
4. Jefferson to Thomas Mann Randolph, January 23, 1801, Library of Congress, 18668.
5. Jefferson to Stephens T. Mason, October 27, 1799, *Writings*, Ford, VII, 396.
6. La Rochefoucauld-Liancourt, François Alexandre Frédéric, *Travels through the United States of North America, etc., in the years 1795, 1796, and 1797* (London, 1799), quoted in Randall, *Jefferson*, II, 302–7.
7. *"La raison en est que les femmes et les filles noires et mulâtresses, n'étant soumises à aucune censure de moeurs, vivent librement, soit avec les ouvriers blanc du pays, soit avec les bondes ou engagés venus d'Europe, allemands, irlandais, et autres, dont la condition diffère peu de la leur. Les enfants qui en résultent, pour être jaunes ou blancs, n'en sont pas moins esclaves."* Gaulmier, *Un Grand Témoin de la révolution et de l'empire*, 211.
8. Anna B. Dodd, *Talleyrand: The Training of a Statesman, 1754-1838,* (New York, 1927), 318; Allan McLane Hamilton, *The Intimate Life of Alexander Hamilton* (New York, 1910), 255.
9. Edward Long, *History of Jamaica*, III, 328, quoted in Jordan, *White over Black*, 140.
10. Thenia is listed with the other Hemings family slaves in the "roll of the negroes taken in 1783," *Farm Book*, 24, with her birth year as 1767. She does not appear in the next listing of slaves in 1794, *Farm Book*, 30, nor again thereafter.
11. Johnston, *Race Relations in Virginia*, x.
12. *Farm Book*, Betts' Commentary [15]. Jefferson to Thomas Mann Randolph, December 26, 1794, Library of Congress, 16733.
13. Martha Jefferson Randolph to Jefferson, January 15, 1795, *Family Letters*, 131.
14. Jefferson to Martha Jefferson Randolph, June 8, 1797, *Family Letters*, 145. For the promise to free Robert Hemings, and the deed of manumission, see *Farm Book*, Bett's Commentary [15]. Jefferson noted the gift of $30 in his account book January 26, 1798. The deed was formally recorded February 6, 1795.
15. See Charles Moran, *Black Triumvirate* (New York, 1957); Herbert Aptheker, *American Negro Slave Revolts* (New York, 1943).
16. For a summary of his *Dissertation on Slavery: With a Proposal for the Gradual Abolition of It, in the State of Virginia*, and a discussion of his proposals, see Jordan, *White over Black*, 555–60.
17. Jefferson to St. George Tucker, August 28, 1797, *Writings*, L. and B., IX, 418.
18. See *Farm Book*, 31, and Martha Jefferson Randolph to Jefferson, January 22, 1798, *Family Letters*, 153.
19. *Farm Book*, 50–51.
20. For the slave inventory of 1794, see *Farm Book*, 30. Two slaves named Tom appear on the bread distribution list for 1796 (*Farm Book*, 50), but it would seem

that one was Tom Shackleford and the other a hired slave, who appears with other slaves as "hired" on page 52. An important listing in 1810 shows Sally Hemings with one "grown" child and three "children" (*Farm Book*, 135), which would seem to be Beverly (grown), Harriet, Madison, and Eston. But a "Tom" appears separately in this same listing, along with other "grown" children, Laravia, Shepherd, Indridge, Thruston, and Sukey, who are listed separately from their parents. No Arabic numeral appears after Tom's name, as with the others, and he is not counted in the totaling of the slaves, which numbered twenty-three. So he appears as a person but not a slave, possible evidence that Jefferson counted him free, but nevertheless, whether deliberately or by accident, saw to it in this important year, as he approached twenty-one, that Tom appeared in the written record. The name Tom appears also on an 1810 list as "hired," along with a Tom Buck and a Tom Lee (*Farm Book*, 136), and on a distribution list for "summer clothes" dated June 16, 1811 (*Farm Book*, 136). Jefferson's account books show his hiring two slaves named Tom, one from William Chamerlayne, the other from Sarah Dangerfield. It is the third "hired" Tom who could be Tom Hemings. It is possible that he had left Monticello before 1810 and 1811, and came back for these two summers.

21. For the Madison Hemings and Israel Jefferson reminiscences, see Appendix I. Israel's birth date appears on page 130 of the *Farm Book*. The letter from Ellen Coolidge to Joseph Coolidge, Jr., dated October 24, 1858, is in the possession of Harold Jefferson Coolidge, who permitted me to quote a small portion only of what is altogether a remarkable letter. For the full text, see pp. 498ff.

22. Polly Sneed may have been the wife of the schoolteacher "Mr. Sneed," mentioned by Martha Randolph in her letter to her father May 12, 1798. She writes of "Mr. Sneed opening school and Jeffy being hurried out of bed every morning at sunrise . . . to walk 2 miles to school" (*Family Letters*, 161). Mrs. Sneed's services were clearly given at Monticello. The account book notes are as follows: "Mrs. Sneed Sept. 14, 1792 3.2"; November 7, 1795, "paid Mrs. Sneed in full for services to the negro women 11.11"; November 19, 1796, "paid Mrs. Sneed in full for Tamar, Ned, Jenny, Iris, and Minerva 6 D"; October 11, 1797, "Mrs. Sneed fees for Rachael, Isabel, and Minerva 6 D"; August 7, 1798, "pd (Sylvanus?) Meeks for Mrs. Sneed in full 20 D"; December 16, 1799, "Pd Mrs. Sneed 2 D. which with (?) lb wool a 2/-42 makes 3 D for her services with Isabel and 6 D for 6 months schooling of Thos Jefferson"; April 25, 1801, "pd Lilly for Mrs. Sneed 6 D"; September 27, 1801, "left with (?) for Mrs. Sneed for Sally 3 D"; May 20, 1802, "pd Mrs. Sneed 10 D."

23. Malone, *Jefferson and the Ordeal of Liberty*, 235.

24. Jefferson to Maria Jefferson Eppes, April 11, 1801, *Family Letters*, 201.

25. Maria Jefferson Eppes to Jefferson, April 18, 1801, *Family Letters*, 202.

26. As described by Madison Hemings. See Appendix I.

27. Thomas Jefferson Randolph, "Last Days of Jefferson," Ms., cited in *Jefferson at Monticello*, 135, note 3. Mrs. William Thornton, who visited Monticello from September 18 through September 22, 1802, observed that Jefferson's master bedroom was always kept locked. Malone, *Jefferson the President*, 168. Margaret Bayard Smith, visiting Monticello in 1809, noted that the door to his "apartments . . . is never opened but by himself and his retirement seems so sacred that I told him it was his sanctum sanctorum." *First Forty Years of Washington Society*, 70.

28. Jefferson to Maria Jefferson, March 11, 1797, *Family Letters*, 141. Jefferson's letter to Randolph on the same date is in Library of Congress, 17321.

29. Jefferson to Martha Jefferson Randolph, March 27, 1797, *Family Letters*, 142.

30. Martha Jefferson Randolph to Jefferson, March 31, 1797, *Family Letters*, 143.

31. Randall to James Parton, June 1, 1868. See Appendix III.

32. For a discussion of the possibility that the Carr brothers did father Sally Hemings' children, see Appendix III.

33. Quoted in Randall, *Jefferson*, II, 307.

34. *Jefferson at Monticello*, 38–39.

35. Jefferson to Martha Jefferson Randolph, June 8, 1797, *Family Letters*, 145–47.

36. Jefferson to Maria Jefferson, June 14, 1797, *Family Letters*, 148. A draft of the marriage contract is in the Huntington Library.

37. Martha Jefferson Randolph to Jefferson, January 22, 1798, *Family Letters*, 153. *Farm Book* references to Harriet, under Sally's name, disappear after 1797, until replaced by a new child named Harriet in May 1801.

38. James A. Bear, Jr., editor of the *Family Letters*, identifies "Tom" and "Goliah" as the older slave laborers, 154n. But the *Farm Book* mentions a Goliah, son of Molly, on pages 30 and 130. He disappears from the *Farm Book* after 1799. His birth date is listed as May 1791.

39. See the Malone chronology, *Jefferson and the Ordeal of Liberty*, xxvi.

40. Martha Jefferson Randolph to Jefferson, January 22, 1798, *Family Letters*, 154.

41. Jefferson to Martha Jefferson Randolph, February 8, 1798, *Family Letters*, 155–56. Martha had written to her father on January 22 and January 28, but only the former letter appears in the *Family Letters*, which suggests that some letters may have been destroyed or are still retained by Jefferson heirs. See Jefferson's mention of the two letters in his letter of February 8, 1798, *Family Letters*, 156.

42. *Farm Book*, 57, 128. Dumas Malone's chronology, *Jefferson and the Ordeal of Liberty*, xxvi, shows that Jefferson had been in Monticello eight months and twenty days earlier, having arrived from Philadelphia on July 11, 1797.

43. Martha Jefferson Randolph to Jefferson, May 12, 1798, *Family Letters*, 160

44. Jefferson to Martha Jefferson Randolph, May 17, 1798, *Family Letters*, 161.

45. Martha Jefferson Randolph to Jefferson, July 1, 1798, *Family Letters*, 166.

46. Maria Jefferson Eppes to Jefferson, April 21, 1802, *Family Letters*, 224.

47. Maria Jefferson Eppes to Jefferson, May 27, 1798, *Family Letters*, 163.

48. Jefferson to Edward Rutledge, June 24, 1797, *Writings*, L. and B., IX, 411.

CHAPTER XXII Candidate à Contre Coeur

1. Jefferson to Madison, December 17, 1796, *Writings*, L. and B., IX, 351.

2. Jefferson to Madison, December 17, 1796, *Writings*, L. and B., IX, 351; Miller, *The Federalist Era*, 103; Koch, *Jefferson and Madison*, 63; Charles, *Origins of the American Party System*, 85.

3. Margaret Bayard Smith, *First Forty Years of Washington Society*, 235.

4. Rush, *Autobiography*, 181.

5. Jefferson to Thomas C. Flournoy, October 1, 1812, *Writings*, L. and B., XIII, 190; *Autobiography*, 55.

6. Malone, *Jefferson and the Ordeal of Liberty*, 276.

7. Hamilton to an unknown correspondent, letter dated simply 1796, Hamilton, *Works*, Lodge, ed., X, 195–96.

8. John Adams to Abigail Adams, January 7, 20, 1796, Page Smith, *John Adams*, II, 880.

9. John Adams to John Quincy Adams, June 10, 1796, Page Smith, *John Adams*, II, 893.

10. John Adams to Abigail Adams, March 1, 1796, Page Smith, *John Adams*, II, 881.

11. Abigail Adams to John Adams, December 31, 1796, Page Smith, *John Adams*, II, 908.

12. William L. Smith, writing under the pseudonym "Phocion," *The Pretensions of Thomas Jefferson to the Presidency Examined* (Philadelphia, 1796).

13. Jefferson to Peregrine Fitzhugh, February 23, 1798, Jefferson to Edward Rutledge, December 27, 1796, *Writings*, L. and B., X, 1, IX, 353.

14. Jefferson to Thomas Mann Randolph, November 28, 1796, *Writings*, L. and B., IX, 201.

15. Jefferson to the Comte de Volney, January 8, 1797, *Writings*, L. and B., IX, 363.

16. Jefferson to Madison, December 17, 1796, *Writings*, L. and B., IX, 351–52.
17. Jefferson to Edward Rutledge, December 27, 1796, *Writings*, L. and B., IX, 353–54.
18. Jefferson to Madison, January 30, 1797, *Writings*, Ford, VII, 116.
19. John Adams to Abigail Adams, March 9, 1797, Page Smith, *John Adams*, II, 917–18.
20. John Adams to Abigail Adams, March 5, 9, 1797, Page Smith, *John Adams*, II, 920, 917.
21. Jefferson to the Comte de Volney, April 9, 1797, *Volney et l'Amérique*, Chinard, ed., 80.
22. Ketcham, *James Madison*, 387.
23. Anas, *Writings*, L. and B., I, 414.
24. Anas, *Writings*, L. and B., I, 415.
25. Jefferson to Benjamin Rush, January 22, 1797, *Writings*, L. and B., IX, 374.
26. Jefferson to Martha Jefferson Randolph, December 27, 1797, *Family Letters*, 150.
27. Jefferson to Maria Jefferson, June 14, 1797, February 7, 1799, Jefferson to Martha Jefferson Randolph, February 8, 1798, June 8, 1797, *Family Letters*, 148. 173, 155, 146.
28. Jefferson to Edward Rutledge, June 24, 1797, *Writings*, L. and B., IX, 411.
29. Adams to General Uriah Forrest, June 20, 1787, Adams, *Life and Works*, VIII, 546–47. Malone, *Jefferson and the Ordeal of Liberty*, 322, notes that the date is erroneous, and should be later.
30. Washington to Adams, July 4, 1798, Washington to Charles Carroll, August 2, 1798, *Writings*, Fitzpatrick, ed., XXXVI, 313, 384.
31. February 4, 1818, Anas, *Writings*, L. and B., I, 283.
32. Jefferson to Madison, March 2, 1798, *Writings*, L. and B., X, 9; February 15, 1798, Anas, *Writings*, L. and B., I, 421.
33. See Jefferson to Thomas Mann Randolph, May 9, 1798, Library of Congress, 17758; Jefferson to Madison, May 3, 1798, Jefferson to Monroe, May 21, 1798, *Writings*, L. and B., X, 35, 38; Peterson, *Jefferson and the New Nation*, 604.
34. Jefferson to Archibald Stuart, June 8, 1798, *Writings*, Ford, VII, 270; Jefferson to Thomas Lomax, March 12, 1799, *Writings*, L. and B., X, 124; Jefferson to Peregrine Fitzhugh, February 23, 1798, *Writings*, L. and B., X, 3.
35. Jefferson to John Taylor, June 4, 1798, *Writings*, L. and B., XVIII, 209.
36. Anas, *Writings*, L. and B., I, 279. See also Malone, *Jefferson and the Ordeal of Liberty*, 386–94; Peterson, *Jefferson and the New Nation*, 606–7; Miller, *The Federalist Era*, 231; James Morton Smith, *Freedom's Fetters: The Alien and Sedition Laws and American Civil Liberties* (Ithaca, N.Y., 1956), 145; Zechariah Chafee, *Free Speech in the United States* (Boston, 1948), 240.
37. Jefferson tells us he was here drawing upon Thwaites' Heptateuch. See "An Essay towards Facilitating Instruction in the Anglo-Saxon and Modern Dialects of the English Language for the Use of the University of Virginia," originally written in reply to a letter from Herbert Croft, and dated Monticello, October 30, 1798. The essay was added to by Jefferson in 1825. *Writings*, L. and B., XVIII, 362–411.
38. Jefferson to John Taylor, November 26, 1798, *Writings*, L. and B., X, 65; Peterson, *Jefferson and the New Nation*, 611.
39. *Writings*, Ford, VII, 289–308.
40. Malone, *Jefferson and the Ordeal of Liberty*, 411.
41. Jefferson to Elbridge Gerry, January 6, 1799, *Writings*, L. and B., X, 74–86.
42. Jefferson to Thaddeus Kosciusko, June 1, 1798; Jefferson to Edmund Randolph, August 18, 1799, *Writings*, L. and B., X, 49, 129.
43. *Works of Alexander Hamilton*, J. C. Hamilton, ed., VI, 502; Malone, *Jefferson and the Ordeal of Liberty*, 305.
44. He included the note in his Anas, *Writings*, L. and B., I, 425.
45. Malone, *Jefferson and the Ordeal of Liberty*, 308–11. Randall, *Jefferson*, II,

371–74. Jefferson spoke of his "malignant neighbor" in his Anas, *Writings*, L. and B., I, 283. See also Flexner, *Washington: Anguish and Farewell*, 384–88.
    46. Jefferson to Dr. Walter Jones, January 2, 1814, *Writings*, L. and B., XIV, 46–52.

CHAPTER XXIII   Callender

1. Worthington Chauncey Ford, "Thomas Jefferson and James Thomson Callender," *New England Historical and Genealogical Register* (1896–97), L, 330.
    2. Callender's *Deformities of Dr. Samuel Johnson* (1782), was reprinted in the Augustan Reprint Society series, nos. 147–48, by Gwin J. Kolb and J. E. Congleton in 1971. Callender said he released the material because of the vitriolic Federalist attacks on James Monroe, recently returned from France, who was being called a Jacobin and Francophile conspirator. See Callender's *Sketches of the History of America*, 101–2.
    3. Callender, *Sketches of the History of America*, 35, 97.
    4. *The History of the United States for the Year 1796*, 219–21, 228, and *Sketches of the History of America*, 97.
    5. "Minutes of an Interview between Col. Monroe and Col. Hamilton reported by David Gelston, 11 July 1797," Gratz Collection, quoted in *Papers*, Boyd, XVIII, 663, and Ammon, *James Monroe*, 159.
    6. Callender, *Sketches*, 101–2.
    7. William Burwell memoir, Ms., Library of Congress.
    8. *Richmond Examiner*, quoting the *Aurora*, October 16, 1802.
    9. *Observations on Certain Documents Contained in Nos. V and VI of "The History of the United States for the Year 1796," in Which the Charge of Speculation against Alexander Hamilton, Late Secretary of the Treasury Is Fully Refuted* (Philadelphia, 1797), 9. The full document was reprinted in Hamilton, *Works*, Lodge, ed., VI, 449–535.
    10. Julian Boyd is the first reputable historian to agree with Callender that Hamilton probably did forge the Maria Reynolds letters, which he calls "incredibly naive inventions" (*Papers*, XVIII, 681). He bases his belief on the misspellings in the Reynolds letters, which he holds are those of a literate man trying to fake those of an illiterate woman. Though normally I deeply respect Julian Boyd's scholarship, here I must part company and agree with the traditional view held by all Hamilton biographers, that these letters were genuine. The fact that the originals disappeared and only copies remain proves little. Erratic spellings were the order of the day (Jefferson himself spelled some words in three different fashions). I believe Maria Reynolds' letters could only have been written by a foolish, unhappy, and despairing woman, as Hamilton described her in his *Observations*, "truly fond and neglected" (p. 20). She no doubt cared more for the attractive Hamilton than for her husband, but she was corrupt, and her husband easily cowed her by threatening her with the loss of her daughter. If Hamilton was innocent of Treasury fraud, it would have been absolute imbecility of him to have forged such letters; if he was guilty, as Boyd hints, it is odd that no evidence has been uncovered. Hamilton himself stoutly denied the forgery charge, insisting "that Mrs. Reynolds' own letters contradict absolutely this artful explanation of hers; if indeed she ever made it. . . . The variety of shapes which this woman could assume was endless," and he presented an affidavit from her former landlady testifying to the authenticity of Maria's handwriting. (For the affidavit of Mary Williams, see Hamilton, *Observations*, xlix.) Hamilton quoted also from a mutual friend Richard Folwell, who said Mrs. Reynolds "made a voluntary confession of her belief, and even knowledge, that I was innocent of all that had been laid to my charge by Reynolds . . . spoke of me in exalted terms of esteem and respect, declared in the most solemn manner her extreme unhappiness lest I should suppose her accessory to the trouble" (Hamilton, *Observations*, 35). Boyd

makes much of the fact that Hamilton failed to exhibit the written Folwell evidence in Maria's hand. But Hamilton had something special to lose by encouraging Folwell's testimony, for the latter believed Reynolds "had urged his wife to make assig-nations with 'certain high influential characters . . . to gull Money from them' " (*Papers*, Boyd, XVIII, 676). Hamilton preferred to believe—what man would not? —that Maria Reynolds' original affection for him had been real, and that the black-mailing had been begun by her husband who compelled his wife to assist in it. For Boyd's entire discussion see "The First Conflict in the Cabinet," *Papers*, XVIII, Appendix, 611–88.

11. Miller, *Hamilton and the Growth of the New Nation*, 523.

12. Jefferson to John Taylor, October 8, 1797, quoted in *Papers*, Boyd, XVIII, 685n.

13. Miller, *The Federalist Era*, 205.

14. *Writings*, L. and B., I, 266.

15. Anas, *Writings*, L. and B., I, 278–79.

16. Callender wrote that he first met Jefferson in Philadelphia at the printing office of Snowden and McCorkle, this in June or July 1797. He also mentioned meeting Jefferson at the Franklin Hotel, Ford, "Thomas Jefferson and James Thomson Callender," *New England . . . Register*, L, 326.

17. Jefferson to James Monroe, May 29, 1801. Ford, "Jefferson and Callender," *New England . . . Register*, LI, 157. Jefferson to James Monroe, July 15, 1802, *Writings*, L. and B., X, 330; Jefferson to Thomas Man Randolph, February 15, 1798. Library of Congress, 17581.

18. June 20, 1797, "paid Callender for Hist of US 15.14"; October 8, "desired J. Barnes to pay James Thomson Callender 20 D for his pamphlets"; December 12, "Paid Callender 16."; December 14, "Callender for pamphlet 4.33"; December 23, "pd Callender for books and pamphlets 5 D"; January 19, 1798, "Gave Thos Lieper ord. on J. Barnes for 25 D in charity"; February 9, "pd T. Lieper for Callender for 5 copies of his Sketches for 97 5 D"; May 28, "Pd Callender for books 5 D"; June 25, "Paid Callender for his next book 5 D"; September 6, 1799, "wrote to G. Jefferson to pay J. T. Callender 50D"; September 23, 1800, "directed G. Jefferson to pay Callender 50 D". The original of this account book is in the New York Public Library.

19. Article in the *Aurora*, republished in the *Richmond Examiner*, September 25, 1802. See also the *Examiner* of September 18 for a similar account. Callender was accused of "stealing some mahogany."

20. Ford, "Jefferson and Callender," *New England . . . Register*, L, 448.

21. Jefferson to Monroe, July 15, 1802, *Writings*, L. and B., X, 331; Jefferson to Callender, October 6, 1799, Ford, "Jefferson and Callender," *New England . . . Register*, L, 449.

22. *Friend of the People, National Magazine, Staunton Scourge of Aristocracy*, and *Petersburg Republican*.

23. Callender to Jefferson, August 10, 1799, Ford, "Jefferson and Callender," *New England . . . Register*, L, 446.

24. Jefferson to Callender, October 6, 1799, *Writings*, Ford, VII, 394–95.

25. *Ibid.*, 395.

26. Callender, *The Prospect before Us* (Richmond, 1800), Preface, Part I, 179, III, 58.

27. See her indignant letter of July 1, 1804, describing Callender's writings as "the blackest calumny, and foulest falshoods," *Adams-Jefferson Letters*, 272.

28. Quoted in Miller, *The Federalist Era*, 233.

29. James Morton Smith, *Freedom's Fetters*, 325. Smith, in this excellent mono-graph, writes that the Sedition Law "reduced the limits of speech and the press in the United States to those set by the English common law in the days before the American Revolution," 424.

30. Francis Wharton, *State Trials of the United States during the Administrations of Washington and Adams* (Philadelphia, 1849), 678–721. See also the report of

the trial in the *Virginia Gazette*, June 6, 1800, reprinted in Ford, "Jefferson and Callender," *New England . . . Register*, L, 453–55.

31. Meriwether Jones' article was reproduced in W. A. Rind's *Virginia Federalist* with the accompanying contemptuous comment on October 5, 1799.

32. *The Prospect before Us*, vol. II; Smith, *Freedom's Fetters*, 358.

33. Callender to Jefferson, October 27, 1800, Ford, "Jefferson and Callender," *New England . . . Register*, LI, 21.

34. Jefferson to Monroe, May 29, 1801, *Writings*, Ford, IX, 389–90.

35. *Richmond Recorder*, September 2, 1802. There is no complete file of the *Virginia Federalist*, the most complete being at the Harvard Library, which has the issue quoted above.

36. Callender to Madison, April 27, 1801, Ford, "Jefferson and Callender," *New England . . . Register*, LI, 154.

37. Henry Randall wrote to Hugh Blair Grigsby, February 15, 1856, that Callender was "helped by some of Mr. Jefferson's *neighbors*." *Correspondence between Henry Stephens Randall and Hugh Blair Grigsby, 1856–1861*, edited with an introduction and notes by Frank J. Klingberg, University of California Publications in History (Berkeley, 1952), XLIII, 29–30.

CHAPTER XXIV   Jason

1. Jefferson to Lafayette, March 1, 1801, *Writings*, L. and B., X, 214.

2. Martha Jefferson Randolph to Jefferson, January 13, 1801, *Family Letters*, 193.

3. *Virginia Federalist* (Richmond), July 19, 1800.

4. *New York Commercial Advertiser*, September 25, 1800.

5. *Life, Journals, and Correspondence of Rev. Manasseh Cutler*, William P. Cutler and Julia Cutler, eds., 2 vols. (Cincinnati, 1888), II, 56, January 1, 1802, diary entry reporting a visit with Martha Washington at Mount Vernon.

6. July 3, 7, 1800, Malone, *Jefferson and the Ordeal of Liberty*, 478.

7. Jefferson to Uriah McGregory, August 13, 1800, *Writings*, L. and B., X, 171.

8. Jefferson to Dr. Joseph Priestley, January 18, 1800, *Writings*, L. and B., X, 139.

9. Jefferson to Benjamin Rush, September 23, 1800, *Writings*, L. and B., X, 174–75.

10. Jefferson to Thomas Mann Randolph, April 9, 1797, Library of Congress, 17358.

11. Jefferson to William Short, April 13, 1800, Short Papers, William and Mary College, and Jefferson to Thomas Mann Randolph, May 7, 1800, Massachusetts Historical Society, I, 76–78, as cited by Schachner, *Jefferson*, 643.

12. Martha Jefferson Randolph to Jefferson, May 15, 1800, *Family Letters*, 188.

13. Martha Jefferson Randolph to Jefferson, January 31, 1801, *Family Letters*, 192–94.

14. Jefferson to Thomas Mann Randolph, sending his love to "My ever dear Martha," *Writings*, L. and B., X, 207–8.

15. Jefferson to Martha Jefferson Randolph, May 28, 1801, *Family Letters*, 202.

16. Maria Jefferson Eppes to Jefferson, December 28, 1800, *Family Letters*, 190.

17. Jefferson to Maria Jefferson Eppes, February 12, 1800, *Family Letters*, 185–86.

18. John Eppes, in a letter to Jefferson February 7, 1800, described the problem with her breasts, saying she was unable to use her arms for several weeks; and a later letter, July 14, 1802, described the continual two-year back pain as deriving from "the unfortunate accident . . . of her miscarriage." University of Virginia Library.

19. Ellen Randolph Coolidge to Henry Randall, January 15, 1856, quoted in Randall, *Jefferson*, III, 102.

20. Maria Jefferson Eppes to Jefferson, February 2, 1801, *Family Letters*, 194.

21. Jefferson to Maria Jefferson Eppes, February 15, 1801, *Family Letters*, 196.
22. *Ibid.*, 197.
23. Jefferson to Thomas Lomax, *Writings*, L. and B., X, 211.
24. Burr to Jefferson, December 23, 1800, received January 1, 1801, Malone, *Jefferson and the Ordeal of Liberty*, 496.
25. Jefferson to Maria Jefferson Eppes, January 4, 1801, *Family Letters*, 190.
26. See Burr's letter to Samuel Smith, December 29, 1800, where he wrote that if chosen president he would not resign in Jefferson's favor, quoted in J. S. Pancake, "Aaron Burr: Would-Be Usurper," *William and Mary Quarterly*, 3rd series, VIII (April 1951); also Anas, January 2, 1804, *Writings*, L. and B., I, 442–43, and B. Hichborn to Jefferson, January 5, 1801, Library of Congress, 18589. The best summary of the episode is Malone, *Jefferson and the Ordeal of Liberty*, 490–506.
27. John Adams to Elbridge Gerry, February 7, 1802, *Life and Works*, IX, 98, quoted in Randall, *Jefferson*, II, 588.
28. Adams to Elbridge Gerry, December 30, 1800, *Life and Works*, IX, 577–78, quoted in Malone, *Jefferson and the Ordeal of Liberty*, 500. And when Henry Lee attacked Jefferson in his presence Adams is said to have flared up in anger, saying, "Jefferson was a better friend than many whose displays of cordiality he had finally come to hate," quoted in Stephen G. Kurtz, *The Presidency of John Adams* (Philadelphia, 1957), 237.
29. Edward Coles to Henry Randall, May 11, 1857, Randall, *Jefferson*, III, 640.
30. Anas, *Writings*, L. and B., I, 452.
31. Jefferson to Martha Jefferson Randolph, February 5, 1801, Jefferson to Maria Jefferson Eppes, February 15, 1801, *Family Letters*, 195, 196.
32. Jefferson to Governor Thomas McKean, March 9, 1801, *Writings*, L. and B., X, 221.
33. Jefferson to Monroe, February 15, 1801, *Writings*, L. and B., X, 201–2.
34. Hamilton, "The Public Conduct and Character of John Adams, Esq., President of the United States," Hamilton, *Works*, Lodge, ed., VII, 309–64.
35. Hamilton to Bayard, August 6, 1800, January 16, 1801; Hamilton to Oliver Wolcott, December 16, 1800, *Works*, Lodge, ed., X, 387, 393–94, 412–19. See also similar letters to Theodore Sedgewick and James Ross.
36. Hamilton, *Works*, Lodge, ed., VI, 276.
37. Samuel Eliot Morison, *Life and Letters of Harrison Gray Otis*, 2 vols. (Boston, 1913), I, 207–8.
38. Margaret Bayard Smith, *First Forty Years of Washington Society*, 23.
39. Bayard to Hamilton, March 8, 1801, Hamilton, *Works*, J. C. Hamilton, ed., VI, 522–24, quoted in Schachner, *Jefferson*, 658. See also Morton Borden, *The Federalism of James A. Bayard* (New York, 1955), chap. 7.
40. Jefferson to John Dickinson, December 19, 1801, *Writings*, L. and B., X, 301.
41. Samuel Adams to Jefferson, quoted in Miller, *Sam Adams: Pioneer in Propaganda*, 400.
42. Jefferson to John Dickinson, December 19, 1801, *Writings*, L. and B., X, 301.
43. Page Smith, *John Adams*, II, 1055.
44. *Ibid.*, 1015.
45. As Merrill Peterson points out, one was John Adams' nephew, one a former Tory who had been captain of a Loyalist regiment during the Revolution, and three were brothers or brothers-in-law of John Marshall. *Jefferson and the New Nation*, 694.
46. Page Smith, *John Adams*, II, 1067, 1015.
47. John Adams to William Tudor, February 3, 1801, Page Smith, *John Adams*, II, 1053.
48. Adams to Jefferson, March 24, 1801, *Adams-Jefferson Letters*, 264.
49. Jefferson to Benjamin Rush, March 24, 1801, *Writings*, L. and B., X, 242.
50. December 14, 1800, Gouverneur Morris, *Diary and Letters*, Anne Cary Morris, ed., II, 395; Jefferson to Thomas Mann Randolph, June 4, 1801. Library of Congress 19390.
51. Henry Adams, *History of the United States*, I, vii, 185–86.

52. Jefferson to Levi Lincoln, August 26, 1801, *Writings*, L. and B., X, 275.
53. Jefferson to Martha Jefferson Randolph, February 5, 1801, *Family Letters*, 195.
For the first inaugural address, see *Writings*, L. and B., III, 317–23.
54. Adams to William Tudor, February 3, 1801, Page Smith, *John Adams*, II, 1053.
55. Jefferson to Elbridge Gerry, March 29, 1801, *Writings*, L. and B., X, 255.
56. Jefferson to Lafayette, March 1, 1801, Jefferson to John Dickinson, March 6, 1801, *Writings*, L. and B., X, 214, 217.

CHAPTER XXV Betrayal

1. Jefferson to Wilson C. Nicholas, *Writings*, L. and B., XII, 288.
2. Peterson, *Thomas Jefferson and the New Nation*, 759.
3. Jefferson to William Short, October 3, 1801, *Writings*, L. and B., X, 287. See James Morton Smith, *Freedom's Fetters*, for an excellent account of this whole episode.
3. Jefferson to William Short, October 3, 1801, *Writings*, L. and B., X, 287.
4. Peterson, *Jefferson and the New Nation*, 727.
5. Margaret Bayard Smith, *First Forty Years of Washington Society*, 5–6, 12.
6. Henry Adams, *History of the United States*, Agar ed., 75.
7. Jefferson to William Short, October 3, 1801, *Writings*, L. and B., X, 287.
8. Jefferson to Dr. Hugh Williamson, April 30, 1803, *Writings*, L. and B, X, 386.
9. Jefferson to Sir John Sinclair, June 30, 1803, *Writings*, L. and B., X, 397.
10. Jefferson to Anne Cary, Thomas Jefferson, and Ellen Wayles Randolph, March 2, 1802, *Family Letters*, 218.
11. Aptheker, *American Negro Slave Revolts*, 222–26; Johnston, *Race Relations in Virginia*, 33–35.
12. Jefferson to James Monroe, September 20, 1800, *Writings*, Ford, 457–58.
13. Callender to Jefferson, September 13, 1800, Ford, "Jefferson and Callender," *New England . . . Register*, L, 456. See also Peterson, *Jefferson and the New Nation*, 638.
14. Jefferson to Rufus King, July 13, 1802, *Writings*, L. and B., X, 328.
15. Peterson, *Jefferson and the New Nation*, 749–50; Malone, *Jefferson the President*, 252; C. L. Lokke, "Jefferson and the Leclerc Expedition," *American Historical Review*, XXXIII (January 1928), 322–28.
16. Henry Adams, *History of the United States*, Agar ed., 61.
17. *Farm Book*, 128. Jefferson had been in Monticello from May 29 to November 24, 1800. See chronology, Malone, *Jefferson and the Ordeal of Liberty*, xxix-xxv.
18. Callender to Madison, April 27, 1801, Ford, "Jefferson and Callender," *New England . . . Register*, LI, 154.
19. Callender to Madison, May 7, 1801, *ibid.*, 156.
20. *Richmond Recorder*, February 9, 1803.
21. Jefferson to Monroe, May 29, 1801, Ford, "Jefferson and Callender," *New England . . . Register*, LI, 157.
22. Monroe to Jefferson, June 1, 1801, *ibid.*, 157.
23. Jefferson fired Randolph from office "on the ground that he had packed juries and withheld money from the government." Malone, *Jefferson the President*, 208, notes that the decision to remove Randolph was made by March 8, 1801.
24. Dabney Carr to Peachy Gilmer, August 12, 1801, Peachy Ridgway Gilmer Papers, Library of Congress.
25. Jefferson to Martha Jefferson Randolph, October 19, 1801, *Family Letters*, 209.
26. Martha Jefferson Randolph to Jefferson, November 27, 1801, *Family Letters*, 213.
27. Maria Jefferson Eppes to Jefferson, November 6, 1801, January 24, 1802, April 21, 1802, *Family Letters*, 211, 217, 224.

28. *Port Folio*, July 10, 1802, later printed in the *Richmond Recorder*, September 1, 1802. The author signed himself Asmodio. Asmodio, also spelled Asmodeus and Ashmedai, was the name of the Biblical "king of demons," known in the Talmudic legends of Solomon as "the genius of matrimonial unhappiness," who fell in love with the beautiful Sara, daughter of Raguel, and slew her seven husbands one by one on their respective bridal nights. The choice of pseudonym is a curiosity, since "Sally" is the nickname for "Sara," and the intent of the ballad maker was clearly the destruction of Sara's "husband." It suggests that the author was a man of considerable erudition.

29. Callender reported this story in the *Richmond Recorder*, September 22, 1802.

30. Jefferson to Monroe, July 14, 1802, *Writings*, L. and B., X, 330.

31. Abigail Adams to Jefferson, July 1, 1804, *Adams-Jefferson Letters*, 271–74.

32. *Richmond Examiner*, August 18, 1802.

33. *Richmond Recorder*, September 1, 22, 1802.

34. *Richmond Examiner*, September 18, 22, 1802.

35. *Ibid.*, September 25, 1802.

36. *Richmond Recorder*, September 15, 1802.

37. See pp. 272, 294, 297–98.

38. *Richmond Recorder*, September 15, 1802. For Madison Hemings' reminiscences, see Appendix I.

39. *Richmond Recorder*, September 22, 1802.

40. Meriwether Jones, in the *Richmond Examiner* of October 16, 1802, accused Hamilton of leaking the story to Bronfon through David Dagget.

41. Reprinted in the *Richmond Recorder*, September 22, 1802.

42. Reprinted in the *New York Evening Post*, December 8, 1802.

43. Jefferson to Samuel Smith, August 22, 1798, *Writings*, L. and B., X, 58.

44. For the discovery that this was actually Jefferson's article, see Noble E. Cunningham, Jr., *The Jeffersonian Republicans in Power: Party Operations, 1801–1809* (Chapel Hill, N.C., 1963), 257. The charge was false, and Jefferson had the documents to prove it.

45. Burwell acknowledged authorship of the articles titled "Vindication of Mr. Jefferson" in his unpublished memoir, now in the Library of Congress. They were printed in the *Richmond Enquirer* in August and September 1805, written in response particularly to the accusations of a Virginia planter, Tom Turner, who had accused Jefferson of a whole list of misdemeanors, and who insisted that the Sally Hemings story was "unquestionably true." The Tom Turner letters appeared in the *Boston Repertory* in 1805.

46. *Richmond Recorder*, September 29, December 1, 1802.

47. *Ibid.*, September 22, 1802.

48. *Ibid.*, September 29, 1802, December 1, 1803.

49. *Frederick-Town Herald*, reprinted in the *Richmond Recorder* September 29, 1802. See *Measure for Measure*, I: 4, 57–61. In the original, Shakespeare used the word "sense" at the end of the third line, rather than "female."

50. Reprinted in the *Richmond Recorder*, December 8, 1802.

51. Reprinted in the *Richmond Recorder*, November 3, 1802.

52. Quoted in Page Smith, *John Adams*, II, 1094.

53. John Adams to Abigail Adams, November 18, 1877, *Adams Family Correspondence*, I, 327.

54. Adams, *Diary and Autobiography*, III, 260.

55. Abigail Adams to Jefferson, July 1, 1804, *Adams-Jefferson Letters*, 274.

56. Jefferson to Abigail Adams, July 22, 1804, *Adams-Jefferson Letters*, 275.

57. "The Discoveries of Captain Lewis," *Boston Review and Monthly Anthology*, IV (March 1807), 143–44. Partly a lampoon on the so-called miraculous discoveries of Meriwether Lewis on his trip to the Pacific, the verses referred to Jefferson as follows:

> Let dusky Sally henceforth bear
> The name of Isabella;

And let the mountain, all of salt,
Be christen'd Monticella—
Adams was embarrassed when this ballad was dredged up in his own presidential campaign in 1828 and his authorship disclosed. Sam Houston read it in the House of Representatives on February 1827, and it was printed in several pro-Jackson newspapers in 1828. Peterson, *The Jefferson Image in the American Mind*, 462. Richard Dillon's *Meriwether Lewis* (New York, 1965), 269–70, has the entire ballad.

58. The *Port Folio* at this point quoted in a footnote from *Notes on the State of Virginia*, p. 205: "They (the blacks) secrete less by the kidneys, and more by the glands of the skin, which gives them *a very strong and disagreeable odor*," October 2, 1802, 312.

59. *Richmond Recorder*, October 27, 1802.
60. *Richmond Examiner*, November 3, 1802.
61. *Ibid.*, October 16, 1802.
62. *Richmond Recorder*, September 1, 1802.
63. *Ibid.*, January 12, 1803.
64. *Richmond Examiner*, July 31, 1802.

CHAPTER XXVI   Jefferson under Attack

1. "Refutation of the Argument that the Colonies Were Established at the Expense of the British Nation," Ms. unpublished until 1940. See *Papers*, Boyd, I, 283–84, 284n.
2. Randall quotes this from a Philadelphia paper, unnamed, originally printed in a Boston paper, also unnamed, *Jefferson*, III, 19n.
3. Reprinted in the *Richmond Recorder*, November 3, 1802.
4. *Ibid.*, September 29, 1802.
5. See Madison Hemings' reminiscences, Appendix I. The date he gives for his birth is corroborated by the *Farm Book*, 128. Dumas Malone's chronology, *Jefferson the President*, xxviii-xxix, shows that Jefferson had been in Monticello from April 4 to May 11, 1804.
6. Appendix I.
7. Jefferson to Martha Jefferson Randolph, July 2, 1802, *Family Letters*, 231.
8. Henry Randall to James Parton, June 1, 1868, reporting a conversation with Thomas Jefferson Randolph, Flower, *James Parton*, 238; see Appendix III.
9. Ellen Randolph Coolidge to Joseph Coolidge, Jr., October 24, 1858, Ms., owned by Harold Jefferson Coolidge.
10. Gaines, *Thomas Mann Randolph*, 46.
11. Jefferson to Martha Jefferson Randolph, October 7, 1802, *Family Letters*, 236.
12. Jefferson to Martha Jefferson Randolph and Maria Jefferson Eppes, October 18, 1802, *Family Letters*, 237.
13. Jefferson to Robert Livingston, October 10, 1802, *Writings*, L. and B, X, 336.
14. Jefferson to Levi Lincoln, October 25, 1802, *Writings*, L. and B., X, 339.
15. *American Citizen*, July 23–24, 1805, republished in *Complete Writings of Thomas Paine*, Foner, ed., II, 983. The phrase had been used by Tom Turner in the *Boston Repertory* May 31, 1805, in describing Callender's attacks on Washington and Adams.
16. *Port Folio*, December 4, 18, 1802.
17. *Port Folio*, April 9, 1803, p. 120, reprinted from the *Boston Gazette*.
18. See the ballad on p. 354.
19. Margaret Bayard Smith, *First Forty Years of Washington Society*, 34–35.
20. *Port Folio*, January 21, 1802; Cutler, *Life, Journals, and Correspondence*, December 13, 1802, January 3, 1803, II, 113, 119.
21. William Plumer to Jeremiah Smith, December 9, 1802, Plumer Mss., Library of Congress, quoted in Schachner, *Jefferson*, 721.

22. Maria Jefferson Eppes to Jefferson, January 11, 1803, *Family Letters*, 240.
23. Second Annual Message, December 15, 1802, *Writings*, L. and B., III, 340.
24. As reported in the *Richmond Recorder*, June 15, 1803.
25. Cutler, *Life, Journals, and Correspondence*, December 2, 1804, II, 172.
26. *Richmond Recorder*, October 13, 27, 1802.
27. The challenge was reported in the *Richmond Recorder*, May 28, 1803. Callender reported that the letter Jefferson had sent to Walker "confessed that his fault was such that it was impossible for the injured husband ever to forgive him," *Richmond Recorder*, November 17, 1802. Though the editor threatened again on February 2 and May 28, 1803, to publish it, and similar threats appeared in other Federalist papers in 1805, Walker never gave permission and the letter seems to have disappeared.
28. *Richmond Recorder*, May 28, 1803.
29. For details, see James Morton Smith, *Freedom's Fetters*.
30. As Callender noted in the *Richmond Recorder*, February 2, 1803.
31. John W. Eppes to Jefferson, January 4, 1803, University of Virginia.
32. See the account of Jefferson's suit against John Henderson, in which Hay acted as attorney for Jefferson, Ms., University of Virginia.
33. As reprinted in the *Richmond Recorder*, January 26, 1803. The *Washington Federalist*, edited by W. A. Rind, was a successor to the *Virginia Federalist*, Richmond, 1800.
34. *Richmond Recorder*, February 9, 1803.
35. *Ibid.*, March 16, 1803. For a discussion of the Langhorne letter episode, see p. 313.
36. Jefferson to Peter Carr, August 10, 1787, *Papers*, Boyd, XII, 15.
37. Jefferson to John Page, March 18, 1803, Library of Congress, 22505.
38. John Page to Jefferson, April 25, 1803, Library of Congress 22632–33.
39. James Madison to James Monroe, April 20, 1803, Madison, *Writings*, Hunt, ed., VII, 48n. The italicized portions were originally in code.
40. The copy of this letter, certified to be exact by Bishop James Madison and John Marshall on May 13, 1806, may now be seen in the Virginia Historical Society, which kindly furnished me a copy. The letter also explained that a letter from Walker to Jefferson, sent to Paris on May 15, 1788, just after his wife's confession, had miscarried.
41. *Richmond Recorder*, May 28, 1802.
42. Thomas Mann Randolph to Jefferson, May 22, 1803, Library of Congress, 22736. Randolph was replying to "your letter preceding that of the 5th inst." The letter to which he refers is in neither the Library of Congress nor the Massachusetts Historical Society.
43. Ellen Randolph Coolidge memories, Ms., University of Virginia. See the curious manner in which Randall handles this story, *Jefferson*, III, 118–19.
44. Jefferson to Benjamin Rush, April 23, 1803, *Writings*, L. and B., X, 379–80.
45. Jefferson to Dr. Joseph Priestley, March 21, 1801, *Writings*, L. and B., X, 228. Jefferson sent a copy of Priestley's work to his daughter Martha in April 1803, urging her to read it "because it establishes the groundwork of my view of this subject." Jefferson to Martha Jefferson Randolph, April 23, 1803, *Family Letters*, 244.
46. Priestley, "Socrates and Jesus Compared," in *Theological and Miscellaneous Works*, J. T. Rutt, ed., 25 vols. in 26 (London, 1817–32), XVII, 400–439.
47. "Syllabus of an Estimate of the Doctrines of Jesus, Compared with Those of Others," *Writings*, L. and B., X, 381–85.
48. *Ibid.*, 381.
49. Jefferson to Martha Jefferson Randolph, April 23, 1803, *Family Letters*, 244.
50. Jefferson to Benjamin Rush, April 21, 1803, *Writings*, L. and B., X, 380–81.
51. Jefferson to John Adams, October 12, 1813, *Adams-Jefferson Letters*, 384.
52. See *The Jefferson Bible*, edited by O. I. A. Roche, with an introduction by H. W. Foote and a foreword by D. S. Harrington (New York, 1964).

53. Jefferson to Charles Thomson, January 9, 1816, *Writings*, L. and B., XIV, 385-86.
54. Jefferson to Horatio G. Spafford, 1816, *Writings*, Ford, X, 13.
55. *Richmond Examiner*, July 27, 1803.
56. *Ibid.*, July 8, 16, 1803.
57. *Ibid.*, July 20, 1803.
58. *Ibid.*, August 10, 1803, July 27, 1803.
59. *Defence of Young and Minns, Printers to the State* (Boston, 1805), 14-15.
60. See John Walker to Henry Lee, March 28, 1805, Library of Congress, 25833: "For you must remember, that by an express article of that negotiation, some mode was to be devised, whereby it might be made known to the world, that satisfaction had been given me. This was regarded as *indispensable*. How has it been complied with? And untill it is, the only possible mode of self defence that occurs to me, is the showing of our correspondence to friends."
61. Huntington Library. First published in *Thomas Jefferson's Correspondence, Printed from the Originals in the Collection of William K. Bixby*, W. C. Ford, ed. (Boston, 1916), 114-15. This covering letter has been mistakenly thought to be a letter discussing the charges concerning Sally Hemings as well as Mrs. Walker. It was on the contrary a letter discussing only Walker's specific charges, published in full here on pp. 75-76. When Malone published this statement, he omitted the reference to Walker's charge that Jefferson had fabricated a letter concerning an old debt to Walker's father. It is important to note that Jefferson here denied this charge, which had been made much of by Tom Turner in the *Boston Repertory* of May 31, 1805. See also Turner's later letter in the *Virginia Gazette and General Advertiser*, October 26, 1805, written in reply to Burwell's "Vindication of Mr. Jefferson," published in the *Richmond Enquirer* in the preceding months.
62. Henry Lee to Jefferson, September 8, 1806, Library of Congress, 28252-53.
63. Malone, *Jefferson the Virginian*, 448.

CHAPTER XXVII   Death, Hatred, and the Uses of Silence

1. Jefferson to John Page, June 24, 1801, *Writings*, L. and B., XI, 31.
2. Jefferson to Thomas Mann Randolph, Jr., February 4, 1800, Library of Congress, 18179; Jefferson wrote also to Maria Eppes, February 12, 1800, "You have perhaps heard of the loss of Jupiter. With all his defects, he leaves a void in my domestic arrangements which cannot be filled." *Family Letters*, 185. For the mention of James Hemings' death, see Jefferson to Thomas Mann Randolph December 4, 1801, Library of Congress, 20356.
3. Jefferson to Benjamin Rush, December 20, 1801, *Writings*, L. and B., X, 304.
4. Jefferson wrote to James Madison, November 30, 1809, of "the catastrophe of poor Lewis," *Writings*, L. and B., XII, 330. See also Dillon, *Meriwether Lewis*, 335.
5. Jefferson to Rev. Isaac Story, December 5, 1801, *Writings*, L. and B., X, 299.
6. Maria Jefferson Eppes to Jefferson, December 8, 1797; Jefferson to Maria Jefferson Eppes, January 7, 1798, *Family Letters*, 150-52.
7. Jefferson to Maria Jefferson Eppes, November 7, 1803, December 26, 1803, *Family Letters*, 248, 250.
8. Maria Jefferson Eppes to Jefferson, February 10, 1804, *Family Letters*, 256. Jefferson after her death did have the artist, C. B. J. F. de Saint-Mémin, make such a portrait.
9. Martha Jefferson Randolph to Jefferson, January 14, 1804, *Family Letters*, 252.
10. Ellen Randolph Coolidge memoirs, Ms., University of Virginia; Malone, *Jefferson the President*, 408-9.
11. Jefferson to Maria Jefferson Eppes, February 26, 1804, *Family Letters*, 258.
12. Jefferson to Maria Jefferson Eppes, March 3, 8, 1804, *Family Letters*, 258-59.

13. See John Eppes to Jefferson, March 12, 19, 23, 1804, University of Virginia Library, and Jefferson to Eppes, March 15, 1804, Randall, *Jefferson*, III, 98–99.

14. Malone, *Jefferson the President*, 415.

15. *Ibid.*

16. Jefferson to Madison, April 23, 1804, *Writings*, Ford, VIII, 300.

17. Jefferson to John Page, June 25, 1804, *Writings*, L. and B., XI, 31–32.

18. Jefferson to Gideon Granger, April 16, 1804, *Writings*, L. and B., XI, 25–26.

19. See Jordan, *White over Black*, 177–78.

20. Jefferson to John Page, June 25, 1804, *Writings*, L. and B., XI, 32.

21. See Appendix I. The accuracy of Madison's birth date, given in these reminiscences as January 19, 1805, is borne out by the *Farm Book*, 128.

22. Jefferson was in Washington in January 1805. Dolley Madison had a warm affection for Martha Jefferson Randolph, and frequently filled her requests for purchases in Philadelphia, as the *Family Letters* indicate. As yet I have seen no evidence that she was visiting at Monticello in late January 1805.

23. James was born in the President's House, where his mother spent the six months between December 2, 1805, and May 1806. The Randolphs named their sons Thomas Jefferson, James Madison, Benjamin Franklin, Lewis Meriwether, and George Wythe. See Gaines, *Thomas Mann Randolph*, 59, Randall, Jefferson III, 563.

24. Abigail Adams to Jefferson, May 20, 1804, *Adams-Jefferson Letters*, 268–69.

25. Jefferson to John Eppes, June 4, 1804, Randall, *Jefferson*, III, 99–100.

26. Jefferson communicated his suspicions to Benjamin Rush, December 5, 1811, by which time he realized that Abigail had been telling the truth, that Adams did not see either his or his wife's letters during the period of the correspondence, *Writings*, L. and B., XIII, 115.

27. Jefferson to Abigail Adams, June 13, 1804, *Adams-Jefferson Letters*, 269–71.

28. Abigail Adams to Jefferson, July 1, 1804, *Adams-Jefferson Letters*, 271–74.

29. Jefferson to Abigail Adams, July 22, 1804, *Adams-Jefferson Letters*, 274–76.

30. Abigail Adams to Jefferson, August 18, July 1, 1804, *Adams-Jefferson Letters*, 276–78, 274.

31. Abigail Adams to Jefferson, October 25, 1804, *Adams-Jefferson Letters*, 281.

32. Jefferson to Benjamin Rush, January 16, 1811, *Writings*, L. and B., XIII, 8.

33. *Adams-Jefferson Letters*, 282.

34. Jefferson to Benjamin Rush, December 5, 1811, *Writings*, L. and B., XIII, 117.

35. Miller, *Hamilton and the Growth of the New Nation*, 573.

36. Schachner, *Alexander Hamilton*, 404.

37. Aaron Burr wrote to his daughter Theodosia November 26, 1801, "You have learned from the newspapers (which you never read) the death of Philip Hamilton. Shot in a duel with Eacker, the lawyer. Some dispute at a theatre, arising, as is said, out of politics." *Correspondence of Aaron Burr with His Daughter Theodosia,* Mark Van Doren, ed. (New York, 1929), 74.

38. Allan M. Hamilton, *The Intimate Life of Alexander Hamilton*, 219.

39. Miller, *Hamilton and the Growth of the New Nation*, 549–50.

40. Douglass Adair and Marvin Harvey, "Was Alexander Hamilton a Christian Statesman?" in *Alexander Hamilton, A Profile*, Cooke, ed., 251–52.

41. Miller, *Hamilton and the Growth of the New Nation*, 544, 552, 567, 556.

42. During 1803 two editors were brought to trial, Harry Croswell and Joseph Dennie, the latter with Jefferson's explicit approval. Dennie was editor of the *Port Folio*, which had published most of the ballads concerning Sally Hemings, and which openly glorified monarchy. When Governor McKean of Pennsylvania had written urging Jefferson's consent to prosecute him, the President had replied, "I have therefore long thought that a few prosecutions of the most prominent offenders would have a wholesome effect in restoring the integrity of the presses. Not a general prosecution, for that would look like persecution: but a selected one . . ." Dennie was brought to trial, however, not for libeling Jefferson but for a tirade against democracy. Not surprisingly, he was acquitted. See Malone, *Jefferson the President*, 231;

Leonard W. Levy, *Legacy of Suppression: Freedom of Speech and Press in Early American History* (Cambridge, Mass., 1960), 299; and Harold M. Ellis, *Joseph Dennie and His Circle* (Austin, Texas, 1915), chap. 10.

43. "Speech on the Law of Libel," Hamilton, *Works*, Lodge, ed., VIII, 378–425.

44. "Narrative of Col. Robert Troup," Nathan Schachner, "Alexander Hamilton as Viewed by his Friends," *William and Mary Quarterly*, 3rd series, IV (April 1947), 216–17.

45. Jefferson had made this clear in a difficult interview with Burr on January 26, 1804.

46. Quoted in Edward P. Power, *Nullification and Secession* (New York, 1897), 133.

47. Henry Adams, *History of the United States*, II, 189.

48. Harold C. Syrett and Jean G. Cooke, *Interview in Weehawken: The Burr-Hamilton Duel, as Told in the Original Documents* (Middletown, Conn., 1960), 102, 111, 133.

49. John Adams to Jefferson, September 3, 1816, *Adams-Jefferson Letters*, 488.

50. William Plumer, *Memorandum of Proceedings in the United States Senate, 1803–1807* (New York, 1923), 213.

51. Henry Adams, *History of the United States*, I, 216.

52. William Duval to Thomas Jefferson, June 4, 1806, Library of Congress, 27874.

53. William Duval to Jefferson, June 8, 19, 29, July 12, 1806, Library of Congress, 27882, 27915, (unnumbered), 28044.

54. Jefferson to William Duval, June 14, 1806, Library of Congress, 27898.

55. Jefferson to William Duval, June 22, 1806, Library of Congress, 27941.

56. Jefferson to William Duval, July 17, 1806, Library of Congress, 28601; Duval to Jefferson, November 21, 1806, Library of Congress, 28475; Jefferson to Duval, December 4, 1806, Library of Congress, 28523; Duval to Jefferson, December 10, 1806, Library of Congress, 28533.

57. Julian Boyd, "The Murder of George Wythe," *William and Mary Quarterly*, 3rd series, XII, no. 4 (October 1955), 513–75; Helen T. Catterall, ed., *Judicial Cases Concerning Slavery and the Negro*, 5 vols. (Washington, D.C., 1926–37), I, 108–9. For a copy of Wythe's will, see Library of Congress, 27971–72.

58. See Paul Leicester Ford's chronology, *Writings*, Ford, IX, xxvii–xxviii, and *Farm Book*, 128.

59. Ford's chronology states that Jefferson was in Monticello from May 12 to June 8, 1808, *Writings*, Ford, IX, xxix.

CHAPTER XXVIII   Jefferson and Burr

1. Jefferson to Du Pont de Nemours, July 14, 1807, *Writings*, L. and B., XI, 275.

2. Herbert S. Parmet and Marie B. Hecht, *Aaron Burr: Portrait of an Ambitious Man* (New York, 1967), 297.

3. Henry Adams, *History of the United States*, II, 271.

4. Jefferson to Edmund P. Gaines, July 23, 1807, *Writings*, Ford, IX, 122.

5. John Adams to Benjamin Rush, February 2, 1807, *Old Family Letters* (Philadelphia, 1892), 129–29, *The Spur of Fame: Dialogues of John Adams and Benjamin Rush, 1805–1813*, 76.

6. Benjamin Rush to John Adams, July 9, 1807, Rush, *Letters*, Butterfield, ed., II, 951.

7. Parmet and Hecht, *Aaron Burr*, 265.

8. Benjamin Rush to Jefferson, January 2, 1811, Rush, *Letters*, II, 1074; Jefferson to Benjamin Rush, January 16, 1811, *Writings*, Ford, IX, 294.

9. Jefferson to Thomas Mann Randolph, June 23, 1806, University of Virginia. William Plumer's diary noted that Randolph accused John Randolph of revealing secrets and exciting clamor. Plumer, *Memorandum of Proceedings*, 490, 622–23.

10. Henry Adams, *History of the United States*, III, 164.

11. Jefferson to Thomas Mann Randolph, February 18, 1807, Library of Congress, 29008.
12. William Burwell to Jefferson, February 18, 20, 28, March 3, 1807, University of Virginia Library.
13. Plumer, Memorandum of Proceedings, 622.
14. Jefferson to Thomas Mann Randolph, February 19, 1807, February 28, 1807, April 3, 1807, Library of Congress, 29024, 29081, 29259.
15. Plumer, Memorandum of Proceedings, 642. Randolph's excellent biographer, William H. Gaines, Jr., describing this crisis, seems to have missed the Burwell correspondence, and the hints of threatened suicide. Thomas Mann Randolph, 65–66.
16. Jefferson to Ellen Randolph, June 29, 1807, Family Letters, 309.
17. Martha Jefferson Randolph to Jefferson, March 20, 1807, Family Letters, 303.
18. Jefferson to Caesar A. Rodney, December 5, 1806, Writings, Ford, VIII, 497.
19. Burr's father and grandmother died of dysentery. His mother and grandfather were inoculated against smallpox, but Jonathan Edwards contracted the disease in a virulent form from the inoculation and died. Family legend has it that Esther Burr recovered from the inoculation but died in shock and sorrow over her father's death. Parmet and Hecht, Aaron Burr, 11.
20. Benjamin Rush heard this oration, and described it to John Adams April 3, 1807, when Burr was on trial for treason. Rush, Letters, Butterfield, ed., II, 938.
21. Mathew L. Davis, Memoirs of Aaron Burr, 2 vols. (New York, 1836–37), I, 32.
22. Parmet and Hecht, Aaron Burr, 251.
23. Ibid., 21.
24. Davis, Memoirs of Aaron Burr, I, iii.
25. Ibid., 408.
26. Anas, January 26, 1804, Writings, L. and B., I, 448.
27. Esther Burr to Jonathan Edwards, Davis, Memoirs of Aaron Burr, I, 23.
28. Davis, Memoirs of Aaron Burr, I, 91.
29. Theodosia P. Burr to Aaron Burr, March 22, 1784, Davis, Memoirs of Aaron Burr, I, 247.
30. Burr to Theodosia P. Burr, May 1795, Davis, Memoirs of Aaron Burr, I, 256.
31. Burr to Theodosia Burr, January 29, 1800; Theodosia Burr Alston to Burr, July 20, 1803, Correspondence of Aaron Burr with His Daughter Theodosia, Van Doren, ed., 56, 122.
32. George Troup to Rufus King, December 12, 1802, Albert J. Beveridge, Life of John Marshall, 4 vols. (Boston, 1919), III, 280n.
33. The Richmond Enquirer in 1807 published the cipher code Wilkinson and Burr used in their correspondence, saying it had begun in 1800 or 1801. The article was reproduced in full in William H. Safford, The Life of Harman Blennerhassett (Chillicothe, Ohio, 1850), 214–17.
34. Burr to Theodosia Burr Alston, February 23, 1802, Correspondence, 85.
35. Burr to Theodosia Burr Alston, August 2, 3, 1804, Correspondence, 172–73.
36. Burr to Theodosia Burr Alston, January 15, 1805, Correspondence, 200.
37. Anthony Merry to Harrowby, August 6, 1804, March 29, 1805, Henry Adams, History of the United States, II, 395, 403.
38. Louis Marie Turreau to Talleyrand, March 9, 1805, Henry Adams, History of the United States, II, 407.
39. A great many writers, including James Parton, Albert Beveridge, and Nathan Schachner, have tried to prove that Burr was not guilty of treasonous intentions against the United States. The matter was solved long ago by Henry Adams, but his findings have been reinforced with additional impeccable scholarship by Thomas Perkins Abernethy (The Burr Conspiracy [New York, 1954]), and Herbert S. Parmet and Marie B. Hecht (Aaron Burr: Portrait of an Ambitious Man). See also Life of the Late General William Eaton, Charles Prentiss, ed. (Brookfield, Mass., 1813), Annals of Congress, 10th Congress, 1st session, "Trial of Aaron Burr" (Washington, D.C., 1852).

40. *Annals of Congress*, 10th Congress, 1st session, I, 425–28.
41. Jefferson had had a detailed letter from the Federal prosecutor of Kentucky, Joseph H. Daviess, who had been made suspicious by Burr's activities in the West in 1805, in Jan. 10, 1806. He warned the president that both Burr and Wilkinson were in the pay of the Spanish government, and that they were also planning a secret expedition against Mexico. See Joseph H. Daviess, "A View of the President's Conduct Concerning the Conspiracy of 1806," *Quarterly Publications of the Historical and Philosophical Society of Ohio*, XII (1917), 53–128. This was first published as a pamphlet in 1807. Spain had in fact turned over $2,500 to Burr and Jonathan Dayton.
42. Jefferson described his suspicions in a letter to Gideon Granger, March 9, 1814, *Writings*, L. and B., XIV, 113.
43. Parmet and Hecht, *Aaron Burr*, 230–31.
44. Anas, April 15, 1806, reporting the conversation as having taken place "about a month ago," *Writings*, L. and B., I, 449.
45. See Jefferson's comments to Granger on this letter, Jefferson to Granger, March 9, 1814, *Writings*, L. and B., XIV, 115. Benjamin Rush, writing to John Adams, January 23, 1807, reported that Eaton made this statement to "a large dining company." See Rush, *Letters*, Butterfield, ed., II, 937.
46. Anas, October 22, 1807, *Writings*, L. and B., I, 459–60.
47. Parmet and Hecht, *Aaron Burr*, 251–52; General James Wilkinson, *Memoirs of My Own Times*, 3 vols. (Philadelphia, 1816), II, 316–17.
48. Daviess, "A View of the President's Conduct Concerning the Conspiracy of 1806," 102. Daviess became incensed because he believed Jefferson did not heed his warnings, and after his criticisms of the President cost him his job as federal prosecutor for Kentucky, he wrote the bitter pamphlet of 1807, publishing his entire correspondence with Jefferson.
49. Jefferson to Robert Smith, December 23, 1806, Henry Adams, *History of the United States*, III, 331.
50. Thomas Abernethy holds that though the conspiracy ended in a fiasco, "its potentialities were so portentous that it seems reasonable to say that next to the Confederate War it posed the greatest threat of dismemberment which the American Union has ever faced." *The Burr Conspiracy*, 274.
51. Dayton to Wilkinson, July 24, 1806, *Annals of Congress*, 10th Congress, 1st session, I, 560. Burr told Matthew Davis that Wilkinson decided to abandon him when he learned of the death of William Pitt in England on January 6, 1806. This meant the end of any possible naval support for Burr's enterprise. Davis, *Memoirs of Aaron Burr*, II, 381–82. Jefferson had been contemplating supplanting Wilkinson by either James Monroe or Meriwether Lewis, as there was a strong sentiment in the country that the governor of a territory should not be a military man.
52. As quoted by prosecution lawyer Alexander MacRae, *Trial of Aaron Burr for Treason, Printed from the Report Taken in Short Hand by David Robertson*, 2 vols. (Jersey City, 1879), II, 41.
53. Parmet and Hecht, *Aaron Burr*, 295.
54. Jefferson's son-in-law, Randolph, tried to persuade him to fire Wilkinson, warning him that unless he did his own administration would fall. This disagreement in his own family became open Washington gossip. Parmet and Hecht, *Aaron Burr*, 282; Gaines, *Thomas Mann Randolph*, 65. Jefferson later defended Wilkinson's arbitrary arrests in New Orleans on the grounds that while "we knew here that there was never danger of a British fleet from below, and that Burr's band was crushed before it reached the Mississippi . . . General Wilkinson's information was very different, and he could act on no other." Jefferson to J. B. Colvin, September 20, 1810, *Writings*, L. and B., XII, 421.
55. Jefferson to Joseph R. Nicholson, February 20, 1807, *Writings*, Ford, IX, 31–32.
56. *Annals of Congress*, 9th Congress, 2nd Session, 40.
57. John Adams to Benjamin Rush, February 2, 1807, *Old Family Letters*, 128–29.

58. Burr to Theodosia Burr Alston, July 24, 1807, *Correspondence*, 223.
59. Beveridge, *Life of Marshall*, II, 165.
60. Jefferson to Madison, November 26, 1795, *Writings*, Ford, VIII, 197–98.
61. Peterson, *Jefferson and the New Nation*, 699.
62. As pointed out by Henry Adams, *History of the United States*, II, 156.
63. William H. Safford, *The Blennerhassett Papers* (Cincinnati, 1864), 355.
64. Jefferson to William Branch Giles, April 20, 1807, *Writings*, L. and B., XI, 187–91.
65. May 25, 1807, *Trial of Aaron Burr*, I, 51.
66. *Trial of Aaron Burr*, I, 51–52.
67. Jefferson to George Hay, June 17, 1807, *Writings*, L. and B., XI, 231–33. Later Jefferson privately denounced the attempt to subpoena him as "preposterous," Jefferson to George Hay, September 7, 1807, *Writings*, L. and B., XI, 365. Abernethy found evidence that Burr and Wilkinson even protected each other, each withholding cipher letters that would have illuminated the conspiracy. *The Burr Conspiracy*, 241.
68. Safford, *The Blennerhassett Papers*, 320.
69. William Cranch, *Reports of Cases Argued and Adjudicated in the Supreme Court of the United States in the Years 1807 and 1808* (New York, 1812), IV, 122. Wirt repeated this ruling in his attack on Burr. See *Trial of Aaron Burr*, II, 75–76. The underlining is Wirt's.
70. Jefferson to Albert Gallatin, September 27, 1810, quoted in Schachner, *Jefferson*, 901.
71. *Oxford History of the American People*, 370.
72. *Trial of Aaron Burr*, I, 51.
73. Jefferson to Lafayette, July 14, 1807, *Writings*, Ford, IX, 113.
74. When Congress tried to suspend the right of habeas corpus to ease the legal restraints on Burr's prosecutors, Jefferson' son-in-law, John Eppes, led the successful fight against this in the House. The Senate had passed the measure. Henry Adams, *History of the United States*, III, 339.
75. Jefferson to Thomas Mann Randolph, June 28, 1808, Library of Congress, 31618.
76. *Private Journal of Aaron Burr*, 2 vols. (Rochester, N.Y., 1903), 11, 401.
77. Parmet and Hecht, *Aaron Burr*, 340.

CHAPTER XXIX   A Genius for Peace

1. Jefferson to John Langdon, August 2, 1808, *Writings*, L. and B., XVI, 310.
2. Jefferson to James Monroe, February 18, 1808, *Writings*, L. and B., XI, 444–45; Ammon, *James Monroe: The Quest for National Identity*, 270–83; Ketcham, *James Madison*, 438.
3. November 3, 1803, *Writings*, Ford, X, 47–48; Peterson, *Jefferson and the New Nation*, 730–34.
4. Jefferson to Charles Carroll, April 15, 1791, *Writings*, L. and B., VIII, 177–78. Jefferson to Meriwether Lewis, August 21, 1808, *Writings*, L. and B., XII, 143.
5. Beloff, *Thomas Jefferson and American Democracy*, 10.
6. Henry Adams, *History of the United States*, IV, 356, 130, 136.
7. Merrill Peterson, *Jefferson and the New Nation*, 806–11.
8. Jefferson to Henry Innes, January 23, 1800, *Writings*, L. and B., X, 145.
9. Jefferson to John Langdon, August 2, 1808, *Writings*, Ford, IX, 201. Jefferson to Col. John Taylor, August 1, 1807, *Writings*, L. and B., XI, 305.
10. Turreau to Champagny, May 20, 1808, quoted in Henry Adams, *History of the United States*, IV, 231.
11. Jefferson to Dr. Robert Morrell, February 5, 1813; to John Adams, July 5, 15, 1814; to Benjamin Austin, February 9, 1816, *Writings*, L. and B., XIII, 216; XIV, 145–46, 436.

12. Jefferson to Caesar A. Rodney, February 10, 1810, *Writings*, L. and B., XII, 358.

13. Henry Adams, *History of the United States*, IV, 26.

14. Jefferson to Du Pont de Nemours, July 14, 1807, *Writings*, L. and B., XI, 274.

15. Jefferson to Thomas Mann Randolph, July 13, 1807, New York Public Library.

16. Turreau to Talleyrand, July 18, 1808, quoted in Henry Adams, *History of the United States*, IV, 36–37.

17. Henry Adams, *History of the United States*, IV, 74.

18. Jefferson to James Madison, April 27, 1809, *Writings*, L. and B., XII, 277.

19. Jefferson to John Langdon, August 2, 1808, *Writings*, Ford, IX, 201.

20. Jefferson to Gen. John Armstrong, May 2, 1808, *Writings*, L. and B., XII, 43.

21. Jefferson to Thomas Leiper, January 21, 1809, *Writings*, L. and B., XII, 238.

22. Henry Adams, *History of the United States*, IV, 138.

23. Jefferson to Thomas Jefferson Randolph, November 24, 1808, *Writings*, L. and B., XII, 200.

24. Henry Adams, *History of the United States*, IV, 139.

25. Jefferson to Levi Lincoln, March 23, 1808, *Writings*, L. and B., XII, 21.

26. "Circular Letter from the Secretary of War to the Governors," January 17, 1809, *Writings*, Ford, IX, 237.

27. William Cullen Bryant, *The Embargo*, with introduction and notes by Thomas O. Mabbott (Gainesville, Fla., 1955).

28. Jefferson to William Branch Giles, December 25, 1825, *Writings*, L. and B., XVI, 144.

29. Jefferson to Madison, August 1809, *Writings*, H. A. Washington, ed., V, 463.

30. Jefferson to Henry Dearborn, June 14, 1809, *Writings*, L. and B., XII, 292.

31. Jefferson to James Maury, June 16, 1816, *Writings*, L. and B., XIV, 316; see also Alfred Mahan, *Sea Power and Its Relation to the War of 1812*, 2 vols. (Boston, 1905), I, 300.

32. Jefferson to William Wirt, May 3, 1811, *Writings*, L. and B., XIII, 56.

33. Jefferson to William Short, November 1814, *Writings*, Washington, ed., VI, 398.

34. Jefferson to Thomas Leiper, June 11, 1815, *Writings*, Ford, IX, 521. See also George Dangerfield, *The Era of Good Feelings* (New York, 1952), 43.

35. Jefferson to James Maury, April 25, 1812, *Writings*, L. and B., XIII, 148.

36. Jefferson to John Adams, June 1, 1822, *Adams-Jefferson Letters*, 579.

CHAPTER XXX   Like a Patriarch of Old

1. Margaret Bayard Smith, *First Forty Years of Washington Society*, 79.

2. See McColley, *Slavery in Jeffersonian Virginia*; Matthew T. Mellon, *Early American Views on Negro Slavery* (New York, 1934); and John H. Russell, *The Free Negro in Virginia, 1619-1865* (Baltimore, 1913).

3. Augustus John Foster, *Jeffersonian America: Notes on the United States of America, Collected in the Years 1805-6-7 and 11-12*, Richard Beale Davis, ed. (San Marino, Calif., 1954), 155-56.

4. *Annals of Congress*, 1806-7, 168; Henry Adams, *History of the United States*, III, 359, Plumer, *Memorandum of Proceedings*, January 21, 1805; Foster, *Jeffersonian America*, 307.

5. Mellon, *Early American Views on Negro Slavery*, 118; Lambert, *Travels*, II, 165, quoted in Lofton, *Insurrection in South Carolina*; Daniel P. Mannix and Malcolm Cowley, *Black Cargoes: A History of the Atlantic Slave Trade* (New York, 1962), 196.

6. Jefferson to Dr. Walter Jones, March 31, 1801, *Writings*, L. and B., X, 256.

7. Jefferson to Edward Coles, August 24, 1814, *Writings*, Ford, IX, 478.

8. Jefferson to Elizabeth Trist, December 27, 1807, *Garden Book*, 359.

9. Jefferson to Charles Willson Peale, February 6, 1809, James Monroe Law Office Papers, courtesy of the University of Virginia.
10. Jefferson to Alexander von Humboldt, March 6, 1809, *Garden Book*, 409.
11. Margaret Bayard Smith, *First Forty Years of Washington Society*, 55–59, 412.
12. *Ibid.*, 385.
13. Jefferson to Du Pont de Nemours, March 2, 1809, *Writings*, L. and B., XII, 266.
14. Jefferson to Madison, March 17, 1809, *Writings*, L. and B., XII, 266.
15. Jefferson to A. C. V. C. Destutt de Tracy, January 26, 1811, *Writings*, L. and B., XIII, 18.
16. See the Edmund Bacon memoir in *Jefferson at Monticello*.
17. "To the Inhabitants of Albemarle County, in Virginia," April 3, 1809, *Writings*, L. and B., XII, 269–70. The Biblical quotation is from 1 Samuel, 12:3.
18. Margaret Bayard Smith, *First Forty Years of Washington Society*, 65, 70.
19. Jefferson to Benjamin Rush, September 22, 1809, Library of Congress, 33495.
20. Jefferson to John Langdon, March 5, 1810, *Writings*, L. and B., XII, 378.
21. George Ticknor, *Life, Letters, and Journals*, 2 vols. Boston, 1909), I, 34–36.
22. Jefferson to Charles Willson Peale, May 5, 1809, Monroe Law Office Papers, courtesy of the University of Virginia; Jefferson to Peale, August 20, 1811, *Writings*, L. and B., XIII, 78–79.
23. *Jefferson at Monticello*, 13.
24. Ellen Randolph Coolidge memoirs, Ms. 36, University of Virginia.
25. See especially Jefferson to Thomas Earle, September 24, 1823, *Writings*, L. and B., XV, 470.
26. Jefferson to John Armstrong, February 8, 1813, *Writings*, L. and B., XIII, 220.
27. Jefferson to Dr. John Manners, June 12, 1817, *Writings*, L. and B., XV, 124–25.
28. Unpublished memoir, University of Virginia.
29. Ellen Randolph Coolidge memoir, University of Virginia.
30. "The sale of my library to Congress for 23,950 D. being concluded I drew on the 18th inst. on the Treasury of the U.S. in favor of Wm. Short for 10,500 for my bonds . . . Thaddeus Kozciewko 4,870 principle and Int due him," account book, April 29, 1815.
31. Jefferson to John Adams, June 10, 1815, *Adams-Jefferson Letters*, 443.
32. Jefferson to Thomas Mann Randolph, January 6, 1809, University of Virginia.
33. Jefferson to John Eppes, June 30, 1820, Massachusetts Historical Society, reproduced in part in the *Farm Book* [46].
34. Louis Filler, *The Crusade against Slavery, 1830–1860* (New York, 1960), 8.
35. Jefferson to Edward Coles, August 25, 1814, *Writings*, Ford, IX, 478–79.
36. Ralph L. Ketcham, "The Dictates of Conscience: Edward Coles and Slavery," *Virginia Quarterly Review*, XXXVI (1960), 47–52.
37. Jefferson to Francis C. Gray, March 4, 1815, *Writings*, L. and B., XIV, 267–71.
38. *Writings*, L. and B., XV, 452.
39. Leland W. Meyer, *Colonel Richard M. Johnson of Kentucky* (New York, 1932), 321–22.
40. Jefferson to Maria Cosway, December 27, 1820, Bullock, *My Head and My Heart*, 176.
41. Jefferson to Amos J. Cooke, January 21, 1816, *Writings*, L. and B., XIV, 404.
42. See Appendix I.
43. *Jefferson at Monticello*, 4.
44. Edmund Bacon to Jefferson, July 20, 1820, University of Virginia.
45. See Appendix I.
46. The editor of the memoir, Pierson, expunged the name, but since the original manuscript of this memoir has disappeared, it is impossible to discover what name was deleted. See *Jefferson at Monticello*, vi, 102.
47. See Appendix I. Pearl N. Graham in 1948 interviewed four sisters in New Jersey and Massachusetts whom she believed to be descendants of Harriet Hemings,

and published her findings in "Thomas Jefferson and Sally Hemings," *Journal of Negro History,* XLIV (1961), 89–103. Miss Graham was good enough to let me see and copy the notes of her original interview, and all her correspondence with these women. In the light of these documents, one of which, a letter from Mrs. Lucy Williams, speaks of "John Heming my great Grand.," I am convinced that these four sisters, all of whom had been born in Charlottesville and were still members of a black community, were descendants of John rather than Sally Hemings. Miss Graham's notes of her original interview state that "they did not recall ever having been told their grandmother's first name. In the family, she was always, simply 'Gramma.' " She was first married to a man named Captain at Keswick, near Monticello; later she went to Canada and married a Reuben Coles. Their own mother, Mary Frances Captain Coles, was born in 1837. All had heard the story of "the slave girl who had attended Maria Jefferson to France," whom they believed to be their "grandmother" and they possessed small items of furniture from Monticello. Miss Graham had not seen the reminiscences of Madison Hemings, with its data which I believe rules out the possibility of Harriet Hemings having three or four granddaughters born in Charlottesville. Since John Hemings did remain in that area, it seems likely that these were indeed his great-granddaughters, as Mrs. Williams stated. Mrs. Anna Ezell in 1948 was eighty-four, Mrs. Lucy C. Williams seventy-two, and Mrs. Minnie Arbuckle about sixty.

48. *Jefferson at Monticello,* 4.
49. See Appendix I, part 2.
50. Jefferson to Peale, July 18, 1824, Monroe Law Office Papers, courtesy of the University of Virginia.
51. Ellen Randolph Coolidge to Joseph Coolidge, Jr., October 24, 1858, courtesy of Harold Jefferson Coolidge.
52. Frances Trollope, *Domestic Manners of the Americans* (1927 ed.), 59.
53. See Appendix III.
54. See Appendix III.
55. *Jefferson at Monticello,* 54.
56. See Appendix I. A copy of the 1830 census for Albemarle County may be seen on film at the University of Virginia Library.
57. Jefferson to John Holmes, April 22, 1820, *Writings,* L. and B., XV, 248–50.
58. Fawn M. Brodie, *Thaddeus Stevens, Scourge of the South* (New York, 1959), 141.
59. Jefferson to Lafayette, December 26, 1820, *Writings,* L. and B., XV, 300–301.

CHAPTER XXXI Writer of Letters

1. Adams to Jefferson, September 10, 1816, *Adams-Jefferson Letters,* 489.
2. Jefferson to William Short, March 25, 1815, Huntington Library.
3. Jefferson to Bernard Peyton, September 3, 1824, Jefferson Papers, Massachusetts Historical Society, quoted in Schachner, *Jefferson,* 993.
4. Richard Beale Davis, *Francis Walker Gilmer: Life and Learning in Jefferson's Virginia* (Richmond, 1939), 354.
5. Jefferson to Samuel Kercheval, July 12, 1816, *Writings,* L. and B., XV, 34, 39.
6. Jefferson to Henry Lee, August 10, 1824, *Writings,* L. and B., XVI, 73.
7. Jefferson to Mann Page, August 30, 1795, *Writings,* L. and B., IX, 306.
8. Jefferson to John Adams, October 28, 1813, *Adams-Jefferson Letters,* 388.
9. Jefferson to Mr. Delaplaine, February 9, 1816, from facsimile in the New York Public Library.
10. Jefferson to Josephus B. Stuart, May 10, 1817, *Writings,* L. and B., XV, 113.
11. John Adams to Benjamin Rush, July 23, 1806; April 12, 1809, *The Spur of Fame,* 60, 142.
12. Foster, *Jeffersonian America,* 155.

13. Jefferson to Du Pont de Nemours, April 25, 1816, Writings, L. and B., XIV, 491.

14. Ackerman, Palladio, 80, 177; Kenneth Clark, Civilization: A Personal View (New York, 1969), 264-68.

15. Jefferson to M. Correa de Serra, quoted in Peterson, Jefferson and the New Nation, 978-79.

16. Jefferson to William Roscoe, December 27, 1820, Writings, L. and B., XV, 303.

17. Jefferson to Nathanial Burwell, March 14, 1818, Writings, L. and B., XV, 165-67.

18. Jefferson to Samuel Kercheval, September 5, 1816, Writings, L. and B., XV, 72.

19. Jefferson to Benjamin Rush, December 5, 1811, Writings, L. and B., XIII, 116; Randall, Jefferson, III, 639-40.

20. Jefferson to Adams, January 21, 1812, Adams-Jefferson Letters, 291.

21. Benjamin Rush to John Adams, February 17, 1812, Rush, Letters, Butterfield, ed., II, 1127.

22. Adams to Jefferson, September 10, 1816, July 15, 1813, Adams-Jefferson Letters, 489, 357-58.

23. Jefferson to Benjamin Rush, December 5, 1811, Writings, L. and B., XIII, 117.

24. Benjamin Rush to John Adams, September 20, 1811, Rush, Letters, II, 1104.

25. Abigail Adams' quotation is from The Comedy of Errors, V:1, 297-99. Abigail Adams to Jefferson, September 20, 1813; John Adams to Jefferson, August 16, 1813, Adams-Jefferson Letters, 377-78, 366.

26. Jefferson to Adams, October 12, 1813, Adams-Jefferson Letters, 386.

27. Adams to Jefferson, February 3, June 28, 1812, Adams-Jefferson Letters, 295, 310.

28. Jefferson to Adams, June 27, 1813, Adams-Jefferson Letters, 337.

29. Adams to Jefferson, February 2, 1817, Adams-Jefferson Letters, 508.

30. Adams to Jefferson, April 19, 1825, Adams-Jefferson Letters, 611.

31. Jefferson to Adams, March 25, 1826, Adams-Jefferson Letters, 614.

32. Adams to Jefferson, June 25, 1813, July 3, 1813, Adams-Jefferson Letters, 333, 349. The reference is to Alexander Pope's "Most Women have no Characters at All," Epistles to Several Persons (Moral Essays), F. W. Bateson, ed. (New Haven, 1951), 45.

33. Adams to Jefferson, December 8, 1818, Adams-Jefferson Letters, 530.

34. Jefferson to Adams, December 10, 1819, Adams-Jefferson Letters, 550.

35. Adams to Jefferson, August 14, 1813, Adams-Jefferson Letters, 365.

36. Jefferson to Adams, October 28, 1813, Adams-Jefferson Letters, 387-88.

37. Adams to Jefferson, November 15, 1813, Adams-Jefferson Letters, 398-99.

38. Adams to Jefferson, October 20, 1818, Adams-Jefferson Letters, 529.

39. Jefferson to Adams, November 13, 1818, Adams-Jefferson Letters, 529.

40. Adams to Jefferson, September 14, 1813, Adams-Jefferson Letters, 375.

41. Jefferson to Dr. Robert Peterson, December 27, 1812, Writings, L. and B., XIII, 192.

42. Jefferson to Alexander Smyth, January 17, 1825, Writings, L. and B., XVI, 101.

43. Jefferson to Adams, January 8, 1825, Adams-Jefferson Letters, 606.

44. Jefferson to Adams, January 11, 1817, Adams-Jefferson Letters, 506; to Ezra Stiles, June 25, 1819, Writings, L. and B., XV, 203.

45. Adams to Jefferson, March 2, 1816, Jefferson to Adams, April 8, 1816, Adams-Jefferson Letters, 464, 467.

46. Adams to Jefferson, May 3, 1816, Adams-Jefferson Letters, 469.

47. Jefferson to Adams, August 1, 1816, Adams-Jefferson Letters, 483.

48. Adams to Jefferson, December 1, 1825, Adams-Jefferson Letters, 611.

49. Jefferson to Adams, December 18, 1825, Adams-Jefferson Letters, 612.

CHAPTER XXXII The Monticello Tragedy

1. Jefferson to Adams, August 1, 1816, *Adams-Jefferson Letters*, 484.
2. Jefferson to Madison, quoted in Kimball, *Jefferson: The Scene of Europe*, 10.
3. The account book, February 1, 1826, shows his having received 150 bottles.
4. Edmund Morgan, "Slavery and Freedom: The American Paradox," *Journal of American History*, LIX (June 1972), 8.
5. Jefferson to Madison, February 17, 1826, *Writings*, L. and B., XVI, 157.
6. H. B. Trist to N. P. Trist, October 10, 1819, Nicholas P. Trist Papers, Library of Congress, quoted in Schachner, *Jefferson*, 969.
7. Jefferson to Thomas Mann Randolph, August 9, 1819, October 8, 1820, July 30, 1821, Library of Congress.
8. Statement of debts, July 4, 1826, Nicholas P. Trist Papers, Library of Congress.
9. Thomas Jefferson Randolph reminiscences, Ms., University of Virginia.
10. Jefferson to Thomas Mann Randolph, August 9, 1819, Library of Congress, 33533.
11. Thomas Mann Randolph to Jefferson, November 21, 1822, Library of Congress, 39825.
12. Gaines, *Thomas Mann Randolph*, 155.
13. *Ibid.*, 157.
14. Randolph to Jefferson, July 8, 1825, Gaines, *Thomas Mann Randolph*, 159.
15. Jefferson to Randolph, June 5, 1825, Library of Congress, 41034. See also Jefferson to Randolph, July 9, 1825, January 8, 1826, Library of Congress, 41076, 41300.
16. Ellen Randolph Coolidge memoirs, Ms., University of Virginia.
17. Bacon reminiscences, *Jefferson at Monticello*, 94, 136; Joseph Vance, "Knives, Whips, and Randolphs on the Court House Lawn," *Albemarle County Historical Society Papers* (1955-56), 28-35.
18. Thomas Jefferson Randolph memoirs, Ms., University of Virginia.
19. Bacon's reminiscences, *Jefferson at Monticello*, 94, 136; Gaines, *Thomas Mann Randolph*, 108.
20. Jefferson to Thomas Jefferson Randolph, February 11, 1826, *Family Letters*, 470.
21. Ellen Randolph Coolidge memoirs, Ms., University of Virginia.
22. Jefferson to Adams, October 12, 1823, June 1, 1822, *Adams-Jefferson Letters*, 599, 577.
23. Jefferson to Charles Willson Peale, October 23, 1822, James Monroe Law Office Papers, University of Virginia.
24. Ticknor, *Life, Letters, and Journals*, I, 348-49.
25. Jefferson to Adams, June 1, 1822, *Adams-Jefferson Letters*, 577.
26. Thomas Jefferson Randolph memoirs, Ms., University of Virginia.
27. The menu was preserved, and the dinner reproduced at the sesquicentennial celebration of the University of Virginia in 1969.
28. Frances Wright to Lafayette, quoted in a letter to her sister Camilla, June 10, 1824, in William Randall Waterman, *Frances Wright* (New York, 1924), 81.
29. A. J. G. Perkins and Theresa Wolfson, *Frances Wright: Free Enquirer* (New York, 1939), 115.
30. See Appendix I, part 2.
31. O. B. Emerson, "Frances Wright and Her Nashoba Experiment," *Tennessee Historical Quarterly*, VI (December, 1947).
32. Frances Wright, *A Plan for the Gradual Abolition of Slavery in the United States without Danger of Loss to the Citizens of the United States* (Baltimore, 1825).

33. Jefferson to Frances Wright, August 7, 1825, *Writings*, L. and B., XVI, 119–21.
34. Waterman, *Frances Wright*, 129.
35. Jefferson's last letter to Maria Cosway, describing the building of the University of Virginia, had been written October 24, 1822. For this, and Maria Cosway's last two letters, July 18, 1823, and September 24, 1824, see Bullock, *My Head and My Heart*, 181–87.
36. Randall, *Jefferson*, III, 503.
37. Jefferson to Joseph Cabell, February 7, 1826, *Writings*, Ford, XII, 450–53.
38. Jefferson to Madison, February 17, 1826, *Writings*, L. and B., XVI, 158–59.
39. Martha Jefferson Randolph to Ellen Randolph Coolidge, April 5, 1826, University of Virginia.
40. Dunglison's memoirs are published in Randall, *Jefferson*, III, 513–17.
41. Martha Jefferson Randolph, November 26, 1825, April 5, 1826, University of Virginia.
42. Jefferson to Adams, March 14, 1820, *Adams-Jefferson Letters*, 562.
43. *Jefferson at Monticello*, 102.
44. Jefferson to Madison, February 17, 1826, *Writings*, L. and B., XVI, 158.
45. See the Hemings family genealogy, *Jefferson at Monticello*, 25. Mary Hemings, born in 1753, gave birth to "Joe Fosset" in 1780 (*Farm Book*, 31, 130). The late John Cook Wyllie, expert on the Monticello slaves, believed that Joe Fosset's father was an apprentice white man employed at Monticello named William Fosset. Jefferson's account book for September 1, 1779, shows that he was working at Monticello at that date. Martha Jefferson was still alive in 1780, and it is therefore most unlikely that Joe Fosset was Jefferson's son. One should also note that Fosset was treated differently from Sally Hemings' sons. First of all, he was given the last name Fosset, which can be considered evidence that Fosset was the father. Second, Sally Hemings' children were permitted to "run away" at twenty-one; Joe Fosset was not. In 1806 he ran away to Washington because of his affection for Edy, a slave Jefferson had taken to Washington. The President's hostler, Joseph Daugherty, alerted by Jefferson, caught him in the "yard" of the President's House on August 3, 1806, and returned him to Monticello. See "Slaves and Slavery," *Farm Book* [22–23]. The belief that Joe Fosset was Jefferson's son gained some credence in 1954 when Lerone Bennett, in "Thomas Jefferson's Negro Grandchildren," *Ebony*, November 1954, published photographs of elderly blacks who traced their ancestry back to Fosset. But the article gave no evidence to indicate that Fosset was indeed Jefferson's son. Joe Fosset's mother, Mary Hemings, according to evidence gathered by John Cook Wyllie at the University of Virginia, was sold in 1792 at her own request to Colonel Thomas Bell, and apparently spent her last years in freedom in Philadelphia.
46. See Appendix I, part 2.
47. C. Vann Woodward, *The Burden of Southern History*, 25.
48. Jefferson to Roger C. Weightman, June 24, 1826, *Writings*, L. and B., XVI, 181–82. See also Julian Boyd's discussion of the emendations in this letter, *New York Times Magazine*, April 10, 1949.
49. Randall, *Jefferson*, III, 546, and Nicholas P. Trist to Joseph Trist, July 4, 1826, University of Virginia.
50. Gaines, *Thomas Mann Randolph*, 184–86.
51. A film of this census may be seen at the University of Virginia. Eston is listed as having in his household two whites (age 20–30) [doubtless himself and Madison], one white (50–60) [his mother], three colored males under 10, one colored male (35–36), one colored female under 10, and one colored female (35–36). Since Eston had married a free black woman, something of the family relationships can be worked out, especially when checked with Madison Hemings' reminiscences. See Appendix I.
52. See Appendix I, part 2.
53. *The Jefferson Image in the American Mind*, 388.

Bibliography

Manuscript Collections

Library of Congress. The largest collection of letters to and from Jefferson. Microfilm edition.

Massachusetts Historical Society. The so-called Coolidge Collection has the majority of the private letters of Jefferson, especially those relating to his family. Microfilm edition.

University of Virginia. A useful guide is Constance E. Thurlow and Francis L. Berkeley, Jr., *The Jefferson Papers of the University of Virginia.* Of special value in this collection is James A. Beard's typescript and photocopy of the collection of Jefferson account books, which are otherwise scattered. Here, too, one may see copies of the memoirs of Martha Jefferson Randolph, Thomas Jefferson Randolph, and Ellen Randolph Coolidge. The Edgehill Randolph Papers, the Carr and Cary Papers, and a recently acquired collection of letters by Ellen Coolidge are useful for providing information about Jefferson's kin. The McGregor Library has on file a film of the Albemarle County census of 1830, with information about the Hemings family, as well as Jefferson's relatives.

The Henry E. Huntington Library. This is the fourth most valuable collection of Jefferson manuscripts, with his 1775 account book, his earliest *Fee Book*, and numerous letters.

Writings of Thomas Jefferson

PUBLISHED EDITIONS

The Writings of Thomas Jefferson. H. A. Washington, ed. 9 vols. New York, 1853–54.

The Writings of Thomas Jefferson. Paul L. Ford, ed., 10 vols. New York, 1892–99.

The Writings of Thomas Jefferson. Andrew A. Lipscomb and Albert E. Bergh, eds., 20 vols. Washington, D.C., 1903.

The Papers of Thomas Jefferson. Julian P. Boyd, ed., 18 vols. to date. Princeton, 1950–72.

OTHER PUBLISHED WORKS

The Adams-Jefferson Letters: The Complete Correspondence between Thomas Jefferson and John and Abigail Adams. Lester J. Cappon, ed. Chapel Hill, N.C., 1959.

Autobiography of Thomas Jefferson, with an Introductory Essay by Dumas Malone. Boston, 1948.
Catalogue of the Library of Thomas Jefferson. E. M. Sowerby, ed., 5 vols. Washington, D.C., 1952.
The Commonplace Book of Thomas Jefferson. Gilbert Chinard, ed. Baltimore, 1926.
The Complete Anas of Thomas Jefferson. F. B. Sawvel, ed. New York, 1903.
Correspondence between Thomas Jefferson and Pierre Samuel Du Pont de Nemours, 1798–1817. Dumas Malone, ed. New York, 1930.
Correspondence of Jefferson and Du Pont de Nemours, with an Introduction on Jefferson and the Physiocrats. Gilbert Chinard, ed. Baltimore, 1931.
Correspondence of Thomas Jefferson and Francis Walker Gilmer, 1814–1826. Richard Beale Davis, ed. Columbia, S.C., 1946.
The Family Letters of Thomas Jefferson. Edwin M. Betts and James A. Bear, eds. Columbia, Mo., 1966.
The Jefferson Bible: The Life and Morals of Jesus of Nazareth. O. I. A. Roche, ed. New York, 1964.
The Jefferson Cyclopedia. John P. Foley, ed. New York, 1900.
The Jefferson-Dunglison Letters. John M. Dorsey, ed. Charlottesville, Va., 1960.
The Letters of Lafayette and Jefferson. Gilbert Chinard, ed. Baltimore, 1929.
The Literary Bible of Thomas Jefferson. Gilbert Chinard, ed. Baltimore, 1928.
"A Memoir on the Discovery of Certain Bones of a Quadruped of the Clawed Kind in the Western Parts of Virginia," American Philosophical Society Transactions, IV (1799).
Notes on the State of Virginia. William Peden, ed. Chapel Hill, N.C., 1955.
Thomas Jefferson and James Thomson Callender. Worthington C. Ford, ed.; originally in the New England Historical and Genealogical Register, LI–LII (1896–97); published separately in 1897.
Thomas Jefferson's Correspondence, printed from the originals in the Collection of William K. Bixby. W. C. Ford, ed. Boston, 1916.
Thomas Jefferson's Farm Book, with Commentary and Relevant Extracts from Other Writings. Edwin Morris Betts, ed. Princeton, 1953.
Thomas Jefferson's Garden Book, 1766–1824, with Relevant Extracts from His Other Writings. Edwin Morris Betts, ed. Philadelphia, 1944.
Volney et l'Amérique, d'après des documents inédits et sa correspondance avec Jefferson. Gilbert Chinard, ed. Baltimore, 1923.

Newspapers Consulted

Aurora (Philadelphia), 1802–5
Boston Repertory, 1805
Boston Review and Monthly Anthology, 1807
Gazette of the United States, 1802–5
New York Commercial Advertiser, 1800
New York Evening Post, 1802–4
Port Folio (Philadelphia), 1802–7
Richmond Enquirer, 1804–5
Richmond Examiner, 1802–4
Richmond Recorder, 1802–3
Virginia Federalist (Richmond), 1800
Virginia Gazette (Lynchburg), 1800

Selected Books and Articles

Abernethy, Thomas P. *The Burr Conspiracy.* New York, 1954.

Ackerman, James S. *Palladio.* London, 1966.

Adams, Abigail. *Letters of Mrs. Adams, the Wife of John Adams.* Charles Francis Adams, ed., 2 vols. Boston, 1848.

———. *New Letters of Abigail Adams, 1788–1801.* Stewart Mitchell, ed. Boston, 1947.

Adams, Henry. *History of the United States during the Administrations of Jefferson and Madison.* 9 vols. New York, 1891–93. See also *The Formative Years,* a condensed edition edited by Herbert Agar. Boston, 1947.

———. *John Randolph.* Boston, 1887.

Adams, John. *Life and Works.* Charles Francis Adams, ed., 10 vols. Boston, 1850–56.

———. *Adams Family Correspondence.* Lyman H. Butterfield, ed., 2 vols. Cambridge, Mass., 1963.

———. *The Adams-Jefferson Letters.* Lester Cappon, ed., 2 vols. Chapel Hill, N.C., 1959.

———. *Familiar Letters of John Adams and His Wife Abigail Adams during the Revolution, with a Memoir of Mrs. Adams by Charles Francis Adams.* Boston, 1875.

———. *Old Family Letters, Copied from the Originals for Alexander Biddle.* Series A. Philadelphia, 1892.

———. *The Spur of Fame: Dialogues of John Adams and Benjamin Rush, 1805–1813.* John A. Schutz and Douglass Adair, eds. San Marino, Calif., 1966.

Adams, John Quincy. *Memoirs.* Charles Francis Adams, ed., 12 vols. Philadelphia, 1874–77.

Aldridge, Alfred O. *Man of Reason: The Life of Thomas Paine.* Philadelphia, 1959.

Allison, John M. *Adams and Jefferson: The Story of a Friendship.* Norman, Okla., 1966.

Ammon, Harry. *James Monroe: The Quest for National Identity.* New York, 1971.

Aptheker, Herbert. *American Negro Slave Revolts.* New York, 1943.

Atherton, Gertrude. *A Few of Hamilton's Letters.* New York, 1903.

Bailyn, Bernard. "Boyd's Jefferson: Notes for a Sketch," *New York England Quarterly,* XXXIII (1960), 380–401.

———. *Ideological Origins of the American Revolution.* Cambridge, Mass., 1967.

Becker, Carl. *The Declaration of Independence.* New York, 1922.

Beeson, Paul B., and Walsh McDermott. *Textbook of Medicine.* Philadelphia, 1963.

Beloff, Max. *Thomas Jefferson and American Democracy.* New York, 1949.

Bemis, Samuel F. *American Secretaries of State and Their Diplomacy.* 2 vols. New York, 1927.

———. *John Quincy Adams and the Foundations of American Foreign Policy.* New York, 1949.

Bennett, Lerone. "Thomas Jefferson's Negro Grandchildren," *Ebony,* X (November 1954), 78–79.

Beveridge, Albert J. *Life of John Marshall,* 4 vols. Boston, 1919.

Binger, Carl. *Thomas Jefferson: A Well-Tempered Mind.* New York, 1970.

Boorstin, Daniel. *The Americans: The Colonial Experience.* New York, 1958.

———. *The Lost World of Thomas Jefferson.* New York, 1948.

Borden, Morton. *The Federalism of James A. Bayard.* New York, 1955.

Bowers, Claude G. *Jefferson and Hamilton.* Boston, 1925.

———. *Jefferson in Power.* Boston, 1936.

———. *The Young Jefferson.* Boston, 1945.

Boyd, Julian. *The Declaration of Independence: The Evolution of the Text* . . . Washington, D.C., 1943.

————. "The Murder of George Wythe," *William and Mary Quarterly*, 3rd series, XII (October 1955), 513–80.

————. *Number 7, Alexander Hamilton's Secret Attempts to Control Foreign Policy.* Princeton, 1964.

Brant, Irving. *James Madison.* 5 vols. Indianapolis, 1941–53.

Brodie, Fawn M. "The Great Jefferson Taboo," *American Heritage*, XXII (June 1972), 48–57, 97–100.

————. *Thaddeus Stevens, Scourge of the South.* New York, 1959.

————. "Jefferson Biographers and the Psychology of Canonization," *Journal of Interdisciplinary History*, II (Summer 1971), 155–71.

Bruce, Philip A. *History of the University of Virginia.* 5 vols. New York, 1920–22.

Bryant, William Cullen. *The Embargo.* Facsimile reproductions of the editions of 1808 and 1809, with an introduction and notes by Thomas O. Mabbott. Gainesville, Fla., 1955.

Buffon, George Louis. *Natural History.* 10 vols. in 5. London, 1792.

Bullock, Helen D. *My Head and My Heart: A Little Chronicle of Thomas Jefferson and Maria Cosway.* New York, 1945.

Burke, Edmund. *Speech on Conciliation with America.* Daniel V. Thompson, ed. New York, 1911.

Burnett, Edmund C., ed. *Letters of Members of the Continental Congress.* 8 vols. Washington, D.C., 1921.

Burr, Aaron. *Correspondence of Aaron Burr with His Daughter Theodosia.* Mark Van Doren, ed. New York, 1929.

————. *Memoirs of Aaron Burr, with Miscellaneous Selections from His Correspondence.* By Matthew L. Davis. 2 vols. New York, 1836–37.

————. *Private Journal of Aaron Burr, Reprinted in Full from the Original Manuscript in the Library of Mr. William K. Bixby.* 2 vols. Rochester, N.Y., 1903.

Burrows, Edwin C., and Michael Wallace. "The American Revolution: The Ideology and Psychology of National Liberation," *Perspectives in American History*, VI (1972), 167–306.

Burwell, William. "Private Memoir . . ." Ms., Library of Congress.

Bush, Alfred L. *The Life Portraits of Thomas Jefferson: Catalogue of an Exhibition at the University Museum of Fine Arts, April 12–26.* Charlottesville, Va., 1962.

Butterfield, Lyman H., and Howard C. Rice. "Jefferson's Earliest Note to Maria Cosway with Some New Facts and Conjectures on His Broken Wrist," *William and Mary Quarterly*, 3rd series, V (1948), 26–33, 620–21.

Callender, James Thomson. *American Annual Register; or, Historical Memories of the United States for the Year 1796.* 1797.

————. *Deformities of Dr. Samuel Johnson.* London, 1782. Reprinted in the Augustan Reprint Society series, nos. 147–48, by Gwin J. Kolb and J. E. Congleton, 1971.

————. *The Political Progress of Britain* . . . Philadelphia, 1795.

————. *The Prospect before Us.* Richmond, 1800.

————. *Sketches of the History of America.* Philadelphia, 1798.

Cassirer, Ernst. *The Philosophy of the Enlightenment.* Boston, 1951.

Catterall, Helen T. *Judicial Cases Concerning Slavery and the Negro.* 5 vols. Washington, D.C., 1926–37.

Charles, Joseph. *The Origins of the American Party System.* Williamsburg, Va., 1951.

Chastellux, Marquis de [François-Jean de Beauvoir]. *Travels in North America, 1780, 1781, and 1782.* Howard C. Rice, Jr., ed., a revised translation. Chapel Hill, N.C., 1963. An earlier edition was published in Dublin in 1787.

Cheetham, James. *Life of Thomas Paine.* New York, 1809.

Chesnut, Mary Boykin. *A Diary from Dixie.* Ben Ames Williams, ed. Boston, 1949.

Chinard, Gilbert. *Thomas Jefferson: The Apostle of Americanism.* Boston, 1939.

————, ed. *Volney et l'Amérique.* Baltimore, 1923.

Clark, Kenneth. *Civilization: A Personal View*. New York, 1969.
Clayton, Ellen C. *English Female Artists*. 2 vols. London, 1876.
Conant, James B. *Thomas Jefferson and the Development of American Public Education*. Berkeley, Calif., 1962.
Cooke, Jacob E., ed. *Alexander Hamilton: A Profile*. New York, 1967.
Cranch, William. *Reports of Cases Argued and Adjudicated in the Supreme Court of the United States in the Years 1807 and 1808*. New York, 1812.
Cresson, William P. *James Monroe*. Chapel Hill, N.C., 1946.
Cunningham, Allan. *The Lives of the Most Eminent British Painters, Sculptors, and Architects*. 6 vols. London, 1829-33.
Cunningham, Noble E., Jr. *The Jeffersonian Republicans: The Formation of Party Organization, 1789-1801*. Chapel Hill, N.C., 1957.
Cutler, Mannasseh. *Life, Journals, and Correspondence*. William P. Cutler and Julia P. Cutler, eds., 2 vols. Cincinnati, 1888.
Cyclopedia of American Literature. Everet and George L. Duyckinck, eds., 2 vols. New York, 1856.
Dangerfield, George. *The Awakening of American Nationalism*. New York, 1965.
———. *The Era of Good Feelings*. New York, 1952.
Daniell, Frederick B. *A Catalogue Raisonné of the Engraved Works of Richard Cosway, with a Memoir of Cosway by Sir Philip Currie*. London, 1890.
Daviess, Joseph H. "A View of the President's Conduct Concerning the Conspiracy of 1806," *Quarterly Publications of the Historical and Philosophical Society of Ohio*, XII (1917), 69ff.
Davis, David Brion. *The Problem of Slavery in Western Culture*. Ithaca, N.Y., 1966.
———. *Was Thomas Jefferson the Authentic Enemy of Slavery?* Oxford, 1970.
Davis, Matthew L. *Memoirs of Aaron Burr, with Miscellaneous Selections from His Correspondence*. 2 vols. New York, 1836-37.
Davis, Richard Beale. *Francis Walker Gilmer: Life and Learning in Jefferson's Virginia*. Richmond, 1939.
Defence of Young and Minns, Printers to the State, before the Committee of the House of Representatives, with an Appendix Containing the Debate, etc. Boston, 1805.
Dennie, Joseph. *Letters of Joseph Dennie*. Laura G. Pedder, ed. Orono, Maine, 1936.
Dillon, Richard. *Meriwether Lewis*. New York, 1965.
Dodd, Anna B. *Talleyrand: The Training of a Statesman, 1754-1838*. New York, 1927.
Dumbauld, Edward. *Thomas Jefferson: American Tourist*. Norman, Okla., 1946.
Du Pont de Nemours, Pierre Samuel. *Correspondence . . . Jefferson*. Dumas Malone, ed. Boston, 1930.
Eckenrode, Hamilton J. *The Randolphs*. New York, 1946.
Ellis, Harold M. *Joseph Dennie and His Circle*. University of Texas Bulletin, July 15, 1915.
Ellis, Richard E. *The Jeffersonian Crisis: Courts and Politics in the Young Republic*. New York, 1971.
Erikson, Erik. *Gandhi's Truth*. New York, 1969.
———. *Young Man Luther*. New York, 1958.
Farington, Joseph. "Joseph Farington's Anecdotes of Walpole, 1793-1807," in *Horace Walpole's Correspondence*, W. S. Lewis, ed., vol. XV. London, 1952.
Farrison, William E. "Origin of Brown's *Clotel*," *Phylon*, XV (December 1954), 347-54.
Filler, Louis. *The Crusade against Slavery, 1830-1860*. New York, 1960.
Fleming, Thomas. *The Man from Monticello: An Intimate Life of Thomas Jefferson*. New York, 1969.
Flexner, James T. *George Washington: Anguish and Farewell, 1793-1799*. Boston, 1972.
———. *George Washington: The Forge of Experience, 1732-1775*. Boston, 1965.
———. *George Washington in the American Revolution, 1775-1783*. Boston, 1967.

————. *George Washington and the New Nation, 1783-1793.* Boston, 1969.
Flower, Milton E. *James Parton: The Father of Modern Biography.* Durham, N.C., 1951.
Fontaine, John. *Memoirs of a Huguenot Family.* Ann Maury, ed. New York, 1907; a reprint of the 1852 edition.
Ford, Worthington Chauncey, ed., "Thomas Jefferson and James Thomson Callender," *New England Historical and Genealogical Register,* LI–LII (1896–97).
Foster, Augustus John. *Jeffersonian America: Notes on the United States of America, Collected in the Years 1805-6-7 and 11-12.* Richard Beale Davis, ed. San Marino, Calif., 1954.
Franklin, Benjamin. *Writings.* Albert H. Smyth, ed., 10 vols. New York, 1906-7.
Frary, I. T. *Thomas Jefferson: Architect and Builder.* Richmond, 1931.
Freehling, William W. "The Founding Fathers and Slavery," *American Historical Review,* LXXVII (1972), 81–94.
Fried, Albert, ed. *The Jeffersonian and Hamiltonian Traditions in American Politics.* New York, 1968.
Gaines, William H., Jr. *Thomas Mann Randolph: Jefferson's Son-in-Law.* Baton Rouge, La., 1966.
Garlick, Richard C., Jr. *Philip Mazzei, Friend of Jefferson: His Life and Letters.* Baltimore, 1933.
Gaulmier, Jean. *Un Grand Témoin de la révolution et de l'empire.* Paris, 1959.
Gay, Peter. *The Enlightenment.* 2 vols. New York, 1967–69.
Genovese, Eugene D. *The World the Slaveholders Made.* New York, 1969.
Gottschalk, Louis. *Lafayette and the Close of the American Revolution.* Chicago, 1942.
————. *Lafayette Joins the American Army.* Chicago, 1937.
Graham, Pearl N. "Thomas Jefferson and Sally Hemings," *Journal of Negro History,* XLIV (1961), 89–103.
Hamilton, Alexander. *Papers.* Harold Syrett and others, eds., 17 vols. New York, 1961-73.
————. *Works.* Henry Cabot Lodge, ed., 12 vols. New York, 1904.
Hamilton, Allan McLane. *The Intimate Life of Alexander Hamilton.* New York, 1910.
Hamilton, John Church. *Life of Alexander Hamilton.* 2 vols. New York, 1840.
Harrell, Isaac S. *Loyalism in Virginia: Chapters in the Economic History of the Revolution.* Durham, N.C., 1926.
Hart, Freeman, H. *The Valley of Virginia in the American Revolution.* Chapel Hill, N.C., 1942.
Hawke, David. *A Transaction of Free Men: The Birth and Career of the Declaration of Independence.* New York, 1964.
Hazelton, John H. *The Declaration of Independence: Its History.* New York, 1906.
Hazlitt, William. *Conversations with James Northcote.* Edmund Gosse, ed. London, 1894.
Healey, Robert M. *Jefferson on Religion in Public Education.* New Haven, 1962.
Heslep, Robert D. *Thomas Jefferson and Education.* New York, 1969.
Hitchcock, Henry Russell. *Architecture, Nineteenth and Twentieth Centuries.* Baltimore, 1958.
Hofstadter, Richard. *American Political Tradition.* New York, 1948.
————. *The Idea of a Party System: The Rise of Legitimate Opposition in the United States, 1780-1840.* Berkeley, Calif., 1969.
Honeywell, Roy J. *The Educational Work of Thomas Jefferson.* Cambridge, Mass., 1931.
Howe, John R., Jr. *The Changing Political Thought of John Adams.* Princeton, 1966.
————. "Republican Thought and Political Violence of the 1790s," *American Quarterly,* XIX (1967), 148–65.
Humphreys, David. *Life and Times of David Humphreys,* 2 vols. New York, 1917.
Jackson, Luther P. *Negro Soldiers and Seamen in the American Revolution.* Norfolk, Va., 1944.

Jacobs, James R. *Tarnished Warrior: Major General James Wilkinson.* New York, 1938.

Jacobson, David L., ed. *Essays on the American Revolution.* New York, 1970.

Jefferson at Monticello. Edited, with an introduction, by James A. Bear, Jr. Charlottesville, Va., 1967.

[Jefferson], Isaac. "Memoirs of a Monticello Slave, as Dictated to Charles Campbell by Isaac." Rayford W. Logan, ed. Charlottesville, Va., 1951. Republished in *Jefferson at Monticello*, James A. Bear, Jr., ed. Charlottesville, Va., 1967.

Jellison, Charles A. "That Scoundrel Callender," *Virginia Magazine of History and Biography*, LXVII (1959), 295–306.

Johnston, James Hugo. *Race Relations in Virginia, and Miscegenation in the South, 1776–1860.* Amherst, Mass., 1970.

Jordan, Winthrop. "Familial Politics: The Killing of the King." Ms.

——. *White over Black: American Attitudes Toward the Negro, 1550–1812.* Chapel Hill, N.C., 1968.

Journals of the American Congress from 1774 to 1788, 4 vols. Washington, D.C., 1823.

Kapp, Friedrich. *The Life of Frederick William von Steuben.* New York, 1959.

Kerber, Linda K. *Federalists in Dissent: Imagery and Ideology in Jeffersonian America.* Ithaca, N.Y., 1970.

Ketcham, Ralph. "The Dictates of Conscience: Edward Coles and Slavery," *Virginia Quarterly Review*, XXXVI (1960), 47–52.

——. *James Madison: A Biography.* New York, 1971.

Kimball, Fiske. *The Life Portraits of Jefferson and their Replicas.* Philadelphia, 1944.

——. *Thomas Jefferson: Architect.* Boston, 1916.

Kimball, Marie. *Jefferson: The Road to Glory.* New York, 1943.

——. *Jefferson: The Scene of Europe.* New York, 1950.

——. *Jefferson: War and Peace.* New York, 1947.

Knudson, Jerry W. "The Jefferson Years: Response by the Press, 1801–1809." Ms. University of Virginia dissertation, 1962.

Koch, Adrienne. *Jefferson and Madison: The Great Collaboration.* New York, 1950.

——. *The Philosophy of Thomas Jefferson.* New York, 1943.

——. *Power, Morals, and the Founding Fathers.* Ithaca, N.Y., 1961.

Kurtz, Stephen G. *The Presidency of John Adams: The Collapse of Federalism, 1795–1800.* Philadelphia, 1957.

La Rochefoucauld-Liancourt, François A. F., Duc de. *Travels through the United States of North America.* 2 vols. London, 1799.

Lee, Henry. *Memoirs of the War in the Southern Department of the United States.* 2 vols. Philadelphia, 1812.

Lefebvre, George. *The Coming of the French Revolution.* New York, 1960.

Lehman, Karl. *Thomas Jefferson: American Humanist.* Chicago, 1947.

Levasseur, A. *Lafayette in America in 1824 and 1825.* 2 vols. Philadelphia, 1829.

Levy, Leonard W. *Jefferson and Civil Liberties: The Darker Side.* Cambridge, Mass., 1963.

——. *Legacy of Suppression: Freedom of Speech and Press in Early American History.* Cambridge, Mass., 1960.

Lewis, Thomas. *The Fairfax Line: Thomas Lewis's Journal of 1746.* J. W. Wayland, ed. New Market, Va., 1925.

Lincoln, Abraham. *Collected Works.* Roy P. Basler, ed., vol. New Brunswick, N.J., 1953–55.

Lokke, C. L. "Jefferson and the LeClerc Expedition," *American Historical Review*, XXXIII (January 1928), 322–28.

Maass, John. Letter in "Postscripts to History," *American Heritage*, XXIV (December, 1972), iii.

McColley, Robert. *Slavery in Jeffersonian Virginia.* Urbana, Ill., 1964.

Mackesy, Piers. *The War for America, 1775–1783.* Cambridge, Mass., 1964.

McKitrick, Eric. "The View from Jefferson's Camp," *New York Review of Books*, December 17, 1970.

Maclay, William. *Journal*. E. S. Maclay, ed. New York, 1890.
Madison, James. *Papers*. William T. Hutchinson and William M. E. Rachal, eds. 6 vols. Chicago, 1962–72.
———. *Writings*. Gaillard Hunt, ed. 9 vols. New York, 1900–1910.
Mahan, Alfred. *Sea Power and Its Relation to the War of 1812*. 2 vols. Boston, 1905.
Malone, Dumas. *Jefferson and the Ordeal of Liberty*. Boston, 1962.
———. *Jefferson and the Rights of Man*. Boston, 1951.
———. *Jefferson the President: First Term, 1801–1805*. Boston, 1970.
———. *Jefferson the Virginian*. Boston, 1948.
———. *The Public Life of Thomas Cooper*. New York, 1926.
Mannix, Daniel P., and Malcolm Cowley. *Black Cargoes: A History of the Atlantic Slave Trade*. New York, 1962.
Marsh, Philip M. *Monroe's Defense of Jefferson and Freneau against Hamilton*. Oxford, Ohio, 1948.
Marshall, John. *The Life of George Washington*. 5 vols. Philadelphia, 1804–7.
Martin, Edwin T. *Thomas Jefferson: Scientist*. New York, 1952.
Martineau, Harriet. *Retrospect of Western Travel*. 2 vols. London, 1838.
———. *Society in America*. 3 vols. London, 1837.
Mason, Frances Norton. *My Dearest Polly: Letters of Chief Justice John Marshall to His Wife, with Their Background, Political and Domestic*. Richmond, 1961.
Maury, Anne Fontaine, ed. *Intimate Virginiana*. Richmond, 1941.
Maury, James. *To Christians of Every Denomination among Us, Especially Those of the Established Church*. Annapolis, 1771.
Mayo, Bernard. *Myths and Men: Patrick Henry, George Washington, Thomas Jefferson*. Athens, Ga., 1959.
———. *Thomas Jefferson and His Unknown Brother, Randolph*. Charlottesville, Va., 1942.
Mazzei, Philip. *Memoirs of the Life and Peregrinations of the Florentine, Philip Mazzei*. Translated by Howard R. Marraro. New York, 1942.
Meade, Robert D. *Patrick Henry: Patriot in the Making*. New York, 1957.
———. *Patrick Henry: Practical Revolutionary*. New York, 1969.
Meade, William. *Old Churches, Ministers, Families of Virginia*. Philadelphia, 1857.
Mellon, Matthew T. *Early American Views on Negro Slavery*. New York, 1934.
Meyer, Leland W. *Colonel Richard M. Johnson of Kentucky*. New York, 1932.
Miller, John C. *Alexander Hamilton and the Growth of the New Nation*. New York, 1959.
———. *The Federalist Era, 1789–1801*. New York, 1960.
———. *Origins of the American Revolution*. Stanford, Calif., 1943.
———. *Sam Adams: Pioneer in Propaganda*. Boston, 1936.
Minnigerode, Meade. *Jefferson, Friend of France, 1793*. New York, 1928.
Mitchell, Broadus. *Alexander Hamilton*. 2 vols. New York, 1962.
Monroe, James. *Writings*. S. M. Hamilton, ed., 7 vols. New York, 1893–1903.
Moore, Thomas. *Poetical Works*. A. D. Godley, ed. London, 1910.
Moran, Charles. *Black Triumvirate: A Study of L'Ouverture, Dessalines, Christophe, the Men Who Made Haiti*. New York, 1957.
Morgan, Edmund S. *Birth of the Republic*. Chicago, 1956.
———. "Slavery and Freedom: The American Paradox," *Journal of American History*, LIX (1972), 5–30.
———. *Virginians at Home*. Williamsburg, Va., 1952.
Morgan, Edmund S., and Helen M. Morgan. *The Stamp Act Crisis*. Chapel Hill, N.C., 1953.
Morison, Samuel Eliot. *Life and Letters of Harrison Gray Otis*. 2 vols. Boston, 1913.
———. *Oxford History of the American People*. New York, 1965.
Morris, Gouverneur. *Diary and Letters*. Anne Cary Morris, ed., 2 vols. New York, 1888.
Mott, Frank L. *Jefferson and the Press*. Baton Rouge, La., 1943.

Mullin, Gerald W. *Flight and Rebellion: Slave Resistance in Eighteenth Century Virginia*. New York, 1972.
Nock, Albert J. *Jefferson*. New York, 1926.
"Old Virginia Correspondence," *Atlantic Monthly*, LXXXIV (1899), 538ff.
Padover, Saul. *Jefferson*. New York, 1942.
Paine, Thomas. *Common Sense and the Crisis*. New York, 1960.
———. *Complete Writings*. Philip S. Foner, ed., 2 vols. New York, 1945.
———. *Life and Works of Thomas Paine*. William M. Van der Weyde, ed., 10 vols. New York, 1925.
Pancake, J. S., "Aaron Burr: Would-Be Usurper," *William and Mary Quarterly*, 3rd series, VIII (April 1951).
Parmet, Herbert S., and Marie B. Hecht. *Aaron Burr: Portrait of an Ambitious Man*. New York, 1967.
Parton, James. *Life of Thomas Jefferson*. Boston, 1874.
Pearce, John. *Migraine*. New York, 1969.
Perkins, A. J. G., and Theresa Wolfson. *Frances Wright: Free Enquirer*. New York, 1939.
Perkins, Bradford. *The First Rapprochement: England and the United States, 1795–1805*. Philadelphia, 1955.
Peterson, Merrill D. *The Jefferson Image in the American Mind*. New York, 1960.
———. *Thomas Jefferson and the New Nation*. New York, 1970.
Pierson, Hamilton W. *Jefferson at Monticello*. New York, 1862.
Plumer, William. *Memorandum of Proceedings in the United States Senate 1803–1807*. New York, 1923.
Power, Edward P. *Nullification and Secession*. New York, 1897.
Prentiss, Charles, ed. *Life of the Late General William Eaton*. Brookfield, Mass., 1813.
Priestley, Joseph. *History of the Corruptions of Christianity*. 2 vols. London, 1782.
———. *Theological and Miscellaneous Works*. J. T. Rutt, ed., 25 vols. in 26. London, 1817–32.
Prince, Carl E. "The Passing of the Aristocracy: Jefferson's Removal of the Federalists, 1801–1805," *Journal of American History*, LVII (1970), 563–76.
Quarles, Benjamin. *The Negro in the American Revolution*. Chapel Hill, N.C., 1961.
Randall, Henry S. *Correspondence between Henry Stephens Randall and Hugh Blair Grigsby, 1851–61*. Frank J. Klingberg, ed. Berkeley, Calif. 1952.
Randolph, Sarah N. *The Domestic Life of Thomas Jefferson*. Dumas Malone, ed. New York, 1958.
Records of the Federal Convention of 1787. Max Farrand, ed. New Haven, 1937.
Robinson, Donald L. *Slavery in the Structure of American Politics, 1765–1820*. New York, 1971.
Rossiter, Clinton. *Alexander Hamilton and the Constitution*. New York, 1964.
Rush, Benjamin. *Autobiography*. George W. Corner, ed. Princeton, 1948.
———. *Letters*. Lyman H. Butterfield, ed., 2 vols. Princeton, 1951.
Safford, William H. *The Blennerhassett Papers*. Cincinnati, 1864.
———. *The Life of Harman Blennerhassett*. Chillicothe, Ohio, 1850.
Schachner, Nathan. *Aaron Burr: A Biography*. New York, 1937.
———. *Alexander Hamilton*. New York, 1946.
———. *Thomas Jefferson: A Biography*. New York, 1951.
Schlesinger, Arthur M. *Prelude to Independence: The Newspaper War on Britain, 1764–1776*. New York, 1957.
Schutz, John A., and Douglass Adair, eds. *The Spur of Fame: Dialogues of John Adams and Benjamin Rush, 1805–1813*. San Marino, Calif., 1966.
Smith, Abigail Adams. *Journal and Correspondence of Miss Adams, Daughter of John Adams*. Caroline De Windt, ed. New York, 1841.
Smith, James Morton. *Freedom's Fetters: The Alien and Sedition Laws and American Civil Liberties*. 2 vols. Ithaca, N.Y., 1956.
Smith, John Thomas. *Nollekens and His Times*. Edmund Gosse, ed. London, 1894.

Smith, Margaret Bayard. *The First Forty Years of Washington Society*. Gaillard Hunt, ed. New York, 1906.
Smith, Page. *John Adams*. 2 vols. New York, 1962.
Smith, William Loughton (Phocion). *The Pretensions of Thomas Jefferson to the Presidency Examined*. Philadelphia, 1796.
Steen, Marguerite. *The Lost One: A Biography of Mary (Perdita) Robinson*. London, 1937.
Syrett, Harold C., and Jean G. Cooke, eds. *Interview in Weehawken: The Burr-Hamilton Duel, as Told in the Original Documents*. Middletown, Conn., 1960.
Tarleton, Banastre. *History of the Campaign of 1780 and 1781*. London, 1787.
Ticknor, George. *Life, Letters, and Journals*. 2 vols. Boston, 1909.
"Trial of Aaron Burr," *Annals of Congress*. 10th Congress, 1st Session. Washington, D.C., 1852.
Trial of Aaron Burr for Treason, Printed from the Report Taken in Short Hand by David Robertson. 2 vols. Jersey City, 1879.
Trollope, Frances. *Domestic Manners of the Americans*, Michael Sadleir, ed. London, 1927.
Trumbull, John. *The Autobiography of Colonel John Trumbull, Patriot-Artist, 1756–1843*. Theodore Sizer, ed. New Haven, 1953. First published in 1841.
Tucker, George. *The Life of Thomas Jefferson*. 2 vols. Philadelphia, 1837.
Tucker, St. George. *A Dissertation on Slavery*. Philadelphia, 1796.
Vance, Joseph. "Knives, Whips, and Randolphs on the Court House Lawn," *Albemarle County Historical Society Papers* (1955–56), 28–35.
Van Doren, Carl. *Benjamin Franklin*. New York, 1941.
Van Pelt, Charles E. "Thomas Jefferson and Maria Cosway," *American Heritage*, XXII (1971), 24–29, 102–3.
Walpole, Horace. *Anecdotes of Painting in England, 1760–1795*. F. W. Hilles and P. B. Daghlian, eds., 5 vols. New Haven, 1937. *Works*, W. S. Lewis, ed., 34 vols. New Haven, 1965.
Wardle, Ralph M. *Hazlitt*. Lincoln, Nebr., 1971.
Warren, Robert Penn. *Brothers to Dragons: A Tale in Verse and Voices*. New York, 1953.
Washington, George. *Writings*. John C. Fitzpatrick, ed., 39 vols. Washington, D.C., 1931–44.
Waterman, William Randall. *Frances Wright*. New York, 1924.
Wecter, Dixon. *The Hero in America*. New York, 1945.
Weld, Isaac, Jr. *Travels through the States of North America . . . 1795, 1796, and 1797*. 2 vols. London, 1800.
Wharton, Francis. *State Trials of the Unied States during the Administrations of Washington and Adams*. Philadelphia, 1849.
White, Leonard D. *The Federalists: A Study in Administrative History*. New York, 1948.
———. *The Jeffersonians*. New York, 1951.
Wilkinson, James. *Memoirs of My Own Times*. 3 vols. Philadelphia, 1816.
Williamson, George C. *Richard Cosway, R. A.* London, 1905.
———. *Richard Cosway, R. A., and His Wife and Pupils. Miniaturists of the Eighteenth Century*. London, 1897.
Wilstach, Paul. *Jefferson and Monticello*. Garden City, N.Y., 1925.
Wirt, William. *Sketches of the Life and Character of Patrick Henry*. Hartford, Conn., 1852.
Wolfenstein, Martha. "How Is Mourning Possible?," *Psychoanalytic Study of the Child*, XXI (1966), 93–123.
Wolff, Harold, G. *Headache and Other Pain*. New York, 1948.
Wood, Gordon S. *The Creation of the American Republic, 1776–1787*. Chapel Hill, N.C., 1969.
Woodfin, Maude H. "Contemporary Opinion in Virginia of Thomas Jefferson," in *Essays in Honor of William E. Dodd*, Avery Craven, ed. Chicago, 1935.

Woodward, C. Vann. *The Burden of Southern History.* Baton Rouge, La., 1960.
Wright, Esmond. *Washington and the American Revolution.* New York, 1962.
Wright, Frances. *A Plan for the Gradual Abolition of Slavery in the United States.*
  Baltimore, 1825.
Young, Alfred. *The Jeffersonian Republicans of New York: The Origins, 1763–1797.*
  Chapel Hill, N.C., 1967.

Index